How to Use This Book

Teach Yourself Borland C++Builder in 21 Days contains 21 chapters, as the title implies. It is expected that you can complete 1 chapter each day. However, you should work at your own rate. If you think you can complete 2 or more chapters a day, then go for it! Also, if you think that you should spend more than 1 day on a certain chapter, spend as much time as you need.

Each day ends with a Q&A section with questions related to that day's material. There is also a quiz that tests your knowledge of the concepts presented that day. One or more exercises are included as well so that you can put your new skills to use. We urge you to complete these sections to reinforce your new knowledge.

Who Should Read This Book

Although you need no previous programming knowledge to read this book, you may find that you need to spend more time on some topics. This is natural and you shouldn't feel disheartened. Just keep at it until you master the details. Of course if you have some prior programming experience, you will find the code sections much easier to follow.

There are two phases to developing programs using the modern GUI-based tools. The first phase involves building the user interface using drag-and-drop components. This part is easy and is similar to the way you build drawings using the Paintbrush program that comes with Windows. The second phase is more difficult and the reason for books such as *Teach Yourself Borland C++Builder in 21 Days*. This phase involves writing the C++ code that is the glue joining the components on the form. This code also serves as the basis for customizing the operation of your program. You don't need to know this code ahead of time. This book teaches you all you need as you work through the book. In no time at all you will be well on your way to becoming a Borland C++Builder programmer.

Conventions Used in This Book

This book contains special features to help highlight important concepts and information.

NOTE

These provide essential background material or different ways of viewing the information to help you understand the concepts behind the implementations.

TIP

These give you ideas of different ways that you might apply what you've learned or point out a way to become a little more productive.

WARNING

These are used to share with you some of the author's experience so that you can avoid some of the pitfalls as you become experienced.

Teach
Yourself
BORLAND
C++BUILDER™
in 21 Days

Teach Yourself
BORLAND
C++BUILDER™
in 21 Days

Kent Reisdorph
Ken Henderson

PUBLISHING

201 West 103rd Street
Indianapolis, Indiana 46290

This book is dedicated to my wife, Teresa, who is my life force, and to my three children, Nicole, Ryan, and Amanda, who make me smile even when they're far away.—K.H.

Copyright © 1997 by Sams Publishing

International Standard Book Number: 0-672-31020-1

Library of Congress Catalog Card Number: 96-71194

2000   99   98   97   4   3   2   1

Interpretation of the printing code: the rightmost double-digit number is the year of the book's printing; the rightmost single-digit, the number of the book's printing. For example, a printing code of 97-1 shows that the first printing of the book occurred in 1997.

Composed in AGaramond and MCPdigital by Macmillan Computer Publishing

Printed in the United States of America

Trademarks

Week 1 in Review

Publisher and President   Richard K. Swadley
Publishing Manager   Greg Wiegand
Director of Editorial Services   Cindy Morrow
Managing Editor   Kitty Wilson Jarrett
Assistant Marketing Managers   Kristina Perry, Rachel Wolfe

Acquisitions Editor
Christopher Denny

Development Editor
Anthony Amico

Production Editor
Kitty Wilson Jarrett

Copy Editor
Kimberly K. Hannel

Indexer
Benjamin Slen

Technical Reviewers
Anduin Withers
Jeff Cottingham
Joe Overton
John Q. Huang
John McCloskey
John Phillips
Wade Evans

Editorial Coordinator
Katie Wise

Technical Edit Coordinator
Deborah Frisby

Editorial Assistants
Carol Ackerman
Andi Richter
Rhonda Tinch-Mize

Cover Designer
Tim Amrhein

Book Designer
Gary Adair

Copy Writer
Peter Fuller

Production Team Supervisors
Brad Chinn
Charlotte Clapp

Production
Georgiana Briggs
Elizabeth Deeter
Brad Lenser
Janet Seib

Overview

Contents

Acknowledgments

I would like to thank some of the people who made this book possible. First, I would like to thank the folks of Delphi TeamB. These guys put up with a "C++ nerd" and answered a lot of questions for me. In particular I would like to thank Bob Arnson for his help. Bob was my "go to" guy when I had a question and needed a quick answer.

Certainly the folks at Borland deserve a word of thanks for making this book possible because without C++Builder there would be no book. I want to thank Brian Myers for encouraging me to pursue this book when it was no more than a gleam in my eye. And thanks to the C++Builder development team, who answered plenty of questions for me as well. Thanks also to the many Borland tech support people who were coerced into doing technical editing.

Also, thanks to the folks at Sams who had faith that I could write this book.

Finally, I want to give special thanks to my wife, Jennifer. She had to endure many weeks of my being there in body but absent in thought and deed. Without her support and understanding, this book would not have been possible.

—Kent Reisdorph

Special thanks to my friend and mentor, Neil Coy, who taught me software craftsmanship; to all the wonderful people at Sams Publishing, especially Chris Denny, for making this project happen; to my friend Doug Tingler, for the good times we've had together; to my staff, who has had to deal with the tremendous demands this project has made on my time; and, finally, to my parents, who gave me the means of writing this book in the first place and who encourage me to press on.

—Ken Henderson

About the Authors

Kent Reisdorph

Kent Reisdorph is a senior software engineer for TurboPower Software. He is also a freelance author. He is a member of TeamB, Borland's volunteer online support group. As a member of TeamB, Kent puts in many hours each week answering questions on Windows programming for Borland C++ users. You can usually find him on the various Borland C++ forums of CompuServe. Kent lives in Colorado Springs with his wife, Jennifer, and their children.

Ken Henderson

Ken Henderson is a database developer and DBA with more than 10 years' experience. He is the author of several commercial software packages, including programmer productivity aids and software libraries. He is also a frequent speaker at industry trade shows. Currently, he is a consultant specializing in database administration and client/server architecture. Ken may be reached at 74763.2305@compuserve.com.

Tell Us What You Think!

As a reader, you are the most important critic and commentator of our books. We value your opinion and want to know what we're doing right, what we could do better, what areas you'd like to see us publish in, and any other words of wisdom you're willing to pass our way. You can help us make strong books that meet your needs and give you the computer guidance you require.

Do you have access to CompuServe or the World Wide Web? Then check out our CompuServe forum by typing GO SAMS at any prompt. If you prefer the World Wide Web, check out our site at http://www.mcp.com.

NOTE

> If you have a technical question about this book, call the technical support line at 800-571-5840, ext. 3668.

As the publishing manager of the group that created this book, I welcome your comments. You can fax, e-mail, or write me directly to let me know what you did or didn't like about this book—as well as what we can do to make our books stronger. Here's the information:

Fax: 317-581-4669

E-mail: programming_mgr@sams.mcp.com

Mail: Greg Wiegand
           Sams Publishing
           201 W. 103rd Street
           Indianapolis, IN 46290

Introduction: You Are Here

Isn't it helpful when the arrow on the map points out just exactly where you are? So you are here! But why are you here? Maybe you're here because you've been a C++ programmer for years and you are attracted to C++Builder's promises of rapid application development (RAD). Maybe you are here because you have been using Borland's Delphi and you want to leverage that knowledge in a C++ programming environment. Maybe you are here because your boss told you to be here. Or maybe you are here as a complete beginner who would like to begin to explore the wonderful world of Windows programming.

Regardless of why you are here, welcome! I can assure you that the trip will be an interesting one. You will no doubt find it enjoyable, too. It will involve some work, but there will be some fun thrown in from time to time. There's nothing quite like taking a passing thought and turning it into a working Windows program.

I encourage you to experiment as you read this book. Putting the book down and playing around for a while can prove more valuable than the best teacher. I also want to encourage you to explore the various online resources at your disposal. The Borland forums on CompuServe are a tremendous resource. There you will find members of Borland's TeamB (a volunteer group) and other Borland users answering questions for beginning and experienced users alike. Just jump in and join the fray. Also be sure to check out Borland's Web site (http://www.borland.com). There you will find additional information on C++Builder and also a discussion group where you can ask questions regarding programming with C++Builder.

So regardless of why you are here, I hope you enjoy your experience. Relax, put your feet up, and have fun learning how to use C++Builder. I know I did.

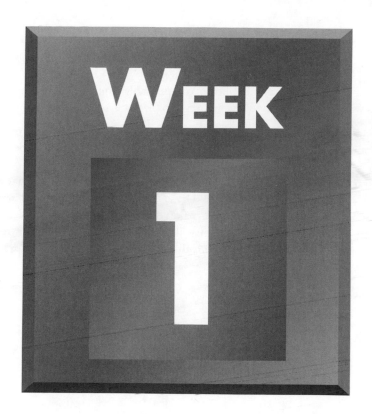

WEEK

1

At a Glance

In Week 1 you will get a start on learning how to write Windows programs in C++. The C++ language is not an easy language to learn. It is, however, the standard programming language in many corporations and governments around the world. Learning C++ might not be the easiest task you could attempt to tackle, but it should be very rewarding, both intellectually, and, eventually, monetarily.

Your first four days this week will be spent learning about the basics of the C++ language. As you work through the first four chapters, you will write simple test programs to help solidify your understanding of particular features of the C++ language. I'll warn you, though, that these programs will probably not be the type of program that you purchased C++Builder to write. The test programs for the first four days will be console applications. These programs work just like DOS programs.

1

2

3

4

5

6

7

They won't have any flash and no glitter. You probably won't be terribly impressed. These programs will, however, help to teach you the basics of C++.

Starting on Day 5 you'll begin to learn about some of the things that make the visual programming aspect of C++Builder the great tool that it is. We will talk about frameworks and what a framework means to you as a Windows programmer. On Day 5 you will build a simple test program using C++Builder's visual programming tools. After that we will spend a couple days going over the C++Builder IDE so that you can become familiar with how the entire C++Builder IDE works together to make your programming tasks easier. This is where things start to get more interesting. You will get an opportunity to write some working Windows programs in the last part of this first week. So, with that in mind, let's get to it.

Day 1

Getting Your Feet Wet

by Kent Reisdorph

Congratulations—you've chosen one of today's hottest new programming tools! Before you can jump into using all of what C++Builder has to offer, though, you'll need to learn a little about C++ first. In this chapter you will find

- ☐ A quick tour of C++Builder
- ☐ Information about how to write a Win32 console-mode application
- ☐ An introduction to the C++ language
- ☐ Facts about C++ variables and data types
- ☐ Information about functions in C++ (including the `main()` function)
- ☐ A discussion of arrays

What Is C++Builder?

By now you know that C++Builder is Borland's hot new rapid application development (RAD) product for writing C++ applications. With C++Builder you can write C++ Windows programs more quickly and more easily than was ever possible before. You can create Win32 console applications or Win32 GUI (graphical user interface) programs. When creating Win32 GUI applications with C++Builder, you have all the power of C++ wrapped up in a RAD environment. What this means is that you can create the user interface to a program (the *user interface* means the menus, dialog boxes, main window, and so on) using drag-and-drop techniques for true rapid application development. You can also drop OCX controls on forms to create specialized programs such as Web browsers in a matter of minutes. C++Builder gives you all of this, but you don't sacrifice program execution speed because you still have the power that the C++ language offers you.

I can hear you saying, "This is going to be so cool!" And guess what? You're right! But before you go slobbering all over yourself with anticipation, I also need to point out that the C++ language is not an easy one to master. I don't want you to think that you can buy a program like C++Builder and be a master Windows programmer overnight. It takes a great deal of work to be a good Windows programmer. C++Builder does a great job of hiding some of the low-level details that make up the guts of a Windows program, but it cannot write programs for you. In the end, you must still be a programmer, and that means you have to learn programming. That can be a long, uphill journey some days. The good news is that C++Builder can make your trek fairly painless and even fun. Yes, you can work and have fun doing it!

So roll up your sleeves and get your hiking shoes on. C++Builder *is* cool, so have fun.

A Quick Look at the C++Builder IDE

This section contains a quick look at the C++Builder IDE. We'll give the IDE a once-over here, and we'll examine it in more detail on Day 6, "The C++Builder IDE Explored: Projects and Forms." Because you are tackling Windows programming, I'll assume you are advanced enough to have figured out how to start C++Builder. When you first start the program, you are presented with both a blank form and the IDE, as shown in Figure 1.1.

The C++Builder IDE (which stands for *integrated development environment*) is divided into three parts. The top window might be considered the main window. It contains the speedbar on the left and the Component Palette on the right. The speedbar gives you one-click access to tasks like opening, saving, and compiling projects. The Component Palette contains a wide array of components that you can drop onto your forms. (*Components* are things like text labels, edit controls, list boxes, buttons, and the like.) For convenience, the components are divided into groups. Did you notice the tabs along the top of the Component Palette? Go ahead and click on the tabs to explore the different components available to you. To place a component on your form, you simply click the component's button in the Component Palette and then click on your form where you want the component to appear. Don't worry about the fact that you don't yet know how to use components. We'll get to that in due time. When you are done exploring, click on the tab labeled Standard, because you'll need it in a moment.

Figure 1.1.

The C++Builder IDE and the initial blank form.

NEW TERM A *component* is a self-contained piece of binary software that performs some specific predefined task, such as a text label, an edit control, or a list box.

Below the speedbar and Component Palette and glued to the left side of the screen is the Object Inspector. It is through the Object Inspector that you modify a component's properties and events. You will use the Object Inspector constantly as you work with C++Builder. The Object Inspector has one or two tabs, depending on the component currently selected. It always has a Properties tab. A component's *properties* control how the component operates. For example, changing the Color property of a component will change the background color of that component. The list of available properties varies from component to component, although components usually have several common elements (Width and Height properties, for instance).

NEW TERM A *property* determines the operation of a component.

Usually the Object Inspector has an Events tab in addition to the Properties tab. Events occur as the user interacts with a component. For example, when a component is clicked, an event fires and tells Windows that the component was clicked. You can write code that responds to those events, performing specific actions when an event occurs. As with properties, the events that you can respond to vary from component to component.

NEW TERM An *event* is a method that is invoked in a component as a result of that component's interaction with the user.

To the right of the Object Inspector is the C++Builder workspace. The workspace initially displays the Form Editor. It should come as no surprise that the Form Editor allows you to create forms. In C++Builder a form represents a window in your program. The form might be the program's main window, a dialog box, or any other type of window. You use the Form Editor to place, move, and size components as part of the form creation process. Hiding behind the Form Editor is the Code Editor. The Code Editor is where you type code when writing your programs. The Object Inspector, Form Editor, Code Editor, and Component Palette work interactively as you build applications.

Now that you've had a look at what makes up the C++Builder IDE, let's actually do something.

Hello World

It's tradition. Almost all programming books start you off by having you create a program that displays `Hello World` on the screen. I'm tempted to do something else, but tradition is a force to be reckoned with, so `Hello World` it is. You've got some work ahead of you in the next few chapters, so I thought I'd give you a taste of C++Builder's goodies before putting you to work on learning the seemingly less-glamorous basics of C++. You'll have a little fun before you have to go on the chain gang. C++Builder (and its cousin, Delphi) possibly allow you the quickest route to `Hello World` of any Windows programming environment to date.

Right now you should have C++Builder running, and you should be looking at a blank form. By default, the form is named Form1. (The form name is significant in C++Builder, but I'll address that a little later.) To the left of the form, the Object Inspector shows the properties for the form. Click on the title bar of the Object Inspector. The `Caption` property is highlighted, and the cursor is sitting there waiting for you to do something. (If the `Caption` property is not in view, you might have to scroll the Object Inspector window to locate it. Properties are listed in alphabetical order.) Type `Hello World!` to change the form's caption.

but you need not be concerned about that right now. So, without further ado, let's create Hello World as a Win32 console program with C++Builder.

 A Win32 *console application* is a 32-bit program that runs in a DOS box under Windows 95 or Windows NT.

From the main menu, choose File | New. C++Builder displays the Object Repository. Curiously enough, the Object Repository's title bar says New Items, but don't be thrown by that. The Object Repository contains predefined projects, forms, dialog boxes, and other objects you can add to your applications or use to begin a new project. I will discuss the Object Repository in detail on Day 9, "Creating Applications in C++Builder." For now, click on the New tab in the Object Repository and double-click Console App to start a new console application project. C++Builder creates the project and displays the Code Editor so that you can enter code for the program. Figure 1.4 shows the Code Editor as it appears when starting a new console-mode application.

Figure 1.4.

The C++Builder Code Editor window.

You will notice a couple of differences between the C++Builder IDE now and how it looked earlier when we created a GUI application. First, there is no Form Editor. That's because a console application can't display forms (well, that's not completely true, but it's accurate enough for this discussion). Also notice that the Object Inspector is blank. You can only place components on a form, so the Object Inspector is useless in a console application.

 TIP

When writing console applications, you can close the Object Inspector to make more room for the Code Editor window. Close the Object Inspector by clicking the Close button on the Object Inspector's title bar. To bring back the Object Inspector, press F11 or choose View | Object Inspector from the main menu.

When you examine the Code Editor, you should see the following text displayed in the editor window:

```
//--------------------------------
#include <condefs.h>
#include <stdio.h>
#include <stdlib.h>

#pragma hdrstop
//--------------------------------
int main(int argc, char **argv)
{
return 0;
}
//--------------------------------
```

ANALYSIS This is a do-nothing C++ program, but a valid C++ program nonetheless. We'll modify the code in just a moment to make this program actually do something, but first I want you to notice the lines that begin with //. These are comment lines that, in this program, serve no purpose other than to divide the program's code visually. (You will normally use comment lines to document your code.) C++Builder adds these comment lines automatically when a new console application is first created. (In future code listings I will eliminate the comment lines to save space.) Notice also that the single statement in this code ends in a semicolon. (I know it doesn't make sense right now, but there is only one actual executable statement in this program.) The semicolon is used at the end of each statement in a C++ program.

Very early in the process of learning the C and C++ languages, the budding programmer must learn the difference between an expression and a statement. The "official" definition of a statement is "an expression that is followed by a semicolon." The semicolon closes an expression and makes it a kind of single-line block of code. I'll get into the code block soon, but for now you should realize that an *expression* is a unit of code that evaluates to some quantity. A *statement* is an expression that is closed. For example, consider the following statement:

```
c = a + b;
```

In this example, the portion to the right of the equal sign, a + b, is an expression. The entire line is a statement. I know this may be a bit confusing at the moment, but it should become clearer as we go along. I'll try to be very careful when I use these two terms. For now, though, just remember that a statement is followed by a semicolon and is a closed expression.

Also notice the opening and closing braces in the program. In C++, a block of code begins with the opening brace ({) and ends with the closing brace (}). The braces are used to delineate the beginning and end of code blocks associated with loops, functions, if statements, and in other cases as well. In this program there is only one set of braces because it is a simple program.

In order to display `Hello World!` on the screen, we need to make use of a C++ class called `iostream`, so a quick tutorial on that class is needed. (You don't know about classes yet, but don't worry about that right now.) The `iostream` class uses *streams* to perform basic input and output, such as printing text on the screen or getting input from the user. The `cout` stream is used to send data to the standard output stream. In a console application, the standard output stream means the console, or the screen. The `cin` stream is used to get data from the console, such as user input. `iostream` implements two special operators to place information on a stream or to extract information from a stream. The *insertion operator* (<<) is used to insert data into an output stream, and the *extraction operator* (>>) is used to extract data from an input stream. To output information to the console, you would use

```
cout << "Do something!";
```

This tells the program to insert the text `Do something!` onto the standard output stream. When this line in the program executes, the text will be displayed on the screen.

NOTE

> `cout` is for use in console-mode applications only. A Windows GUI application does not have a standard output stream (everything in a GUI app is graphics based), so the output from `cout` goes nowhere in a Windows GUI program. Standard Windows programs use `DrawText()` or `TextOut()` to display text on the screen. C++Builder programs can also use `DrawText()` and `TextOut()`, either using the Windows API or via the `TCanvas` class.

Before you can use `cout`, you need to tell the compiler where to find the description (called the *declaration*) of the `iostream` class. The declaration for `iostream` is located in a file called `IOSTREAM.H`. This file is called a *header file*.

 NEW TERM A header file (or *header* for short) contains the class declaration of one or more classes.

To tell the compiler to look in `IOSTREAM.H` for the class definition of `iostream`, use the `#include` directive as follows:

```
#include <iostream.h>
```

NEW TERM A *declaration* is a statement of intention or a foreshadowing of an event. It precedes a *definition* of that event. For example, a voter *declares* himself to be a Democrat or Republican. He then *defines* himself to be a member of that party by voting in that party's primary election. In C and C++, the distinction between these two separate states is very important.

Now the compiler will be able to find the iostream class and will understand what to do when it encounters the cout statement.

 TIP

> If you forget to include the header file for a class or a function your program references, you will get a compiler error. The compiler error will say something to the effect of Undefined symbol 'cout'. If you see this error message, you should immediately check to be sure that you have included all of the headers your program needs. To find out what header file a class or function's declaration is in, click on the function or class name and press the F1 key. Windows help will run, and the help topic for the item under the cursor will be displayed. Toward the top of the help topic you will see a reference to the header file in which the function or class is declared.

There's one more thing I'll mention before we write the console version of Hello World. The iostream class contains special *manipulators* that can be used to control how streams are handled. The only one we are concerned with right now is the endl (end line) manipulator, which is used to insert a new line in the output stream. We'll use endl to insert a new line after we output text to the screen.

Now that you have some understanding of the iostream class, we can proceed to write Hello World as a console application. Edit the program until it looks like Listing 1.1. Each of the lines in the listing has a number that I've put there for identification. Be sure to skip that number and the space after it when you type in the lines.

Listing 1.1. HELLO.CPP.

```
1: #include <condefs.h>
2: #include <stdio.h>
3: #include <stdlib.h>
4: #include <iostream.h>          // add this line
5: #pragma hdrstop
6:
7: int main(int argc, char **argv)
8: {
9:   cout << "Hello World!" << endl;   // add this line
10:   return 0;
11: }
```

NOTE

In C++, whitespace is ignored. For the most part, it doesn't matter where you put spaces or new lines. Obviously you cannot insert spaces in the middle of keywords or variable names, but other than that just about anything goes. For example, the following bits of code are equivalent:

```
int main(int argc, char **argv)
{
cout << "Hello World!";
return 0;
}
```

is the same as

```
int main(int argc,char** argv){cout<<"Hello World!";return 0;}
```

Obviously, the first form is more readable and is much preferred. While coding styles vary, if you emulate the coding conventions you see in this book, you should be okay when it comes to programming in the real world.

ANALYSIS   Now click the Run button on the speedbar. The program compiles and runs. When the program runs you will see a DOS box pop up and the words Hello World!...whoops! What happened? You probably saw the application for a split second and then watched as it disappeared. The reason for this is that at the end of the main() function the program terminates and the console window immediately closes. To remedy this we need to add a couple of lines to our program to prevent the console window from closing until we're done with it. The standard C library includes a function called getch() that is used to get a keystroke from the keyboard. We'll use that as a means of preventing the console window from closing. Again, edit the program in the editor window until it looks like Listing 1.2. You don't need to add the comment lines if you don't want to. Remember to skip the line numbers.

Listing 1.2. HELLO.CPP (revised).

```
1: #include <condefs.h>
2: #include <stdio.h>
3: #include <stdlib.h>
4: #include <iostream.h>
5: #include <conio.h>          // add this line
6: #pragma hdrstop
7:
8: int main(int argc, char **argv)
```

continues

Listing 1.2. continued

```
 9: {
10:    cout << "Hello World!" << endl;
11:    // add the following two lines
12:    cout << endl << "Press any key to continue...";
13:    getch();
14:    return 0;
15: }
```

ANALYSIS This time the application runs, Hello World! is displayed, and the console window stays visible. To end the program and close the console window, you can press any key on the keyboard.

You can also find the programs listed in the text on the CD-ROM that accompanies this book. The examples need to be installed on your hard drive before they can be compiled. While it's good practice early on to enter short programs by hand, you may want to load the longer sample programs from your hard drive in order to avoid inevitable typing errors and the compiler errors that are sure to follow.

That's all there is to it. Hello World, Part II isn't too exciting, but you'll make good use of console-mode applications as you explore the C++ language in the following pages. That's why it is necessary for you to understand how to create and run a console-mode application. Now let's move on to the basics of the C++ language.

C++ Language Overview

C++ is a powerful language. It allows you to do things that are not possible in other languages. As is true in most of life, that kind of power does not come without responsibility. It could be said that C++ gives you just enough rope to hang yourself—and while starting out learning C++, you often *will* hang yourself. This usually comes in the form of memory overruns and access violations that will cause crashes in your programs.

I will do my best to describe C++ in the short space allotted. Entire books have been written on the C++ language (and big ones at that!), so do not expect that I can cover it all in a couple chapters. I strongly suggest that, after you read this book and experiment with C++Builder for a period of time, you buy a book that explains C++ in greater detail.

C++ allows you to take advantage of object-oriented programming (OOP) to its fullest. OOP is not just a buzzword. It has real benefits because it allows you to create objects that can be used in your current program and reused in future programs.

NEW TERM An *object*, like components described earlier, is a piece of binary software that performs a specific programming task. (Components are objects, but not all objects are components. I'll get into that later.)

An object reveals to the user (the programmer using the object) only as much of itself as needed in order to simplify its use. All internal mechanisms that the user doesn't need to know about are hidden from sight. All of this is rolled up in the concept of object-oriented programming. OOP allows you to take a modular approach to programming, thus keeping you from constantly re-inventing the wheel. C++Builder programs are OOP-oriented due to C++Builder's heavy use of components. Once a component is created (either one of your own or one of the built-in C++Builder components), it can be reused in any C++Builder program. A component can also be extended by inheritance to create a new component with additional features. Best of all, components hide their internal details and let the programmer concentrate on getting the most out of the component. Objects and C++ classes are discussed in detail on Day 4, "Totally Immersed: C++ Classes and Object-Oriented Programming."

Humble Beginnings

In the beginning there was C…as far as C++ is concerned, anyway. C++ is built on the C programming language. It has been described as "C with classes." This foundation in C is still very prevalent in C++ programs written today. It's not as if C++ were written to replace C, but rather to augment it. The rest of this chapter and much of the next chapter focus primarily on the part of the C++ language that has its roots in C. Actually, we will be dealing with the C language here and moving to C++ later, on Day 2, "Wading In Deeper." You don't have to be concerned with which of the information presented is from C and which is from C++ because it's all rolled up into the language we call C++.

It would be nice if presenting the C++ language could be handled sequentially. That's not the case, though, because all of the features we will be discussing are intertwined. Presenting the C++ language sequentially is not possible, so I'll take the individual puzzle pieces one at a time and start fitting them together. Toward the end of Day 3, "Up to Your Neck in C++," you'll have a fairly complete picture of the C++ language. Don't be concerned if you do not instantly grasp every concept presented. Some of what is required to fully understand C++ can only come with real-world experience.

Variables

Well, we have to start somewhere, so let's take a look at variables. A *variable* is essentially a name assigned to a memory location. Once you have declared a variable, you can then use it to manipulate data in memory. That probably doesn't make much sense to you, so let me give you a few examples. The following code snippet uses two variables. At the end of each line of code is a comment that describes what is happening when that line executes:

```
int x;          // variable declared as an integer variable
x = 100;        // 'x' now contains the value 100
x += 50;        // 'x' now contains the value 150
int y = 150;    // 'y' declared and initialized to 150
x += y;         // 'x' now contains the value 300
x++;            // 'x' now contains the value 301
```

 NEW TERM A *variable* is a location set aside in computer memory to contain some value.

Notice that the value of x changes as the variable is manipulated. I'll discuss the C++ operators used to manipulate variables a little later.

WARNING

Variables that are declared but are not initialized will contain random values. Because the memory to which the variable points has not been initialized, there is no telling what that memory location contains. For instance, look at the following code:

```
int x;
int y;
x = y + 10;  // oops!
```

In this example the variable x could contain any value because y was not initialized prior to use.

The exception to this rule is that global variables and variables declared with the static modifier are initialized to 0. All other variables contain random data until initialized or assigned a value.

Variable names can mix upper- and lowercase letters and can include numbers and the underscore (_), but they cannot contain spaces or other special characters. The variable name must start with a character or the underscore. Generally speaking, it's not a good idea to begin a variable name with an underscore because compilers often start special variable and function names with the underscore. The maximum allowed length of a variable name will vary from compiler to compiler. If you keep your variable names to 31 characters or less, you'll be safe. In reality, anything more than about 20 characters is too long to be useful anyway.

C++ Data Types

NEW TERM In C++ a *data type* defines the way the compiler stores information in memory.

1

In some programming languages you can get by with assigning any type of value to a variable. For example, look at the following examples of BASIC code:

```
x = -1;
x = 1000;
x = 3.14
x = 457000;
```

In BASIC the interpreter takes care of allocating enough storage to fit any size or type of number. In C++, however, you must declare a variable's type before you can use the variable:

```
int x1 = -1;
int x = 1000;
float y = 3.14;
long z = 457000;
```

This allows the compiler to do type-checking and to make sure that things are kept straight when the program runs. Improper use of a data type will result in a compiler error or warning that can be analyzed and corrected so that you can head off a problem before it starts. Some data types can have both signed and unsigned versions. A *signed* data type can contain both negative and positive numbers, whereas an *unsigned* data type can contain only positive numbers. Table 1.1 shows the basic data types in C++, the amount of memory they require, and the range of values possible for that data type.

Table 1.1. Data types used in C++ (32-bit programs).

Data Type	Size in Bytes	Possible Range of Values
char	1	-128 to 126
unsigned char	1	0 to 255
short	2	-32,768 to 32,767
unsigned short	2	0 to 65,535
long	4	-2,147,483,648 to 2,147,483,648
unsigned long	4	0 to 4,294,967,295
int	4	Same as long
unsigned int	4	Same as unsigned long
float	4	1.2E-38 to 3.4E381
double	8	2.2E-308 to 1.8E3082
bool	1	true or false

NOTE

In C++Builder (as well as in Borland C++ 5.0), `bool` is a true data type. Some C++ compilers have a `BOOL` keyword, but `bool` is not a data type in those compilers. In those cases `BOOL` is a `typedef` that makes the `BOOL` equivalent to an `int`. A `typedef` in effect sets up an alias so that the compiler can equate one symbol with another. A `typedef` looks like this:

```
typedef int BOOL;
```

This tells the compiler, "`BOOL` is another word for `int`."

NOTE

Only the `double` and `float` data types use floating-point numbers (numbers with decimal places). The other data types deal only with integer values. Although it's legal to assign a value containing a decimal fraction to an integer data type, the fractional amount will be discarded and only the whole-number portion will be assigned to the integer variable. For example,

```
int x = 3.75;
```

will result in x containing a value of 3. Note that the resulting integer value is not rounded to the nearest whole number; rather, the decimal fraction is discarded altogether. By the way, you'd be surprised how few times you need floating-point numbers in most Windows programs.

C++ will perform conversion between different data types when possible. Take the following code snippet for an example:

```
short result;
long num1 = 200;
long num2 = 200;
result = num1 * num2;
```

In this case I am trying to assign the result of multiplying two `long` integers to a `short` integer. Even though this formula mixes two data types, C++ is able to perform a conversion. Would you like to take a guess at the result of this calculation? You may be surprised to find out that the result is -25,536. This is due to *wrapping*. If you look at Table 1.1, you'll see that a `short` can have a maximum value of 32,767. What happens if you take a `short` with a value of 32,767 and add 1 to it? You will end up with a value of -32,768. This is essentially the same as the odometer on a car turning over from 99,999 to 00,000 when you drive that last mile. To illustrate, type in and run the program contained in Listing 1.3.

Listing 1.3. WRAPME.CPP.

```
 1: #include <iostream.h>
 2: #include <conio.h>
 3: #pragma hdrstop
 4:
 5: int main(int argc, char **argv)
 6: {
 7:    short x = 32767;
 8:    cout << "x = " << x << endl;
 9:    x++;
10:    cout << "x = " << x << endl;
11:    getch();
12:    return 0;
13: }
```

The output will be

```
x = 32767
x = -32768
```

You won't go too far wrong if you use the int data type as your data type of choice. You are unlikely to run into the problem of wrapping because the int data type gives you a range of -2 billion to +2 billion, plus change. Your programs will be slightly larger, however, because you will be using more memory than required in many situations.

Okay, where was I? Oh, yes, I was talking about automatic type conversion. In some cases, C++ cannot perform a conversion. If that is the case, you will get one of several possible compiler errors that essentially say Cannot convert from X to Y. You may also get a compiler warning that says, Conversion may lose significant digits.

 TIP

> Learn to treat compiler warnings as errors because the compiler is trying to tell you that something is not quite right. Ultimately, you should strive for warning-free compiles. In some cases a warning cannot be avoided, but be sure to examine all warnings closely. Do your best to understand the reason for the warning and correct it if possible.

C++ Operators

Operators are used to manipulate data. Operators perform calculations, check for equality, make assignments, manipulate variables, and other more esoteric duties most programmers never get into. There are a lot of operators in C++. Rather than present them all here, I will list only those most commonly used. Table 1.2 contains a list of those operators.

Table 1.2. Commonly used C++ operators.

Operator	Description	Example
Mathematical Operators		
+	Addition	x = y + z;
-	Subtraction	x = y - z;
*	Multiplication	x = y * z;
/	Division	x = y / z;
Assignment Operators		
=	Assignment	x = 10;
+=	Assign and sum	x += 10; (same as x = x + 10;)
-=	Assign and subtract	x -= 10;
*=	Assign and multiply	x *= 10;
\=	Assign and divide	x \= 10;
&=	Assign bitwise AND	x &= 0x02;
¦=	Assign bitwise OR	x ¦= 0x02;
Logical Operators		
&&	Logical AND	if (x && 0xFF) {...}
¦¦	Logical OR	if (x ¦¦ 0xFF) {...}
Equality Operators		
==	Equal to	if (x == 10) {...}
!=	Not equal to	if (x != 10) {...}
<	Less than	if (x < 10) {...}
>	Greater than	if (x > 10) {...}
<=	Less than or equal to	if (x <= 10) {...}
>=	Greater than or equal to	if (x >= 10) {...}

Operator	Description	Example
	Unary Operators	
*	Indirection operator	`int x = *y;`
&	Address of operator	`int* x = &y;`
~	Bitwise NOT	`x &= ~0x02;`
!	Logical NOT	`if (!valid) {...}`
++	Increment operator	`x++; (same as x = x + 1;)`
--	Decrement operator	`x--;`
	Class and Structure Operators	
::	Scope resolution	`MyClass::SomeFunction();`
->	Indirect membership	`myClass->SomeFunction();`
.	Direct membership	`myClass.SomeFunction();`

As you can see, the list of operators is a bit overwhelming, so don't worry about trying to memorize each one. As you work with C++ you will gradually learn how to use all of the operators.

It should be noted that in some cases an operator can be used either pre-increment (++x) or post-increment (x++). A *pre-increment* operator tells the compiler, "Increment the variable's value and then use the variable." A *post-increment* operator tells the compiler, "Use the variable first and then increment its value." For example, this code

```
int x = 10;
cout << "x = " << x++ << endl;
cout << "x = " << x << endl;
cout << "x = " << ++x << endl;
cout << "x = " << x << endl;
```

will result in the following output:

```
x = 10
x = 11
x = 12
x = 12
```

A lot of this won't make sense until you've worked with C++ for a while, but be patient and it will eventually come to you. As Pontius said to Augustus, "Relax, Augie. Rome wasn't built in a day, ya know."

NOTE

> In C++, operators can be *overloaded*. This is a technique by which a programmer can take one of the standard operators and make it perform in a specific manner for a specific class. For example, you could overload the ++ operator for one of your classes and have it increment the value of a variable by 10, rather than by 1. Operator overloading is an advanced C++ technique and won't be covered in any detail in this book.

You will notice that some of the operators use the same symbol. The meaning of the symbol is different depending on the context. For instance, the asterisk (*) can be used to perform multiplication, declare a pointer, or dereference a pointer. This can be confusing at first, and to be honest, it can be confusing at times no matter how long you've been programming in C++. Just keep plugging away and eventually it will start to sink in.

You will see many examples of these operators as you go through this book. Rather than trying to memorize the function of each operator, try instead to learn through careful study of the example programs and code snippets.

Functions in C++

Functions are sections of code separate from the main program. These code sections are called (executed) when needed to perform specific actions in a program. For example, you might have a function that takes two values, performs a complex mathematical calculation on those two values, and returns the result. Or you might need a function that takes a string, parses it, and returns a portion of the parsed string.

Functions are sections of code, separate from the main program, that perform a single, well-defined service.

Functions are an important part of any programming language, and C++ is no exception. The simplest type of function takes no parameters and returns void (meaning it returns nothing at all). Other functions may take one or more *parameters*, and may return a value. Rules for naming functions are the same as those discussed earlier for variables. Figure 1.5 shows the anatomy of a function.

A *parameter* is a value passed to a function that is used to alter its operation or indicate the extent of its operation.

Before a function can be used, it must have first been declared. The *function declaration*, or *prototype*, tells the compiler how many parameters the function takes, the data type of each parameter, and the data type of the return value for the function. Listing 1.4 illustrates this concept.

NEW TERM A *prototype* is a declaration of a function's appearance or a foreshadowing of its definition.

Figure 1.5.
Anatomy of a function.

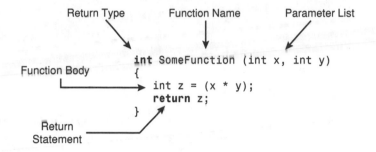

Listing 1.4. MULTIPLY.CPP.

```
 1: #include <iostream.h>
 2: #include <conio.h>
 3: #pragma hdrstop
 4:
 5: int multiply(int, int);
 6: void showResult(int);
 7:
 8: int main(int argc, char **argv)
 9: {
10:    int x, y, result;
11:    cout << endl << "Enter the first value: ";
12:    cin >> x;
13:    cout << "Enter the second value: ";
14:    cin >> y;
15:    result = multiply(x, y);
16:    showResult(result);
17:    cout << endl << endl << "Press any key to continue...";
18:    getch();
19:    return 0;
20: }
21:
22: int multiply(int x, int y)
23: {
24:    return x * y;
25: }
26:
27: void showResult(int res)
28: {
29:    cout << "The result is: " << result << endl;
30: }
```

This program asks for two numbers from the user (using the standard input stream, cin) in lines 11 through 14, calls the multiply() function to multiply the two numbers together (line 15), and then calls the showResult() function to display the result (line 16). Notice the function prototypes for the multiply() and showResult() functions on lines 5 and 6, just above the main program. The prototypes list only the return type, the function name, and the data type of the function's parameters. That is the minimum requirement for a function declaration.

If desired, the function prototype may contain variable names that can be used to document what the function does. For example, the function declaration for the multiply() function could have been written like this:

```
int multiply(int firstNumber, int secondNumber);
```

In this case it's pretty obvious what the multiply() function does, but it can't hurt to document your code both through comments and through the code itself.

Look again at Listing 1.4. Notice that the function definition for the multiply() function (lines 22 through 25) is outside of the block of code defining the main function (lines 8 through 20). The function definition contains the actual body of the function. In this case the body of the function is minimal because the function simply multiplies the two function parameters together and returns the result.

The multiply() function in Listing 1.4 could be called one of several ways. You can pass variables, literal values, or even the results of other function calls:

```
result = multiply(2, 5);      // passing literal values
result = multiply(x, y);      // passing variables
showResult(multiply(x,y));    // return value used as a
                              // parameter for another function
multiply(x, y);               // return value ignored
```

Notice in this example that the return value is not used. In this case it doesn't make much sense to call the multiply() function and ignore the return value, but ignoring the return value is something that is done frequently in C++ programming. There are many functions that perform a specific action and then return a value indicating the status of the function call. In some cases the return value is not relevant to your program, so you can just ignore it. If you don't do anything with the return value, it is simply discarded and no harm is done. For example, we have been ignoring the return value of the getch() function (which returns the ASCII value of the key that was pressed) in our sample programs.

Functions can (and frequently do) call other functions. Functions can even call themselves. This is called *recursion*, and is one way to get into trouble in C++ programming. Recursion is best left alone until you've put in some time with the C++ language.

NEW TERM   *Recursion* is the process by which a function calls itself.

The material on functions presented in this section deals with standalone functions in a C or C++ program (they are *standalone* in that they are not members of a class). Standalone functions can be used in C++ exactly as they can be used in C. However, C++ takes functions a bit further. I'll leave that discussion for now and pick it up again later when we look deeper into C++.

HOUSE RULES FOR FUNCTIONS

- ☐ A function can take any number of parameters or no parameters at all.
- ☐ A function can be written to return a value, but it is not mandatory that a function return a value.
- ☐ If a function has a return type of void, it cannot return a value. If you attempt to return a value from a function with a return type of void, a compiler error will be issued. A function that returns void need not contain a return statement at all, but it may if desired. Either way is acceptable. If no return statement is provided, the function returns automatically when it gets to the end of the function block (the closing brace).
- ☐ If the function prototype indicates that the function returns a value, the function body should contain a return statement that returns a value. If the function does not return a value, a compiler warning is issued.
- ☐ Functions can take any number of parameters but can return only one value.
- ☐ Variables can be passed to functions by value, by pointer, or by reference. (I'll discuss this a little later.)

SYNTAX

The function statement, in declaration (prototype) format:

```
ret_type function_name(argtype_1 arg_1, argtype_2 arg_2, ..., argtype_n arg_n);
```

The function declaration identifies a function that will be included in the code. It shows the return data type (`ret_type`) of the function and the name of the function (`function_name`), and identifies the order (`arg_1, arg_2, ..., arg_n`) and types (`argtype_1, argtype_2, ..., argtype_n`) of data arguments the function will expect.

The function statement, in definition format:

```
ret_type function_name(argtype_1 arg_1, argtype_2 arg_2, ..., argtype_n arg_n) {
statements;
    }
```

The function definition identifies the code block (`statements`) that makes up the function and shows the return data type (`ret_type`) of the function. `function_name` identifies the function. The parameters supplied to the function (`arg_1, arg_2, ..., arg_n`) and their types (`argtype_1, argtype_2, ..., argtype_n`) are included.

The `main()` Function

A C++ program must have a `main()` function. This function serves as the entry point into the program. You have seen this in each of the sample programs you've seen thus far. Not all C++ programs have a traditional `main()` function, however. Windows programs written in C and C++ have an entry-point function called `WinMain()` rather than the traditional `main()` function.

NOTE

> A C++Builder GUI application has a `WinMain()`, but it is hidden from you. C++Builder frees you from having to worry about the low-level details of a Windows program and allows you to concentrate on creating the user interface and the remainder of the program.

`main()` is a function like any other function. That is, it has the same basic anatomy. You already saw that for a 32-bit console application C++Builder creates a default `main()` function with the following prototype:

```
int main(int argc, char** argv);
```

This form of `main()` takes two parameters and returns an integer value. As you learned earlier, you pass values to a function when you call the function. In the case of `main()`, though, you never call the function directly—it's automatically executed when the program runs. So how does the `main()` function get its parameters? The answer: From the command line. Let me illustrate.

Let's assume that you have a Win32 console application that you execute from a DOS prompt with the following command line:

```
grep WM_KILLFOCUS -d -i
```

In this case you are starting a program called `grep` with command-line arguments of `WM_KILLFOCUS`, `-d`, and `-i`. Given that example, let me show you how that translates to `argc` and `argv` inside the `main()` function. First of all, the integer variable `argc` will contain the number of parameters passed in the command line. This will always be at least 1 because the program name counts as a parameter. The variable `argv` is an array of pointers to strings. This array will contain each string passed in the command line. For this code example, the following are true:

`argv`	contains 4
`argc[0]`	contains c:\bc5\bin\grep.com
`argc[1]`	contains WM_KILLFOCUS
`argc[2]`	contains -d
`argc[3]`	contains -i

Let's prove that this works with a little sample program. Create a new console application in C++Builder and enter the program shown in Listing 1.5.

Listing 1.5. ARGSTEST.CPP.

```
 1: #include <iostream.h>
 2: #include <conion.h>
 3: #pragma hdrstop
 4:
 5: int main(int argc, char **argv)
 6: {
 7:   cout << "argc = " << argc << endl;
 8:   for (int i=0;i<argc;i++)
 9:     cout << "Parameter " << i << ": " << argv[i] << endl;
10:   getch();
11:   return 0;
12: }
```

Save the project as ARGSTESTCPP. Rather than clicking the Run button, choose Project | Build All from the main menu. This will build the project but won't execute the program. When the project has finished building, choose Run | Parameters from the main menu. Type the following in the Run parameters dialog box:

```
one two three "four five" six
```

Now click the Run button, and the program will run using the command-line parameters you specified. An alternative is to run the program from an MS-DOS prompt by using the following command line:

```
argstest one two three "four five" six
```

When the program runs it will display the number of arguments passed and then list each of the arguments. The output should match that of Figure 1.6. Run the program several times, providing different command-line arguments each time, and observe the output.

Figure 1.6.

Sample output from ARGSTEST.EXE.

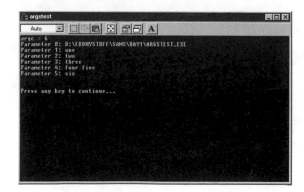

In most programs the value returned from `main()` is irrelevant because the return value is not typically used. In fact, you don't need your `main()` function to return a value at all. There is more than one form of `main()`. The following all represent valid declarations:

```
main();
int main();
int main(int argc, char** argv);
void main();  // same as the first form above
void main(int argc, char** argv);
```

Believe it or not, there are even more possibilities than those listed here. If you are not going to be using the command-line arguments and are not returning a value from `main()`, you can use the first form of `main()` listed here. This form returns a `void` and takes no parameters (signified by the empty parentheses). In other words, the most basic form of the `main()` function takes no parameters and returns no value.

Arrays

You can place any of the intrinsic C++ data types into an array. An *array* is simply a collection of values. For example, let's say you wanted to keep an array of `int`s that held five integer values. You would declare the array as follows:

```
int myArray[5];
```

In this case the compiler allocates memory for the array as illustrated in Figure 1.7. Because each `int` requires 4 bytes of storage, the entire array will take up 20 bytes in memory.

Figure 1.7.

Memory allocation for an array of five `int`s.

myArray[0]	myArray[1]	myArray[2]	myArray[3]	myArray[4]
baseAddr	baseAddr+4	baseAddr+8	baseAddr+12	baseAddr+16

Now that you have the array declared, you can fill it with values using the *subscript operator* (`[]`) as follows:

```
myArray[0] = -200;
myArray[1] = -100;
myArray[2] = 0;
myArray[3] = 100;
myArray[4] = 200;
```

Later in your program you can access the individual elements of the array again using the subscript operator:

```
int result = myArray[3] + myArray[4];  // result will be 300
```

There is a shortcut method to declaring and filling an array all at one time. It looks like this:

```
int myArray[5] = { -200, -100, 0, 100, 200 };
```

To take this one step further, if you know exactly how many elements your array will have, and if you fill the array when you declare it, you can even leave out the array size when you declare the array. In that case you would use the following:

```
int myArray[] = { -200, -100, 0, 100, 200 };
```

This works because the compiler can figure out from the list of values being assigned how many elements are in the array and how much memory to allocate for the array.

Arrays can be multidimensional. To create a two-dimensional array of integers, you would use code like this:

```
int mdArray[3][5];
```

This allocates storage for 15 ints (a total of 60 bytes, if you're keeping score). You access elements of the array like you do a simple array, with the obvious difference that you must supply two subscript operators:

```
int x = mdArray[1][1] + mdArray[2][1];
```

Figure 1.8 illustrates how a two-dimensional array might look in memory.

Figure 1.8.

A two-dimensional array in memory.

	myArray[][0]	myArray[][1]	myArray[][2]	myArray[][3]	myArray[][4]
Array[0][]	baseAddr	baseAddr+4	baseAddr+8	baseAddr+12	baseAddr+16
Array[1][]	baseAddr+20	baseAddr+24	baseAddr+28	baseAddr+32	baseAddr+36
Array[2][]	baseAddr+40	baseAddr+44	baseAddr+48	baseAddr+52	baseAddr+56

WARNING

You must be careful not to overwrite the end of an array. One powerful feature of C++ is direct access to memory. Because of this feature, C++ will not prevent you from writing to a particular memory location even if that location is memory your program isn't supposed to have access to. The following code is legal, but will result in a crash in your program (or in Windows):

```
int array[5];
array[5] = 10;
```

This is a common error to make because you might think the last element of this array is 5 when it is really 4. If you overwrite the end of an array, you have no idea what memory you are overwriting. The

results will be unpredictable at best. At worst, you will crash your
program and maybe even crash Windows, too. This type of problem
can be difficult to diagnose because often the affected memory is not
accessed until much later, and the crash occurs at that time (leaving you
wondering what happened). Be careful when writing to an array.

HOUSE RULES FOR ARRAYS

☐ Arrays are 0 based. The first element in the array is 0, the second element is 1, the
third element is 2, and so on.

☐ Array sizes must be compile-time constants. The compiler must know at compile
time how much space to allocate for the array. You cannot use a variable to assign
an array size, so the following is not legal and will result in a compiler error:

```
int x = 10;
int myArray[x];    // compiler error here
```

☐ Be careful not to overwrite the end of an array.

☐ Allocate large arrays from the heap rather than from the stack. (You'll learn more
about this later.)

Character Arrays

Odd as it may seem, there is no support in C++ for a string variable (a variable that holds text).
Instead, strings in C++ programs are represented by arrays of the char data type. For instance,
you could assign a string to a char array as follows:

```
char text[] = "This is a string.";
```

This allocates 18 bytes of storage in memory and stores the string in that memory location.
Depending on how quick you are, you may have noticed that there are only 17 characters in
this string. The reason that 18 bytes are allocated is that at the end of each string is a
terminating null, and C++ accounts for the terminating null when allocating storage.

NEW TERM The *terminating null* is a special character that is represented with /0, which equates
to a numerical 0.

When the program encounters a 0 in the character array, it interprets that location as the end of the string. To see how this is done, enter and run Listing 1.6 as a console application.

Listing 1.6. NULLTEST.CPP.

```
 1: #include <iostream.h>
 2: #include <conio.h>
 3: #pragma hdrstop
 4:
 5: int main(int argc, char **argv)
 6: {
 7:   char str[] = "This is a string.";
 8:   cout << str << endl;
 9:   str[7] = '\0';
10:   cout << str << endl;
11:   getch();
12:   return 0;
13: }
```

Figure 1.9 shows the output from the program in Listing 1.6.

Figure 1.9.

The output from NULLTEST.CPP.

ANALYSIS   Initially, the character array contains the characters, This is a string. followed by the terminating null. That string is sent to the screen via cout. The next line assigns the seventh element of the array to \0, which is, of course, the terminating null. The string is again sent to the screen, but this time only This is is displayed. The reason for this is that as far as the computer is concerned, the string ends at element 7 in the array. The rest of the characters are still in storage but can't be displayed because of the terminating null. Figure 1.10 illustrates how the character array looks before and after the line that changes element 7 to the terminating null.

Figure 1.10.

The contents of a character array.

Before

| T | h | i | s | | i | s | | a | | s | t | r | i | n | g | . | \0 |

After

| T | h | i | s | | i | s | \0 | a | | s | t | r | i | n | g | . | \0 |

I could have simply assigned a 0 in place of '\0' in Listing 1.6. Either is acceptable because a numerical 0 and the char data type version, '\0', are equivalent.

> **NOTE**
>
> There is a difference between single and double quotes in a C++ program. When assigning the terminal null (or any other character value) to an element of an array, you must use single quotes. The single quotes effectively turn the character within the quotes into an integer value (the ASCII value of the character) that is then stored in the memory location. When assigning strings to character arrays, you must use double quotes. If you get it wrong in either case, the compiler will let you know by issuing a compiler error.

String-Manipulation Functions

If you are coming from a programming language that has a string data type, all of this might seem like a pain. The truth is, it takes very little time to get used to. You're not completely on your own, by the way. In order to aid in string operations, the standard C library has several functions for string manipulation. Table 1.3 lists the most frequently used string-manipulation functions and a description of each. For a complete description of each of these functions and examples of their use, see the C++Builder online help.

Table 1.3. String-manipulation functions.

Function	Description
strcat()	Concatenates (adds) a string to the end of the target string.
strcmp()	Compares two strings for equality.
strcmpi()	Compares two strings for equality without case sensitivity.
strcpy()	Copies the contents of one string to the target string.
strstr()	Scans a string for the first occurrence of a substring.

Function	Description
strlen()	Returns the length of the string.
strupr()	Converts all characters in a string to uppercase.
sprintf()	Builds a string based on a variable number of parameters.

NOTE

The string operations discussed here are how strings are handled in C. Most C++ compilers provide a cstring class that simplifies the difficulties inherent in the C way of handling strings. (C++Builder's Visual Component Library contains a class called Strings that handles string operations. Check the C++Builder online help for more information on Strings.) Although the C way of handling strings is a little quirky, it is by no means obsolete. C++ programmers use C-style string operations on a daily basis as well as string classes such as cstring.

I won't go into examples of all of the string-manipulation functions listed in the table, but I'll touch on a couple of the more widely used ones. The strcpy() function is used to copy one string to another. The source string can be a variable or a string literal. Take the following code, for example:

```
// set up a string to hold 29 characters
char buff[30];
// copy a string literal to the buffer
strcpy(buff, "This is a test.");
// display it
cout << buff << endl;
// initialize a second string buffer
char buff2[] = "A second string.";\
// copy the contents of this string to the first buffer
strcpy(buff, buff2);
cout << buff << endl;
```

Accidentally overwriting the end of a character array is even easier to do than with the numeric arrays discussed earlier. For instance, imagine you had done the following:

```
char buff[10] = "A string";
// later....
strcpy(buff, "This is a test.");    // oops!
```

Here we set up a character array to hold 10 characters and initially assigned a string that requires 9 bytes (don't forget about the terminating null). Later on, possibly forgetting how large the array was, we copied a string to the buffer that requires 16 bytes, overwriting the array by 6 bytes. Six bytes of some memory location somewhere just got tromped on by our little faux pas. Be careful when copying data to character arrays.

Another frequently used string function is sprintf(). This function allows you to build a formatted string by mixing text and numbers together. Here is an example that adds two numbers and then uses sprintf() to build a string to report the result:

```
char buff[20];
int x = 10 * 20;
sprintf(buff, "The result is: %d", x);
cout << buff;
```

When this section of code executes, the program will display this:

```
The result is: 200
```

In this example, the %d tells the sprintf() function, "An integer value will go here." At the end of the format string the variable x is inserted to tell sprintf() what value to put at that location in the string (the contents of the variable x). sprintf() is a unique function in that it can take a variable number of arguments. You must supply the destination buffer and the format string, but the number of arguments that come after the format string is variable. Here is an example of sprintf() that uses three additional arguments:

```
int x = 20;
int y = 5;
sprintf(buff, "%d + %d = %d", x, y, x + y);
cout << buff;
```

When this piece of code executes, the result displayed on the screen will be this:

```
20 + 5 = 25
```

 NOTE

> The single slash is used in strings to indicate special characters. For example, '\n' is for a new line, and '\t' represents a tab character. To put an actual backslash character into a string, you must use a double backslash:
>
> ```
> strcpy(fileName, "c:\\windows\\system\\win.ini");
> ```
>
> Forgetting this simple fact has caused many programmers sleepless nights trying to find a bug in their program. This is a very common mistake to make. Don't say I didn't tell you!

sprintf() has a cousin called wsprintf() that is a Windows version of sprintf(). You might see either of these two functions used in Windows programs. wsprintf() is functionally the same as sprintf(), with one major difference: It does not allow you to put floating-point numbers in the formatted string. You can use either function in your C++Builder programs, but `sprintf()` is preferred because it has full floating-point support (and it's one less character to type!). To get a real appreciation of what `sprintf()` can do for you, consult the C++Builder online help.

Arrays of Strings

Not only can you have character arrays, but you can have an array of character arrays (effectively an array of strings). That might sound complicated, but you have already seen this type of array in the ARGSTEST program we looked at earlier. You can allocate this kind of array as follows:

```
char strings[][20] = {
"This is string 1",
"This is string 2",
"This is string 3",
"This is string 4"
  };
```

Although you can use this type of string array, there are easier ways to handle arrays of strings in C++Builder. (I'll save that discussion for after you've had a chance to learn more about C++Builder.)

NOTE

> If you are going to use arrays of strings extensively, you should look into the Standard Template Library (STL). STL provides C++ classes that allow you to store and manipulate arrays of strings much more easily than is possible using C-style character arrays. STL also includes a `string` class.

Summary

You've covered a lot of ground today. First you tinkered with the C++Builder IDE by creating a GUI Hello World program. Following that you were introduced to console mode applications where you created Hello World, Part II. After the initial playing around, you were put to work learning the basics of C as a foundation to learning C++. You have learned about the following C and C++ features:

- ☐ Variables
- ☐ Operators
- ☐ Data types

☐ Functions

☐ The main() function

☐ Arrays

☐ How strings are handled in C and C++

There is a lot of material to absorb in this chapter. Don't feel bad if it didn't all sink in. Go back and review if you are unclear about anything presented in this chapter.

Workshop

The Workshop contains quiz questions to help you solidify your understanding of the material covered and exercises to provide you with experience in using what you have learned. You can find answers to the quiz questions in Appendix A, "Answers to Quiz Questions."

Q&A

Q What's the difference between a Win32 GUI application and a Win32 console-mode application?

A A GUI application is a traditional Windows program. It usually has a title bar, menu, and window area. A console-mode application is a 32-bit application that runs in an MS-DOS box in Windows. The console application looks like a DOS program.

Q Do my functions have to take parameters and return values?

A Functions you write may take parameters and may return a value, but they are not required to do either. Once a function has been written to return a value, you must provide a return statement that returns a value or the compiler will issue a warning.

Q Can I assign a number containing decimal places to an integer data type variable?

A Yes, but the decimal fraction will be dropped (not rounded) and only the whole number portion will be assigned to the integer variable.

Q Will C++ make sure I don't overwrite memory somewhere if I accidentally write past the end of an array?

A No. One of the strengths of C++ is that it gives you the power to access memory directly. With that power comes responsibility. It's up to you, the programmer, to be sure that the memory you are accessing is memory that your program owns. If you accidentally overwrite memory that you are not supposed to have access to,

Windows will issue a general protection fault (GPF) or an access-violation error. The GPF might come immediately, or it may not come until later when the overwritten memory is used by another part of your program, by another program, or by Windows itself.

Quiz

1. What is wrong with this program?

```
#include <iostream.h>
#include <conio.h>
#pragma hdrstop

void displayText();
displayText()
{
cout << "Hello Bubba!" << endl;
}
```

2. How many return values can a function return?

3. What does the strcpy() function do?

4. What value does a variable have when it is initially declared?

5. How many functions can a program have?

6. Can a function call another function?

7. What is wrong with this program?

```
#include <iostream.h>
#include <conio.h>
#pragma hdrstop

int main(int argc, char** argv)
{
doSomething();
return 0;
}

void doSomething()
{
cout << "I'm doing something now" << endl;
}
```

8. How many functions called main() can a program have?

9. Look at this line of code:

```
char buff[20];
```

How many characters can this string hold?

10. What is the index number of the first element of an array, 0 or 1?

Exercises

1. Write a Windows GUI program that displays the words "Welcome to C++Builder!" on the window when the program runs.

2. Rewrite the program you wrote in exercise 1 and change the displayed text to Hello There! (**Hint:** You only have to change the Caption property of the Label component.)

3. Write a Windows console-mode application that outputs This is a test to the screen.

4. Write a Windows console-mode application. In the program, declare two variables and assign values to those variables. Multiply the two numbers together and display the result on the screen.

5. Write a console-mode application that calls a function to display Function entered, sir!! on the screen.

6. Write a console-mode application that takes an integer as a parameter, multiplies it by itself, and returns the result.

7. Enter and compile the following program:

```
#include <iostream.h>
#include <conio.h>
#include <math.h>
#include <stdio.h>
#pragma hdrstop

void getSqrRoot(char* buff, int x);
int main(int argc, char** argv)
{
int x;
char buff[30];
cout << "Enter a number: ";
cin >> x;
getSqrRoot(buff, x);
cout << buff;
getch();
}

void getSqrRoot(char* buff, int x)
{
sprintf(buff, "The sqaure root is: %f", sqrt(x));
}
```

What does the program do?

Day 2

Wading In Deeper

by Kent Reisdorph

You've now got a pretty good start on learning C++. In this chapter you will continue to learn about the C++ language by examining more of the fundamentals of C++ that have their roots in C. Today you will learn about

- ☐ The `if` and `else` keywords
- ☐ Loops: `for`, `do`, and `do-while`
- ☐ The `switch` statement
- ☐ Scope
- ☐ Structures

If...

There are some aspects of programming that are common to all programming languages. One such item that C++ has in common with other programming languages is the `if` statement. The `if` statement is used to test for a condition and then execute sections of code based on whether that condition is `true` or `false`. Here's an example:

```
int x;
cout << "Enter a number: ";
cin >> x;
if (x > 10)
  cout << "You entered a number greater than 10." << endl;
```

This code asks for input from the user. If the user enters a number greater than 10, the expression `x > 10` evaluates to `true` and the message is displayed; otherwise nothing is displayed. Note that if the conditional expression evaluates to `true`, the statement immediately following the `if` expression is executed.

 The `if` statement is used to test for a condition and then execute sections of code based on whether that condition is `true` or `false`.

 Be sure not to follow the `if` expression with a semicolon. A semicolon by itself represents a blank statement in code. If you accidentally follow your `if` expression with a semicolon, the compiler will interpret the blank statement as the statement to execute if the expression evaluates to `true`. Here's an example:

```
if (x == 10);          // Warning! Extra semi-colon!

  DoSomething(x);
```

In this case, the `DoSomething()` function will always be executed because the compiler does not see it as being the first statement following the `if` expression. Because this code is perfectly legal (albeit useless), the compiler will not warn you that anything is amiss.

If you have multiple lines of code that should be executed if the conditional expression is `true`, you would need braces to block those lines:

```
if (x > 10) {
  cout << "The number is greater than 10" << endl;
  DoSomethingWithNumber(x);
}
```

If the conditional expression evaluates to `false`, the code block associated with the `if` expression is ignored, and program execution continues with the first statement following the code block.

NOTE

C++ contains a lot of shortcuts. One of those shortcuts involves using just the variable name to test for `true`. Look at this code:

```
if (fileGood) ReadData();
```

This method is a shortcut for the longer form, which is illustrated with this line:

```
if (fileGood == true) ReadData();
```

This example uses a `bool` variable, but any data type will do. The expression evaluates to `true` as long as the variable contains any non-zero value. You can test for `false` by applying the logical NOT (`!`) operator to a variable name:

```
bool fileGood = OpenSomeFile();
if (!fileGood) ReportError();
```

Learning the C++ shortcuts will help you write code that contains a degree of elegance. Knowing the shortcuts also helps you understand C++ code that you read in examples and sample listings.

In some cases you want to perform an action if the conditional expression evaluates to `true` and perform some other action if the conditional expression evaluates to `false`. In this case you can implement the `else` statement:

```
if (x == 20) {
  DoSomething(x);
}
else {
  DoADifferentThing(x);
}
```

NEW TERM The `else` statement is used in conjunction with the `if` statement and identifies sections of code that are executed when the `if` statement fails (that is, evaluates to `false`).

In this example one of the two functions will be called, but not both.

WARNING

Note that the equality operator is the double equal sign (==) and that the assignment operator is the single equal sign (=). A common coding mistake is to use the assignment operator where you meant to use the equality operator. For instance, if the previous example were inadvertently written like this:

```
if (x = 20) {
    DoSomething(x);
}
```

x would be assigned the value of 20. Because this operation would be successful, the expression would evaluate to true. A bug like this, although seemingly obvious, can be hard to spot, so take care when testing for equality.

You can nest if statements if needed. Nesting is nothing more than following an if statement with one or more additional if statements. Here's an example:

```
if (x > 10)
  if (x < 20)
    cout << "X is between 10 and 20" << endl;
```

Keep in mind that these are simplified examples. In the real world you can get lost in the maze of braces that separate one function block from the next. Take a look at this code snippet, for instance:

```
if (x > 100) {
  y = 20;
  if (x > 200) {
    y = 40;
    if (x > 400) {
      y = 60;
      DoSomething(y);
    }
  }
}
else if (x < -100) {
  y = -20;
  if (x < -200) {
    y = -40;
    if (x < -400) {
      y = -60;
      DoSomething(y);
    }
  }
}
```

Even this is a fairly simple example, but you get the idea.

TIP

The C++Builder Code Editor has a handy function to help you find matching braces. Position the cursor on the brace for which you want to find the corresponding brace. Press either the Alt+[or the Alt+] key combination, and the cursor will be positioned at the brace you are looking for. It doesn't matter whether you start on the opening brace or the closing brace. In either case, the matching brace will be located.

2

TIP

If a section of code contains more than two or three consecutive `if` statements testing for different values of the same variable, it might be a candidate for a `switch` statement. The `switch` statement is discussed later in this chapter in the section "The `switch` Statement."

Earlier I mentioned C++ shortcuts. There is a shortcut for the `if-else` combination. Look at the following code:

```
if (direction == EAST) lost = true;
else (lost = false);
```

These two lines can be condensed into a single line:

```
direction == EAST ? lost = true : lost = false;
```

Although this shortcut notation might look a little odd at first, you will quickly learn to recognize it when you see it. The `if` statement is heavily used in C++. It's pretty straightforward, so you won't have any trouble with it. The main thing is keeping all of the braces straight.

The `if` statement, Form 1:

SYNTAX

```
if (cond_expr) {
    true_statements;
    }
else {
    false_statements;
    }
```

If the conditional expression, `cond_expr`, is true (nonzero), the block of code represented by `true_statements` is executed. If the optional `else` clause is specified, the block of code represented by `false_statements` is executed when the conditional expression, `cond_expr`, is false.

The if statement, Form 2:

```
if (cond_expr_1) {
    true_statements_1;
    }
else if (cond_expr_2) {
    true_statements_2;
    }
else {
    false_statements;
    }
```

If the conditional expression *cond_expr_1* is true (nonzero), the block of code represented by *true_statements_1* is executed. If it is false and the conditional expression *cond_expr_2* is true, the block of code represented by *true_statements_2* is executed. If both *cond_expr_1* and *cond_expr_2* are false, the block of code represented by *false_statements* is executed.

Thrown for a Loop

The loop is a common element in all programming languages. A loop can be used to iterate through an array, to perform an action a specific number of times, to read a file from disk…the possibilities are endless. I will examine several types of loops here, and for the most part they work in very similar ways. All loops have these common elements:

☐ A starting point

☐ A body, usually enclosed in braces, that contains the statements to execute on each pass

☐ An ending point

☐ A test for a condition that determines when the loop should end

☐ Optional use of the break and continue statements

NEW TERM   A *loop* is an element in a programming language that is used to perform an action a specific number of times.

The starting point for the loop is one of the C++ loop statements (for, while, or do) followed by an opening brace. The body contains the statements that will execute each time through the loop. The body can contain any valid C++ code. The ending point for the loop is the closing brace.

Most loops work something like this: The loop is entered and the test condition is evaluated. If the test condition is not met, the body of the loop is executed. When program execution reaches the bottom of the loop (usually the closing brace), it jumps back to the top of the loop, where the test condition is again evaluated. If the test condition is not met, the whole process is repeated. If the test condition is met, program execution jumps to the line of code immediately following the loop code block. The exception to this description is the do-while loop, which tests for the condition at the bottom of the loop rather than at the top.

The test condition tells the loop when to stop executing. In effect the test condition says, for example, "Keep doing this until x is equal to 10," or, "Keep reading the file until the end-of-file is reached." Once the loop starts it continues to execute the body of the loop until the test condition is met.

WARNING

It's easy to accidentally write a loop so that the test condition is never met. This will result in a program that is locked up or hung. Your only recourse at that point is to press Ctrl+Alt+Del and kill the task. The Windows Close Program box will come up and will display the name of your program with (Not Responding) next to it. You'll have to select your program from the list and click End Task to terminate the runaway program.

TIP

In C++Builder you typically run a program using the Run button on the Speed Bar or by pressing F9. If you need to kill a runaway program that was run from the IDE, you can choose Run | Reset Process from the main menu or press Ctrl+F2 on the keyboard.

Given that general overview, let's take a look at each type of loop individually.

The for Loop

The for loop is probably the most commonly used type of loop. It takes three parameters: the starting number, the test condition that determines when the loop stops, and the increment expression.

The for loop statement:

```
for (initial; cond_expr; adjust) {
    statements;
    }
```

The for loop repeatedly executes the block of code indicated by *statements* as long as the conditional expression, *cond_expr*, is true (nonzero). The state of the loop is initialized by the statement *initial*. After the execution of *statements*, the state is modified using the statement indicated by *adjust*.

That won't make much sense until you see some examples. First take a look at a typical `for` loop:

```
for (int i=0;i<10;i++) {
  cout << "This is iteration " << i << endl;
}
```

This code will result in the statement inside the braces being executed 10 times. The first parameter, `int i=0`, tells the `for` loop that it is starting with an initial value of `0`. (In this case I am declaring and assigning a variable inside the `for` statement. This is perfectly legal and is common in `for` loops.) The second parameter, `i<10`, tells the loop to keep running as long as the variable `i` is less than `10`. Because I'm starting with `0`, I need to stop *before* `i` is equal to `10`. The last parameter, `i++`, increments the variable `i` by one each time through the loop.

NOTE   The use of the variable name `i` (presumably for *iterator*) is traditional in `for` loops. Naturally, any variable name can be used, but you will often see `i` used in `for` loops.

Let's look at a variation of this code. The following code snippet will achieve exactly the opposite effect as the first example:

```
for (int i=10;i>0;i--) {
  cout << "This is iteration " << i << endl;
}
```

This time I'm starting with `10`, stopping when `i` is equal to `0`, and decrementing `i` by one on each pass. This is an example of a loop that counts backward.

NOTE   In the previous examples, the opening and closing braces are not strictly required. If no opening and closing braces are supplied, the statement immediately following the `for` statement is considered the body of the loop. It's not a bad idea to include the braces for clarity and readability even when they aren't strictly required.

Let's write a little program that illustrates the use of the `for` loop. You can enter, compile, and run the program found in Listing 2.1. It's called `FORLOOP.CPP`, and you can find it on the CD-ROM that accompanies this book. The output from `FORLOOP.CPP` is shown in Figure 2.1.

Listing 2.1. `FORLOOP.CPP.`

```
 1: #include <iostream.h>
 2: #include <conio.h>
 3: #pragma hdrstop
 4:
 5: int main(int argv, char** argc)
 6: {
 7:   cout << endl << "Starting program..." << endl << endl;
 8:   int i;
 9:   for (i=0;i<10;i++) {
10:     cout << "Iteration number " << i << endl;
11:   }
12:   cout << endl;
13:   for (i=10;i>0;i--) {
14:     cout << "Iteration number " << i << endl;
15:   }
16:   getch();
17:   return 0;
18: }
```

Figure 2.1.

The output from
FORLOOP.CPP.

By now you know that the loop starting number can be any value you like (assuming it fits the range of the data type selected, of course). The test condition can be any C++ expression that eventually evaluates to true. The test value could be a numeric constant as used in the examples here, it could be a variable, or it could be the return value of a function call. The following are examples of valid test conditions:

```
for (int i=0;i < 100;i++) {...}
for (int i=1;i == numberOfElements;i++) {...}
for (int i=0;i <= GetNumberOfElements();i+=2) {...}
```

Take a look at the last example. Notice the last parameter of the `for` statement. In this case I am incrementing the counter by 2 each time through the loop. The increment parameter can increment by any amount you want. For instance, this loop counts by 10s:

```
for (int i=0;i<100;i+=10) {...}
```

Now that you've seen the for loop in action, it won't be too difficult to apply the same concepts to the while and do-while loops. Let's take a look at those now.

The while Loop

The while loop differs from the for loop in that it contains only a test condition that is checked at the start of each iteration. As long as the test condition is true, the loop keeps running. Here's an example:

```
int x;
while (x < 1000) {
  x = DoSomeCalculation();
}
```

In this example I am calling a function that I assume will eventually return a value greater than 1,000. As long as the return value from this function is less than 1,000, the while loop continues to run. When the variable x contains a value greater than or equal to 1,000, the test condition yields false, and program execution jumps to the first line following the while loop's ending brace. A common implementation of a while loop uses a bool as a test variable. The state of the test variable can be set somewhere within the body of the loop:

```
bool done = false;
while (!done) {
  // some code here
  done = SomeFunctionReturningABool();
  // more code
}
```

At some point it is expected that the variable done will be false and the loop will terminate. The program in Listing 2.2 illustrates the use of the while loop.

Listing 2.2. WHILETST.CPP.

```
 1: #include <iostream.h>
 2: #include <conio.h>
 3: #pragma hdrstop
 4: int main(.int argv, char** argc)
 5: {
 6:   cout << endl << "Starting program..." << endl << endl;
 7:   int i = 6;
 8:   while (i-- > 0) {
 9:     cout << endl << "Today I have " << i;
10:     cout << " problems to worry about.";
11:   }
12:   cout << "\b!\nYipee!";
13:   cout << endl << endl << "Press any key to continue...";
14:   getch();
15:   return 0;
16: }
```

SYNTAX

The `while` loop statement:

```
while (cond_expr) {
    statements;
    }
```

The `while` loop repeatedly executes the block of code indicated by `statements` as long as the conditional expression, `cond_expr`, is `true` (nonzero). The state of the loop must be initialized prior to the `while` statement, and modification of the state must be explicit in the block of code. When the conditional expression, `cond_expr`, evaluates to `false` the loop terminates.

The `do-while` Loop

The `do-while` loop is nearly identical to the `while` loop. The distinction between the two is important, though. As you can see from Listing 2.2, the `while` loop checks the conditional expression at the top of the loop. In the case of the `do-while` loop, the conditional expression is checked at the bottom of the loop:

```
bool done = false;
do {
  // some code
  done = SomeFunctionReturningABool();
  // more code
} while (!done)
```

Whether you use a `while` or a `do-while` loop depends on what the loop itself does.

SYNTAX

The `do-while` loop statement:

```
do {
    statements;
    } while (cond_expr)
```

The `do` loop repeatedly executes the block of code indicated by `statements` as long as the conditional expression, `cond_expr`, is `true` (nonzero). The state of the loop must be initialized prior to the `do` statement, and modification of the state must be explicit in the block of code. When the conditional expression, `cond_expr`, evaluates to `false`, the loop terminates.

goto

I'll mention `goto` just so you know it exists. The `goto` statement allows you to jump program execution to a label that you have previously declared by using a term followed by a colon. The following code snippet illustrates this:

```
bool done = false;
startPoint:
// do some stuff
if (!done) goto(startPoint);
// loop over, moving on...
```

It is not necessary to use braces here because all lines of code between the goto statement and the label will be executed.

NOTE

> The goto statement is considered bad form in a C++ program. Just about anything you can accomplish with goto you can accomplish with a while or do-while loop. Very few self-respecting C++ programmers have goto in their code. If you are moving to C++ from another language that uses goto statements, you will find that the basic structure of C++ makes the goto statement unnecessary.

SYNTAX

The goto statement:

```
goto label
  .
  .
  .
label:
```

The goto statement unconditionally transfers the program execution sequence to the label represented by label.

continue **and** break

Before we leave this discussion of loops, you need to know about two keywords that help control program execution in a loop. The continue statement is used to force program execution back to the top of the loop. For example, you might have part of a loop that you don't want to execute if a particular test returns true. In that case you would use continue to jump back to the start of the loop and avoid execution of any code below the continue statement:

```
bool done = false;
while (!done) {
  // some code
  bool error = SomeFunction();
  if (error) continue;  // jumps to the top of the loop
  // other code that will execute only if no error occured
}
```

The break statement is used to halt execution of a loop prior to the loop's normal test condition being met. For example, you might be searching an array of ints for a particular number. By breaking execution of your search loop when the number is found, you can obtain the array index where the number is located:

```
int index = 0;
int searchNumber = 50;
```

```
for (int i=0;i<numElements;i++) {
  if (myArray[i] == searchNumber) {
    index = i;
    break;
  }
}
if (index)
  cout << "Number found at index " << index << endl;
else
  cout << "Number not found in array." << endl;
```

There are many situations in which the continue and break statements are useful. As with most of what I've been talking about, it will take some experience programming in C++ before you discover all the possible uses for continue and break.

The switch Statement

The switch statement could be considered a glorified if statement. It allows you to execute one of several code blocks based on the result of an expression. The expression might be a variable, the result of a function call, or any valid C++ expression that evaluates to an expression. Here is an example of a switch statement:

```
switch(amountOverSpeedLimit) {
  case 0  : {
    fine = 0;
    break;
  }
  case 10 : {
    fine = 20;
    break;
  }
  case 15 : {
    fine = 50;
    break;
  }
  case 20 :
  case 25 :
  case 30 : {
    fine = amountOverSpeedLimit * 10;
    break;
  }
  default : {
    fine = GoToCourt();
    jailTime = GetSentence();
  }
}
```

Several parts make up a switch statement. First, you can see that there is the expression, which in this example is the variable amountOverSpeedLimit (remember, I warned you about long variable names!). Next, the case statements test the expression for equality. If amountOverSpeedLimit equals 0 (case 0 :), the value 0 is assigned to the variable fine. If amountOverSpeedLimit is equal to 10, a value of 20 is assigned to fine, and so on. In each of the first three cases you see a break statement. The break statement is used to jump out of the switch block—it means that a case matching the expression has been found, and the rest of the switch statement can be ignored. Finally, you see the default statement. The code block following the default statement will be executed if no matching cases are found.

Notice that cases 20 and 25 have no statements following them. If the expression amountOverSpeedLimit evaluates to 20 or 25, those cases fall through and the next code block encountered will be executed. In this situation, the values 20, 25, or 30 will all result in the same code being executed.

WARNING

Don't forget your break statements! Without break statements the switch will continue on even after finding a match and may execute code you didn't intend to be executed. Sometimes that is how you want your switch to perform, but most of the time it is not.

Inclusion of the default statement is not mandatory. You could write a switch without a default statement:

```
switch (x) {
  case 10 : DoSomething(); break;
  case 20 : DoAnotherThing(); break;
  case 30 : TakeABreak();
}
```

Note that there is no break statement following the last case statement. Because this is the last line of the switch, there is no point in including the break statement for this line.

As I said earlier, you might want to use a switch if you find that you have several if statements back-to-back. The switch is a bit clearer to others reading your program.

SYNTAX

The switch statement:

```
switch (expr) {
    case value_1:
        statements_1;
        break;
    case value_2:
        statements_2;
        break;
    .
    .
    .
    case value_n:
        statements_n;
        break;
```

2

```
default:
    dflt_statements;
    break;
}
```

The switch statement offers a way to execute different blocks of code depending on various values of an expression (*expr*). The block of code represented by *statements_1* is executed when *expr* is equal to *value_1*, the block of code represented by *statements_2* when *expr* is equal to *value_2*, and so on through the block of code represented by *statements_n* when *expr* is equal to *value_n*. When *expr* is not equal to any of *value_1* through *value_n*, the block of code at *dflt_statements* is executed. The break statements are optional.

Learning About Scope

The term *scope* refers to the visibility of variables within different parts of your program. Most variables have *local scope*. This means that the variable is visible only within the code block in which it is declared. Take a look at the program in Listing 2.3.

NEW TERM The term *scope* refers to the visibility of variables in different parts of your program.

Listing 2.3. SCOPE.CPP.

```
1: #include <iostream.h>
2: #include <conio.h>
3: #pragma hdrstop
4: int x = 20;
5: void CountLoops(int);
6: int main(int, char**)
7: {
8:   int x = 40;
9:   int i = 0;
10:   cout << "In main program x = " << x << endl;
11:   bool done = false;
12:   while (!done) {
13:     int x;
14:     cout << endl << "Enter a number (-1 to exit): ";
15:     cin >> x;
16:     if (x != -1) {
17:       cout << endl << "In while loop x = " << x;
18:       CountLoops(++i);
19:     }
20:     else
21:       done = true;
22:   }
23:   cout << "Global x = " << ::x << endl;
24:   cout << endl << "Press any key to continue...";
25:   getch();
```

continues

Listing 2.3. continued

```
26:    return 0;
27: }
28: void CountLoops(int x)
29: {
30:   cout << ", While loop has executed "
31:      << x << " times" << endl;
32: }
```

The first thing you might notice (if you're still awake by this time) is that the variable x is declared four times. It is declared on line 4 outside the main() function, on line 8 inside the main() function, on line 13 inside the while loop, and in the CountLoops() function on line 28. If you accidentally declare a variable more than once, the compiler spits out an error that says Multiple declaration for 'x' and the compile stops. Yet this program compiles and runs just fine. Why? Because each of the x variables in Listing 2.3 is in a different scope.

Take a closer look at Listing 2.3. The declaration for x on line 13 is inside the body of the while loop and is local to that block of code. Effectively, it does not exist outside that block. This variable has local scope. Likewise, the declaration for x on line 28 is local to the CountLoops() function and does not exist outside the function. In this case the declaration for x is less obvious because it's part of the function's parameter list, but it's a variable declaration nonetheless.

Now look at the variables x and i declared inside the main() function. These variables are local to the code block in which they are declared, *plus* they are available (in scope) in any code blocks within the code block in which they are declared. In other words, the x and i variables are in scope both in the main() function *and* inside the while loop. That's easy enough to figure out in the case of i because there is only one variable named i. But what about x? Once inside the while loop, there are two variables named x (the one declared in main() and the one declared in the while loop), and both are in scope. Which one is being used? The one within the while loop, because it has the most immediate scope.

 NOTE

> A recent C++ draft rule change affects the visibility of a variable that is declared inside a statement like a for statement. (The C++ draft is a document that the C++ standards committee issues. It defines the rules for the C++ language.) For example, the following code will generate a compiler error:
>
> ```
> for (int i=0;i<10;i++) {
>   if (array[i] == 40) break;
> }
> index = i;
> ```

This code generates a compiler error because the variable i is visible only inside the for loop code block. In order to get this code to compile, you would have to declare i outside the for statement:

```
int i;
for (i=0;i<10;i++) {
  if (array[i] == 40) break;
}
index = i;
```

Although this change won't affect you if you are just learning C++, it threw many old C++ programmers for a loop when it was first announced. In the end, it doesn't really matter which form is the standard as long as we programmers know what the rules are.

Finally, we get to the declaration of the x that falls outside the main() function (line 4). Because this variable is declared outside any function, it is called a *global variable* and is said to have *global scope*. What this means is that the global variable x is available anywhere in the program: inside the main() function, inside the while block, and inside the CountLoops() function.

As mentioned earlier, a local variable will have precedence over a global variable. But what if you want to access the global variable x from inside the main() function? You use the *scope-resolution operator*, ::. Line 23 of Listing 2.3 contains this line:

```
cout << "Global x = " << ::x << endl;
```

The scope-resolution operator tells the compiler, "Give me the global variable x and not the local variable x." (The scope-resolution operator is also used with classes, but I'll get to that when I talk about classes later.)

extern **Variables**

A real-world application usually has several source files containing the program's code. (The terms *module, source file,* and *unit* can be used interchangeably. I'll talk about programs using multiple source files in just a bit.) A global variable declared in one source file is global to that file but is not visible in any other modules. There are times, however, when you need to make a variable visible to all modules in your program. Doing this is a two-step process. First, declare the variable in one source file as you would any global variable. Then, in any other source file that needs to access the global variable, you declare the variable again, this time with the extern keyword:

```
extern int countChickens;
```

The extern keyword tells the compiler, "I'm going to be using a variable in this source file that you will find declared in another source file." The compiler sorts it all out at compile time and makes sure you get access to the correct variable.

While global variables are convenient, they aren't particularly OOP friendly. Usually there are better solutions (which you will learn about when I discuss classes). In addition, global variables consume memory for the life of the program. Local variables use up memory only while they are in scope. Use local variables whenever possible, and keep the use of global variables to a minimum.

Structures

A *structure* is a collection of related data rolled up into a single storage unit. For instance, let's say you wanted to keep a mailing list. It would be convenient to be able to have a single data variable that could be used to hold all the fields needed in a typical mailing list. A structure will allow you to do that. You first declare a structure and then later create an *instance* of that structure when you want to put the structure to use. A structure is declared with the struct keyword:

```
struct mailingListRecord {
  char firstName[20];
  char lastName[20];
  char address[50];
  char city[20];
  char state[4];
  int zip;
  bool aFriend;
  bool aFoe;
};
```

Each of the elements of a structure is called a *data member*. You will notice that each of the data members must be declared just as it would be if it were a variable in a code block. In this example I have five char arrays, one int, and two bool data members. (My apologies to my friends around the world if this looks like a U.S.-slanted mailing-list record.) Finally, make note of the semicolon following the closing brace of the structure declaration. This is a requirement for structure and class declarations.

 A *structure* is a collection of related data identified as a single storage unit. After a structure has been declared, an *instance* of that structure can be created for use. Each of the elements of a structure is called a *data member*.

NOTE You can create instances of a structure when you declare the structure. At the end of the structure declaration, insert a variable name (one or more) between the closing brace and the semicolon that follows the structure declaration. Here's an example:

```
struct point {
    int x;
    int y;
} upperLeft, lowerRight;
```

This code declares the structure and creates two instances of the structure with variable names upperLeft and lowerRight.

Now that I have the structure declared, I need to put it to use. I first need to create an instance of the structure. Here's how that looks:

```
mailingListRecord record;
```

This statement allocates memory for the structure (120 bytes, give or take) and assigns that memory to a variable named record. Now that I have an instance of the structure set up, I can assign values to the data members:

```
strcpy(record.firstName, "Bruce");
strcpy(record.lastName, "Reisdorph");
strcpy(record.address, "123 Inspiration Pt.");
strcpy(record.city, "Merced");
strcpy(record.state, "CA");
record.zip = 95031;
record.aFriend = true;
record.aFoe = false;
```

There is something you haven't seen yet in this code. In order to access the data members of a structure, you need to employ the *structure member operator*, which is a period placed between the variable name and the data member. (If you forget to add the structure member operator, you will probably have the compiler whining about undefined symbols.) The structure member operator allows you to access a particular member of the structure—either to read the value of the data member or to change the value of the data member.

If you want to, you can instantiate an object and supply its members all at one time:

```
mailingListRecord rec = {
    "Bruce",
    "Reisdorph",
    "123 Inspiration Pt.",
    "Merced",
    "CA",
    95031,
    true,
    false
};
```

This saves you some typing over the first method I showed you, but is not always practical in real-world situations. In a real-world program a structure would likely be filled out as a result of user input or possibly with data read from a file. Assigning data to the structure like you see here is not practical in those situations.

The struct statement:

```
struct name {
    data_member_1;
    data_member_2;
    .
    .
    .
    data_member_n;
    } instance;
```

The struct statement declares a grouping of data members (*data_member_1*, *data_member_2*, ..., *data_member_n*) and provides a name for this grouping (*name*). The optional *instance* statement creates an occurrence of this grouping.

Arrays of Structures

Just as you can have arrays of ints, chars, or longs, you can also have arrays of structures. Declaring and using an array of structures is not terribly complicated:

```
mailingListRecord listArray[5];
strcpy(listArray[0].firstName, "Chuck");
listArray[4].aFoe = true;  // grrrrr!!
// etc.
```

This is only slightly more complicated than using an array of one of the integral data types. You will notice that the subscript operator and the structure member operator are used back-to-back.

Headers and Source Files

The *source file* is an ASCII text file that contains the program's source code. The compiler takes the source code file, parses it, and produces machine language that the computer can execute.

One of the problems with books on programming is that they use simple examples to communicate concepts and ideas. You will undoubtedly find that things are never that simple. So far, we have been dealing with very short programs contained in a single source file. In the real world, a program of any consequence will have several source files. A program's code is divided into different source files for a number of reasons. One of the primary reasons is organization. By keeping related chunks of code together, you can more easily find a certain section of code when needed.

So how do the source files all get tied together? First, the compiler compiles each source file (.cpp) into an object file (.obj). After each module has been compiled, the linker links all the object files together to make a single executable file (the .exe). The linker also may link in other needed files such as resource files (.res) and library files (.lib).

 NEW TERM The declarations for classes and structures are often kept in a separate file called a *header file*. Headers have a filename extension of .h or .hpp. (I touched on headers briefly when I discussed the iostream class in Day 1, "Getting Your Feet Wet.") A header file should contain only class, structure, and function declarations. You should never put any code statements in a header.

2

> **NOTE**
>
> There is an exception to the rule that no code should be placed in headers. You may put *inline functions* in headers. An inline function is a special function in terms of the way the compiler generates code for the function. You'll learn more about inline functions on Day 4, "Totally Immersed: C++ Classes and Object-Oriented Programming," when I discuss classes.

Once you have created a header file for a class or structure, you can include that header in any source code module that needs to see the class or structure declaration. To do that you use the #include directive:

```
#include "structur.h"
```

When you use the #include directive, it is as if the contents of the file being included were pasted into the source file at that point. Listing 2.4, in the next section, contains a program that uses the #include directive. The header file used in Listing 2.4 is contained in Listing 2.5.

> **TIP**
>
> Header files typically implement a *sentry* to ensure that the header is included only once for a program. A sentry essentially tells the compiler, "I've already been included once, so don't include me again." A sentry looks like this:
>
> ```
> #ifndef _MYCLASS_H
> #define _MYCLASS_H
> class MyClass {
>   // class declared here
> };
> #endif
> ```

C++Builder automatically adds sentries to units that you create as a result of creating new forms or components. You should add sentries to any headers you create for classes used outside the C++Builder VCL framework.

A header file can contain more than one class or structure declaration. Using a separate header for each class or structure helps keep your project organized and makes it easier to reuse classes and structures in other programs. Sometimes you will group related classes together in one header. For instance, you may have a class that implements a helper class to carry out its duties. In that case, both the main class and the helper class would be declared in the same header. Ultimately, it's up to you how you organize your headers.

Don't be too concerned if this is all a little fuzzy right now. It will probably take some experience writing real programs for all this to come together for you.

An Example Using Structures

Listing 2.4 contains a program that has the user input three names and addresses and stores those records in an array of structures. After the names are input, they are displayed on the screen. The user is asked to choose one of the records. When the user chooses one of the records, it is displayed on the screen. Listing 2.5 contains the header file for the mailingListRecord structure used in the MAILLIST program shown in Listing 2.4.

Listing 2.4. MAILLIST.CPP.

```
 1: #include <iostream.h>
 2: #include <conio.h>
 3: #include <stdlib.h>
 4: #pragma hdrstop
 5: #include "structur.h"
 6: void displayRecord(int, mailingListRecord mlRec);
 7: int main(int, char**)
 8: {
 9:   //
10:   // create an array of mailingListRecord structures
11:   //
12:   mailingListRecord listArray[3];
13:   cout << endl;
14:   int index = 0;
15:   // get three records
16:   //
17:   do {
18:     cout << "First Name: ";
19:     cin.getline(listArray[index].firstName,
```

```
20:         sizeof(listArray[index].firstName) - 1);
21:      cout << "Last Name: ";
22:      cin.getline(listArray[index].lastName,
23:         sizeof(listArray[index].lastName) - 1);
24:      cout << "Address: ";
25:      cin.getline(listArray[index].address,
26:         sizeof(listArray[index].address) - 1);
27:      oout << "City: ";
28:      oin.getline(listArray[index].city,
29:         sizeof(listArray[index].city) - 1);
30:      cout << "State: ";
31:      cin.getline(listArray[index].state,
32:         sizeof(listArray[index].state) - 1);
33:      char buff[10];
34:      cout << "Zip: ";
35:      cin.getline(buff, sizeof(buff) - 1);
36:      listArray[index].zip = atoi(buff);
37:      index++;
38:      cout << endl;
39:   }
40:   while (index <`3);
41:   //
42:   // clear the screen
43:   //
44:   clrscr();
45:   //
46:   // display the three records
47:   //
48:   for (int i=0;i<3;i++) {
49:      displayRecord(i, listArray[i]);
50:   }
51:   //
52:   // ask the user to choose a record
53:   //
54:   cout << "Choose a record: ";
55:   char rec;
56:   //
57:   // be sure only 1, 2, or 3 was selected
58:   //
59:   do {
60:     rec = getch();
61:     rec -= 49;
62:   } while (rec < 0 || rec > 2);
63:   //
64:   // assign the selected record to a temporary variable
65:   //
66:   mailingListRecord temp = listArray[rec];
67:   clrscr();
68:   cout << endl;
69:   //
70:   // display the selected record
71:   //
72:   displayRecord(rec, temp);
73:   getch();
74:   return 0;
```

continues

Listing 2.4. continued

```
75: }
76: void displayRecord(int num, mailingListRecord mlRec)
77: {
78:   cout << "Record " << num + 1 << ":" << endl;
79:   cout << "Name:    " << mlRec.firstName << " ";
80:   cout << mlRec.lastName;
81:   cout << endl;
82:   cout << "Address: " << mlRec.address;
83:   cout << endl << "         ";
84:   cout << mlRec.city << ", ";
85:   cout << mlRec.state << "   ";
86:   cout << mlRec.zip;
87:   cout << endl << endl;
88: }
```

Listing 2.5. STRUCTUR.H.

```
 1: #ifndef _STRUCTUR_H
 2: #define _STRUCTUR.H
 3: struct mailingListRecord {
 4:   char firstName[20];
 5:   char lastName[20];
 6:   char address[50];
 7:   char city[20];
 8:   char state[5];
 9:   int zip;
10: };
11: #endif
```

There are a couple new things presented in this program and some variations on material we've already covered.

First, this program uses the getline() function of the cin class to get input from the user (on line 19, for instance). I did this because the cin extraction operator, >>, is not very friendly when it comes to whitespace. The second parameter of getline() is used to limit the number of characters that will be placed in the buffer (in this case the buffer is a data member of the mailingListRecord structure). I supply a value here because I don't want to overwrite the end of the arrays in the structure. The sizeof() operator is used to determine the size of the destination buffer so we know how many characters we can safely store in the buffer.

The atoi() function on line 36 is also new to you. This function takes a character string and converts it to an integer value. This is necessary to convert the text in the zip code field (which I got from the user as a string) to an integer value that can be stored in the zip data member of the mailingListRecord structure.

The displayRecord() function, which begins on line 76, takes two parameters. The first parameter, num, is an int that contains the index number of the record to display. This variable is used only to display the record number. On line 78 I add 1 to num when I display it because users are accustomed to lists beginning with 1 rather than with 0. (I aim to please!) The second parameter of the displayRecord() function is an instance of the mailingListRecord structure. Inside the displayRecord() function I use the local instance of the structure passed in (which represents a copy of the structure) to display the contents of the structure.

NOTE

> In this case I am passing the mailingListRecord structure *by value.* What this means is that a copy of the structure is created each time the displayRecord() function is called. This is not very efficient because of the overhead required to pass a structure by value. The overhead comes in the form of the extra time and memory required to make a copy of the structure each time the function is called. It would be better to pass the structure *by reference*, but I haven't talked about that yet, because the structure is passed by value in this program. You will learn about passing by reference tomorrow when we discuss functions in C++.

Note that the displayRecord() function is called from both the for loop when all the records are displayed (line 49) and again from the main body of the program to display the actual record chosen (line 72). That's precisely why the code to display a record has been placed in a function. By putting it in a function, I only have to write the code once and can avoid duplicating the code unnecessarily.

TIP

> Any time you find yourself repeating code more than a couple times in your programs, think about moving that code to a function. Then you can call the function when you need that code executed.

There is another segment of this program that deserves mention. Look at this do-while loop, which begins on line 59:

```
do {
  rec = getch();
  rec -= 49;
} while (rec < 0 || rec > 2);
```

This code first gets a character from the keyboard using the getch() function. As you have seen, I have been using getch() at the end of my programs to keep the program from closing prematurely, but have been ignoring the return value. The getch() function returns the ASCII value of the key pressed. Because the ASCII value of the 1 key is 49, I want to subtract 49 from the value of the key pressed to obtain the equivalent index number for that record in the records array. If the user presses 1, an ASCII 49 is returned, and 49–49 is 0, which is the first index of the array. If the user presses 2, the calculation yields 1 (50–49), and so on. The do-while loop ensures that the user presses a key between 1 and 3. If a key other than 1, 2, or 3 is pressed, the loop continues to fetch keystrokes until a valid key is pressed.

Finally, I want to point out line 66 in Listing 2.4:

```
mailingListRecord temp = listArray[rec];
```

This code is not necessary in this program, but I included it to illustrate a point. This code creates an instance of the mailingListRecord structure and assigns to it the contents of one of the structures in the array. A simple assignment is possible here because the compiler knows how to copy one structure to another. It does a simple member-to-member copy and copies all structure members to the newly created instance of the structure.

NOTE

Our discussion of structures up to this point describes how a structure works in C. In C++ a structure operates like it does in C, but C++ extends structures to allow them to contain functions as well as data members. In fact, a structure in C++ is essentially a class where all data members and functions have public access. That won't make sense until later on when I discuss classes on Day 4, but you can file this tidbit away for future reference.

Now you know about structures. Chances are you won't use a lot of structures in your programs. This section is important, though, because it serves as sort of a primer for discussing classes in Day 3, "Up to Your Neck in C++."

Summary

This chapter contains essential information on some of C++'s basic operations. You need what is presented here in order to program in C++Builder. First you learned about the different types of loops in C++; then you learned about the switch statement and how to use it. I talked a little about scope and what that means to your variables. Then you found out what structures are and how they can be used in your programs. Tomorrow we'll tackle some of the big stuff.

Workshop

The Workshop contains quiz questions to help you solidify your understanding of the material covered and exercises to provide you with experience in using what you have learned. You can find answers to the quiz questions in Appendix A, "Answers to Quiz Questions."

Q&A

Q How many levels deep can I nest if statements?

A There's no limit. There is, however, a practical limit. If you have too many nested if statements it gets very hard to keep all those brackets straight!

Q Will loops automatically terminate if something goes wrong?

A No. If you accidentally write an endless loop, that loop will continue to run until you do something to stop it. You can stop a program stuck in an endless loop by bringing up the Windows Task Manager (or the Close Program box) and ending the errant task. If you executed the program via the C++Builder IDE, you can choose Run | Reset Program from the main menu to kill the program.

Q Does a switch statement have to include a default section?

A No. The default section is optional.

Q Can I have more than one variable with the same name?

A Yes, provided they are in different scopes. You cannot have two variables named x that are both declared within a code block. You can, however, have a global variable named x and a local variable with the same name.

Q Can I use a structure by itself, without an object?

A No. Before you can use a structure you have to create an instance of the structure and access the structure through the instance variable.

Quiz

1. What statements are executed in the event that an if expression evaluates to true?
2. What do the three parameters of a for statement represent?
3. Besides syntax, what is the difference between a while loop and a do-while loop?
4. What do the break and continue statements do?
5. What is a global variable?
6. Can a structure contain a mixture of data types (char, int, long, and so on)?

7. How do you access the members of a structure?

8. Is it legal to have arrays of structures?

Exercises

1. Write a program that counts from 200 to 300 by 5s and displays the results.

2. Write a program that asks the user to input the day of the week and then displays the name of the day using a `switch` statement.

3. See if you can figure out what the \b and \n do in this line from Listing 2.2:

   ```
   cout << "\b!\nYipee!";
   ```

   (**Hint:** Check the C++ Programmer's Guide Help file for the section about escape sequences.)

4. Write a structure containing data members representing employee information. Include first name, last name, address, hire date, and a data member indicating whether the employee is in the company's insurance plan.

Day **3**

Up to Your Neck in C++

by Kent Reisdorph

"Don't worry, I've got you." Do you remember hearing those words when you were learning to ride a bike? The C++ language is often unforgiving. With the information in this chapter, you will be branching out into the concepts of C++ that most people trip over. Although I can't promise to be there to pick you up if you fall, I can at least point out some of the bumps in the road you might encounter. Today you will learn about

- ☐ Pointers
- ☐ References
- ☐ The `new` and `delete` operators
- ☐ Functions in C++

Pointers: Welcome to My Nightmare

Pointers are one of the most confusing aspects of the C++ language. They are also one of the most powerful features of C++. My goal in this section is not to teach you the textbook definition of pointers, but rather to teach you pointers in the context of how you will use them in your C++Builder programs. So what is a pointer? It's a variable that holds the address of another variable. There, that wasn't so bad, was it? I wish it were that simple! Because a pointer holds the address of another variable, it is said to "point to" the second variable. This is called *indirection* because the pointer does not have a direct association with the actual data, but rather an indirect association.

NEW TERM   A *pointer* is a variable that holds the address of another variable.

NEW TERM   Because the pointer does not have a direct association with the actual data, *indirection* is the term used when referring to this indirect association.

Let's look at an example. Earlier we talked about arrays. Let's say that you had an array of `int`s. You could access the individual elements of the array using the subscript operator, as I talked about on Day 1, "Getting Your Feet Wet":

```
int array[] = { 5, 10, 15, 20, 25 };
int someVariable = array[3];    // the value 20
```

You could also use a pointer to accomplish the same thing:

```
int array[] = { 5, 10, 15, 20, 25 };
int* ptr = array;
int someVariable = ptr[3];
```

In this example, the memory location of the beginning of the array is assigned to the pointer named `ptr`. Note that the pointer is a pointer of the data type `int` and that the *indirection operator* (the * symbol) is used when you declare a pointer. You can declare a pointer to any of the integral data types (`int`, `char`, `long`, `short`, and so on), as well as a pointer to objects (structures or classes). After the assignment the pointer contains the memory address of the start of the array, and as such points to the array.

NOTE   The name of an array variable, when used without the subscript operator, returns the memory address of the first element of the array. Put another way, the variable name of an array is a pointer, to the start of the array. That makes it possible to assign an array to a pointer, as in the preceding example.

3

In this case you can now use the pointer, ptr, just as you would the array name itself. I can hear you wondering, though: "But why would you want to?" The truth is that in this example there is no real benefit to using a pointer. The real benefit of pointers is when it comes to creating objects dynamically in memory. In that case, a pointer is necessary to access the object. I really can't go on with this discussion, though, until I digress a moment and talk about the two ways you can create variables and objects.

Local Versus Dynamic Memory Usage

So far all my sample programs have used local allocation of objects—that is, the memory required for a variable or object is obtained from the program's stack.

NEW TERM   *Local allocation* means that the memory required for a variable or object is obtained from the program's stack.

NEW TERM   The *stack* is an area of working memory set aside by the program when the program starts.

Any memory the program needs for things such as local variables, function calls, and so on is taken from the stack. This memory is allocated as needed and then freed when it is no longer needed. Usually this happens when the program enters a function or other local code block. Memory for any local variables the function uses is allocated when the function is entered. When the function returns, all of the memory allocated for the function's use is freed. It all happens for you automatically; you don't have to give any thought to how or if the memory is freed.

Local allocation has its good points and its bad points. On the plus side, memory can be allocated from the stack very quickly. The downside is that the stack is of a fixed size and cannot be changed as the program runs. If your program runs out of stack space, weird things start to happen. Your program might just crash, it might start behaving oddly, or it might seem to perform normally but crash when the program terminates. This is less of a problem in the 32-bit world than it is in 16-bit programming, but it's still a consideration.

For things like variables of the built-in data types and small arrays, there is no point in doing anything other than local allocation. But if you are going to be using large arrays, structures, or classes, you will probably want to use dynamic allocation from the heap. This amounts to your free physical RAM plus all of your free hard disk space. In other words, you could easily have 100MB of heap memory available on a typical Windows system. The good news here is that you have virtually unlimited memory available for your programs. The bad news is that memory allocated dynamically requires some additional overhead, and as such is just a smidgen slower than memory allocated from the stack. In most programs the extra overhead is not noticed in the least. An additional drawback of dynamic allocation is that it requires more from the programmer. Not a lot more, mind you, but a little.

Dynamic allocation means that memory required for an object is allocated from the heap.

 The *heap* in a Windows program refers to all of your computer's virtual memory.

Dynamic Allocation and Pointers

NEW TERM In a C++ program, memory is allocated dynamically by using the new operator.

I'm going to talk about new a little later in the chapter, but you need a little sampler as I continue the discussion about pointers. Earlier I talked about structures and used the mailingListRecord structure as an example. Allocating a structure from the stack looks like this:

```
mailingListRecord listArray;
strcpy(listArray.firstName, "Ian");
strcpy(listArray.lastName, "Spencer");
// etc.
```

That's what I did earlier when I talked about structures. Now I'll create the array dynamically rather than locally:

```
mailingListRecord* listArray;
listArray = new mailingListRecord;
strcpy(listArray->firstName, "Ian");
strcpy(listArray->lastName, "Spencer");
// etc.
```

The first line declares a pointer to a mailingListRecord structure. The next line initializes the pointer by creating a new instance of a mailingListRecord structure dynamically. This is the process by which you dynamically create and access objects in C++.

And Now Back to Our Program

Now you begin to see where pointers fit into the scheme of things. When you create an object dynamically, the new operator returns a pointer to the object in memory. You need that pointer to be able to do anything with the object. Figure 3.1 illustrates how the pointer points to the object in memory. Note that although the memory for the dynamically created object is allocated from heap memory, the actual pointer is a local variable and is allocated from the stack.

Figure 3.1.

A pointer to an object in memory.

mailingListRecord
structure in memory

mailingListRecord*
listArray

listArray points to
address 0x00780E50,
which is an instance
of the mailingListRecord
structure in memory

Let's go back to a code snippet you saw earlier:

```
mailingListRecord* listArray;
listArray = new mailingListRecord;
strcpy(listArray->firstName, "Ian");
strcpy(listArray->lastName, "Spencer");
// etc.
```

On the third line you see that the firstName data member of the structure is accessed using the *indirect member* operator (->) rather than the structure member operator. (We discussed the structure member operator yesterday in the section titled "Structures." The term *direct member operator* is also used and is more representative than structure member operator, so I will use direct member operator from now on.) When you create an object dynamically, you must access the object's data members and functions using this operator.

Creating an array of structures dynamically requires a bit more work. Again, here's the stack-based version:

```
mailingListRecord listArray[3];
listArray[0].zip = 57441;
```

And the dynamic version:

```
mailingListRecord* listArray[3];
for (int i=0;i<3;i++)
  listArray[i] = new mailingListrecord;
listArray[0]->zip = 57441;
```

Note that I have to create a new instance of the structure for each element of the array. Notice also that to access a data member of the array, I use the indirect membership operator combined with the subscript operator.

Uninitialized pointers contain random values just like any other uninitialized variable. Attempting to use an uninitialized pointer can wreak havoc on a program. In many cases, a pointer is declared and immediately initialized:

```
MyArray* array = new MyArray;
```

Sometimes, however, you will declare a pointer and then not initialize it until sometime later in the program. If you attempt to use the pointer before initializing it, the pointer will point to some random memory location, and modifying that memory could cause all sorts of nasty problems. Often the problems caused by modifying unknown memory do not show up immediately, making the bug appear to be random. To be safe, you should initialize a pointer to 0 when you declare it:

```
MyArray* array = 0;
```

If you attempt to use a NULL pointer (any pointer set to NULL or 0), you will immediately get an access violation or GPF from Windows. Although this may not sound like a good thing, it is certainly the lesser of two evils. It is far better to have an immediate error at the point of the infraction than to have a random problem that may show up further down the road.

Dereferencing a Pointer

Frequently you will need to dereference a pointer in order to retrieve the contents of the memory location (the object) that a pointer points to. Take the following example:

```
int x = 20;
int* ptrx = &x;
// later...
int z = *ptrx;
```

I can just imagine your frustration right now. What a mess! Take heart; it's not quite as bad as it might appear. The first line in this example declares an int variable called x and assigns it a value of 20. The next line declares a pointer to an int and assigns to the pointer the *address of the variable* x. This is done by using the *address-of operator* (&). In this example, the address-of operator tells the compiler, "Give me the address of the variable x, not the value of x itself." After the assignment, ptrx contains the memory address of x. Later on in the program you might need to get the value of the object pointed to by ptrx. You might think to try this:

```
int z = ptrx;    // wrong!
```

3

That won't work, however, because you are trying to assign a memory address to a regular variable. When you try to compile this line, the compiler will spit back an error stating, Cannot convert int* to int. That makes sense because you are dealing with two different types of variables. So you need to dereference the pointer using the indirection operator:

```
int z = *ptrx;
```

This could be considered the opposite of the address-of operator. Here you don't want the actual value of ptrx because the actual value is a memory address. Instead you want the value of the object pointed to by that memory address. So, in this case, the indirection operator tells the compiler, "Give me the value of the object ptrx points to, not the actual value of ptrx."

 Dereferencing a pointer means to retrieve the contents of the memory location (the object) that a pointer points to.

 NOTE

As you can see, the indirection operator is used to declare a pointer (int* x;) and also to dereference a pointer (int z = *x;). The compiler can tell from the context in which the indirection operator is used what to do in each case. You don't have to worry that the compiler won't know what you intend.

 NOTE

C++ syntax is largely a personal thing. I prefer to use the indirection operator next to the data type when declaring a pointer, and next to the pointer when dereferencing a pointer:

```
int* x;
SomeClass* aClass = new SomeClass;
char* s = new char[256];
int z = *x;
SomeClass temp = *aClass;
```

Others prefer to place the indirection operator next to the variable name:

```
int *x;
// or even...
int * x;
```

I happen to think that the syntax I use makes the most sense, but others could probably argue that their way is best, too. In the end, settle on the method you like best and then stick to it.

Putting It Together

Let's try to tie together what you have learned in the previous section. I'll take the MAILLIST program from Day 2, "Wading In Deeper," and modify it so that it uses dynamic memory allocation. This will require a few changes. First, take a look at the modified program, and then I'll explain the changes. Listing 3.1 contains the modified MAILLIST program.

Listing 3.1. POINTER.CPP.

```
 1: #include <iostream.h>
 2: #include <conio.h>
 3: #include <stdlib.h>
 4: #pragma hdrstop
 5: #include "structur.h"
 6: void displayRecord(int, mailingListRecord mlRec);
 7: int main(int, char**)
 8: {
 9:   //
10:   // create an array of pointers to
11:   // the mailingListRecord structure
12:   //
13:   mailingListRecord* listArray[3];
14:   //
15:   // create an object for each element of the array
16:   //
17:   for (int i=0;i<3;i++)
18:     listArray[i] = new mailingListRecord;
19:   cout << endl;
20:   int index = 0;
21:   //
22:   // get three records
23:   //
24:   do {
25:     cout << "First Name: ";
26:     cin.getline(listArray[index]->firstName,
27:       sizeof(listArray[index]->firstName) - 1);
28:     cout << "Last Name: ";
29:     cin.getline(listArray[index]->lastName,
30:       sizeof(listArray[index]->lastName) - 1);
31:     cout << "Address: ";
32:     cin.getline(listArray[index]->address,
33:       sizeof(listArray[index]->address) - 1);
34:     cout << "City: ";
35:     cin.getline(listArray[index]->city,
36:       sizeof(listArray[index]->city) - 1);
37:     cout << "State: ";
38:     cin.getline(listArray[index]->state,
39:       sizeof(listArray[index]->state) - 1);
40:     char buff[10];
41:     cout << "Zip: ";
```

3

```
42:     cin.getline(buff, sizeof(buff) - 1);
43:     listArray[index]->zip = atoi(buff);
44:     index++;
45:     cout << endl;
46:   }
47:   while (index < 3);
48:   //
49:   // display the three records
50:   //
51:   clrscr();
52:   //
53:   // must dereference the pointer to pass an object
54:   // to the displayRecord function.
55:   //
56:   for (int i=0;i<3;i++) {
57:     displayRecord(i, *listArray[i]);
58:   }
59:   //
60:   // ask the user to choose a record
61:   //
62:   cout << "Choose a record: ";
63:   char rec;
64: do {
65:     rec = getch();
66:     rec -= 49;
67:   } while (rec < 0 || rec > 2);
68:   //
69:   // assign the selected record to a temporary variable
70:   // must dereference here, too
71:   //
72:   mailingListRecord temp = *listArray[rec];
73:   clrscr();
74:   cout << endl;
75:   //
76:   // display the selected recrord
77:   //
78:   displayRecord(rec, temp);
79:   getch();
80:   return 0;
81: }
82: void displayRecord(int num, mailingListRecord mlRec)
83: {
84:   cout << "Record " << num + 1 << ":" << endl;
85:   cout << "Name:    " << mlRec.firstName << " ";
86:   cout << mlRec.lastName;
87:   cout << endl;
88:   cout << "Address:  " << mlRec.address;
89:   cout << endl << "            ";
90:   cout << mlRec.city << ", ";
91:   cout << mlRec.state << "   ";
92:   cout << mlRec.zip;
93:   cout << endl << endl;
94: }
```

ANALYSIS   First, on line 13 I declared the `listArray` array as an array of pointers. Following that, I created objects for each element of the array. This takes place in the `for` loop on lines 17 and 18. After that, I changed the direct membership operators (.) to indirect membership operators (->). I also have to dereference the pointers on line 57 and again on line 72. This is necessary because an object is expected and we cannot use a pointer in place of an object. Notice that the `displayRecord` function (starting on line 82) doesn't change. I haven't changed the fact that the `mailingListRecord` structure is passed to the function by value, so the code in the function doesn't need to be modified.

If you've had previous experience with C++, you may have noticed that this program has a bug in it. I'll let you in on the secret before the end of the chapter.

References

NEW TERM   A *reference* is a special type of pointer that allows you to treat a pointer like a regular object.

References, like pointers, can be confusing. A reference is declared using the *reference operator*. The symbol for the reference operator is the ampersand (&) which is the same symbol used for the address-of operator (don't worry, the compiler knows how to keep it all straight). As I said, a reference allows you to treat a pointer like an object. Here's an example:

```
MyStruct* pStruct = new MyStruct;
MyStruct& ref = *pStruct;
ref.X = 100;
```

Notice that with references you use the direct member operator rather than the indirect member operator as you do with pointers. Now you can get rid of all of those pesky -> operators! Although you won't use references a lot, they can be very handy when you need them. By the way, this code snippet could be condensed a little. Here's how I would write it in a real program:

```
MyStruct& ref = *new MyStruct;
ref.X = 100;
```

Although this might look odd, it does exactly the same thing as the first example. Combining statements like this is common and avoids unnecessary overhead.

Let's go once more to the `MAILLIST` example. This time I'll modify it by implementing a reference in the `do-while` loop. Actually, I'll be modifying the `POINTER` example found in Listing 3.1. The new program, found in Listing 3.2, illustrates this change.

Listing 3.2. REFERENC.CPP.

```
 1: #include <iostream.h>
 2: #include <conio.h>
 3: #include <stdlib.h>
 4: #pragma hdrstop
 5: #include "structur.h"
 6: void displayRecord(int, mailingListRecord mlRec);
 7: int main(int, char**)
 8: {
 9:   cout << endl;
10:   //
11:   // create an array of mailingListRecord structures
12:   //
13:   mailingListRecord* listArray[3];
14:   //
15:   // create objects for each record
16:   //
17:   for (int i=0;i<3;i++)
18:     listArray[i] = new mailingListRecord;
19:   int index = 0;
20:   //
21:   // get three records
22:   //
23:   do {
24:     // create a reference to the current record
25:     mailingListRecord& rec = *listArray[index];
26:     cout << "First Name: ";
27:     cin.getline(rec.firstName, sizeof(rec.firstName) - 1);
28:     cout << "Last Name: ";
29:     cin.getline(rec.lastName, sizeof(rec.lastName) - 1);
30:     cout << "Address: ";
31:     cin.getline(rec.address, sizeof(rec.address) - 1);
32:     cout << "City: ";
33:     cin.getline(rec.city, sizeof(rec.city) - 1);
34:     cout << "State: ";
35:     cin.getline(rec.state, sizeof(rec.state) - 1);
36:     char buff[10];
37:     cout << "Zip: ";
38:     cin.getline(buff, sizeof(buff) - 1);
39:     rec.zip = atoi(buff);
40:     index++;
41:     cout << endl;
42:   }
43:   while (index < 3);
44:   //
45:   // display the three records
46:   //
47:   clrscr();
48:   //
49:   // must dereference the pointer to pass an object
50:   // to the displayRecord function.
51:   //
```

continues

Listing 3.2. continued

```
52:    for (int i=0;i<3;i++) {
53:      displayRecord(i, *listArray[i]);
54:    }
55:    //
56:    // ask the user to choose a record
57:    //
58:    cout << "Choose a record: ";
59:    char rec;
60: do {
61:      rec = getch();
62:      rec -= 49;
63:    } while (rec < 0 || rec > 2);
64:    //
65:    // assign the selected record to a temporary variable
66:    // must dereference here, too
67:    //
68:    mailingListRecord temp = *listArray[rec];
69:    clrscr();
70:    cout << endl;
71:    //
72:    // display the selected recrord
73:    //
74:    displayRecord(rec, temp);
75:    getch();
76:    return 0;
77: }
78: void displayRecord(int num, mailingListRecord mlRec)
79: {
80:    cout << "Record " << num + 1 << ":" << endl;
81:    cout << "Name:     " << mlRec.firstName << " ";
82:    cout << mlRec.lastName;
83:    cout << endl;
84:    cout << "Address:  " << mlRec.address;
85:    cout << endl << "          ";
86:    cout << mlRec.city << ", ";
87:    cout << mlRec.state << "   ";
88:    cout << mlRec.zip;
89:    cout << endl << endl;
90: }
```

ANALYSIS   The only real change is in the do-while loop. Notice that a reference to a mailingListRecord structure is declared. Each time through the loop, the reference is assigned a different object (the next element in the array). Notice that I got rid of the indirect membership operators and replaced them with the direct membership operators. As I said earlier, a reference allows you to treat a pointer as an object. What that does for us in this case is clean up the code a little and make it easier to read. Oh, for those of you keeping score, this program has the same bug in it as does the POINTER example. I'll remedy that at the end of the chapter.

3

Although it might appear that references are preferred over pointers, that is not the case. References have some peculiarities that make them unsuitable in many cases. For one thing, references cannot be declared and then later assigned a value. They must be initialized when declared. For instance, the following code snippet will result in a compiler error:

```
MyStruct* pStruct = new MyStruct;
MyStruct& ref;
ref = *pStruct;
ref.X = 100;
```

Another problem with references is that they cannot be set to 0 or NULL as pointers can. That means you'll have to take special care to ensure that a reference is not deleted twice. References and pointers can often serve the same purpose, but neither is perfect in every programming situation.

Passing Function Parameters by Reference and by Pointer

Earlier I talked about passing objects to functions by value. I said that in the case of structures and classes, it is usually better to pass those objects by reference rather than by value. Any object can be passed by reference. This includes the primitive data types such as int and long, as well as instances of a structure or class. To review, when you pass function parameters by value, a copy of the object is made, and the function works with the copy. When you pass by reference, a *pointer to the object* is passed and not the object itself. This has two primary implications. First, it means that objects passed by reference can by modified by the function. Second, passing by reference eliminates the overhead of creating a copy of the object.

The fact that an object can be modified by the function is the most important aspect of passing by reference. Take this code, for instance:

```
void IncrementPosition(int& xPos, int& yPos)
{
  xPos++;
  yPos++;
}
int x = 20;
int y = 40;
IncrementPosition(x, y);
// x now equals 21 and y equals 41
```

Notice that when the function returns, both of the parameters passed have been incremented by one. This is because the function is modifying the actual object via the pointer (remember that a reference is a type of pointer).

> **TIP**
>
> Remember that a function can return only one value. By passing parameters by reference you can achieve the effect of a function returning more than one value. The function still only returns one value, but the objects passed by reference are updated, so the function effectively returns multiple values.

As I said, the other reason to pass parameters by reference is to eliminate the overhead of making a copy of the object each time the function is called. When dealing with primitive data types, there is no real overhead involved in making a copy. When dealing with structures and classes, however, the overhead is something to be considered. You should pass structures of any consequence by reference, as the following code demonstrates:

```
// structure passed by reference
void someFunction(MyStructure& s)
{
  // do some stuff with 's'
  return;
}
MyStructure myStruct;
// do some stuff, then later...
someFunction(myStruct);
```

Notice that the function call looks exactly the same whether the object is being passed by reference or by value.

Do you see a potential problem with passing by reference? If you pass by reference, you avoid the overhead of making a copy of the object, but now the object can be modified by the function. Sometimes you don't want the object to be modified by the function. So what if you want to pass by reference but make sure the object is not modified? Read on and I'll tell you.

The const **Keyword**

NEW TERM   The const keyword will allow you to declare a variable as constant.

Once a variable is declared with const, it cannot be changed. The solution, then, is to pass by reference *and* make the object const:

```
void someFunction(const MyStruct& s)
{
  // do some stuff with 's'
  return;
}
MyStructure myStruct;
// later
someFunction(myStruct);
```

Now you are free to pass by reference and not worry that your object might be modified by the function. Note that the function call itself stays the same and that only the function definition (and declaration) is modified with the const keyword.

NOTE

> If you attempt to modify a const object, you will get a compiler error stating, Cannot modify a const object. The following code will generate that error message:
>
> ```
> void someFunction(const MyStruct& s)
> {
>   s.dataMember = 100;    // cannot modify a const object
>   return;
> }
> ```
>
> Once you declare an object as const, the compiler will make sure you don't modify the object.

Note that the object is const only within the function. The object can be modified both before and after the function returns (provided it was not initially declared as const).

Passing by pointer is essentially the same as passing by reference. Passing by pointer has a couple of syntactical headaches that make it less desirable than passing by reference. Let's take the IncrementPosition() function from the first example in this section and modify it to pass by pointer rather than by reference:

```
void IncrementPosition(int* xPos, int* yPos)
{
  *xPos++;    // dereference, then increment
  *yPos++;
}
```

Note that the pointer has to be dereferenced before it can be incremented. Most of the time your needs will be best served by passing by reference, but you may pass by pointer if a situation dictates the need. When passing char arrays, you will usually pass by pointer rather than by reference because you can use a pointer to a char array and the name of the array interchangeably. When passing character arrays, it is better to pass by pointer.

The new and delete Operators

Up to this point I have been talking primarily about aspects of the C++ language that come from C. From this point on we'll be looking at features that are specific to the C++ language. The new and delete operators are two important C++ language features.

As mentioned in the preceding section, memory in a C++ program is allocated dynamically using operator new. You free memory using the delete operator. Unless you have previously programmed in C, you might not appreciate the simplicity of new and delete. In C programs, you use malloc(), calloc(), realloc(), and free() to dynamically allocate memory. Windows really complicates things by offering a whole raft of local and global memory-allocation functions. Although this is not exactly difficult, it can be confusing to say the least. C++ removes those headaches through the use of new and delete.

A new **World Order**

You've already seen new in action, so let's review. As discussed earlier, you can allocate memory locally (from the stack) or dynamically (from the heap). The following code snippet shows examples of allocating two character arrays. One is allocated from the stack (local allocation), and the other is allocated from the heap (dynamic allocation):

```
char buff[80];
char* bigBuff = new char[4096];
```

In the first case the buffer size is insignificant, so it doesn't really matter whether the stack or the heap is used. In the second case a large char array is needed, so it makes sense to allocate it from the heap rather than from the stack. This preserves stack space. In the case of arrays (remember, a string is just an array of type char), the dynamic and local flavors can be used interchangeably. That is, they use the same syntax:

```
strcpy(buff, "Ricky Rat");
strcpy(bigBuff, "A very long string that goes on and on...");
// later on...
strcpy(bigBuff, buff);
```

Remember that the name of an array when used by itself points to the first memory location of the array. A pointer also points to the first memory location of the array, so that is why the two forms can be used interchangeably.

NOTE

If the new operator fails to allocate the requested memory, it returns NULL. In theory, you should check the pointer after calling new to ensure that it contains a non-zero value:

```
char* buff = new char[1024];
if (buff) strcpy(buff, "Buteo Regalis");
else ReportError();  // something went wrong
```

In reality, if the new operator fails in a 32-bit Windows program, the entire system is in trouble, and neither your program nor any other will be running for long.

3

If you are attempting to allocate very large chunks of memory (several megabytes in size) or are trying to allocate memory at critical points in your program, you should check the pointer for validity before continuing. For routine memory-allocation chores, you can probably get by without checking to ensure that the new operator succeeded.

delete

All memory allocated must be deallocated (released or freed) after you are done with the memory. With local objects, this happens for you automatically, and you don't have to worry about it. The memory manager allocates the memory your object needs from the stack and then frees that memory when the object goes out of scope (usually when a function returns or when the code block in which the object was declared ends). When using dynamic memory allocation, the programmer must take the responsibility of freeing any memory allocated with the new operator.

 Freeing memory allocated with new is accomplished with the delete operator.

 All calls to new need to have a matching delete. If you do not free all memory allocated with the new operator, your program will leak memory. You need to be diligent in matching new/delete pairs.

Using the delete operator is frightfully easy:

```
SomeObject* myObject = new SomeObject;
// do a bunch of stuff with myObject
delete myObject;    // so long!
```

That's all there is to it! There isn't a lot to the delete operator, but there are a couple of things about pointers and delete that you should be aware of. The first is that you must not delete a pointer that has already been deleted, or you will get access violations and all sorts of other fun stuff. Second, it is okay to delete a pointer that has been set to 0. So what does that mean in the real world? Let me explain.

Sometimes you declare a pointer just in case it might be used, but you don't know for sure whether it will be used in a given instance of your program. For example, let's say you have an object that is created if the user chooses a certain menu item. If the user never chooses that menu item, the object never gets created. So far, so good. The problem is that you need to delete the pointer if the object was created, but not delete the pointer if the object was not created. Deleting an initialized pointer is asking for trouble because you have no idea what memory the pointer points to. There are two ways to work around this.

I said earlier that it is a good idea to initialize pointers to 0 if you don't use them right away. This is a good idea for two reasons. The first reason I explained earlier (uninitialized pointers contain random values, which is undesirable). The second reason is because it's okay to delete a NULL pointer—you can call delete for that pointer and not worry about whether it was ever used:

```
Monster* swampThing = 0;
// later when it's time to exit the program...
delete swampThing;  // so long, sucker!
```

In this case you don't really care whether memory for the object was ever allocated because the call to delete is safe whether the pointer points to an object or is NULL.

TIP

You may run into situations where delete could be called more than once for an object. For instance, you may create an object in one part of your program and delete it in another part of the program. A situation might exist where the section of code that deletes the object might never be executed. In that case you will also want to delete the object when the program closes (for insurance). To avoid the possibility of a pointer getting deleted twice, get into the habit of setting the pointer to NULL or 0 after deleting it:

```
Monster* borg = new Monster;
// later....
delete borg;
borg = 0;
```

Now, if delete is called twice for the object, it won't matter because it's okay to delete a NULL pointer.

Another way around the double-delete problem is to check the pointer for a non-zero value before calling delete:

```
if (swampThing) delete swampThing;
```

This assumes that you have been diligent in setting deleted pointers to 0 in other parts of the program. It doesn't matter which method you use, but be sure to use one of them in any case where a pointer could accidentally be deleted twice.

NOTE

> If you use a reference when dynamically creating an object, the syntax for `delete` requires a twist. Here's an example that illustrates this point:
>
> ```
> MyStruct& ref = *new MyStruct;
> ref.X = 100;
> // later...
> delete &ref;
> ```
>
> Note that you need the address-of operator to delete the pointer in the case of a reference. Remember that a reference cannot be set to 0, so you must be careful not to delete a reference twice.

Another Mystery Solved

Have you figured it out yet? "Huh?" you say? The bug in the POINTER and REFERENC programs... have you figured out what it is? You got it! The program leaks memory. I created an array of structures allocated from the heap but never freed the memory. So what I need is a couple of lines to clean things up just before the program ends:

```
getch();  // existing line
for (int i=0;i<3;i++)
  delete listArray[i];
```

There! Now I have a properly behaving program. I just ran through the array of pointers and deleted each one. Nuthin' to it.

new[] **and** delete[]

When you call `new` to create an array, you are actually using the `new[]` version of the `new` operator. It's not important that you know the inner details of how that works, but you do need to know how to properly delete arrays that are dynamically allocated. Earlier I gave you an example of dynamically creating a character array. Here is the same code snippet except with the `delete[]` statement added:

```
char buff[80];
char* bigBuff = new char[4096];
strcpy(buff, "Ricky Rat");
strcpy(bigBuff, "Some very long string.");
// later on...
delete[] bigBuff;
```

Notice that the statement calls `delete[]` and not just plain `delete`. I won't go into a technical description of what happens here, but this ensures that all elements in the array get properly deleted. Be sure that if you dynamically allocate an array you call the `delete[]` operator to free the memory.

> **HOUSE RULES: POINTERS AND DYNAMIC MEMORY ALLOCATION**
>
> ☐ Be sure to initialize pointers to 0 if they are not used right away.
> ☐ Be sure not to delete a pointer twice.
> ☐ It is okay to delete pointers set to NULL or 0.
> ☐ Set pointers to NULL or 0 after deleting them.
> ☐ Dereference pointers to obtain the object the pointer points to.

Functions in C++

A function in C++ can do everything that a function can do in C. In addition, C++ functions can do things that functions in C cannot. Specifically, this section looks at the following:

☐ Function overloading
☐ Default parameters
☐ Class member functions
☐ Inline functions

Function Overloading

C++ allows you to have functions that have the same name but take different parameters.

NEW TERM *Function overloading* is when you have two or more functions with the same name but with different parameter lists.

NEW TERM Functions that share a common name are called *overloaded functions*.

On Day 1 I showed you an example program which contained a function called `multiply()`. Not surprisingly, this function multiplied two values together. The function took two integers, multiplied them, and returned the result. But what if you wanted to have the function multiply two floating-point numbers? In C you would have to have two functions:

```
// declarations for a program written in c
int multiplyInt(int num1, int num2);
float multiplyFloat(float num1, float num2);
short multiplyShort(short num1, short num2);
```

Wouldn't it be a lot easier if you could just have a function called `multiply()` that would be smart enough to know whether you wanted to multiply `short`s, `int`s, or `long`s? In C++ you can create such a scenario thanks to function overloading. Here's how the declarations for an overloaded function look:

```
// declarations in C++
int multiply(int num1, int num2);
float multiply(float num1, float num2);
short multiply(short num1, short num2);
```

You still have to write separate functions for each of these declarations, but at least you can use the same function name. The compiler takes care of calling the correct function based on the parameters you pass the function. For example:

```
float x = 1.5;
float y = 10.5;
float result = multiply(x, y);
```

The compiler sees that two `floats` are passed to the function and calls the version of the `multiply()` function that takes two floating-point values for parameters. Likewise, if two `ints` are passed, the compiler calls the version of `multiply()` that takes two integers.

NOTE

It is the parameter list that makes overloaded functions work. You can vary either the type or the number of parameters a function takes (or both), but you cannot create an overloaded function by changing just the return value. For example, the following does not constitute an overloaded function:

```
int  DoSomething();
void DoSomething();
```

If you try to compile a program containing these lines, you will get a compiler error that says, `Type mismatch in redeclaration of 'DoSomething()'`. The two functions need to vary by more than just the return value in order to have overloaded functions.

NOTE

Compilers keep track of overloaded functions internally through a process called *name mangling*. Name mangling means that the compiler creates a function name that takes into account the parameter list of the function. Internally, the compiler refers to the mangled name rather than the plain text name you would recognize. For example, for the `multiply` function taking two float values, the mangled name might be `multiply$qff`.

Let's take a quick detour and talk about something you will need to use on occasion when dealing with overloaded functions.

Meet the Cast

Using overloaded functions works fine as long as you use the proper data types when calling an overloaded function. But what if you mix and match? In this case, you will need to cast a variable or literal value.

NEW TERM   A *cast* tells the compiler to temporarily treat one data type as if it were another.

A cast looks like this:

```
float x = (float)10 * 5.5;
```

In this case the cast tells the compiler, "Make the number 10 a float." (The second number is automatically interpreted as a float because it contains a decimal place.) Take a look at the following code snippet:

```
int anInt = 5;
float aFloat = 10.5;
float result = multiply(anInt, aFloat);
```

In this case you will get a compiler error because there is an ambiguity between the parameters passed and the function declarations. The compiler error, in effect, says, "I can't figure out from the parameters passed which version of multiply() to call." The same error will be produced if you use code like this:

```
int result = multiply(10, 10);
// is 10 a float, int or short?
```

Here the compiler cannot figure out whether the numeric constants are to be interpreted as floats, ints, or shorts. When this occurs, you basically have two choices. First, you can simply avoid using literal values in the function call. If you want to multiply two ints, you can declare two int variables and pass those to the function:

```
int x = 10;
int y = 10;
int result = multiply(x, y);
```

Now there is no ambiguity because x and y are both obviously ints. That's probably overkill for simple situations, though. The other thing you can do is to cast the numeric constants to tell the compiler what type to expect:

```
int result = multiply((int)10, (int)10);
```

3

Now the compiler knows to treat the literal values as ints. A cast is also used to temporarily force the compiler to treat one data type as if it were something else. Let's go back to the first example in this section and this time cast one of the variables to remove the ambiguity:

```
int x = 5;
float y = 10.5;
float result = multiply((float)x, y);
```

In this case x is an int, but you are casting it to a float, thereby telling the compiler to treat it as a float. The compiler happily calls the float version of multiply() and goes on its way.

Ultimately, you want to write overloaded functions so that ambiguities do not exist and casting is not necessary. In some cases that is not possible, and in those cases casting will be required.

Default Parameters for Functions

 A function in C++ can have *default parameters* which, as the name implies, supply a default value for a function if no value is specified when the function is called.

A function implementing a default parameter might look like this:

```
// declaration, parameter 'eraseFirst' will be false by default
void Redraw(bool eraseFirst = false);
// definition
void Redraw(bool eraseFirst)
{
  if (eraseFirst) {
    // erase code
  }
  // drawing code
}
```

When this function is called, it can be called with or without a parameter. If the parameter is supplied at the time the function is called, the function behaves as a regular function would. If the parameter is not supplied when the function is called, the default parameter is used automatically. Given this example, the following two lines of code are identical:

```
Redraw();
Redraw(false);
```

Note that when a parameter has a default value, it can be omitted from the function call altogether. You can mix default and non-default parameters in the same function:

```
int PlaySound(char* name, bool loop = false, int loops = 10);
// call function
int res;
res = PlaySound("chime.wav");           // does not loop sound
res = PlaySound("ding.wav", true);      // plays sound 10 times
res = PlaySound("bell.wave", true, 5); // plays sound 5 times
```

Default parameters are helpful for many reasons. For one thing, they make your life easier. You may have a function that you call with the same parameters 99 percent of the time. By giving it default parameters, you shorten the amount of typing required each time you make a call to the function. Whenever you want to supply parameters other than the defaults, all you have to do is plug in values for the default parameters.

NOTE Any default parameters must come at the end of the function's parameter list. The following is not a valid function declaration:

```
int MyFunction(int x, int y = 10, int t = 5, int z);
```

In order for this function declaration to compile, the default parameters must be moved to the end of the function list:

```
int MyFunction(int x, int z, int y = 10, int t = 5);
```

If you don't put the default parameters at the end of the parameter list, the compile will generate a compiler error.

Class Member Functions

 As you will find out in this section, classes can contain their own functions. Such functions are called *member functions* because they are members of a class.

Class member functions follow the same rules as regular functions: They can be overloaded, they can have default parameters, they can take any number of parameters, and so on.

Class member functions can be called only through an object of the class to which the function belongs. To call a class member function, you use the direct member operator (in the case of local objects) or the indirect member operator (for dynamically created objects) just like you did when accessing data members of a structure on Day 2. For example, let's say that you had a class called Airplane that was used to track an airplane for aircraft-control software. That class would probably have the capability to retrieve the current speed of a given aircraft via a function called GetSpeed(). The following example illustrates how you would call the GetSpeed() function of an Airplane object:

```
Airplane plane;   // create a class instance
int speed = plane.GetSpeed();
cout << "The airplane's current speed is " << speed << endl;
```

This code uses the direct membership operator to call the GetSpeed() function. Class member functions are defined like regular functions except that the class name and scope-resolution operator precede the function name. For example, the definition of the GetSpeed() function might look like this in the source file:

```
int Airplane::GetSpeed()
{
  return speed;  // speed is a class member variable
}
```

In this case, the scope-resolution operator tells the compiler that the `GetSpeed()` function is a member of the `Airplane` class. I'll talk more about class member functions when I discuss classes tomorrow.

 NOTE Tradition has it that class member function names begin with upper-case letters. There is no hard and fast rule about this, but you will find that most C++ programs follow this tradition. As a further note, I am not a fan of the underscore character in function names. For example, I much prefer the function name `GetVideoRect()` over the name `get_video_rect()`. Regardless of what naming convention you use for your functions, be consistent and use the same naming convention throughout your programs.

Inline Functions

Normally a function only appears in the executable file once. Each section of code that uses the function *calls* the function. This means that program execution jumps from the point of the function call to the point in the program where the function resides. The statements in the function are executed, and then the function returns. When the function returns, program execution jumps back to the statement following the function call.

 NEW TERM An *inline function,* as its name implies, is placed inline in the compiled code wherever a call to that function occurs.

Inline functions are declared like regular functions but are defined with the `inline` keyword. Each time the compiler encounters a call to an inline function in the source code, it places a separate copy of the function's code in the executable program at that point. Inline functions execute quickly because no actual function call takes place (the code is already inlined in the program).

 NOTE Inline functions should be reserved for functions that are very small or for those that need to be executed very quickly. Large functions or those that are called from many places in your program should not be inlined because your executable file will be larger as a result.

Inline functions are usually class member functions. Often the inline function definition (the function itself) is placed in the header file following the class declaration. (This is the one time that you can place code in your header files.) Because the `GetSpeed()` function mentioned previously is so small, it can be inlined easily. Here's how it would look:

```
inline int Airplane::GetSpeed() {
  return speed;  // speed is a class member variable
}
```

An inline function can also be defined within a class declaration. Because I haven't talked about classes yet, though, I'll hold that discussion for tomorrow.

Summary

Wow, that's some pretty heavy stuff! Because you are reading this, you must still be left standing. That's good news. Today we got out the big guns and took on pointers and references. Once you get a handle on pointers, you are well on your way to understanding C++. As part of the discussion on pointers you learned about local versus dynamic memory allocation, which led to a discussion about the `new` and `delete` operators. Today ends with an explanation of how C++ extends the use of functions over what the C language provides.

Workshop

The Workshop contains quiz questions to help you solidify your understanding of the material covered and exercises to provide you with experience in using what you have learned. You can find answers to the quiz questions in Appendix A, "Answers to Quiz Questions."

Q&A

Q Pointers and references confuse me. Am I alone?

A Absolutely not! Pointers and references are complicated and take some time to fully understand. You will probably have to work with C++ a while before you get a handle on pointers and references.

Q Do I always have to delete an object that I created dynamically with the `new` operator?

A Yes and no. All objects created with `new` must have a corresponding `delete`, or the program will leak memory. Some objects, however, have parent objects that will take the responsibility for deleting them. So the question is not whether an object created with `new` should be deleted, but rather who should delete it. You will always want to call `delete` for classes you write. Later, when you learn about VCL (on

Day 5, "C++ Class Frameworks and the Visual Component Model"), you will see that VCL parent objects take the responsibility for deleting their children.

Q Should I create my objects on the stack or on the heap?

A That depends on the object. Large objects should be created on the heap in order to preserve stack space. Small objects and primitive data types should be created on the stack for simplicity and speed of execution.

Q What's the point of having overloaded functions?

A Overloaded functions provide you a means by which you can have several functions that perform the same basic operation and have the same function name, but take different parameters. For example, you might have an overloaded function called DrawObject(). One version might take a Circle class as a parameter, another might take a Square class as a parameter, and a third could take a class called Polygon as a parameter. By having three functions with the same name, you avoid the need to have three different function names.

Q Should I use a lot of inline functions?

A That depends on the function, of course. In general, though, the answer is no. Inline functions should be reserved for functions that are very small or seldom used, or where execution speed is critical.

Quiz

1. What is a pointer?
2. What does it mean to dereference a pointer?
3. What is the return value of operator new?
4. Should instances of classes and structures be passed to functions by reference or by value?
5. What does the const keyword do?
6. Does the following qualify as an overloaded function? Why or why not?
   ```
   void MyFunction(int x);
   long MyFunction(int x);
   ```
7. Which is better to use, a reference or a pointer?
8. What is a class member function?
9. How does the compiler treat an inline function as opposed to a regular function?
10. What, if anything, is wrong with the following code snippet?
    ```
    char* buff = new char[200];
    // later...
    delete buff;
    ```

Exercises

1. Write a program that declares a structure, dynamically creates an instance of the structure, and fills the structure with data. (**Hint:** Don't forget to delete the pointer.)

2. Modify the program from exercise 1 to use a reference rather than a pointer.

3. Rewrite the REFERENC program in Listing 3.2 so that the mailingListRecord structure is passed to the displayRecord() function by reference rather than by value.

4. What is wrong with the following function declaration?

   ```
   void SomeFunction(int param1, int param2 = 0, int param3);
   ```

5. Explain to a five-year-old the difference between pointers and references.

Day 4

Totally Immersed: C++ Classes and Object-Oriented Programming

by Kent Reisdorph

Today you get to the good stuff. In this chapter you will learn about classes. Classes are the heart of C++ and a major part of object-oriented programming. Classes are also the heart of the Visual Component Library (VCL), which you will use when you start writing Windows GUI applications. (VCL is discussed in detail on Day 5, "C++ Class Frameworks and the Visual Component Model.") First you will find out what a class is and how it's expected to be used. Along the way you will learn the meaning of C++ buzzwords like inheritance, object, and data abstraction. At the end of the chapter you will get an introduction to file input and output in C++.

So, uh...What's a Class?

A *class*, like a structure, is a collection of data members and functions that work together to accomplish a specific programming task. In this way a class is said to *encapsulate* the task. Classes have the following features:

- ☐ The capability to control access
- ☐ Constructors
- ☐ Destructors
- ☐ Data members
- ☐ Member functions
- ☐ A hidden, special pointer called this

Before diving into an examination of those features, let me give you a quick example of how a class might work. Let's use a typical Windows control as an example—a check box, for instance. A class that represents a check box could have data members for the caption of the check box and for the state (checked or unchecked). This class would also have functions that would allow you to set and query both the check box caption and the check state. These functions might be named GetCheck(), SetCheck(), GetCaption(), and SetCaption(). Once the class has been written, you can create an instance of the class to control a check box in Windows. (It's not quite that simple, but this is just an example, after all.) If you have three check boxes, you could have three instances of the CheckBox class that could then be used to control each check box individually. Here's an example:

```
MyCheckBox check1(ID_CHECK1);
MyCheckBox check2(ID_CHECK2);
MyCheckBox check3(ID_CHECK3);
check1.SetCaption("Thingamabob Option");
check1.SetCheck(true);
check2.SetCaption("Doohickey Options");
check2.SetCheck(false);
check3.SetCaption("Whodyacallum Options");
check3.SetCheck(true);
if (check1.GetCheck()) DoThingamabobTask();
if (check2.GetCheck()) DoDoohickeyTask();
// etc.
```

In this example, each instance of the class is a separate object. Each instance has its own data members, and the objects operate independently of one another. They are all objects of the same type, but are separate instances in memory. With that brief introduction, let's roll up our sleeves once more and go to work on understanding classes.

4

Anatomy of a Class

A class, like a structure, has a declaration. The class declaration is usually contained in a header file. In simple cases, both the class declaration and the definition can be contained in a single source file, but you typically won't do that for real applications. Usually you create a class source file with a filename closely matching the class name and with a .cpp extension. Because Windows 95 and Windows NT both support long filenames, you can use filenames that exactly match your class name if you want. The header file for the class usually has the same name as the source file but with the extension .h. For example, if you had a class called MyClass, you would have a source file named MYCLASS.CPP and a header named MYCLASS.H.

Class Access Levels

 Classes can have three levels of access: *private*, *public*, or *protected*. Each of these access levels is defined in this section.

Class access levels control how a class is utilized by users of the class. As a sole programmer, you might be the class's creator but also a user of the class. In team programming environments, one programmer might be the creator of the class and other programmers are users of the class.

NOTE

Let me clarify a couple comments I made on Day 2, "Wading In Deeper." I said that a structure is a class in which all data members and functions are public. In fact, in C++ this is the only thing that distinguishes a structure from a class. A structure can have functions as well as data members. A structure cannot use the access-modifier keywords (private, protected, and private) because a structure can only have public access. I also said that you probably won't use structures very much in your C++ programs. Because a class and a structure are nearly the same, you will probably prefer to use classes over structures.

To understand what role levels of access play in class operation, you first need to understand how classes will be used. In any class there is the *public* part of the class, which the outside world has access to, and there is the private part of a class. The *private* part of a class is the internal implementation of the class—the inner workings, so to speak.

Part of a well-designed class includes hiding anything from public view that the user of the class doesn't need to know.

 Data abstraction is the hiding of internal implementations within the class from outside view.

Data abstraction prevents the user from knowing more than he or she needs to know about the class, but also prevents the user from messing with things that shouldn't be messed with. For instance, when you get in your car and turn the key to start the car, do you want to know every detail about how the car operates? Of course not. You only want to know as much as you need to know to operate the car safely. So in this analogy the steering wheel, pedals, gear shift lever, speedometer, and so on represent the public interface between the car and the driver. The driver knows which of those components to manipulate in order to make the car perform the way he wants.

Conversely, the engine, drive train, and electrical system of the car are hidden from public view. The engine is tucked neatly away where you never have to look at it if you don't want to. (That's what service stations are for!) It's a detail that you don't need to know about, so it is hidden from you—kept private, if you prefer. Imagine how much trouble driving would be if you had to keep track of everything the car was doing at all times: Is the carburetor getting enough gas? Does the differential have enough grease? Is the alternator producing adequate voltage for both the ignition and the radio to operate? Are the intake valves opening properly? Arggghhhh!!! Who needs it! In the same way, a class keeps its internal implementation private so the user of the class doesn't have to worry about what's going on under the hood. The internal workings of the class are kept private, and the user interface is public.

The *protected* access level is a little harder to explain. Protected class members, like private class members, cannot be accessed by users of the class. They can, however, be accessed by classes that are derived from this class. I will talk about protected access more a little later, in the section "Member Functions."

The C++ language has three keywords that pertain to class access. The keywords are (not surprisingly) `public`, `private`, and `protected`. You specify a class member's access level when you declare the class. A class is declared with the `class` keyword. A class declaration looks like a structure declaration with the access modifiers added:

```
class Vehicle {
  public:
    bool haveKey;
    bool Start();
    void SetGear(int gear);
    void Accelerate(int acceleration);
    void Break(int factor);
    void Turn(int direction);
```

```
      void ShutDown();
  protected:
      void StartupProcedure();
  private:
      void StartElectricalSystem();
      void StartEngine();
      int currentGear;
      bool started;
      int speed;
};
```

Notice how you break the class organization down into the three access levels. You may not use all three levels of access in a given class. You are not required to use any of the access levels if you don't want, but typically you will have a public and a private section at the least.

NOTE

> Class-member access defaults to `private`. If you do not add any access keywords, all data and functions in the class will be private. A class where all data members and functions are private is not very useful in most cases.

Constructors

Classes in C++ have a special function called the *constructor*.

NEW TERM   The *constructor* is a function that is automatically called when an instance of a class is created.

The constructor is used to initialize any class member variables, allocate memory the class will need, or do any other startup tasks. The `Vehicle` example you just saw does not have a constructor. If you do not provide a constructor, the C++Builder compiler will create a *default constructor* for you. While this is OK for simple classes, you will almost always provide a constructor for classes of any significance. The constructor must have the same name as the name of the class. This is what distinguishes it as a constructor. Given that, let's add a constructor declaration to the `Vehicle` class:

```
class Vehicle {
  public:
      Vehicle();        // constructor
      bool haveKey;
      bool Start();
      void SetGear(int gear);
      void Accelerate(int acceleration);
      void Break(int factor);
      void Turn(int direction);
      void ShutDown();
```

```
protected:
   void StartupProcedure();
private:
   void StartElectricalSystem();
   void StartEngine();
   int currentGear;
   bool started;
   int speed;
};
```

Notice that the constructor does not have a return type. A constructor cannot return a value, so no return type is specified. If you try to add a return type to the constructor declaration, you will get a compiler error.

A class can have more than one constructor. This is possible through function overloading, which I discussed on Day 3, "Up to Your Neck in C++." For instance, a class might have a constructor that takes no parameters (a default constructor) and a constructor that takes one or more parameters in order to initialize data members to certain values. For example, let's say you have a class called Rect that encapsulates a rectangle (rectangles are frequently used in Windows programming). This class could have several constructors. It could have a default constructor that sets all the data members to 0, and another constructor that allows you to set the class's data members through the constructor. First, let's take a look at how the class declaration might look:

```
class Rect {
  public:
    Rect();
    Rect(int _left, int _top, int _bottom, int _right);
    int GetWidth();
    int GetHeight();
    void SetRect(int _left, int _top, int _bottom, int _right);
  private:
    int left;
    int top;
    int bottom;
    int right;
};
```

The definitions for the constructors, then, would look something like this:

```
Rect::Rect()
{
  left = 0;
  top = 0;
  bottom = 0;
  right = 0;
}
Rect::Rect(int _left, int _top, int _bottom, int _right)
{
  left = _left;
  top = _top;
  bottom = _bottom;
  right = _right;
}
```

The first constructor is a default constructor by virtue of the fact that it takes no parameters. It simply initializes each data member to 0. The second constructor takes the parameters passed and assigns them to the corresponding class data members. The variable names in the parameter list are local to the constructor, so each of the variable names begins with an underscore to differentiate between the local variables and the class data members.

TIP

> Remember that an uninitialized variable will contain random data. This is true for class data members as well as other variables. To be safe, you should set class member variables to some initial value.

NEW TERM *Instantiation* is the creation of an object, an instance, or a class.

It's important to understand that you can't call a constructor directly. So how do you use one of these constructors over the other? You do that when you create or *instantiate* an object or a class. The following code snippet creates two instances of the Rect class. The first uses the default constructor, and the second uses the second form of the constructor:

```
Rect rect1;              // object created using default constructor
Rect rect2(0, 0, 100, 100); // created using 2nd constructor
```

You can have as many constructors as you like, but be sure that your constructors don't have ambiguous parameter lists (as per the rules on function overloading).

Initializer Lists

NEW TERM C++ provides a means by which you can initialize class data members in what is called an *initializer list*.

The following is the proper way to initialize data members of a class. Rather than trying to explain how to use an initializer list, let me show you an example. Let's take the two constructors for the Rect class and initialize the data members with an initializer list rather than in the body of the function as I did before. It looks like this:

```
Rect::Rect() :
  left(0),
  top(0),
  bottom(0),
  right(0)
{
}
```

4

```
Rect::Rect(int _left, int _top, int _right , int _bottom) :
  left(_left),
  top(_top),
  bottom(_bottom),
  right(_right)
{
}
```

Notice two things in this code snippet. First, notice that the initializer list is preceded by a colon. (The colon is at the end of the function header, so you may not have noticed it.) Notice also that each variable in the initializer list is followed by a comma *except* the last variable. Forgetting either of these two things will cause compiler errors.

NOTE

On Day 3 I talked about references. You can have a class data member that is a reference, but the reference can only be initialized in the initializer list of the class and nowhere else. Here's an example:

```
class MyClass {
  public:
    MyClass();
    // other public stuff
  private:
    OtherClass& other;
    // other private stuff
};
MyClass::MyClass() :
  other(*new OtherClass)  // must do this here!
{
}
```

Attempts to initialize the reference anywhere else will result in compiler errors.

In most cases it doesn't matter whether you initialize your data members in the body of the constructor or the initializer list. I have done it both ways, but I prefer the initializer list.

Destructors

NEW TERM The *destructor* is a special function that is automatically called just before the object is destroyed.

The destructor could be considered the opposite of the constructor. It is usually used to free any memory allocated by the class or do any other cleanup chores. A class is not required to have a destructor, but if it does, it can have only one. A destructor has no return value and takes no parameters. The destructor's name must be the name of the class preceded by a tilde (~).

4

As mentioned, the destructor is called just before the class is destroyed. The class may be destroyed because it was allocated from the stack and is going out of scope, or it might be destroyed as a result of delete being called for the class (if the class was created dynamically). In either case, the destructor will be called as the last thing before the class breathes its last breath.

The following shows the updated code for the Rect class:

```
class Rect {
  public:
    Rect();
    Rect(int _left, int _top, int _bottom, int _right);
    ~Rect();            // destructor added
    int GetWidth();
    int GetHeight();
    void SetRect(int _left, int _top, int _bottom, int _right);
  private:
    int left;
    int top;
    int bottom;
    int right;
    char* text;        // new class member added
};
Rect::Rect() :
  left(0),
  top(0),
  bottom(0),
  right(0)
{
  text = new char[256];
  strcpy(text, "Any Colour You Like");
}
// code omitted
Rect::~Rect()
{
  delete[] text;
}
```

The modified version of the Rect class allocates storage for a char array named text in its constructor and frees that storage in the destructor. (I can't think of a good reason for a class that handles rectangles to have a text data member, but you never know!) Again, use the destructor for any cleanup tasks that need to be done before the instance of the class is destroyed.

Data Members

Data members of a class are simply variables that are declared in the class declaration. They could be considered variables that have class scope. Data members in classes are essentially the same as data members in structures except that you can control their access by declaring them as private, public, or protected. Regardless of a data member's access, it is available for use in all functions of the class. Depending on the data member's access level, it might be visible outside the class as well. Private and protected data members, for instance, are private to the class and cannot be seen outside the class. Public data members, however, can be accessed from outside the class, but only through an object. Take the Rect class declared previously, for example. It has no public data members. You could try the following, but you'd get a compiler error:

```
Rect rect(10, 10, 200, 200);
int x = rect.left;  // compiler error!
```

The compiler error will say Rect::left is not accessible. The compiler is telling you that left is a private data member and you can't get to it. If left were in the public section of the class declaration, this code would compile.

You can use getters and setters to change private data members. That is, *getters* are functions that get the value of a private data member, and *setters* are functions that set the value of a private data member. Both getters and setters are public member functions that act on private data members.

To illustrate, let's say that for the Rect class you had the following getters and setters for the left data member:

```
int Rect::GetLeft()
{
   return left;
}
void Rect::SetLeft(int newLeft)
{
   left = newLeft;
}
```

Now, when you want to obtain the value of the left member of the Rect class, use this:

```
TRect rect;
int x = rect.GetLeft();
```

In some cases this is overkill. Setters have one main advantage, though—they allow you to validate input. By validating input, you can control the values your data members contain.

 NOTE

> Some OOP extremists say that data members should never be public. They would say that you should use getters and setters to access all data members. On the other end of the spectrum is the group that says to make all your data members public. The truth lies somewhere in between. Some data members are noncritical and may be left public if it is more convenient. Other data members are critical to the way the class operates and should not be made public. If you are going to err, it is better to err on the side of making data members private.

Each instance of your class gets its own copy of the class's data members in memory. The exception to this is that if any class data members are declared with the static storage modifier, all instances of the class will share the same copy of that data member in memory. In that case only one copy of that data member will exist in memory. If any one instance of the class changes a static data member, it changes in all the classes. Use of static data members in classes is not common, so don't worry about it if this doesn't make sense right now.

HOUSE RULES: CLASS DATA MEMBERS

☐ Use as many data members as you need for vital class operations, but use local variables where possible.

☐ Don't make all data members public.

☐ Use getters and setters for data members that you want to remain private but that you need to be able to access.

☐ Validate data in your setters to ensure that improper values are not being input.

☐ Initialize all data members either in the initializer list or in the body of your constructor.

☐ Don't forget to delete any data members that dynamically allocate memory.

Member Functions

Class member functions are functions that belong to your class. They are local to the class and do not exist outside the class. Class member functions can be called only from within the class itself or through an instance of the class. They have access to all public, protected, and private data members of the class. Member functions can be declared in the private, protected, or public sections of your class. Good class design requires that you think about which of these sections your member functions should go into.

Public member functions represent the user interface to the class. It is through the public member functions that users of the class access the class in order to gain whatever functionality the class provides. For example, let's say you have a class that plays and records wave audio. Public member functions might include functions like Open(), Play(), Record(), Save(), Rewind(), and so on.

Private member functions are functions that the class uses internally to do its thing. These functions are not intended to be called by users of the class; they are private in order to be hidden from the outside world. Frequently a class has startup chores to perform when the class is created. (For example, you have already seen that the constructor is called when a class is created.) In some classes the startup processing might be significant, requiring many lines of code. To remove clutter from the constructor, a class might have an Init() function that is called from the constructor to perform those startup tasks. This function would never be called directly by a user of the class. In fact, more than likely bad things would happen if this function were to be called by a user at the wrong time, so the function is private in order to protect both the integrity of the class and the user.

Protected member functions are functions that cannot be accessed by the outside world but can be accessed by classes that are derived from this class. I haven't talked yet about classes being derived from other classes, so I'll save this discussion for a little later when it will make more sense. I discuss deriving classes in the section "Inheritance."

The inline function, Form 1:

```
ClassName {
  public:
    ReturnType FunctionName();
};

inline ReturnType ClassName::FunctionName() {
  statements
}
```

The function *FunctionName* is declared within the body of the class *ClassName*. The function definition (the function itself) is defined outside the class declaration using the inline keyword. *FunctionName* must be proceeded by *ClassName* and the scope resolution operator.

The inline function, Form 2:

```
ClassName {
  public:
    ReturnType FunctionName()
    {
      statements
    }
};
```

The function *FunctionName* is declared and defined entirely within the *ClassName* declaration. The function is an inline function by virtue of the fact that it is contained within the *ClassName* declaration. The inline keyword is not required.

As with data members, member functions can be declared with the static modifier. A *static member function* operates more like a regular function than a member function. Specifically, a static member function cannot access data members of the class. (I'll tell you why this restriction exists in just a bit.) Most of the time you will not use static member functions, but sometimes you will be required to. For instance, some Windows API functions use *callbacks* to perform repeated tasks. If you used this kind of function in your class, the callback function would have to be declared as static.

4

> **HOUSE RULES: CLASS MEMBER FUNCTIONS**
>
> ☐ Make public only those functions that users will need in order to properly utilize the class.
>
> ☐ Make private any functions that users do not need to know about.
>
> ☐ Make protected any functions that derived classes may need access to but that users do not need to know about.
>
> ☐ Use static member functions only under special circumstances.
>
> ☐ Declare any class member functions that have to be executed quickly as inline functions. Remember to keep inline functions short.
>
> ☐ Place any code duplicated more than twice in a function.

What's this?

NEW TERM   All classes have a hidden data member called this. this is a pointer to the instance of the class in memory. (A discussion on the this pointer quickly starts to look like a "Who's on First?" comedy sketch, but I'll try anyway.)

Obviously this (pun intended) will require some explanation. First, let's take a look at how the Rect class would look if this were not a hidden data member:

```
class Rect {
  public:
    Rect();
    Rect(int _left, int _top, int _bottom, int _right);
    ~Rect();
    int GetWidth();
    int GetHeight();
    void SetRect(int _left, int _top, int _bottom, int _right);
  private:
    Rect* this;        // if 'this' were not invisible
    int left;
    int top;
    int bottom;
    int right;
    char* text;
};
```

This is effectively what the Rect class looks like to the compiler. When a class object is created, the this pointer automatically gets initialized to the address of the class in memory:

```
TRect* rect = new TRect(20, 20, 100, 100);
// now 'rect' and 'rect->this' have the same value
// because both point to the object in memory
```

"But," you ask, "what does this mean?" Remember that each class instance gets its own copy of the class's data members. But all class instances share the same set of functions for the class (there's no point in duplicating that code for each instance of the class). How does the compiler figure out which instance goes with which function call? Each class member function has a hidden this parameter that goes with it. To illustrate, let's say you have a function for the Rect class called GetWidth(). It would look like this (no pun intended):

```
int Rect::GetWidth()
{
  return right - left;
}
```

That's how the function looks to you and me. To the compiler, though, it looks something like this:

```
int Rect::GetWidth(Rect* this)
{
  return this->right - this->left;
}
```

That's not exactly accurate from a technical perspective, but it's close enough for this discussion. From this code you can see that this is working behind the scenes to keep everything straight for you. You don't have to worry about *how* that happens, but only that it *does* happen.

WARNING

Never modify the this pointer. You can use it to pass a pointer to your class to other functions, or as a parameter in constructing other classes, but don't change its value. Learn to treat this as a read-only variable.

Although this works behind the scenes, it is still a variable that you can access from within the class. As an illustration, let's take a quick peek into VCL. Most of the time you will create components in VCL by dropping them on the form at design time. When you do that, C++Builder creates a pointer to the component and does all sorts of housekeeping chores on your behalf, saving you from concerning yourself with the technical end of things. Sometimes, however, you will create a component at runtime. VCL has this funny insistence (as all good frameworks do) on wanting to keep track of which child objects belong to which parent. For instance, let's say you wanted to create a button on a form when another button is clicked. You need to tell VCL who the parent of the new button is. The code would look like this:

```
void __fastcall TMyForm::Button1Click(TObject *Sender)
{
  TButton* button = new TButton(this);
  button->Parent = this;
```

4

```
button->Caption = "New Button";
button->Left = 100;
button->Top = 100;
button->Show();
// more code
}
```

In this code you can see that this is used in the constructor (this sets the Owner property of the button, but I'll get into that later when I cover VCL components on Day 8, "VCL Components") and also that it is assigned to the Parent property of the newly created button. This will be how you use the this pointer the vast majority of the time in your C++Builder applications.

NOTE

Earlier I said that static member functions can't access class data members. This is true because static member functions do not have a hidden this parameter as regular class member functions do. Without this, a function cannot access class members.

Don't get too hung up on this…er, this (whatever!). When you begin to use VCL, it will quickly become clear when you are required to use this in your C++Builder applications.

An Example

Right now it would be nice if you had an example that uses classes. The following listings contain a program that implements classes. This program allows you to play air traffic controller by issuing commands to three aircrafts. Listing 4.1 is the header for the Airplane class, Listing 4.2 is the source code for the Airplane class, and Listing 4.3 is the main program.

Listing 4.1. AIRPLANE.H.

```
 1: //------------------------------------------------
 2: #ifndef airplaneH
 3: #define airplaneH
 4: #define AIRLINER      0
 5: #define  COMMUTER     1
 6: #define  PRIVATE      2
 7: #define  TAKINGOFF    0
 8: #define  CRUISING     1
 9: #define LANDING       2
10: #define ONRAMP        3
11: #define  MSG_CHANGE   0
```

continues

Listing 4.1. continued

```
12: #define  MSG_TAKEOFF  1
13: #define  MSG_LAND     2
14: #define  MSG_REPORT   3
15: class Airplane {
16:   public:
17:     Airplane(const char* _name, int _type = AIRLINER);
18:     ~Airplane();
19:     virtual int GetStatus(char* statusString);
20:     int GetStatus()
21:     {
22:     return status;
23:     }
24:      int Speed()
25:     {
26:       return speed;
27:     }
28:     int Heading()
29:     {
30:       return heading;
31:     }
32:     int Altitude()
33:     {
34:       return altitude;
35:     }
36:     void ReportStatus();
37:     bool SendMessage(int msg, char* response,
38:       int spd = -1, int dir = -1, int alt = -1);
39:     char* name;
40:   protected:
41:     virtual void TakeOff(int dir);
42:     virtual void Land();
43:   private:
44:     int speed;
45:     int altitude;
46:     int heading;
47:     int status;
48:     int type;
49:     int ceiling;
50: };
51: #endif
```

Listing 4.2. AIRPLANE.CPP.

```
1: #include <stdio.h>
2: #include <iostream.h>
3: #include "airplane.h"
4: //
5: // Constructor performs initialization
6: //
```

```
 7: Airplane::Airplane(const char* _name, int _type) :
 8:   type(_type),
 9:   status(ONRAMP),
10:   speed(0),
11:   altitude(0),
12:   heading(0)
13: {
14:   switch (type) {
15:     case AIRLINER : ceiling = 35000; break;
16:     case COMMUTER : ceiling = 20000; break;
17:     case PRIVATE  : ceiling = 8000;
18:   }
19:   name = new char[50];
20:   strcpy(name, _name);
21: }
22: //
23: // Destructor performs cleanup.
24: //
25: Airplane::~Airplane()
26: {
27:   delete[] name;
28: }
29: //
30: // Gets a message from the user.
31: //
32: bool
33: Airplane::SendMessage(int msg, char* response,
34:   int spd, int dir, int alt)
35: {
36:   //
37:   // Check for bad commands.
38:   //
39:   if (spd > 500) {
40:     strcpy(response, "Speed cannot be more than 500.");
41:     return false;
42:   }
43:   if (dir > 360) {
44:     strcpy(response, "Heading cannot be over 360 degrees.");
45:     return false;
46:   }
47:   if (alt < 100 && alt != -1) {
48:     strcpy(response, "I'd crash, bonehead!");
49:     return false;
50:   }
51:   if (alt > ceiling) {
52:     strcpy(response, "I can't go that high.");
53:     return false;
54:   }
55:   //
56:   // Do something base on which command was sent.
57:   //
58:   switch (msg) {
```

4

continues

Listing 4.2. continued

```
59:        case MSG_TAKEOFF : {
60:          // Can't take off if already in the air!
61:          if (status != ONRAMP) {
62:            strcpy(response, "I'm already in the air!");
63:            return false;
64:          }
65:          TakeOff(dir);
66:          break;
67:        }
68:        case MSG_CHANGE : {
69:          // Can't change anything if on the ground.
70:          if (status == ONRAMP) {
71:            strcpy(response, "I'm on the ground");
72:            return false;
73:          }
74:          // Only change if a non-negative value was passed.
75:          if (spd != -1) speed = spd;
76:          if (dir != -1) heading = dir;
77:          if (alt != -1) altitude = alt;
78:          status == CRUISING;
79:          break;
80:        }
81:        case MSG_LAND : {
82:          if (status == ONRAMP) {
83:            strcpy(response, "I'm already on the ground.");
84:            return false;
85:          }
86:          Land();
87:          break;
88:        }
89:        case MSG_REPORT : ReportStatus();
90:    }
91:    //
92:    // Standard reponse if all went well.
93:    //
94:    strcpy(response, "Roger.");
95:    return true;
96: }
97: //
98: // Perform takeoff.
99: //
100: void
101: Airplane::TakeOff(int dir)
102: {
103:    heading = dir;
104:    status = TAKINGOFF;
105: }
106: //
107: // Perform landing.
108: //
109: void
110: Airplane::Land()
111: {
```

4

```
112:    speed = heading = altitude = 0;
113:    status == ONRAMP;
114: }
115: //
116: // Build a string to report the airplane's status.
117: //
118: int
119: Airplane::GetStatus(char* statusString)
120: {
121:   sprintf(statusString, "%s, Altitude: %d, Heading: %d, "
122:     "Speed: %d\n", name, altitude, heading, speed);
123:   return status;
124: }
125: //
126: // Get the status string and output it to the screen.
127: //
128: void
129: Airplane::ReportStatus()
130: {
131:   char buff[100];
132:   GetStatus(buff);
133:   cout << endl << buff << endl;
134: }
```

Listing 4.3. AIRPORT.CPP.

```
 1: //-----------------------------------------------------
 2: #include <vcl\condefs.h>
 3: #include <iostream.h>
 4: #include <conio.h>
 5: #pragma hdrstop
 6: USERES("Airport.res");
 7: USEUNIT("airplane.cpp");
 8: #include "airplane.h"
 9: int getInput(int max);
10: void getItems(int& speed, int& dir, int& alt);
11: int main(int argc, char **argv)
12: {
13:   char returnMsg[100];
14:   //
15:   // Set up an array of  Airplanes and create
16:   // three Airplane objects.
17:   //
18:   Airplane* planes[3];
19:   planes[0] = new Airplane("TWA 1040");
20:   planes[1] = new Airplane("United Express 749", COMMUTER);
21:   planes[2] = new Airplane("Cessna 3238T", PRIVATE);
22:   //
23:   // Start the loop.
24:   //
```

continues

Listing 4.3. continued

```
25:  do {
26:     int plane, message, speed, altitude, direction;
27:     speed = altitude = direction = -1;
28:     //
29:     // Get a plane to whom a message will be sent.
30:     // List all of the planes and let the user pick one.
31:     //
32:     cout << endl << "Who do you want to send a message to?";
33:     cout << endl << endl << "0. Quit" <<  endl;
34:     for (int i=0;i<3;i++)
35:       cout << i + 1 << ". " << planes[i]->name << endl;
36:     //
37:     // Call the getInput() function to get the plane number.
38:     //
39:     plane = getInput(4);
40:     //
41:     // If the user chose item 0 then break out of the loop.
42:     //
43:     if (plane == -1) break;
44:     //
45:     // The plane acknowledges.
46:     //
47:     cout << endl << planes[plane]->name << ", roger.";
48:     cout << endl << endl;
49:     //
50:     // Allow the user to choose a message to send.
51:     //
52:     cout << "What message do you want to send?" << endl;
53:     cout << endl << "0. Quit" << endl;;
54:     cout << "1. State Change" << endl;
55:     cout << "2. Take Off" << endl;
56:     cout << "3. Land" << endl;
57:     cout << "4. Report Status" << endl;
58:     message = getInput(5);
59:     //
60:     // Break out of the loop if the user chose 0.
61:     //
62:     if (message == -1) break;
63:     //
64:     // If the user chose item 1 then we need to get input
65:     // for the new speed, direction, and altitude. Call
66:     // the getItems() function to do that.
67:     //
68:     if (message == 0)
69:       getItems(speed, direction, altitude);
70:     //
71:     // Send the plane the message.
72:     //
73:     bool goodMsg = planes[plane]->SendMessage(
74:       message, returnMsg, speed, direction, altitude);
```

```
75:    //
76:    // Something was wrong with the message
77:    //
78:    if (!goodMsg) cout << endl << "Unable to comply.";
79:    //
80:    // Display the plane's response.
81:    //
82:    cout << endl << returnMsg << endl;
83:  } while (1);
84:    //
85:    // Delete the Airplane objects.
86:    //
87:    for (int i=0;i<3;i++) delete planes[i];
88: }
89: int getInput(int max)
90: {
91:    int choice;
92:    do {
93:      choice = getch();
94:      choice -= 49;
95:    } while (choice < -1 || choice > max);
96:    return choice;
97: }
98: void getItems(int& speed, int& dir, int& alt)
99: {
100:   cout << endl << "Enter new speed: ";
101:   getch();
102:   cin >> speed;
103:   cout << "Enter new heading: ";
104:   cin >> dir;
105:   cout << "Enter new altitude: ";
106:   cin >> alt;
107:   oout << endl;
108: }
```

ANALYSIS   Let's look first at the header file in Listing 4.1. First notice all the lines that begin with #define. What I am doing here is associating one text string with another. At compile time, the compiler just does a search-and-replace and replaces all occurrences of the first string with the second. #defines are used because it's much easier to remember a text string than it is to remember a number. Which of the following do you prefer?

```
if (type == AIRLINER) ...
// or
if (type == 0) ...
```

Tradition has it that names for #defines be in uppercase, but you can use any mixture of upper- and lowercase letters. I like all uppercase because it tells me at a glance that this is a defined constant and not a variable.

> **NOTE**
>
> Another way of declaring constants is to declare a variable using the
> const modifier. Here's an example:
>
> ```
> const int airliner = 0;
> ```
>
> Using a `const` variable is probably the more modern method of
> defining constants.

The next thing to note in the header is that the class includes some inline functions. These functions are so small that it makes sense to inline them. You might also notice that the Airplane class has one overloaded function called GetStatus(). When called with a character array parameter, it will return a status string as well as the status data member. When called without a parameter, it just returns status. Note that there is only one public data member. The rest of the data members are kept private. The only way to access the private data members is via the public functions. For instance, you can change the speed, altitude, and heading of an airplane only by sending it a message. To use an analogy, consider that an air traffic controller cannot physically change an aircraft's heading. The best he can do is send a message to the pilot and tell him to change to a new heading.

Now turn your attention to Listing 4.2. This is the definition of the Airplane class. The constructor performs initialization, including dynamically allocating storage for the char array that holds the name of the airplane. That memory is freed in the destructor. The SendMessage() function does most of the work. A switch statement determines which message was sent and takes the appropriate action. Notice that the TakeOff() and Land() functions cannot be called directly (they are protected), but rather are called through the SendMessage() function. Again, you can't make an aircraft take off or land; you can only send it a message telling it what you want it to do. The ReportStatus() function calls GetStatus() to get a status string, which it outputs.

The main program is shown in Listing 4.3. The program first sets up an array of Airplane pointers and creates three instances of the Airplane class. Then a loop starts. You can send messages to any of the airplanes by calling the object's SendMessage() function. When you send a message, you get a response back from the airplane. The do-while loop cheats a little in this program. Notice that the test condition is simply 1. This means that the loop will keep running indefinitely. In this case it's not a problem because I am using the break statement to break out of the loop rather than relying on the test condition. Run the program and play with it to get a feel for how it works.

Inheritance

One of the most powerful features of classes in C++ is that they can be extended through inheritance.

Inheritance means taking an existing class and adding functionality by deriving a new class from it.

The class you start with is called the *base class*, and the new class you create is called the *derived class*.

Let's take the `Airplane` class as an example. The civilian and military worlds are quite different, as you know. In order to represent a military aircraft, I can derive a class from `Airplane` and add functionality to it:

```
class MilitaryPlane : public Airplane {
  public:
    MilitaryPlane(char* name, int _type);
    virtual int GetStatus(char* statusString);
  protected:
    virtual void TakeOff();
    virtual void Land()
    virtual void Attack();
    virtual void SetMission();
private:
    Mission theMission;
};
```

A `MilitaryPlane` has everything an `Airplane` has, plus a few more goodies. Note the first line of the class definition. The colon after the class name is used to tell the compiler that I am inheriting from another class. The class name following the colon is the base class from which I am deriving. The `public` keyword, when used here, means that I am claiming access to all the public functions and data members of the base class.

NOTE

When you derive a class from another class, the new class gets all the functionality of the base class plus whatever new features you add. You can add data members and functions to the new class, but you cannot remove anything from what the base class offers.

You'll notice that in the private section there is a line that declares a variable of the `Mission` class. The `Mission` class could encapsulate everything that deals with the mission of a military aircraft: the target, navigation waypoints, ingress and egress altitudes and headings, and so on. This illustrates the use of a data member that is an instance of another class. In fact, you'll see that a lot when programming in C++Builder.

There's something else here that I haven't discussed yet. Note the `virtual` keyword. This specifies that the function is a virtual function.

4

NEW TERM A *virtual function* is a function that will be automatically called if a function by that name exists in the derived class.

For example, note that the `TakeOff()` function is a virtual function in the `Airplane` class. Refer to Listing 4.2. Notice that `TakeOff()` is called by `SendMessage()` in response to the `MSG_TAKEOFF` message. If the `MilitaryPlane` class did not provide its own `TakeOff()` function, the base class's `TakeOff()` function would be called. Because the `MilitaryPlane` class does provide a `TakeOff()` function, that function, rather than the function in the base class, will be called.

NEW TERM Replacing a base class function in a derived class is called *overriding* the function.

In order for overriding to work, the function signature must exactly match that of the function in the base class. In other words, the return type, function name, and parameter list must all be the same as the base class function.

You can override a function with the intention of replacing the base class function, or you can override a function to enhance the base class function. Take the `TakeOff()` function, for example. If you wanted to completely replace what the `TakeOff()` function of `Airplane` does, you would override it and supply whatever code you wanted:

```
void MilitaryPlane::TakeOff(int dir)
{
  // new code goes here
}
```

But if you wanted your function to take the functionality of the base class and add to it, you would first call the base class function and then add new code:

```
void MilitaryPlane::TakeOff(int dir)
{
  Airplane::TakeOff(dir);
  // new code goes here
}
```

By calling the base class function, you get the original functionality of the function. You could then add code before or after the base class call to enhance the function. The scope-resolution operator is used to tell the compiler that you are calling the `TakeOff()` function of the `Airplane` class. Note that the `TakeOff()` function is in the `protected` section of the `Airplane` class. If it were in the `private` section, this would not work because even a derived class cannot access the private members of its ancestor class. By making the `TakeOff()` function protected, it is hidden from the outside world but still accessible to derived classes.

NOTE

The scope-resolution operator is required only when you have derived and base class functions with the same name and the same function signature. You can call a public or protected function of the base class at any time without the need for the scope-resolution operator, provided they aren't overridden. For example, if you wanted to check the status of the aircraft prior to takeoff, you could do something like this:

```cpp
void MilitaryPlane::TakeOff(int dir)
{
  if (GetStatus() != ONRAMP) Land(); // gotta land first!
  Airplane::TakeOff(dir);
  // new code goes here
}
```

In this case, the GetStatus() function exists only in the base class, so there is no need for the scope-resolution operator. In the case of the Land() function, the MilitaryPlane version will be called because it has the most immediate scope.

When you derive a class from another class, you must be sure to call the base class's constructor so that all ancestor classes are properly initialized. Calling the base class constructor is done in the initializer list. Here's how the constructor for MilitaryPlane might look:

```cpp
MilitaryPlane:: MilitaryPlane(char* _name)
  : Airplane(_name, MILITARY)           // call base class
{
  // body of constructor
}
```

Be sure to call the base class constructor whenever you derive a class from a base class. Figure 4.1 illustrates the concept of inheritance.

Figure 4.1.
An example of inheritance.

You can see from Figure 4.1 that the class called F16 is descended from the class called MilitaryFighter. Ultimately, F16 is derived from Airplane since Airplane is the base class for all classes.

Multiple Inheritance

 The act of deriving a class from two or more base classes is called *multiple inheritance*.

Multiple inheritance is not used frequently, but it can be very handy when needed. For example, let's say you had a class called Armaments that kept track of the armaments for a particular aircraft. It might look like this:

```
class Armaments {
  public:
    Armaments();
    LoadArms();
  private:
    bool isArmed;
    int numSidewinders;
    int numSparrows;
    // etc.
};
```

Now let's say that you were to create a class to represent a military fighter. You could inherit from both MilitaryPlane and Armaments:

```
class Fighter : public MilitaryPlane, public Armaments {
  public:
    Fighter(char* name);
  private:
    // other stuff
};
```

Now you have a class that contains all the public elements of MilitaryPlane and all the public elements of Armaments. This would allow you to do the following:

```
Fighter fighter("F16");
fighter.LoadArms();
fighter.SendMessage(...);
// etc.
```

The two base classes are blended to form a single class.

> **NOTE**
>
> You should call the base class constructor for all base classes. The following illustrates:
>
> ```
> F16::F16(char* _name)
>   : MilitaryPlane(_name, F16), Armaments()
>   {
> ```

```
    // body of constructor
}
```

If a class has a default constructor, it is not strictly necessary to call the base class constructor for that class. In most situations, though, you will call the base class constructor for all ancestor classes.

Let me give you one other example. In the United States, the Military Air Command (MAC) is responsible for moving military personnel from place to place. MAC is sort of like the U.S. military's own personal airline. Since personnel are ultimately cargo, this requires a military cargo plane. But since people are special cargo, you can't just throw them in the back of a cargo plane designed to haul freight (not usually, anyway). So what is needed is a military cargo plane that also has all the amenities of a commercial airliner. Look back to Figure 4.1. It appears that to get what we want, we can derive from both MilitaryCargo and Airliner—and we can. Figure 4.2 illustrates.

Figure 4.2.

*An example of
multiple inheritance.*

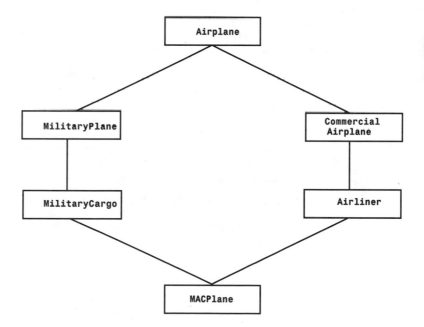

While you may not use multiple inheritance very often, it is a very handy feature to have available when you need it.

NOTE

Classes in VCL do not support multiple inheritance. You can still use multiple inheritance in any classes you write for use in your C++Builder applications.

Basic File I/O

It won't be long before you are going to need the ability to read and write files in your applications. I saved this discussion for now because you needed an understanding of classes in order to understand how file input and output is handled in C++.

If you are going to be doing heavy database operations with C++Builder, you might be relieved to know that you don't have to worry about dealing with reading and writing database files directly. That is all handled for you behind the scenes through C++Builder's VCL database components. VCL also provides support for reading and writing the contents of edit controls, list boxes, and other basic Windows controls. The Windows API provides functions for reading configuration files (.INI files). Many OCX and ActiveX controls know how to save and load files specific to the type of action the control performs.

As you can see, many of the objects you will use in C++Builder will handle file I/O for you. Still, there will be times when you have to read and write your own files, and you'll need a basic understanding of file I/O in order to do that.

Basic file I/O is accomplished via three C++ classes:

☐ The ofstream class, which handles file output

☐ The ifstream class, which handles file input

☐ The fstream class, which handles both file input and output

These classes are derived from the iostream class. You have had some experience with iostream already, although you may not know it. The cout and cin classes I have been using for console input and output are also derived from iostream. iostream itself is derived from a class called ios, which is the base class for all stream input and output in C++.

Does this sound complicated? Well, it is. Sometimes the labyrinth of the streaming classes can be pretty confusing. What I am going to do here is give you a cursory glance at file I/O, but then we'll have to move on. You'll be relieved to know that basic file I/O is not terribly complicated. If you need to do sophisticated file operations, you'll need to dig into the class library help files or get a good book on C++ (such as *Teach Yourself Borland C++ 4.5 in 21 Days, Second Edition* by Sams Publishing) that deals with file I/O in detail.

4

Basic File Input

Reading a text file in C++ is a fairly painless task. Listing 4.4 contains a program that reads its own source file and displays each line as it reads it from disk. First, enter the program as it appears in the listing (remember, don't type the line numbers). Then save the project with the name READFILE. If you don't save the program with this name, the program will not run properly. Compile and run the program. Since the program reads its own source file, the output from the program will be the contents of Listing 4.4.

Listing 4.4. READFILE.CPP.

```
 1: #include <condefs.h>
 2: #include <stdio.h>
 3: #include <stdlib.h>
 4: #include <iostream.h>
 5: #include <fstream.h>
 6: #include <conio.h>
 7: #pragma hdrstop
 8:
 9: int main(int argc, char **argv)
10: {
11:   char buff[80];
12:   ifstream infile;
13:   infile.open("readfile.cpp");
14:   if (!infile) return 0;
15:   while (!infile.eof()) {
16:     infile.getline(buff, sizeof(buff));
17:     cout << buff << endl;
18:   }
19:   infile.close();
20:   cout << endl << "Press any key to continue...";
21:   getch();
22:   return 0;
23: }
```

ANALYSIS The code on line 12 creates an instance of the ifstream class called infile. Line 13 opens the file READFILE.CPP for input. Line 14 checks to see if the file was opened successfully. If it wasn't, the program terminates. Line 15 starts a loop. Notice that the loop expression is a call to the eof() function of the istream class. This function returns true when the file encounters the end of the file. On line 16, one line of text is read from the file using the getline() function. The line of text is placed in the character array called buff. After that, the contents of the character array are sent to the screen. Finally, line 19 closes the file. Notice that on line 4 I #include the IOSTREAM.H header file so the compiler can see the declaration for the ifstream class. As you can see from this example, reading a text file does not require a lot of programming, thanks to C++ and the ifstream class.

One of the `ifstream` constructors takes a `char*` as a parameter so that you can provide a filename when you instantiate the class. Using this constructor, lines 12 and 13 could be condensed into a single line:

```
ifstream infile("readfil.cpp");
```

If you create the object this way, the call to `open()` is unnecessary because the file will automatically be opened from the constructor.

TIP

Don't forget about the double backslash in constant strings! For example, if you wanted to open the WIN.INI file in the Windows directory, you would have to use this:

```
ifstream infile("c:\\windows\\win.ini");
```

I know I've mentioned this before, but I'll guarantee you that at some point you'll goof this up, so I want to drill it into your head while I've got the opportunity.

The call to `close()` on line 19 of Listing 4.4 is not strictly needed. The `ifstream` destructor checks whether the file was left open. If it was, the destructor calls `close()` to ensure that the file is closed before the instance of the class is destroyed. In my programs I almost always call `close()` even though it is not strictly required. Explicitly calling `close()` has the added benefit of documenting that the file is no longer needed.

NOTE

The program in Listing 4.4 contains a minor bug. Due to the way the end of the file is determined, the program will print one blank line before the loop terminates. In order to avoid the extra line, the loop would have to be written like this:

```
while (!infile.getline(buff, sizeof(buff)).eof()) {
  cout << buff << endl;
}
```

Chaining functions like this is perfectly legal, but it's confusing to new C++ programmers. To make the code easier to understand, I allowed the bug to live rather than squashing it.

Because the file-handling classes are derived from `iostream`, you can use the insertion and extraction operators just as you do when writing to the console using `cout` and reading from the console using `cin`. The reason `getline()` is used in Listing 4.4 is because the extraction operator (>>) stops at the first whitespace it encounters. (*Whitespace* includes blank spaces, tabs, and so on.) The `getline()` function, on the other hand, reads from the file until an EOL (end-of-line) character is detected, which is what you want when reading lines of text. When reading single values without whitespace, the extraction operator is very useful. The following code snippet reads a file containing numbers and outputs the numbers to the screen:

```
ifstream infile("somefil.dat");
while (!infile.eof()) {
  int x;
  infile >> x;    // read number from file and assign it to x
  cout << x << endl;
}
```

Note that the file being read is still a text file and not a binary file. The extraction operator knows how to read text from the file and convert it into an integer.

Basic File Output

In some ways, file output is easier than file input. The insertion operator (<<) makes it easy. The procedure is nearly identical to what is done when reading a file. Instead of creating an instance of the `ifstream` class, you create an instance of the `ofstream` class and start throwing things at it. Listing 4.5 contains a program that creates a new file, writes 10 lines of text to it, and closes it. Following that, the file is reopened in read mode, and the contents are read and displayed.

Listing 4.5. WRITEFIL.CPP.

```
 1: #include <condefs.h>
 2: #include <stdio.h>
 3: #include <stdlib.h>
 4: #include <iostream.h>
 5: #include <fstream.h>
 6: #inolude <oonio.h>
 7:
 8: #pragma hdrstop
 9:
10: int main(int argc, char **argv)
11: {
12:   char buff[81];
13:   cout << "Creating File..." << endl;
14:   ofstream outfile("test.dat");
15:   if (!outfile) return 0;
16:   cout << "Writing File..." << endl;
17:   for (int i=0;i<10;i++) {
18:     outfile << "This is line #" << i + 1 << endl;
19:   }
```

continues

Listing 4.5. continued

```
20:   outfile.close();
21:   cout << "Opening File for Input..." << endl;
22:   ifstream infile("test.dat");
23:   if (!infile) return 0;
24:   cout << "Reading File..." << endl << endl;
25:   while (!infile.eof()) {
26:     infile.getline(buff, sizeof(buff));
27:     cout << buff << endl;
28:   }
29:   infile.close();
30:   cout << endl << "Press any key to continue...";
31:   getch();
32:   return 0;
33: }
```

ANALYSIS Line 14 creates an instance of the ofstream class and creates a file called TEST.DAT. Once the file has been created, a loop writes 10 lines of text to the file. Line 18 illustrates the use of the insertion operator to write to the file. Notice that a text string is written, followed by an integer value (i + 1). The integer is converted to a string and inserted in the output stream. Last but not least, the endl manipulator is inserted to terminate the string. This is repeated for each iteration of the loop. Line 20 closes the file after the loop ends. In this case it is necessary to close the file because we are going to reopen it to read the file. If we do close the file, it cannot be opened for reading. In lines 25–28 I use code similar to what was used in the READFILE.CPP example to display the contents of the file. When the program in Listing 4.5 runs, the output looks like this:

OUTPUT
```
Creating File...
Writing File...
Opening File for Input...
Reading File...
This is line #1
This is line #2
This is line #3
This is line #4
This is line #5
This is line #6
This is line #7
This is line #8
This is line #9
This is line #10
Press any key to continue...
```

Specifying File Modes

Files can be opened in several different modes. For example, the default action when a file is opened using the ofstream class is to create a new file. This means that if you use the default open mode, you will overwrite the file if it already exists. Often that is not what you want.

For example, sometimes you want to append data to the end of an existing file rather than create a new file. In that case you can append data to the end of a file by opening the file in append mode. To specify append mode, you must use one of the ios class's open_mode specifiers in the ofstream constructor when you create the object:

```
ofstream outfile("test.dat", ios::app);  // open in append mode
```

This file will be opened in append mode and any new data written to the file will be written to the end of the file. There are several specifiers you can use when opening files. Table 4.1 lists the open_mode enumeration's values and their descriptions.

Table 4.1. ios **class** open_mode **specifiers.**

Specifier	Description
app	The file is opened and any new data will be appended to the end of the file.
ate	Seek to the end of the file when the file is opened.
in	The file is opened for input (reading). This is the default for the ifstream class.
out	The file is opened for output (writing). This is the default for the ofstream class.
binary	The file is opened in binary mode. The default is to open the file in text mode. In text mode, when the file is read, carriage-return/linefeed (CR/LF) pairs are converted to a single linefeed character (LF). When the file is written, linefeed characters are converted to CR/LF pairs before being written to the file. In binary mode no conversion of CR/LR pairs takes place.
trunc	Opens the file and clears the contents. If neither app nor ate are specified, trunc is the default.
nocreate	The file will not be created if it does not exist. Open() will fail if the file does not exist. Opening an ifstream with this flag can be used to check for the existence of a file.
noreplace	Similar to nocreate except that Open will fail unless either app or ate is specified.

You can or together two or more of the values listed in Table 4.1 if needed. For example, let's say you wanted to open a file in binary mode and that you wanted to append data to the end of the file. In that case the constructor would look like this:

```
ofstream outfile("test.dat", ios::app | ios::binary);
```

This will open the file in binary mode and move the file pointer to the end of the file. Any new data will be written to the end of the file.

> Binary files are treated differently than text files (see the binary specifier in Table 4.1). To read binary files, you will have to have an understanding of the read(), write(), put(), and get() functions. We don't have the time to go into each of those functions at this point. If you need more information on binary file operations, you might want to get a good book on C++ that covers file I/O in detail.

Basic file I/O is pretty easy, really. But as I said earlier, if you need to do complicated file I/O, you are going to have to tie into the online help or get hold of a good book on file I/O in C++ (again, *Teach Yourself Borland C++ 4.5 in 21 Days, Second Edition* by Sams Publishing is a good bet).

Summary

Today you have learned about classes in C++. A well-designed class is easy to use and saves many programming hours. I'd even go so far as to say that a well-designed class is a joy to use—especially when it's of your own creation. Early in the chapter you learned about some of the features of functions that are specific to C++. You learned about function overloading, virtual functions, inline functions, and default parameters in functions. All these are heavily used in designing classes in C++. Finally, the chapter finished up with an introduction to basic file I/O operations.

The lessons of these first four days are important to understand as you continue through this book. If it doesn't make complete sense to you, don't despair. As we continue through the following days, you will see these concepts repeated and put to use in programs that have more practical application than the console apps we've been working with thus far.

> Learning C++ can and will lead to brain overload! It's natural, and you shouldn't worry about it. You might put down this book for the evening, turn out the lights, and think, "I'll never get it." Trust me, you will.

Sometimes it's necessary to take a couple days off and let it all soak in. In fact, if I thought I could get by with it I'd make Day 5 a blank chapter called "A Day of Rest." Take it a little at a time, and one of these days you'll be just like Archimedes—you'll be running around your office or your house shouting "Eureka!" because the light just came on in your noggin. But keep track of your clothes, will you? The neighbors could be watching.

Workshop

The Workshop contains quiz questions to help you solidify your understanding of the material covered and exercises to provide you with experience in using what you have learned. You can find answers to the quiz questions in Appendix A, "Answers to Quiz Questions."

Q&A

Q How can I keep a class member function private to the outside world but allow derived classes to call it?

A Make it protected. A protected function is not accessible to users of your class but is accessible to derived classes.

Q What does *data abstraction* mean?

A Data abstraction means hiding the details of the class that the users of the class don't need to see. A class might have dozens of data members and functions, but only a few that the user can see. Make visible (public) only the functions that a user needs to know about to use the class.

Q What is an object?

A Effectively speaking, an object is any block of code that can be treated as a separate entity in your programs. An object in C++ generally means a class. In C++Builder, that definition is expanded to include VCL components. OCX and ActiveX controls could also be considered objects.

Q Can my class have more than one constructor?

A Yes. Your class can have as many constructors as needed, provided that you follow the rules of function overloading.

4

Q Do I have to understand every aspect of file I/O to program in C++Builder?

A No. C++Builder has plenty of built-in file I/O through its use of components. A basic understanding of file I/O is a good idea in any case. As always, it depends on what your program does.

Q Can I open a file in such a way that I can read from and write to the file as needed?

A Yes. In addition to the file I/O classes I discussed in this chapter, there is also a class called `fstream`. This class allows you to read from a file, write to the file, and reposition the file pointer as needed.

Quiz

1. How do classes and structures differ in C++?

2. What is the purpose of having private data members and functions?

3. How can you keep data members private, yet allow users to read and set their values?

4. How and when is a class's destructor called?

5. What does it mean to override a function of the base class?

6. How can you override a base class function and still get the benefit of the operation the base class function performs?

7. What does an initializer list do?

8. Can a class contain other class instances as data members?

9. How can you get the functionality of two separate classes all rolled into a single class?

Exercises

1. Write a class that takes a person's height in inches and returns the height in feet.

2. Derive a class from the class in exercise 1 that also returns the height in meters, centimeters, or millimeters. (**Hint:** There are 25.4 millimeters in an inch.)

3. Write a program that takes user input and writes it to a data file.

4. Modify the program in exercise 3 so that it reads the data file and displays the output after the file is written.

5. Take a day off from work. You've earned it!

Day 5

C++ Class Frameworks and the Visual Component Model

by Kent Reisdorph

Today I am going to talk about class frameworks. I will tell you what a framework is and let you know what your options are for writing Windows programs in today's fast-paced software industry. In doing so, I will look at the following:

- ☐ Borland's Object Windows Library (OWL)
- ☐ Microsoft's Microsoft Foundation Class Library (MFC)
- ☐ Borland's Visual Component Library (VCL)

Frameworks 101

"In the beginning there was C...." If you recall, I started my discussion of the C++ programming language with that statement. The same is true of Windows programming—in the beginning, the vast majority of Windows programs were written in C. In fact, the Windows Application Programming Interface (API) is just a huge collection of C functions—hundreds of them. There are still undoubtedly thousands of programmers out there writing Windows programs in C.

Somewhere along the line, some folks at Borland decided, "There has *got* to be an easier way!" (Actually, the framework revolution may have started on several different fronts at once, but Borland was certainly a leader in the field.) It was apparent that Windows programming was very well suited to the C++ language, and vice versa. By creating classes that encapsulate common Windows programming tasks, a programmer could be much more productive. Once a class was created to encapsulate the various duties of a window, for instance, that class could be used over and over again. The framework revolution began.

But I haven't actually told you what a framework is yet.

 NEW TERM   A *framework* is a collection of classes that simplifies programming in Windows by encapsulating often-used programming techniques. Frameworks are also called *class libraries*.

Popular frameworks have classes that encapsulate windows, edit controls, list boxes, graphics operations, bitmaps, scrollbars, dialog boxes, and on and on.

So What's the Big Deal?

That's a good question. The bottom line is that frameworks make Windows programming much easier than it would be in straight C. Let me give you an example. Listing 5.1 contains a portion of a Windows program written in C. This section of code loads a bitmap file from disk and displays the bitmap in the center of the screen. None of this will make sense to you right now, but that's not the point.

Listing 5.1. C code to load and display a bitmap.

```
1: HPALETTE hPal;
2: BITMAPFILEHEADER bfh;
3: BITMAPINFOHEADER bih;
4: LPBITMAPINFO lpbi = 0;
5: HFILE hFile;
6: DWORD nClrUsed, nSize;
7: HDC hDC;
```

```
 8: HBITMAP hBitmap;
 9: void _huge *bits;
10: do
11: {
12:    if ((hFile = _lopen(data.FileName, OF_READ)) == HFILE_ERROR) break;
13:    if (_hread(hFile, &bfh, sizeof(bfh)) != sizeof(bfh)) break;
14:    if (bfh.bfType != 'BM') break;
15:    if (_hread(hFile, &bih, sizeof(bih)) != sizeof(bih)) break;
16:    nClrUsed =
17:       (bih.biClrUsed) ? bih.biClrUsed : 1 << bih.biBitCount;
18:    nSize =
19:       sizeof(BITMAPINFOHEADER) + nClrUsed * sizeof(RGBQUAD);
20:    lpbi = (LPBITMAPINFO) GlobalAllocPtr(GHND, nSize);
21:    if (!lpbi) break;
22:    hmemcpy(lpbi, &bih, sizeof(bih));
23:    nSize = nClrUsed * sizeof(RGBQUAD);
24:    if (_hread(hFile, &lpbi->bmiColors, nSize) != nSize) break;
25:    if (_llseek(hFile, bfh.bfOffBits, 0) == HFILE_ERROR) break;
26:    nSize = bfh.bfSize-bfh.bfOffBits;
27:    if ((bits = GlobalAllocPtr(GHND, nSize)) == NULL) break;
28:    if (_hread(hFile, bits, nSize) != nSize) break;
29:    hDC = GetDC(hWnd);
30:    hBitmap = CreateDIBitmap(hDC, &(lpbi->bmiHeader), CBM_INIT,
31:                       bits, lpbi, DIB_RGB_COLORS);
32:    if (hBitmap) {
33:      LPLOGPALETTE lppal;
34:      DWORD nsize = sizeof(LOGPALETTE)
35:         + (nClrUsed-1) * sizeof(PALETTEENTRY);
36:      lppal = (LPLOGPALETTE)  GlobalAllocPtr(GHND, nSize);
37:      if (lppal) {
38:        lppal->palVersion = 0x0300;
39:        lppal->palNumEntries = (WORD) nClrUsed;
40:        hmemcpy(lppal->palPalEntry, lpbi->bmiColors,
41:           nClrUsed * sizeof(PALETTEENTRY));
42:        hPal = CreatePalette(lppal);
43:        (void) GlobalFreePtr(lppal);
44:      }
45:    }
46: } while(FALSE);
47: if (hFile != HFILE_ERROR) _lclose(hFile);
48: HPALETTE oldPal = SelectPalette(hDC, hPal, FALSE);
49: RealizePalette(hDC);
50: HDC hMemDC = CreateCompatibleDC(hDC);
51: HBITMAP oldBitmap =(HBITMAP)SelectObject(hMemDC, hBitmap);
52: BitBlt(hDC, 0, 0, (WORD)bih.biWidth, (WORD)bih.biHeight,
53:    hMemDC, 0, 0, SRCCOPY);
54: SelectObject(hMemDC, oldBitmap);
55: DeleteDC(hMemDC);
56: SelectPalette(hDC, oldPal, FALSE);
57: ReleaseDC(hWnd, hDC);
58: if (bits) (void) GlobalFreePtr(bits);
59: if (lpbi) (void) GlobalFreePtr(lpbi);
```

5

That looks just a little intimidating, doesn't it? The fact is, I even had to get some help from my friends on the BCPPLIB forum of CompuServe (thanks, Paul!). Now look at the equivalent using Borland's Object Windows Library, shown in Listing 5.2.

Listing 5.2. OWL code to load and display a bitmap.

```
1: TDib dib("test.bmp");
2: TPalette pal(dib);
3: TBitmap bitmap(dib, &pal);
4: TClientDC dc(*this);
5: dc.SelectObject(pal);
6: dc.RealizePalette();
7: TMemoryDC memdc(dc);
8: memdc.SelectObject(bitmap);
9: dc.BitBlt(0, 0, bitmap.Width(), bitmap.Height(), memdc, 0, 0);
```

So which would you rather use? You don't even have to know what these code snippets do to make that decision. It's easy to see that the OWL version is shorter and more readable. (VCL makes the task even easier by providing a bitmap component that you drop on a form. I don't want to get ahead of myself, though, so I'll save that discussion for a little later.)

These examples sum up what frameworks are all about. Frameworks hide details from you that you don't need to know about. Everything that is contained in Listing 5.1 is performed behind the scenes in the OWL code in Listing 5.2. You don't need to know every detail about what goes on behind the scenes when OWL does its thing, and you probably don't want to know. All you want to do is take the objects that make up a framework and put them to use in your programs.

A good framework takes full advantage of OOP. Some do that better than others. Borland's Object Windows Library and Visual Component Model are tremendous examples of object-oriented programming. They provide the proper abstraction needed for you to rise above the clutter and get down to the serious business of programming.

So What's the Catch?

A little skeptical, are you? Good. You're bright enough to figure out that if you have all of that ease of use, you must be giving something up. Truth is, you are right. You might think that a program written with a framework will be larger and slower than its counterpart written in C. That's partially correct. Applications written with frameworks don't necessarily have to be slower than programs written in C, though. There is some additional overhead inherent in the C++ language, certainly, but for the most part it is not noticeable in a typical Windows program.

The primary trade-off is that Windows programs written in C++ tend to be larger than their straight C counterparts. For example, let's say you had a simple Windows program written in C that was 75KB in size. The equivalent program written with one of the framework libraries might end up being 200KB in size. That's a significant difference, yet this example demonstrates the worst-case scenario. The difference in final program size between a C application and a C++ application written with a framework is going to be most noticeable in very small programs. As your programs increase in size and become more sophisticated, the difference in size is much less noticeable.

One of the differences is simply the difference between C and C++. C++ carries additional overhead for features such as exception handling, runtime type information (RTTI), and other C++ goodies. In my opinion, the difference in code size is an acceptable trade-off for the features that C++ provides. Now, before you label me as a code-bloat proponent, let me say that I am as conscientious as the next guy when it comes to code bloat. I believe that we should all write the tightest code we can, given the tools we use. I am also a realist, and I understand that time-to-market is a driving force in the software industry today. I am willing to trade some code size for the power that C++ and an application framework give me.

Frameworks Teach Object-Oriented Programming and Design

If you end up getting serious about this crazy game we call Windows programming, you will eventually end up peeking into the source code of your favorite framework. Sooner or later you'll want to know how the big boys do things. The OWL or VCL source code is a great place to go for that kind of information.

 NOTE

> The MFC source code is probably not the best place to go to see good object-oriented design in action. MFC lacks the elegance, abstraction, and overall design that make a top-notch framework. In addition, it tends to break OOP rules from time to time. MFC may well be the most popular framework, but that doesn't mean it is the best framework from an OOP standpoint.

Some weekend when the leaves are all raked, the house trim has been painted, the laundry is all done, the kids are shipped off for a weekend at grandma's, and you think you have a pretty good handle on C++, you should spend some time browsing your favorite framework's source code. It can be intimidating at first, but after a while you start to see what the designers were up to. Don't strain yourself. Attempt to understand the things that bump up against the limits of your knowledge regarding C++. Leave the complicated stuff for next month. But notice how the framework designers use private, protected, and public access in classes. Notice how and when they implement inline functions. Notice how things that should be kept hidden from the user aren't in public view. Studying a good C++ class library can teach you a great deal about C++ and object-oriented design.

The C++ Framework Wars

The frameworks need to be separated into two categories: C++ frameworks and VCL. First I'll discuss the C++ frameworks and then I'll move on to VCL. There are really only two viable C++ frameworks, and they are Borland's OWL and Microsoft's MFC.

Borland's Object Windows Library

Borland took the lead role in the framework race with OWL a few years back. First there was OWL 1.0. This first version of OWL was a separate product sold by Borland for use with its Borland C++ 3.0 compiler. (Actually, the very first OWL was written for Turbo Pascal and was later converted to C++.) OWL 1.0 was a good framework, but because of some proprietary syntax and other issues, it wasn't the design that Borland would eventually stick with for the future of OWL. OWL 1.0 did, however, do the entire Windows programming community a service—it got the framework ball rolling. Although OWL 1.0 was not the first framework ever written, it certainly was the first to gain mass-market appeal.

After OWL 1 came OWL 2.0. OWL 2 was a masterpiece. It implemented many of the latest C++ language features—not because they were new, but because they made sense. Best of all, OWL 2 was included as part of the Borland C++ 4.0 compiler. From this point on, Borland would include OWL as part of its Borland C++ package. Borland C++ compilers have always been first to implement new C++ features, and OWL 2 put those features to good use. OWL 2 also did away with the proprietary syntax that plagued OWL 1. OWL 2 was all standard C++ that could be compiled with any C++ compiler—at least in theory. As it was, there were few C++ compilers implementing the latest and greatest C++ features, so OWL 2 was typically used only with Borland compilers.

Borland released a revision to OWL 2.0 called OWL 2.5. For the most part, the changes were minor. They were minor in the sense that they didn't add a lot to OWL 2 itself; a few bug fixes here and there and a few new classes. But in one way OWL 2.5 was a major release— it added OLE (object linking and embedding) support in a new set of classes called the Object Components Framework (OCF). OCF is not technically part of OWL. It works very well with OWL, but at the same time it can be used independently of OWL.

5

The latest and greatest OWL is 5.0. OWL 5 represents significant enhancements to OWL 2.5. The primary changes come in new OWL classes that encapsulate the new Win32 custom controls. OCF was also updated in the OWL 5.0 release.

OWL's strengths are considerable. First, it is an architectural wonder. It is obvious that OWL was very well thought out from the beginning. I can't say enough about my admiration for OWL designers Carl Quinn, Bruneau Babet, and the other OWL team members. OWL is very OOP friendly and follows all the OOP rules. Its level of abstraction strikes a good balance between ease of use and power. OWL has one major advantage over its competitors: It can be used in both 16-bit and 32-bit programs. Borland has even emulated some of the 32-bit custom controls for use in 16-bit programs. While these emulations are not perfect in all cases, they are usable and give you a method of getting the 32-bit look and feel even in 16-bit programs.

OWL also has its weaknesses. Ironically, one of OWL's strengths leads, in some people's minds, to one of its weaknesses. OWL has done a great job of encapsulating the Windows environment and that is certainly a strength. Part of the problem with that level of encapsulation is that OWL is complex, and it is sometimes difficult to find your way around when you are first learning OWL. The complexity of OWL is considered by some to be one of its weaknesses. It takes time to master, no question about it. But once you have mastered OWL, you can be very efficient in writing Windows programs.

The Microsoft Foundation Class Library

Sometime between OWL 1 and OWL 2, the Microsoft Foundation Class (MFC) Library was born. MFC is included as part of Microsoft's Visual C++ compiler package. Actually, versions of MFC ship with compilers by Symantec, Watcom, and, believe it or not, Borland (there may be others as well). Typically Microsoft has not licensed the most current version of MFC to other compiler vendors (Symantec and Watcom), but Borland C++ 5.01 included MFC version 4.1, which at the time was the latest version of MFC (a newer version, 4.2, came out shortly thereafter).

It could be said that MFC is a different type of class library than OWL. MFC is less abstract and lies closer to the Windows API. MFC's strengths come in three primary areas. First, it is relatively easy to learn. (Understand that no C++ framework dealing with Windows programming is going to be *easy* to learn, but MFC is a little easier to pick up than the competition.) It is easier to learn primarily because it is less abstract in some areas. If you are new to Windows programming, you will probably find OWL and MFC about equal when it comes to learning the framework. If you are coming from a C programming background and already know the Windows API, MFC is almost certainly going to be easier to learn.

5

Another strength of MFC, according to some, is that it is a thin wrapper around the Windows API. Again, for Windows programmers who are moving from programming in C to programming in C++ with MFC, this is an advantage. They can begin to use MFC and feel somewhat at home.

Finally, MFC has the distinct advantage of belonging to Microsoft. The advantage is that as new Windows features and technologies come along, MFC can be first to implement them. Microsoft can release a new technology, and MFC can already have support for that technology when it is announced. That certainly doesn't hurt!

MFC has its weaknesses too. First and foremost, it is a thin wrapper around the Windows API. "Wait a minute!" you say. "I thought you said that was one of MFC's strengths!" Yes, I did. It's also one of its weaknesses. Some folks would consider MFC's close tie to the API a strength. I consider it a weakness. The whole idea behind a class library is to shield the user from things he or she doesn't need to know about. MFC fails that test in many cases. Folks who are coming from Windows programming in C consider that a strength. You can form your own opinion. Along those same lines, MFC is not OOP friendly. Sometimes it appears to be a hastily implemented collection of classes that don't work and play well together rather than something planned and designed from the ground up to work as a unit.

Another problem with MFC is that the latest version is 32-bit only, as is the Visual C++ 4.0 compiler. Although you can still write 16-bit programs using Microsoft's Visual C++ 1.5 (which comes with Visual C++ 4.0), you will likely find a disappointing development environment.

So Who's Winning?

Without question, MFC is more widely used than OWL. Part of the reason is that both MFC and the Visual C++ compiler bear the Microsoft name. It's no secret that Microsoft is king of the hill in the PC software industry. It is also no secret that Microsoft has marketing power that other companies can only dream about. In addition, there is a prevailing attitude of (to slightly modify a coined phrase) "No one ever got fired for buying Microsoft."

I firmly believe that OWL is the better framework. Few who have used both OWL and MFC extensively would argue that point. But MFC is undoubtedly the C++ framework of choice today. There are many reasons, some of which I've alluded to already. Other reasons include a perceived lack of direction on Borland's part in recent years. Some managers prefer to play it safe and buy a product produced by "the big M" regardless of technical merit. Hopefully that attitude won't eventually lead us to a software industry with a gross lack of competition. This industry desperately needs companies like Borland that will push the envelope.

So what is the future of C++ frameworks? It's nearly impossible to guess at this point. It could be that both MFC and OWL are losing to the new kid on the block—components. Let's take a look at the Visual Component Library now.

The Visual Component Library: The New Kid on the Block

In 1995 Borland introduced a revolutionary new product called Delphi. It was an instant hit. Delphi offered rapid application development (RAD) using something called *components*. Components are objects that can be dropped on a form and manipulated via properties, methods, and events. It's visual programming, if you will.

The concept of form-based programming was first popularized by Microsoft's Visual Basic. Unlike Visual Basic, though, Delphi used a derivative of Pascal as its programming language. This new language, called *Object Pascal*, introduced OOP to the Pascal language. In a sense, Object Pascal is to Pascal what C++ is to C. Delphi and Object Pascal represented the marriage of object-oriented programming and form-based programming. In addition, Delphi could produce standalone executables. *Real* programs. Programs that did not require a runtime DLL in order to run; programs that were compiled, not interpreted; programs that ran tens of times faster than Visual Basic programs. The programming world was impressed.

Delphi didn't just throw Object Pascal at you and let you flounder. It also introduced the Visual Component Library (VCL). VCL is an application framework for Windows programming in Object Pascal. But VCL is not really comparable to OWL and MFC. Yes, it is a framework, but the core is very different. It is different primarily because it was designed around the concept of properties, methods, and events.

You may be wondering why I'm talking about Delphi. The reason is simple—it's because the very same VCL that is the heart of Delphi is also the heart of C++Builder. That may come as a shock to you. If you are coming from a C++ background, you might be scratching your head right now, wondering how that works. If you are coming from a Pascal background, you're probably grinning from ear to ear. If you are coming to C++Builder from any other type of background, you probably don't care either way. In the end, it doesn't really matter because it works. Let's look a little deeper into VCL.

Components

As I talked about on Day 1, "Getting Your Feet Wet," VCL components are objects that perform a specific programming task. VCL components are wrapped up in Object Pascal classes. From this point on in this book, we will be encountering components on a daily basis. I won't spend a lot of time explaining every detail of components right now because you will see by example how components work as you go through the rest of the book. Tomorrow I'll explain components in more detail.

Properties, Methods, and Events

On Day 1 I gave you a brief introduction to the properties, methods, and events model. These three ingredients make up the public interface of components in VCL (the part of the component the user will see). Let's take a look at these elements one at a time.

Properties

Properties are elements of a component that control how the component operates. Many components have common properties. All visual components, for example, have a Top and a Left property. These two properties control where the component will be positioned on a form. In the case of form components, the Top and Left properties control where the form will be placed on the screen when the form is displayed. All components have an Owner property, which VCL uses to keep track of the child components a particular parent form or component owns.

A picture is always worth a thousand words, so let's fire up C++Builder again and I'll show you properties in action. When you start C++Builder, you are greeted with a blank form and the Object Inspector.

NOTE

If you have the C++Builder options configured to save the desktop when you close C++Builder, you may see the last project you were working on when you start C++Builder. If that's the case, choose File | New Application from the main menu to get a blank form.

Right now the Object Inspector should look something like Figure 5.1. If necessary, click on the Properties tab of the Object Inspector window so that the form's properties are displayed. The component's properties are arranged in alphabetical order. If more properties exist than can be displayed at one time, the Object Inspector will have a scrollbar so that you can view additional properties. The Object Inspector window can be moved and sized. I like my Object Inspector as tall as my screen permits so that I can see the maximum number of properties at one time. Scroll down through the properties until you locate the Left property and then click on it. Change the value for the Left property (any number between 0 and 600 will do) and press Enter on the keyboard. Notice how the form moves as you change the value.

This illustrates an important aspect of properties—they are more than simple data members of a class. Each property has an underlying data member associated with it, but the property itself is not a class data member. Changing a property often leads to code executed behind the scenes.

5

Figure 5.1.

The Object Inspector window.

 Properties are often tied to *access methods* that execute when the property is modified.

> **NOTE**
>
> Things start to get a little confusing at this point. As I said, VCL is written in Pascal. Pascal uses the term *method* where C++ uses the term *function*. To further muddy the waters, Pascal uses the term *function* to refer to a method that returns a value, and the term *procedure* to refer to a method that does not return a value. I would be happy enough to call them all functions (being the old C++ hacker that I am), but when discussing VCL I will use the Pascal parlance. For the most part I will use the generic term *method*.

Properties can be changed at design time (when you are designing your form) and at runtime (when the program is running through code you write). In either case, if the property has an access method, that access method will be called and executed when the property is modified. You have already seen an example of changing a property at design time when you changed the Left property and watched the form move on the screen. That is one of the strengths of VCL and how it is used in C++Builder: You can instantly see on the screen what the result of your design change will be. Not all properties are able to show a visible change on the form at design time, however, so this does not happen in every case. Still, when possible the results of the new property value are immediately shown on the form.

To change a property at runtime, you simply make an assignment to the property. When you make an assignment, VCL works behind the scenes to call the access method for that property. To change the Left property at runtime, you would use code like this:

```
MainForm->Left = 200;
```

In the case of the Left property (as well as the Top property), VCL moves and repaints the form. (You Windows API programmers can figure out that this eventually translates into calls to the Windows API functions SetWindowPos() and InvalidateRect().)

NOTE
> Notice that the previous code line uses the indirect member operator (->) to set the property. All VCL components are allocated from the heap. The indirection operator is always used to access a component's properties and methods. Classes you write for use in your C++Builder applications can be allocated either from the heap or from the stack, but all VCL component classes, and all classes derived from them, must be allocated from the heap.

NEW TERM Properties actually have two access *specifiers*, which are used when properties are read or modified. There is a *read specifier* and a *write specifier*.

Suffice it to say that the access specifiers associate read and write methods (functions) with the property. When the property is read or written to, the functions associated with the property are called automatically. When you make an assignment as in the previous example, you are accessing the write specifier. In effect, VCL checks to see whether an access method exists for the write specifier. If so, the access method is called. If no access method exists, VCL simply assigns the new value to the data member associated with the property.

When you reference a property (use the property as the right side of an equation), you are accessing the read specifier:

```
int x = MainForm->Left;
```

In this case, VCL calls the read specifier to read the value of the Left property. In many cases, the read specifier does very little more than return the current value for a property.

The properties of the property (sorry, I couldn't resist!) are determined by the writer of the component. A property can be read-only. A read-only property can be read—its value can be retrieved—but not written to. In other words, you can fetch the value of the property, but you can't change it. In rare cases, a property could be made write-only (a property that can be written to but not read is not very useful in most cases). This is obviously the opposite of a read-only property.

Finally, some properties can be specified to be runtime-only. A runtime-only property is one that can only be accessed at runtime but not at design time. Since a runtime-only property does not apply at design time, it is not displayed in the Object Inspector. A runtime-only property can be declared as read-only, too, which means that it can only be accessed at runtime and can only be read (but not written to).

Some properties use an array as the underlying data member. To illustrate let's put a memo component on our blank form. Go to the C++Builder Component Palette, choose the Standard tab, and click on the Memo button. (The tool tip will tell when you are over the Memo button.) Now move to the form and click on the form where you want the top-left corner of the memo to appear. As soon as you place the memo component on the form, the Object Inspector switches to show you the properties of the component just placed on the form, in this case a TMemo. Locate the Lines property and click on it. Notice that the property value contains the text (TStrings) and that there is a little button with an ellipsis (...) to the right of the property value.

NOTE

> The ellipsis button tells you that this property can be edited by invoking a property editor dialog box. For an array of strings, for instance, a dialog box will be displayed in which you can type the strings. In the case of the Font property, clicking the ellipsis button will invoke the Choose Font dialog box. The exact type of the property editor is property specific, although certain properties can share a common editor. You can bring up the property editor by clicking the ellipsis button or by double-clicking the property value.

The Lines property for a memo component is an array of strings. When you double-click the Value column, the string editor is displayed and you can then type the strings you want to be displayed in the memo component when the application runs. If you don't want any strings displayed in the memo component, you will need to clear the property editor of any strings.

Properties can be instances of other VCL classes. The Font property is an obvious example. A *font* includes things like the typeface, the color, the font size, and so on. Locate the Font property in the Object Inspector. (It doesn't matter whether you have the memo component or the form selected.) Notice that there is a plus sign before the word "Font." This tells you that there are individual properties within this property that can be set. If you double-click on the property name, you will see that the Object Inspector expands the property to reveal the individual elements of that property. You can now edit the elements of the Font property individually. The same settings can be edited by invoking the Property Editor. Either method can be used, and in the end the results are the same.

NEW TERM   Some properties are *sets*, or collections of other properties.

The Style property within the Font object is a good example of a set. Notice that Style has a plus sign in front of it. If you double-click on the Style property, you will see that the Style node expands to reveal the contents of the set. In this case the set consists of the various styles available for fonts: bold, italic, underline, and strikeout. By double-clicking a style, you can turn that style on or off (set the value to `true` or `false`). Some properties can be *enumerations*.

NEW TERM   An *enumeration* is a list of possible choices for a property.

When you click on an enumeration property, a drop-down arrow button appears to the right of the value. To see the choices in the enumeration, click the drop-down button to display the list of choices. Alternatively, you can double-click the value column for the property. As you double-click on the property's value, the Object Inspector will cycle through (or enumerate) the choices. The `Cursor` property gives a good example of an enumerated property. Locate the `Cursor` property and click the arrow button to expose the list of possible cursors you can choose from.

As long as you've got C++Builder running and a blank form displayed, you might as well spend some time examining the various components and their properties. Go ahead; I'll wait.

HOUSE RULES: PROPERTIES

☐ Properties appear to be class data members and are accessed like class data members.

☐ Properties are *not* class data members. They are a special category of class member.

☐ Properties often invoke an access method when they are written to (assigned a value), but not always. It depends on how the particular component is written.

☐ Properties cannot be used as parameters in function calls.

☐ Properties usually have default values. The default value is the value that initially shows up in the Object Inspector when a component is first utilized and is the value that will be used if no specific value is assigned.

☐ Properties can be designed as read-only, write-only, or runtime-only.

☐ Runtime-only properties do not show up in the Object Inspector and can be modified only at runtime.

☐ Properties can include

　　☐ Simple data types

　　☐ Arrays

　　☐ Sets

　　☐ Enumerations

　　☐ VCL class objects

Methods

Methods in VCL components are functions (ahem...*procedures* and functions) that can be called to make the component perform certain actions. For example, all visual components have a method called Show(), which displays the component, and a method called Hide(), which hides the component. Calling these methods is exactly the same as calling class member functions as we did on Day 3, "Up to Your Neck in C++":

```
MyWindow->Show();
// do some stuff, then later...
MyWindow->Hide();
```

In C++ parlance, methods are member functions of a component class. Methods in VCL can be declared as public, protected, or private just as functions in C++ can be public, protected, or private. These keywords mean the same thing in Object Pascal classes as they do in C++ classes. Public methods can be accessed by users of the component. In this example, both the Show() and Hide() methods are public. Protected methods cannot be accessed by users of the component, but can be accessed by classes (components) derived from a component. And, of course, private methods can be accessed only within a class itself.

Just like C++ functions, some methods take parameters and return values, and others do not. It depends entirely on how the method was written by the component writer. For example, the GetTextBuf() method retrieves the text of a TEdit component. This method could be used to get the text from an edit control as follows:

```
char buff[256];
int numChars = EditControl->GetTextBuf(buff, sizeof(buff));
```

As you can see, this particular method takes two parameters and returns an integer. When this method is called, the contents of the edit control are placed in buff, and the return value will be the number of characters retrieved from the edit control.

For now, that's all you need to know to use methods. I'll get into more detail later when I talk about writing components.

5

HOUSE RULES: METHODS

- ☐ Methods can be private, protected, or public.
- ☐ Methods are called using the indirect membership operator.
- ☐ Methods may take parameters and may return values.
- ☐ Some methods take no parameters and return no value.
- ☐ A procedure is a method that does not return a value.
- ☐ A function is a method that returns a value.
- ☐ Only public methods can be called by component users.

Events

 Windows is said to be an *event-driven* environment. Event-driven means that a program is driven by events that occur within the Windows environment. Events include mouse movements, mouse clicks, and keypresses.

Programmers moving from DOS or mainframe programming environments may have some difficulty with the concept of something being event driven. A Windows program continually polls Windows for events. Events in Windows include a menu being activated, a button being clicked, a window being moved, a window needing repainting, a window being activated, and so forth. Windows notifies a program of an event by sending a Windows *message*. There are somewhere in the neighborhood of 175 possible messages that Windows can send to an application. That's a lot of messages! Fortunately, you don't have to know about each and every one of them to program in C++Builder; there are only a couple dozen that are used frequently.

In VCL, an event is anything that occurs in the component that the user might need to know about. Each component is designed to respond to certain events. Usually this means a Windows event, but it can mean other things as well. For example, a button component is designed to respond to a mouse click, as you would expect. But a nonvisual control such as a database component might respond to non-Windows events such as the user reaching the end of the table.

 When you respond to a component's event, you are said to *handle* the event. Events are handled through functions called *event handlers*.

VCL makes it incredibly easy to handle events. The events that a component has been designed to handle are listed under the Events tab in the Object Inspector window. An event name is descriptive of the event to which it responds. For instance, the event to handle a mouse click is called OnClick.

 NOTE

> You don't have to handle every event that a component defines. In fact, you rarely do. If you do not respond to a particular event, the event message is either discarded or handled in a default manner, as described by either VCL or the component itself. You can handle any events you have an interest in and ignore the rest.

This will make more sense if you can put it into practice. To begin, let's start a new application from scratch. Choose File | New Application from the main menu. If you are prompted to save the current project, click No. Now you should again have a blank form. First, let's set up the main form:

1. Change the Name property to PMEForm (PME for "properties, methods, and events").
2. Change the Caption property to PME Test Program.

Next we need to add a memo component to the form:

1. Choose the Standard tab on the Component Palette and click the Memo button.
2. Click on the form to place a memo component on the form.
3. Change the Name property to Memo. Be sure the memo component is selected so you don't accidentally change the name of the form rather than the memo component.
4. Double-click on the Lines property in the value column. The String list editor will be displayed.
5. Delete the word Memo and type A test program using properties, methods, and events. Click OK to close the String list editor.
6. Resize the memo component so that it occupies most of the form. Leave room for a button at the bottom.

Your form should now look something like the form shown in Figure 5.2.

Figure 5.2.

The form with a memo component added.

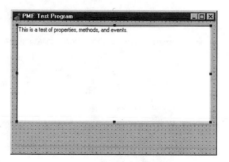

Now let's place a button on the form:

1. Choose the Standard tab on the Component Palette and click the Button component button.
2. Click on the form below the memo component to place the button on the form.
3. Change the Name property for the button to Button.
4. Change the Caption property to Show/Hide.
5. Center the button on the form.

TIP

> You can center components visually, but for a more exact method you can use the Alignment Palette. Choose View | Alignment Palette from the main menu and then click the Center horizontally in window button on the Alignment Palette to center a component horizontally on the form.

We will use this button to alternately show and hide the memo component. Now we need to write some code so that the button does something when clicked. Be sure the button component is selected and then click on the Events tab in the Object Inspector. A list of the events that a button component is designed to handle is presented. The top event should be the OnClick event. Double-click on the value column of the OnClick event. What happens next is one of the great things about visual programming. The Code Editor comes to the top and displays the OnClick function, ready for you to type code. Figure 5.3 shows the Code Editor with the OnClick handler displayed.

Figure 5.3.

The C++Builder Code Editor with the OnClick *handler displayed.*

NOTE

> This function looks like the class member functions I discussed on Day 3 and, in fact, that's exactly what it is. The only difference is that C++Builder functions use the __fastcall keyword (note that two

> underscores proceed the `fastcall` keyword). It's not important that
> you understand what __`fastcall` does, but just that every C++Builder
> function uses this calling convention.

You'll probably want to make the Code Editor window a little wider so you can see all of the text that is displayed. Before you go on, save the project. Choose File | Save from the main menu. The first thing you are prompted for is the name of the unit (source file). Type PMEMain and click OK. Next you are prompted for a filename for the project. Type PMETest and press Enter or click OK. Now on to the good stuff....

Notice that the function is already set up for you and all you have to do is type the code. If you take a good look at the function, you will see that the function is called ButtonClick, that it is a member function of the TPMEForm class, that it returns void, and that it takes a pointer to a TObject called Sender as a parameter. (I'll talk about the Sender parameter in just a bit.) All that is left to do now is type code that alternately shows or hides the button each time the button is clicked. We'll borrow a little code from our earlier discussion of methods. Edit the ButtonClick function until it looks like this:

```
void __fastcall TPMEForm::ButtonClick(TObject *Sender)
{
  static bool isVisible;
  isVisible = !isVisible;
  if (isVisible) Memo->Hide();
  else Memo->Show();
}
```

This code sets up a static variable named isVisible.

NEW TERM   A *static* variable is one that retains its value between function calls.

Static variables are the exception to the rule regarding uninitialized variables—static variables are initially set to 0. In this case, isVisible is a bool variable, so it is initially set to false.

The second line of code in this function flips the bool variable between true and false by applying a logical NOT to the present value of the variable. It works like this: Initially the static variable is set to false. The first time the function executes, the variable is assigned NOT false, which is, of course, true. The next time the function executes, the variable is assigned NOT true, and so on. So each time the function executes, isVisible contains the opposite value it had on the previous function call. After that, the if/else pair calls either Show() or Hide() depending on the value of isVisible.

5

NOTE

Remember when you changed the Name property of the memo component to Memo? When you did that, C++Builder went to work behind the
scenes. C++Builder first derived a class from TMemo. Then it created a
dynamic instance of the new class and gave it the variable name Memo.
In the code in this section, Memo is a pointer to the object. That is why
the Show() and Hide() functions are accessed using the indirect member
operator.

That's all there is to it! But does it work? Let's find out. Click the Run button on the speedbar.
After being compiled, the program runs and is displayed. It's the moment of truth. Click the
button, and the memo component is hidden. Click the button again, and the memo
component is again displayed. It works! Hallelujah! After playing with that for a minute, close
the program (use the Close Program button in the upper-left corner of the title bar) and you
are back to the Code Editor.

Hmmm…all that messing with the static bool variable is a bit cumbersome. Think back to
the discussion about properties. Wouldn't it be nice if the memo component had a property
that could tell us whether the component was currently visible? Is there such a beast? Of
course there is! It's called, predictably, Visible. Let's make use of it. Again, edit the function
until it looks like this:

```
void __fastcall TPMEForm::ButtonClick(TObject *Sender)
{
  if (Memo->Visible) Memo->Hide();
  else Memo->Show();
}
```

Again click the Run button. The program is displayed and, lo and behold, the button does
what it's supposed to. How about that? We managed to use properties, methods, and events
in the same example.

Are you getting the fever yet? Hold on, because there's lots more to come. Oh, and wipe that
silly grin off your face…your boss thinks you're *working*!

As you can see, the ButtonClick() function takes a pointer to a TObject called Sender. Every
event-handling function will have at least a Sender parameter. Depending on the event being
handled, the function might have one or more additional parameters. For instance, the
OnMouseDown event handler looks like this:

```
void __fastcall TPMEForm::ButtonMouseDown(TObject *Sender,
  TMouseButton Button, TShiftState Shift, Integer X, Integer Y)
{
}
```

5

In this case, you are getting information on the button that was pressed, which keyboard keys were pressed at the time the mouse was clicked, and the x,y coordinate of the cursor when the mouse button was clicked. The event-handling function contains all the information you need to deal with the particular event that the event handler is designed to handle.

So what exactly is Sender? Sender is a pointer to the component that is sending the message to the message handler. In this example, the Sender parameter is extra baggage because we know that the Show/Hide button is the sender. Sender exists to allow you to have more than one component use the same event handler. To illustrate, let's create a new button and have one of our buttons be the Show button and the other be the Hide button:

1. If the Code Editor is on top, press F12 to switch back to the Form Editor.

2. Click on the Show/Hide button to select it. Change both the Name and Caption properties to Show.

3. Add a new button to the form to the right of the Show button. Arrange the buttons, if desired, to give an even look to the form.

4. Change the Name property for the new button to Hide. The Caption property will also change to Hide (you'll have to press Enter before the Caption property will change).

5. Click the Show button and then click on the Events tab in the Object Inspector. Notice that the OnClick event now says ShowClick. Edit it to say ButtonClick again. (The initial event handler name is a default name. You can change it to any name you like.)

6. Click the Hide button and find the OnClick event in the Object Inspector (it should be selected already). Next to the value is a drop-down arrow button. Click the arrow button and then choose ButtonClick from the list that drops down (there should only be one function name in the list at this point).

7. Double-click on the value ButtonClick. You are presented with the Code Editor with the cursor in the ButtonClick() function. Modify the code so that it reads like this:

```
void __fastcall TPMEForm::ButtonClick(TObject *Sender)
{
  if (Sender == Hide) Memo->Hide();
  else Memo->Show();
}
```

8. Bake at 425 degrees for 1 hour or until golden brown. (Just making sure you're still awake.)

Right now your form should look similar to Figure 5.4. Compile and run the program. Click each of the buttons to be sure that they do as advertised.

Figure 5.4.

The form with all components added.

What we have done here is create a single event-handling function that handles the OnClick event of both buttons. We use the Sender parameter to determine which of the two buttons sent the OnClick event and then either hide or show the memo component as needed. We could have created a separate OnClick handler for each button, but with this method the code is a little more compact. Besides, it's a good illustration of how Sender can be used.

You can see from this exercise that once you have created an OnClick event handler for a particular component, you can attach that same handler to the OnClick event of any component on the form. I'll discuss more of the details of events as we move through the book.

HOUSE RULES: EVENTS

- [ ] You may respond to any of a component's events as needed.
- [ ] You are not required to respond to all events a component defines.
- [ ] Events are handled by event-handling functions called *event handlers*.
- [ ] Several components may share a common event handler.
- [ ] Event handler names produced by C++Builder are default names and may be changed by the programmer.
- [ ] Be sure to change an event handler's name only in the Object Inspector.
- [ ] The Sender parameter of an event handler can be used to determine which component fired the event.

☐ Double-clicking the event handler's name in the Object Inspector will display the Code Editor and take you to the section of code containing the event handler.

☐ Each event handler contains the function parameters needed to properly handle that event.

C++Builder and VCL

As I have said, VCL is a library written in Object Pascal. VCL is written in Object Pascal because it was written for Delphi. It made perfect sense for the people at Borland to take an already-existing class library and adapt it for use in C++Builder. There was no point in starting from scratch to build C++Builder when they could hit the ground running by implementing Delphi's VCL. An added benefit is that users of Delphi can easily move to C++Builder, and vice versa. Because both are using the same VCL, you don't have to learn a new framework when moving around in the Delphi/C++Builder family.

C++Builder is a C++ compiler, and VCL is an Object Pascal library. How does that work, exactly? Truthfully, you shouldn't be concerned about how it works at the compiler level, but rather how it affects the way you program in C++Builder. The bottom line is that VCL is Object Pascal and is nearly invisible. Take the following code snippet, for instance:

```
int screenW = GetSystemMetrics(SM_CXSCREEN);
int screenH = GetSystemMetrics(SM_CYSCREEN);
int h = MainForm->Height;
int w = MainForm->Width;
MainForm->Top = (screenH / 2) - (h / 2);
MainForm->Left = (screenW / 2) - (w / 2);
TPoint cPt;
GetCursorPos(cPt);
h -= 150;
w -= 150;
MainForm->Height = h;
MainForm->Width = w;
for (int i=0;i<150;i+=6) {
  MainForm->Height = h + i;
  MainForm->Width = w + i;
  SetCursorPos(
    MainForm->Left + MainForm->Width,
    MainForm->Top + MainForm->Height);
}
SetCursorPos(cPt.x, cPt.y);
```

Now, in this code, which is Object Pascal and which is C++? As far as you are concerned, it's all C++. VCL and C++ work together seamlessly to give you rapid application development using C++. VCL gives you RAD through components, and the rest of your code can be written in C++.

5

VCL for C++ Programmers

This section is for current C++ programmers moving to C++Builder, but will also be of interest to new C++ programmers. Although the following is not terribly advanced, it is aimed at C++ programmers, so if you get lost, muddle your way through and meet us on the other side.

There are a couple things C++ programmers might find odd when moving to C++Builder. First, don't forget that VCL is Object Pascal and not C++. Don't try to make it C++. The system works very well as long as you understand that and work within those parameters. All the code you write will be C++, but remember that VCL itself is not C++. With that in mind, let me give you a couple things to consider when using VCL.

All VCL Objects Must Be Allocated Dynamically

When you drop components on a form, C++Builder automatically writes code that dynamically creates the components, so you don't have to think about it. However, you may need to create and use VCL classes at runtime. For instance, let's say you needed to display a File Open dialog box and you didn't have a TFileOpen component on your form. No problem—you can just create the object on-the-fly. The code would look something like this:

```
TOpenDialog* dlg = new TOpenDialog(this);
dlg->Title = "Open a New File";
dlg->Execute();
```

Note that the object must be created using the new operator. If you attempt to use local allocation, you will get a compiler error that says VCL classes must be constructed using operator new.

NOTE

> Most VCL components can be created at runtime as well as at design time. It's easier to create the components at design time because it is much easier to set the properties using the Object Inspector than it is to set the properties through code. Still, there are times when you need to create components at runtime, and C++Builder allows you to do that.

Object Pascal Does Not Support Overloaded Functions; Hence, VCL Classes Have No Overloaded Constructors

In fact, VCL constructors typically do very little. Take the VCL version of the TRect class, for instance. In order to construct and set up a TRect object in VCL, you would use code like this:

5

```
TRect rect;
rect->left = 20;
rect->top = 20;
rect->right = 220;
rect->bottom = 220;
```

OWL also has a TRect class. In OWL you can create a TRect object and supply the top, left, bottom, and right members through the constructor:

```
TRect rect(20, 20, 220, 220);
```

Obviously, specifying the rectangle's parameters in the constructor saves you some typing. In addition, the OWL version of TRect has several constructors to create TRect instances in different ways. MFC's CRect class has basically the same type of constructors as OWL's TRect. What this means is that in some cases you have to give up the flexibility that C++ allows you when constructing VCL classes. It's a minor sacrifice in most cases.

VCL Does Not Have Default Parameters for Functions

To illustrate, let's examine the Windows API function MessageBox(). This function takes four parameters: the window handle of the window that is displaying the message box, the message box text, the message box title, and a Flags parameter that controls which buttons and icons are displayed on the message box. In MFC or OWL, you can call a message box by just specifying the message box text:

```
MessageBox("This is a message.");
```

This is possible because the OWL and MFC versions of MessageBox() have default parameters for the message box title and style flags. You can specify the additional parameters, but if you don't, the default values will be used. This is convenient for throwing up message boxes with a minimum of fuss. Here is the VCL equivalent to the previous line:

```
Application->MessageBox("This is a message", "Message", MB_OK);
```

Because VCL does not have default parameters, you have to specify all the parameters. It's not convenient, but not the end of the world, either. Note that in all three cases (MFC, OWL, and VCL), the framework takes care of supplying the window handle parameter.

VCL Classes Do Not Support Multiple Inheritance

This means that you cannot create a new component derived from two existing components. I don't see this as a serious restriction because multiple inheritance is not widely used. Regular C++ classes that you write for use in your C++Builder applications may use multiple inheritance.

5

VCL Explored

The Visual Component Library is a well-designed framework. As with most good frameworks, VCL makes maximum use of inheritance. The bulk of the VCL framework is made up of classes that represent components. Other VCL classes are not related to components. These classes perform housekeeping chores, act as helper classes, and provide some utility services.

The VCL class hierarchy dealing with components is fairly complex. Fortunately, you don't have to know every detail of VCL to begin programming in C++Builder. At the top of the VCL chain you will find TObject. Figure 5.5 shows some of the main base classes and classes derived from them.

Figure 5.5.

The VCL class hierarchy.

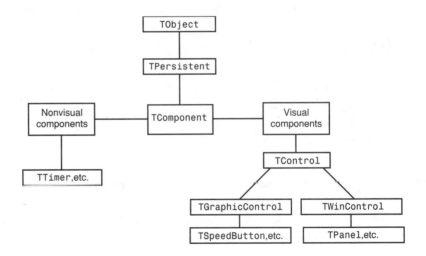

TObject is the granddaddy of all component classes in VCL. Below TObject you see TPersistent. This class deals with a component's ability to save itself to files and to memory as well as taking care of other messy details we don't need to know about. I'm thankful (and you should be, too) that we don't need to know much about TPersistent to program most applications in C++Builder.

The TComponent class serves as a more direct base class for components. This class provides all the functionality that a basic component requires. Nonvisual components are derived from TComponent itself. Visual components are derived from TControl, which, as you can see from Figure 5.5, is derived from TComponent. TControl provides additional functionality that visual components require. The individual components, then, are derived from either TGraphicControl or TWinControl.

5

When you drop a component on a form, C++Builder creates code that inherits a class from the VCL class that represents that component. A pointer to the object is created so that you can access the objects in your code. C++Builder uses the Name property in the class name and for the pointer variable's name. When we created the sample application earlier, we placed a memo component on the form. At that point C++Builder derived a class from TMemo and created an instance of that class. Similarly, when we created a button on the form, C++Builder derived a class from TButton and created an instance of that class. Before any of that took place, C++Builder had already derived a class from TForm and, of course, created an instance of that class to represent the form.

Some understanding of the VCL classes is obviously required to begin working with VCL. Although I cannot review each and every class in VCL, I can hit the high points. Let's take a look at some of the classes that you will use most frequently.

Form and Application Classes

Form and application classes represent forms and the Application object in VCL. These classes are all derived from TComponent and indeed are components themselves. They are listed separately to distinguish them from the controls you drop on a form.

TApplication

The TApplication class encapsulates the basic operations of a Windows program. TApplication takes care of things like managing the application's icon, providing context-sensitive help, and doing basic message handling. Every C++Builder application has a pointer to the TApplication object called Application. You will use the TApplication class primarily to execute message boxes, manage context-sensitive help, and set hint text for buttons and status bars. TApplication is a bit of an oddity in VCL in that some of its properties (Icon, HelpFile, and Title) can be set via the Application page of the Project Options dialog box.

TForm

The TForm class encapsulates forms in VCL. Forms are used for main windows, dialog boxes, secondary windows, and just about any other window type you can imagine. TForm is a workhorse class in VCL. It has nearly 60 properties, 45 methods, and about 20 events it can respond to. I am going to discuss forms in detail tomorrow, so I won't go into a lot of detail right here.

Component Classes

This group encompasses a wide range of classes. This group could be further broken down into separate categories, which I've done in the following sections.

Standard Component Classes

The standard components are those components that encapsulate the most common Windows controls. The standard component classes include TButton, TEdit, TListBox, TMemo, TMainMenu, TPopupMenu, TCheckBox, TRadioButton, TRadioGroup, TGroupBox, and TPanel.

Most of these classes encapsulate a Windows control, so I won't discuss all of them right now. The TMainMenu class encapsulates an application's main menu. At design time, double-clicking the MainMenu component's icon brings up the Menu Editor. TMainMenu has properties that control whether the menu item is grayed out, whether it is checked, the help context ID, the item's hint text, and others. Each menu item has a single event, OnClick, so that you can attach a function to a menu item being selected. I'll discuss menus and the Menu Editor in more detail on Day 7, "Working with the Form Designer and the Menu Designer."

Another of the standard components of interest is TPanel.

NEW TERM A *panel* represents a rectangular region on a form, usually with its own components, that can be treated as a single unit.

For instance, if you wanted to build a speedbar for an application, you would start with a panel and then place speed buttons on the panel. If you move the panel, the speed buttons move with it. Panels can be used for a wide variety of tasks in C++Builder. You could use a panel to build a status bar, for example. Panels have properties that control what type of edge the panel should have; whether the panel is raised, sunken, or flat; and the width of the border. Combinations of these properties can be used to create a variety of 3D panels.

C++Builder has another group of components that I'll throw in with the standard controls. These controls can be found under the Additional tab on the Component Palette. The classes representing these components include TBitBtn, TSpeedButton, TMaskEdit, TStringGrid, TDrawGrid, TImage, TShape, TBevel, and TScrollBox. The TBitBtn class represents a button that has an image on it. TSpeedButton is also a button with an image, but this component is designed to be used as a speed button on a control bar. A TSpeedButton is not a true button, but rather a graphical depiction of a button. This allows you to have a large number of speed buttons and not consume Windows resources for each of the buttons. The TImage component allows you to place an image on a form that can then be selected from a file on disk. The TBevel component can be used to create boxes and lines that are raised (bumps) or lowered (dips). Bevels can be used to divide up a form into visual regions and generally to provide an aesthetically pleasing form.

Windows 95 Custom Control Classes

VCL has component classes that encapsulate many of the Windows 32-bit custom controls. These classes include TListView, TTreeView, TProgressBar, TTabControl, TPageControl,

TRichEdit, TImageList, TStatusBar, and a few others. Some of these controls are, by nature, complicated, and the VCL classes that represent them are fairly complicated as well. Trust me when I say that VCL does a great deal to ease the burden of working with these common controls. You'll have to spend some time with these classes before you fully understand them.

Database Component Classes

VCL has a host of database components, which include both visual and nonvisual classes. Nonvisual database components include TDataSource, TDatabase, TTable, and TQuery. These classes encapsulate behind-the-scenes database operations.

Visual database component classes are the part of the VCL database operations that users can see and interact with. For instance, a TDBGrid component is used to give users access to a database table that might be represented as a TTable component. In this way, the TDBGrid acts as the interface between the user and the TTable. Through the TDBGrid, the user can view and edit the database table on disk.

The TDBNavigator component provides buttons that allow the user to move through a database table. This class includes buttons for next record, previous record, first record, last record, cancel edit, accept edit, and undo edit.

Other data-aware component classes hook standard Windows controls to database fields. These classes include TDBText, TDBEdit, TDBListBox, and TDBImage, among others.

Common Dialog Classes

As you are no doubt aware, Windows has common dialog boxes for things like opening files, saving files, choosing fonts, and choosing colors. VCL encapsulates these common dialog boxes in classes representing each type. The classes are TOpenDialog, TSaveDialog, TFontDialog, TColorDialog, TPrintDialog, and TPrinterSetupDialog. VCL also adds the TFindDialog and TReplaceDialog classes to this group of components. These components are nonvisual in that they do not have a design-time interface that you can see. The dialog boxes are visible when displayed at runtime, of course.

System Component Classes

The System tab on the Component Palette contains a mixture of visual and nonvisual components. The TTimer class is used to represent a Windows system timer. Its single event is OnTimer, which is called each time the timer fires. The timer interval is set through the Interval property. TTimer is a nonvisual component.

VCL includes several component classes that allow you to build your own custom File Open or File Save dialog box. The classes are TFileListBox, TDirectoryListBox, TDriveComboBox, and TFilterComboBox.

Tucked into this group of classes is the TMediaPlayer class. This class allows you to play media files like WAV audio, AVI video, and MIDI audio. The media can be played, stopped, paused, or positioned at a particular point in the file, as well as many other operations. This class has many properties and events that greatly simplify the complex world of the Windows Media Control Interface (MCI).

The System group includes OLE and dynamic data exchange (DDE) classes as well.

GDI Classes

The GDI (graphics device interface) classes typically get a lot of work in Windows GUI applications. These classes encapsulate the use of bitmaps, fonts, device contexts (DCs), brushes, and pens. It is through these GDI objects that graphics and text are displayed on a window. The GDI classes are not associated with a specific component, but many components have instances of these classes as properties. For example, an edit control has a property called Font that is an instance of the TFont class.

The term *device context* is well known by Windows programmers whether they program in C or with one of the C++ frameworks. In VCL, though, the term is not widely used. This is because VCL calls DCs *canvases* and encapsulates the complex world of DCs in the TCanvas class. A canvas provides a surface that you can draw on using methods like MoveTo(), LineTo(), and TextOut(). Bitmaps can be displayed on the canvas using the Draw() or StretchDraw() methods. The concept of a canvas that you draw on makes more sense than the archaic term device context, don't you think?

The TCanvas class contains instances of the other GDI classes. For example, when you do a MoveTo()/LineTo() sequence, a line is drawn with the current pen color. The Pen property is used to determine the current pen color and is an instance of the TPen class. TPen has properties that determine what type of line to draw: the line width, the line style (solid, dashed, dotted, and so on), and the mode with which to draw the line.

The TBrush class represents a brush that is used as the fill pattern for canvas operations like FillRect(), Polygon(), and Ellipse(). TBrush properties include Color, Style, and Bitmap. The Style property allows you to set a hatch pattern for the brush. The Bitmap property allows you to specify a bitmap that will be used for the fill pattern.

TBitmap encapsulates bitmap operations in VCL. Properties include Palette, Height, Width, and TransparentColor. Methods include LoadFromFile(), LoadFromResourceID(), and SaveToFile(). TBitmap is used by other component classes such as TImage, TBitBtn, and TSpeedButton in addition to TCanvas.

The TFont class handles font operations. Properties include Color, Height, and Style (bold, italic, normal, and so on). The TFont class is used by all component classes that display text.

In addition to the GDI classes listed here, there are others that either work as helper classes or extend a base class to provide extra functionality. As you work with C++Builder you will learn more about these classes and how to use them. Figure 5.6 shows the hierarchy of the VCL classes that encapsulate GDI operations.

Figure 5.6.

VCL GDI class hierarchy.

Utility Classes

So far I have discussed component classes. VCL also contains utility classes you can use in your applications. A utility class simplifies some tasks in Windows programming. For instance, the TIniFile class eases the use of writing and reading Windows configuration files (.INI files). Conventional wisdom has it that the use of .INI files is out and the Registry is in. To aid in Registry operations, VCL has the TRegistry and TRegKeyInfo classes.

The TRect and TPoint classes (which are really just structures) aid in using various VCL and Windows functions requiring a point or rectangle parameter.

The TStrings class is used to manipulate strings, and the TStringList class allows for arrays of strings. These classes are used by many of the component classes to store strings. For instance, the TMemo class uses a TStringList object for its Lines property. TStringList has the capability to save its list of strings to file or load strings from a file using the LoadFromFile() and SaveToFile() methods.

And That's Not All...

By no means did I cover all of the VCL classes here. I did, however, touch on the classes that you are most likely to use in your applications.

Flip back a few pages and take another look at Listing 5.1 and the OWL example that performs the equivalent code in Listing 5.2. If you recall, I said that placing a bitmap image on a window is even easier in C++Builder. Let me show you what I mean. First, begin a new application in C++Builder. You should be looking at a blank form. Perform the following steps:

1. Change the Caption property of the form to Bitmap Test Program.

2. Click on the Additional tab on the Component Palette, choose the Image component, and place the component on the form.

3. Locate the `Align` property and change it to `alClient`. The picture component fills the client area of the form.

4. Locate the `Stretch` property and change it to `true`.

5. Locate the `Picture` property and double-click the Value column.

6. The Picture Editor dialog box is displayed. Click the Load button. The File Open dialog box is displayed.

7. Navigate to the `\CBUILDER\IMAGES\SPLASH\256COLOR` directory and choose an image from those presented (I like `HANDSHAKE.BMP`). Click OK.

8. You are now back to the Image Editor dialog box, and the bitmap you chose is displayed in the preview window. Click OK. (If you want to choose a different bitmap, click the Load button again.) The bitmap now fills the client area of the form.

9. Click the Run button. When the application runs you can size the window, and the bitmap will always fill the client area of the window.

See how easy it is? It would have been even easier if we hadn't bothered to make the image fill the client area of the form. Figure 5.7 shows the bitmap test program running.

Figure 5.7.

The bitmap test program running.

Summary

Today you have learned about frameworks. You first learned about OWL and MFC and the role they have had in shaping Windows programming today. After that you learned about VCL and how it differs from the C++ frameworks. We discussed properties, methods, and events, and you got a little hands-on experience in the process. We finished up today with an overview of the VCL classes that you are likely to encounter when programming in C++Builder. I didn't cover them all, but I gave you a brief look at the most commonly used classes.

5

So where is this industry going? The wave of the future appears to be components, but it is apparent that there will be a need for class libraries like MFC and OWL for quite some time to come. Some of you who are now using MFC or OWL will abandon them in favor of programs like C++Builder and Delphi. Others of you will use both your old tool and the new RAD tools. Still others will stick with what you know best. In any event, it is important to realize that each of these frameworks is a tool. My advice is simple: Use the most appropriate tool for the current job.

If you have never used OWL or MFC, you don't have to worry about what you are missing. C++Builder and VCL allow you to build robust applications in much less time than you could with one of the C++ frameworks. This is particularly true when you take into account the learning curve of VCL compared to that of MFC or OWL. Programming in C++Builder is much easier to learn, and you can write programs faster, too.

Workshop

The Workshop contains quiz questions to help you solidify your understanding of the material covered and exercises to provide you with experience in using what you have learned. You can find answers to the quiz questions in Appendix A, "Answers to Quiz Questions."

Q&A

Q What is a framework?

A A framework, also called a class library, is a set of classes that simplifies Windows programming. A good framework implements object-oriented design and object-oriented programming to apply an object-oriented approach to writing Windows applications.

Q Is VCL a C++ framework?

A No. VCL is a framework that works with C++ in C++Builder, but it is written in Object Pascal rather than C++. VCL is written in Object Pascal because it was initially created for Borland's Delphi.

Q Am I supposed to know how to program in Pascal and C++ in order to write Windows programs with C++Builder?

A No. The fact that VCL is Pascal is virtually transparent to you. As far as you are concerned, you are just programming in C++. Advanced C++ users might notice some situations where VCL limits their choices, but most users of C++Builder will not.

5

Q It seems like the component way of doing things is the best approach. Is that true?

A It is true for many applications, but certainly not for all. In some cases a framework such as OWL or MFC will be better suited to the task. For applications that use a lot of dialog boxes and windows, and for database applications, VCL is probably a very good choice. Overall, C++Builder is much easier to learn and easier to use than the C++ class libraries.

Q Are properties just class data members?

A No. Properties are special creatures. Some properties simply set a data member in the class. Other properties, when modified, invoke a method that performs special operations with that property. In these cases, a property does more than just set a data member.

Q Do I have to respond to each and every event a component defines?

A No. You can respond to as many events as is appropriate for your application, or not respond to any events at all.

Q There sure are a lot of VCL classes. I thought programming with C++Builder was going to be easy.

A Programming with C++Builder is much easier than programming Windows in C, and easier than programming with a C++ framework like OWL or MFC. Windows programming, no matter how good the programming tool, requires a lot of experience and knowledge to master. Over time, you will master it if you keep at it.

Q Can I use C++Builder forms in my OWL and MFC programs?

A Yes. Later in the book I'll show you how you can do that.

Quiz

1. Are all components visible at design time and runtime?
2. Which is better—OWL, MFC, or VCL?
3. Can VCL objects be allocated locally (from the stack) as well as dynamically?
4. Are methods in VCL components equivalent to functions in C++?
5. Are all VCL classes ultimately derived from TObject?
6. Name one nonvisual VCL component.
7. Do all components share certain common properties?
8. Name two common properties that all visual components share.
9. Can two or more components share the same event-handling function?
10. What is the VCL terminology for a Windows device context? What is the name of the VCL class that encapsulates device contexts?

Exercises

1. Write a paragraph describing how properties and class data members differ.
2. Create a C++Builder application that displays a bitmap **on the main form** when a button is clicked.
3. Create a C++Builder application that displays a message box that displays the text `Hello, Bubba!` when the main form is clicked.
4. Create a C++Builder application that displays the text `I've been resized!` in red letters when the application is resized.
5. **Extra credit:** Modify the program in exercise 4 so that the text disappears again after 5 seconds.

5

Day **6**

The C++Builder IDE Explored: Projects and Forms

by Kent Reisdorph

One of the most difficult aspects of learning how to use a new program is finding your way around: getting to know the basic menu structure, what all the options do, and how the program works as a whole. If you are new to programming or new to C++, this task is complicated by the fact that you have to learn a new program (the C++Builder IDE) *and* learn a new language at the same time. It can be a bit overwhelming at times. I'll do my best to make learning the C++Builder IDE a painless experience. For the most part, you will learn by example, which is more interesting (not to mention more effective). So, without further ado, and referring to Figure 6.1, let's get on with it.

Figure 6.1.

The C++Builder IDE windows.

The C++Builder IDE consists of these main parts:

☐ The main menu and toolbar

☐ The Component Palette

☐ The Form Designer

☐ The Code Editor

☐ The Object Inspector

☐ The Project Manager

I can't cover all these in a single chapter, so over the next several chapters I will show you around the C++Builder IDE and examine each of these features in detail. I'll start today by discussing projects and how they are used in writing C++Builder applications. After that, we'll look at the C++Builder toolbar and the Component Palette. Then I'll move to discussing forms in greater detail than I have up to this point. Along the way we'll create some sample programs to illustrate various aspects of C++Builder. We'll close the day by looking at the Object Inspector. This will be a warm-up for tomorrow, when you will learn all about the C++Builder Form Designer.

For starters, let's look at the way C++Builder views applications and how it has simplified the process of creating programs.

Projects in C++Builder

As you know by now, a lot goes on behind the scenes as you write a C++Builder application. In fact, more goes on than I have told you about up to this point. It's not vital that you know every detail about what happens behind the scenes as you write a C++Builder application, but it is a good idea to have a general overview.

 A *project* is a collection of files that work together to create a standalone executable file or DLL.

Files Used in C++Builder Projects

C++Builder manages a project through the use of several support files. To illustrate, let's create a simple application to get a look at some of what goes on when C++Builder builds an executable file for your program. Do the following:

1. Before you begin, create a fresh directory on your hard drive.

2. Now choose File | New Application from the main menu. A blank form is displayed.

3. Before you do anything else, choose File | Save Project from the main menu.

4. First, you will be prompted for the name of the unit file. Be sure to switch to the empty directory you just created.

5. Next, type in the name MyUnit for the unit filename and click OK.

6. Now you are prompted for the project name. Type TEST in the File name field and click OK.

7. Now choose Project | Build All from the main menu. C++Builder displays the compile status box and goes to work compiling the program.

8. After a while, the compile status box reports that it is done compiling, and the OK button is enabled. Click OK to close the compile status dialog box

9. Now choose Project | Close All from the main menu. (Yes, this exercise does have a purpose.)

10. Now run Windows Explorer and locate the directory where you saved the project. You should see a number of files.

Wow! All that to create just one little program that does nothing? Yep, it's true. First, let me tell you what happens when C++Builder builds an application; then I'll explain what each of these files is for.

NOTE Files with extensions that begin with a tilde (~) are backup files. C++Builder may create several backup files, depending on the number of source files in the project and the project options you have set. Project options are discussed on Day 10, "More on Projects."

When you first create a project, C++Builder creates a minimum of six files (assuming a typical C++Builder GUI application):

- [ ] The project source file
- [ ] The main form source file
- [ ] The main form header file
- [ ] The main form resource file
- [ ] The application resource file
- [ ] The project makefile

The *project source file* is the file that contains the WinMain() function and other C++Builder startup code. You can view the project source file by choosing View | Project Source from the main menu. The *main form source file* and *main form header file* are files that contain the class declaration and definition for the main form's class. C++Builder will create an additional source file and header for each new form you create. The *main form resource file* and *application resource file* are binary files that describe the main form and the application's icon. I'll explain that in more detail a little later, in the section titled "Dialog Boxes in Traditional Windows Programs."

Somewhere in this process, C++Builder creates the project makefile. The *makefile* is a text file that contains information about the compiler options you have set, the names of the source files and forms that make up the project, and what library files have to be included.

NOTE There are two types of library files. A *static library* contains common code that an application needs in order to run. An *import library* is needed when your application references functions in a DLL, such as the Windows API functions. The number and exact filenames of the library files required depend on the features your application uses. Fortunately, you don't have to worry about managing the library files because C++Builder takes care of that detail for you. Library files have an .LIB extension and are tucked away in your C++Builder \lib directory.

6

There are a few more odds and ends, but that's the bulk of what is contained in the makefile. When you tell C++Builder to compile the project, it hands the makefile to the compiler. (Technically, the makefile is read by the Make utility, but why quibble over details?) The compiler reads the makefile and begins compiling all the source files that make up the project.

Several things happen during this process. First, the C++ compiler compiles the C++ source files into binary object files. Then the resource compiler compiles any resources, such as the program's icon and form files, into binary resource files. Next, the linker takes over. The linker takes the binary files the compilers created, adds any library files the project needs, and binds them all together to produce the final executable file. Along the way it produces more files that perform some special operations (I'll get to that in a minute). When it's all over, you have a standalone program that can be run in the usual ways.

Okay, but what are all those files for? Table 6.1 lists the file extensions C++Builder uses, with a description of the role that each file type plays.

Table 6.1. Types of files used in C++Builder.

Extension	Description
.CPP	The C++ source files. There will usually be one for each unit and one for the main project file, as well as any other source files that you add to the project.
.DFM	The form file. This file is actually a binary resource file (.RES) in disguise. It is a description of the form and all its components. Each form has its own .DFM file.
.DSK	The desktop file. This file keeps track of the way the desktop appeared when you last saved (or closed) the project. All the open windows' sizes and positions are saved so that when you reopen the project it looks the same as it did when you left it.
.EXE	The final executable program.
.H	C++ header files that contain class declarations. These could be C++Builder-generated files or your own class headers.
.IL?	The four files whose extension begins with .IL are files created by the incremental linker. The incremental linker saves you time by linking only the parts of the program that have changed since the last build.

continues

Table 6.1. continued

Extension	Description
.OBJ	The compiled binary object files. These are the files that the compiler produces when it compiles your C++ source files.
.MAK	The project makefile. This is a text file that contains a description of which files C++Builder needs to compile and link.
.RES	A compiled binary resource file produced by the resource compiler.
.TDW	The debugger symbol table. This file is used by the debugger during debugging sessions.

NOTE C++Builder database applications will use other database-specific file types as well. Database applications are discussed in detail in later chapters.

The files that C++Builder produces can be broken down into two categories: files that C++Builder relies on to build the project and files that it will create when it compiles and links a project. If you were to move all your source files to another computer, for instance, you wouldn't have to move all the files, just the files C++Builder needs to build the application. Conveniently, the source files happen to be the smallest files in the project. It does not take a lot of disk space to back up just the project source files.

The minimum set of files consists of the .CPP, .H, .DFM, and .MAK files. All other files are files that C++Builder will re-create when you compile the program. The desktop file (.DSK) is one that you may want to hang on to because it keeps track of the state your project was in when you last worked on it.

NOTE In addition to the source files I've mentioned, some applications use a *resource script file*. Resource scripts have an .RC extension. Resource scripts are text files that are used to define resources like bitmaps, icons, or cursors. If you use a resource script, be sure to keep it with the project if you move the project to another location.

6

Figure 6.2 illustrates how C++Builder takes source files and compiles and links them to form the final executable file.

Figure 6.2.

The C++Builder compile/link process.

TIP

If you find yourself running low on hard disk space, you can delete some of the C++Builder files from projects you are not currently working on. It is safe to delete the files with the .OBJ, .RES, and .TDW extensions, as well as any files with extensions beginning with .IL. Some of these files can grow quite large, and there is no use keeping them for noncurrent projects.

6

WARNING

Do not delete any files from the C++Builder directories other than the Examples directory. If in doubt, *don't delete*!

Source Code Units

Earlier I mentioned that most applications of any size have several source files, which Borland calls *units*. The use of the term *unit* in C++Builder is a holdover from Pascal and Delphi. C++Builder has its roots in the Delphi IDE, and *unit* is used throughout both VCL and the C++Builder IDE itself. C++ programmers would typically refer to a file containing a program's source as a *module*. While using the term *module* would have been more C++ friendly (and less Pascal-like), replacing the word *unit* with *module* would have required major changes to the C++Builder infrastructure, so the term *unit* was left in. If you are coming from a C++ programming background, it might seem odd to refer to modules as units, but you will get used to it soon enough. In the end, there's no point in getting hung up over terminology.

NEW TERM   C++Builder uses the term *unit* to refer to source files.

Each time you create a new form, C++Builder does the following:

- [ ] Creates a form file (.DFM)
- [ ] Derives a class from TForm or from another form class
- [ ] Creates a header (.H file) containing the class declaration
- [ ] Creates a unit (.CPP file) for the class definition
- [ ] Adds the new form information to the project makefile

Initially C++Builder assigns the default name Form1 to the form, Unit1.cpp for the associated unit, and Unit1.h for the header. The second form created for the project would have the default name Form2, and so on.

NOTE

As soon as you create a new project, you should save it with a meaningful name. Likewise, every time you create a new form, you should save it with a descriptive name. This makes it easier to locate forms and units when you need to make modifications.

When doing a technical book, a nasty situation often arises. I want to use meaningful examples to reinforce the presentation of information. In order to complete those examples, I have to use techniques or methods that I haven't talked about yet. But I can't talk about those methods until I've given you some good, meaningful examples. But I can't... well, you see my dilemma. So I'm going to digress a little here and talk about the main menu, toolbar, and Component Palette. As you read this section, remember that we're off on a tangent.

The C++Builder Main Menu and Toolbar

The C++Builder main menu has all the choices necessary to make C++Builder work. Because programming in C++Builder is a highly visual operation, you may not use the main menu as much as you might in other programming environments. Still, just about anything you need is available from the main menu if you prefer to work that way. I'm not going to go over every item on the main menu here because you will encounter each item as you work through the next several chapters.

The C++Builder toolbar is a convenient way of accomplishing often-repeated tasks. A button is easier to locate than a menu item, not to mention that it requires less mouse movement. The C++Builder toolbar's default configuration is illustrated in Figure 6.3.

Figure 6.3.
The C++Builder toolbar.

If you are like me, you often forget to use the toolbar. But I'm telling you: Don't forget to learn to use the toolbar. As the old saying goes, "Do as I say, not as I do." If you take the time to learn the toolbar, it will save you time and make you more efficient in the long run. One of the reasons you bought C++Builder was to produce Windows applications quickly, so you might as well make the most of it.

The C++Builder toolbar is fully customizable. As you saw back in Figure 6.1, between the toolbar and the Component Palette is a vertical line that acts as a sizing bar. When you place the mouse cursor over the sizing bar, you will see the sizing cursor (a double-headed black arrow). Once you have the sizing cursor, you can drag the sizing bar right or left to make the toolbar take more or less room on the C++Builder main window.

Customizing the toolbar is remarkably easy. C++Builder allows you to add buttons to the toolbar, remove buttons, and rearrange buttons however you see fit. To configure the toolbar, you must use the toolbar speed menu. To display the speed menu, place your mouse cursor over the toolbar and click the secondary mouse button. The speed menu choices are listed in Table 6.2.

Table 6.2. Items on the toolbar's speed menu.

Menu Item	Description
Show Hints	Controls whether the hints (tool tips) are displayed for the toolbar buttons.
Hide	Hides the toolbar.
Help	Invokes C++Builder help with the toolbar page displayed.
Properties	Displays the Toolbar Editor dialog box, which allows you to customize the toolbar.

> **NOTE**
>
> If you have hidden the toolbar, you will have to choose View | Toolbar from the main menu to display the toolbar again.

To customize the toolbar, choose Properties from the speed menu. When you choose this menu item, the Toolbar Editor dialog box is displayed. This dialog box contains all the possible toolbar buttons. To add a button to the toolbar, just locate it in the Toolbar Editor and drag it to the place you want it to occupy on the toolbar. To remove a button, grab it and drag it off the toolbar. It's as simple as that. If you really make a mess of things, just click the Reset button in the Toolbar Editor dialog box (see Figure 6.4), and the toolbar will revert to its default settings.

If you want to make room for more buttons, drag the sizing bar to the right to make the toolbar wider. Now just drag any buttons you want from the Toolbar Editor to the toolbar. The toolbar has an invisible grid that aids you when dropping new buttons; just get the buttons close to where you want them and they will snap into place. I happen to like the Cut,

Copy, and Paste buttons on the toolbar, so I have customized my toolbar to include those buttons. Figure 6.4 illustrates the process of dragging the Paste button to the toolbar (the Cut, Copy, and Undo buttons have already been placed).

Figure 6.4.
Customizing the toolbar.

Feel free to customize the C++Builder IDE any way you like. It's your development environment, so make it work for you.

Using the Component Palette

The C++Builder Component Palette is used to select a component or other control (such as an ActiveX control) in order to place that control on a form. The Component Palette is a multipage window. Tabs are provided to allow you to navigate between pages. Clicking on a tab will display the available components or controls on that page.

Placing a component on a form is a two-step process. First, go to the Component Palette and select the button representing the component you want to use. Then click on the form to place the component on the form. The component appears with its upper-left corner placed where you clicked with the mouse.

You have already seen the Component Palette's basic operations, but it has a couple other features that you haven't seen yet. The following sections explain these features.

Placing Multiple Copies of a Component

So far you have only placed one component at a time on a form. You can easily place multiple components of the same type without selecting the component from the Component Palette each time. To place multiple components on the form, press and hold the Shift key when selecting the component from the Component Palette. After you select the component, you can release the Shift key. The component's button on the Component Palette will appear pressed and will be highlighted with a blue border. Click on the form to place the first component. Notice that the button stays pressed in the Component Palette. You can click as many times as you like; a new component will be placed each time you click the form. To stop placing components, click the selector button on the Component Palette (the arrow button). The component button pops up to indicate that you are done placing components.

Seeing is believing, so follow these steps:

1. Create a new project.
2. Press and hold the Shift key on the keyboard and click on the Label component button in the Component Palette.
3. Click three times on the form, moving the cursor each time to indicate where you want the new component placed.
4. Click the arrow button on the Component Palette to end the process and return to form design mode.

 TIP

> It's fastest to place all components of a particular type on your form at one time using this technique. Components can always be rearranged and resized at a later time.

 NOTE

> When placing multiple copies of a particular component, it's easy to forget to click the arrow button when you're done. If you accidentally place more components than you intended, you can simply delete any extras.

Placing and Centering a Component on the Form

C++Builder provides a shortcut method of placing a component on a form. Simply double-click the component's button in the Component Palette, and the component will be placed on the form. The component will be centered on the form both horizontally and vertically. Components placed with this method can be moved to another location on the form just like components placed in the usual method.

NOTE

Each time you double-click a button on the Component Palette, a component is placed on the center of the form in the component's default size. If you repeatedly double-click the component button, multiple copies of the component will be placed on the form. Each component will be placed in the center of the form and will be stacked on top of the previous one. It will appear as if you have a single component, so you may not realize that you have several components occupying the same space. If you accidentally place multiple components, just click on the extra components and delete them from the form.

The Component Palette Speed Menu

When you place the mouse cursor over the Component Palette and click the right mouse button, you will see a speed menu specific to the Component Palette. (See Figure 6.5.)

Figure 6.5.

The Component Palette speed menu.

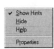

The Show Hints item toggles the tool tips on and off for the component buttons. Unless you really dislike tool tips, this should be left on. The Hide item on the speed menu hides the Component Palette. In order to show the Component Palette again, you will have to choose View | Component Palette from the main menu. The Help item on the speed menu brings up C++Builder help with the Component Palette page displayed. The Properties item brings up the Palette page of the Environment Options dialog box, where you can customize the Component Palette. Here you can add and remove pages of the Component Palette. You can also add, remove, or rearrange the order of components on the individual pages. I'll discuss this in more detail on Day 10, when we look at setting the environment options.

Navigating the Component Palette

As mentioned earlier, you can drag the sizing bar, located between the toolbar and the Component Palette, to make the Component Palette occupy more or less room on the C++Builder main window. If the Component Palette is sized small enough so that it cannot display all its tabs, you will see scroll buttons in the upper-right corner of the Component

6

Palette. Click these scroll buttons to display tabs not currently in view. Likewise, if a particular page of the Component Palette contains more buttons than will fit the width of the display window, scroll buttons will be enabled to allow you to scroll through the available buttons. Figure 6.6 shows the Component Palette with both types of scroll buttons enabled.

Figure 6.6.

The Component Palette scroll buttons.

The Component Palette is not terribly complicated, but a basic understanding of its use is vital for programming with C++Builder. Now that we've finished with these little tasks, we can get back to the main topic again.

Back on Track—A Multiple-Form Application

To illustrate how C++Builder uses units, let's create an application with multiple forms. We'll create a simple application that displays a second form when you click a button:

1. Create a new project by choosing File | New Application from the main menu.

2. Change the Name property to MainForm and the Caption property to Multiple Forms Test Program.

3. Save the project. Save the unit as Main and the project as Multiple.

4. Now place a button on the form. Make the button's Name property ShowForm2 and the Caption property Show Form 2.

5. Choose File | New Form from the main menu (or click the New Form button on the speed menu) to create a new form.

At this point the new form has a name of Form1 and is placed exactly over the main form. We want the new form to be smaller than the main form and more or less centered on the main form. Continuing on, then....

6. Size and position the new form so that it is about 50 percent the size of the main form and centered on the main form. Use the title bar to move the new form. Size the form by dragging the lower-right corner.

7. Change the new form's Name property to SecondForm and the form's Caption property to A Second Form.

8. Choose File | Save from the main menu (or click the Save File button on the toolbar) and save the file with the name Second.

9. Choose a Label component and drop it on the new form. Change the label's Caption property to This is the second form. Change the label's size and color as desired. Center the label on the form. Your form should now look roughly similar to the one in Figure 6.7.

Figure 6.7.

The form up to this point.

10. Click on the main form. Notice that the second form is covered by the main form. Double-click the Show Form 2 button. The Code Editor is displayed, and the cursor is placed just where you need it to begin typing code.

11. Type in code so that the function looks like this (you have to type only one line of code):

```
void __fastcall TMainForm::ShowForm2Click(TObject *Sender)
{
  SecondForm->ShowModal();
}
```

12. Run the program.

At this point you will get a compiler error that says Undefined symbol 'SecondForm'. Hmmm...SecondForm should be a valid symbol because that's the name of the second form we created...I wonder...Aha! Remember that we have two source files with a header for each source file. The problem is that the MainForm unit can't see the declaration for the SecondForm variable (which is a pointer to the TSecondForm class). We have to tell it where to find the class declaration. (Recall Day 2, "Wading In Deeper." We have to #include the header for

6

SecondForm in MainForm's source file.) Switch to the Code Editor and click on the Main.cpp tab to display the unit for the main form. Scroll up to the top of the file. The first few lines look like this:

```
//--------------------------------
#include <vcl.h>
#pragma hdrstop
#include "Main.h"
//--------------------------------
```

You can see the #include for Main.h, but there isn't one for Second.h. That's because we haven't yet told C++Builder to add it. Let's do that now:

1. Choose File | Include Unit Hdr from the main menu. The Include Unit dialog box is displayed. Figure 6.8 shows the Include Unit dialog box as it looks at this point.

2. You will see a list of available units. In this case, the only unit in the list is Second. Click on Second and then click OK to close the dialog box.

Figure 6.8.

The Include Unit dialog box.

NOTE
The Include Unit dialog box will show only those units that exist in the project *and* have not yet been included in this unit. Units that have already been included do not show in the list of available units.

If you blinked, you missed it, but C++Builder added the #include for Second.h when you clicked OK. Now the first few lines of the file show this:

```
//--------------------------------
#include <vcl.h>
#pragma hdrstop
#include "Main.h"
#include "Second.h"
//--------------------------------
```

Now the Main unit can see the class declaration for the Second unit. Click the Run button to run the program. This time the compile goes off without a hitch, and the program runs. When you click the Show Form 2 button on the main form, the second form is displayed. You can close the second form by clicking the system close box on the form's title bar.

6

As you can see, C++Builder does a good job of managing units for you. You have to be sure that you use the Include Unit Hdr option so that one unit can see the class declarations of other units, but for the most part, C++Builder frees you from having to worry about your source files. Later, when your programming needs are more sophisticated, you'll have to do a little more source file management, but at this stage of the game, C++Builder does most of the work for you.

Now let's take a moment to look at the different compiling options available to you when you're writing programs in C++Builder.

Compiling, Building, and Linking

Each time you click the Run button, C++Builder compiles and links your program. But it doesn't necessarily compile every unit in the project. It only compiles any units that have changed since the last compile. This feature saves you time because you don't have to wait for the compiler to compile files that haven't changed. C++Builder keeps track of which files have changed and which haven't, so you don't need to do anything special to use this feature—it's automatic.

Most of the time you want to see in action the results of any changes you have made. In those cases you click the Run button and the program is compiled, linked, and executed. Sometimes, however, you don't want to run the program. For instance, you might want to compile the program just to see whether there are any errors. C++Builder has three menu items in addition to Run that allow you to control the compile/link process. If you choose the Project menu item on the main menu, you will see three menu items called Compile Unit, Make, and Build All. Let's take these in order of simplest to most complex (from the compiler's perspective).

The Compile Unit option is one I really like. This feature causes C++Builder to compile the current unit in the Code Editor and report any errors and warnings. This is the fastest way to check for errors in your code. C++Builder only compiles the file—it does not perform a link. The purpose of the Compile Unit option is to check your code for syntax errors as quickly as possible. Because the link phase takes extra time, the Compile Unit option skips that step.

The Make option compiles any units that have changed since the last compile just as the Compile Unit options does, but it also links the entire project. Naturally, this takes slightly longer than the Compile Unit option. Use the Make option when you want to be sure the program will compile and link but you don't want to run the program.

6

TIP

> The keyboard shortcut for Make is Ctrl+F9.

The Build All option takes the longest to perform. This option compiles every unit in the project regardless of whether it has changed since the last build. After compiling all units, C++Builder links the entire project. So far we have been letting C++Builder add units to our projects. Further on down the road you may have to do some hand editing of your source files to add headers and other needed directives. You may even end up editing the makefile. From time to time, you know, things can get goofed up (we all make mistakes). Performing a Build All will bring everything up-to-date so you can better sort out any problems you might be running into. Sometimes a Build All will resolve compiler and linker errors without requiring you to do anything further.

TIP

> Any time you get unexpected (out of the ordinary) compiler or linker errors, first try a Build All. It could just be that something is out of sync, and a Build All may cure it. If performing a Build All doesn't fix the problem, you'll have to go to work figuring out where the problem lies.

Regardless of the method chosen to compile the project, if errors are detected the compile status dialog box will report There are errors. and will list the number of errors that were detected as well as any warnings. Figure 6.9 shows the compile status dialog box after errors are detected.

Figure 6.9.

The compile status dialog box showing warnings and errors.

After you click OK to dismiss the compile status dialog box, the Code Editor will come to the top with the first error line highlighted. The message window at the bottom of the Code Editor is displayed, and the errors and warnings are listed there. After a successful Compile Unit, Make, or Build All you can immediately run the program via the Run button if you choose.

Compiling and Building Other C++ Programs

C++Builder's strength is in its visual programming environment. That environment is tied directly to VCL and cannot be separated from it. To get the most out of C++Builder, you will most likely be writing applications based on VCL. There are times, however, when you want to write other types of applications. C++Builder is a standard C++ compiler, so you can compile any type of 32-bit C++ program with C++Builder.

Probably the most obvious type of "other" program you may want to build is a *dynamic link library* (DLL). DLLs might seem a bit like black magic, but they are really not very complicated; they are simply bits of compiled code that you can call from your application. Once you have the DLL created and your main program's source file has the needed header, calling a function contained in a DLL is no different than calling a function contained in your main program.

Another type of application you might write with C++Builder is the *console application*. Earlier we built several Win32 console applications when you were learning about the C++ language. Console applications are useful in teaching situations and for quick test programs. They can also be very useful for small utility programs, servers such as Web servers or mail servers, and a whole host of other possibilities. Basically, any application that does not require a graphical interface is a good candidate for a console application. Earlier in the chapter I talked about the C++Builder C++ compiler, the resource compiler, and the C++Builder linker. All these programs are Win32 console applications that are executed from within C++Builder.

You can also compile programs written in either MFC or OWL. This allows you to use a single compiler for all of your development regardless of what framework you are using. Although you probably won't develop full-scale MFC or OWL applications with C++Builder, there is certainly no reason you could not do so if you chose to. Of course, you would have to have the OWL or MFC library files and headers in order to build an OWL or MFC application. Listing 6.1 contains an OWL version of the Hello World program. First, set up C++Builder to build an OWL application (see the C++Builder documentation on how to configure C++Builder to build an OWL application). Then enter the program from the keyboard or load it from this book's CD-ROM. Compile and run, and you've got an OWL program built with C++Builder.

6

Listing 6.1. OWLHELLO.CPP.

```
 1: #include <owl\applicat.h>
 2: #include <owl\framewin.h>
 3: #pragma hdrstop
 4: class TestWindow : public TWindow {
 5:   public:
 6:     TestWindow() : TWindow(0, 0, 0) {}
 7:   protected:
 8:     void Paint(TDC&, bool, TRect&);
 9: };
10: void
11: TestWindow::Paint(TDC& dc, bool, TRect&)
12: {
13:   TRect rect = GetClientRect();
14:   dc.DrawText("HelloWorld!", -1,
15:     rect, DT_CENTER | DT_VCENTER | DT_SINGLELINE);
16: }
17: class TestApp : public TApplication {
18:   public:
19:     TestApp() : TApplication("") {}
20:     void InitMainWindow()
21:     {
22:       TFrameWindow* frame = new TFrameWindow(
23:         0, "OWL Hello World", new TestWindow);
24:       SetMainWindow(frame);
25:     }
26: };
27: int OwlMain(int, char* [])
28: {
29:   return TestApp().Run();
30: }
```

More About C++Builder Forms

Before I continue with the discussion about the C++Builder IDE, I need to spend some time explaining forms. You have seen several forms in action as you have worked through this book, and tomorrow you are going to learn all about the Form Designer. Before we get there, you need some more background information on forms, so I'll cover that base now.

Main Window Forms

Forms are the main building block of a C++Builder application. Every GUI application has at least one form that serves as the main window. The main window form might be just a blank window, it might have controls on it, or it might have a bitmap displayed on it. In a typical Windows program, your main window would have a menu. It might also have decorations such as a toolbar or a status bar. Just about anything goes when you're creating the main window of your application. Each application is unique, and each has different requirements.

Dialog Box Forms

Forms are also used where traditional Windows programs use dialog boxes. In fact, to the user there is no difference between a C++Builder form acting as a dialog box and a true dialog box. Dialog boxes usually have several traits that distinguish them from ordinary windows:

- Dialog boxes are not usually sizable. They usually perform a specific function, and sizing of the dialog box is neither useful nor desirable.
- Dialog boxes almost always have an OK button. Some dialog boxes have a button labeled Close that accomplishes the same thing. Simple dialog boxes like an About dialog box typically have only the OK button.
- Dialog boxes may also have a Cancel button and a Help button.
- Dialog boxes typically have only the system close button on the title bar. They do not usually have minimize and maximize buttons.
- Some dialog boxes are tabbed dialog boxes that display several tabs from which the user can choose. When a tab is clicked on, a different page of the dialog box is displayed.
- The Tab key can be used to move from one control to the next in most dialog boxes.

There are certainly exceptions to every rule. Most dialog boxes have the usual characteristics, but some perform specialty tasks and therefore depart from the norm in one way or another.

Dialog boxes in C++Builder are slightly different than in other programming environments. First, let's take a look at how other programming environments handle dialog boxes; then we'll look at how they are implemented in C++Builder.

Dialog Boxes in Traditional Windows Programs

In a traditional Windows program (one written in C or with one of the frameworks), a dialog box is created with a dialog box editor. In most cases, the dialog box editor is a visual tool that works somewhat like the C++Builder Form Editor. When the user is done designing the dialog box, the visual representation of the dialog box is converted into a dialog box definition in a resource script. (A *resource script* is a text file that is later compiled into a binary resource file by the resource compiler.) To illustrate, take a look at the dialog box in Figure 6.10.

6

Figure 6.10.

*A typical About
dialog box.*

Figure 6.10 represents a typical About dialog box. It contains the program name, the copyright information, and the application's icon. The resource script definition for the dialog box is shown in Listing 6.2.

Listing 6.2. A dialog box resource definition.

```
 1: IDD_ABOUT DIALOG 58, 53, 194, 119
 2: STYLE DS_MODALFRAME ¦ WS_POPUP ¦
 3:   WS_VISIBLE ¦ WS_CAPTION ¦ WS_SYSMENU
 4: CAPTION "About TMMPlayer Example Program"
 5: FONT 8, "MS Sans Serif"
 6: {
 7:   DEFPUSHBUTTON "OK", IDOK, 72, 96, 50, 14
 8:   CTEXT "TMMPlayer Example Program", -1, 48, 22, 128, 8
 9:   CTEXT "Copyright © 1996, by Kent Reisdorph", -1, 32, 47, 136, 8
10:   CTEXT "March 15, 1996", -1, 24, 59, 146, 8
11:   CONTROL "", 99, "button", BS_GROUPBOX ¦
12:     WS_CHILD ¦ WS_VISIBLE ¦ WS_GROUP, 12, 4, 176, 70
13:   OONTROL 1, 1, "static", SS_ICON ¦
14:     SS_SUNKEN ¦ WS_CHILD ¦ WS_VISIBLE, 24, 17, 20, 20
15: }
```

The resource script contains information that Windows uses to build the dialog box at runtime. This information includes the number and type of controls on the dialog box, as well as their size, position, text, options, and so on. Of course, the resource script also includes the same type of information for the dialog box itself.

Some Windows programmers don't use a dialog box editor at all, but prefer to write the dialog box definition from scratch with a text editor. While I can't fault those programmers for creating dialog boxes in this manner, I can say that for most programmers to take that approach would be, er, less than 100 percent efficient. It would take many times longer to create a dialog box in that manner than with the visual approach.

Usually all of the application's dialog box definitions are contained in a single resource script file that has the filename extension .RC. At some point in the program-creation process, the resource script is compiled into an .RES file (the binary resource file), which then gets linked to the .EXE by the linker. At runtime the dialog box is displayed either modally or modelessly, depending on the dialog box's intended purpose. When the dialog box is executed, Windows loads the dialog box resource from the executable file, builds the dialog box, and displays it.

NOTE

A *modal* dialog box is one that must be dismissed before the user can continue using the application. The main window of an application is disabled while this type of dialog box is open. Most dialog boxes are modal. The Compile Status dialog box in C++Builder is an example of a modal dialog box.

A *modeless* dialog box is one that allows the user to continue to work with the application while the dialog box is displayed. The Find dialog box in some word-processing programs is an example of a modeless dialog box.

Now, with that background information on how dialog boxes are handled in a traditional Windows program, let's take a look at how C++Builder handles dialog boxes.

Dialog Boxes in C++Builder

In C++Builder, a dialog box is simply another form. You create a dialog box just like you do a main window form or any other form. To prevent the dialog box from being sized, you can change the BorderStyle property to bsDialog or bsSingle. If you use bsDialog, your dialog box will have only the close box on the title bar, which is traditional for dialog boxes. Other than that, you don't have to do anything special to get a form to behave like a dialog box. All C++Builder forms have tabbing support built in. You can set the tab order by altering the TabOrder property of the individual controls on the dialog box.

A C++Builder dialog box (any C++Builder form, actually) is modal or modeless, depending on how it is displayed. To execute a modal dialog box, you call the ShowModal() method of TForm. To create a modeless dialog box, you call the Show() method.

Let's add an About box to the multiple-forms project we created earlier. If you don't have that project open, choose File | Open from the main menu or click the Open Project button on the toolbar and locate the file (you should have saved it with the project name Multiple).

6

> **TIP**
>
> C++Builder keeps a list of the files and projects you have used most recently. Chose File | Reopen to view the MRU (most recently used) list. The MRU list is divided into two parts. The top part shows the projects you have used most recently, and the bottom part shows the individual files that you have used most recently. Just click on one of the items to reopen that project or file.

First we'll add a button to the form that will display the About dialog box:

1. Bring the main form into view. Choose the button component from the Component Palette and drop a button on the form.

2. Arrange the two buttons that are now on the form to balance the look of the form.

3. Change the Name property of the new button to AboutButton and the Caption property to About....

4. Double-click the AboutButton you just created on the form. The Code Editor is displayed with the cursor placed in the event-handler function. Add this line of code at the cursor:

```
AboutBox->ShowModal();
```

We haven't actually created the About box yet, but when we do we'll name it AboutBox so we know enough to go ahead and type the code to display the About box.

Now we'll create the dialog box itself:

1. Create a new form (click the New Form button on the toolbar). Size the form to the size of a typical About box (roughly the same size as the form named SecondForm that we created earlier).

2. Change the Name property to AboutBox and change the Caption property to About This Program.

3. Locate the BorderStyle property (it's just above Caption) and change it to bsDialog.

4. Now add three text labels to the box. Edit the labels so that the About box resembles that in Figure 6.11. (You can type any text you want, of course.) You can leave the default names C++Builder generates for the text labels' Name properties. We aren't actually going to do anything with the Name property, so we don't need a descriptive name.

6

TIP

The copyright symbol (©) has an ASCII value of 169. To create the copyright symbol, press and hold the Alt key and type the numbers 0169 on the numeric keypad (be sure Num Lock is on). When you let go of the Alt key, the copyright symbol appears. You can insert the ASCII value of any character this way. You must type all four numbers, though. For example, the ASCII value of a capital A is 65. To insert an A, you would have to hold down Alt and type 0065 on the numeric keypad.

Figure 6.11.

The About box with text labels added.

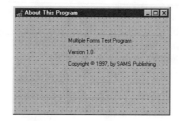

Next we'll add an icon to the About box:

1. Click on the Additional tab on the Component Palette and choose the Image component. Place the component to the left of the text on the form.

2. Locate the AutoSize property for the Image component and change it to true.

3. Locate the Picture property and double-click the Value column. The Picture Editor dialog box is displayed.

4. Click the Load button. In the File Open dialog box, navigate to the \CBuilder\Images\Icons directory and choose an icon from the icon files listed. Click OK. The icon you selected is displayed in the Picture Editor window. Click OK again to close the Picture Editor. The icon is displayed on the form. Note that the Image component has sized itself to the size of the icon.

5. Position the icon as desired.

At this point we need an OK button on the form. I'll be a little creative and show you a new component:

1. If you're not already there, click on the Additional tab on the Component Palette. Select the BitBtn component and place a BitBtn on the form near the bottom and centered horizontally.

2. Locate the Kind property and change it to bkOK. Notice that a green check mark has appeared on the button, and the Caption property has changed to OK. That's all we

have to do with the button. The BitBtn component already includes code to close the form when the OK button is clicked.

Let's add one final touch to the About box:

1. Locate the Bevel button (on the Additional tab in the Component Palette) and click it.
2. Move to the form, but rather than clicking on the form, drag a box around the three text labels. The Bevel component appears when you stop dragging. If you didn't get it quite right, you can resize or reposition the component.
3. Locate the Shape property and change it to bsFrame. You now have a 3D frame around the static text.

Your form should now look something like the one shown in Figure 6.12. Save the unit (File | Save) and give it the name About.

Figure 6.12.

The finished
About box.

Are we ready to compile and run the program? Not yet. We need to tell the main form to #include the About unit:

1. Switch to the Code Editor (press F12) and select the Main.cpp tab.
2. Choose File | Include Unit Hdr from the main menu.
3. Choose the About unit from the Include Unit dialog box and click OK.

Now you're ready to run the program. Click the Run button. When the program runs, click the About button, and the About dialog box is displayed. Note that the dialog box is modal (you can't go back to the main window while the dialog box is displayed) and that it cannot be sized. The About form behaves in every way like a regular Windows dialog box.

 NOTE

The common dialog box classes (TOpenDialog, TSaveDialog, TFontDialog, and so on) do not represent dialog boxes created as C++Builder forms. Windows provides these dialog boxes as a set of common dialog boxes that all Windows applications can use (the actual dialog boxes are contained in a file called COMDLG32.DLL). The VCL dialog box classes encapsulate the common dialog boxes to make using them easier.

NOTE

C++Builder includes several prebuilt forms that you can choose from to help you build dialog boxes as quickly as possible. I'll discuss those on Day 9, "Creating Applications in C++Builder."

Secondary Windows Versus Dialog Boxes

A *secondary window* is a form that you display from your main window. So when is a form a secondary window and when is it a dialog box? When it really comes down to it, there is no difference between a secondary window and a dialog box in C++Builder. You might have dialog box–looking windows, and you may have other windows that resemble traditional windows. In the grand scheme of things, they are all forms and it doesn't make much sense to differentiate between the terms *dialog box* and *secondary form*. It's all the same in the end. In traditional programming environments, you have to specifically create a dialog box or specifically create a secondary window in an application. C++Builder frees you from that restriction and allows you to treat both dialog boxes and windows exactly the same.

The Multiple-Document Interface Model

So far we have built only *single-document interface* (SDI) applications. An SDI application has a single main window and typically displays dialog boxes as needed, but does not otherwise display child windows.

Some programs follow the *multiple-document interface* (MDI) model. MDI applications consist of a main window (the MDI parent) and child windows (the MDI children). Examples of programs that use the MDI model are the Windows System Configuration Editor (SYSEDIT) and the Windows 3.1 Program Manager. One of the most obvious characteristics of the MDI model is that the MDI child windows are confined to the parent. You can drag the child windows within the parent window, but you cannot drag them outside the parent. MDI applications almost always have a Window pop up on their main menu. The pop-up menu usually contains items named Cascade and Tile, which allow you to display the MDI child windows in either a cascaded or tiled arrangement. When an MDI child is minimized, its icon is contained within the MDI parent's frame. When a regular (non-MDI) child window is minimized, its icon is placed on the Windows desktop.

To create an MDI application in C++Builder, you must set the main form's `FormStyle` property to `fsMDIForm`. Each of the MDI child windows must have the `FormStyle` property set to `fsMDIChild`. Aside from that restriction, there is very little to creating an MDI application in C++Builder. You simply create the main window form and one or more forms to be used as child windows, and you're off and running.

Key Properties for Forms

The `TForm` class has a lot of properties. Some of these properties are obscure and rarely used; others are widely used. I'll touch on the most widely used properties here. I won't include obvious properties like `Color`, `Left`, `Top`, `Width`, and `Height` unless they have a particular feature you should be aware of.

Runtime and Design-Time Properties

The properties outlined in this section can be set at design time and also at runtime. Almost all of these properties can be read at runtime as well.

ActiveControl

The `ActiveControl` property is used to set the control that will have focus when the form is activated. For instance, you may want a particular edit control to have focus when a dialog box form is displayed. At design time the Value column for the `ActiveControl` property contains a list of components on the form. You can choose one of the components from this list to make that component the active control when the form is first displayed.

AutoScroll, HorzScrollBar, **and** VertScrollBar

Together, the `AutoScroll`, `HorzScrollBar`, and `VertScrollBar` properties control the scrollbars for a form. If `AutoScroll` is set to `true` (the default), scrollbars automatically appear when the form is too small to display all of its components. The `HorzScrollBar` and `VertScrollBar` properties each have several properties of their own that control the scrollbar operations.

BorderStyle

The `BorderStyle` property indicates what type of border the form will have. The default value is `bsSizeable`, which creates a window that can be sized. Nonsizable styles include `bsDialog` and `bsNone`.

ClientWidth **and** ClientHeight

You can specify the client area width and height rather than the full form's width and height by using the ClientWidth and ClientHeight properties. (The *client area* of the form is the area inside the borders and below the title bar and menu bar.) Use these properties when you want the client area to be a specific size and the rest of the window to adjust as necessary. Setting the ClientWidth and ClientHeight properties makes automatic changes to the Width and Height properties.

Font

The Font property specifies the font that the form uses. The important thing to understand here is that the form's font is inherited by any components placed on the form. This also means that you can change the font used by all components at one time by changing just the form's font. If an individual control's font had been manually changed, that control's font will not be changed when the main form's font changes.

FormStyle

This property is usually set to fsNormal. If you want a form to always be on top, use the fsStayOnTop style. MDI forms should use the fsMDIForm style and MDI child forms should use the fsMDIChild style. MDI forms and MDI child windows were discussed previously in the chapter, in the section "The Multiple-Document Interface Model."

HelpContext

The HelpContext property is used to set the help context ID for a form. If context help is enabled for a form, the Windows Help system will activate when the F1 key is pressed. The context ID is used to tell the Help system which page in the help file to display.

Icon

The Icon property sets the icon that is used on the title bar for the form when the form is displayed at runtime, and also when the form is minimized. In some cases, setting this property has no effect. For instance, when the FormStyle is set to fsDialog, the Icon property is ignored.

Position

The Position property determines the size and position of the form when the form is initially displayed. The three basic choices are poDesigned, poDefault, and poScreenCenter. poDesigned causes the form to be displayed in the exact position it was in when it was designed. poDefault allows Windows to set the size and position according to the usual Windows Z-ordering

6

algorithm. (Z-ordering is what Windows uses to decide where it displays a new window on the screen. If the new window does not have specific placement information, it will be displayed just below and to the right of the last window displayed on the screen.) The poScreenCenter option causes the form to be displayed in the center of the screen each time it is shown.

Visible

The Visible property controls whether the form is initially visible. This property is not particularly useful at design time, but at runtime it can be read to determine whether the form is currently visible. It can also be used to hide or display the form.

WindowState

The WindowState property can be read to determine the form's current state (maximized, minimized, or normal). It can also be used to indicate how the form should initially be displayed. Choices are wsMinimized, wsMaximized, and wsNormal.

Runtime-Only Properties

Some properties can be accessed only at runtime through code. The following are the most commonly used runtime properties.

ActiveMDIChild

When read, the ActiveMDIChild property returns a pointer to the currently active MDI child window. This property is read-only.

Canvas

The form's canvas represents the drawing surface of the form. The Canvas property gives you access to the form's canvas. By using the Canvas property you can draw bitmaps, lines, shapes, or text on the form at runtime. Most of the time you will use a Label component to draw text on a form, an Image component to display graphics, and a Shape component to draw shapes. However, there are times when you need to draw on the canvas at runtime and the Canvas property allows you to do that. The Canvas property can also be used to save an image of the form to disk.

ClientRect

The ClientRect property contains the top, left, right, and bottom coordinates of the client area of the form. This is useful in a variety of programming situations. For instance, you may need to know the client area's width and height in order to place a bitmap on the center of the form.

Handle

The `Handle` property returns the window handle (HWND) of the form. Use this property when you need the window handle to pass to a Windows API function.

ModalResult

The `ModalResult` property is used to close a modal window. If you have a dialog box that has OK and Cancel buttons, you can set `ModalResult` to `mrOK` when the user clicks the OK button, and to `mrCancel` when the user clicks the Cancel button. The calling form can then read `ModalResult` to see which button was clicked to close the form. Other possibilities include `mrYes`, `mrNo`, and `mrAbort`.

Owner

The `Owner` property is a pointer to the owner of the form. The owner of the form is the object that is responsible for deleting the form when the form is no longer needed. The parent of a component, on the other hand, is the window (a form or another component) that acts as the container for the component. In the case of a main form, the application object is both the owner of the form and the parent of the form. In the case of components, the owner would be the form, but the parent could be another component, such as a panel.

Parent

The `Parent` property is a pointer to the parent of the form. See the previous section about `Owner` for an explanation of `Owner` versus `Parent`.

Form Methods

Forms are components, too. As such, forms have many methods in common with components. Common methods include `Show()`, `ShowModal()`, and `Invalidate()`, to name just a few. There are some methods, however, that are specific to forms. As before, I'll discuss only the most commonly used methods.

BringToFront()

The `BringToFront()` method causes the form to be brought to the top of all other forms in the application.

Close() and CloseQuery()

The `Close()` method closes a form after first calling `CloseQuery()` to be sure that it's okay to close the form. The `CloseQuery()` function, in turn, calls the `OnCloseQuery` event handler. If

6

the `bool` variable passed to the `OnCloseQuery` handler is set to `false`, the form is not closed. If it is set to `true`, the form closes normally. You can use the `OnCloseQuery` event handler to prompt the user to save a file that needs saving and to control whether a form can close.

Print()

The `Print()` method prints the contents of the form. Only the client area of the form is printed, not the caption, title bar, or borders. `Print()` is handy for quick screen dumps of a form.

ScrollInView()

The `ScrollInView()` method scrolls the form so that the specified component is visible on the form.

SetFocus()

The `SetFocus()` method activates the form and brings it to the top. If the form has components, the component specified in the `ActiveControl` property will receive input focus (see the `ActiveControl` property in the section "Runtime and Design-Time Properties").

Show() **and** ShowModal()

The `Show()` and `ShowModal()` methods display the form. The `Show()` method displays the form as modeless, so other forms can be activated while the form is visible. The `ShowModal()` method executes the form modally. A modal form must be dismissed before the user can continue to use the application.

MDI Methods

Several form methods deal specifically with MDI operations. The `ArrangeIcons()` method arranges the icons of any minimized MDI children in an MDI parent window. The `Cascade()` method cascades all non-minimized MDI child windows. The `Tile()` method tiles all open MDI child windows. The `Next()` method activates (brings to the top) the next MDI child in the child list, and the `Previous()` method activates the previous MDI child in the child list. The MDI methods apply only to MDI parent windows.

Form Events

Forms can respond to a wide variety of events. Some of the most commonly used are listed in the following sections.

OnActivate

The OnActivate event occurs when the form is activated. The form might be activated as a result of its initial creation, when the user switches from one form to another, or when the user switches from another application.

OnClose and OnCloseQuery

When an application is closed, the OnClose event is sent. OnClose calls the OnCloseQuery event to see whether it is okay to close the form. If the OnCloseQuery event returns false, the form is not closed.

OnCreate

The OnCreate event occurs when the form is initially created. Only one OnCreate event will occur for any instance of a particular form. Use the OnCreate handler to perform any startup tasks that the form needs in order to operate.

OnDestroy

The OnDestroy event is the opposite of OnCreate. Use this event to clean up any memory a form allocates dynamically or to do other cleanup chores.

OnDragDrop

The OnDragDrop event occurs when an object is dropped on the form. Respond to this event if your form supports drag-and-drop.

OnMouseDown, OnMouseMove, and OnMouseUp

Respond to the OnMouseDown, OnMouseMove, and OnMouseUp events to respond to mouse clicks on a form.

OnPaint

The OnPaint event occurs whenever the form needs repainting, which could happen for a variety of reasons. Respond to this event to do any painting that your application needs to display at all times. In most cases, individual components will take care of painting themselves, but in some cases you may need to draw on the form itself.

OnResize

The OnResize event is sent every time the form is resized. You may need to respond to this event to adjust components on the form or to repaint the form.

6

OnShow

The OnShow event occurs just before the form becomes visible. You could use this event to perform any processing that your form needs to do just before it is shown.

The Object Inspector

An integral part of the C++Builder IDE is the Object Inspector. This window works in conjunction with the Form Designer to aid in the creation of components. I'm going to discuss the Form Designer tomorrow, but before I do, I want to talk a little about the Object Inspector.

The Object Inspector is where you set the design-time properties that affect how the component acts at runtime. The Object Inspector has three main areas:

☐ The Component Selector

☐ The Properties page

☐ The Events page

You have been using the Object Inspector quite a bit up to this point, so I'll review what you already know and show you a few things you don't know.

The Component Selector

The Component Selector is a drop-down combo box that is located at the top of the Object Inspector window. The Component Selector allows you to choose a component to view or modify.

 NOTE | Usually the quickest way to select a component is by clicking on the component on the form. Choosing the component from the Component Selector is convenient if the component you are looking for is hidden beneath another component or is off the visible area of the form.

The Component Selector displays the name of the component and the class from which it is derived. For example, a memo component named Memo would appear in the Component Selector as

```
Memo: TMemo
```

The class name does not show up in the drop-down list of components, but only in the top portion of the Component Selector. To select a component, click the drop-down button to reveal the list of components and then click on the one you want to select.

NOTE The Component Selector shows only the components available on the current form and the name of the form itself. Other forms and their components will not be displayed until they're made the active forms in the Form Designer.

After you select a component in the Component Selector, the component is selected on the form as well. The Properties and Events tabs change to display the properties and events for the selected component. (Remember that a form is a component, too.) Figure 6.13 shows the Object Inspector with the Component Selector list displayed.

Figure 6.13.

The Component Selector list.

The Properties Page

The Properties page of the Object Inspector displays all the design-time properties for the currently selected control. The Properties page has two columns. The Property column is on the left side of the Properties page and shows the property name. The Value column is on the right side of the Properties page and is where you type or select the value for the property.

If the component selected has more properties than will fit in the Object Inspector, a scrollbar will be provided so you can scroll up or down to locate other properties.

NOTE If you have multiple components selected on the form, the Object Inspector shows all the properties that those components have in common. You can use this feature to modify the properties of several components at one time. For example, to change the width of several components at one time, you can select all the buttons and then modify the Width property in the Object Inspector. When you press Enter or move to another property, all the components you selected will have their Width property modified.

Figure 6.14 shows the Object Inspector when a Memo component is selected.

Figure 6.14.

The Object Inspector showing Memo *component properties.*

On Day 5, "C++ Class Frameworks and the Visual Component Model," I talked about properties. I discussed how properties can be integer values, enumerations, sets, other objects, strings, and other types. The Object Inspector deals with each type of property according to the data type of the property. C++Builder has several built-in property editors to handle data input for the property. For example, the Top property accepts an integer value. Because an int is a basic data type, no special handling is required, so the property editor is fairly basic. The property editor for this type of property allows you to type a value (such as Top, Left, Width, and Height) directly in the Value column for integer properties.

NOTE

In most cases, the property editor does parameter checking for any properties in which you can enter an integer value. The Width property, for instance, cannot be a negative number. If you attempt to enter a negative number for the width of a control, C++Builder will force the width to the minimum allowed for that control (usually 0). If you enter a string value for a property that expects an integer value, C++Builder will display an error message. It is the job of the property editor to do parameter checking.

In many cases, the property editor for the property contains a list of items from which you can choose. Properties that have an enumeration or boolean value as their base data type fall into this category. When you click on the Value column with this type of property editor, you will see a drop-down button on the right side of the Value column. Clicking this button will display the list of possible values.

TIP

If you double-click the Value column for this type of property, the property editor will cycle through the possible choices. To quickly change a `bool` property, for instance, simply double-click its value. Because the only choices are `true` and `false` double-clicking the value has the effect of toggling the property's value.

If you look closely at the Object Inspector, you will see that some properties have a plus sign preceding the property name. Properties that are sets and properties that are objects both have the plus sign in front of their names. The plus sign indicates that the property node can be expanded to show the set or, in the case of properties that are objects, the properties of that object. To expand a node, double-click on the Property column for that property (on the property name) or choose Expand from the Object Inspector speed menu. To collapse the node, double-click on it again or choose Collapse from the Object Inspector speed menu.

To see an example of a set, choose a form and then double-click on the `BorderIcons` property. The node expands and you see four boolean members of the set. You can turn on or off any of the four members as needed.

In the case of properties that are objects (instances of a VCL class), you have two choices in editing the property. First, you can click on the Value column for the property and then click the button to the right side of the value. This button is indicated by an ellipsis (...) on its face. Clicking this button will invoke the property editor for that particular control. For example, click on the `Font` property and then click the ellipsis button. The Choose Font dialog box is displayed so that you can select the font. The second way you can edit this type of property is by expanding the property node. The property's properties (yes, it's true) will be displayed, and you can edit them just like any other property. Again, locate the `Font` property and double-click on it. The `TFont` properties will be displayed. You can now modify the font's `Height`, `Color`, or `Name` properties.

For some properties you can use only the ellipsis button as a means of editing the property. Earlier you used the `Image` component to select an icon for the `Multiple` program's About box. As you found out then, the `Image` component's `Picture` property can be changed only by invoking that property's property editor. In that case, the property editor is the C++Builder Image Editor.

6

Rest assured that each property knows what it needs to do to present you with the correct property editor. You will see different types of property editors as you are introduced to new components and new properties.

The Events Page

The Events page lists all the events that the property is designed to handle. Using the Events page is pretty basic. In order to create an event handler for an event, you simply double-click in the Value column next to the event you want to handle. When you do, C++Builder creates an event-handling function for you with all the parameters needed to handle that event. The Code Editor is displayed, and the cursor is placed in the event handler. All you have to do is start typing code. The name of the function is generated based on the Name property of the component and the event being handled. If, for instance, you had a button named OK and were handling the OnClick event, the function name generated would be OKClick().

You can let C++Builder generate the name of the event-handling function for you or you can provide the function name for C++Builder to use. To provide the function name yourself, type the name in the Value column next to the event and press Enter. The Code Editor is displayed, and so is the event-handling function, complete with the name you supplied.

Once you have created an event-handling function for a component, you can use that event handler for any component that handles the same event. Sometimes it's convenient to have several buttons use the same OnClick event, for instance. To take it a step further, you might have a main menu item, a pop-up menu item, and a speedbar button all use the same OnClick handler. You will learn to appreciate this kind of code reuse as you gain experience with C++Builder. Even though you are dealing with three different components, they can still share a common OnClick handler. The Value column of the Events page contains a drop-down button that can be used to display a list of all event handlers compatible with the current event. All you have to do is choose an event from the list.

An MDI Sample Program

To help solidify today's discussion of projects and forms, let's create an MDI application. This application will allow you to open and save graphics files like bitmaps, icons, and metafiles. In order to complete our task, we'll have to have a master plan. Here's what we need to do:

1. Create the main window form (an MDI parent), including a menu.
2. Write code for the File | Open and File | Save menu selections.
3. Write code for the Cascade, Tile, and Arrange All items on the Window menu.

4. Create the MDI child forms.

5. Create an About box.

6. Stand back and admire our work.

There's no point in dawdling (time is money!), so let's get right to it.

Step 1: Create the Main Window Form

First we'll create the main window form. The main window for an MDI application must have the `FormStyle` property set to `fsMDIForm`. We will also need to add a menu to the application, as well as File Open and File Save dialog boxes:

1. Start C++Builder and choose File | New Application from the main menu.

2. For the main form, change the `Name` property to `MainForm`.

3. Change the `Caption` property to `Picture Viewer`.

4. Change the `Height` to `450` and the `Width` to `575`.

5. Change the `FormStyle` to `fsMDIForm`.

Okay, now we've got the main part of the form done. Next we'll add a menu to the form. Because I haven't discussed the Menu Editor yet, we'll take the easy route to creating a menu. To do that, we'll take advantage of a C++Builder feature that allows us to import a predefined menu:

1. Click on the Standard tab of the Component Palette and click the MainMenu button.

2. Drop a `MainMenu` component on the form. It doesn't matter where you drop it because the icon representing the menu is just a placeholder and won't show on the form at runtime.

3. Change the `Name` property to `MainMenu`.

4. Double-click on the `MainMenu` component. The Menu Editor is displayed. (We'll look at the Menu Editor in more detail tomorrow.)

5. Place your cursor over the Menu Editor and click your right mouse button. The Insert Template dialog box appears. Choose Insert from template... from the speed menu. Figure 6.15 shows the Insert Template dialog box with the Menu Editor behind it.

6. Choose MDI Frame Menu and click OK. The menu is displayed in the Menu Editor.

7. Click the system close box on the Menu Editor to close it.

6

Figure 6.15.

The Menu Editor with the Insert Template dialog box open.

Now you should be back to the main form. Notice that you have a menu on the form. You can click on the top-level items to see the full menu. Don't click on any menu subitems at this point—we'll do that in a minute. Notice that there are a lot of menu items. For now we'll just leave the extra items where they are.

Now we need to prepare the File Open and File Save dialog boxes:

1. Click on the Dialogs tab on the Component Palette. Choose an `OpenDialog` component and place it on the form. The `OpenDialog` component's icon can be placed anywhere on the form.

2. Change the `Name` property of the open dialog box to `OpenDialog`.

3. Change the `Title` property to `Open a Picture for Viewing`.

4. Add a `SaveDialog` component.

5. Change the `Name` property of the component to `SaveDialog` and the `Title` property to `Save a Picture`.

Your form should now look like the one in Figure 6.16.

Figure 6.16.

The form up to this point.

Step 2: Write Code for the File | Open and File | Save As Menu Items

So far, so good. Now let's write the code to implement the File | Open and File | Save As menu items. C++Builder provides a slick way of writing menu handlers with a minimum amount of fuss. Keep in mind that we haven't created the MDI child form yet, but we know enough about it to write the code for the menu handlers. Here goes:

1. On the main form, choose File | Open from the menu. An event handler is created for that menu item, and the Code Editor is displayed.

2. Type code so that the event handler looks like this:

```
void __fastcall TMainForm::Open1Click(TObject *Sender)
{
  if (OpenDialog->Execute())
  {
    TChild* child = new TChild(this);
    child->SetParent(this);
    child->Image->Picture->LoadFromFile(OpenDialog->FileName);
    child->ClientWidth = child->Image->Picture->Width;
    child->ClientHeight = child->Image->Picture->Height;
    child->Caption = OpenDialog->FileName;
    child->Show();
  }
}
```

This code first executes the File Open dialog box and gets a filename. If the Cancel button on the File Open dialog box is clicked, the function returns without doing anything further. If the OK button on the File Open dialog box is clicked, a new TChild object is created (TChild will be the name of the MDI child class we're going to create later). The image file is loaded into the Image component on the child form; then the MDI child's client area is sized to match the size of the image. Finally, the Caption property is set to the filename selected and the child window is displayed.

NOTE

Remember our earlier discussion about calling delete for all objects created with new? Notice that I appear to be violating that rule in the preceding code. In reality I am not, because VCL will take the responsibility of freeing the memory allocated for the MDI child windows. Notice that the single parameter in the TChild constructor is this. That tells VCL that the Owner of the MDI child is the MDI form window. When the MDI form is destroyed (when the application closes), it will be sure to delete all of its MDI child objects.

6

3. Press F12 to switch back to the form. Now choose File | Save As from the menu. The File | Save As event handler is displayed.

4. Type code so that the File | Save As event handler looks like this:

```
void __fastcall TMainForm::SaveAs1Click(TObject *Sender)
{
  TChild* child = dynamic_cast<TChild*>(ActiveMDIChild);
  if (!child) return;
  if (SaveDialog->Execute())
  {
    child->Image->Picture->SaveToFile(SaveDialog->FileName);
  }
}
```

The code for the File | Save menu item is pretty simple. The first two lines check to see whether an MDI child window is active. If, so the File Save dialog box is displayed. If the user clicks OK, the image is saved to disk using the TPicture class's SaveToFile() method.

NOTE

In the preceding code you see a special C++ operator called dynamic_cast. dynamic_cast is used to cast a pointer of a base class to a pointer of a derived class. The ActiveMDIChild property returns a pointer to a TForm object. What we actually need in this case is a pointer to a TChild object (our MDI child class, derived from TForm) so that we can access the Image property of the MDI child form.

If dynamic_cast is unable to perform the cast, it returns NULL. Attempting to use a NULL pointer will result in an access violation, but the debugger will conveniently point out the offending line so you know exactly where the problem lies. This is much better than the alternative of attempting to use the old-style cast, where a bad cast could result in some random memory location being overwritten.

Before we go on, it would be a good idea to save the project. Choose File | Save All from the main menu. Save Unit1 (the default name C++Builder assigns to a new unit) as ViewMain and the project as ViewPict.

Step 3: Write Code for the Window Menu

Now we'll add code to the Window menu. This part is simple:

1. Switch back to the form by pressing F12. Choose Window | Tile from the form's menu.

2. You need to enter only a single line of code for the event handler. The finished event handler will look like this:

```
void __fastcall TMainForm::Tile1Click(TObject *Sender)
{
  Tile();
}
```

3. Switch back to the form and repeat the process for Window | Cascade. The finished function looks like this:

```
void __fastcall TMainForm::Cascade1Click(TObject *Sender)
{
  Cascade();
}
```

4. Repeat the steps for the Window | Arrange All menu item. The single line of code to add for the function body is

```
ArrangeIcons();
```

Okay, now we're done with the main form. We can now move on to creating the MDI child form.

Step 4: Create the MDI Child Form

The MDI child form is surprisingly simple. In fact, we don't have to write any code at all:

1. Create a new form using the New Form button on the toolbar or by choosing File | New Form from the main menu.

2. Change the Name property to Child. The Caption property can be ignored because we will be setting the dialog box's caption at runtime.

3. Change the FormStyle property to fsMDIChild. This is necessary for the form to be treated as an MDI child window.

That's it for the form itself. Now let's put an Image component on the form. The Image component will display the graphics file selected by the user.

1. Click on the Additional tab on the Component Palette. Click the Image button and place an Image component anywhere on the form.

2. Change the Name property to Image.

3. Change the Stretch property to true.

4. Change the Align property to alClient. The Image component expands to fill the client area of the form.

5. Choose File | Save and save the form's unit as MDIChild.

6. Switch to the Code Editor (press F12). Click on the ViewMain.cpp tab. Now choose File | Include Unit Hdr from the main menu, select the MDIChild unit, and click OK. This is so the compiler is happy when we reference the TChild object.

The form is pretty unimpressive at this point, but it should look similar to Figure 6.17.

Figure 6.17.

The MDI child form with an Image *component.*

We still have to create the About box, but right now you're probably eager to try the program. Go ahead and click the Run button. After a while, the program is displayed. You can choose File | Open and open any graphics file (any file with a .bmp, a .wmf, or an .ioo extension, that is). Notice that the MDI child window sizes itself to the graphic it contains. Open several files and then try the Cascade and Tile options under the Window menu. If you want, you can save a file with a different name using the File | Save As menu item.

Step 5: Create the About Box

By now you should know enough about C++Builder to create the About box on your own. Create the About box so that it looks something like Figure 6.18. If you get stuck, you can jump back a few pages and review the steps you took to create the About box earlier in the chapter. Feel free to make your About box as personalized as you like.

Figure 6.18.

*The About box for the
application.*

After you have the box created, you can take these steps to call the box from the menu:

1. Change the Name property to AboutBox.

2. Save the unit as PVAbout.

NOTE

C++Builder has full support for long filenames. I use the 8.3 file-
naming convention in this book for reasons related to electronic
publishing. For applications you write, you can take advantage of long
filenames.

3. Switch to the ViewMain.cpp tab in the Code Editor (press F12). Choose
File | Include Unit Hdr from the main menu and include the PVAbout header.

4. Press F12 to switch back to the main form. Choose Help | About from the menu.
You are taken to the Code Editor with the OnClick handler for the menu item
displayed.

5. Add this line to the event handler:

```
AboutBox->ShowModal();
```

That should do it for now. Click the Run button and try out the About item on the Help
menu. Figure 6.19 shows the Picture Viewer program running with several child windows
open.

6

Figure 6.19.

The Picture Viewer program running.

At this point the program is functional, but it isn't polished by any means. Still, for a 30-minute programming job, it's not too bad! There are a few problems with the program as it stands right now. If you try to open a file that is not a graphic, you will find that the program will throw an exception. We'll deal with that later. Also, we have a lot of extra menu items that we need to get rid of. You'll learn how to do that tomorrow as we work more with the Menu Designer.

There is one problem that I think we should deal with because it's easy to fix. Did you notice that a blank MDI child window was displayed when the application started? That's because a C++Builder application automatically creates all forms when the application runs. In the case of an MDI child, that means the window is displayed when the application becomes visible. We are creating each MDI child as needed, so we don't need to have C++Builder auto-create the form for us.

Fortunately, removing the MDI child window form from the auto-create list is easy. Choose Project | Options from the main menu. The Project Options dialog box is displayed. If necessary, click on the Forms tab. The list of forms to auto-create is displayed. Click on the child form and then click the > button. This removes the child form from the Auto-create list and puts it in the Available forms list. Figure 6.20 shows the Project Options dialog box after you move the child form to the Available forms list.

Figure 6.20.

The Project Options dialog box.

Now run the program again. This time the blank MDI child is not displayed.

WARNING

If you remove a form from the auto-create list, you must be sure to specifically create the form before using it. If you do not create the form, the pointer to the form is uninitialized, and attempting to use the pointer will result in an access violation or erratic program behavior. Once you remove a form from the auto-create list, it is your responsibility to make sure the form has been created before using it.

Summary

The C++Builder IDE can be intimidating until you become familiar with it. If you learn it a little at a time, it's not nearly so daunting. Today you learned about how projects are used to create an executable file. You also learned more about forms. You found out how C++Builder deals with dialog boxes and other child windows. After that you got to create a program that actually does something interesting. Finally, you ended up with a look at the C++Builder Object Inspector. Tomorrow we'll go after the Form Designer and the Menu Designer.

Workshop

The Workshop contains quiz questions to help you solidify your understanding of the material covered and exercises to provide you with experience in using what you have learned. You can find answers to the quiz questions in Appendix A, "Answers to Quiz Questions."

Q&A

Q **The C++Builder toolbar doesn't have buttons for the features I use most often. Can I change the toolbar?**

A Absolutely. The toolbar is fully customizable. You can add or remove buttons as you see fit.

Q **I placed multiple `Label` components on a form and then attempted to select them all by dragging. Instead I just got another big `Label` component. What have I done wrong?**

A You forgot to turn off the multiple placement option. After placing multiple components on the form, you need to click the arrow button on the Component Palette to turn off the multiple placement option.

Q **I have several components on a panel. I'm trying to select the components by dragging, but I keep moving the panel instead. What must I do to select a group of components on a panel?**

A Either use Shift+click to select each component or hold down the Ctrl key and drag a bounding rectangle around the components.

Q **Can I write, compile, and run a simple C++ program without a project?**

A No. In order to create an executable file, you need a project. The project makes sure that all needed library routines are linked to the final executable.

Q **What are library files for?**

A There is a common set of routines used in C++ programs. The string manipulation functions I discussed on Day 1, "Getting Your Feet Wet," are examples of such routines. If your program calls a C++ function, that function must be included in the executable file for your program. These functions are contained in a library file (`.LIB`). The linker makes a copy of the function found in the library file and places it in your executable. Any VCL methods your program calls are handled in the same way.

Q **Why does C++Builder use the term _unit_ to refer to a source file?**

A C++Builder uses the term _unit_ because C++Builder was created from Borland's Delphi. Delphi is based on Pascal, and _unit_ is a Pascal term for a source file.

Q **What do I need to do in order for my application to be an MDI application?**

A Just be sure that the main form has a `FormStyle` of `fsMDIForm` and that any MDI child forms have a `FormStyle` of `fsMDIChild`.

Q **What's the difference between a dialog box and a child window in C++Builder?**

A There is no real difference. A dialog box form might have certain traits such as a dialog box border rather than a sizing border; OK, Cancel, and Help buttons; and no Minimize or Maximize buttons. But a dialog box is still just a form like any other. A form might have the appearance of a dialog box or of a child window, but a form is just a form.

Q **Can I check my program for errors without running the program?**

A Yes. Just choose Project | Syntax Check from the main menu. C++Builder will compile any units that have changed since the last compile and will report any errors encountered.

Q **Can I build OWL or MFC applications with C++Builder?**

A Yes. Because C++Builder's strengths lie in its use of VCL, you probably won't want to develop complex applications in C++Builder using OWL or MFC, but you certainly may if you want.

Quiz

1. How do you invoke the Toolbar Editor dialog box?
2. Once you have the Toolbar Editor dialog box, how do you add buttons to the toolbar?
3. How do you remove buttons from the toolbar?
4. What's the easiest way to place multiple components of the same type on a form?
5. What's the easiest way to place a component in the center of the form?
6. List the file types needed to build an application in C++Builder.
7. What VCL method do you use to display a form modelessly?
8. What VCL method do you use to display a form modally?
9. How can you attach an event to an event handler that has been previously defined?
10. When using the Object Inspector, how can you enumerate the choices for a particular property?

Exercises

1. Remove the Pause, Step Over, and Trace Into buttons from the toolbar. Add Cut, Copy, and Paste buttons to the toolbar.

2. Reset the toolbar to its default settings.

3. Spend some time looking over the components on each page of the Component Palette. Place any components you are curious about on a form and experiment with them.

4. Create a new directory on your hard drive. Create a new application in C++Builder. Add three new forms to the project (they can be blank if you want). Save the project to the new directory you created and run the program. Close the program. Now examine the directory where the project was saved. Compare the files you see there with the file types listed in Table 6.1.

5. Run the Picture Viewer program you created earlier. Open several graphics files. Drag the MDI child windows around in the parent window. Attempt to move a child window outside of the parent. What happens?

6. With the Picture Viewer program still running, minimize all windows. Drag the minimized windows to random locations on the screen and then choose Window | Arrange All from the menu.

7. Start a new application. Place several components on the form. Click on each component and observe the properties for each component in the Object Inspector.

8. Create a blank form. Double-click in the Value column next to the Color property to invoke the Color dialog box. Choose a color and click OK.

9. Get some rest. Tomorrow is going to be a big day.

Day **7**

Working with the Form Designer and the Menu Designer

by Kent Reisdorph

As you know by now, C++Builder is heavily form based, a model that takes maximum advantage of the visual programming environment. In this chapter you will explore

- ☐ The Form Designer
- ☐ The Menu Designer

To illustrate the use of the Form Designer, we will build an application that approximates the Windows Notepad program. Along the way you will gain valuable experience working with the Form Designer. Later in the chapter you'll explore the Menu Designer in detail.

Working with the Form Designer

The C++Builder Form Designer is a powerful visual programming tool. It allows you to place, select, move, resize, and align components, and much more. The Form Designer also allows you to size and position the form itself, add menus, and create specialized dialog boxes—everything you need to create the user interface to a typical Windows program.

We'll examine each of the features of the Form Designer in the following sections. As you read, I encourage you to stop and experiment any time you are curious about how something works. Sometimes a few minutes of playing around can teach you a technique that you can carry with you for a long time to come.

The Form Designer's Speed Menu

The Form Designer, like most C++Builder windows, has a speed menu associated with it. Table 7.1 lists the items on the Form Designer speed menu and provides a description of each.

Table 7.1. The Form Designer's speed menu items.

Item	Description
Align To Grid	Aligns selected components to the Form Designer grid.
Bring To Front	Brings selected components to the front its components layer.
Send To Back	Sends selected components behind its component layer.
Revert to Inherited	When you are working with a form you have inherited from the Object Repository, choosing this menu item will cause the form to revert back to its original state. (Inheriting forms from the Object Repository is covered on Day 9, "Creating Applications in C++Builder.")
Align	Displays the Alignment dialog box.
Size	Displays the Size dialog box.
Scale	Displays the Scale dialog box.
Tab Order	Displays the Edit Tab Order dialog box.
Creation Order	Displays the Creation Order dialog box.
Add to Repository	Adds this form to the Object Repository. Custom forms can be saved to be used later. (The Object Repository is discussed on Day 9.)

Item	Description
View as Text	Shows the form description as text in the Code Editor. You may edit the text version of the form if you like. Choose View as Form from the Code Editor speed menu to go back to the form. You can also use Alt+F12 to switch from the View As Text and View As Form options.

NOTE

C++Builder creates a form file (DFM) for every form you create and places it in your project's directory. The form file is a binary resource file that can't be read by mere humans. When you choose the View As Text speed menu item, C++Builder converts the binary resource to readable form. When you switch back to the View as Form option, C++Builder recompiles the form file to implement any changes you have made.

Most of the speed menu options are discussed in the following sections. Others are discussed in later chapters when we discuss the particular aspect of C++Builder that they pertain to.

Placing Components

The act of placing a component on a form is trivial. You simply select the component you want from the Component Palette and click on the form to place the component. When you click on the form, the component's upper-left corner is placed at the location you clicked. Notice that when you click a button on the Component Palette, the button appears as pressed. When you click on the form to place the component, the button on the Component Palette pops up again to indicate that the action is completed.

TIP

As you learned in the last chapter, to place a component on a form multiple times, press and hold Shift when you first select the component's button on the Component Palette. Each time you click on the form, a new component will be added. Click the Arrow button on the Component Palette to stop placing components.

7

Most components can be sized. You can place a component on a form and then size it, or you can size the component at the same time you place it on the form. To size while placing the component, click on the form where you want the top-left corner to be placed and then drag with the mouse until the component is the desired size. When you release the mouse button, the component will be placed with the size you specified.

NOTE   Not all components will allow sizing in this manner. Nonvisual components, for instance, are represented on the form by an icon. Although you can click-and-drag to place a nonvisual component, the drag size will be ignored. Another example is a single-line edit component. The edit component can be placed by dragging, but only the drag width will be used. The drag height will be ignored because a single-line edit component's height defaults to the height of a single-line edit control.

TIP   If you change your mind while placing the control via the dragging method, you can press the Esc key on the keyboard before you release the mouse button to cancel the operation. The component's button will still be pressed on the Component Palette, however, so you may need to click the Arrow button to return to component-selection mode.

Placing components is simple enough that we don't need to spend a lot of time on the subject. You had some experience with placing components yesterday, so let's move on to other things.

The Form Designer Grid

The Form Designer has a built-in grid that aids in designing forms. By default, C++Builder shows the grid. The grid size is initially set to 8 pixels horizontally and 8 pixels vertically. When the Form Designer is set to display the grid, a dot is placed at the intersection of each grid point. Components placed on a form will snap to the nearest grid point. By *snap to* I mean that the component's top-left corner will automatically jump to the nearest grid point. This is an advantage because you frequently want a group of controls to be aligned either on their left, right, top, or bottom edges. When the Snap to Grid option is on, you can simply get close enough to the correct location and the Form Designer will automatically place your component at the nearest grid point. This saves you time by saving you from tweaking the individual component's size or position on the form.

The grid settings can be modified via the Preferences page of the Environment Options dialog box. (I'll discuss the Environment Options in detail on Day 10, "More on Projects.") Here you can change the grid size or turn off the Snap to Grid feature. You can also turn the grid display on or off. When the grid display is off, the grid is still active (assuming that Snap to Grid is on), but the dots marking grid points are not drawn on the form.

Selecting Components

After you place a component on a form, you often have to select the component in order to modify it in some way. You may have to select a component in order to perform one of the following actions:

- ☐ Move the component
- ☐ Change the component's properties
- ☐ Align the component
- ☐ Size the component
- ☐ Cut or copy the component
- ☐ Order the component (bring to front or move to back)
- ☐ Delete the component

Selecting Individual Components

To select a single component, just click on it. When you select the component, eight black sizing handles appear around the component to indicate that it is selected. (I'll discuss the sizing handles in a moment.) Figure 7.1 shows a form with a button component selected.

As soon as you select a component, the Object Inspector changes to show the properties and events for the control selected. To deselect a control, click on the form's background or Shift+click on the control. (Shift+click is described in the next section.)

TIP

Each component has a default event handler associated with it. When you double-click a component on a form, the Code Editor displays the default event handler for that component, ready for you to type code. In most cases, the default event handler is the OnClick handler. Exactly what happens when the component is double-clicked depends on how the component is designed. For example, in the case of the Image component, double-clicking will display the Picture Editor dialog box.

7

Figure 7.1.

A form with a button component selected.

Group Selection

You can also select multiple components so that you can act on them as a group. You can select multiple components in one of three ways:

- ☐ Shift+click with the keyboard and mouse
- ☐ Drag with the mouse
- ☐ Choose Edit | Select All from the main menu

To select all components on the form, choose Edit | Select All from the main menu. All components on the form are then selected.

Selecting Components with Shift+Click

To use the Shift+click sequence, first select one control. Then press and hold the Shift key on the keyboard and click on any other controls you want to include in the selection. Each control you click is bound by four gray boxes to indicate that it is part of the selection.

You can remove a control from the selection by continuing to hold the Shift key and clicking on the component again. In other words, the Shift+click sequence toggles a component's inclusion in the selection.

To illustrate, first start with a blank form and then perform the following steps:

1. Place three button components anywhere on the form. They will automatically be labeled Button1, Button2, and Button3.

2. Click Button1. The black sizing rectangles are placed around the component.

3. Press and hold the Shift key on the keyboard. Click Button2. It is added to the selection. Gray boxes now appear at the corners of both Button1 and Button2.

4. Shift+click on Button3. Now all three buttons are part of the selection.

5. Shift+click again on Button2. Button2 is removed from the selection (the gray boxes disappear), but Button1 and Button3 are still in the selection.

6. Shift+click on Button1. Now Button3 is the only component in the selection. The gray boxes are replaced with the black sizing rectangles.

7. Shift+click on Button1 and Button2. All three buttons are now part of the selection again.

Figure 7.2 shows the form as it should look at the end of this sequence. Keep in mind that your buttons could have been placed anywhere on the form.

Figure 7.2.

A form with three buttons selected.

Keep the form handy because you'll use it again in the next exercise.

NOTE

If you click on a component that is part of a group selection, nothing will happen. In order to select a single control that is currently part of a group selection, you need to first click on the form's background or press the Esc key to remove the group selection. Then you can click on the individual control you want to select.

7

Multiple Selection by Dragging

You can select multiple controls by dragging a bounding rectangle around the controls to be selected. The *bounding rectangle* is a dashed (or is it dotted?) gray rectangle that changes size as you drag. In fact, you don't have to drag the bounding rectangle completely around the components. You only have to touch a component with the bounding rectangle in order for it to be included in the selection.

Be sure that you start by placing the mouse cursor over the background of the form and not on a component. Hold the primary mouse button down and begin dragging. You will see the bounding rectangle as you drag. Surround or touch the components you want selected and release the mouse button. Any components that were inside the bounding rectangle (or touching it) are included in the selection.

When you have a group of controls selected, you can use the Shift+click technique explained in the previous section to add other controls from the selection or to remove controls from the selection. For example, you might want to select all controls in one area of your form except for one. Surround the controls and then deselect the control you want to exclude from the selection.

Go back to the form with the three buttons you created earlier (if you've already discarded that form, create a new one and place three buttons on it). Start at the top-left corner and drag down and to the right to surround the buttons. Let go of the mouse button, and the controls will be selected. Figure 7.3 shows the form and the bounding rectangle being dragged.

Figure 7.3.

*Controls being selected
by dragging.*

TIP

> You can use Shift+drag to select non-adjacent groups of controls. If, for instance, you had two separate groups of controls in separate areas on your form, you could drag around the first set of controls and then hold the Shift key down and drag around the second set of controls. Both groups of controls will be selected.

NOTE

> You don't have to drag down and to the right. You can drag in any
> direction to select components.

Selecting Multiple Items: Components Within Components

Frequently you will have components placed within other components. The Panel component is frequently used as a container for other components. Speedbars are built this way, for
example. To select a group of components on a panel, you have to hold down the Ctrl key
on the keyboard while you drag to select the components. (Try it without holding down the
Ctrl key and see what happens!) In case you're wondering, yes, you can use a combination
of Ctrl+Shift+drag. (I suppose the Borland designers could have figured out some way of
working the Alt key in there, too.)

To illustrate, first start with a blank form. Then do the following:

1. Select a Panel component from the Component Palette and place it on the form
   using the drag method. Drag it so that it occupies most of the form.

2. Now select a Button component and place six buttons on the form. Your form
   should look something like Figure 7.4.

3. Drag a bounding rectangle around Button1, Button2, and Button3. You will
   notice that you moved the panel, which is not what you expected (and not what
   you wanted). Move the panel back to where it was.

4. Hold down the Ctrl key and drag a rectangle around Button1, Button2, and
   Button3. The buttons are selected.

5. Now hold down both the Ctrl and Shift keys and drag the bounding rectangle
   around Button5 and Button6. Now all buttons are selected except Button4.

Figure 7.4.

*The form with a
panel and six buttons.*

Using the Ctrl+drag sequence is the only way to select a group of components that are contained within another component if you are using the drag method. You can use the Shift+click method to select components contained within another component just as you do when selecting components on a form.

Moving Components

Moving components is a common and fairly simple task. To move an individual component, simply place the mouse cursor over the component and drag. As you drag, a white rectangle that represents the component moves with the mouse cursor. When you have the white rectangle where you want it, let go of the mouse button, and the component will be moved to that location.

NOTE   When you move a control via drag-and-drop, the Left and Top properties of the control are automatically updated.

NOTE   It's easiest to move a component by drag-and-drop. If you need finer control, you can modify the Left and Top properties of the component. You can also use various alignment options, which I'll discuss later in the chapter in the section "Aligning Components."

If you have the Snap to Grid option on, the white dragging rectangle will snap to the nearest grid point as you drag.

TIP   If you change your mind while dragging, you can press the Esc key on the keyboard before you release the mouse button to cancel the drag operation. The component will return to its original position.

Dragging a group of controls works the same way. After you have a group of components selected, place the mouse cursor over any one of the controls and begin dragging. The white dragging rectangle will be displayed for each of the controls in the group. This allows you to visualize where the group will be placed when you release the mouse button.

NOTE

You cannot move a group of components if components in the group have different parent controls. For instance, let's say you had selected both a Button component on the main form and a SpeedButton on a panel. Since these two components have different parent controls, you cannot move them as a group.

TIP

Once you have a control selected, you can nudge the control by holding down the Ctrl key while using the arrow keys on the keyboard. This allows you to move the control one pixel at a time. This technique works for both groups of controls and individual controls. The Snap to Grid feature is overridden when you use this technique.

After you have moved a component using this method, the component is no longer on a grid point—it is offset by some amount. If you now drag the component, it will maintain its offset from the grid point as you drag.

TIP

If you have moved a control using the Ctrl+arrow method and want to again align it to the grid, choose Edit | Align to Grid from the main menu or choose Align to Grid from the local menu. The control's top-left corner will snap to the nearest grid point.

A control cannot be dragged outside its parent. If you drag a component off the left or top edge of the form, you will see that the component is clipped at the edge of the form. If, however, you drag the component off the right or bottom of the form and drop it, scrollbars will appear on the form to allow you to scroll to see the rest of the form. The Width and Height properties of the form are not altered. If you drag the component back onto the visible part of the form, the scrollbars disappear again. This is the default behavior and will occur unless you change the AutoScroll property of the form to False. Figure 7.5 shows a Memo component that has been dragged partially off the left edge of the form. Notice the scrollbar that appears at the bottom of the form.

7

Figure 7.5.
A form with
`AutoScroll` *in*
action.

Preventing Components from Being Moved or Sized

Components can be locked into place so that they cannot be moved. Locking components is useful if you know that a form's design is final and you don't want to worry about accidentally moving controls. To lock a form's controls, choose Edit | Lock Controls from the main menu. Locked controls cannot be moved or sized. When controls are locked, their sizing handles are gray with a black border. To unlock the controls again, choose Edit | Lock Controls again. The controls can now be moved as before.

Ordering, Cutting, Copying, and Pasting Components

You will place some components on top of one another in order to achieve a visual effect. For example, you can create a shadowed box by placing a white box over a black box (both would be Shape components). Obviously, you can't have the shadow on top of the box, so you have to have some way of ordering the controls to tell C++Builder which controls go on top and which go on the bottom. Let's do a simple exercise that illustrates this. Along the way you will also see how you can use Copy and Paste with components. First (as always), start with a blank form. Now do this:

1. Click on the Additional tab on the Component Palette and choose the Shape component. Click on the form to place the shape. A white square appears on the form.

2. Size the shape as desired (mine ended up being 209 pixels by 129 pixels).

3. Be sure the Shape component is selected. Choose Edit | Copy from the main menu.

4. Choose Edit | Paste from the main menu. A copy of the shape is placed below and to the right of the original shape. Conveniently, this is exactly where we want it.

NOTE

> After a paste operation, the component just pasted will be selected.

5. Double-click the `Brush` property and change the `Color` property under `Brush` to `clBlack`. The new shape is now black, but it is on top of the original shape. Can't have that!

6. Click the secondary mouse button and choose Send to Back from the speed menu (you could also choose Edit | Send to Back from the main menu). The black shape is moved behind the white shape. You now have a box with a shadow. (As an alternative, we could have clicked on the white shape and used Bring to Front to move it on top of the black shape.)

This exercise illustrates two features of the Form Designer. It shows how you can change the stacking order of controls, and also that you can use Copy and Paste to copy components. The original component's properties are copied exactly and pasted in as part of the pasting process. Each time you paste a component, it is placed below and to the right of the previous component pasted.

NOTE

> If a component that can serve as a container is selected when you perform a paste, the component in the Clipboard will be pasted as a child of the container component. For instance, you might want to move a button from the main form to a panel. You could select the button and then choose Edit | Cut from the main menu to remove the button from the form and place it in the Clipboard. Then you could select the panel and choose Edit | Paste from the main menu to paste the button onto the panel.

I don't need to go into a lot of detail on the cut operation. When you cut a component, the component disappears from the form and is placed in the Clipboard. Later you can paste the component onto the form or onto another component, such as a `Panel` component.

Sizing Components

With some components, you drop them on a form and accept the default size. Buttons are a good example. A standard button has a height of 25 pixels and a width of 75 pixels. For many situations, the default button size is exactly what you want. With some components, however, the default size is rarely exactly what you need. For example, a `Memo` component nearly always has to be sized to fit the specific form on which you are working.

7

Sizing by Dragging

When you select a control, eight black sizing handles appear around the control. When you place the mouse cursor over one of the sizing handles, the cursor changes to a black, double-headed arrow known as the *sizing cursor*. Once you see the sizing cursor, you can begin dragging to size the control. How the component is sized depends on which of the sizing handles you grab.

The sizing handles centered on the component at the top and bottom can be used to size the component vertically (to make the selected control taller or shorter). Likewise, the right and left sizing handles can be used to size the component horizontally (to make the selected control wider or narrower). If you grab one of the sizing handles at the corners of the component, you can size both horizontally and vertically at the same time. As with moving a component, a sizing rectangle appears as you drag. When you have the sizing rectangle at the desired size, let go of the mouse button and the component will be resized. Figure 7.6 illustrates a memo component being sized by dragging; Figure 7.7 shows the form after the drag operation.

Figure 7.6.

A memo component being sized.

Figure 7.7.

The form after the memo component is sized.

 NOTE Sizing applies to visual components only. A nonvisual component appears on the form as an icon that cannot be sized. The sizing handles appear on nonvisual components, and the handles can be dragged, but the results of the dragging operation will be ignored.

Groups of controls cannot be sized by dragging. The sizing handles (black squares) are replaced by selection indicators (gray squares) when you select more than one component.

TIP

To size all the components in a group at one time, modify the Width or Height property in the Object Inspector or use the Size dialog box (the Size dialog is discussed in the section "Sizing Components"). All components in the selection will take on the new values.

TIP

To size a control or group of controls one pixel at a time, hold down the Shift key and press any of the arrow keys on the keyboard. The up and down arrows will size the control vertically, and the right and left arrows will size the control horizontally. Only the Width and Height properties of the component are affected. The Top and Left properties are not modified.

Sizing with the Size Dialog Box

Another sizing option is the Size dialog box. You can bring up the Size dialog box by choosing Edit | Size from the main menu. Figure 7.8 shows the Size dialog box.

Figure 7.8.

The Size dialog box.

This dialog box is used when you want to force a group of controls to the same width or height. For instance, let's say you had six edit components on a form, all with different widths. To make the form appear more balanced, you might want to make all the edit components the same width. You would first select the components and then invoke the Size dialog box. From there you could choose Shrink to Smallest in the Width column to make all the components the width of the shortest edit component, or Grow to Largest to make all the components the width of the longest component in the group. You could also enter an exact width in the Width box, in which case you would leave the Height set on No Change. When you click OK, the components will all be the same width.

TIP

> The Size dialog box can also be invoked from the Form Designer speed menu.

Sizing with the Scale Dialog Box

Another sizing tool is the Scale dialog box, shown in Figure 7.9. This dialog box allows you to specify a scaling percentage. To make the components twice as large as they currently are, enter 200 in the Scaling Factor box. To reduce the components' size by half, enter 50 in the Scaling Factor box. The Scale dialog box is convenient for quickly changing the size of all components on the form. You can bring up the Scale dialog box by choosing Edit | Scale from the main menu or Scale from the Form Designer speed menu.

Figure 7.9.

The Scale dialog box.

A control can also be sized and moved by using the various alignment options. Let's take a look at those now.

NOTE

> Remember that you can always move components by modifying their Left and Top properties, and you can size them by modifying their Width and Height properties.

Aligning Components

Regardless of whether you have the Snap to Grid option turned on, you sometimes need to align components after placing them. Aligning components could mean aligning several components along a common edge, centering components on the form, or spacing components. There are two different ways to go about aligning components:

☐ Using the Alignment Palette and Alignment dialog box

☐ Modifying a component's `Align` property

The following sections explain the use of these two methods.

NOTE

> You might have noticed the `Alignment` property for some components. This property only pertains to the way the text in the component is aligned (centered, right-justified, or left-justified) and has nothing to do with aligning components on a form.

The Alignment Palette and the Alignment Dialog Box

It is often necessary to move or size components relative to the form or relative to one another. The Alignment Palette contains several buttons that aid in that task. The Alignment dialog box performs the same operations as the Alignment Palette, but in a different format. To display the Alignment Palette, choose View | Alignment Palette from the main menu. Figure 7.10 shows the Alignment Palette and a description of each button.

Figure 7.10.

The Alignment Palette.

TIP

> The Alignment Palette can save you a lot of work. Don't spend too much time trying to get controls to line up exactly. Place the components on the form and then use the Alignment Palette to line them up.

The Align Left Edges button is used to line up components on their left edges. Start with a blank form and then do the following:

1. Place five button components vertically on the form without regard to where their left edges fall.

7

2. Select the buttons by dragging a bounding rectangle around them (or just touching them). The selection indicators show that all of the buttons are selected. The form should now look something like the one in Figure 7.11.

3. Choose View | Alignment Palette from the main menu. The Alignment Palette is displayed. Move the Alignment Palette if necessary so that it does not obscure the form.

4. Click the Align Left Edges button on the Alignment Palette. The buttons are all lined up.

Figure 7.11.

The form with the buttons randomly placed.

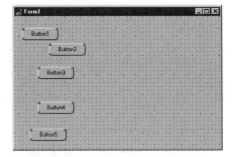

See how easy that is? As long as we have the buttons selected, let's look at another alignment option. The Space Equally Vertically alignment option can now be used to space the buttons evenly. The buttons should still be selected, so all you have to do is click the Space Equally Vertically button on the Alignment Palette, and voilà! the buttons are perfectly spaced. The form should now look like Figure 7.12.

Figure 7.12.

The form with the buttons aligned and equally spaced.

 NOTE

The Space Equally Vertically alignment option will space the components equally between the first component in the column (the top component) and the last component in the column (the bottom component). Be sure to set the first and last components where you want them before choosing the Space Equally Vertically alignment option. This is true of the Space Equally Horizontally alignment option as well.

The Center Horizontally in Window and Center Vertically in Window alignment options do exactly as their names indicate. These options are convenient for centering a single control, such as a button, on the form or for centering a group of controls. As long as you still have the group of buttons selected, click both the Center Horizontally in Window and Center Vertically in Window buttons on the Alignment Palette. The buttons will be centered on the form both vertically and horizontally.

NOTE

When you have a group of controls selected and you click one of the centering buttons, the controls will be treated *as a group*. If you were to choose each control individually and center it both horizontally and vertically on the form, all the controls would be stacked on top of one another in the middle of the form. By selecting the group and then centering, you will get the entire group centered as you intended.

The form should now look like the one in Figure 7.13.

Figure 7.13.

The form with the buttons centered.

NOTE

The two window-centering alignment options can be used to align components that are contained within other components, such as buttons on a panel. The components will be centered horizontally or vertically on their parent component whether the parent is a panel or a form.

The Align Tops, Align Bottoms, and Align Right Edges options work just like the Align Left Edges option we used earlier. There's not much point in going over all the possibilities that exist for their use.

TIP

The first component selected will be the anchor point when you're using any of the edge-alignment options. Refer to Figure 7.4. Let's say you had selected Button3 first and then used Shift+click to select the remaining buttons. When you chose Align Left Edges, Button3 would remain where it is and all other buttons would be lined up with Button3's left edge because Button3 is the anchor component.

The Align Horizontally Across Centers and Align Vertically Across Centers options can be used to center components relative to one another. This is best illustrated with shapes. Start with a new form (or delete the buttons from the form you have been working on). Now do the following:

1. Click on the Additional tab on the Component Palette and choose the Shape component. Click somewhere on the upper left of the form to add the shape.

2. Change the Shape property to stCircle.

3. Change the Width property to 150.

4. Double-click the Brush property and change the Color property of the Brush property to clBlack.

5. Place another Shape component on the form.

6. Change the second shape's Shape property to stCircle as well. Now you have two circles of different sizes on the screen—a white circle and a black circle.

7. Click on the black circle. Hold the Shift key and click on the white circle. Both shapes are selected.

8. Choose View | Alignment Palette from the main menu, if necessary (it may already be displayed). Arrange the Alignment Palette so you can see the two shapes on the form. Observe the shapes as you perform the following two steps.

9. Click the Align Vertically Across Centers button on the Alignment Palette. The vertical centers are aligned.

10. Click the Align Horizontally Across Centers button on the Alignment Palette. The horizontal centers are aligned. Congratulations—you made a tire!

Did you see the impact as you performed the last two steps? Notice that because you selected the black circle first, it did not move (it is the anchor component), but the white circle moved as you clicked the alignment buttons. You can use these alignment options to center any number of controls on one another. These two alignment options have no effect when used on a single control.

Like the Component Palette, the Alignment Palette has a speed menu associated with it. Place the mouse cursor over the Alignment Palette and click the secondary mouse button. The speed menu is displayed. Table 7.2 lists the items on the Alignment Palette's speed menu and explains their use.

Table 7.2. The Alignment Palette's speed menu items.

Menu Item	Description
Stay on top	Forces the Alignment Palette to always be on top. This is useful if you are frequently switching back and forth between the Form Designer and the Code Editor. Because the Alignment Palette is a small window, it's easy to lose it.
Show Hints	Turns the hints (tool tips) for the Alignment Palette buttons on and off.
Hide	Hides the Alignment Palette. (You can also use the close box on the Alignment Palette to hide it.) In order to show the Alignment Palette again, you have to choose View | Alignment Palette from the main menu.
Help	Brings up C++Builder Help with the Alignment Palette page displayed.

The Alignment dialog box performs the same actions as the Alignment Palette. To bring up the Alignment dialog box, choose Edit \| Align from the main menu or Align from the Form Designer's speed menu. Figure 7.14 shows the Alignment dialog box.

Figure 7.14.

The Alignment dialog box.

In most cases, the Alignment Palette is easier to use, but you may certainly use the Alignment dialog box if you prefer.

The `Align` Property

The `Align` property controls how a component is aligned with its parent. The possible values for the `Align` property and a description of each are listed in Table 7.3.

Table 7.3. Possible values for the `Align` property.

Value	Description
alBottom	The component will be aligned at the bottom of the parent window. A status bar is an example of a component aligned along the bottom of a main form.
alClient	The component will expand to fill the client area of the parent window. If other components occupy part of the client area, the component will fill what client area remains. Examples include `Memo` components, `Image` components, and `RichEdit` components.
alLeft	The component will be aligned along the left edge of the parent window. A horizontal speedbar is an example of a left-aligned component.
alNone	The component will be placed as designed with no special relationship to the parent. This is the default for most components.
alRight	The component will be aligned along the right edge of the parent.
alTop	The component will be aligned along the top of the parent's window. A speedbar is an example of this type of alignment.

An illustration will help explain alignment. Start with a blank form. Then perform these steps:

1. Click on the Standard tab on the Component Palette and choose a `Panel` component. Place the panel anywhere on the form.
2. Locate the `Align` property in the Object Inspector (it's at the top of the list). Notice that it is set on `alNone`. Change the `Align` property to `alTop`. The panel is aligned at the top of the form, and it expands to fill the width of the form.
3. Try to move the panel back to the middle of the form. The panel will snap back to the top of the form.
4. Try to make the panel narrower. Notice that the panel retains its width.
5. Change the panel's height. Note that the panel's height can be changed (while the width cannot).
6. Change the `Align` to `alBottom`. Now the panel is glued to the bottom of the form.
7. Change the `Align` to `alRight` and then `alLeft`. Notice how the panel keeps its original shape. The width is now the same as the height was before. In effect, the panel is rotated. Again, attempts to vertically move or size the panel fail.

8. Change the `Align` property to `alClient`. The panel expands to fill the entire client area of the form. The panel cannot be resized in any dimension.

9. Change the `Align` property to `alNone`. The panel can again be sized and moved.

As you can see, changing `Align` to anything other than `alNone` effectively glues the panel to one edge of the form. In the case of `alClient`, the panel is glued to all four edges of the form. To illustrate how different components work together, let's build a prototype of an application that resembles Windows Notepad.

NEW TERM A *prototype* is an application that has the appearance of a working application but lacks full functionality.

NOTE

> C++Builder is perfect for quick prototyping of an application. You can have the main screens and dialog boxes designed and able to be displayed in much less time than it would take with traditional C++ Windows programming tools like OWL or MFC. That is not, however, to say that C++Builder is just for prototyping. C++Builder is fully capable of handling *all* your 32-bit Windows programming needs.

Step 1: Starting a New Application

1. Choose New Application from the main menu. If you're prompted to save the current project, click No.

2. Change the `Name` property to `ScratchPad`.

3. Change the `Caption` to `ScratchPad 1.0`.

4. Choose Project | Options from the main menu. Click on the Application tab and enter `ScratchPad 1.0` for the application's title. Click OK to close the Project Options dialog box.

Step 2: Building a Speedbar

Most Windows applications these days have a speedbar. Building a speedbar requires several steps itself. First, we'll put a spacer at the top of the window. (You'll see the benefit of the spacer later, when we add a menu to the application.) Here we go:

1. Choose a `Bevel` component from the Component Palette and place it on the form (it's located on the Additional tab).

2. Change the `Height` property to 2.

3. Change the `Align` property to `alTop`. The bevel is placed along the top of the form's client area.

Step 3: Creating the Speedbar Container

Now we can add the panel that will serve as the container for the speedbar buttons:

1. Choose a `Panel` component from the Component Palette and place it anywhere on the form.
2. Change the `Name` property to `SpeedBar`.
3. Change the `Height` property to 32.
4. Change the `BevelOuter` property to `bvNone`.
5. Clear the `Caption` property.
6. Change the `Align` property to `alTop`. The panel moves to the top, but just underneath the bevel we placed there earlier.

NOTE

> The last step in this sequence illustrates a point about the `Align` property. If you make a component's `Align` property `alTop`, it will move to the top of the client area or to the bottom edge of the first component it encounters. This allows you to place several components on the top of a form and have them adjust automatically as the form is sized.

Step 4: Decorating the Panel

Now all that's left to do is add a button or two to the panel:

1. Click on the Additional tab of the Component Palette and choose a `SpeedButton` component.
2. Place a speed button on the panel (not on the main form). Don't worry about its exact placement.
3. Change the `Name` property to `FileOpenBtn`.
4. Change the `Left` property to 5.
5. Choose View | Alignment Palette from the main menu. Click the Center Vertically in Window button.
6. Locate the `Glyph` property and double-click the Value column. The Image Editor is displayed.
7. Click the Load button on the Image Editor. The Load picture dialog box is displayed. Navigate to the `\Images\Buttons` subdirectory of C++Builder and choose the `fileopen.bmp` file. Click OK.

8. Repeat the first seven steps to add a File Save button. Place it to the right of the File Open button. Name it `FileSaveBtn` and use the `filesave.bmp` file for the glyph.

The form should now look like Figure 7.15.

Figure 7.15.

The `ScratchPad`
form up to this point.

Step 5: Adding a Status Bar

Okay, so far, so good. Windows Notepad doesn't have a status bar (or a speedbar, for that matter), but we'll put one in our application (we're cooler!):

1. Click on the Win95 tab on the Component Palette and choose the `StatusBar` component.

2. Click anywhere on the form. The status bar is automatically placed at the bottom of the form. The status bar has a default `Align` value of `alBottom`.

3. Change the `Name` property to `StatusBar`.

Step 6: Adding the Memo Component

We need some component in which to type text, so we'll use a memo component (believe it or not, we're almost done with our prototype):

1. Click on the Standard tab on the Component Palette and choose a `Memo` component. Place the memo anywhere on the client area of the form.

2. Change the `Name` property to `Memo`.

3. Change the `WordWrap` property to `True` (if necessary).

4. Double-click the Value column next to the `Lines` property. The String List Editor is displayed. Delete the word `Memo` and click OK.

5. Change the `Scrollbar` property to `ssVertical`. (Initially, we only want a vertical scrollbar on the memo.)

7

6. Change the Name property of the Font property to Fixedsys. (Because this is a Notepad copycat, we'll use the system font.)

7. Change the Align property to alClient. The memo expands to fill the client area between the speedbar and the status bar.

Hey, this is starting to look like a real application! Before we go on, let's do one more thing so you can see the value of the Align property. We need to make the main form a little larger. Grab the lower-right corner of the form with the mouse and drag the form to a larger size. If you want to be exact, you can change the form's Height property to 375 and the Width property to 575.

TIP

> The client area of our form is completely covered by components. This makes it impossible to select the form by clicking on it if you want to change the form's properties. To make the form the active component in the Object Inspector, select any component on the form and then press the Esc key on the keyboard. You can also choose the form from the Component Selector combo box on the Object Inspector.

Notice that all the controls automatically resize themselves to retain their relationship with the parent window—the form, in this case. That is one of the main advantages of the Align property. The form now looks like the one in Figure 7.16.

Figure 7.16.

The completed prototype.

Run, Baby, Run

You can now click the Run button to run the program. You can type text in the client area of the window, and you can press the speedbar buttons (although they don't do anything at this point). Keep in mind that this is a prototype and is mostly for show right now. We'll add more to the program by the end of the chapter.

We better save the project because we're going to use it later in the chapter. Choose File | Save All from the main menu. Save the main form's source unit as SPMain and the project as Scratch.

Setting the Tab Order

 The *tab order* refers to the order in which components will receive input focus when the user presses the Tab key on the keyboard.

C++Builder forms automatically support component navigation using the Tab key. You can move forward from component to component using Tab and backward using Shift+Tab.

> There are two types of visual components. *Windowed* components are components that accept focus. Windowed components include the Edit, Memo, ListBox, ComboBox, and Button components, as well as many more.
>
> *Non-windowed* components are components that do not accept keyboard focus. Components such as Image, SpeedButton, Label, Shape, and many others are non-windowed components.
>
> The tab order applies only to windowed components. Non-windowed components are excluded from the tab order.

The tab order is initially set based on the order the components were placed on the form when the form was designed. You can modify the tab order by changing the TabOrder property for each control in the Object Inspector. That method is tedious because you have to go to each control individually. An easier way is provided via the Edit Tab Order dialog box. (See Figure 7.17.)

Figure 7.17.
The Edit Tab Order dialog box.

The Edit Tab Order dialog box displays all windowed components currently on the form. Non-windowed components are not displayed. To change the tab order, click on the name of the component you want to move in the tab order and then click the up or down buttons as needed. You can also drag the component to its new position in the tab order. Once you get the tab order set the way you want it, click OK and the tab order will be set. You can confirm the new settings by viewing the TabOrder property of each control.

NOTE

> The tab order starts with 0. The first component in the tab order is 0, the second is 1, and so on.

May I See a Menu, Please?

Menus are a big part of most Windows applications. Some Windows programs do not have menus, but the vast majority do. C++Builder makes creating menus easy with the Menu Designer. The Menu Designer has the following features:

☐ It can create both main menus and pop-up menus (speed menus).

☐ It provides immediate access to the Code Editor to handle the OnClick events for menu items.

☐ It can insert menus from templates or from resource files.

☐ It can save custom menus as templates.

All of the Menu Designer's commands are accessed via the Menu Designer speed menu or by interacting with the Object Inspector. Figure 7.18 shows the Menu Designer's speed menu.

Figure 7.18.

The Menu Designer's speed menu.

For the most part these menu items are self-explanatory, so I'm not going to go over each one right now. Rather, you will learn about each item on the speed menu via the hands-on approach. To begin, let's add a main menu to the ScratchPad application we created earlier. After that we'll add a speed menu.

Creating a Main Menu

The Menu Designer allows you to quickly build any menu. The menu structure for a main menu consists of a MainMenu component, which is represented by the VCL class TMainMenu. Each item on the menu is a MenuItem component that is encapsulated in the TMenuItem class. You don't need to be too concerned about the intricacies of how these classes work together because the Menu Designer makes creating menus easy. With that brief overview, let's add a main menu to the ScratchPad application.

Adding a Main Menu to the Form

The first thing you must do is add a MainMenu component to your form:

NOTE By this time you have had some experience with C++Builder. From this point on I will abbreviate some of the steps that you need to take to perform certain actions. For example, from here on I'll say, "Place a MainMenu component on the form" rather than "Click on the Standard tab on the Component Palette. Click the MainMenu button and click on the form to place the component." Don't worry; I'll still give plenty of detail when new operations are introduced.

1. Open the ScratchPad project created earlier in the chapter.
2. Place a MainMenu component on the form and change its Name property to MainMenu. Notice that a MainMenu component has very few properties and no events. All the work of a menu is done by the MenuItem component.
3. Double-click on the main menu icon. The Menu Designer is displayed.

The Menu Designer looks like a blank form without grid points. The Menu Designer can be sized in any way you want. The size is just for your convenience and has no bearing on how the menu operates at runtime. At this point, the Menu Designer is waiting for you to begin building the menu. Once you have created your first menu, you will find that menu creation is fairly easy and intuitive.

Creating a Menu by Hand

Although there are easier ways to create a File menu, you will create your first menu by hand. The Menu Designer always has a blank menu item that acts as a placeholder for any new menu items you create. When you first start the Menu Designer, the blank item is selected:

1. Change the `Name` property to `FileMenu`.
2. Click on the `Caption` property in the Object Inspector, type `&File`, and press Enter.

NOTE

The ampersand (&) is used to create the underlined character for a menu item. The underlined character is the *accelerator* the user can type, in combination with the Alt key, to navigate a menu using the keyboard. You can put ampersands anywhere in the menu item's text. For instance, the customary text string for the Exit menu item is `E&xit`. All you have to do is provide the ampersands where appropriate and Windows will take it from there.

At this point, several things happen. First, the File menu shows up in the Menu Designer. It also shows on the main form behind the Menu Designer. (Remember when we added the `Bevel` component to the `ScratchPad` main form to use as a spacer? Now you can see why. The bevel provides visual distinction between the menu and the speedbar.) The other thing that happens is that a new, blank placeholder is added below the File menu you just created, plus a new, pop-up placeholder is created to the right of the File menu. The Object Inspector is displaying a blank `MenuItem` component, waiting for you to enter the `Caption` and `Name` property values. Figure 7.19 shows the Menu Designer as it appears at this point.

Figure 7.19.

The Menu Designer and Object Inspector after the File menu is created.

Let's continue with the creation of the menu:

1. Change the `Name` property for the new item to `FileNew`.

2. Change the `Caption` property to `&New` and press Enter. Again, a blank item is created in the Menu Designer.

3. Repeat steps 1 and 2 and create menu items for Open, Save, and Save As. If you need help knowing where to place the ampersand, refer to Figure 7.20. Don't worry that you might not get it exactly right. You can always go back later and fix any errors.

 TIP Make your menus as standard as possible. Be sure that your accelerators (the underlined character) are the same as in other Windows programs. Also, remember that an ellipsis (...) following a menu is a visual cue that indicates to the user that choosing the menu item will invoke a dialog box.

At this point, we need a menu separator.

 NEW TERM A *separator* is the horizontal line on a menu that separates groups of menu items.

Adding a separator is easy with the C++Builder Menu Designer. All you have to do is put in a hyphen for the `Caption` property. Move to the blank menu item under Save As, type a hyphen for the `Caption`, and press Enter. A separator is placed in the menu. Continue adding menu items until your menu looks like the one in Figure 7.20. If you need to modify any of the menu items, just click on the item you want to modify and then change properties in the Object Inspector as needed.

Figure 7.20.

The Menu Designer with the finished File menu.

NOTE

> The Menu Designer always provides a blank menu item at the bottom of each pop-up menu and on the right side of the menu bar. You cannot delete these blank items, but there's no need to—they are only used in the Menu Designer and won't show on the menu when your program runs.

Now that the File menu is done, we need to create an Edit menu and a Help menu.

Inserting a Menu from a Template

This time we'll take the easy approach. First, click on the blank pop-up menu placeholder to the right of the File menu. Now click your secondary mouse button and choose Insert From Template from the speed menu. The Insert Template dialog box is displayed, as shown in Figure 7.21.

Figure 7.21.

The Insert Template dialog box.

This dialog box shows a list of templates from which you can choose. You can use the predefined templates or create your own. In this case, we are only interested in adding an Edit menu, so choose Edit Menu and click OK. A full Edit menu is immediately inserted into the Menu Designer. In fact, it's a little too full. We'll deal with that in a moment.

As long as we're here, let's add the Help menu, too. Click on the placeholder to the right of the Edit menu. Choose Insert From Template again, and this time insert a Help menu. (Don't choose the Expanded Help menu, though.) We'll tidy up both the Edit and Help menus in the next section. Notice that the main form has been updating to show the new menu items as they are placed.

 NOTE

> You can insert templates to create pop-up menus as easily as you can when creating main menu items.

Yes, inserting from a template is really that easy. After using C++Builder for a period of time, you will no doubt have your own custom templates that you can choose from to build menus quickly and easily. You still have to update the Name properties to meaningful names, but it's a whole lot easier than creating the entire menu from scratch.

NOTE   The Insert From Resource choice works essentially the same as Insert From Template, except that it expects a resource script file (a resource script file has the extension .RC) containing a valid menu definition. You won't use this option as much as Insert From Template except when converting existing C or C++ programs to C++Builder.

Deleting Menu Items

The process of creating a Windows application is a living, breathing thing. Rarely will you get everything exactly right the first time. Users will request new features, the boss will come up with a few of his own, and some features will even be dropped. Your application's menus will often need to be updated as these changes take place. For example, the Edit menu that we inserted earlier is a tad verbose for our needs. Specifically, there are several items on the Edit menu that we just don't need. No problem—we'll just delete them:

1. Click on the Edit menu.
2. Click on the item called Repeat <command>.
3. Press Delete on the keyboard or choose Delete from the Menu Designer speed menu to delete the item. The item disappears, and the remaining items move up.
4. Delete the Paste Special menu item as well.

There, that was easy! We're not quite done with the Edit menu, but before we go on I want to mention a feature of the Menu Designer that is really handy. You are probably familiar with using Shift+click and Ctrl+click when selecting items in other Windows programs. These techniques can be used in Windows Explorer to select files, for instance. The Menu Designer supports Shift+click and Ctrl+click with one caveat—these combinations can be used to select multiple menu items, but they cannot be used to deselect an item. As always, an exercise will illustrate better than I can explain:

1. The Edit menu should still be displayed. If it's not, click on Edit to reveal the Edit menu.
2. Click on the menu item called Goto.
3. Hold down the Shift key and click on the menu item called Object. All items between those two points are selected.

7

4. Press Delete on the keyboard to delete all the items at one time.

5. Move to the Help menu and delete the two middle items. Only the Contents and About items will remain.

As you can see, the Shift+click technique can be used to quickly delete unwanted menu items. Now we have the menus trimmed back to the way we want them to appear in the ScratchPad application.

Inserting Menu Items

Inserting menu items is pretty straightforward. Just click on the menu item above which you want to insert a new item and press the Insert key on the keyboard (or choose Insert from the Menu Designer's speed menu). A blank menu item is inserted, and you can now modify the Name and Caption properties just as you did earlier. Let's insert an item into the Edit menu:

1. Drop down the Edit menu.

2. Click on the Find menu item.

3. Press the Insert key on the keyboard. A new menu item is provided, and all other menu items below the new item move down.

4. Change the Name property to EditSelectAll and change the Caption property to Select &All.

5. Click on the empty placeholder at the bottom of the Edit menu. Add a menu separator (remember, just enter a hyphen for the Caption property).

6. Click on the placeholder again and add a new item. Make the Name property EditWordWrap and the Caption property &Word Wrap.

Moving Menu Items

You can easily move menu items as needed. You can move them up or down within the pop-up menu they are already in, or you can move them across pop-ups. There are two ways to move a menu item. The first is by using Cut and Paste. Cut and Paste work as you would expect, so there's no need to go over that. The other way to move a menu item is by dragging it to a new location and dropping it. Let's try it out. We really want the Select All menu item just below the Undo item. No problem—just move it:

1. Click on Edit to display the Edit menu.

2. Click on the Select All item and drag it up until the separator under the Undo item is highlighted.

3. Let go of the mouse, and the menu item is moved.

Too easy, right? Yep, but that's what C++Builder is all about!

Batch Modification of Properties

Sometimes you want to modify several menu items' properties at one time. For example, we have a few menu items in the ScratchPad application that we are not ready to implement at this time. We aren't ready for printing support, for instance, nor are we ready to implement the help system. We need to gray out (disable) those menu items:

1. Choose Help | Contents in the Menu Designer.
2. Change the Enabled property to False. The menu item is grayed out.
3. Click on the File menu.
4. Click on the Print menu item, hold down the Shift key, and click on the Print Setup menu item. Both items are selected.
5. In the Object Inspector, change the Enabled property to False. Both menu items are disabled.
6. Repeat steps 4 and 5 to disable the Find and Replace items on the Edit menu.

You can modify a group of menu items at one time with this method. Simply select the items you want to modify and then change the property you want to modify. All menu items currently selected will have the new property value.

Creating Submenus

There's nothing special or tricky about creating submenus. A *submenu* is a menu item that, when clicked, expands to show more menu choices. A submenu is denoted by a right-pointing arrow next to the menu item text. You can create a submenu by choosing Create Submenu from the Menu Designer speed menu or by holding down the Ctrl key and pressing the right-arrow key. When you create a submenu, a blank menu item is placed to the right of the submenu. You can add menu items to the submenu just as you did when creating the main menu. You can create a submenu by inserting a menu template as well.

Adding Shortcuts

You can easily add keyboard shortcuts to your menu items by changing the ShortCut property of the menu item in the Object Inspector. The Edit menu that we inserted earlier already had keyboard shortcuts built in. For instance, the customary shortcut for Cut is Ctrl+X. If you look at the Edit menu, you will see Ctrl+X listed next to the Cut item. Click on the Cut menu item, and you will see that the ShortCut property says Ctrl+X. Click on the Value column next to the ShortCut property. On the right side of the Value column you will see a drop-down button. Click on the button to display the list of available shortcuts. The list you see there contains just about any keyboard shortcut you would need. To set the keyboard shortcut for a menu item, simply pick one of the shortcuts from the list.

7

The standard shortcut for Select All is Ctrl+A, so let's add that as a shortcut for our Select All menu item:

1. Choose Edit | Select All from your menu in the Menu Designer.
2. Click on the ShortCut property in the Object Inspector.
3. Choose Ctrl+A from the list of available shortcuts. Now the Select All menu item shows Ctrl+A next to it.

That's all you have to do; C++Builder takes care of it from there. The shortcuts function without you having to write any code.

Odds and Ends

Let's tie up a few loose ends to finish off our menu. First, we'll turn on the Word Wrap menu item by default. This menu item is going to be used to turn word wrapping on or off. When word wrapping is on, the Word Wrap menu item will have a check mark next to it. When word wrapping is off, it will not have a check mark next to it. Click on the Word Wrap menu item and then change the Checked property to True. A check mark shows up to indicate that the word wrap feature is on.

Another thing we need to do is change the Name property on all the menu items we inserted from a template. They were given default names, and we want to change them to more meaningful names. Select the Edit | Undo menu item. Change the Name property from Undo1 to EditUndo. Notice that you append the pop-up menu name, Edit, to the front of the menu item name and remove the 1 at the end. You can use any naming convention you like, but be consistent. Repeat the process for the Cut, Copy, Paste, Find, and Replace menu items. Now move to the Help menu and modify the Name property of the Contents item to HelpContents, and that of the About menu item to HelpAbout.

That about wraps up our menu. Run through the menu to check it over once more. If you find any errors, make the necessary changes. When you are satisfied that the menu is correct, click the close box to close the Menu Designer.

NOTE

> You can access the Code Editor directly from the Menu Designer by double-clicking on any menu item. When you double-click a menu item, the Code Editor will display the OnClick event for that item, and you can start typing code. In this case, we are going to go back to the main form and do our code editing there.

Writing the Code

Okay, so we have all these menu items but no code to make them work. It's going to be a lot of work to implement all these menu items, right? Actually, it's pretty easy. Most of the code required is already part of the TMemo class. All we have to do is call the appropriate TMemo methods in our menu handlers. We'll have to do a few other things, but most of what we will add is code you have seen before.

Before we write the code, we need to add the usual OpenDialog and SaveDialog components to the form:

1. Place an OpenDialog component on the form.
2. Change the Name property to OpenDialog.
3. Place a SaveDialog component on the form.
4. Change the Name property to SaveDialog.
5. Line up the MainMenu, OpenDialog, and SaveDialog icons on the form.

That was easy enough. Now let's get on with writing the code for the menu items. We'll start with the File Exit menu item (hey, it's the easiest!). Be sure that the Menu Designer is closed so you don't confuse the Menu Designer with the Form Designer.

1. Choose File | Exit from the main menu. The Code Editor comes to the top, and the FileExitClick() event handler is displayed.
2. The cursor is positioned and ready to go. Type the following at the cursor:

```
Close();
```

NOTE

In step 2 I had you use the Close() function to close the form. This works fine here because this is the main form of the application. But if you want to terminate the application from anywhere in the program you should use this:

```
Application->Terminate();
```

This will ensure that the application is terminated regardless of which form is currently open.

That's it. I told you it was the easiest! Let's do one more; then I'm going to turn you loose to finish the rest on your own.

7

1. Choose Edit | Cut from the main menu. The Code Editor comes to the top, and the `EditCutClick()` event handler is displayed.

2. Type the following at the cursor:

```
Memo->CutToClipboard();
```

And that's all there is to that particular menu item! You may not fully realize it, but VCL does a lot for you behind the scenes. The whole idea of a framework is to take the burden of the low-level details off the programmer's back. Life is good.

One of the interesting aspects of a program like C++Builder is that you rarely view your program as a whole. C++Builder conveniently takes you to the section of code you need to work on to deal with a particular event, so you usually only see your program in small chunks. Listing 7.1 contains the header for the ScratchPad program up to this point. The header is entirely C++Builder generated. The entire SPMAIN.CPP program is shown in Listing 7.2. Follow the examples you've just worked through to write code for each of the remaining menu items. Copy the code for each of the menu OnClick handlers from Listing 7.2. (The comment lines are there to explain to you what the code is doing. You don't have to include them when you type the code.)

NOTE

The event handlers appear in the source file in the order in which they were created. Don't be concerned if the order of the event handlers in your source file does not exactly match Listing 7.2. The order in which the functions appear makes no difference to the compiler.

Listing 7.1. SPMAIN.H.

```
 1: //------------------------------------------------------------
 2: #ifndef SPMainH
 3: #define SPMainH
 4: //------------------------------------------------------------
 5: #include <Classes.hpp>
 6: #include <Controls.hpp>
 7: #include <StdCtrls.hpp>
 8: #include <Forms.hpp>
 9: #include <ExtCtrls.hpp>
10: #include <Buttons.hpp>
11: #include <ComCtrls.hpp>
12: #include <Menus.hpp>
13: #include <Dialogs.hpp>
14: //------------------------------------------------------------
15: class TScratchPad : public TForm
16: {
```

```
17: __published:    // IDE-managed Components
18:     TPanel *Panel1;
19:     TBevel *Bevel1;
20:     TSpeedButton *SpeedButton1;
21:     TSpeedButton *SpeedButton2;
22:     TStatusBar *StatusBar;
23:     TMainMenu *MainMenu;
24:     TMenuItem *FileMenu;
25:     TMenuItem *FileOpen;
26:     TMenuItem *FileSave;
27:     TMenuItem *FileSaveAs;
28:     TMenuItem *N1;
29:     TMenuItem *FilePrintSetup;
30:     TMenuItem *N2;
31:     TMenuItem *FileExit;
32:     TMenuItem *FilePrint;
33:     TMenuItem *Edit1;
34:     TMenuItem *EditReplace;
35:     TMenuItem *EditFind;
36:     TMenuItem *N4;
37:     TMenuItem *EditPaste;
38:     TMenuItem *EditCopy;
39:     TMenuItem *EditCut;
40:     TMenuItem *N5;
41:     TMenuItem *EditUndo;
42:     TMenuItem *Help1;
43:     TMenuItem *HelpAbout;
44:     TMenuItem *HelpContents;
45:     TMenuItem *EditSelectAll;
46:     TMenuItem *N3;
47:     TMenuItem *EditWordWrap;
48:     TOpenDialog *OpenDialog;
49:     TSaveDialog *SaveDialog;
50:     TMenuItem *FileNew;
51:     TMemo *Memo;
52:     void __fastcall FileOpenClick(TObject *Sender);
53:     void __fastcall FileSaveClick(TObject *Sender);
54:     void __fastcall FileSaveAsClick(TObject *Sender);
55:     void __fastcall FileExitClick(TObject *Sender);
56:     void __fastcall EditSelectAllClick(TObject *Sender);
57:     void __fastcall EditCutClick(TObject *Sender);
58:     void __fastcall EditCopyClick(TObject *Sender);
59:     void __fastcall EditPasteClick(TObject *Sender);
60:
61:
62:     void __fastcall EditWordWrapClick(TObject *Sender);
63:     void __fastcall FileNewClick(TObject *Sender);
64: private:        // User declarations
65: public:         // User declarations
66:     virtual __fastcall TScratchPad(TComponent* Owner);
67: };
68: //------------------------------------------------------------
69: extern TScratchPad *ScratchPad;
70: //------------------------------------------------------------
71: #endif
```

7

Listing 7.2. SPMAIN.CPP.

```
 1: //-------------------------------------------------------------
 2: #include <vcl.h>
 3: #pragma hdrstop
 4: #include "SPMain.h"
 5: //-------------------------------------------------------------
 6: #pragma resource "*.dfm"
 7: TScratchPad *ScratchPad;
 8: //-------------------------------------------------------------
 9: __fastcall TScratchPad::TScratchPad(TComponent* Owner)
10:    : TForm(Owner)
11: {
12: }
13: //-------------------------------------------------------------
14: void __fastcall TScratchPad::FileNewClick(TObject *Sender)
15: {
16:    //
17:    // Open a file. First check to see if the current file
18:    // needs to be saved.
19:    //
20:    if (Memo->Modified) {
21:      //
22:      // Display a message box.
23:      //
24:      int result = Application->MessageBox(
25:        "The current file has changed. Save changes?",
26:        "ScratchPad Message", MB_YESNOCANCEL);
27:      //
28:      // If Yes was clicked then save the current file.
29:      //
30:      if (result == IDYES) FileSaveClick(Sender);
31:      //
32:      // If No was clicked then do nothing.
33:      //
34:      if (result == IDCANCEL) return;
35:    }
36:    //
37:    // Delete the strings in the memo, if any.
38:    //
39:    if (Memo->Lines->Count > 0) Memo->Clear();
40:    //
41:    // Set the FileName property of the Save Dialog to a
42:    // blank string. This lets us know that the file has
43:    // not yet been saved.
44:    //
45:    SaveDialog->FileName = "";
46: }
47: //-------------------------------------------------- -- -- -- --
48: void __fastcall TScratchPad::FileOpenClick(TObject *Sender)
49: {
50:    //
51:    // Open a file. First check to see if the current file needs
52:    // to be saved. Same logic as in FileNewClick() above.
53:    //
```

```
54:    if (Memo->Modified) {
55:      int result = Application->MessageBox(
56:        "The current file has changed. Save changes?",
57:        "ScratchPad Message", MB_YESNOCANCEL);
58:      if (result == IDYES) FileSaveClick(0);
59:      if (result == IDCANCEL) return;
60:    }
61:    //
62:    // Execute the File Open dialog. If OK was pressed then
63:    // open the file using the LoadFromFile() method. First
64:    // clear the FileName property.
65:    //
66:    OpenDialog->FileName = "";
67:    if (OpenDialog->Execute())
68:    {
69:      if (Memo->Lines->Count > 0) Memo->Clear();
70:      Memo->Lines->LoadFromFile(OpenDialog->FileName);
71:      SaveDialog->FileName = OpenDialog->FileName;
72:    }
73: }
74: //-------------------------------------------------- -- -- -- --
75: void __fastcall TScratchPad::FileSaveClick(TObject *Sender)
76: {
77:    //
78:    // If a filename has already been provided then there is
79:    // no need to bring up the File Save dialog. Just save the
80:    // file using SaveToFile().
81:    //
82:    if (SaveDialog->FileName != "")
83:    {
84:      Memo->Lines->SaveToFile(SaveDialog->FileName);
85:      //
86:      // Set Modified to false since we've just saved.
87:      //
88:      Memo->Modified = false;
89:    }
90:    //
91:    // If no filename was set then do a SaveAs().
92:    //
93:    else FileSaveAsClick(Sender);
94: }
95: //-------------------------------------------------- -- -- -- --
96: void __fastcall TScratchPad::FileSaveAsClick(TObject *Sender)
97: {
98:    //
99:    // Display the File Save dialog to save the file.
100:   // Set Modified to false since we just saved.
101:   //
102:   SaveDialog->Title = "Save As";
103:   if (SaveDialog->Execute())
104:   {
105:     Memo->Lines->SaveToFile(SaveDialog->FileName);
106:     Memo->Modified = false;
107:   }
108: }
```

continues

Listing 7.2. continued

```
109: //------------------------------------------------------------
110: void __fastcall TScratchPad::FileExitClick(TObject *Sender)
111: {
112:   //
113:   // All done. Close the form.
114:   //
115:   Close();
116: }
117: //------------------------------------------------------------
118: void __fastcall TScratchPad::EditUndoClick(TObject *Sender)
119: {
120:   //
121:   // TMemo doesn't have an Undo method so we have to send
122:   // a Windows WM_UNDO message to the memo component.
123:   //
124:   SendMessage(Memo->Handle, WM_UNDO, 0, 0);
125: }
126: //------------------------------------------------------------
127: void __fastcall TScratchPad::EditSelectAllClick(TObject *Sndr)
128: {
129:   //
130:   // Just call TMemo::SelectAll().
131:   //
132:   Memo->SelectAll();
133: }
134: //------------------------------------------------------------
135: void __fastcall TScratchPad::EditCutClick(TObject *Sender)
136: {
137:   //
138:   // Call TMemo::CutToClipboard().
139:   //
140:   Memo->CutToClipboard();
141: }
142: //------------------------------------------------------------
143: void __fastcall TScratchPad::EditCopyClick(TObject *Sender)
144: {
145:   //
146:   // Call TMemo::CopyToClipboard().
147:   //
148:   Memo->CopyToClipboard();
149: }
150: //------------------------------------------------- -- -- -- --
151: void __fastcall TScratchPad::EditPasteClick(TObject *Sender)
152: {
153:   //
154:   // Call TMemo::PasteFromClipboard().
155:   //
156:   Memo->PasteFromClipboard();
157: }
158: //------------------------------------------------------------
```

```
159: void __fastcall TScratchPad::EditWordWrapClick(TObject *Sender)
160: {
161:    //
162:    // Toggle the TMemo::WordWrap property. Set the Checked
163:    // property of the menu item to the same value as WordWrap.
164:    //
165:    Memo->WordWrap = !Memo->WordWrap;
166:    EditWordWrap->Checked = Memo->WordWrap;
167:    //
168:    // If WordWrap is on then we only need the vertical scroll
169:    // bar. If it's off, then we need both scroll bars.
170:    //
171:    if (Memo->WordWrap) Memo->ScrollBars = ssVertical;
172:    else Memo->ScrollBars = ssBoth;
173: }
174: //-----------------------------------------------------------
```

And Now, the Moment You've All Been Waiting For

After you have created the event handlers for the menu items, you are ready to run the program. Click the Run button, and the program should compile and run. If you get compiler errors, carefully compare your source code with the code in Listing 7.2. Make any changes and click the Run button again. You might have to go through this process a few times before the program will compile and run. Eventually, though, it will run (I promise!).

When the program runs you will find a program that, although not 100 percent feature-complete yet, acts a lot like Windows Notepad. Although we have a few things to add before we're finished, we have a pretty good start—especially when you consider the actual time involved up to this point. Figure 7.22 shows the ScratchPad program running.

Figure 7.22.

The ScratchPad *program in action.*

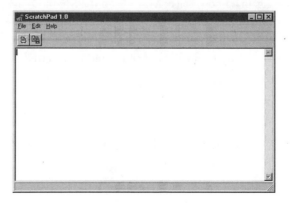

7

Pop-up Menus (Speed Menus)

We're not quite done with our discussion of menus. In C++Builder, you can create pop-up menus as easily as you can create a main menu. A nice feature of C++Builder is that you can assign a particular pop-up menu to a component via the PopupMenu property of the component. When the cursor is placed over the component and the secondary mouse button is clicked, that pop-up will automatically be displayed. Writing event handlers for pop-up menus is exactly the same as writing event handlers for main menus.

A common feature of text-editing programs is that the Cut, Copy, and Paste operations are on a speed menu. We'll add that capability to ScratchPad. To create the pop-up, we'll cheat and copy part of the main menu. Here we go:

1. Choose a PopupMenu component from the Component Palette and place it on the form.

2. Change the Name property to MemoPopup.

3. Double-click the PopupMenu icon to run the Menu Designer.

4. Click the secondary mouse button to bring up the Menu Designer speed menu. Choose Select Menu from the speed menu. A dialog box is displayed that shows the menus available for your application. Choose MainMenu and click OK.

5. Click on the Edit menu. Click on the Cut menu item, hold down the Shift key, and click on the Paste menu item. Cut, Copy, and Paste are all now highlighted.

6. To copy the selected items to the Clipboard, choose Edit | Copy from the C++Builder main menu (don't choose Edit | Copy from the menu you are creating in the Menu Designer) or press Ctrl+C.

7. Again, choose Select Menu from the Menu Designer speed menu. This time, choose MemoPopup and click OK. The Menu Designer shows a blank pop-up menu.

8. Choose Edit | Paste from the main menu or type Ctrl+V on the keyboard. The Cut, Copy, and Paste menu items are inserted into the pop-up.

Okay, just a few more things and we'll be done. We need to change the Name property for the new menu items:

1. For the Cut menu item, change the Name property to PopupCut.

2. Change the Name property for the Copy menu item to PopupCopy.

3. Finally, change the Name property for the Paste menu item to PopupPaste.

The final step is to write event handlers for the pop-up menu items. Hmmm...we already have code written for the main menu's Cut, Copy, and Paste items. It would be a shame to duplicate that code (even if it is just a single line in each case). It would be nice if we could just use the same event handlers that we created earlier. Can we? Sure we can! Just follow these steps:

1. Click on the Cut menu item.

2. Click on the Events tab in the Object Inspector.

3. Click the drop-down arrow button in the `Value` column next to the `OnClick` event (the only event in the list). A list of event handlers that you have created up to this point is displayed.

4. Choose the `EditCutClick` event handler from the list. Now, when the Cut pop-up menu item is clicked, the Edit | Cut handler will be called. No code duplication is required. Cool.

5. Repeat steps 1 through 4 for the Copy and Paste items on the pop-up menu. When you are done, close the Menu Designer.

6. On the main form, click on the `Memo` component. Change the `PopupMenu` property to `MemoPopup` (by choosing it from the list).

You can attach just about any event to any event handler using this method. Now run the program again to test the new speed menu. Of course it works!

TIP

> You can attach a speed button `OnClick` event to an existing event handler just as easily as you did with the pop-up menu. Click the File Open speed button on your form. Locate the `OnClick` event in the Object Inspector and select the `FileOpenClick` event handler. Repeat this for the File Save speed button, except choose the `FileSaveClick` event handler.

Creating and Saving Menu Templates

C++Builder provides you with several menu templates that you can insert into your main menus and pop-ups. You can also create and save your own templates for future use in your programs. First, start the Menu Designer and create the menu.

NOTE

> When creating menus to use as templates, you first must have a main menu or a pop-up menu on a form in order to start the Menu Designer. You can use a temporary, blank form if you want. Start with a blank form, place a `MainMenu` component on it, and double-click the menu component's icon to start the Menu Designer. When you are done creating menu templates, discard the blank form without saving.

7

After you have the menu created, choose Save As Template from the Menu Designer's speed menu. The Save Template dialog box is displayed. Give the menu a meaningful name and click the OK button, and the menu is saved as a template. To insert the menu, choose Insert From Template from the Menu Designer's speed menu just as you did earlier. Any menus you have created will show up along with C++Builder's prebuilt templates.

To remove a template that you have previously created, choose Delete Templates from the Menu Designer's speed menu. The Delete Templates dialog box is displayed, and you can choose the templates you want to delete. When you click the OK button, the selected menu templates will be deleted. Press Cancel to close the dialog box without deleting any templates.

Summary

Congratulations! You have just covered the bulk of the visual programming features of C++Builder. Hopefully it was enjoyable for you as well as educational. The Form Designer is a powerful tool that allows you to do as much of your programming as possible visually. If you haven't had to place controls on a window in C or C++, you may not fully appreciate this advantage. Trust me, it's significant. The Menu Designer is also a powerful tool, particularly because of the capability to import menus, which makes menu creation easy and actually fun with C++Builder. The Menu Designer also makes updating existing menus a snap.

Workshop

The Workshop contains quiz questions to help you solidify your understanding of the material covered and exercises to provide you with experience in using what you have learned. You can find answers to the quiz questions in Appendix A, "Answers to Quiz Questions."

Q&A

Q I'm using the Alignment Palette a lot, and every time I switch from the Code Editor back to the Form Designer, the Alignment Palette gets lost somewhere. Is there anything I can do about that?

A Locate the Alignment Palette (it's there somewhere!) and click your secondary mouse button to bring up the Alignment Palette's speed menu. Choose the Stay on Top item from the speed menu. Now the Alignment Palette will always be on top where you can find it.

Q I am trying to select a group of components on a panel by dragging the selection rectangle around them, but I keep moving the panel. What's wrong?

A You need to hold down the Ctrl key while dragging when you are selecting components contained on a panel.

Q I've moved my components around my form several times and now the tab order is erratic. What can I do to fix that?

A Choose Tab Order from the Form Designer's speed menu. Arrange the tab order the way you want it. When you click OK, the new tab order will be implemented.

Q The templates provided are nice, but they've got so much stuff on them that I don't need. What can I do about that?

A Basically, you can do two things. First, you can import a menu and then simply delete the items you don't want. Using the click, Shift+click method you can get rid of unwanted menu items in just a few seconds. Deleting items from a menu inserted from a template has no adverse effects. The second thing you can do is to follow the click, Shift+click method and then, when you have the menu just the way you want it, you can save it as a new template. That way you can keep the original C++Builder-supplied template and have your customized template as well.

Q Can I save my own menus as templates?

A Yes. First create the menu and then choose Save As Template from the Menu Designer speed menu. Give the template a name, click OK, and the template is saved. Now all you have to do to reuse the menu later is insert the menu using the Insert From Template feature.

Quiz

1. When do you use Ctrl+drag in selecting components?
2. What significance does the first component selected have when you're aligning a group of components?
3. What is the quickest method of selecting a group of components?
4. How can you make a group of components all have the width of the widest component in the group?
5. What happens when you double-click a component on a form?
6. What does the alClient option of the Align property do?
7. What does the ellipsis following a menu item mean?
8. What two ways can you move a menu item?
9. How do you add keyboard shortcuts to menu items?
10. How do you initially disable a menu item?

Exercises

1. Place five edit components on a form and arrange them so that they are stacked vertically with their left edges aligned.

2. Turn off the Snap to Grid option (choose Tools | Options from the main menu). Place five controls of your choice on a form and align their right edges.

3. Place a ListBox component on a blank form and modify it so that it always occupies the entire client area of the form.

4. Add an About box to the ScratchPad program. Use the Alignment Palette to quickly align the text labels.

5. Add an Undo item and a menu separator to the speed menu for the ScratchPad program.

6. Start a new application. Place six edit components on a form in random fashion. Now arrange the tab order so that tabbing proceeds from top to bottom. Run the program to test the tabbing order.

7. Add speedbar buttons for Cut, Copy, and Paste to the ScratchPad program, as well as any others you want to add. Assign the menu event handlers for the same functions to the speed buttons.

8. Add the Ctrl+S keyboard shortcut to the File | Save menu item in the ScratchPad program.

9. Open the Picture Viewer project you created on Day 6, "The C++Builder IDE Explored: Projects and Forms." Remove all unused menu items.

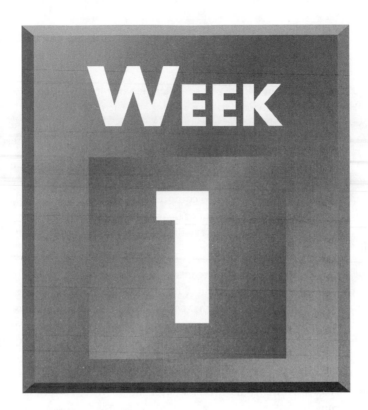

In Review

You covered a lot of ground this week! In some ways this was the toughest week in the book. C++ is not an easy language to learn. But there is no doubt that you can learn to be a C++ programmer if you stay with it. Don't forget to take a break now and then. This book is titled *Teach Yourself Borland C++Builder in 21 Days*, but that doesn't mean they have to be consecutive days! Sometimes it's good to take a few days off to let it all soak in.

If you are confused by some of the C++ syntax, don't think you are alone. Pointers and references; * versus &; direct and indirect operators…it can all be pretty confusing at first. Don't worry, though, because you will start to get the hang of it before long. As you work with C++Builder, little by little it begins to make sense. What you probably lack at this point is

1
2
3
4
5
6
7

real-world experience. That is where you really learn. Knowledge gained by experience is the kind that really sticks. My advice is to take an idea and turn it into a working program. You can't necessarily do that at this point, but you can get a good start. The program doesn't have to be a Word, a Netscape Navigator, or an Excel program, mind you. It just needs to be a little something to help you tie your education in with some experience.

The first part of this week you worked on C++ language keywords and syntax. Things like loops and `if` statements are fairly easy to comprehend. Don't be concerned, though, if you have to go back and look up the syntax once in a while. There is a lot to learn and you aren't expected to be able to memorize every keyword and its syntax. Later on you will, but at this stage of the game it isn't expected.

Toward the middle of the week you were introduced to structures and then to C++ classes. Classes are the bulk of what C++ is about. The things we discussed on Days 1, 2, and 3 are primarily features of the C++ language that come from the C language. Classes, though, are pure C++. Sometimes it takes a while for you to grasp where classes can be used in your programs. For a long time you might only deal with the classes that the VCL provides and not write any classes of your own. Later on you will probably find situations where a class would fit perfectly with a particular task you have to accomplish. When that time comes, you will be ready to tackle writing your own class. After you've written one or two, you will likely be off and running.

On Day 5 you got an introduction to class libraries, also known as *frameworks*. VCL is a framework. A framework makes your life easier by encapsulating difficult Windows programming tasks into classes that you can deal with on a more rational level. Believe me, sometimes the raw Windows API appears to be anything but rational. VCL takes care of dealing with those issues for you and provides you with a higher level of programming objects that you can easily incorporate in your applications. No, VCL is not easy, but it is much easier than dealing with the API that VCL works to shield you from. As part of the discussion on frameworks, you were introduced to the PME (properties, methods, and events) model. You learned a bit about properties, methods, and events, and how you will use them to build Windows programs in C++Builder.

At the end of this first week you were able to play around with the IDE a little. You learned about the IDE: how to customize it to your liking, how the Component Palette works, what the Object Inspector is for, and how to use the Menu Designer. This part of the week you got into the fun stuff. It's okay to use the word *fun*. I find all kinds of programming a great deal of fun. That's why I do it. Hopefully, you find it fun, too.

Finally, you ended the week by learning all about the Form Designer. The Form Designer is where the bulk of your C++Builder applications will be designed—the graphical part of the application, anyway. Working with the Form Designer can be fun, too. Using the Form Designer you can create great-looking forms. Remember, a form represents a window in your applications. Most applications have a main window and several dialog boxes that are displayed based on user interaction with the program. The Form Designer gives you an advantage that you can't appreciate unless you have had to design dialog boxes with more traditional programming tools. As great as the resource editors that come with Borland C++ or Visual C++ are, they are no match for C++Builder when it comes to building forms. Being able to place forms and set their properties at design time gives you a big edge when it comes to beating the competition to market. C++Builder's visual programming model is both powerful and easy to use. What could be better?

On Day 7 you created a simple, but useful, program. This program, ScratchPad, got you started on how to build an application with C++Builder. We are going to use ScratchPad throughout the book. As you build your programming knowledge, we will add new features to ScratchPad to solidify the techniques presented. If you are developing an application of your own, I encourage you to add new features to your program as you learn about them.

I hope this week hasn't left you too worn out. If it has, take a short break and jump right back into the game. If you found this week exhilarating and energizing, just keep on turnin' those pages! I'm ready if you are!

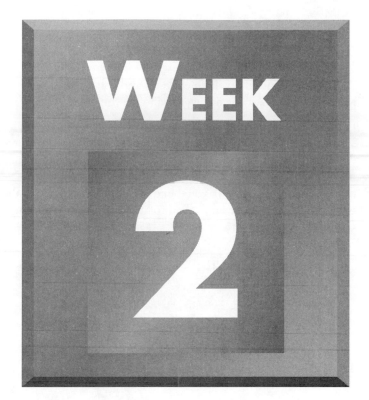

WEEK

2

8

9

10

11

12

13

14

At a Glance

Are you ready for the fun stuff? This week you are going to learn about Windows programming in earnest. You are going to start off with a discussion of components that will go well beyond the introduction you had during Week 1. You are going to find out about specific components and how to use them. You will spend some time reading and, hopefully, a lot of time experimenting. Reading this book is not a race. The first one done does not receive a prize. Better to be the tortoise than the hare when it comes to learning programming. Take time to experiment!

This week you will learn about creating applications using C++Builder's experts. These experts help you get a program up and running in the minimum amount of time. After that, you will learn about debugging your programs. Yes, your programs will have bugs. Don't fight it. Just learn how to find those nasty critters in your programs and squash them.

Debugging is a vital application development tool, and you must learn how to debug your programs. Knowing how to use the debugger will save you hours and hours of time in the long run.

Finally, late in the week you will get into more advanced programming techniques. At that time you will learn about things like status bars, speedbars, and printing. On Day 14 you will learn how to implement context help and how to use the Windows registry to store information for your program. I think you'll like what you find there. By the time you get to the end of the week, you will be on a steam roller that can't be stopped!

Day 8

VCL Components

by Kent Reisdorph

As you know by now, components are much of what gives C++Builder its power. Components are designed using the properties, methods, and events model. Using the Form Designer, you can place a component on a form and modify its design-time properties. In some cases, that's all you have to do. If needed, you can also manipulate the component at runtime by changing its properties and calling its methods. Further, each component is designed to respond to certain events. I discussed properties, methods, and events on Day 5, "C++ Class Frameworks and the Visual Component Model," so I'm not going to go over that again here.

Today you will find out more about components. You will learn about often-used components and, as a result, learn about the VCL classes that represent those components. As you go through this chapter, feel free to experiment. If you read something that you want to test, by all means do so. Learning by experience is as valuable as anything you can do, so don't be afraid to experiment.

Review

Let's review some of what you already know about components. But first, I want to take a moment to explain the differences between a VCL component and a Windows control. Windows controls include things such as edit controls, list boxes, combo boxes, static controls (labels), and buttons, not to mention all the Windows 95 controls. Windows controls, by nature, do not have properties, methods, and events. Instead, messages are used to tell the control what to do or to get information from the control. To say that dealing with controls on this level is tedious and cumbersome would be an understatement.

A VCL component is a class that encapsulates a Windows control (not all VCL components encapsulate controls, though). A VCL component in effect adds properties, methods, and events to a Windows control to make working with the control easier. You might say that VCL takes a fresh approach to working with Windows controls. It could be said that all VCL components are controls, but not all controls are components. A VCL Edit component, for instance, is a control, but a standard Windows edit control is not a VCL component. VCL components work with Windows controls to raise the job of dealing with those controls to a higher level.

Given that discussion, then, I will use the terms *control* and *component* interchangeably when referring to VCL components. (But I will never call a Windows control a component!)

Visual and Nonvisual Components

Some components are visual components; others are nonvisual components.

NEW TERM A *visual component*, as its name implies, is one that can be seen by the user at design time.

Visual components include things like edit controls, buttons, list boxes, labels, and so on. Most components you use in a C++Builder application are visual components. Visual components, as much as possible, show you at design time what the component will look like when the program runs.

NEW TERM A *nonvisual component* is one that cannot be seen by the user at design time.

Nonvisual components work behind the scenes to perform specific programming tasks. Examples include system timers, database components, and image lists. Common dialog boxes like File Open, File Save, choose Font, and so on are considered nonvisual components. They are nonvisual because they don't show themselves at design time. At runtime, they become visible when they are invoked. When you place a nonvisual component on a form,

C++Builder displays an icon representing the component on the form. This icon is used to access the component at design time in order to change the component's properties, but the icon does not show up when the program runs. Nonvisual components have properties, methods, and events just like visual components do.

The Name Property

The Name property serves a vital role in components. As mentioned earlier, when you place a component on a form, C++Builder goes to work in the background while you ponder your next move. One thing C++Builder does is create a pointer to the component and assign the Name property as the variable name. For example, let's say you place an Edit component on a form and change the Name property to MyEdit. At that point C++Builder places the following in the header file for the form:

```
TEdit* MyEdit;
```

When the application runs, C++Builder creates an instance of the TEdit class and assigns it to MyEdit. You can use this pointer to access the component at runtime. To set the text for the edit control, you would use

```
MyEdit->Text = "Jenna Lynn";
```

C++Builder also uses the Name property when creating event handler names. Let's say that you wanted to respond to the OnChange event for an Edit component. Normally, you double-click the Value column next to the OnChange event to have C++Builder generate an event handler for the event. C++Builder creates a default function name based on the Name property of the component and the event being handled. In this case, C++Builder would generate a function called MyEditChange().

You can change the Name property at any time, provided that you change it *only* via the Object Inspector. When you change a component's Name property at design time, C++Builder goes through all the code that C++Builder had previously generated and changes the name of the pointer and all event-handling functions.

NOTE

C++Builder will change all the code generated by C++Builder to reflect the new value of the component's Name property, but it will not modify any code you wrote. In other words, C++Builder will take care of modifying the code it wrote, but it is up to you to update and maintain the code you wrote. Generally speaking, you should change the Name property when you initially place the component on the form and leave it alone after that.

Continuing with this example, if you change the `Name` property of the edit control from `MyEdit` to `FirstName`, C++Builder will change the pointer name to `FirstName` and the `OnChange` handler name to `FirstNameChange()`. It's all done automatically; you don't have to do anything but change the `Name` property and trust that C++Builder will do its thing.

WARNING

Never change the `Name` property at runtime. Never manually change a component's name (the name that C++Builder assigned to the component's pointer) or event handler names in the Code Editor. If you do either of these, C++Builder loses track of components, and the results are not good, to say the least. You might even lose the ability to load your form. The only safe way to change the `Name` property of a component is through the Object Inspector.

C++Builder assigns a default value to the `Name` property for all components placed on a form. If you place an `Edit` component, for example, C++Builder assigns `Edit1` to the `Name` property. If you place a second `Edit` component on the form, C++Builder assigns `Edit2` to that component's `Name` property, and so on. You should give your components meaningful names as soon as possible to avoid confusion and extra work later on.

NOTE

You can leave the default names for components that will never be referenced in code. For example, if you have several label components that contain static (unchanging) text, you can leave the default names because you won't be accessing the components at runtime.

HOUSE RULES: THE `Name` PROPERTY

- ☐ Change the `Name` property of a component from the default name to a meaningful name as soon as possible.
- ☐ Components not referenced at runtime can be left with the C++Builder-supplied name.
- ☐ Never change the `Name` property of a component in code or at runtime.
- ☐ Make your components' names meaningful but not overly long.

Important Common Properties

All components have certain properties in common. For instance, all visual components have Left and Top properties that determine where the component is placed on the form. Properties such as Left, Top, Height, and Width are self-explanatory, so I won't go over them. A few of the common properties, however, warrant a closer look.

The Align Property

On Day 7, "Working with the Form Designer and the Menu Designer," I discussed the Align and Alignment properties, so I won't go over those again in detail. Refer to Day 7 for complete information on Align. It should be noted here, however, that not all components expose the Align property at design time. A single-line edit control, for instance, should occupy a standard height, so the features of the Align property do not make sense for that type of component. As you gain experience with C++Builder, and depending on the type of applications you write, you will probably rely heavily on the Align property.

Color My World

The Color property sets the background color for the component. (The text color is set through the Font property.) Although the Color property is simple to use, there are a few aspects of component colors that should be pointed out.

The way the Color property is handled in the Object Inspector is somewhat unique. If you click on the Value column, you will see the drop-down arrow button indicating that you can choose from a list of color values. That is certainly the case, but there's more to it than that. If you double-click on the Value column, the Color dialog box is displayed. This dialog box allows you to choose a color from one of the predefined colors or to create your own colors by clicking the Define Custom Colors button. Figure 8.1 shows the Color dialog box after the Define Custom Colors button has been clicked.

NOTE This is the same Color dialog box that will be displayed if you implement the ColorDialog component in your application.

If you choose a color from the Color dialog box, you will see that the value of the Color property changes to a hexadecimal string. This string represents the red, green, and blue (RGB) values that make up the color. If you know the exact RGB value of a color (not likely!), you can type it in.

Figure 8.1.

The Color dialog box.

Most of the time you will probably choose a color from the list of color values provided. When you click the drop-down button to display the list of possible values, you will see what essentially amounts to two groups of values. The first group of colors begins with clBlack and ends with clWhite. These are the C++Builder predefined colors; this list represents the most commonly used colors. To choose one of the listed colors, simply click on the color in the list. If you can't find a color in the list that suits your needs, you can invoke the Color dialog box, as discussed.

The second group of colors in the list begins with clScrollBar. This group of colors represents the Windows system colors. If you use colors from this list, your application will automatically adjust its colors when the user changes color schemes in Windows. If you want your application to follow the color scheme the user has chosen for his or her system, you should choose colors from this list rather than from the first list.

Use of color should be carefully considered. Proper use of color provides an aesthetically pleasing environment for the user. Abuse of color makes for an obnoxious application that is annoying to use. Color is like a magnet to new programmers. It is common to want to throw lots of colors on a form because it's fun and easy, but don't get caught up in the fun at the expense of your users.

HOUSE RULES: COLORS

☐ Use color for accent and emphasis.

☐ Don't use loud colors that are hard on the eyes.

☐ Use the system colors in your application where appropriate. If the user changes color schemes, your application will follow suit.

☐ Be consistent in your use of colors across your forms.

Cursors

The Cursor property controls the cursor that is displayed when the user moves the mouse cursor over the component. Windows automatically changes cursors for some components. For example, Windows changes the cursor to an I-beam when the cursor is moved over an Edit, a Memo, or a RichEdit component, to name just a few. To let Windows manage the cursor, leave the Cursor property set to crDefault. If you have specialized windows (components), you can specify one of the other cursors. When the mouse is moved over that component, Windows will change the cursor to the one you have specified.

Frequently you will need to change cursors at runtime. A long process, for instance, should be indicated to the user by displaying the hourglass cursor. When you reset the cursor you need to be sure to set the cursor back to whatever it was originally. The following code snippet illustrates:

```
TCursor oldCursor = Cursor;
Cursor = TCursor(crHourGlass);
// do some stuff which takes a long time
Cursor = oldCursor;
```

This ensures that the cursor that was originally set for the application is properly restored.

Another cursor property, DragCursor, is used to set the cursor that is used when the mouse cursor is being dragged from the component and the target can accept the drag. As with colors, you should be prudent in your use of cursors. Use custom cursors when needed, but don't overdo it.

Enabled

Components can be enabled or disabled through the Enabled property. When a component is disabled, it cannot accept focus (clicking on it has no effect), and usually it gives some visual cue to indicate that it is disabled. In the case of buttons, for instance, the button text is grayed out as is any bitmap on the button. Enabled is a boolean property—set it to true to enable the component, or set it to false to disable the component. Enabling and disabling windows (remember that windowed components are windows, too) is a feature of Windows itself.

NOTE   Some components show their disabled state at design time, but most do not. The BitBtn component is one that does show its disabled state at design time.

The Enabled property applies mostly to windowed components, but can apply to non-windowed components as well. The SpeedButton component is an example of a non-windowed component that can be disabled.

NOTE

> Modifying the Enabled property for a panel component has additional implications. Panels are often used as containers for other controls. Therefore, they become the parents of the controls that are placed within them. If you disable a panel, the components on the panel will not show as disabled, but will not function because their parent (the panel) is disabled.

Although components can be disabled at design time, enabling and disabling components is something that is usually done at runtime. Menu items, for instance, should be enabled or disabled according to whether they apply at a given time. The same is true of buttons. There are a variety of reasons why you might want to disable other types of controls as well.

To disable a component at runtime, just assign false to its Enabled property, and to enable a component assign true to Enabled. The following code snippet enables or disables a menu item based on some condition:

```
if (saveEnabled) FileSave->Enabled = true;
else FileSave->Enabled = false;
```

This process is often referred to as *command enabling* and is an important part of a professional-looking Windows program.

The Font Property

The Font property is a major property and therefore needs to be included here, but there is not a lot that needs to be said about it. The Font property is an instance of the TFont class, and as such has its own properties. You can set the Font properties by double-clicking on the font name in the Object Inspector (which will expand the Font node and show the Font properties) or by invoking the Font dialog box. (The Font dialog box is discussed in more detail later in the chapter in the section "The Font Dialog Box.") Figure 8.2 shows the Object Inspector with the Font property node expanded to reveal the TFont properties.

The Color property sets the color of the font, and the Name property allows you to choose the typeface for the font.

The Height and Size properties of TFont deserve special mention. The Height property is used to specify the height of the font in pixels, whereas the Size property is used to specify the height of the font in points. When you change one of these properties, the other will change automatically. The Height is often specified as a negative number. Refer to the online help for TFont for an explanation of why this is the case.

8

Figure 8.2.

The Object Inspector showing the Font *property.*

The Pitch property is not particularly useful. I'll explain it in just a moment, but first a quick tutorial on fonts. A font can be either proportionally spaced or fixed space. Most fonts are proportionally spaced. This means that each letter takes only as much space as needed. For example, an uppercase M takes up much more space than a lowercase i. Take a look at the letters in this book, and you will see what I mean. Examples of proportional fonts include Times New Roman, Arial, and Bookman. With a fixed-space font (typically called a fixed-pitch font), on the other hand, all characters take exactly the same amount of space. This is convenient for windows such as code editors (the C++Builder Code Editor, for instance) or any other window where a fixed-pitch font is desired. Courier New is probably the most commonly used fixed-pitch font, although Fixedsys is the Windows fixed-pitch font of choice.

In theory, the Pitch property can be used to force a proportionally spaced font to fixed space and vice versa. The problem is that Windows might perform font substitutions in order to carry out the conversion. In other words, you really don't know what you might get. It is far better to pick exactly the font you require than to rely on the Pitch property.

Finally, the Style property of TFont can be used to toggle bold, italic, underline, or strikethrough. These styles are not mutually exclusive, so you can mix styles in any way you choose.

TIP

Although you can use the Object Inspector to change font properties, the Font dialog box has the added benefit of showing you a sample of what the font looks like as you choose different font options. To simply change the font's Style property or Size property, use the Object Inspector. But if you are looking for just the right font, the Font dialog box is a better choice.

Give Me a Hint

The Hint property is used to set hint text for a component. The hint text has two parts. The first part is sometimes called the *short hint*. This is the hint text that is displayed when the user places the cursor over the component and pauses. The pop-up window that displays the hint text is called a *tool tip*.

The second part of the hint text is sometimes called the *long hint*. The long hint is the optional hint text that will show in the status bar when the user moves the mouse cursor over the component. The short and long hint texts are separated by a pipe (¦). For example, to specify both the short hint text and the long hint text for a File Open speed button, you would enter the following for the Hint property:

```
File Open¦Open a file for editing
```

In order for short hints to show, you must have the Application object's ShowHint property set to true (the default) as well as the component's ShowHint property. Displaying the long hint in the status bar requires a little more work, so I'll save that discussion for tomorrow.

NOTE

You can specify the short hint text, the long hint text, or both. You can use the pipe to tell C++Builder which hint text you are supplying. If you do not use the pipe, both the short hint and the long hint will use the same text.

ParentColor, ParentCtl3D, ParentFont, and ParentShowHint

The ParentColor, ParentCtl3D, ParentFont, and ParentShowHint properties all work the same way, so I'll discuss them at the same time. When these properties are set to true, the component takes its Color, Ctl3D, Font, or ShowHint settings from its parent. For example, for most components the ParentFont property is set to true by default. This means the component will inherit the font that its parent is currently using. To illustrate, do this exercise:

1. Create a blank form. Set the Font property's Size property to 16.
2. Place a Label component on the form. Notice that the label automatically uses a 16-point type size.
3. Place a Button component on the form. It also uses a 16-point type size.

You can set this property to false, but by the time the component is placed, it is already too late and you will have to change the font manually to the font you want for the component.

The Tag Property

The Tag property is nothing more than a 4-byte variable set aside for your use. You can use the Tag property to store any data that your component might need. The data stored might be a pointer to another class, an index value, or any number of other possibilities. Using the Tag property would probably be considered an advanced programming technique.

Other Common Properties

Table 8.1 lists other common properties that are frequently used. These properties don't require as much explanation, so I just listed them here for your reference. Not all components have each of the properties listed.

Table 8.1. Additional component properties.

Property	Description
BorderStyle	Can be bsSingle or bsNone. Use bsNone when you want the component to blend in with the background.
Caption	Sets the component's caption. Many components do not have captions, so for those components the Caption property is not exposed.
Ctl3D	Indicates whether the control should be drawn with a 3D border. If BorderStyle is set to bsNone, this property has no effect.
Height	Sets the component's height.
HelpContext	The HelpContext property is used to associate an index number in a help file with a particular component.
Left	Sets the x coordinate of the component.
PopupMenu	Specifies the pop-up menu that will be displayed when the user clicks the secondary mouse button.
TabOrder	For windowed components. Sets this component's position in the tab order.
TabStop	For windowed components. Indicates that this component can be tabbed into. Setting this property to false removes the component from the tab order.

continues

Table 8.1. continued

Property	Description
Top	Sets the y coordinate of the component.
Visible	When read, indicates whether the component is currently visible. When written to, Visible either hides or shows the component.
Width	Sets the width of the component.

Primary Methods of Components

There are more than 20 methods that most components have in common. Windowed components have more than 40 common methods from which you can choose. Interestingly, not many of these are widely used. Much of the functionality of components is accomplished via properties. For example, to hide a component, you can call the Hide() method, or you can set the Visible property to false. In addition, components typically have methods specific to their purpose, and it will likely be those methods that you use most when dealing with a particular component.

There are a few methods worthy of note, however, which are listed in Table 8.2. Note that some of these methods are not available to all controls. These are not the most often-used methods common to every component, but rather the most commonly used methods of components in general. Also, this list concentrates on components representing controls (components placed on forms) rather than components as forms. Methods particular to forms were discussed on Day 6, "The C++Builder IDE Explored: Projects and Forms."

Table 8.2. Common methods of components.

Method	Description
Broadcast	Used to send a message to all windowed child components.
ClientToScreen	Converts client window coordinates into screen coordinates.
ContainsControl	Returns true if the specified component is a child of the component or form.
HandleAllocated	Returns true if the Handle property for the component has been created. Simply reading the Handle property automatically creates a handle if it hasn't already been created, so HandleAllocated() can be used to check for the existence of the handle without creating it.
Hide	Hides the component. The component is still available to be shown again later.

Method	Description
Invalidate	Requests that the component be redrawn. The component will be redrawn at Windows's earliest convenience.
Perform	Allows a component to send a message to itself directly rather than going through the Windows messaging system.
Refresh	Requests that a component be redrawn immediately and erases the component prior to repainting.
Repaint	Requests that a component be redrawn immediately. The component's background is not erased prior to repainting.
SetBounds	Allows you to set the Top, Left, Width, and Height properties all at one time. This saves time over having to set them individually.
SetFocus	Sets the focus to a component and makes it the active component. Applies only to windowed components.
Update	Forces an immediate repaint of the control. Typically, you should use Refresh or Repaint to repaint components.

Now let's take look at some of the events to which a component is most likely to respond.

Common Events

As with properties and methods, there are some events that will be responded to most often. Components cover a wide variety of possible Windows controls, so each component will have individual needs. Events specific to forms are not covered here because I covered that information on Day 6. The most commonly used events are listed in Table 8.3.

Table 8.3. Commonly handled component events.

Event	Description
OnChange	This event is triggered when a control changes in one way or another. Exact implementation depends on the component.
OnClick	Sent when the component is clicked with either mouse button.
OnDblClick	This event occurs when the user double-clicks the component.
OnEnter	This event occurs when a windowed component receives focus (is activated).
OnExit	This event occurs when a windowed component loses focus as the result of the user switching to a different control. It does not occur,

continues

Table 8.3. continued

Event	Description
	however, when the user switches forms or switches to another application.
OnKeyDown	This event is triggered when the user presses a key while the control has focus. Keys include all alphanumeric keys as well as keys such as the arrow keys, Home, End, Ctrl, and so on.
OnKeyPress	This event is also triggered when the user presses a key, but only when alphanumeric keys or the Tab, backspace, Enter, or Esc keys are pressed.
OnKeyUp	This event occurs whenever a key is released.
OnMouseDown	This event is triggered when the mouse button is pressed while over the component. The parameters passed to the event handler give you information on which mouse button was clicked, special keys that were pressed (Alt, Shift, Ctrl), and the x,y coordinate of the mouse pointer when the event occurred.
OnMouseMove	This event occurs any time the mouse is moved over the control.
OnMouseUp	This event is triggered when the mouse button is released while over a control. The mouse button must first have been clicked while on the control.
OnPaint	This event is sent any time a component needs repainting. You can respond to this event to do any custom painting a component requires.

DEALING WITH MOUSE EVENTS

Mouse events have a couple peculiarities that you should be aware of. If you are responding just to a mouse click on a component, you will want to keep it simple and only respond to the OnClick event. If you must use OnMouseDown and OnMouseUp, you should be aware that the OnClick event will be sent as well as the OnMouseDown and OnMouseUp events. For example, a single click will result in these events occurring (and in this order):

OnMouseDown
OnClick
OnMouseUp

Similarly, when the user double-clicks with the mouse, it could result in the application getting more events than you might think. When a component is double-clicked, the following events occur:

```
OnMouseDown
OnClick
OnDblClick
OnMouseUp
```

The point I am trying to make is that you need to take care when responding to both double-click and single-click events for a component. Be aware that you will get four events for a double-click event.

Multiple events will occur when a key is pressed, too. A keypress in an edit control, for instance, will result in OnKeyDown, OnKeyPress, OnChange, and OnKeyUp events occurring.

 The CD-ROM that accompanies this book contains a program called EventTst that illustrates the fact that multiple events occur on mouse clicks and keypresses. Run this program and you will see how multiple events can be triggered based on certain user actions.

In just a moment we're going to look at some of the VCL components in more detail. First, however, I want to introduce you to a class that is used by certain VCL components.

TStrings

The TStrings class is a VCL class that manages lists of strings. Several VCL components use instances of TStrings to manage their data (usually text). For example, on Day 7 you used TStrings when you built the ScratchPad application. "Hmmm...I don't recall using a TStrings class," you say. Well, you did, but you just weren't aware of it. Remember when we saved and loaded files? You used something like this:

```
Memo->Lines->SaveToFile(SaveDialog->FileName);
```

The Lines property of TMemo is an instance of the TStrings class. The SaveToFile() method of TStrings takes the strings and saves them to a file on disk. You can do the same thing to load a list box from a file on disk or save the contents of a list box to disk. In the case of the

TListBox class, the property that holds the list box items is called Items. For example, do this exercise:

1. Create a new application and place a ListBox component on the form. Size the list box as desired.
2. Change the Name property of the list box to ListBox.
3. Double-click on the background of the form (not on the list box). The Code Editor displays the FormCreate() function.
4. Type the following code in the FormCreate() function:

```
char winDir[256], fileName[256];
GetWindowsDirectory(winDir, sizeof(winDir));
sprintf(fileName, "%s\\win.ini", winDir);
ListBox->Items->LoadFromFile(fileName);
```

5. Click the Run button to compile and run the program.

When the program runs, the list box will contain the contents of your WIN.INI file. Using this method, it's easy to load a list box from any ASCII text data file. The ComboBox component also has an Items property, and it works in exactly the same way.

You can add, delete, insert, and move items in a list box, combo box, or memo by calling the Add(), Append(), Delete(), Insert(), and Move() methods of the TStrings class.

NOTE

> How Add() performs depends on the value of the Sorted property. If the Sorted property is set to true, Add() will insert the string where it needs to be in the list of items. If Sorted is false, the new string will be added at the end of the list.

You can clear a component of its contents by calling the Clear() method. You can access an individual string by using the Strings property of TStrings and the array subscript operator. For example, to retrieve the first string in a list of strings, you would use

```
Edit->Text = ListBox->Items->Strings[0];
```

Each string in a TStrings array contains the string itself and 4 bytes of extra storage. This extra storage can be accessed through the Objects property. You can use the extra storage any way you like. Let's say, for example, that you were creating an owner-drawn list box that displayed bitmaps. You could store the string in the usual way, plus store a pointer to the TBitmap object in the Objects array.

TIP

There may be a time when you need to manage a list of strings unrelated to a component. The TStringList class is provided for exactly that purpose. This class works just like TStrings but can be used outside components.

NOTE

In reality TStrings is what is called an *abstract base class*. An abstract base class is never used directly, but only serves as a base class from which to derive other classes. Technically, the Lines property of the Memo component is an instance of the TMemoStrings class and not an instance of the TStrings class as I said in this section. I didn't mean to lead you astray, but I thought it was best to make this distinction after the discussion on TStrings rather than confuse you with this information during that discussion.

Standard Windows Control Components

Back in the Jurassic age, there was something called Windows 3.0. Windows 3.0 gave us things like edit controls (single line and multiline), list boxes, combo boxes, buttons, check boxes, radio buttons, and static controls. These controls must have been pretty well designed because they are very prevalent in Windows programs today—even considering all the new Win32 controls.

I'm not going to go over every Windows control and its corresponding VCL component. There are a few things, though, that you should know regarding the standard components.

Edit Controls

C++Builder comes with four edit-control components. The Edit, Memo, and MaskEdit components are based on the standard Windows edit control. The RichEdit component is based on the Win32 rich edit control, which is not one of the standard Windows controls. Still, I will discuss RichEdit here because it has many things in common with the other edit controls.

The Edit component encapsulates the basic single-line edit control. This component has no Align or Alignment property. It has no Alignment property because the text in a single-line edit control can only be left-justified. The Edit component has no Align property because it cannot (or more accurately, should not) be expanded to fill the client area of a window.

TIP

If you need text in an edit component to be right-justified or centered, use a Memo component but make its height the height of a standard Edit component. Then set the Alignment property as needed.

NOTE

Keep your forms standard whenever possible. Although you can make an Edit component as tall as you like, it will confuse users if you make its height greater than a standard Windows edit control (it might appear to the user to be a multiline edit).

The MaskEdit component is an Edit component with an input filter, or mask, attached. The MaskEdit does not represent a Windows control per se, but rather is just a VCL extension of a standard edit control. A mask is used to force input to a specific range of numbers or characters. In addition, the mask can contain special characters that are placed in the edit control by default. For example, a date is commonly formatted as follows:

10/25/97

An edit mask for a date can already have the slashes in place so that the user only has to enter the numbers. The edit mask would specify that only numbers can be entered to avoid the possibility of the user entering a nonnumeric character.

The EditMask property controls the mask used. When you press the ellipsis (...) button in the Value column for the EditMask property, the Input Mask Editor is displayed. This dialog box allows you to choose one of the predefined masks or to create your own. You can choose prebuilt masks from several countries. Figure 8.3 shows the Input Mask Editor displaying the United Kingdom set of predefined input masks.

For more information on building your own masks, see the C++Builder online help.

The Memo component encapsulates a multiline edit control. The Lines property is the most significant property in a Memo component. As mentioned earlier in the discussion on TStrings, the Lines property allows you to save the contents of the Memo component to disk or load the Memo with text from a file, as well as other things. The ScrollBars property is unique to the Memo component. This property allows you to specify whether your component has a horizontal scrollbar, a vertical scrollbar, or both. You used the ScrollBars property on Day 7 when you wrote the ScratchPad application. The Memo component is a very versatile component that you will probably find yourself using frequently.

Figure 8.3.

The Input Mask Editor.

The RichEdit component is the biggest and the best of all the edit components. It is based on the Win32 rich edit control. The RichEdit component allows you to change fonts; use indentation; set text to bold, italic, or underlined; and much more. Basically, the RichEdit component is a mini word processor in one neat package. RichEdit has surprisingly few design-time properties compared to the Memo component. Key runtime properties include SelAttributes and Paragraph. The RichEdit component is fairly complex, but still easy to use considering its complexities. See the C++Builder online help for full details on the RichEdit component.

Table 8.4 lists the properties specific to components based on edit controls.

Table 8.4. Properties for edit controls.

Item	Applies To	Description
		Properties
AutoSelect	Edit, MaskEdit	When set to true, text in the edit control will automatically be selected when the user tabs to the control. Default: true
AutoSize	Edit, MaskEdit	When set to true, the edit control will automatically resize itself when the font of the edit control changes. Otherwise, the edit control does not change size when the font changes. Default: true

continues

Table 8.4. continued

Item	Applies To	Description
		Properties
CharCase	Edit, MaskEdit	Determines whether the edit control displays uppercase (ecUpperCase), lowercase (ecLowerCase), or mixed text (ecNormal). Default: ecNormal
HideScrollBars	RichEdit	When set to true, the scrollbars will be shown when needed but hidden otherwise. When set to false, the scrollbars are shown as determined by the value of the ScrollBars property.
HideSelection	Edit, Memo, RichEdit	When set to true, any text selected will not show as selected when the user tabs to another control. Default: false
Lines	Memo, RichEdit	The text contained in the component. Lines is an instance of the TStrings class.
MaxLength	All	Specifies the maximum number of characters that the component will hold. When set to 0, the amount of text that can be input is unlimited (limited only by system considerations). When set to any nonzero value, limits the number of characters to that value. Default: 0
OEMConvert	Edit, Memo	Set to true when the text input will consist of filenames. Default: false
PasswordChar	Edit, MaskEdit	When this property is set to a value other than ASCII #0, any text entered will be echoed with the character provided. The actual text in the edit control is unaffected. Most password edits use the asterisk (*) as the password character. Default: #0

Item	Applies To	Description
		Properties
PlainText	RichEdit	When set to true, RTF (rich text format) files will be shown as plain text without character and paragraph formatting. When set to false, RTF files are displayed with full formatting. Default: false
ReadOnly	All	When set to true, the component will display its text, but new text cannot be entered. The user can, however, highlight text and copy it to the Clipboard. Default: false
ScrollBars	Memo, RichEdit	Determines which scrollbars to display. Choices are ssNone, ssBoth, ssHorizontal, and ssVertical. Default: ssNone
Text	Edit, MaskEdit	Contains the text in the component.
WantReturns	Memo, RichEdit	When set to true, the component keeps the return character, and a new line is inserted in the edit control when the user presses Enter. When set to false, return characters go to the form and are not placed in the edit control. If you have a form with a default button and WantReturns set to false, pressing Enter will cause the form to close. Default: true
WantTabs	Memo, RichEdit	When set to true, a tab character is placed in the edit control when the user presses the Tab key. When set to false, tab characters go to the form, which would allow tabbing out of the edit control. Default: false
WordWrap	Memo, RichEdit	When set to true, text entered will wrap to a new line when the right edge of the edit control is reached. When set to false, the edit control automatically scrolls as new text is entered. Default: true

continues

8

Table 8.4. continued

Item	Applies To	Description
		Runtime Properties
Modified	All	Indicates whether the contents of the edit control have changed since the last time the Modified property was set. After saving the contents of a Memo or RichEdit component to a file, you should set Modified to false.
SelLength	All	Contains the length of the text currently selected in the edit control.
SelStart	All	Contains the starting point of the selected text in the edit control. The first character in the edit control is 0.
SelText	All	Contains the currently selected text in an edit control.

Edit controls have many common methods; they are too numerous to list here. The CutToClipboard(), CopyToClipboard(), PasteFromClipboard(), and Clear() methods deal with Clipboard operations and text manipulation. The GetSelTextBuff() and GetTextBuff() methods retrieve the selected text in the component and the entire text in the component, respectively. See the C++Builder online help topics TEdit, TMaskEdit, TMemo, and TRichEdit for a complete list of methods pertaining to each type of edit component.

The edit component events that you are most likely to be interested in are dependent on the type of edit control you are using. In general, though, the OnEnter, OnExit, OnChange, OnKeyDown (or OnKeyPress), and OnKeyUp events will be the most widely used.

The ListBox and ComboBox Components

The ListBox and ComboBox components are also widely used. The ListBox component represents a standard Windows list box, which simply presents a list of choices that the user can choose from. If the list box contains more items than can be shown at one time, scrollbars appear to allow access to the rest of the items in the list box.

NEW TERM   Some list boxes are *owner-drawn* list boxes. In an owner-drawn list box, the programmer takes the responsibility for drawing the items in the list box.

You can use owner-drawn list boxes if needed. Owner-drawn list boxes are fairly common, although you may not realize it. On Day 6 I talked about customizing the C++Builder speedbar. As part of that discussion, we looked at the C++Builder Speedbar Editor dialog box, which was shown in Figure 6.2. Go back and take another look at that figure. The Speedbar Editor dialog box contains two list boxes. The list box on the left is a regular list box. It lists the possible button groups you can choose from. The list box on the right is an owner-drawn list box. It shows the actual button as it will appear on the speedbar, as well as a textual description of what function the button performs.

Combo boxes are specialized list boxes. Actually, a combo box is a combination of a list box and an edit control. The user can choose from the list or type in a value in the edit portion. When the user chooses an item from the list, that item is placed in the edit control. There are three different types of combo boxes. Table 8.5 lists the types of combo boxes and gives a description of each.

Table 8.5. Types of combo boxes.

Item	Description
Simple	The simple style of the combo box is nothing more than an edit control placed on top of a list box. The user can choose from the list or type text in the edit portion.
Drop-down	Similar to the simple style, except the list box portion is not initially displayed. A drop-down button is provided so that the user can view the list and choose an item. The user can also type text in the edit portion.
Drop-down list	This is the most restrictive type of combo box. As with the drop-down style, the list is not initially exposed. The user can click the drop-down button to expose the list and choose an item from the list, but cannot enter text in the edit portion. Use this style when you want the user to select only from a predetermined set of choices.

 The CD-ROM that accompanies this book contains a program called ComboBox Test that illustrates the different types of combo boxes. Figure 8.4 shows the test program running. Run the program and try out the combo boxes to get a feel for how each works.

Table 8.6 lists the properties common to list boxes and combo boxes.

Figure 8.4.

The ComboBox Test program.

Table 8.6. Properties for list boxes and combo boxes.

Property	Applies To	Description
		Properties
Columns	ListBox	Contains the number of columns in the list box. You can make a list box have multiple columns by making this property greater than 1. Default: 0
ExtendedSelection	ListBox	Determines whether extended selection is allowed. *Extended selection* allows the user to select items using Shift+click and Ctrl+click. Has no effect if MultiSelect is set to false. Default: true
IntegralHeight	ListBox	When true, the list box height will be resized to be sure that no partial lines are displayed. When false, the list box may show partial lines. Default: false
ItemHeight	Both	For use with owner-drawn list boxes and combo boxes. Sets the height of the items in the control. Default: 13
Items	Both	A TStrings instance that contains the list of items in the list box. (See the section on TStrings earlier in this chapter for a description of available properties and methods.)
MaxLength	ComboBox	The maximum number of characters the user can type in the edit portion of the combo box. Same as MaxLength in edit controls. Default: 0 (no limit)
MultiSelect	ListBox	When true, the list box allows multiple items to be selected. Default: false
Sorted	Both	When set to true, the list box items are sorted in ascending order. When set to false, the items are not sorted at all. Default: false

Property	Applies To	Description
		Properties
Style	ComboBox	The style of the combo box. Choices are csSimple, csDropDown, csDropDownList, lbOwnderDrawFixed, and csOwnerDrawVariable. (See Table 8.5 for a description of the three basic styles.) Default: csDropDown
	ListBox	Style choices for list boxes are lbStandard, lbOwnderDrawFixed, and csOwnerDrawVariable. Default: lbStandard
TabWidth	ListBox	List boxes can use tabs. This property sets the tab width, in pixels. Default: 0
Text	ComboBox	Contains the text in the edit portion of the combo box.
		Runtime Properties
ItemIndex	ListBox	Contains the index of the currently selected item, with 0 being the first item in the list. Returns -1 if no item is selected. When written to, selects the specified index.
SelCount	ListBox	Contains the number of items selected in a multiple-selection list box.
Selected	ListBox	Returns true if the specified item is selected or false if it is not.
SelLength	ComboBox	Contains the length of the text currently selected in the edit control part of the combo box.
SelStart	ComboBox	Contains the starting point of the selected text in the edit control. The first character in the edit control is 0.
SelText	ComboBox	Contains the currently selected text in the edit control.
TopIndex	ListBox	Returns the list box item that is at the top of the list box. Can be used to set the top item to a certain list box item.

8

As with the edit components we looked at earlier, there are very few ListBox and ComboBox methods. The Clear() method will clear the control of all data. The ItemAtPos() methods will return the list box item at the specified x and y coordinates. The SelectAll() method will select the text in the edit control portion of a combo box.

Easily the most-used event when dealing with combo boxes and list boxes is the OnClick event. Use this event to determine when a selection has been made in the list box.

NOTE

Clicking on the edit portion of a combo box or the drop-down button does not result in an OnClick event being sent. Only when the list box portion of a combo box is clicked will the OnClick event occur.

The OnChange event can be used to detect changes to the edit portion of a combo box just as it is used with edit controls. The OnDropDown event is used to detect when the drop-down button on a combo box has been clicked. The OnMeasureItem and OnDrawItem events are used with owner-drawn list boxes and owner-drawn combo boxes.

Button, Button, Who's Got the Button?

VCL contains several types of buttons that you can use in your applications. Although not all of them could be considered to be based on the standard Windows button control, I will still address all the button types here. Before we look at the specific button components, though, let's cover some of the basics.

NOTE

When setting the Caption property of a button, use the ampersand (&) just as you would when setting the Caption property of menu items. The character after the ampersand will be underlined and will be the accelerator for the button.

Button Basics

The button components only have about three properties of note.

The ModalResult Property

The ModalResult property is used to provide built-in form closing for forms displayed with ShowModal(). By default, ModalResult is set to mrNone (which is #defined as 0). Use this value

8

for buttons that are used as regular buttons on the form and that do not close the form. If you use any nonzero value for ModalResult, pressing the button will close the form and return the ModalResult value. For example, if you place a button on a form and set the ModalResult property to mrOk, pressing the button will close the form, and the return value from ShowModal() will be mrOk (1). Given that, then, you can do something like the following:

```
int result = MyForm->ShowModal();
if (result == mrOK) DoSomething();
if (result == mrCancel) return;
```

Table 8.7 lists the ModalResult constants that VCL defines.

Table 8.7. VCL ModalResult constants.

Constant	Value
mrNone	0
mrOk	1
mrCancel	2
mrAbort	3
mrRetry	4
mrIgnore	5
mrYes	6
mrNo	7
mrAll	8

NOTE   You don't have to use one of the predefined ModalResult constants for your buttons. You can use any value you like. Let's say, for example, you had a custom dialog box that could be closed by using a variety of buttons. You could assign a different ModalResult value to each button (100, 150, and 200, for example), and you would then know which button closed the dialog box. Any nonzero number is valid, up to the maximum value of an int.

The CD-ROM that accompanies this book contains a program called ButtnTst that demonstrates the use of ModalResult. The program allows you to execute a form containing several buttons. When you click a button, the ModalResult will be reported back on the main form.

The Default **Property**

The Default property is another key property of buttons. Windows has a standard mechanism for dealing with dialog boxes. One of the features of this mechanism is as follows: If a control other than a button has keyboard focus and the user presses the Enter key on the keyboard, the dialog box will behave as if the user had clicked the *default button*. The default button is the button that has the BS_DEFPUSHBUTTON style set (usually the OK button). This feature has been the bane of programmers and the curse of data-entry personnel for years. The Default property is used to set a button as the default button for a form. The default value for this property is false. To make a button the default button, set its Default property to true. If you don't specifically set any button's Default property to true, the form will not close when the user presses the Enter key.

 NOTE

> When the user closes the form by pressing the Enter key, the OnClick handler of the default button (if one exists) will be called before the form closes.

The Cancel **Property**

The Cancel property works with the Esc key in much the same way as the Default property works with the Enter key. When the user presses the Esc key to close a form, the return value from ShowModal() will be the ModalResult value of the button whose Cancel property is set to true. If no button has its Cancel property set to true, mrCancel will be returned if the user uses the Esc key to close the form (mrCancel is equal to 2; see Table 8.7).

 NOTE

> Closing a form by clicking the system close box or by pressing Alt+F4 will result in mrCancel being returned from ShowModal() as you would expect. Pressing the Esc key, however, will result in a return value of the ModalResult property being set to whatever button has the Cancel property set to true. The OnClick handler for the Cancel button will be called before the form closes. No OnClick handler is called if the user uses the system close box or Alt+F4 to close the form. Be sure to anticipate the different ways users might use (or abuse) your forms.

 NOTE

> You may have more than one button with a Default property set to true. Likewise, you may have more than one button with the Cancel

property set to true. However, when the user presses Enter on the keyboard, the first button in the tab order that has its Default property set to true will be invoked. Similarly, when the user presses the Esc key to close the form, the return value from ShowModal() will be the ModalResult value of the first button in the tab order that has its Cancel property set to true.

The Enabled Property

Earlier I discussed the Enabled property when I discussed components in general. This property is used a lot with buttons to enable or disable the button depending on the current state of the program or of a particular form. When a button is disabled (its Enabled property is set to false), its text is grayed out, and the button does not function. In the case of buttons with bitmaps on them (BitBtn and SpeedButton), the bitmap will also be grayed out automatically.

Button components have only one method of interest: the Click() method, which simulates a mouse click. When you call Click() for a button, the OnClick event of the button is executed just as if the user had clicked the button. As for events, typically only the OnClick event is used.

Now let's take a look at the different button components C++Builder provides.

The Button Component

The standard Button component is sort of like actor Danny DeVito—he ain't pretty, but he sure gets a lot of work. There really isn't anything to add concerning the standard Button component. It has a default Height property value of 25 pixels and a default Width property value of 75. Typically you will place a button on a form and respond to its OnClick event, and that's about it.

The BitBtn Component

The BitBtn component is a perfect example of how a component can be extended to provide additional functionality. In this case the standard Button component is extended to allow a bitmap to be displayed on the face of the button.

The BitBtn component has several properties over what the Button component provides. All these properties work together to manage the bitmap on the button and the layout between the bitmap and the button's text. They are explained in the following sections.

The `Glyph` **Property**

The `Glyph` property represents the bitmap on the button. The value of the `Glyph` property is a picture, or glyph.

NEW TERM   A *glyph* is a picture that is typically in the form of a Windows bitmap file (BMP).

The glyph itself consists of one or more bitmaps that represent the four possible states a button can be in: up, down, disabled, and stay down. If you are creating your own buttons, you can probably get by with supplying just one glyph, which the `BitBtn` component will then modify to represent the other three possible states. The bitmap will move down and to the left when the button is clicked and will be grayed out when disabled. The glyph in the stay-down state will be the same as in the up state, although the button face will change to give a pressed look.

If you provide more than one glyph, the glyphs must all be the same height and width and must be contained in a bitmap strip. The bitmaps that ship with C++Builder provide two glyphs. Figure 8.5 shows the bitmap for the print button that comes with C++Builder (`PRINT.BMP`) in both its actual size and zoomed in to show detail. Note that the two glyphs each occupy the same width in the bitmap.

Figure 8.5.

The `PRINT.BMP` *bitmap.*

 TIP

The pixel in the lower-left corner of the bitmap is the color that will be used for the transparent color. Any pixels in the bitmap having that color will be transparent when the glyph is displayed on the button. You must keep this in mind when designing your bitmaps. If you are not using transparency, you will need the pixel in the lower-left corner to be a color not present anywhere else on the bitmap.

To set the glyph for a BitBtn, double-click the Value column in the Object Inspector next to the Glyph property. The Image Editor will be displayed, and you can choose the bitmap that will be used for the glyph.

NOTE

> The standard button glyphs that come with C++Builder are 15×15 pixels in size. This size fits well with the standard button height of 25 pixels. Your glyphs can be any size you like, but the BitBtn component makes no effort to size the button according to the size of the bitmap. If you use larger glyphs, you will have to size the button accordingly.

The Kind Property

The Kind property is a nice feature of the BitBtn component that allows you to choose from several predefined kinds of buttons. The default value for the Kind property is bkCustom, which means that you will supply the glyph and set any other properties for the button. Choosing any of the other predefined kinds will result in these five things happening:

☐ The Glyph property is automatically set for the kind of button chosen.

☐ The Cancel or Default properties are modified according to the kind of button chosen.

☐ The Caption property is modified for the type of button chosen.

☐ The ModalResult property is set according to the kind of button chosen.

☐ The button on the form is updated to reflect all these settings.

For instance, if you set the value of Kind to bkOK, the button will become an OK button. The glyph is set to a green check mark, the Cancel property is set to false, the Default property is set to true, the ModalResult property is set to mrOk, the Caption property is set to OK, and the results show up on the form. You can always override any of the properties modified by changing the Kind property, but it is not usually necessary to do so. Figure 8.6 shows the Button Test program from the CD-ROM that comes with this book, with the BitBtn Test form displayed. The form contains each of the predefined button types available plus one custom button.

The Layout Property

The Layout property determines where the button is placed relative to the text. The default is blGlyphLeft. You can also choose to place the glyph on the face of the button to the right of the text, above the text, or below the text.

Figure 8.6.

The predefined
BitBtn *types.*

The Margin **Property**

The Margin property specifies the margin between the glyph and the edge of the button (which edge this property affects is determined by the value of the Layout property). The default is -1, which centers the glyph and the text in the button. Enter any positive value to set an absolute margin (in pixels).

The NumGlyphs **Property**

The NumGlyphs property specifies the number of glyphs you have in your bitmap strip for a particular button. You can supply from one to four glyphs, as mentioned. The glyphs must appear in the bitmap strip in this order: Up, Disabled, Down, Stay Down.

The Spacing **Property**

The Spacing property controls the distance, in pixels, between the glyph and the button's text. The default value is 4 pixels.

The SpeedButton **Component**

The SpeedButton component was designed to be used on speedbars. It is different from the Button and BitBtn components in that it is not a windowed component. This means that a speed button cannot receive input focus and cannot be tabbed to. On the other hand, the SpeedButton component has several things in common with the BitBtn component. The way in which the Glyph property is handled by the SpeedButton component is exactly the same as with the BitBtn component, so I'm not going to go over that ground again. There are a couple major differences, though, so let's go over those.

By default, speed buttons are square and are 25×25 pixels. Your speed buttons may be any size you like and can contain text, although typically speed buttons do not contain text. There are some properties specific to speed buttons that you should be aware of, which I've broken down in the following sections.

The GroupIndex **Property**

Speed buttons can be grouped to make them behave like radio buttons (radio buttons are discussed later in the chapter in the section "Radio Buttons and Check Boxes"). When one button in the group is pressed, it stays down, and the button that was previously pressed pops up again. To group speed buttons, simply assign the same value to the GroupIndex property for all buttons in a group. (The default value of 0 indicates that the button is not part of any group.) To illustrate, do the following exercise:

1. Create a blank form and place five speed buttons on the form. (I won't bother with adding glyphs to the buttons in this simple exercise, but you certainly may if you want.)

2. Select all the buttons and change the value of the GroupIndex property to 1. The GroupIndex for all buttons will be changed to 1.

3. Optional: Change the Down property of one of the buttons to true.

4. Click the Run button to compile and run the program.

When you run the program, click on several of the buttons. You will notice that only one button can be in the down state at one time. As you can see when you assign a nonzero value to GroupIndex, the speed buttons change their behavior. A speed button with a GroupIndex of 0 pops back up when you click it, whereas a speed button that is part of a group stays down when clicked.

The AllowAllUp **Property**

By default, one button in the group must be down at all times. You can change that behavior by setting the AllowAllUp property to true. Doing this for one button automatically changes the AllowAllUp property for all other buttons in the group to true as well. Now you can have any one button in the group selected or no buttons at all.

TIP

Sometimes you want a speed button to act as a toggle button. A toggle button is used to turn an option on or off and is not part of a button group. To make an individual speed button a toggle button, assign a nonzero value to its GroupIndex property and set its AllowAllUp property to true. Be sure to set the GroupIndex property to a value not used by any other components on the form. When the user clicks the button, it stays down. When the button is clicked again, it pops back up.

The Down Property

The Down property, when read, returns true if the button is currently down and false if it is not. When written to, the Down property can be used to toggle a button as pressed or not pressed. Writing to the Down property has no effect unless the speed button is part of a group.

Radio Buttons and Check Boxes

Radio buttons and check boxes are specialized buttons but are, in the end, still buttons. I'm not going to spend a lot of time discussing these two buttons because implementing them is pretty straightforward. Both the RadioButton and CheckBox components have a property called Checked that can be used to set the check state and can be read to retrieve the current check state.

The radio button is usually used in a group of buttons. A radio button typically signifies a group of options, only one of which can be selected at one time (like a group of speed buttons, which you just learned about). Although you can use a radio button by itself, it is not recommended because it is confusing to your users. When tempted to use a radio button by itself, use a check box instead—that's what a check box is for, after all.

Any buttons placed on a form will automatically be considered part of the same group. If you have more than one group of radio buttons, and those groups need to operate independently of one another, you need to use a RadioGroup component. This component allows you to quickly set up a group of radio buttons with a 3D frame around the buttons and a caption as well. To illustrate this concept, do the following exercise:

1. Create a blank form or use the form you created in the previous exercise. Place a RadioGroup component on the form.

2. Locate the Items property and double-click the Value column.

3. The String list editor is displayed. Type the following lines in the String list editor:

   ```
   Redtailed Hawk
   Peregrine Falcon
   Gyrfalcon
   Northern Goshawk
   ```

4. Click OK to close the String list editor. The group box is populated with radio buttons containing the text you typed.

5. Change the Caption property of the radio group box to Apprentice Falconers Can Legally Possess:.

6. Click Run to compile and run the program.

When you click one of the radio buttons, the previously selected button pops up as expected. Using the RadioGroup component, you can put more than one group of radio buttons on a form. Like the ListBox and ComboBox components discussed earlier, the RadioGroup component has an ItemIndex property that you can read at runtime to determine which item in the group is selected. Oh, by the way—the answer to the quiz is Redtailed Hawk (American Kestrel would also have been an acceptable answer, but it was not presented in the list).

 NOTE

> You can also use a GroupBox component to hold radio buttons. The GroupBox component is less convenient to use than the RadioGroup component, but it has more flexibility. You can place any type of control in a group box. Once placed in the group box, the controls and the group box itself can be moved as a unit at design time.

The CheckBox component is used to allow users to turn an option on or off or to indicate to a user that an option is currently on or off. A check box can have up to three states, depending on its style: on, off, or grayed. If the check box's AllowGrayed property is false, it can only be checked or unchecked. When the AllowGrayed property is true, the check box can be any one of the three states. The grayed, or indeterminate, state is handled programmatically. In other words, it's up to you to decide what the grayed state means for your application. If the AllowGrayed property is false (the default), you can use the Checked property to determine whether the check box is checked or unchecked. If the AllowGrayed property is true, you must use the State property to determine (or set) the check box state. State will return either cbChecked, cbUnchecked, or cbGrayed.

 TIP

> To make a check box read-only but not grayed, place it on a panel and change the panel's Enabled property to false.

The Label Component

The Label component is used to display text on a form. Sometimes the label text is determined at design time and never changed. In other cases, the label is dynamic and is changed at runtime as the program dictates. Use the label's Caption property to set the label text at runtime. The Label component has no specialized methods or events beyond what is available with other components. Table 8.8 lists the properties specific to the Label component.

Table 8.8. Properties for the `Label` component.

Property	Description
AutoSize	When set to `true`, the label will size itself according to the text contained in the `Caption` property. When set to `false`, text will be clipped at the right edge of the label.
FocusControl	A label is a non-windowed component, so it cannot receive input focus and it cannot be tabbed to. Sometimes, however, a label serves as the text for a control such as an edit control. In those cases you could assign an accelerator key to the label (using the ampersand) and then change the `FocusControl` property to the name of the control you want to receive focus when the label's accelerator key is pressed.
ShowAccelChar	Set this property to `true` if you want an actual ampersand to show up in the label rather than the ampersand serving as the accelerator key.
Transparent	When this property is set to `true`, the `Color` property is ignored and anything beneath the label shows through. This is useful for placing labels on bitmap backgrounds, for instance.
WordWrap	When set to `true`, text in the label will wrap around to a new line when it reaches the right edge of the label.

The `ScrollBar` Component

The `ScrollBar` component represents a standalone scrollbar. It's standalone in the sense that it is not connected to an edit control, a list box, a form, or anything else. I have not found that the scrollbar is a control I use very frequently. Certain types of applications use scrollbars heavily, of course, but for day-in, day-out applications its use is fairly uncommon. The scrollbar's performance is set by setting the `Min`, `Max`, `LargeChange`, and `SmallChange` properties. The scrollbar's position can be set or obtained via the `Position` property. The `Kind` property allows you to specify a horizontal or vertical scrollbar.

 This book's CD-ROM contains a program called `Scroller` that illustrates the use of scrollbars. Run this program and examine how it works to learn more about the `ScrollBar` component.

The `Panel` Component

The `Panel` component is sort of a workhorse in C++Builder. There is almost no limit to what you can use panels for. Panels can be used to hold speedbar buttons, to display text labels such

8

as a title for a form, display graphics, and to hold regular buttons as well. One of the advantages to a panel is that components placed on the panel become children of the panel. As such, they go with the panel wherever the panel goes. This can be a great aid at runtime and at design time.

Much of the power of the Panel component lies in its Align property. For instance, let's say you want a title to be displayed on the top of a form. Let's further assume that you want it centered no matter how the user sizes the window. By setting the Align property to alTop and the Alignment property to taCenter, your title will always be centered. It's a simple as that.

A panel can have many different appearances. You can alter the panel's appearance by changing the BevelInner, BevelOuter, BorderStyle, and BorderWidth properties. The book's CD-ROM contains a program called PanelEx that demonstrates how the different styles can be used in combination to achieve various visual effects. Figure 8.7 shows the PanelEx program running.

Figure 8.7.

The panel styles example showing different styles.

The Panel component is so versatile that it will take you a while to discover all its possible uses.

And That's Not All...

Unfortunately, there isn't sufficient space here to go over all the components C++Builder provides. You saw the Image component on Day 6, when you created the Picture Viewer program. You also got a brief glimpse at the Bevel component on Day 6 when you built an About dialog box, and the Shape component on Day 7 as part of an exercise on aligning components. These represent just a sampling of the components that are waiting for you. You need to test drive each one of them to determine its usefulness for you.

There is one other group of components that I need to discuss before we move on: the Dialog group.

The Common Dialog Boxes

Windows provides a set of common dialog boxes that any Windows program can use, including

☐ File Open

☐ File Save

☐ Font

☐ Color

☐ Print

☐ Printer Setup

☐ Find

☐ Replace

The common dialog boxes are found on the Dialogs tab of the Component Palette. These components are nonvisual because they do not have a visual design-time interface. The following sections discuss each of these dialog boxes with one exception—I'll leave the discussion of the Print and Printer Setup dialog boxes for later, when I discuss printing.

The Execute Method

One thing that all the common dialog boxes have in common is the Execute() method, which is used to create and display the dialog box. The dialog box is displayed modally except for the Find and Replace dialog boxes, which are displayed modelessly. Execute() returns true if the user clicked the OK button, double-clicked a file name, or pressed Enter on the keyboard. Execute() returns false if the user clicked the Cancel button, pressed the Esc key, or closed the dialog box with the system close box. A common dialog box is often implemented like this:

```
if (OpenDialog->Execute()) {
  // user pressed OK so use the filename
  Memo->Lines->LoadFromFile(OpenDialog->FileName);
}
return;
```

This code displays the File Open dialog box and gets a filename from the user. If the user clicked the OK button, the code inside the if block is executed and the file is loaded in to a Memo component. If OK was not pressed, the code inside the if block is ignored and no action takes place.

NOTE The code used in the previous snippet is another example of C++ shortcut syntax. The first line:

```
if (OpenDialog->Execute()) {
```
is equivalent to this:
```
if (OpenDialog->Execute() == true) {
```
Use either method, but the first is preferred.

The File Open and File Save Dialog Boxes

The File Open and File Save dialog boxes have several properties in common. File Open is used when you want to allow the user to open a file in your application (see Figure 8.8). It is encapsulated in the OpenDialog component. You use the File Save dialog box when getting a filename from the user in order to save a file. It is also used as the Save As dialog box. The File Save dialog box is encapsulated by the SaveDialog component.

Figure 8.8.
A typical File Open dialog box.

The File dialog boxes are fairly easy to use in their most basic form. They do have a few features, however, that need to be explained in order for you to get the full benefit of using them. The following sections examine the properties that are specific to the File dialog boxes.

NOTE

The OpenDialog and SaveDialog components merely retrieve a filename from the user. It is up to the programmer to write code that actually does something with the filename.

The DefaultExt Property

Use the DefaultExt property to set the default extension that the dialog box will use. The *default extension* is the extension that will automatically be appended to the filename if the user does not supply an extension.

The `FileName` Property

The `FileName` property is the most obvious of the File dialog box properties; it holds the text of the file that the user chooses. Set this property before calling the dialog box if you want a filename to show in the edit portion of the File dialog box when it is initially displayed. After the user clicks OK to close the dialog box, this property will contain the full path and filename of the file chosen.

The `Files` Property

`Files`, a read-only property, is a `TStrings` instance that contains the list of files selected when multiple file selection is enabled.

The `Filter` Property

The `Filter` property contains a list of the file types from which the user can choose. The file types are displayed in the File of type: combo box in the file dialog box. You can set `Filter` to reflect types of files specific to your application. For instance, a simple text-editing program could have the filter set to show files of type `TXT`, `INI`, and `LOG`, to name just a few. The filter can easily be set at design time through the Filter Editor dialog box. To invoke the Filter Editor, double-click the Value column next to the `Filter` property in the Object Inspector. Figure 8.9 shows the Filter Editor for a File Open dialog box, as described previously.

Figure 8.9.

The Filter Editor dialog box.

The Filter Name column contains a textual description of the file type. The Filter column is the actual file mask that will be used to display files of that type.

Although you can enter the filter string directly in the Value column of the Object Inspector, it is easiest to use the Filter Editor. If you are only using a single filter, you can type it directly into the Value column for the `Filter` property. Separate the description and filter with a pipe. For instance, to have a single filter for all file types, you would enter the following:

```
All Files (*.*)¦*.*
```

The FilterIndex **Property**

The FilterIndex property is used to set the filter that will be used when the dialog box is initially displayed. The index is not zero based as you might expect, however. The first filter in the list is 1, the second is 2, and so on. For example, refer to Figure 8.9. If you wanted the All Files filter to be the one initially displayed, you would set the FilterIndex property to 4.

The InitialDir **Property**

The InitialDir property is used to specify the directory that will be used as the initial directory when the File dialog box is displayed. If no value is supplied for the InitialDir property, the current directory will be used (as determined by Windows).

> **TIP**
>
> A top-notch Windows program keeps track of the last directory the user used both when opening files and when saving them. Usually this information is stored in the Registry. Before displaying a File Open or File Save dialog box, set the InitialDir to the previous directory the user used. After the user selects a file, update the registry to reflect the new directory if necessary.

The Options **Property**

The Options property controls the way the File dialog box is used. The list of options is too long to list here, but common items include whether you allow new files or directories to be created, whether the Help button is shown on the dialog box, whether long filenames are allowed, whether multiple file selection is allowed, and others. See the C++Builder online help for the OpenDialog and SaveDialog components for complete information.

The Title **Property**

The Title property is used to set or read the title of the File dialog box. If no title is specified, the common dialog box defaults of Open for the OpenDialog component and Save for the SaveDialog component will be used.

> **TIP**
>
> A Save As dialog box is nothing more than a SaveDialog component with the Title property set to Save As.

The File dialog boxes have no events associated with them.

> **TIP**
>
> You can implement a File Open dialog box (or any of the common dialog boxes) at runtime without ever placing an `OpenDialog` component on your form. To accomplish this, create an instance of the `TOpenDialog` class and then call its `Execute()` method:
>
> ```
> TOpenDialog openDlg = new TOpenDialog(this);
> if (openDlg->Execute()) {
>   // do something here
> }
> delete openDlg;
> ```
>
> If necessary, you can set any of the `OpenDialog` component's properties before calling `Execute()`.

The Color Dialog Box

The Color dialog box allows the user to choose a color. When the OK button is clicked, the `Color` property will contain the color information. (Refer to Figure 8.1, which shows the Color dialog box.) The Color dialog box, like the file dialog boxes, has no events to respond to.

The Font Dialog Box

The Font dialog box allows the user to choose a font from the list of fonts available on his or her system. Through the `Device` property, you can choose whether you want screen fonts, printer fonts, or both types of fonts to be displayed. You can limit the maximum and minimum font sizes that the user can select by modifying the `MaxFontSize` and `MinFontSize` properties. As with the File dialog boxes, the `Options` property contains a wide variety of options you can use to control how the Font dialog box functions.

If the user clicks OK, the `Font` property will contain all the information you need to implement the new font. Figure 8.10 shows the Font dialog box in the default configuration.

The Font dialog box has a single event, `OnApply`, that will occur when the user clicks the Apply button on the Find dialog box. The Apply button will not be present on the Font dialog box unless you have first created a valid (not empty) event handler for the `OnApply` event.

The Find and Replace Dialog Boxes

The Find and Replace dialog boxes provide users the capability to enter text to search for and text to replace the found text with, and a variety of search and replace options. The Find dialog box is encapsulated in the VCL component FindDialog, and the Replace dialog box is represented by the ReplaceDialog component. The Replace dialog box, which contains everything found on the Find dialog box, plus the extra replace features, is shown in Figure 8.11.

Figure 8.10.
The Font dialog box.

Figure 8.11.
The Replace dialog box.

Major properties of the FindDialog and ReplaceDialog components include FindText (the text to find), ReplaceText (the text with which to replace the found text), and Options. Obviously, the FindDialog does not have a ReplaceText property. The Options property contains a wide variety of information about the various options that the user had set at the time the Find Next, Replace, or Replace All button was clicked.

The Execute() method for the FindDialog and ReplaceDialog components is a little different than it is with the other common Dialog components. First, the Find and Replace dialog boxes are modeless dialog boxes. As soon as the dialog is displayed, the Execute() method returns. Because the dialog is modeless, the return value from Execute() is meaningless (it's always true). Instead, the Find and Replace dialog boxes use the OnFind and OnReplace events along with the Options property to determine what is happening with the dialog box. The OnFind event occurs when the Find Next button is clicked. The ReplaceDialog has an OnFind event, but it also has an OnReplace event that is fired when the Replace or Replace All button is clicked. Use these events to determine when the user has requested a find or replace action. Your programs should read the Options property to determine how the user intended the find or replace operation to be carried out.

Summary

Today you have had a look into some of the basic components that C++Builder provides. You have learned about components in general, and you have learned about some of the specifics of the components that are based on Windows controls. It is important to understand the basic controls available in Windows and the C++Builder components that represent those controls. Today ends with an examination of the Windows common dialog boxes.

Workshop

The Workshop contains quiz questions to help you solidify your understanding of the material covered and exercises to provide you with experience in using what you have learned. You can find answers to the quiz questions in Appendix A, "Answers to Quiz Questions."

Q&A

Q If I change the `Name` property of a component using the Object Inspector, C++Builder will automatically change all references to that component in my code, right?

A Yes and no. C++Builder will change all references to that component name in C++Builder-generated code, but it will not change any user-written code.

Q The `OpenDialog` component is obviously a visible component. Why is it called a nonvisual component?

A Because it is not visible at design time. It is visible only at runtime when you invoke it with the `Execute()` method.

Q Why is it important to change the `Name` property only with the Object Inspector?

A As you work with the Form Designer, C++Builder writes code based on the `Name` property. If you later change the `Name` property either by directly editing the source files or at runtime, all references to that form or component will be incorrect and will likely lead to your program refusing to compile or crashing at runtime.

Q I seem to be using properties more than methods when dealing with my components in code. Is that wrong?

A Not at all. In fact, that's the way VCL components are designed. A well-written component makes maximum use of properties. For this reason you may not use a component's methods very often. Use methods when necessary, but otherwise use properties to manipulate your components at runtime.

8

Q **I'm responding to both the** OnDblClick **and the** OnClick **events for a component. Every time I double-click on a component, both the** OnClick **and the** OnDblClick **event handlers are called. Why?**

A Because when you double-click on a component, Windows will generate both single- and double-click messages. You can't prevent it, so you will have to write code to account for that fact.

Q **I want to use the features of the** TStrings **class to keep a list of strings my program needs in order to operate. The compiler won't let me use a** TStrings **object. What do I do?**

A Use a TStringList object instead. The TStringList class is provided for this purpose.

Q **I need a single-line edit control to be right-justified, but there is no** Alignment **property for the** Edit **component. Can I right-align text in a single-line edit?**

A No. What you can do, though, is use a Memo component and make it appear to be a regular Edit component. Be sure to set the Memo component's WantReturn property to false, its Height to the height of a standard edit component (21 pixels), and its Alignment property to taRightJustify. The component will give all appearances of being a single-line edit control that is right-justified.

Q **I have a form that has several buttons on it. When the user closes the form using the Esc key, I get one return value from** ShowModal()**, and when the user closes the form with the system close box I get a different return value from** ShowModal()**. Why?**

A You have a button on the forum whose Cancel property is set to true. When the user presses the Esc key, the ModalResult value of that button is used as the return value from ShowModal(). When the user closes the form with the system close box, you will always get a return value of mrCancel. You need to be prepared to take into account both ways a form can be closed.

Quiz

1. Can you change the Name property of a component at runtime?
2. What property is used to enable and disable controls?
3. How can you tell at runtime that a button is disabled?
4. What is the difference between the long hint and the short hint?
5. Name three of the four methods that can be used to force a control to repaint itself.

6. How many types of combo boxes are there?

7. How is the `ModalResult` property used for button components?

8. Which component is often used as a container for other components?

9. What is the return value from the `Execute()` method for an `OpenDialog` component if the user clicks OK to close the dialog box?

10. How do you make the `SaveDialog` component into a Save As dialog box?

Exercises

1. Create a program that contains two edit components. When the user types information in the first control, make it appear in the second edit control as it is entered.

2. Create a program with a list box. Write code to load the list box from a text file prior to the application being visible.

3. Add an edit component to the program in exercise 2. When the user selects an item in the list box, have the item's text appear in the edit control.

4. Add a button to the program in exercises 2 and 3. Write code so that when the button is clicked, any text in the edit control is added as a new item in the list box.

5. Create a program that has a `RadioGroup` with four items in the group. Add a label component whose text changes depending on which radio button is clicked.

6. Create a program that has a title on the form that is centered at the top of the form regardless of how the program's window is sized.

7. Modify the program in exercise 6 so that the font of the title can be changed to any font available on the system by clicking a button.

8. Reopen the Picture Viewer program created on Day 5. Modify the `OpenDialog` and `SaveDialog` components so that their `Filter` properties allow for selection of Bitmap (`*.bmp`), Metafile (`*.wmf`), Icon (`*.ico`), and All Files (`*.*`).

Day 9

Creating Applications in C++Builder

by Kent Reisdorph

C++Builder provides a variety of tools that aid in creating forms, dialog boxes, and applications. Today you will learn about

- ☐ The Object Repository
- ☐ The Dialog Wizard
- ☐ The Application Wizard
- ☐ Adding functions and data members to your code
- ☐ Using resources in your C++Builder applications

For starters, I'll spend some time discussing the Object Repository, which is where C++Builder stores any prebuilt forms or applications for you to reuse. Following that discussion, you will meet the Wizards, which guide you step-by-step through the creation process. You provide the details, and C++Builder builds the form or application based on the information you provided. The Wizards are a powerful tool for rapid application development. Finally, we'll close the day talking about how you can use resources in your C++Builder applications. So let's get to it.

Working with the Object Repository

The Object Repository dialog box is the means by which you can select predefined objects to use in your applications.

> **NOTE**
>
> The Object Repository is a text file that contains the information that the Object Repository dialog box displays. For the sake of simplicity, I will refer to the Object Repository dialog box and the repository file collectively as simply the Object Repository.

The Object Repository allows you to do the following:

- ☐ Choose a predefined application, form, or dialog box to implement in your application
- ☐ Add your own forms, dialog boxes, and applications to the Object Repository
- ☐ Add other objects to your application such as ASCII text files and additional source code units
- ☐ Manage data modules
- ☐ Create new components
- ☐ Invoke Wizards to help you build a dialog box or an application

Object Repository Pages and Options

The Object Repository is displayed automatically whenever you choose File | New from the main menu. Figure 9.1 shows the Object Repository window as it initially appears if you choose File | New with no project open.

Figure 9.1.
The Object Repository window.

NOTE

Strange as it may seem, the Object Repository dialog box is titled New Item, and the Object Repository configuration dialog box is titled Object Repository. To say that this is confusing is a bit of an understatement.

The Object Repository has several pages, each of which contains different objects that you can incorporate into your applications. As you can see from Figure 9.1, the New tab is what is initially selected when the Object Repository is displayed. Table 9.1 lists the Repository pages and a description of the items you will find on each page.

Table 9.1. The Object Repository pages.

Page/Tab	Description
New	Allows you to create a new application, console app, form, or source code unit for use in your application. Also allows you to create advanced objects such as DLLs, components, and data modules.
Forms	Allows you to create standard forms from prebuilt forms such as an About box, a database form, or Quick Reports.
Dialogs	Presents choices of several different basic dialog box types from which you can choose. Also contains the Dialog Wizard.
Data Modules	Allows you to choose from data modules in your application.
Projects	Displays full projects that you can choose from to initially set up an application. Also contains the Application Wizard.

NOTE

If you invoke the Object Repository when you already have a project open, you will see an additional tab in the Object Repository. The tab will have the name of your project on it. Clicking on this tab will display a page that contains all the objects currently in the project. This allows you to quickly reuse a form or other object by simply selecting it from the Object Repository.

Across the bottom of each page you see three radio buttons. These buttons, labeled Copy, Inherit, and Use, determine how the selected object is implemented.

NOTE

Depending on the object selected, some (or all) of the radio buttons may be disabled. For example, all three radio buttons are always grayed out when the New page is displayed. This is because Copy is the only option available for objects on this page, so C++Builder grays out all choices and applies the Copy option automatically.

Copy

When you choose the Copy radio button, C++Builder creates a copy of the object selected and places it in your application. At that point you are free to modify the object in any way you choose. The original object in the Repository is not altered when you make changes to the new object in your application.

To illustrate, let's say you had an often-used form (a form in the traditional sense, not in the C++Builder sense) printed on paper—a work schedule, for instance. Let's say that you wanted to fill in that form with scheduling information. You wouldn't modify the original form because it would then be unusable for future reuse. Instead, you would put the original form in the copy machine, make a copy, and then return the original to some location for safekeeping. You would then fill out the copy of the form as needed. Making a copy of an object in the Repository works in exactly the same way. You are free to modify the copy in any way you choose while the original remains safely tucked away. Making a copy is the safest method of object usage.

Inherit

The Inherit method of usage is similar to Copy, but with one important distinction: The new object is still tied to the base object. If you modify the base object, the newly created object will be updated to reflect the changes made to the base object. The inverse is not true, however. You can modify the new object without it having any effect on the base object.

To illustrate this type of object usage, consider the following scenario: Frequently, information managers will create a spreadsheet in a spreadsheet program and use the contents of that spreadsheet in a word processing program in order to present a report. They will usually opt to link the data to the spreadsheet when pasting from the Clipboard or importing the spreadsheet into the word processor. That way, when changes are made to the spreadsheet, the word processing document is automatically updated to reflect the new data. In the same way, changes made to a base form will automatically be reflected in all forms inherited from the base form. Use the Inherit option when you want to have several forms based on a common form that might change at some point. Any changes in the base form will be reflected in all inherited forms.

Use

The Use option is not common. When you use an object, you are opening that object directly for editing. Use this option when you have saved an object in the Repository and you want to make permanent changes to that object. In the section "Inherit" I said that changes made to a base form would be reflected in all inherited forms. If you wanted to make changes to a base form, you would open it in the Object Repository with the Use option.

Now What?

Exactly what takes place when you select an object from the Object Repository depends on several factors. The factors include the type of object selected, whether a project is currently open, and the usage type you have selected (Copy, Inherit, or Use). If you have an application open and you choose to create a new application from the Object Repository, you will be prompted to save the current project (if necessary) before the new project is displayed.

 TIP   Choosing File | New Application from the main menu is a shortcut for starting a new application. It is equivalent to choosing New from the main menu and then choosing the Application object from the Object Repository. Similarly, the New Form, New Data Module, and New Unit items on the main menu are shortcuts for their equivalents in the Object Repository.

Creating a new form from the Object Repository is treated differently based on whether a project is open at the time. If a project is open, the new form is added to the application as a form/unit pair. If no project is open, a new form and unit are created as a standalone form. Use this option when creating a new base form to add to the Object Repository.

If you choose to create a new unit or text file, the new file is simply created in the Code Editor (and, in the case of a new unit, added to the current project). You might create a new text file for several reasons. For example, let's say you wanted to implement a configuration file (an .INI file) in your application. You could create a new text file in the Object Repository in order to initially create the configuration file. You create a new unit any time you want to start a new source file for your application that is not associated with a form.

Choosing a new DLL or console application results in a new project being created with the project set up for a DLL or console application target. Creating a new Automation, Component, or Thread object will result in a dialog box being presented that asks for more information about the object you are creating.

The Object Repository Views

The actual Object Repository window is a Win32 list view control similar to the right side of Windows Explorer (where the files are listed). As such, it has several views that you can choose from: Large Icons, Small Icons, List, and Details. By default, the view is set to Large Icons. To change the Object Repository view, right-click on the Object Repository and choose the view you want from the Object Repository speed menu. Figure 9.2 shows the Object Repository with the Dialogs page selected and the view set to Details.

Figure 9.2.

The Object Repository in Details view.

The Object Repository speed menu also shows several sorting options. You can sort by object name, description, date, or author.

TIP | When the Object Repository is in the Details view, you can click on a column header (Name, Description, Date, or Author) to instantly sort by that category.

Creating New Objects from the Object Repository

9

Certainly the most basic use of the Object Repository is creating a new object using an object from the Repository. To illustrate, let's create a simple application with a main form, an About dialog box, and a second form. Follow these steps:

1. Be sure no other application is open. Choose File | New from the main menu. The Object Repository is displayed.

2. Click on the Application icon and click OK to create a new application. A new application is created, and a blank form is displayed.

3. Place two buttons on the form. Change the Caption property of one of the buttons to About... and the Caption property of the other button to Display Form2. Change the Name properties if desired.

4. Choose File | New from the main menu. The Object Repository is again displayed.

5. Click on the Forms tab in the Object Repository.

6. Choose the About box object. Be sure that the Copy radio button is selected, and click OK to create a new About Box form. The About box is displayed. Change any properties as needed.

7. Modify the About box as desired. (Enter your own information, change the icon, change the size and position, and so on.)

8. Select File | New from the main menu again. The Object Repository is displayed for the third time.

9. Click on the Forms tab and choose the Dual list box object. Click OK to close the Object Repository. A dual list box form is displayed. (I had you choose this one just so you could see it.)

10. Write event handlers for the two buttons that display the About box and the second form as required.

11. Compile, run, and test the program.

No, this program doesn't do anything, but it does illustrate how you can use the Object Repository to quickly prototype an application. As time goes on, you will add your own custom objects to the Object Repository and then you can really be effective! Let's look at that next.

Adding Objects to the Object Repository

The Object Repository wouldn't be nearly so effective a tool if you couldn't add your own objects to it. But you can add your own objects and you should. Adding often-used objects to the Object Repository makes you a more efficient and, therefore, a more valuable programmer. There is no point in reinventing the wheel over and over again. Once you have an application, a form, or another object created, save it to the Repository so that you can reuse it whenever you want. Of course, you don't want to save every form you ever created in the Object Repository—just the ones you will reuse most often.

You can set out to create an object with the express purpose of adding it to the Repository, or you can add an object to the Repository during the normal course of application development. (The term *object* is pretty broad, so I'll have to use a specific example in order for this to make sense.) Let's say that you create an About box form while creating an application. Suddenly it dawns on you that you'd like to save this About box to use in all your programs. After all, it has your company name, logo, and all the copyright information laid out just the way you like it, so it'd be a shame to have to re-create the same About box for every application you write. No problem—just add it to the Repository. To add a form to the Object Repository, first save the form (if you don't save the form, you will be prompted to save it before continuing). Next, right-click the mouse anywhere on the form and choose Add To Repository from the Form Designer speed menu. When you do, the Add To Repository dialog box is displayed, as shown in Figure 9.3.

Figure 9.3.

The Add To Repository dialog box.

The Forms list box on the left side of this dialog box lists the current forms as well as any other objects in the application (such as data modules). First, select the form that you want to add to the Object Repository.

NOTE   The active form in the Form Designer will already be selected in the Forms list box in the Add To Repository dialog box.

9

Now enter the object's title. This is the title that will appear below the icon in the Object Repository. The Description field is used to give further information about the object. This description is displayed when the Object Repository view is set to display all object details (refer back to Figure 9.2). The Author field is where you type your name as the author of the object. You can enter your personal name, a company name, or any other identifying name.

NOTE   The prebuilt objects in the Object Repository that come with C++Builder have "Borland" as the author name.

The Page field is used to select the Object Repository page where the new object will be placed. You can choose from one of the existing pages or simply type in the name of a new page in the Page field. If a page with the name you type does not exist, C++Builder will create a new page with that name. Near the bottom of the dialog box is a button labeled Browse that you can use to select the icon used to represent the object.

TIP   You can choose icons from the CBuilder\Images\Icons directory or the CBuilder\Objrepos directory. The icons in the Cbuilder\Objrepos directory are the icons used by C++Builder for the items it places in the Object Repository.

Once you've filled in all the fields and selected an icon, you can click OK to add the object to the Repository. The object is added to the Object Repository on the page you specified. You can now reuse that object any time you want. As you can see, adding an object to the Object Repository is nearly as easy as using an object.

WARNING

When you add an object to the Object Repository, C++Builder makes an entry in the Object Repository file that describes the object. This information includes the pathname where the form and source file for the object are located. If you move or delete an object's form or source file, you will not be able to use the object from the Object Repository.

Adding Projects to the Object Repository

Adding projects to the Object Repository is not much different from adding individual forms. To add a project to the Object Repository, choose Project | Add To Repository from the main menu. The Add To Repository dialog box is displayed just like it is when you're adding objects to the Repository, except the Forms list box is not displayed. Fill in any required information (Title, Description, Author, and so on) and click OK, and the project is added to the Repository.

After you are familiar with C++Builder, you should create an application shell that has the features you use most often in your applications. Each time you start a new standard application, make a copy of the shell from the Object Repository. This way you can have your menus, speedbar, About box, and other standard dialog boxes all set up and ready to go in a matter of seconds. Once the new application has been created, it can then be modified as with any project. You can add new forms, delete any unwanted forms, and so on.

Object Repository Housekeeping

You can manage the pages and objects in the Object Repository by using the Object Repository configuration dialog box.

To view the Object Repository configuration dialog box, choose Options | Repository from the main menu or, if you have the Object Repository open, choose Properties from the Object Repository speed menu. The configuration dialog box is displayed, as shown in Figure 9.4.

This dialog box allows you to delete objects and pages from the Object Repository, move objects from one page to another, change the order of pages in the Object Repository, and more. The list of pages in the Object Repository is displayed in the list box labeled Pages on the left side of the dialog box. When you select one of the pages in the Pages list, the list box on the right (labeled Objects) displays the objects contained on that page.

9

Figure 9.4.

*The Object Repository
configuration dialog
box.*

 NOTE

The Pages list box has two important items of note. First, notice that
the New page, which is always the first page displayed when the Object
Repository is invoked, is not listed here. The New page is fixed and
cannot be altered. Also notice that there is an item labeled [Object
Repository]. This item is actually a list of all items on all pages of the
Repository.

Managing Objects

Before you can edit, delete, or move an object, you must first select it. To select an object,
click on the object in the Objects list box. After you have selected an object, you can edit it
by clicking on the Edit Object button. Editing an object allows you to change the object's
name, description, and author, as well as the page on which the object is displayed.

 TIP

To quickly edit an object, double-click on the object in the Objects
list box.

You can delete an object by selecting it and then clicking the Delete Object button. You are
prompted for confirmation before the object is removed from the page and from the
Repository.

 NOTE

When an object is deleted from the Object Repository, it is removed
from the object repository file and no longer shows up on any page in

> the Object Repository. However, the actual form file and source file that describe the object are not deleted from your hard drive.

Objects can be moved from one page to another by simply dragging the object from the Objects list box to the Pages list box. Drop the object on the page on which you want the object to be located, and the object is moved.

Managing Pages

The previous section deals with editing, deleting, and moving individual objects. You may also add, delete, or remove Object Repository pages through the Object Repository configuration dialog box. Before you can delete a page, you must first delete all the objects on the page. Once a page is empty, you can remove the page by clicking on the page name in the Pages list box and then clicking the Delete Page button. After checking to be sure the page is empty, C++Builder deletes the page from the Object Repository.

You can add a new page by clicking the Add Page button. A dialog box pops up, asking for the name of the new page. Just supply a new page name, and when you click OK the new page appears in the Pages list box. Renaming a page works essentially the same way. When you select a page and click the Rename Page button, a dialog box appears, prompting you for the new page name.

The order in which the pages appear in the Object Repository can be changed. To change a page's position in the page order, click on the page to highlight it and then click the up or down arrow button underneath the Pages list box to move the page up or down in the list. You can also drag a page to its new location if you want.

Setting Default Forms and Projects

The Object Repository configuration dialog box allows you to set three default objects:

- [ ] The default form that will be used when you choose File | New Form from the main menu
- [ ] The default form that will be used as the main form when you choose File | New Application from the main menu
- [ ] The default project that will be used when you choose File | New Project from the main menu

You will notice that, depending on the object you have selected, one or two check boxes appear beneath the Objects list box. If you have selected a form, the New Form and Main Form check boxes appear. If you have selected a project, the New Project check box appears. Making a form or project the default is easy. Let's say you create a main form that you want to be the default main form when a new application is created. Select the form from the Objects list box and click the Main Form check box at the bottom of the screen. When you click OK, that form will now be the default. Similarly, if you have a project that you want to be the default project, first locate it in the Object Repository configuration dialog box, click on it, and then check the New Project check box. From that point on, when you choose File | New Application from the main menu, the project you set as the default will appear.

Building Forms and Applications with the Wizards

C++Builder has two built-in wizards designed to guide you through the application-creation process. The Dialog Wizard aids you in creating dialog boxes, and the Application Wizard helps you create the basic layout of an application.

NOTE

C++Builder has a couple other dialog boxes that it calls wizards. Choosing a new component from the Object Repository, for instance, results in a dialog box that asks you for information regarding the new component. Because that's the extent of the "wizard," I hesitate to group that type of Wizard with the Dialog Wizard and the Application Wizard.

Now let's see what the individual wizards do.

The Dialog Wizard

Truthfully, there isn't very much for a dialog box wizard to do because dialog boxes of any real value will have to be customized with the Form Designer. The Dialog Wizard is started from the Object Repository. First, choose File | New from the main menu to display the Object Repository. Next, switch to the Dialogs page and then double-click the Dialog Wizard icon. The Dialog Wizard is displayed, as shown in Figure 9.5.

Figure 9.5.

The Dialog Wizard.

You can choose to create a single-page dialog box or a tabbed (multipage) dialog box. The icon on the left side of the dialog box shows you what the dialog box will look like at each step. If you choose to create a single-page dialog box, when you click the Next button you will see the next page of the Dialog Wizard (see Figure 9.6).

Figure 9.6.

The second page of the Dialog Wizard.

This page allows you to choose whether you want buttons on the dialog box and, if so, whether you want them on the right side or the bottom of the dialog box. As you can see from Figure 9.6 (see the Finish button?), this is the last page of the Dialog Wizard when you're creating a single-page dialog box. After choosing the button layout you want, click the Finish button to have C++Builder create the dialog box for you.

The new dialog box is displayed on the Form Designer, complete with the features you chose through the wizard. It also has its BorderStyle property set to bsDialog, which is customary for forms used as dialog boxes. Once the Dialog Wizard has created the basic dialog box, you can go to work with the Form Designer to add functionality to the dialog box.

If you choose to create a tabbed dialog box, the second page of the dialog box looks like the one in Figure 9.7.

Figure 9.7.

The Dialog Wizard creating a tabbed dialog box.

This page has a multiline edit control where you can enter the names of the individual tabs you want to see on the dialog box. Enter the text for each tab on a separate line, as illustrated in Figure 9.7. When you click the Next button, you will see the last page of the Dialog Wizard as you saw in Figure 9.6. Choose the location of the buttons, if any, and click the Finish button to have C++Builder create the tabbed dialog box.

 NOTE

The Dialog Wizard is most useful when you're creating tabbed dialog boxes. When you're creating single-page dialog boxes, it is easier to choose one of the predefined dialog boxes from the Object Repository than to go through the Dialog Wizard.

Creating Applications with the Application Wizard

The Application Wizard is a useful tool that can help you quickly set up the shell of an application. To create a new application using the Application Wizard, choose File | New from the main menu. When the Object Repository is displayed, click on the Projects tab and then double-click on the Application Wizard icon.

NOTE

The New Application item on the main menu creates a new application based on the current default project setting. It does not start the Application Wizard as you might expect.

Let's walk through the Application Wizard one page at a time.

Page One: Selecting the Menus

When you start the Application Wizard, the first page is displayed, as shown in Figure 9.8.

Figure 9.8.

Page one of the Application Wizard.

This page allows you to select the items you want on your application's main menu. You can choose to add a File menu, an Edit menu, a Window menu, and a Help menu. Place a check in the box for each menu item you want to appear on your menu bar.

TIP

The Window menu is usually reserved for MDI applications. You probably won't put a Window menu on your SDI application's menu bar unless you have a specialty app that requires it.

NOTE

The menus added by the Application Wizard are a reasonable representation of the menu items that are most commonly used in Windows applications. Remember that the Application Wizard is intended to give you a head start in creating your application. It is up to you to take the basic structure and modify it to make a working application.

After you have chosen the menus you want for your application, click the Next button to move on to the next page.

Page Two: Setting the File Dialog Filters

If you chose to add a File menu to your application, the next page displayed will look like the one in Figure 9.9.

Figure 9.9.

Setting filters for the File dialog boxes.

This page allows you to set the filters that your application's File Open and File Save dialog boxes will use. (Figure 9.9 shows the dialog box after the filters have been added.) Click the Add button to add a new filter. A dialog box is displayed, asking for the description and the filter. Enter the filters exactly as you do when setting the Filter property for the common file dialog box components. Enter the textual description and then the actual file mask (*.bmp, for instance). The Edit, Delete, Up, and Down buttons can be used as necessary to change, delete, or move the filter in the list.

NOTE

Pages two and three will be displayed only if you had previously selected menus on page one of the Application Wizard. More specifically, page two will be displayed only if you selected a File menu on page one.

Page Three: Setting Up the Speedbar

Page three of the Application Wizard aids you in setting up a speedbar for your application. This is possibly the most useful feature of the Application Wizard (not that the other features aren't useful). You can quickly lay out your speedbar using this page. Figure 9.10 shows the third page of the Application Wizard after a speedbar has been created.

Figure 9.10.

Setting up the speedbar.

The list box on the left side of the page, labeled Menus, shows the four menus for which you can add buttons. When you choose one of the menus, the available buttons for that menu are displayed in the list box to the right of the Menus list box (labeled Available commands). To add a speedbar button, click the button in the Available Commands list box and then click the Insert button. The button will be added to the sample speedbar at the top of the page. The Space button can be used to add a separator to the speedbar. Adding separators visually distinguishes groups of buttons. Continue to add buttons and spaces as needed until the speedbar is complete. If you decide to remove a button, just click it in the sample speedbar and then click the Remove button.

NOTE

If you elected not to add a particular menu to your application, no buttons will be shown for that menu group. For instance, if you did not add a Window menu, the Available Commands list box will be empty when you click on the Window item in the Menus list box.

The Application Wizard even takes care of setting the short hint text for the speed buttons. Do you remember creating a speedbar by hand on Day 7, "Working with the Form Designer and the Menu Designer"? Compare that process with the process of creating the speedbar through the Application Wizard. It should be apparent that using the Application Wizard is by far the easiest way to create a speedbar.

TIP

Some specialty applications have a speedbar but do not have a menu. To create a speedbar with the Application Wizard, you must first have created a menu. To work around this, tell the Application Wizard that you want a menu and then build the speedbar. After the application has been generated, you can delete the MainMenu component from the application to remove the menu.

Page Four: Setting the Final Options

The fourth and last page of the Application Wizard allows you to set the program name, the path where the project should be stored on disk, and a few final options. Figure 9.11 shows the last page of the Application Wizard.

Figure 9.11.

The final Application Wizard settings.

The first field on this page is where you specify the name of the application. This is not the name as it appears on the Project Options dialog box, but rather the filename that C++Builder will use to save the project. You will still need to set the application name in the Project Options dialog box. The second field is used to specify the directory where the project should be saved. If you don't know the exact path, click the Browse button to the right of this field and choose the path from the Select Directory dialog box.

TIP

You can use the Select Directory dialog box to create a directory as well as to select a directory. Click the Browse button to display the Select Directory dialog box. Enter the path for the directory you want to create and then click OK or press Enter. C++Builder will prompt you to create the new directory if the directory you entered does not exist.

9

The bottom half of this page gives you three additional options. If you are creating an MDI application, click in the check box marked Create MDI Application. (MDI applications were discussed on Day 6, "The C++Builder IDE Explored: Projects and Forms.") The remaining two check boxes allow you to implement a status bar and hint text for your components.

When you are sure you have made all the choices for your new application, click the Next button. C++Builder creates the application based on the options you specified. C++Builder writes as much code as possible for the application. This doesn't amount to a lot of code, but some of the basic code is already written for you. For example, if you chose a File menu, the `FileOpenClick()` handler has been written and looks like this:

```
void __fastcall TMainForm::FileOpen(TObject *Sender)
{
  if (OpenDialog->Execute())
  {
    //-- Add code to open OpenDialog.FileName --
  }
}
```

The code to execute the File Open dialog box is in place; you only have to write the code that actually deals with the returned filename.

TIP

After you create an Application Wizard project, you can choose Project | Save To Repository to save the project for later use. This will save you the trouble of going through the Application Wizard to create your basic application. You might want to add an About box before saving the project to the Repository.

Using the wizards is fast and easy. You will still need to write the program, of course, but C++Builder gives you a head start by saving you from the tedium of creating the basic application elements. As RAD-friendly as C++Builder is overall, the wizards simplify things even more. The C++Builder wizards are sort of like RAD on RAD!

Adding Functions and Data Members to Code

As you know by now, C++Builder is a great tool for quickly creating the user interface portion of a Windows application. It creates event handlers for you so that you can begin entering code to drive your application. It won't be long, however, before you find the need to start adding more complicated code to your applications. That means adding your own data members and functions to the code that C++Builder generates. For example, a simple application might contain two dozen event handlers of various types. C++Builder creates all these event handlers for you; you simply fill in the blanks with working code. In order to make the application a viable, working application, however, you might have to write another two dozen functions of your own.

Adding your own functions and data members to C++Builder-generated code is not a difficult task, but you need to know the rules or you can get into trouble.

How C++Builder Manages Class Declarations

As you know, when you create a new form in the Form Designer, C++Builder creates three files for you: the form file, the source code unit, and the unit's header. When C++Builder creates the class declaration in the header, it essentially creates two sections. The first section is the part of the class declaration that C++Builder manages. The second section is the part that you manage. On Day 7 you created the ScratchPad program. If you did the exercises at the end of that chapter, you also created an About box for the program and added a few more buttons. Listing 9.1 contains the main form's header as it appears after adding these enhancements.

Listing 9.1. `SPMain.h`.

```
1: class TScratchPad : public TForm
2: {
3: __published:      // IDE-managed Components
4:     TPanel *Panel1;
5:     TBevel *Bevel1;
6:     TSpeedButton *FileOpenBtn;
7:     TSpeedButton *FileSaveBtn;
8:     TStatusBar *StatusBar;
9:     TMainMenu *MainMenu;
10:     TMenuItem *FileMenu;
11:     TMenuItem *FileOpen;
12:     TMenuItem *FileSave;
13:     TMenuItem *FileSaveAs;
14:     TMenuItem *N1;
15:     TMenuItem *FilePrintSetup;
16:     TMenuItem *N2;
```

```
17:        TMenuItem *FileExit;
18:        TMenuItem *FilePrint;
19:        TMenuItem *Edit1;
20:        TMenuItem *EditReplace;
21:        TMenuItem *EditFind;
22:        TMenuItem *N4;
23:        TMenuItem *EditPaste;
24:        TMenuItem *EditCopy;
25:        TMenuItem *EditCut;
26:        TMenuItem *N5;
27:        TMenuItem *EditUndo;
28:        TMenuItem *Help1;
29:        TMenuItem *HelpAbout;
30:        TMenuItem *HelpContents;
31:        TMenuItem *EditSelectAll;
32:        TMenuItem *N3;
33:        TMenuItem *EditWordWrap;
34:        TOpenDialog *OpenDialog;
35:        TSaveDialog *SaveDialog;
36:        TMenuItem *FileNew;
37:        TMemo *Memo;
38:        TPopupMenu *MemoPopup;
39:        TMenuItem *PopupCut;
40:        TMenuItem *PopupCopy;
41:        TMenuItem *PopupPaste;
42:        TSpeedButton *EditCutBtn;
43:        TSpeedButton *SpeedButton2;
44:        TSpeedButton *SpeedButton3;
45:        TSpeedButton *SpeedButton4;
46:        void __fastcall FileOpenClick(TObject *Sender);
47:        void __fastcall FileSaveClick(TObject *Sender);
48:        void __fastcall FileSaveAsClick(TObject *Sender);
49:        void __fastcall FileExitClick(TObject *Sender);
50:        void __fastcall EditSelectAllClick(TObject *Sender);
51:        void __fastcall EditCutClick(TObject *Sender);
52:        void __fastcall EditCopyClick(TObject *Sender);
53:        void __fastcall EditPasteClick(TObject *Sender);
54:        void __fastcall EditWordWrapClick(TObject *Sender);
55:        void __fastcall FileNewClick(TObject *Sender);
56:        void __fastcall EditUndoClick(TObject *Sender);
57:        void __fastcall HelpAboutClick(TObject *Sender);
58:        void __fastcall FormCreate(TObject *Sender);
59: private:         // User declarations
60: public:          // User declarations
61:        virtual __fastcall TScratchPad(TComponent* Owner);
62: };
```

Look at line 3 in the code. Notice the published keyword and the comment that says IDE-managed Components. The section between the published keyword and the private keyword (on line 59 in this case) should be considered off-limits. As they say, don't go there. Leave the published section to C++Builder to manage.

WARNING

Placing any code between the `published` keyword and the `private` keyword can cause problems with your program. In some cases, you might just get compiler or linker errors. In other cases, your program might be beyond repair (unusual but possible). Get in the habit of avoiding the `published` section like the plague.

NOTE

If you're an astute student, you may be scratching your head right now. In the first four chapters we covered the basics of the C++ language. You learned about `private`, `protected`, and `public` class access, but not a word about the `published` keyword. The reason is simple: `published` is not a C++ keyword. The `published` keyword is a Borland extension to C++ and doesn't exist in ANSI standard C++. This keyword was added to allow the C++ language to take advantage of the power of components.

Notice that lines 59 and 60 in Listing 9.1 have comments that say `User declarations`. You can safely place any of your own class data members or class member function declarations in either the `private` or the `public` section of the class declaration.

A Word About Status Bars and Hints

In a moment we're going to add support for hint text displayed in the status bar of the `ScratchPad` program. Before we do, though, you need a brief primer on how hint text is handled.

When the `Application` object's `ShowHint` property is set to `true` (the default), and the mouse cursor is placed over a component that also has its `ShowHint` property set to `true`, a hint event is triggered. The `Application` object has an event called `OnHint` that occurs whenever a hint event is triggered. The Application's `Hint` property will contain the hint text for the control that generated the hint event. An application can use the `OnHint` event to display the hint on a status bar.

The problem is that you can't directly access the `OnHint` event of the `Application` object. What you can do, however, is reassign the value of `OnHint` to point to one of your own functions. Then, when the hint event occurs, the event gets rerouted to your own `OnHint` handler. To do that, you have to write your own event handler for the `OnHint` event. Let's do that next.

Adding a Function to Your Code

 In order to illustrate adding a function to an application, let's implement hint text for the ScratchPad program you wrote earlier. First, reopen the ScratchPad program. If you skipped your homework assignment for Day 7, load ScratchPad from the CD-ROM that accompanies this book.

First, we need to prepare the way. We need to assign hint text to each of the speed buttons and prepare the status bar to receive the hints. Do the following:

1. Be sure the ScratchPad main form is visible. Click the File Open speed button on the main form's speedbar.

2. Locate the Hint property in the Object Inspector and type the following for the hint text:

   New¦Create a New File

3. Change the ShowHint property to true.

4. Repeat steps 2 and 3 for all buttons on the speedbar, adding appropriate hint text for each type of button.

5. Click on the status bar component along the bottom of the main form. Change the SimplePanel property to true. This will allow the full status bar to display a text string through the SimpleText property.

Okay, now we have everything ready to go, so it's time we did what you came here for. We're going to create our own OnHint handler and, not surprisingly, we're going to name the function OnHint(). Let's take this one step at a time. First, we'll add the function declaration to the class declaration. Here goes:

1. Switch to the Code Editor and click on the SPMain.cpp tab.

2. Right-click on the Code Editor window and choose Swap Cpp/Hdr Files from the speed menu. The SPMain.h tab appears next to the SPMain.cpp tab and becomes the active code window.

3. Scroll down through the class declaration for the TScratchPad class until you locate the private section. Add this line of code after the private keyword:

   void __fastcall OnHint(TObject* Sender);

   To give you perspective, the last few lines of the class declaration should now look like this:

```
    void __fastcall FormCreate(TObject *Sender);
private:         // User declarations
    void __fastcall OnHint(TObject* Sender);
public:          // User declarations
    virtual __fastcall TScratchPad(TComponent* Owner);
};
```

So far, so good. Now you've added the function declaration for your new function. Two more steps and we'll be done. First we need to add the actual function to the source unit. After that, we need to assign our new function to the Application object's OnHint event.

1. Click on the SPMain.cpp tab and scroll to the bottom of the file.

2. Enter the following code:

```
void __fastcall TScratchPad::OnHint(TObject* Sender)
{
  StatusBar->SimpleText = Application->Hint;
}
```

3. Go to the Object Inspector. Select the main form, ScratchPad, from the Object Selector.

4. Switch to the Events page in the Object Inspector and double-click in the Value column next to the OnCreate event. The Code Editor is displayed and is ready for you to type code.

5. Enter this code at the cursor:

```
Application->OnHint = &OnHint;
```

The complete FormCreate() function should now look like this:

```
void __fastcall TScratchPad::FormCreate(TObject *Sender)
{
  Application->OnHint = &OnHint;
}
```

6. Compile and run the program. The long hint text you entered will show in the status bar, and the short hint text will be displayed in the tool tip over the button.

Step 2 sets the hint text (from the Hint property of the Application object) to the SimpleText property of the StatusBar class. Step 5 takes the function we created in step 2 and assigns its address to the OnHint event of the Application class. Each time an OnHint event occurs, your OnHint() function is called and the hint text is displayed in the status bar.

Adding a Class Data Member

Adding a class data member to a C++Builder-generated class works in exactly the same way. All you have to do is be sure that you add the data member to the private or public section of the class declaration as you did earlier when adding a class member function.

Deleting C++Builder–Generated Code

There may be a time when you'll need to delete code that C++Builder generated in your application. For instance, you might have a button on a form that, because of design changes, is no longer needed. To delete the button, of course, all you have to do is click it and press the Delete button on the keyboard. No more button. C++Builder deletes the button, but the

OnClick handler associated with that button is still in the code. C++Builder knows that the button associated with that OnClick handler is gone, but it still doesn't delete the event handler because it is possible that other components are using the same event handler. It's up to you to delete the event handler if you want it removed from your code.

The actual deletion of the event handler is an easy task:

- ☐ Delete the function definition from the source unit.
- ☐ Delete the function declaration from the header.

NOTE

> This is the exception to the rule that you should never modify the published section of your form's class declaration.

Before you delete the event handler, you need to make sure that no other components are using that handler. Unfortunately, there is no simple way of determining whether another component is using a particular event handler. You need to be aware of how the components in your application interact.

NOTE

> Some might say that if you are unsure about an event handler being used by other components, just leave it in the code. That's a bad solution, in my opinion. You need to take responsibility for knowing what is in your code and getting rid of any unused functions. Although unused code doesn't hurt anything, it leads to a larger .exe file. In some cases, unused code can lead to performance degradation. Be diligent in paring your programs of unused or inefficient code.

Using Resource Files

Every Windows program uses resources.

NEW TERM *Resources* are the elements of a program that support the program but are not executable code.

A typical Windows program's resources include

- ☐ Accelerators
- ☐ Bitmaps
- ☐ Cursors

- [ ] Dialog boxes
- [ ] Icons
- [ ] Menus
- [ ] Data tables
- [ ] String tables
- [ ] Version information
- [ ] User-defined specialty resources (sound files and AVI files, for example)

Resources are generally contained in a *resource script file* (a text file with an `.rc` extension), which is compiled by a resource compiler and then bound to the application's `.exe` file during the link phase.

Resources are usually thought of as being bound to the executable file. Some resources, such as bitmaps, string tables, and wave files, can be placed in external files (`.bmp`, `.txt`, and `.wav`), or they can be bound to the `.exe` and contained within the application file. You can opt to do it either way. Placing resources in the `.exe` file has two main advantages:

- [ ] The resources can be accessed more quickly because it takes less time to locate a resource in the executable file than it does to load it from a disk file.
- [ ] The program file and resources can be contained in a single unit (the `.exe` file) without the need for a lot of supporting files.

The downside to this approach is that your `.exe` will be slightly larger. The program file won't be any larger than the combined external resource files plus the executable, but the extra size could result in slightly longer load times for the program.

Your exact needs will determine whether you decide to keep your resources in external files or have your resources bound to the `.exe`. The important thing to remember is that you can do it either way (or even both ways in the same program).

A traditional Windows program will almost always contain at least one dialog box and an icon. A C++Builder application, however, is a little different. First, there are no true dialog boxes in a C++Builder application, so there are no dialog box resources per se (C++Builder forms are stored as resources, but they are RCDATA resources and not dialog box resources). A C++Builder application does have a traditional icon resource, though. C++Builder takes care of creating the resource file for the icon for you when you create the application. Similarly, when you choose bitmaps for speed buttons, Image components, or BitBtn components, C++Builder includes the bitmap file you chose as part of the form's resource. The form and all its resources are then bound to the program file when the application is built. It's all more or less handled for you automatically.

There are times, however, when you will want to implement resources aside from the normal C++Builder processes. For instance, if you want to do animation, you will have to have a series of bitmaps that can be loaded as resources for the fastest possible execution speed. In this kind of situation, you are going to need to know how to bind the resources to your C++Builder program file.

The act of binding the resource file to the executable is trivial, actually. It's much more difficult to actually create the resources. Creating basic resources such as bitmaps, icons, and cursors is not difficult with a good resource editor, but creating professional-quality 3D bitmaps and icons is an art. How many times have you seen a pretty decent program with really awful bitmap buttons? I've seen plenty. (Oops, looks like I'm getting off track here.) You can create bitmaps, icons, and cursors with the C++Builder Image Editor. If you are going to create string resources, user data resources, wave file resources, or other specialty resources, you will probably need a third-party resource editor.

NOTE

If you have Borland C++, you can use the Resource Workshop from that package to edit specialty resources. After creating the resources, you will have an .rc file that you can either add to your C++Builder project directly or compile into a .res file using the Borland Resource Compiler (BRCC32.EXE). The Borland Resource Compiler comes with both Borland C++ and C++Builder. Technically, you could create the .rc file with any text editor and compile it with the Resource Compiler, but in reality it is much easier to use a resource editor.

You can add either a .res file or an .rc file to your project via the Project Manager. To add a resource file to a project using the Project Manager, you first choose View | Project Manger from the main menu. When the Project Manager dialog box is displayed, click the Add To Project button. When the File Open dialog box appears, select the resource file you want to add to the project and click OK. The resource file shows up in the Project Manager with the rest of the application's files. I'll discuss the Project Manager in more detail tomorrow.

Listings 9.2 and 9.3 contain the header and main form unit for a program called Jumping Jack. This program shows a simple animation with sound effects. The main form contains just two buttons, an Image component, and a Label component. The Jumping Jack program illustrates several aspects of using resources in a C++Builder application. (The program can be found on the CD-ROM that accompanies this book.) Specifically, it shows how to load a bitmap stored as a resource, how to load and display a string resource, and how to play wave audio contained as a resource. Listing 9.4 is a partial listing of the resource file that is used by the Jumping Jack program. Examine the listings, and then we'll discuss what the program does.

Listing 9.2. `JJMain.h`.

```
 1: //--------------------------------
 2: #ifndef JJMainH
 3: #define JJMainH
 4: //--------------------------------
 5: #include <vcl\Classes.hpp>
 6: #include <vcl\Controls.hpp>
 7: #include <vcl\StdCtrls.hpp>
 8: #include <vcl\Forms.hpp>
 9: #include <vcl\ExtCtrls.hpp>
10: //---------------------------------
11: class TMainForm : public TForm
12: {
13: __published:     // IDE-managed Components
14:     TButton *Start;
15:     TButton *Stop;
16:     TImage *Image;
17:     TLabel *Label;
18:     void __fastcall FormCreate(TObject *Sender);
19:
20:     void __fastcall StartClick(TObject *Sender);
21:     void __fastcall StopClick(TObject *Sender);
22: private:         // User declarations
23:     bool done;
24:     void DrawImage(String& name);
25: public:          // User declarations
26:     virtual __fastcall TMainForm(TComponent* Owner);
27: };
28: //-------------------------------
29: extern TMainForm *MainForm;
30: //-------------------------------
31: #endif
```

Listing 9.3. `JJMain.cpp`.

```
 1: //------------------------------------------------------------
 2: #include <vcl\vcl.h>
 3: //
 4: // have to add this include for the PlaySound() function
 5: //
 6: #include <vcl\mmsystem.hpp>
 7: #pragma hdrstop
 8:
 9: #include "JJMain.h"
10: //------------------------------------------------------------
11: #pragma resource "*.dfm"
12: //
13: // defines for the string resources
14: //
15: #define IDS_UP     101
16: #define IDS_DOWN   102
17:
18: TMainForm *MainForm;
```

```
19: //------------------------------------------------------------
20: __fastcall TMainForm::TMainForm(TComponent* Owner)
21:   : TForm(Owner),
22:   done(false)
23: {
24: }
25: //------------------------------------------------------------
26: void __fastcall TMainForm::FormCreate(TObject *Sender)
27: {
28:   //
29:   // load and display the first bitmap
30:   //
31:   Image->Picture->Bitmap->
32:     LoadFromResourceName((int)HInstance, "ID_BITMAP1");
33: }
34: //------------------------------------------------------------
35: void __fastcall TMainForm::StartClick(TObject *Sender)
36: {
37:   //
38:   // When the Start button is clicked the animation
39:   // loop starts. The bitmap resources are named
40:   // ID_BITMAP1 through ID_BITMAP5 so we'll start with
41:   // a string called "ID_BITMAP" and append the last
42:   // digit when needed.
43:   //
44:   String s = "ID_BITMAP";
45:   //
46:   // a buffer for the string resources
47:   //
48:   char buff[10];
49:   //
50:   // a flag to let us know when we're done
51:   //
52:   done = false;
53:   //
54:   // start the loop and keep looping until the 'Stop'
55:   // button is pressed
56:   //
57:   while (!done) {
58:     //
59:     // loop through the five bitmaps starting with
60:     // 1 and ending with 5
61:     //
62:     for (int i=1;i<6;i++) {
63:       //
64:       // append the value of 'i' to the end of the string
65:       // to build a string containing the resource name
66:       //
67:       String resName = s + String(i);
68:       //
69:       // call a class member function to display the bitmap
70:       //
71:       DrawImage(resName);
72:     }
73:     //
74:     // load the "Up" string resource using the WinAPI
```

continues

Listing 9.3. continued

```
 75:      // function LoadString(), display the string,
 76:      // and tell Windows to repaint the Label
 77:      //
 78:      LoadString(HInstance, IDS_UP, buff, sizeof(buff));
 79:      Label->Caption = buff;
 80:      Label->Refresh();
 81:      //
 82:      // play the 'up' sound using the WinAPI function
 83:      // PlaySound(), play it asynchronously
 84:      //
 85:      PlaySound("ID_WAVEUP",
 86:        HInstance, SND_ASYNC | SND_RESOURCE);
 87:      //
 88:      // pause for a moment at the top of the jump
 89:      //
 90:      Sleep(200);
 91:      //
 92:      // repeat all of the above except in reverse
 93:      //
 94:      for (int i=5;i>0;i--) {
 95:        String resName = s + String(i);
 96:        DrawImage(resName);
 97:      }
 98:      PlaySound("ID_WAVEDOWN",
 99:        HInstance, SND_ASYNC | SND_RESOURCE);
100:      LoadString(HInstance, IDS_DOWN, buff, sizeof(buff));
101:      Label->Caption = buff;
102:      Label->Refresh();
103:      Sleep(200);
104:    }
105: }
106: //----------------------------------------------------------
107: void __fastcall TMainForm::StopClick(TObject *Sender)
108: {
109:    //
110:    // Stop button pressed, so tell the loop to stop executing
111:    //
112:    done = true;
113: }
114: //----------------------------------------------------------
115: //
116: // a class member function to display the bitmap
117: //
118: void
119: TMainForm::DrawImage(String& name)
120: {
121:    //
122:    // load the bitmap from a resource
123:    // using the name passed to us
124:    //
125:    Image->Picture->Bitmap->
126:      LoadFromResourceName((int)HInstance, name);
127:    //
128:    // must pump the message loop so that Windows gets
129:    // a chance to display the bitmap
```

```
130:    //
131:    Application->ProcessMessages();
132:    //
133:    // take a short nap so the animation doesn't go too fast
134:    //
135:    Sleep(20);
136: }
```

Listing 9.4. JJRes.rc.

```
 1: #define IDS_UP      101
 2: #define IDS_DOWN    102
 3:
 4: STRINGTABLE
 5: {
 6:   IDS_UP,  "Up"
 7:   IDS_DOWN, "Down"
 8: }
 9:
10: ID_WAVEUP    WAVE "up.wav"
11: ID_WAVEDOWN WAVE "down.wav"
12:
13: ID_BITMAP1 BITMAP LOADONCALL MOVEABLE DISCARDABLE IMPURE
14: {
15:   '42 4D 76 02 00 00 00 00 00 00 76 00 00 00 28 00'
16:   '00 00 20 00 00 00 20 00 00 00 01 00 04 00 00 00'
17: //
18: //   remainder of bitmap resources follow
```

ANALYSIS Notice lines 23 and 24 in the header for the main form class in Listing 9.2. Line 23 declares a `bool` data member that is used to determine when to stop the animation. The class member function declared on line 24 is used to display the bitmap in the `Image` component.

In Listing 9.3 you will notice that two Windows API functions are used to load the string and wave file resources. On line 78, the `LoadString()` function loads a string resource into a text buffer based on the numerical identifier of the string (see Listing 9.4 to see how the string resources are created). The string is then assigned to the `Caption` property of the label component on the form. On line 83, the `PlaySound()` function is used to play a wave file contained as a resource. The `SND_ASYNC` flag used with the `PlaySound()` function tells Windows to play the sound and immediately return control to the program. This allows the animation to continue while the sound is being played. The `SND_RESOURCE` flag tells Windows that the sound is contained as a resource and not as a file on disk. Both the `LoadString()` and `PlaySound()` functions use the `HInstance` global variable to tell Windows to look in the executable file for the resources.

Lines 1 through 8 of Listing 9.4 illustrate how a string table looks in a resource script file. Creating string tables is very easy with any text editor. On lines 10 and 11, a WAVE resource is created for each of the two wave files, which were previously recorded and reside in the project's directory. When the resource compiler sees the WAVE declaration, it reads the individual sound files and compiles them into the binary resource file.

NOTE

As you can see from Listing 9.4, you can create some resources easily with a text editor. If you have bitmaps or wave audio stored as external files, you can include them in an .rc file as illustrated in Listing 9.4 and have them compiled into the binary resource file using the resource compiler. Later, the binary resource file can be bound to your application's executable file.

Listing 9.4 is a partial listing. Bitmaps are contained in the resource file as numerical data. The resource descriptions for bitmaps can get very long. The rest of the bitmap resource descriptions for the Jumping Jack bitmaps require about 200 lines of resource code, so I decided not to list them all. Figure 9.12 shows Jumping Jack in mid-stride.

Figure 9.12.

Jumping Jack in action.

Creating additional resources for your programs is not rocket science, but it is not exactly trivial, either. It takes some time to realize how it all fits together. You may never need to add additional resources to your applications. If you do, though, it's good to have an idea where to begin. If this section left you a little dazed and confused, don't worry. Over time, it all starts to make sense.

NOTE

Bitmaps, icons, and cursors found in other programs are usually copyrighted material. Do not use resources from any copyrighted program without permission. Further, assume that all programs are copyrighted unless they are specifically said to be freeware. You are free to use the bitmaps, icons, and cursors that are provided with

C++Builder (in the \CBuilder\Images directory) in your applications without permission from Borland.

Summary

The Object Repository is a great tool for reusing previously created forms, dialog boxes, projects, and other objects. The capability to add your own objects to the Repository is a huge advantage when you're doing RAD. The Dialog Wizard and Application Wizard take it a step further and guide you through the creation process. The Application Wizard, in particular, is a very useful tool. In the middle of the chapter you learned how to add data members and functions to the classes that C++Builder generates. The last part of the chapter touches on the different types of resources that you might need to incorporate into your applications and how to add them to your C++Builder projects.

Workshop

The Workshop contains quiz questions to help you solidify your understanding of the material covered and exercises to provide you with experience in using what you have learned. You can find answers to the quiz questions in Appendix A, "Answers to Quiz Questions."

Q&A

Q When would I use the Use option of the Object Repository?

A When you have an object stored in the Object Repository that you want to update or make other changes to.

Q Is there a limit to the number of objects that can be stored in the Object Repository?

A Technically, you can store as many objects as you like. Remember, though, that the purpose of the Object Repository is to help you quickly locate and reuse your forms, dialog boxes, and other objects. If you put too many seldom-used objects in the Object Repository, you will start to lose efficiency because it takes longer to find the specific object you are looking for. It also takes longer for the Object Repository to load and display all those objects.

Q I've got a bunch of old objects in the Object Repository that I don't use any-more. How can I get rid of them?

A Choose Options | Repository from the main menu. The Object Repository configuration dialog box is displayed. To remove an object, first select the object in the Objects list box, and then click the Delete Object button. The object will be removed from the Object Repository.

Q I had an object stored in the Object Repository. Now when I try to use that object I get a message box that says Unable to find both a form and a source file. What's the problem?

A You have either moved or deleted the source and/or form file for the object. The Object Repository keeps track of the directory where the object is stored. If you move or delete the object, the Object Repository is unable to find the object and reports an error.

Q Can I add objects to the New page of the Object Repository?

A No. The New page of the Object Repository is fixed. It cannot be deleted or modified. You'll have to place your objects on another page.

Q I added a function to my main form class. Now I can't compile. What's the problem?

A You probably added the function declaration to the published section of the class declaration accidentally. Be sure that the declaration for your class is in either the public or the private section of the class declaration.

Q I have a resource editor that allows me to decompile resources contained in other programs. This lets me "borrow" bitmaps and other resources from other programs. Is this okay?

A The short answer is "No." You should assume all resources in other programs to be copyrighted material that cannot be freely copied. Consult a lawyer for a qualified opinion.

Q I have a lot of bitmaps and sound files that go with my application. Can I put all those resources in a file other than the program's executable file?

A Yes. You can have resources stored in a dynamic link library (DLL).

Quiz

1. When do you use the Inherit option when selecting an object in the Object Repository?
2. What is the procedure for saving a project to the Object Repository?
3. What happens to inherited forms when you change the base form?
4. Where in the form's class declaration do you place user function declarations?

5. Where do you place the function definition (the function itself) when you add your own functions to C++Builder code?

6. How can you determine who wrote a particular object in the Object Repository?

7. Where do you add and delete pages in the Object Repository?

8. Is it easier to create a basic application from scratch or by using the Application Wizard?

9. What are the two ways you can add a resource file to your project?

10. Can you create a resource script file containing a string table with a text editor?

Exercises

1. Create a new form. Add several components of your choosing to the form. Save the form to the Forms page of the Object Repository with the name BaseForm.

2. Start a new application. Choose File | New to view the Object Repository. Switch to the Forms page. Click the Inherit radio button. Choose the BaseForm object you created in exercise 1 and add it to the application. (Be sure you used the Inherit option.) Save the project and close it.

3. Open the BaseForm object you created in exercise 1. Delete all components on the form and save the form.

4. Reopen the project you created in exercise 2. Display the new form you created in that exercise. Note that the components are all gone. (Remember, you inherited this object, so all changes made to the base form were also made to the inherited form.)

5. Choose Options | Repository from the main menu. Delete the BaseForm created earlier.

6. Create a project using the Application Wizard. Use all menu options and make the application an MDI application. Create a speedbar for the application.

7. Add a multipage dialog box to the application you created in exercise 6. Use the Dialog Wizard.

8. Use the Object Repository to add an About box to the program you created in exercise 6.

9. Create a string table resource with a text editor and compile it with the resource compiler (BRCC32.EXE). **Extra Credit:** Write a program to load the strings and display them on a form.

10. Using a text editor, open the JJRes.rc file contained on the CD-ROM that accompanies this book and examine its contents.

11. Write "I will not borrow bitmaps from other programs." 100 times on the blackboard.

Day 10

More on Projects

by Kent Reisdorph

On Day 6, "The C++Builder IDE Explored: Projects and Forms," you were introduced to C++Builder projects and found out a little about how projects work. Today you will find out about projects in more detail.

You will also learn more about the C++Builder Code Editor. The Code Editor has features that make working with code easier; you'll find out all about those features today.

Everyone Needs a Project

Projects are a fact of life with C++Builder. You cannot create a program without a project. The project makes sure that everything works together to create a working application. In this section I will talk about

☐ The Project Manager

☐ The Project Explorer
☐ The Project Options dialog box
☐ Maintaining and using projects

So, without further ado, let's get to it.

Using the Project Manager

At some point, every project needs some management. It could be that you need to add a new source unit to the project, or maybe you need to remove a source unit. You might need to add other types of files to the project, such as a binary resource file or an import library for a DLL. It is through the Project Manager that you add and remove units and other project files.

The Project Manager Window

The Project Manager window shows you the current files in your project. To view the Project Manager, choose View | Project Manager from the main menu. Figure 10.1 shows the Project Manager window for the ScratchPad program created on Day 6.

The Project Manager window tells you at a glance the state of each file in the project. Files that are up-to-date are displayed in a regular font; files that have been modified but have not yet been saved are shown in a bold font. This serves to remind you which of your files have changed since you last saved the project.

You will notice in Figure 10.1 that the Project Manager file list has three columns. The first column shows the name of the source unit that represents that file. For example, the source unit for the main form of the ScratchPad program is called SPMain.cpp.

The second column shows the name of the form that is associated with that file. The form name is taken from the Name property for the form. In some cases, there is no form associated with a source unit. Each project has a project source file associated with it that contains the VCL startup code for the application. Because there is no form associated with the project source file, the Form column for that file will always be blank. Looking at Figure 10.1, you can see that the project source file for the ScratchPad program is named Scratch.cpp and that the Form column is blank.

The last column in the File list of the Project Manager window contains the path where the file is located. This column is always blank for files that reside in the project's own directory.

The only time this column contains a directory path is when you add a file from a location other than the project's working directory. This column tells you at a glance where each file in your project is located.

Figure 10.1.

The Project Manager window.

>
> **TIP**
>
> The columns in the Project Manager window can be resized. To change a column's width, place your mouse cursor on the dividing line between two columns on the column header. When you see the mouse cursor change to the drag cursor, you can drag right to make the column wider or drag left to make the column narrower.

The status bar of the Project Manager window shows you the project's working directory and the total count of the project's units and forms.

>
> **NOTE**
>
> The status bar text is generous in its count of units contained in the project. The status bar text considers every file in the project a unit whether or not it is actually a source code unit. For example, adding a text file to the project will increment the unit count in the status bar even though the text file does not constitute a code unit.

The Project Manager Speedbar

The Project Manager speedbar can be used to navigate the project. Figure 10.2 shows the Project Manager speedbar buttons.

Figure 10.2.

The Project Manager speedbar.

Add Unit

Use the Add Unit button to add files to the project. When you click this button, the Add To Project dialog box is displayed. The Add To Project dialog box has file filters for the following types of files:

- [ ] C++ source files (`.cpp`)
- [ ] C source files (`.c`)
- [ ] Pascal source files (`.pas`)
- [ ] Library files (`.lib`)
- [ ] Binary object files (`.obj`)
- [ ] Resource script files (`.rc`)
- [ ] Binary resource files (`.res`)

If you add files of any of these types, C++Builder will know what to do with them. For example, if you add a C source file (`.c`), C++Builder will compile it as C rather than C++ (the differences are subtle, and most of you don't care about the differences, but to some programmers it matters). If you add a Pascal file (`.pas`), the Pascal compiler will compile the source file before passing it to the linker. If you add a binary object file (`.obj`), C++Builder passes it to the linker at link time.

NOTE

> You cannot add a unit to a project if a form with the same name already exists in the project. For example, if you have a form called MainForm and try to add a unit from another project that also has a form named MainForm, you will get an error message from C++Builder even if the filenames are different.

NOTE

> Adding files to your project of types other than those listed in this section is not advised. C++Builder will try to compile any unknown file types, and an error message will result.

TIP

You can add more than one source file at a time. To add multiple files, select the files to add in the Add To Project dialog box. When you click OK, all of the files selected will be added to the project.

Remove Unit

Use this option to remove files from the project. Files removed from the project are not deleted from your hard drive, but are just removed from the project compile/link process.

WARNING

Be careful when removing units from your projects. You need to take care not to remove units that are referenced by other units in the project. If you remove units that are required by your project, a compiler or linker error will result. Before removing a unit, be sure that it is not used anywhere in your project.

The Project Manager window itself does not allow multiple selection. If you want to delete several units, you will have to delete them one at a time.

View Unit

When you click the View Unit speed button, the source code for the currently selected unit is displayed in the Code Editor. If no unit is selected or if no source unit exists for the selected unit, this button is disabled. For example, a binary resource file (.res) does not have a source file. If you click on a binary resource file in the Project Manager window, the View Unit button will be disabled.

View Form

The View Form button displays the form associated with the currently selected unit. The form is displayed in the Form Designer. As with the View Unit button, the View Form button will be disabled if no form exists for the selected unit.

TIP

> The Project Manager provides shortcuts for viewing a unit's source file or form. To view a unit's source file, double-click on the unit's filename (in the File column). To view a form, double-click on the form name in the Form column. Double-clicking on units that do not have a source file has no effect.

Project Options

The Project Options speedbar button displays the Project Options dialog box for the project. Project options are discussed later in the chapter, in the section titled "Understanding Project Options."

Update

The Update button updates the project after the project source file has been modified. Normally, this button is disabled. If you manually change the project source file, the Update button is enabled and all files in the Project Manager file list will be grayed out. Clicking the Update button will ensure that all files in the project are reconciled. This button is also enabled after you change the project options.

NOTE

> Saving the project will also resynchronize the project, and you won't need to click the Update speed button.

The Project Manager Speed Menu

The Project Manager has a speed menu to aid you in project management. Many of the items on the speed menu are also available via the speedbar. Figure 10.3 shows the Project Manager speed menu. Table 10.1 lists the speed menu items along with a description of what each item does.

Figure 10.3.

The Project Manager speed menu.

Table 10.1. The Project Manager speed menu items.

Item	Description
Save Project	Saves the project and all source files in the project.
Add Project To Repository	Saves the project to the Object Repository.
New Unit	Creates a blank source code unit and displays the new unit in the Code Editor.
New Form	Creates a blank form and displays the new form in the Form Designer.
Add File	Same as the Add Unit speed button.
Remove File	Same as the Remove Unit speed button.
View Unit	Displays the currently selected unit's source code in the Code Editor.
View Form	Displays the currently selected unit's form in the Form Designer.
View Project Source	Displays the project source file in the Code Editor.
Options	Displays the Project Options dialog box.
Update	Same as the Update speed button.

Several of the speed menu items are also accessible from the main menu, from the Project Manager speedbar, or via keyboard shortcuts.

Exploring Your Projects

The Project Explorer is a nifty little item that gives you a unique look at your project. Figure 10.4 shows the Project Explorer while exploring the ScratchPad program.

Figure 10.4.
The Project Explorer.

The Project Explorer shows all of your project's source units, forms, and components in a tree view. Nodes can be contracted or expanded to reveal more details. Each component is listed under its parent. For example, notice the SpeedBar node in Figure 10.4. In this project, the SpeedBar node is a Panel component that contains several speed buttons. The speed buttons are displayed underneath the panel to show that the panel is the parent of the speed buttons.

The Project Explorer is a hierarchical window. At the top of the Project Explorer you have the project file; under the project file you have the project's source units. Immediately under the project source file is the form file for that unit. Under the form file you have all the components that are direct children of the form. If a component on the form has children, they are listed under their parent, and so on. Figure 10.5 shows how the Project Explorer would look if the component and unit names were replaced with descriptive text.

Figure 10.5.

The Project Explorer hierarchy.

When you click on an item in the Project Explorer, the status bar at the bottom of the Project Explorer window shows information about the item selected. If the item is a source file or form file, the status bar displays the full path and filename of the file. If the item is a component, the status bar displays the class name of the component. For example, if you click a speed button component, the Project Explorer status bar will display TSpeedButton.

Project Explorer Commands

You can do more than just view your objects in the Project Explorer. The Project Explorer has a speed menu that allows you to delete, rename, edit, or select an item. Not all speed menu items are available at all times, however. If you have selected a unit's source file, for example, the Rename speed menu item is disabled because you cannot rename a source file from the Project Explorer. Let's look at the Project Explorer commands individually.

Select

The Select menu item selects the current object and displays the object in the Object Inspector. The effect is the same as if you had selected the object in the Form Designer. If you place the Object Inspector and Project Explorer side by side, you can quickly go through all the objects in your project and view their properties. This command is available only if you have selected a form or a control.

Figure 10.6.
*The Project Explorer
speed menu.*

 NOTE

> Just highlighting (selecting) the control in the Project Explorer tree is
> not the same as selecting it using the Select command. If you want the
> component to be displayed in the Object Inspector, you must first
> select the component in the Project Explorer tree and then choose
> Select from the speed menu.

Edit

The Edit speed menu item allows you to edit the object selected. If the object is a source file,
choosing the Edit menu item will result in the Code Editor being displayed with the selected
file loaded. If the object selected in the Project Explorer window is a form, the Form Designer
comes to the top with the selected form displayed. If the object selected is a component on
a form, the Form Designer is displayed, and the object is selected in the Form Designer as
if you had clicked it with the mouse. In the case of forms and components, the Object
Inspector changes to show the object selected.

Rename

The Rename menu item allows you to change the Name property of a form or a control from
the Project Explorer. To change the name of a component, for example, first select the
component in the Project Explorer window and then choose Rename from the speed menu.
You can then type a new name for the component. As when changing the Name property in
the Object Inspector, the change is immediately reflected throughout your program's source
code.

TIP

The Project Explorer window is a Windows tree view, and as such has the same characteristics as most tree views. Specifically, you can change the text of a particular item in the Project Explorer by clicking once on the item to select it and clicking again to begin editing. This is called *in-place editing*. By using this method you don't have to use the Rename item on the speed menu at all. If you attempt to change the name of an item that cannot be changed via the Project Explorer (a source file, for example), the results of the in-place edit will be ignored.

Delete

The Delete item on the Project Explorer speed menu does exactly as its name indicates. If you select an object in the Project Explorer and choose Delete, that object will be removed from the project.

WARNING

Be careful when deleting objects from the Project Explorer window. The Project Explorer does not have an Undo or Undelete option, so if you delete an object via the Project Explorer by accident, you will have to close the project without saving it and then reopen the project.

The Project Explorer is one of those features that is easy to overlook. Spend some time with the Project Explorer and I'm sure you'll find it a useful feature in application development.

Understanding Project Options

Project options are another of those things that are easy to ignore. For one thing, the defaults are usually good enough when you are just starting out. After all, who has time to worry about all those compiler/linker options when you are just struggling to learn a new programming environment? At some point, though, you will start to become more interested in what all those options do, and it's good to have some reference when the time comes.

In this section we'll look at the Project Options dialog box. You can invoke this dialog box by choosing Options | Project from the main menu, pressing Alt+F6 on the keyboard, or choosing Options from the Project Manager speed menu. The Project Options dialog box is a tabbed dialog box with several pages:

10

☐ Forms
☐ Application
☐ C++
☐ Pascal
☐ Linker
☐ Directories/Conditionals

We'll take a look at each page of the dialog box so that you can understand exactly what each page does. I'll start you out easy by discussing the Forms and Application pages. After that we'll move on to the more complicated stuff.

NOTE

At the bottom of each page of the Project Options dialog box is a check box labeled Default. If you want the current settings to become the default settings for all new projects created, check the Default box. When you click OK, the current settings will become the new default settings.

10

The Forms Page

The Forms page of the Project Options dialog box is where you control how your application handles its forms. You saw this dialog box on Day 5, "C++ Class Frameworks and the Visual Component Model," when you created the Picture Viewer program. Figure 10.7 shows the Forms page of the Project Options dialog box for (what else?) the ScratchPad program.

Figure 10.7.

The Forms page of the Project Options dialog box.

At the top of the Forms page is the Main form combo box. This is where you tell C++Builder which form to display when the application starts. By default, the first form you create will be the main form. If you change your project in such a way that a different form becomes the main form, you will need to change this setting so that the new form becomes the application's main form.

In the middle of the dialog box, you see two list boxes. The list box on the left is labeled Auto-create forms; the one on the right is labeled Available forms. Before I talk about how to use these two list boxes, let's take a moment to talk about auto-creation of forms.

Each time you create a form, C++Builder places that form in the auto-create list for the application. Auto-creation means that C++Builder will construct the form during the application startup process. Forms that are auto-created will display more quickly than forms that are not auto-created. The disadvantage to auto-creation of forms is that your application will use more memory than it would if your forms were not auto-created. Another disadvantage, although probably insignificant, is that your application will take slightly longer to load if you are auto-creating a lot of forms.

NOTE

The first form in the Auto-create forms list box is always the main form. If you change the main form, the new form selected will move to the top of the Auto-create forms list box. Another way to set the main form is to drag-and-drop any one of the forms in the Auto-create forms list box to the top of the list.

The nice thing about auto-creation is that displaying an auto-created form is easy. All you have to do is call that form's Show() or ShowModal() function:

```
AboutBox->ShowModal();
```

If you do not have your forms auto-created by C++Builder, you will have to take the responsibility of creating the form before you use it:

```
TAboutBox* aboutBox = new TAboutBox(this);
aboutBox->ShowModal();
delete aboutBox;
```

This example does not use the C++Builder-generated pointer to the About box. It creates a local pointer, displays the form, and then deletes the pointer as soon as the form is no longer needed. As is often the case in C++ programming, there are several ways to perform this particular task. Because C++Builder always creates a pointer to the form object, I could have written the previous code like this:

10

```
if (!AboutBox->Handle) {
  AboutBox = new TAboutBox(this);
  AboutBox->SetParent(this);
}
aboutBox->ShowModal();
```

This code checks to see if the form has already been created. If it has not, the object is created and then the ShowModal() method is called. This code also calls SetParent() to set the parent of the form to the calling form (the main form, in most cases). It's up to you to decide which method you use, but I prefer the former.

NOTE

Each time you create a form in the Form Designer, C++Builder creates a pointer to the form. If you allow C++Builder to auto-create a form, you don't have to worry about the pointer being valid. If you choose not to have a form auto-created, the pointer to the form will be NULL until you explicitly create the form and initialize the pointer. If you forget and use the pointer before it is initialized, Windows will generate an access-violation error.

Okay, so back to the Project Options dialog box. The Auto-create forms list box contains a list of the forms that will be auto-created. If you do not want a form to be auto-created, drag the form from the Auto-create forms list box to the Available forms list box. You can move forms from one list box to the other using drag-and-drop, too. To move several forms at one time, simply select the forms you want to move (both list boxes support multiple selection) and drag-and-drop them all at once. It's as easy as that.

NOTE

You can use the buttons between the two list boxes to move forms from one list box to the other, but it's usually easier to use drag-and-drop.

The Application Page

The Application page of the Project Options dialog box is very simple. (See Figure 10.8.)

The Title field on this page is used to set the title of the application. The title is the text that will appear on the Windows taskbar when your application is minimized.

Figure 10.8.

The Application page.

NOTE

> The application's title and the caption of the main form are two separate items. If you want your program's name to show up when you minimize your program, you will have to be sure that you set the title for the application in the Project Options dialog box. If you do not provide an application title, the name of the project file will be used by default.

The Help file field of the Application page is used to set the help file that your application will use. This is the help file that the program will load when you press F1 while your application is running. You can use the Browse button to locate the help file if you can't remember the name or location of the help file. If you do not supply a help file, pressing F1 in your application will have no effect.

The Icon option allows you to choose an icon for your application. This is the icon that will be displayed in the Windows taskbar when your application runs and when it is minimized. In addition, this icon will be displayed on your main form's title bar unless you have explicitly set an icon for the main form. To choose an icon, click the Load Icon button and locate the icon file (.ico) using the Application Icon dialog box.

The C++ Page

The C++ page of the Project Options dialog box is where you set the options that the compiler uses to build your project. (See Figure 10.9.)

10

Figure 10.9.

*The C++ page of the
Project Options dialog
box.*

At the top of this page is a section called Speed Settings that contains two buttons. The Full
Debug button sets the default compiler options for a typical debug session. These are the
settings you will be most likely to use while debugging your application. The Release button
sets the compiler options for a typical release build. Use the Release settings after you have
debugged your application and are ready to ship the final product. Be sure that you do a Build
All of your project after changing compiler settings.

NOTE

> The Full Debug and Release buttons set the compiler settings to the
> suggested settings for debugging or final release, respectively. You can
> always change individual options after choosing one of these speed
> buttons.

The remainder of the C++ page is broken down into four sections. Let's examine each section
so that you can better understand the different compiler options.

Code Optimization

The compiler can be configured to perform optimizations on your code. When optimizations
are turned off (the None radio button is selected) in the Code optimization section of the C++
page, the compiler makes no attempts to optimize code in any way.

If you choose the Speed option, the compiler will generate the fastest code possible without
regard to code size. When optimizations are set to Speed with scheduling, the compiler will
optimize to take advantage of Pentium Pipeline Instructions. In most cases you should leave
this option on the default setting chosen when you press either the Full Debug or Release
speed buttons.

NOTE The results of changing optimization settings can vary widely. Each application is different. Sometimes optimizing for size has a big impact on the final executable file size; other times the difference is negligible. The same is true of optimizing for speed.

Debugging

The Debugging section of the C++ page of the Project Options dialog box controls how the compiler generates code for debugging sessions. This section has four options, which are explained in the following sections. (I'll discuss debugging operations in detail tomorrow.)

Debug Information

When the Debug information option is enabled, C++Builder will generate debug information for the project. The debug information is stored in a separate file in the project's directory. The filename of the file containing the debug information has a .TDS extension. For example, if you had a program with a project name MyApp, C++Builder would generate a symbol file called MyApp.tds. This file is read by the debugger during debug sessions. If you do not generate debug information, you will not be able to stop on breakpoints and inspect variables during debugging. Put another way, you can't debug your program unless you tell C++Builder to generate debug information.

Line Number Information

The Line number information option tells C++Builder to generate line number information for the project. Line number information is used by the debugger to allow you to step through your code line by line. This option is automatically enabled when you have the Debug Information option turned on (even though the check box doesn't show it). You can, however, turn debug information off and then turn line number information on. This will allow you to set breakpoints and step through your code, but you won't be able to inspect any variables. The benefit is that your .tds file will be smaller. In reality, it is unlikely that you will opt to turn debug information off and line numbering on.

Automatic Register Variables

When the Automatic Register Variables option is on, the compiler will make use of register variables as it sees fit. The use of register variables allows for much faster code. Register variables can, however, be a bit of a pain while debugging. The compiler might optimize your variables during debugging, making the variable unavailable for inspection. When a variable has been optimized, the watch window will display the message Variable 'x' has been optimized and is not available when you attempt to inspect the variable.

TIP

> To avoid the problem with register variables, you can do one of two things. The first is to turn off the Automatic Register Variables option while debugging your application. Turn it back on again when you are done debugging and before your product ships.
>
> The other thing you can do is to declare a local variable with the `volatile` keyword:
>
> `volatile int x;`
>
> This will prevent the compiler from optimizing the variable, thereby making it available for inspection.

If you turn off the Automatic Register Variables option, you can still force the compiler to treat a particular variable as a register variable by declaring it with the `register` keyword. Here's an example:

```
register int x = 20;
```

Disable Inline Expansions

The Disable Inline Expansions option controls how inline functions are handled by the compiler. By default, inline functions are expanded inline (placed in the code where necessary) as you would expect. If you turn on this option, thereby disabling inline expansion, inline functions will be treated as regular functions rather than as inline functions. Use of this option is rare, but you may need to use it on occasion when debugging certain inline functions.

NOTE

> If you change any of the options on the C++ page, you should do a Build All immediately following. This will ensure that all modules are built using the same compiler settings.

Pre-compiled Headers

Note the Pre-compiled Headers section on the C++ page of the Project Options dialog box. A *pre-compiled header* is essentially an image of the symbol table for a project stored on disk. The first time you build your program, C++Builder creates the pre-compiled header. On subsequent makes, C++Builder can load the pre-compiled header from disk, which is much faster than compiling the headers for each build. In addition, you can opt to cache the pre-compiled header in memory. This increases compile speed even more because the pre-compiled header can be held in memory rather than being loaded from disk when needed.

You can set the Pre-compiled Headers option to None, Use pre-compiled headers, or Cache pre-compiled headers depending on your needs and the hardware available on your system. Generally speaking, you will use pre-compiled headers in one way or another. Turning off pre-compiled headers almost always results in much slower build times.

TIP

> The option to cache pre-compiled headers will dramatically speed up compile and build times *if* you have enough system RAM. If you do not have enough system RAM, caching pre-compiled headers can actually slow down your builds. Do your own tests to determine whether caching of pre-compiled headers is faster or slower on your system. In general, though, I would recommend turning caching off if you have less than 32MB of system RAM.

Compiling

The Compiling group of options on the C++ page is used to control how the C++ compiler performs certain options. For the most part, you should leave these options set at the defaults until you get more familiar with C++Builder and C++ in general. These settings are explained in the following sections.

Merge Duplicate Strings

When the Merge Duplicate Strings option is on, it tells the compiler to merge duplicate strings into one memory location. This saves overall program size but can lead to problems if one of the strings is modified.

Stack Frames

Leave the Stack frames option on when debugging. When you are done debugging, you can turn off this option to have the compiler generate smaller and faster code, but compile times will be slightly longer with the Stack frames option off. Most of the time the speed and size savings are not significant enough to warrant turning off this option. As always, do your own test to be sure.

Show Warnings

When the Show warnings option is on, any compiler warnings are displayed in the Code Editor message window. I always leave this option on. Compiler warnings should not be ignored for the long term. Most of the time compiler warnings can, and should, be resolved.

NOTE

Compiler and linker errors are always displayed in the message window.

Show General Msgs

When the Show general msgs option is on, various status messages are displayed in the message window of the Code Editor. For example, compiling the ScratchPad program with general messages turned on results in the following text being output to the message window:

```
[C++] Compiling: Scratch.cpp
[C++] Compiling: SPMain.cpp
[C++] Loaded cached pre-compiled headers.
[C++] Compiling: SPAbout.cpp
[Linker] Incremental Linking: D:\Projects\Scratch\Scratch.exe
```

Turn on this option if you want to see the status messages in the message window.

The Pascal Page

The Pascal page of the Project Options dialog box is used to set the Pascal compiler options. The Pascal compiler is used if you add Pascal units (.pas) to your C++Builder projects. The Pascal compiler settings are numerous and beyond the scope of this discussion, so I'm not going to go over each one. See the C++Builder online help for details about the settings on this page.

The Linker Page

The Linker page of the Project Options dialog box is where you set options that specify how you want the linker to function. Until you get very familiar with C++Builder, you can leave this page alone and accept the default settings. Figure 10.10 shows the Linker page of the Project Options dialog box. The sections of this page are explained in the following sections.

Figure 10.10.

Project Linker options.

10

Application Target

The Application target section specifies whether the project target is an EXE or a DLL. If you create your projects using the Object Repository, this option is set for you and you don't have to worry about it.

Application Type

The Application type section allows you to set the application type. The available choices are Windows GUI and Console Application. As with the Application target option, if you create a new project using the Object Repository this option will already be set for you.

Map File

The Map file settings control whether a map file is generated and how much detail is included in the map file. (A *map file* is an advanced debugging tool and is something you will not likely use.)

Linking

The Linking section has three linker options. The Use incremental linker option tells C++Builder whether it should use the incremental linker. The incremental linker saves a lot of time when you are developing your applications. For example, let's say you have a project with 20 units. If you change one line of a unit, that unit will have to be recompiled and relinked. When incremental linking is on, only the object file that has changed is relinked. When incremental linking is off, the linker must relink every binary file in the project, regardless of whether it has changed since the last link. Linking takes a fair amount of time, so the incremental linker is a big advantage when working on a project of any significance.

The disadvantage of incremental linking is twofold. First, the initial link takes longer when incremental linking is enabled. Second, the incremental linker sets up several files in order to do its thing. These files can get very large (several megabytes) and use up a lot of disk space. If disk space is a problem, you might want to turn off incremental linking. Otherwise, it's probably just as well to leave incremental linking on.

NOTE

There is actually a third disadvantage to using the incremental linker: It results in slightly larger executable sizes. Before you ship your final product you should do a Build All with the Use incremental linker option turned off.

The Show warnings option tells C++Builder to display any linker warnings in the Code Editor message window.

The Link debug version of VCL option allows you to link to the version of VCL that is built with debug information. This will allow you to step into the VCL source code while debugging your application.

NOTE

Stepping into VCL code is not generally a fruitful endeavor. This is particularly true if you are not an experienced programmer. Any problems you are experiencing in your application are almost certainly in your code and not in the VCL code. There are times when stepping into the VCL source code is useful, but it has been my experience that those times are infrequent. Remember, also, that VCL is written in Object Pascal, so if the VCL source looks like a foreign language, it is.

10

Stack Sizes

The Stack sizes section allows you to set the minimum and maximum stack sizes for the project. It is not usually necessary to change these settings.

The Directories/Conditionals Page

The Directories/Conditionals page of the Project Options dialog box is where you set the directories that your project uses to find things like library files and headers. You can also set the directory where you want the compiler to put the output files. (See Figure 10.11.) The fields on this page are described in the following sections.

Figure 10.11.

*The Directories/
Conditionals page.*

Include Path

The Include Path setting is the path where C++Builder will look for the headers it needs to build your application (the .h and .hpp files). By default this field is set to point to the various C++Builder directories where the system headers are found. You should leave this field set to the default directories unless you have a third-party library that resides in a separate directory. If you need to add directories to the Include Path field, you can add them to the end of the existing directories. Separate each directory with a semicolon and be sure to include the full path.

Library Path

The Library Path field contains the paths where the C++Builder library files (.lib) can be found. As with the Include Path field, you can add directories by separating each with a semicolon.

WARNING

Do not remove the list of default directories in either the Include Path or Library Path fields. If you need to modify these fields, add directories to the end of the directories listed, but do not delete any of the default directories. If you remove the default directories, your application will not compile.

Conditional Defines

The Conditional defines field is used to specify any #defines that you want to add at the project level. For example, to add support for the TRACE and WARN diagnostic macros you would add this text to the Conditional Defines field:

```
__TRACE;__WARN
```

Note that each #define is separated by a semicolon.

Pascal Unit Aliases

The Pascal Unit Aliases field associates a Pascal unit name with a specific C++ header file. The aliases are separated by a semicolon.

The C++Builder Code Editor

There is no question that C++Builder is highly visual in nature. That's one of the great things about programming with it. Still, any program of any significance will have a great deal of code that must be written by hand. After you get the user interface part of your application written with C++Builder's impressive visual tools, you'll likely spend a long stretch with the C++Builder Code Editor. The Code Editor has some features you'll learn to appreciate once you discover them.

In this section you will learn about

- [ ] Basic editor operations
- [ ] Specialized editor features
- [ ] The Code Editor speed menu
- [ ] Changing the editor options

10

NOTE The C++Builder Code Editor allows you to choose from four keyboard-mapping configurations: Default, IDE Classic, BRIEF, and Epsilon. The rest of this chapter assumes Default keyboard mapping. If you are already familiar with one of the other keyboard-mapping configurations, you can ignore any references to specific keystrokes.

Basic Editor Operations

I'm going to assume that you know enough to be able to enter and delete text; highlight text with the mouse; cut, copy, and paste; and so on. I won't spend any time going over things at that level.

NOTE If you have a lot of time in the pilot's seat writing code, you may be a heavy keyboard user. If that is the case, you will likely use the keyboard shortcuts for simple things like cutting, copying, and pasting. If you are not as experienced with the keyboard (or you just prefer using the mouse), you may want to customize your C++Builder speedbar to add speed buttons for operations like cutting, copying, and pasting. Whichever method you choose, you will probably get lots of practice— if you are anything like me, you will do a lot of cut, copy, and paste while writing your programs.

When it comes right down to it, the C++Builder Code Editor is a typical code editor. It features syntax highlighting, which makes it easy to identify keywords, strings, numeric constants, and comments at a glance. We'll look at setting the editor preferences a little later on.

The Code Editor is a tabbed window. You can open as many editor windows as you like; each will be represented by a tab along the top of the editor window. The tab will display the name of the file. To switch to a source file, simply click on the tab corresponding to the file you want to view. If more tabs exist than can be displayed at one time, scroll buttons will appear so that you can scroll among the tabs.

The status bar at the bottom of the Code Editor gives status information (obviously). The current line number and the cursor position on the line are reported in the left panel of the status bar. If the file has changed since it was last saved, the status bar will say Modified in the center panel of the status bar. The right panel of the status bar shows the current mode, either Insert or Overwrite. If the file has been set to read-only, this panel will say Read Only.

The editor window has a left margin that is called the *gutter*. The gutter is used to display icons at different stages of the development process. For example, when you set a debugger breakpoint (discussed tomorrow), a red stop-sign icon is placed in the gutter. When you set a bookmark (discussed in just a bit), an icon representing the bookmark is placed in the gutter.

NOTE

The gutter can be annoying at times. If you accidentally click on the gutter when trying to select text or place the cursor, you will find that a breakpoint is set on that line. Click the gutter again to clear the breakpoint.

Opening and Saving Files

There's nothing too mysterious about opening and saving files in the Code Editor. It should be pointed out, though, that there is a difference between opening a project and opening a source file. When you choose File | Open Project from the main menu, you are prompted for the name of a project file (.mak) to open. When you choose File | Open from the main menu, you can open any text file. (You can also open a form file, but that's a different discussion.) Both the Open and Open Project menu items have corresponding speedbar buttons.

10

NOTE

If you open a source file (.cpp) that is the source code unit for a form, C++Builder will open the source file in the Code Editor and will also open the form in the Form Designer.

You can open multiple files at one time. To open multiple files, choose the files you want to open in the Open dialog box and click OK. Each file selected will be loaded, and a tab for each file will be placed at the top of the editor window.

TIP

You can also use drag-and-drop to open files. For instance, you can choose a file (or a group of files) in Explorer, drag it onto the Code Editor, and drop it. The file will be opened in the Code Editor.

To save a file, choose File | Save or File | Save As from the main menu or type Ctrl+S on the keyboard. If the file has not been previously saved, the Save As dialog box will appear, and you can enter a filename at that time.

Highlighting Text

Although text highlighting is basic text editor stuff, I thought it wouldn't hurt to remind you of a couple basic highlighting techniques you can use in the C++Builder Code Editor.

To highlight a short block of text, you can use the mouse to drag across any text you want to highlight. After you've selected the text, you can cut, copy, or paste as needed. To highlight longer blocks of code, you can use the click+Shift+click method. First, click at the beginning of the block you want to highlight. Next, hold the Shift key on the keyboard, and then click again at the end of the block. All text between the starting point and the ending point is highlighted.

Another useful feature is the capability to quickly select an individual word. To select a keyword, function name, or variable, just double-click on the word. Now you can perform any editing operations you want with the highlighted word.

10

> **TIP**
>
> To select a single line of code with the mouse, click at the beginning of the line and drag straight down to the beginning of the next line. To highlight a single line of code with the keyboard, first press the Home key to move to the beginning of the line and then use Shift+down-arrow key to highlight the line.

There are dozens of keyboard combinations that can be used to highlight text and do other editing chores. For a complete list of all the keyboard shortcuts available, consult the C++Builder online help.

> **TIP**
>
> As you program you often add, delete, or move blocks of text. Sometimes you will need to indent an entire block of code. At other times you will need to un-indent (outdent?) an entire block of code. To indent a block of code, highlight the lines that you want to indent and then press Ctrl+Shift+I on the keyboard. The entire block will be indented. To un-indent a block of code, press Ctrl+Shift+U on the keyboard.

Undo

The Code Editor has a virtually limitless number of undo levels (32,767 by default). Normally, you can only undo commands up to the last time you saved a file. By changing the editor options, you will be able to undo past commands even after saving the file. I'll talk about editor options and preferences later in the chapter, in the section titled "Changing the Editor Options."

In general, it pays to remember this simple maxim: "Undo is your friend."

Find and Replace

Find and Replace are used fairly heavily in programming. Find might be used to find a specific piece of code or a specific variable in your code. Replace might be used to change a variable's name or to change the name of a function. The possibilities are endless.

The C++Builder Find and Replace dialog boxes implement more or less standard find-and-replace operations. To bring up the Find dialog box, choose Search | Find from the main menu or press Ctrl+F. To invoke the Replace dialog box, choose Search | Replace from the menu or press Ctrl+R. Figure 10.12 shows the C++Builder Replace dialog box. With a couple of obvious exceptions, the Find dialog box contains the same options.

Figure 10.12.

The Replace Text dialog box.

For the most part, the options on the Find and Replace dialog boxes do exactly what they indicate. If you choose the Case sensitive option, you need to type in the search text exactly as it appears in the source file.

The Whole words only option requires a word of explanation. C++ code is, obviously, not plain text. Take the following line, for instance:

```
Memo->Caption = GetCaption();
```

In this case neither Memo, Caption, nor GetCaption could be considered a whole word because they are surrounded by special C++ syntax characters. If you search for the word Memo and have the Whole words only option on, the Find operation will ignore syntax characters and will still find Memo in this line.

The Regular expressions option requires explanation as well. When this option is on, you can use special wildcard characters when doing searches. For a complete description of the wildcard characters, see the C++Builder online help under the topic Regular Expressions.

When replacing text, it is safest to leave on the Prompt on replace option. When you do a Replace All operation with this option on, the editor highlights each found word and prompts you whether to replace it. It is easy to miscalculate the results of a Replace All operation, so always use Replace with care. Even then, it still pays to remember that maxim: "Undo is your friend."

The rest of the Find and Replace options are self-explanatory and therefore don't need additional mention.

NOTE

C++Builder comes with a utility that allows you to search for text across source files. The utility is called grep (for Global Regular Expression Print) and can be found in the CBuilder\Bin directory. This command-line program is a powerful search utility. Unfortunately C++Builder does not integrate grep into the IDE as Borland C++ does. Still, you can run grep from the command line or search various online sources for a host of third-party Windows-based grep tools.

Getting Help

One of the most useful features of the Code Editor is its integration with the C++Builder help system. Just place the editor cursor over a C++ keyword, a VCL property or method, or any other C++Builder-specific text and press F1. If a help topic for the text under the cursor exists in the C++Builder help files, WinHelp will run with the appropriate page showing. If no help topic exists for the selected text, an error message will be displayed. This feature is extremely useful when you can't remember how to use a particular aspect of C++Builder, C++, or VCL. Help, as they say, is just a keystroke away.

Specialized Editor Features

The C++Builder Code Editor has a few features that are extremely useful when you are writing a lot of code. They are explained in the following sections.

Using Bookmarks

You can set bookmarks in your code to temporarily mark your place in a source file. For example, you often have to temporarily leave a block of code you are working on to review previously written code or to copy code from another location. By dropping a bookmark at that point in your code before running off to do your other work, you can return to that section of code with a simple keystroke. You can have up to 10 bookmarks set at any one time.

To set a bookmark at a particular location, press Ctrl+Shift and the number of the bookmark to set. For example, to set bookmark 0 (the first bookmark), place the editor cursor at the location you want to mark and then press Ctrl+Shift+0. When you set a bookmark, an icon is placed in the Code Editor gutter to indicate that a bookmark exists on that line. The icon shows the number of the bookmark. Figure 10.13 shows the Code Editor with a bookmark dropped on a line.

Figure 10.13.
The Code Editor with
a bookmark set.

To return to the bookmark, press Ctrl plus the number of the bookmark to which you want to return. Using the same example, you would type Ctrl+0 to go back to the bookmark. To clear a bookmark, place the editor cursor anywhere on the line containing the bookmark and again press Ctrl+Shift+0.

NOTE

Bookmarks can be set for each file you have open in the Code Editor. For instance, you can have bookmark 0 set in one source file and another bookmark 0 set in another source file. This means that bookmarks cannot be found across source files. If you set bookmark 0 in Unit1.opp, you cannot press Ctrl+0 from Unit2.cpp and expect to be taken to the bookmark in Unit1.cpp.

To illustrate the use of bookmarks, do the following:

1. Open any source file in the Code Editor.
2. Scroll almost to the bottom of the file and click on a line of code.
3. Press Ctrl+Shift+0 to set a bookmark. The bookmark icon shows in the Code Editor gutter.
4. Press Ctrl+Home to move to the top of the source file.
5. Now press Ctrl+0 to jump back to the bookmark. The Code Editor changes to show the line of code where the bookmark was set, and the cursor is placed exactly where it was when you set the bookmark.
6. Type Ctrl+Shift+0 again to clear the bookmark. The bookmark is cleared, and the bookmark icon disappears from the Code Editor gutter.

Bookmarks are temporary. When you close the source file and reopen it, the bookmark is not preserved.

Incremental Search

You can use the incremental search option to quickly find a short series of characters. To start an incremental search, choose Search | Incremental Search from the main menu or press Ctrl+E on the keyboard. To understand how the incremental search works, it is easiest to do an exercise. Do the following:

1. Create a new text file from the Object Repository. (It doesn't matter whether you currently have a project open.)

2. Type the following text:

   ```
   Learning to write Windows
   programs a bit at a time
   is not so bad. Isn't it
   time you got back to work?
   ```

3. Move the cursor back to the top of the file (Ctrl+Home).

4. Press Ctrl+E to start the incremental search. You will be searching for the word back. Note that the Code Editor status bar says Searching for:.

5. Type a b on the keyboard. The letter b in the word bit is highlighted. Hmmm… that's not what you are looking for.

6. Now type an a on the keyboard. The next occurrence of ba is found, this time in the word bad. That's still not what you are looking for.

7. Type a c on the keyboard. The letters bac in the word back are highlighted. Now type a k. The Code Editor status bar now says Searching for: back and the word back is highlighted. Congratulations, you found what you were looking for!

8. Press Esc (or Enter) on the keyboard to stop the incremental search. Close the text file without saving it.

That's all there is to it. The incremental search is handy when you're searching for short amounts of text.

 TIP   If you make a mistake when typing in the characters while doing an incremental search, you can use the Backspace key to remove the last character typed from the search string.

Finding Matching Braces

As you have seen, C++ code can often get pretty convoluted when you start nesting if statements, if-else pairs, and so on. To tell the truth, it's easy to get lost. The Code Editor has a feature to help you find a brace that matches the brace the cursor is currently on. To find a matching brace, place the cursor before a brace (it doesn't matter if it's the opening or closing brace). Now press Ctrl+[on the keyboard. The cursor jumps to the brace that matches the brace you started on. Press Ctrl+[again, and the cursor jumps back to where you started. Getting lost in the maze of braces in a long series of if statements is still a possibility, but at least now you know how to find your way out again.

The Code Editor Speed Menu

Like most of the different windows you encounter in C++Builder, the Code Editor has its own speed menu. The Code Editor speed menu can essentially be broken down into two parts: editor items and debugger items. I will leave the debugger items of the speed menu for tomorrow when I discuss debugging, but I'll go over the editor items on the speed menu now. Table 10.2 contains a list of the speed menu items that pertain to the editor, along with a description of each.

Table 10.2. The Code Editor speed menu items.

Item	Description
Swap Cpp/Hdr Files	If the header file corresponding to the current source file is not opened in the Code Editor, choosing this menu item opens the header file, creates a new tab for it, and changes focus to that window. Choosing this option when both the .cpp and .h files are open switches focus back and forth between the two files.
Close Page	Closes the active page in the edit window. If the file on the page has been modified since it was last saved, you will be prompted to save the file.
Open File At Cursor	Opens the file under the cursor. This option has an effect only when the text under the cursor represents a source code file. For example, if you had a header included with #include "myclass.h", you could place the cursor over the filename and choose this menu item to open the file. The file will be placed in a new editor window, and focus will be set to the window.
New Edit Window	Opens a new copy of the Code Editor. This is convenient if you want to compare two source files side-by-side.

continues

Table 10.2. continued

Item	Description
Topic Search	Displays the help topic for the item under the cursor (if it can be found). Same as pressing F1 on the keyboard.
View As Form	If the active source unit in the Code Editor has a corresponding form, choosing this option will switch from the Code Editor to the Form Designer where the form will be displayed. (Same as pressing F12.)
Read Only	Toggles the currently active file between read-only and read/write mode. When set to read-only, the file cannot be modified, although text can be selected and copied to the Clipboard. The status bar displays Read Only to indicate that the file is read only. When the file is closed and reopened, it is again in read/write mode.
Message View	Displays or hides the C++Builder message window. The message window automatically appears when there are compiler or linker errors or warnings, but can be specifically shown or hidden with this command.
Properties	Displays the Environment Options dialog box so that the editor options can be set.

Depending on the current state of the Code Editor and the particular type of file open, some of the items in Table 10.2 may be disabled at any given time.

Changing the Editor Options

The editor options occupy three pages of the Environment Options dialog box. To view this dialog box, choose Options | Environment from the main menu.

TIP

You can also choose Properties from the Code Editor speed menu to view the editor options. The difference with this method is that only the three pages pertaining to the editor options will be displayed in the Environment Options dialog box.

The three pages of the Environment Options that are specific to the Code Editor are the Editor, Display, and Colors pages. We'll examine these pages next.

The Editor Page

The Editor page of the Environment Options dialog box allows you to control how the editor works for you. As you can see from Figure 10.14, there are a lot of options available on this page.

Figure 10.14.

The Editor page of the Environment Options dialog box.

At the top of the page is a combo box labeled Editor SpeedSetting. You can choose Default keymapping, IDE Classic, BRIEF emulation, or Epsilon emulation from the combo box. If you change the setting in this combo box, the Editor Options will change to reflect the defaults for the type you chose.

NOTE

> If you are new to programming or if you have been using other Borland compilers using the Default keymapping, you don't have to worry about what you are missing. For those of you who are accustomed to years of using a particular type of editor, you will be glad to know that you can still use the keyboard shortcuts and editor options you know and love by simply changing the Editor SpeedSetting on this page and on the Display page.

Toward the bottom of the screen you will see the Block indent and Tab stops fields. You can use these two fields to change the amount by which code is indented when you block indent or when you tab to the next tab stop. Block indenting is discussed in the section "Highlighting Text."

NOTE

> *Real* programmers use tab stops of either two or three characters. (I use two-character tabs.)

The Undo limit of 32,767 is probably sufficient for most needs (I hope!), so I doubt you'll feel the need to modify that setting. The Syntax extensions field allows you to select the types of files for which syntax highlighting will be applied. For example, you probably don't want syntax highlighting applied to regular text files (.txt) that you open in the Code Editor, so that file type is not listed by default.

In the middle of the Editor page, you will find a whole gaggle of editor options from which to choose. Because there are so many options available, and because it is difficult to determine exactly which of the available options are the most important, I'll refer you to the C++Builder online help. Simply press F1 while on this page or click the Help button and you will have explanations of each of the editor options you see on this page. As with some of the other options you looked at today, you can probably feel comfortable in accepting the C++Builder defaults. (Except for the tab stops and block indent!)

The Display Page

The Display page of the Environment Options dialog box has additional options from which you can choose. These options pertain to the actual display of the text in the Code Editor window. (See Figure 10.15.)

Figure 10.15.

The Display page.

In the Display and file options section, you will find the BRIEF cursor shapes option. Turn on this option if you want the horizontal cursor in the editor window rather than the vertical cursor. Check the Create backup file option if you want C++Builder to create a backup file every time you save your file or your project. Backup file extensions begin with a tilde (~). For instance, the backup file for a source file called MyApp.cpp would by MyApp.~cp.

I usually get fed up with all those backup files cluttering up my project directories and turn off file backups. Suit yourself.

The Zoom to full screen option controls how the Code Editor acts when maximized. If this option is on, the Code Editor will fill the entire screen when maximized. When this option is off (the default), the top of the Code Editor window will stop at the bottom of the C++Builder main window when maximized. In other words, the C++Builder main window will always be visible when the Code Editor is maximized if this option is off.

You can also choose whether your editor windows have a visible right margin. The right margin is not binding—you can still type text beyond it—but it gives you a visual cue that your lines might be getting too long.

You can also change the Code Editor font and point size. A combo box is provided for you to choose these options. Only fixed-space screen fonts are listed; proportional and printer fonts are not. Choose the typeface and point size that best suit your needs. A preview window is provided so that you can see how the font you have chosen will look.

The Colors Page

The Colors page of the Environment Options dialog box allows you to fully customize the Code Editor's window and syntax highlighting options. (See Figure 10.16.)

Figure 10.16.

The Colors page in the Environment Options dialog box.

At the top of the page is the Color SpeedSetting combo box. This combo box gives you four predefined color schemes from which to choose. You can choose one of these color schemes or use one of them as a base for creating your own color scheme.

10

The Colors page is very easy to use. At the bottom of the page is a text window that contains sample code. If you click on one of the key elements of the code, that element will be selected in the Elements list box, and its current settings will be displayed on the Color grid. To change the foreground, background, and text attributes for that element, simply choose the settings you like. For example, keywords are displayed in bold text with a black foreground and a white background (assuming the Default color scheme). To change the keywords to green, bold text, click on the `void` keyword in the sample code window and then change the foreground color to green. The text colors in the sample window change to reflect the new color you have chosen. Continue changing colors as desired until you have the example window just the way you want it. When you click OK, the Code Editor will change to the new colors you have chosen.

Summary

Today is one of those days when you learned a lot about the kinds of things that often get overlooked. I hope you picked up some tips that you can use as you work with C++Builder projects and the C++Builder Code Editor. You also got an explanation of what some of the project and editor options are for. Even if it didn't make much sense to you now, this chapter is something you can refer to at a later date.

Workshop

The Workshop contains quiz questions to help you solidify your understanding of the material covered and exercises to provide you with experience in using what you have learned. You can find answers to the quiz questions in Appendix A, "Answers to Quiz Questions."

Q&A

Q When I use the Project Manager window, the units in my project seem to alternate between bold and normal text. Why is that?

A Any units that have changed and that have not yet been saved show up in bold text in the Project Manager window. Units that are up-to-date (that do not need to be saved) are shown in normal text.

Q Whenever I try to change the name of my project source code unit in the Project Explorer, it reverts back to its original filename. Why is that?

A You cannot change the filenames of source code units through the Project Explorer. You can only change those objects in the Project Explorer that have a `Name` property. In other words, you can only change the names of forms and components. To change a source code filename, choose File | Save As from the Code Editor main menu.

Q When I start my application, my main form isn't displayed, but instead one of my dialog boxes is displayed. What gives?

A You have accidentally set the main form for the application to be the dialog form. Go to the Project Options dialog box, click on the Forms tab, and select your main form from the Main Form combo box on the top of the page. Run your program again, and the main form will be displayed as you would expect.

Q All those project compiler and linker options confuse me. Do I need to know about each of those options to write programs with C++Builder?

A No. The default project options work well for almost all C++Builder applications. At some point you may get further into the mysteries of the compiler and linker, and at that time you can learn more about the project options. Until then, don't worry about them.

Q When my application is minimized, the icon and caption do not match what I set up in my application's main form. Why not?

A Setting the icon and caption of the main form does not affect the way your application is displayed when minimized. To set the caption and icon for the application, go to the Project Options dialog box, choose the Application page, and supply the application name and icon.

Q Can I open several source files at one time in the Code Editor?

A Yes. You can either choose File | Open and select multiple files to open, or you can select a group of files in Windows Explorer and drop them on the Code Editor.

Q Can I find and replace a variable name across all my source files?

A No. You will have to open each source file and execute the Replace dialog box in each source file. You can, however, use the F3 key to repeat the last find or replace command. Remember not to change any C++Builder-generated variable names.

Q I find that 32,767 undo levels is not enough for my needs. What do you suggest?

A Don't quit your day job.

Quiz

1. How can you quickly switch between a unit's form and source code when working with C++Builder?

2. If you remove a file from your project via the Project Manager, is the file removed from your hard drive?

3. How do you set the main form for an application?

4. What does it mean if you do not have C++Builder auto-create forms?

5. What's the minimum amount of memory your computer should have before you turn on the option to cache pre-compiled headers?

6. What is the significance of generating debug information for your application?

7. If you do not specify an Output Directory in the Project Options, where will C++Builder create your .exe file?

8. What is the keyboard shortcut for saving a file in the Code Editor?

9. How do you set a bookmark in an editor window? How many bookmarks are available?

10. How do you set a file to read-only in the Code Editor?

Exercises

1. Create a new application. Display the Project Manager. Click the Add Unit button to add a new unit to the project. Navigate to the \CBuilder\Examples\Apps\Contacts directory and choose the file called Contacts.cpp. Click OK to add the file to the project.

2. Remove the Contacts.cpp unit from the project in exercise 1.

3. Open the ScratchPad project. Change the main form to the AboutBox form. Close the Project Options dialog box and run the program. The About box will be displayed when the program starts. Close the About box to end the program and change the main form back to the ScratchPad form.

4. Open the RichEdit application that is supplied with C++Builder. Go to the Project Options dialog box and confirm that the Optimization setting on the C++ page is set to Optimize for Speed. Do a Build All to build the program. Check the size of the produced .exe. Go back to the Project Options dialog box and change the optimization to Optimize for Size. Again do a Build All. Check the final .exe size again to compare the difference. How much smaller or larger was the .exe when the compiler optimized for size?

5. Open any source file in the Code Editor. Set four bookmarks at random locations in the source file. Jump from bookmark to bookmark and observe the effects in the Code Editor. When you are finished, clear all the bookmarks.

6. Open the ScratchPad project (or any other project) and switch to the Code Editor. View the project's main form source file. Choose Search | Find from the main menu. Type Click in the Text To Find box and click OK to find the first occurrence of the word Click.

7. Press F3 several times to repeat the search until the entire file has been searched.

8. Continuing with the same project, press Ctrl+Home to go to the top of the file. Press Ctrl+R to display the Replace Text dialog box. Type `Click` in the Text To Find box and `Test` in the Replace With box. Turn off the Prompt On Replace option and then click the Replace All button. Scroll through the file to view the results. **Important:** Select Edit | Undo to undo the Replace operation. Close the project without saving (just to be safe).

9. Open a file in the Code Editor. Choose Properties from the Code Editor speed menu. Change the syntax highlighting for strings, integers, and floats to dark gray. Click OK to view the results in the Code Editor.

10. Change the colors back to the default color scheme.

Day **11**

Using the Debugger

by Kent Reisdorph

A major feature of the C++Builder IDE is the integrated debugger. The debugger allows you to easily set breakpoints, watch variables, inspect objects, and much more. The IDE debugger allows you to see what is going on in your program while the program runs. Using the debugger you can quickly find out what is happening (or not happening) with your program as it runs. A good debugger is vital to efficient program development.

Debugging is one of those things that is easy to overlook. Don't tell anyone, but when I first started Windows programming (not with C++Builder, of course) I ignored the debugger for a long time because I had my hands full just learning how to do Windows programming. When I found out how valuable a good debugger is, I felt a little silly for cheating myself out of the use of that tool for so long. Oh well, live and learn. You have the luxury of learning from my mistakes. Today you will learn about what the debugger can do for you.

The IDE debugger provides several features and tools to help you in your debugging chores. Specifically, the following features are discussed here:

- ☐ Debugger menu items
- ☐ Using breakpoints
- ☐ Inspecting variables with the Watch List
- ☐ Inspecting objects with the Debug Inspector
- ☐ Other debugging tools
- ☐ Stepping through code
- ☐ Debugging techniques

Why Use the Debugger?

The quick answer is that the debugger helps you track down bugs in your program. But the debugging process is not just for finding and fixing bugs—it is a development tool as well. As important as debugging is, many programmers don't take the time to learn how to use all the features of the IDE debugger. As a result, they cost themselves time and money, not to mention the frustration of a bug that can't easily be tracked down.

You begin a debugging session by starting up the program under the debugger. You automatically run your program using the debugger when you click the Run button on the speedbar. You can also choose Run | Run from the main menu or press F9 on the keyboard.

The Debugging Menu Items

Before we get into the details of the debugger, let's go over the menu items that pertain to the debugger. Some of these menu items are on the main menu under Run, and others are on the Code Editor speed menu. Most of these items are discussed in detail as you work through the chapter, so I'll just touch on them here so that you are at least familiar with them. Table 11.1 lists the Code Editor speed menu items that are specific to the debugger and their descriptions.

Table 11.1. The Code Editor speed menu's debugging items.

Item	Shortcut	Description
Toggle Breakpoint	F5	Toggles a breakpoint on or off for the current line in the Code Editor.
Run to Cursor	none	Starts the program (if necessary) and runs it until the line in the editor window containing the cursor is reached.

Item	Shortcut	Description
Inspect	Alt+F5	Opens the Debug Inspect window for the object under the cursor.
Go To Address	none	Allows you to specify a specific address in the program at which program execution will resume.
Evaluate/Modify	none	Allows you to view and/or modify a variable at runtime.
Add Watch at Cursor	Ctrl+F5	Adds the variable under the cursor to the Watch List.

The Run item on the main menu has several selections that pertain to running programs under the debugger. The Run menu items allow you to start a program under the debugger, to terminate a program running under the debugger, and to specify command-line parameters for your program, to name just a few. Some of the items found here are duplicated on the Code Editor speed menu. Table 11.2 shows the Run menu items that control debugging operations.

Table 11.2. The Run menu's debugging items.

Item	Shortcut	Description
Run	F9	Compiles the program (if needed) and then runs the program under the control of the IDE debugger. Same as the Run speedbar button.
Parameters	none	Allows you to enter command-line parameters for your program.
Step Over	F8	Executes the source code line at the execution point and pauses at the next source code line.
Trace Into	F7	Traces into the function at the execution point.
Trace to Next Source Line	Shift+F7	Causes the execution point to move to the next line in the program's source code.
Run to Cursor	F4	Runs the program and pauses when program execution reaches the current line in the source code.

continues

Table 11.2. continued

Item	Shortcut	Description
Show Execution Point	none	Displays the program execution point in the Code Editor. Scrolls the source code window if necessary. Only works when program execution is paused.
Program Pause	none	Pauses program execution as soon as the execution point enters the program's source code.
Program Reset	Ctrl+F2	Closes down the program and returns to the C++Builder IDE.
Inspect	none	Displays the Inspect dialog box so that you can enter the name of an object to inspect.
Evaluate/Modify	Ctrl+F7	Displays the Evaluate/Modify dialog box.
Add Watch	Ctrl+F5	Displays the Watch Properties dialog box.
Add Breakpoint	none	Displays the Edit Breakpoint dialog box to allow you to add a breakpoint.

You will use these menu items a lot when you are debugging your programs. You should also become familiar with the various keyboard shortcuts for the debugging operations.

Now let's take a look at breakpoints and how you use them in your program.

Breakpoints

When you run your program from the C++Builder IDE it runs at full speed, stopping only where you have set breakpoints.

 A *breakpoint* is a marker that tells the debugger to pause program execution when that point in the program is reached.

Setting and Clearing Breakpoints

To set a breakpoint, click in the editor window's gutter to the left of the line on which you want to pause program execution. A stop sign icon appears in the gutter, and the entire line is highlighted in red. To clear the breakpoint, click on the stop sign icon and the breakpoint is removed. You can also press F5 or choose Toggle Breakpoint from the Code Editor speed menu to toggle a breakpoint on or off.

NOTE

A breakpoint can only be set on a line that generates actual code. Breakpoints are not valid if set on blank lines, comment lines, or declaration lines. You are not prevented from setting a breakpoint on these types of lines, but the debugger will warn you about the fact that you have set a breakpoint on a line that contains no code. The following lines will produce an invalid breakpoint warning:

```
// this is a comment followed by a blank line

int x;  // a declaration
```
Breakpoints can be set on `return` statements or on the closing brace of a function.

If you set a breakpoint on an invalid line, the debugger will warn you that the breakpoint may not be valid, but it won't do that until you attempt to run the program. Figure 11.1 shows the warning message that is displayed when the debugger detects an invalid breakpoint.

Figure 11.1.

A warning message for an invalid breakpoint.

If you click the Yes button in the warning dialog box, the program will run and any invalid breakpoints will be ignored. If you click No, you will be taken back to the Code Editor, where you can clear the invalid breakpoint. Any invalid breakpoints will be highlighted in green, and the stop sign icon in the gutter will be grayed out.

When the program is run under the debugger, it behaves as it normally would—until a breakpoint is hit, that is. When a breakpoint is hit, the IDE is brought to the top, and the breakpoint line is highlighted in the source code. If you are using the default colors, the line where the program has stopped is highlighted in red because red indicates a line containing a breakpoint.

NEW TERM The *execution point* indicates the line that will be executed next in your source code.

As you step through the program, the execution point is highlighted in blue and the editor window gutter displays a black arrow glyph. Understand that the line highlighted in blue has not yet been executed but will be executed when program execution resumes.

Once you have stopped at a breakpoint, you can view variables, view the call stack, browse symbols, or step through your code. After you have inspected any variables and objects, you can resume normal program execution by clicking the Run button. Your application will again run normally until the next breakpoint is encountered.

NOTE

> It's common to detect coding errors in your program after you have stopped at a breakpoint. If you change your source code in the middle of a debugging session and then choose Run to resume program execution, the IDE will prompt you with a message box asking whether you want to rebuild the source code. If you choose Yes, the current process will be terminated, the source code will be recompiled, and the program will be restarted.
>
> The problem with this approach is that your program does not get a chance to close normally, and any resources currently in use might not be freed properly, which could result in memory leaks. While Windows 95 and Windows NT handle resource leaks better than 16-bit Windows, it is still advisable to terminate the program normally and then recompile.

The Breakpoint List Window

The C++Builder IDE keeps track of the breakpoints you have set in the Breakpoint list window. To view the breakpoint list, choose View | Breakpoints from the main menu. The Breakpoint list window will be displayed, as shown in Figure 11.2.

Figure 11.2.

The Breakpoint list window.

Filename	Line	Condition	Pass
SPMain.cpp	135		0
SPMain.cpp	133		0
SPMain.cpp	69		3
SPMain.cpp	85	x > 10	0

The Breakpoint list window has four columns. The first column, Filename, shows the filename of the source code unit in which the breakpoint is set. The second column, labeled Line, shows the line number on which the breakpoint is set. The Condition column shows any conditions that have been set for the breakpoint, and the Pass column shows the pass count condition that has been set for the breakpoint. (Breakpoint conditions and pass count conditions are discussed later, in the section "Conditional Breakpoints.") You can size the columns by dragging the dividing line between two columns in the column header.

NOTE

> The Pass column does not show the number of times the breakpoint has been hit; it only shows the pass condition that you have set for the breakpoint.

The Breakpoint list window actually has two speed menus. Table 11.3 lists the speed menu items you will see if you click the right mouse button while over the Filename column. I will refer to this as the window's *primary speed menu*.

Table 11.3. The primary Breakpoint list speed menu.

Item	Description
Enable	Enables or disables the breakpoint. When a breakpoint is disabled, its glyph is grayed out in the Breakpoint list window. In the source window the breakpoint glyph is also grayed, and the breakpoint line is highlighted in green to indicate that the breakpoint is disabled.
Delete	Removes the breakpoint.
View Source	Scrolls the source file in the Code Editor to display the source line containing the breakpoint. (The breakpoint list retains focus.)
Edit Source	Places the edit cursor on the line in the source file where the breakpoint is set and switches focus to the Code Editor.
Properties	Displays the Edit breakpoint dialog box.

TIP

> To quickly edit the source code line on which a breakpoint is set, double-click on the breakpoint in the Filename column of the Breakpoint list window. This is the same as choosing Edit Source from the Breakpoint list speed menu.

The secondary speed menu can be displayed by clicking the right mouse button while the cursor is over any part of the Breakpoint list window except in the Filename column. This speed menu has items called Add, Delete All, Disable All, and Enable All. These items are self-explanatory, so I won't bother to comment on them.

NOTE

> In my opinion, the Add speed menu item is not very useful. It is much easier to set a breakpoint in the Code Editor than it is to add a breakpoint via the Add command in the Breakpoint list window.

Breakpoints can be enabled or disabled any time you like. You might disable a breakpoint if you want to run the program normally for a while; you can then enable the breakpoint again later without having to re-create it. Breakpoints that are disabled are ignored by the debugger.

If you want to modify a breakpoint, you can choose Properties from the primary Breakpoint list speed menu. When you do, the Edit breakpoint dialog box is displayed. (See Figure 11.3.)

Figure 11.3.

The Edit breakpoint dialog box.

The primary reason to modify a breakpoint is to add conditions to the breakpoint. (Conditional breakpoints are discussed in the section "Conditional Breakpoints.") The New button in the Edit breakpoint dialog box works in a curious way. If you click the New button, a breakpoint will be set on the line containing the cursor in the Code Editor. This is not a particularly useful feature, so you can happily ignore the New button in the Edit breakpoint dialog box.

To remove a breakpoint, you can select the breakpoint in the breakpoint list and then press the Delete key on the keyboard. To delete all breakpoints, right-click the mouse to bring up the secondary speed menu and then choose Delete All from the speed menu.

Now let's take a look at the two breakpoint types.

Simple Breakpoints

Breakpoints can be either simple or conditional. A *simple breakpoint* will cause program execution to be suspended whenever the breakpoint is hit. When you initially set a breakpoint, it is, by default, a simple breakpoint. Simple breakpoints don't really require additional explanation. When the breakpoint is encountered, program execution pauses at the breakpoint, and the debugger awaits your bidding. There's no need to belabor the point.

Conditional Breakpoints

In the case of a *conditional breakpoint*, program execution is paused only when predefined conditions are met. To create a conditional breakpoint, first set the breakpoint in the Code Editor. Then choose View | Breakpoints from the main menu to display the Breakpoint list dialog box. Right-click on the breakpoint for which you want to set conditions and choose Properties from the speed menu. When the Edit breakpoint dialog box is displayed, set the conditions for the breakpoint.

Conditional breakpoints come in two flavors. The first type is a *conditional expression breakpoint*. Enter the conditional expression in the Condition field of the Edit breakpoint dialog box (refer to Figure 11.3). When the program runs, the conditional expression is evaluated each time the breakpoint is encountered. When the conditional expression evaluates to true, program execution is halted. If the condition does not evaluate to true, the breakpoint is ignored. For example, look back at the last breakpoint in the Breakpoint list window shown in Figure 11.2. This breakpoint has a conditional expression of x > 10. If at some point in the execution of the program x is greater than 10, the program will stop at the breakpoint. If x is never greater than 10, program execution will not stop at the breakpoint.

The other type of conditional breakpoint is the *pass count breakpoint*. With a pass count breakpoint, program execution is paused only after the breakpoint is encountered the specified number of times. To specify a pass count breakpoint, edit the breakpoint and specify a value for the Pass count field in the Edit breakpoint dialog box. Figure 11.2 shows a breakpoint that has the pass count set to 3. Program execution will stop at this breakpoint the third time the breakpoint is encountered.

NOTE

> The pass count is 1 based and not 0 based. As indicated in the previous example, a pass count of 3 means that the breakpoint will be valid the third time the breakpoint is encountered by the program.

Use pass count breakpoints when you need your program to execute through a breakpoint a certain number of times before you break to inspect variables, step through code, or something similar.

NOTE

> Conditional breakpoints will slow down the normal execution of the program because the conditions need to be evaluated each time a conditional breakpoint is encountered. If your program is acting sluggish during debugging, check your breakpoints in the breakpoint list and see whether you have conditional breakpoints that you have forgotten about.

TIP

> The fact that conditional breakpoints slow down program execution can work in your favor at times. If you have a process that you want to view in slow motion, set one or more conditional breakpoints in that section of code. Set the conditions so that they will never be met and your program will be slowed down but not stopped.

The Run to Cursor Command

There is another debugging command that deserves mention here. The Run to Cursor command (found under the Run menu on the main menu and on the Code Editor speed menu) will run the program until the source line containing the editing cursor is reached. At that point the program stops as if a breakpoint were placed on that line.

Run to Cursor acts like a temporary breakpoint. You can use this command rather than setting a breakpoint on a line that you want to immediately inspect. Just place the cursor on the line you want to break on and choose Run to Cursor (or press F4). The debugger behaves exactly as if you had placed a breakpoint on that line. The benefit is that you don't have to clear the breakpoint after you are done debugging that section of code.

Watching Variables

So what do you do once you've stopped at a breakpoint? Usually you will stop at a breakpoint to inspect the value of one or more variables. You might want to ensure that a particular variable has the value you think it should have, or you may not have any idea what a variable's value is and simply want to find out. The Watch List allows you to do that.

The function of the Watch List is pretty basic: It allows you to inspect the values of variables. This simple but essential feature often gets overlooked because a lot of programmers don't take the time to learn to use the debugger fully. You can add as many variables to the Watch List as you like. Figure 11.4 shows the Watch List during a debugging session.

Figure 11.4.

The Watch List in action.

The variable name is displayed in the Watch List followed by its value. How the variable value is displayed is determined by the data type of the variable and the current display settings for that watch item.

The Watch List Speed Menu

As with every other C++Builder window discussed up to this point, the Watch List has its own speed menu. (You'd be disappointed if it didn't, right?) Table 11.4 lists the Watch List speed menu items and their descriptions.

Table 11.4. The Watch List speed menu.

Item	Description
Edit Watch	Allows you to edit the watch item with the Watch Properties dialog box.
Add Watch	Adds a new item to the Watch List.
Enable Watch	Enables the watch item.
Disable Watch	Disables the watch item.
Delete Watch	Removes the watch item from the Watch List.
Enable All Watches	Enables all items in the Watch List.
Disable All Watches	Disables all items in the Watch List.
Delete All Watches	Deletes all items in the Watch List.

The Edit Watch and Add Watch speed menu items both invoke the Watch Properties dialog box, so let's look at that next.

Using the Watch Properties Dialog Box

You use the Watch Properties dialog box when you add a watch and when you edit a watch. Figure 11.5 shows the Watch Properties dialog box as it looks when you're editing a variable called `buff`.

Figure 11.5.

The Watch Properties dialog box.

The Expression field at the top of the Watch Properties dialog box is where you can enter a variable name to edit or to add to the Watch List. If you are adding a watch by selecting it from the Code Editor window, this field will already be filled in (see the section titled "Adding Variables to the Watch List"). This field is a combo box that can be used to select previously used watch items.

You use the Repeat count field when you are inspecting arrays. For example, let's say you have an array of 20 integers. To inspect the first 10 `int`s in the array, you would enter the first element of the array in the Expression field (`array[0]`, for example) and then enter `10` in the Repeat count field. The first 10 elements of the array would then be displayed in the Watch List.

NOTE

> If you just add the array name to the Watch List, all elements in the array will be displayed. Use the Repeat count field when you want to view only a specific number of array elements.

You use the Digits field only when inspecting floating-point numbers. Enter the number of significant digits you want to see when your floating-point number is displayed in the Watch List. The displayed digits are rounded, not truncated. Another field in this dialog box, the Enabled field, determines whether the watch item is currently enabled.

The remainder of the Watch Properties dialog box is comprised of the various display options from which you can choose. Each data type has a default display type, and that type will be used if you choose the Default viewing option. The Default viewing option is the default. (Sorry, there's just no other way to say it!) Select one of the other viewing options to view the data in other ways. Figure 11.6 shows the Watch List window with two variables added and with various viewing options applied. The `buff` variable is a character array, and the `i` variable is an integer.

Figure 11.6.

The Watch List with various viewing options.

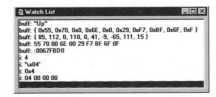

To modify a watch item, click on the item in the Watch List and choose Edit Watch from the Watch List speed menu. The Watch Properties dialog box is displayed, and you can edit the watch item as needed.

TIP

> The fastest way to edit a watch item is to double-click on its name in the Watch List.

Enabling and Disabling Watch Items

As with breakpoints, individual items in the Watch List can be enabled or disabled. When a watch item is disabled, it is grayed and its value shows <disabled>.

To disable a watch item, click on the item's name in the Watch List and choose Disable Watch from the Watch List speed menu. To enable the watch item again, choose Enable Watch from the speed menu.

NOTE

> You may want to disable watch items that you don't currently want to watch but that you will need again later. Having a number of enabled items in the Watch List can slow down program execution during the debugging process because all the variables in the Watch List must be updated each time a line of code executes. It doesn't take many items in the Watch List to slow things down, so don't forget to delete or disable any unused items in the Watch List.

Adding Variables to the Watch List

You can add variables to the Watch List in one of several ways. The quickest is to click on the variable name in the editor window and then select Add Watch at Cursor from the Code Editor speed menu or press Ctrl+F5. The Watch Properties dialog box will be displayed, where you can either select watch options for the watch item or click OK (or press Enter) to accept the defaults. The watch item will be added to the Watch List.

To add a variable to the watch without first locating it in the source file, choose Run | Add Watch from the main menu. When the Watch Properties dialog box comes up, enter the name of the variable you want to add to the Watch List and click OK.

NOTE

> Although you can add a class instance variable to the Watch List, the displayed value will not likely be useful. In the case of pointers to objects, this is useful for determining if the pointer is valid, but often

> you want to view the details of the class. For viewing all the data
> members of a class, you should use the Debug Inspector, which I'll
> discuss in a minute.

Using the Watch List

When a breakpoint is hit, the Watch List will display the current value of any variables that have been added to the Watch List. If the Watch List is not currently open, you can choose View | Watches from the main menu to display it.

Under certain circumstances, a message will be displayed next to the variable rather than the variable's value. If, for instance, a variable is out of scope or not found, the Watch List displays `Undefined symbol 'x'` next to the variable name. If the program is not running or if the program is not stopped at a breakpoint, the Watch List will display `[process not accessible]` for all watch items. A disabled watch item will have `<disabled>` next to it. Other messages may be displayed depending on the current state of the application or the current state of a particular variable.

As I said yesterday, you may on occasion see `Variable has been optimized and is not available` in the Watch List. This is one of the minor disadvantages to having an optimizing compiler. If you need to inspect variables that are subject to optimization, either declare the variable with the `volatile` keyword or turn off the Register Variables option on the Compiler page of the Project Options dialog box. After debugging, remove the `volatile` modifier from the variable.

TIP

The Watch List can be used as a quickie decimal/hexadecimal converter. To convert a hex number to decimal, choose Run | Add Watch from the main menu. Type the hexadecimal number in the Expression field and click OK. Both the hexadecimal number and the decimal equivalent will be displayed in the Watch List. To convert a decimal number to hex, perform the same procedure, except click the Hexadecimal radio button to change the display type to hexadecimal. Because the Expression field will accept a mathematical expression, you can also use the Watch List as a hex calculator. You can even mix hexadecimal and decimal values in the same expression.

The Watch List is a simple but vital tool when you're debugging applications. To illustrate the use of the Watch List, perform this exercise:

1. Create a new application and place a button on the form. Change the button's Name property to WatchBtn and its Caption to Watch Test. Change the Name property of the form to DebugMain and the Caption property to whatever you like.

2. Double-click the button to display its OnClick handler in the Code Editor. Enter the following code at the cursor:

```
String s;
int x = Width;
s = String(x);
int y = Height;
x *= y;
s = String(x);
x /= y;
s = String(x);
Width = x;
Height = y;
```

3. Choose Options | Project from the main menu and click on the C++ page. Change the Optimization option to None. (See the note in the section titled "Stepping Through Your Code" for an explanation of this step.)

4. Save the project. Name the unit DbgMain and the project DebugTst.

5. Set a breakpoint on the second line in the code you entered in step 2. Run the program.

6. Click the Watch Test button. The debugger will stop at the breakpoint.

7. Add watches for the variables s, x, and y. (Initially the variables x and y will display the message Variable 'x' has been optimized, but don't worry about that.)

8. Arrange the Watch List and Code Editor so that you can see both.

9. Switch focus to the Code Editor and press F8 to execute the next line of code. That line is executed, and the execution point moves to the next line. The variable x now shows a value (probably 435).

10. Continue to step through the program by pressing F8. Watch the results of the variables in the Watch List.

11. When the execution point gets to the last line in the function, click the Run button on the speedbar to continue running the program.

12. Click the Watch Test button as many times as you want to get a feel for how the Watch List works. Experiment with different watch settings each time through.

11

NOTE

The code in this example gets the values for the Width and Height properties of the form, performs some calculations, and then sets Width and Height back to where they were when you started. In the end nothing changes, but there is a good reason for assigning values to the Width and Height properties at the end of the function.

If you don't actually do something with the variables x and y, you wouldn't be able to inspect them because the compiler will optimize them and they won't be available to watch. Essentially, the compiler can look ahead, see that the variables are never used, and just more or less discard them. Putting the variables to use at the end of the function avoids having them optimized away by the compiler.

I've brought this up several times now, but I want to make sure you have a basic understanding of how an optimizing compiler works. When you start debugging your applications, this knowledge will help avoid some frustration when you start getting those Variable 'x' has been optimized and is not available messages in the Watch List.

The Debug Inspector

Simply stated, the Debug Inspector allows you to view data objects such as classes and components (components are really just classes, anyway). You can also inspect simple data types such as integers, character arrays, and so on, but those are best viewed with the Watch List. The Debug Inspector is most useful in examining classes and structures.

NOTE

You can use the Debug Inspector only when program execution is paused under the debugger.

To inspect an object, click on the object's name in a source file and choose Inspect from the Code Editor speed menu (or press Alt+F5). You could also choose Run | Inspect from the main menu.

NOTE

> When you use Inspect from the speed menu or use Alt+F5, the Debug Inspector automatically displays the object under the cursor. If you choose Run | Inspect from the main menu, you will first get a dialog box that asks you to input the object to inspect. Enter a variable name and click OK. The Debug Inspector will be shown with the requested object displayed.

The Debug Inspector window comes up with details of the object displayed. If the object is a simple data type, the Debug Inspector window shows the current value (in both decimal and hex for numeric data types), and the status line at the bottom displays the data type. For example, if you inspect an integer variable, the value will be shown and the status bar will say int. At the top of the Debug Inspector is a combo box that initially contains a description of the object being inspected.

If you are inspecting a class, the Debug Inspector will look something like Figure 11.7.

Figure 11.7.

The Debug Inspector inspecting a form class.

In order to better understand the Debug Inspector, do the following:

1. Load the DebugTst program you created earlier (if it's not already loaded).
2. Set a breakpoint somewhere in the WatchBtnClick() function.
3. Run the program and click the Watch button. The debugger stops at the breakpoint you have set.

4. From the main menu, choose Run | Inspect. The Inspect dialog box is displayed.

5. Type this in the Expression field and click OK.

6. The Debug Inspector is displayed.

NOTE You can only inspect this from within a class member function. If you happen to set a breakpoint in a regular function and then attempt to inspect this, you will get an error stating that this is an invalid symbol.

As you can see, when you're inspecting classes the Debug Inspector window contains three pages. The Data page shows all the data members for the class. The list of data members is hierarchical. The first items listed are the data items that belong to the immediate class. The next group of items listed is the data members of that class's immediate ancestor class—in this case, TForm. If you scroll down through the Debug Inspector list, you will see that following the TForm data members are the data members for the TScrollingWinControl class (TForm's immediate ancestor) and on and on.

By using the arrow keys to move up and down through the list of data members, you can tell at a glance what each data member's type is (look at the status bar). To further inspect a data member, double-click on the value column on the line showing the data member. A second Debug Inspector window is opened with the selected data member displayed. You can have multiple Debug Inspector windows open simultaneously.

NOTE The Debug Inspector has a lot of information to load, so scrolling down through the list of items can be slow on some systems.

The Methods page of the Debug Inspector displays the class's methods. As with the data members discussed earlier, the list of methods is hierarchical. The first methods are those in the immediate class, followed by the methods in the ancestor classes. In some cases the Methods tab is not displayed (when inspecting simple data types, for instance).

The Properties page of the Debug Inspector shows the properties for the class being inspected. Inspecting properties through the Debug Inspector is very slow if you are inspecting a VCL inherited class. Most of the time you can accomplish the same thing by inspecting the data member associated with a particular property on the Data page instead. Inspecting the data member is much faster than inspecting properties.

NOTE

> The Methods page and the Properties page of the Debug Inspector are only available when you're inspecting a class. When you're inspecting simple data types, only the Data page will be displayed.

The Debug Inspector speed menu has several items that allow you to work with the Debug Inspector and the individual variables. For example, instead of opening a new Debug Inspector window for each object, you can choose Descend from the speed menu to replace the current object in the Debug Inspector window with the object under the cursor. This method has an added advantage: The IDE will keep a history list of the objects you inspect. To go back to an object you have previously inspected, just choose the object from the combo box at the top of the Debug Inspector window. Choosing one of the objects in the history list will again show that object in the Debug Inspector window.

The Change item on the Debug Inspector speed menu will allow you to change the value of a variable. Change data members with care. Changing the wrong data member or specifying a value that is invalid for that data member could lead to your program crashing. The Inspect item on the speed menu allows you to open a second Debug Inspector window with the item under the cursor displayed. The New Expression speed menu item allows you to enter a new expression to inspect in the Debug Inspector.

The Show Inherited item on the Debug Inspector speed menu is a toggle that determines how much information the Debug Inspector should display. When the Show Inherited option is on, the Debug Inspector shows all data members, methods, and properties of the class being inspected as well as the data members, methods, and properties of all ancestor classes. When the Show Inherited option is off, only the data members, methods, and properties of the class itself are shown. Turning off this option can greatly speed up the Debug Inspector since it does not have as much information to display.

TIP

> If you have a class data member and you don't remember that data member's type, you can click on it when stopped at a breakpoint and press Alt+F5 to display the Debug Inspector. The status bar at the bottom of the Debug Inspector window will tell you the data type of the variable. This also works for Windows and system #defines such as HINSTANCE, HWND, DWORD, and so on.

Other Debugging Tools

C++Builder has some additional debugging tools to aid you in tracking down bugs. Some of these tools are, by nature, advanced debugging tools. Although the advanced debugging tools are not as commonly used as the other tools, they can be very powerful in the hands of an experienced programmer.

Evaluate/Modify

The Evaluate/Modify dialog box allows you to inspect the current value of a variable and to modify the value of a variable if you want. Using this dialog box, you can test for different outcomes by modifying a particular variable. This allows you to play a what-if game with your program as it runs. Figure 11.8 shows the Evaluate/Modify dialog box inspecting an integer variable called x.

Figure 11.8.

The Evaluate/Modify dialog box.

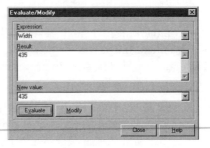

The Evaluate/Modify dialog box works similarly to the Watch List or the Debug Inspector. If you click on a variable in the source code and choose Evaluate/Modify from the Code Editor speed menu, the variable will be evaluated. If you want to enter a value that is not currently showing in the source code, you can choose Run | Evaluate/Modify from the main menu and then type a variable name to evaluate.

The Evaluate field is used to enter the variable name or expression you want to evaluate. When you click the Evaluate button (or press Enter), the expression will be evaluated and the result displayed in the Result field.

TIP

The Evaluate/Modify dialog box can be used as a quickie calculator. You can enter hex or decimal numbers (or a combination) in a mathematical formula and have the result evaluated. For instance, if you type

```
0x400 - 256
```

in the Evaluate field and press Enter, the result, 768, will be displayed in the Result field.

You can also enter logical expressions in the Evaluate field and have the result shown in the Results field. For instance, if you entered

```
20 * 20 == 400
```

the Result field would show true. The only problem with this scenario is that the program must be stopped at a breakpoint for the Evaluate/Modify dialog box to function.

If you want to change the value of a variable, enter a new value for the variable in the New Value field and click the Modify button. The variable's value will be changed to the new value entered. When you click the Run button to restart the program (or continue stepping), the new value will be used.

NOTE   The Evaluate/Modify dialog box does not update automatically when you step through your code as do the Watch List and Debug Inspector. If your code modifies the variable in the Evaluate/Modify dialog box, you must click the Evaluate button again to see the results. A typical interaction with this dialog box would be to evaluate a variable or expression and then immediately close the Evaluate/Modify dialog box.

View Call Stack

While your program is running, you can view the call stack to inspect any functions your program called. From the main menu, choose View | Call Stack to display the Call stack window. This window displays a list of the functions that were called by your program and the order in which they were called. The most recently called function will be at the top of the window. The functions listed will be a combination of functions in your program, VCL methods, and functions contained in Windows DLLs. Figure 11.9 shows the call stack as it appears after you run the DebugTst program you created earlier in the chapter.

Figure 11.9.

The Call stack
window.

In this case the first function on the list is `TMainForm::WatchBtnClick()`. Following that you see calls to some VCL functions and a couple calls to functions (unnamed) in the Windows `KERNEL32.DLL`. Remember that the functions are listed in reverse order—the function executed last shows up first in the call stack list.

Double-clicking on a function name in the Call stack window will take you to the source code line for that function if the function is in your program. In case of functions in Windows DLLs, the Call stack window will contain just an address and the name of the DLL. Double-clicking on a listed function that is contained in a DLL will display the CPU View window (the CPU View is discussed in the next section).

 NOTE

> If you have linked to the debug version of VCL, double-clicking on a VCL method in the Call stack window will display the VCL source code for that method. If you have not linked to the debug version of VCL, double-clicking on a VCL method in the Call stack window will display the CPU View.

Viewing the call stack is most useful after a Windows Access Violation error. By viewing the call stack, you can see where your program was just before the error occurred. Knowing where your program was just before it crashed is often the first step in determining what went wrong.

 TIP

> If the call stack list contains seemingly nonsensical information, it could be that the call stack was corrupted. A corrupted call stack is usually an indicator of a stack problem. This is not as likely to occur in a 32-bit program as it is in a 16-bit program, but it can still happen.

CPU View

The CPU View allows you to view your program at the assembly level. Obviously this is an advanced debugging feature. Using this view you can step into or over instructions one assembly instruction at a time. You can also run the program to a certain assembly instruction just as you can run the program to a certain source line with the regular debugger. The CPU View window has five panes: the disassembly pane, the register pane, the flags pane, the raw stack pane, and the dump pane. Each pane has a speed menu associated with it. The speed menus provide all the functions necessary to utilize that pane. The CPU View requires a knowledge of assembly language to be used effectively. To display the CPU View, choose View | CPU from the main menu.

The Go to Address Command

The Go to Address command is also an advanced debugging tool. When your program crashes, Windows displays an error message showing the address of the violation. You can use the Go to Address command to attempt to find out where in your program the crash occurred. When you get an Access Violation error from Windows, you will see a dialog box similar to the one in Figure 11.10.

Figure 11.10.

A Windows message box reporting an access violation.

When you see this error message, write down the address at which the violation occurred and then choose Search | Go to Address from the main menu to display the Go to Address dialog box. Enter the address you just wrote down in the Address field of the Go to Address dialog box. When you click OK, the debugger will attempt to find the source code line where the error occurred. If the error occurred in your code, the cursor will be placed on the line that generated the error. If the error occurred somewhere outside of your code, you will get a message box saying that the address could not be found. As I said, this is an advanced debugging tool and is something you might never use.

Stepping Through Your Code

Stepping through code is one of the most basic debugging operations, yet it still needs to be mentioned here. Sometimes we fail to see the forest for the trees. (Just like sometimes authors of programming books fail to include the obvious!) Reviewing the basics from time to time may reveal something you were not previously aware of.

When you stop at a breakpoint, you can do many things to determine what is going on with your code. You can set up variables to watch in the Watch List, inspect objects with the Debug Inspector, or view the call stack. You can also step through your code to watch what happens to your variables and objects as each line of code is executed. As you continue to step through your code, you will see that the line in your source code that will be executed next is highlighted in blue. If you have the Watch List and Debug Inspector windows open, they will be updated as each line of code is executed. Any changes to variables or objects will be immediately seen in the watch or inspector window.

NOTE

The compiler optimization option is set to Optimize for Speed by default. (Optimization options were discussed yesterday.) When the compiler optimizes code, it "rearranges" your source code using mysterious means about which mere mortals can only speculate. (Your source code is not rearranged per se, but the resulting assembly code may not exactly match the source code as it appears in your source file.) The end result is that you end up with a program that runs faster—and that is, of course, a good thing.

This benefit does come at a cost, however. Earlier I discussed the fact that variables can be optimized by the compiler making them unavailable for inspection, and this is one of the disadvantages of using optimizations.

Another interesting side effect of using optimizations is that your code gets rearranged as I mentioned. The net result of this rearranging is that when you step through your code, the execution point may not proceed sequentially from line to line as you might expect. Rather, the execution point appears to jump around in your source and may even land on a single line of code multiple times.

This is all perfectly normal, but it can be disconcerting when you are just learning to use the debugger. If you prefer to see the execution point proceed sequentially through your code, turn off optimizations while debugging. Turn optimizations back on again for your final builds. Remember that when you change optimization settings, you need to do a Build All for all modules to be rebuilt using the new settings.

The IDE debugger has two primary stepping commands that you can use to aid in your debugging operations: Step Over and Trace Into. Step Over means to execute the next line in the source code and pause on the line immediately following. Step Over is sort of a misnomer. The name would seem to indicate that you can step over a source line and the line would not be executed. That is not the case, however. Step Over means that the current line will be executed and any functions that that source line calls will be run at full speed. For instance, let's say you have set a breakpoint at a line that calls another function in your program. When you tell the debugger to step over the function, the debugger executes the function and stops on the next line. (Contrast this with how Trace Into works, which you'll learn about in a minute, and it will make more sense.) To use Step Over to step through your program, you can either press F8 or choose Run | Step Over from the main menu.

NOTE   As you step through various source code units in your program, the Code Editor automatically loads and displays the needed source units if they are not already open.

The Trace Into command allows you to trace into any functions that are encountered as you step through your code. Rather than executing the function and returning to the next line as Step Over does, Trace Into will place the execution point on the first source code line in the function being called. You can then step through that function line by line using Step Over or Trace Into as necessary. The keyboard shortcut for Trace Into is F7.

After you have inspected variables and done whatever debugging you need to do, you can again run the program at full speed by clicking the Run button. The program will then function as normal until the next breakpoint is encountered.

TIP   If you have enabled the Link Debug Version of VCL Linker option, when you encounter a VCL method Trace Into will take you into the VCL source code for that method. Once in the VCL source, you can inspect whatever variables you need to see. If you turn on this option, you must do a Build All for it to take effect. As I said earlier, stepping into the VCL source is of doubtful benefit to most programmers.

Another, less frequently used, debugging command is Trace To Next Source Line (Shift+F7 on the keyboard). You will not likely use this command a lot, particularly not until you get more familiar with debugging and Windows programming in general. Some Windows API functions use what is termed a *callback function*. This means that the Windows function calls one of your functions to perform some action. If the execution point is on a Windows API function that uses a callback function, using Trace To Next Source Line will jump the execution point to the first line in the callback function. The effect is similar to that of Trace Into, but the specific situation where Trace To Next Source Line is used is altogether different. If that doesn't make any sense to you, don't worry about it. It's not important for what you need to learn today.

NOTE

When you are stepping through a function, the execution point will eventually get to the closing brace. If the function you are stepping through returns control to Windows when it finishes, pressing F8 when on the closing brace will exit the function and will return control to the program being debugged. There is no obvious indication that the program is no longer paused because the IDE still has focus. This behavior can be confusing the first few times you encounter it unless you are aware of what has happened. To switch back to your program, just activate it like you would any other program (click on its glyph on the Windows taskbar or use Alt+Tab).

As I said, stepping through your code is a basic debugging technique, but it is one that you will use constantly while debugging. Of all the keyboard shortcuts available to you in C++Builder, F7 and F8 should definitely be in your arsenal.

Debugging Techniques

I have touched on a few debugging techniques as we looked at the various aspects of the IDE debugger up to this point in the chapter. I will mention a few more techniques to make your debugging tasks easier.

The Diagnostic Macros: TRACE and WARN

Sometimes it is helpful to track your program's execution. For instance, it would be nice to have a log file that could be used to log events, such as when your program executes certain functions. Or maybe you would like to send the value of a variable to a log file so that you could inspect its value without stopping program execution at a breakpoint. The diagnostic macros, TRACE and WARN, allow you to do exactly that. These macros are convenient debugging tools that many programmers overlook because of sparse documentation and general lack of discussion on the subject.

When you use TRACE or WARN in your programs, the messages produced by these macros go to a log file called OutDbg1.txt. C++Builder automatically creates this text file and displays it in a Code Editor window whenever a TRACE or WARN statement is encountered. You can then browse the log file to see what has happened in your program.

NOTE

The OutDbg1.txt file has a couple interesting characteristics. For one, the file is not considered part of the project. When you do a Save All, the OutDbg1.txt file is not saved as the rest of the files in the project are. Along those same lines, when you close the OutDbg1.txt file, you are not prompted to save the file. If you want the file saved, you must specifically do a Save or Save All prior to closing it.

This might seem a little odd, but it makes sense when you think about it. The log file is almost always used as a temporary debugging tool. Rarely do you need to save the contents of the log file, so by not prompting you to save the file, C++Builder saves you the aggravation of having to deal with another message box.

The TRACE macro simply outputs a line of text to the log file in the Code Editor. For example, you might have the following code in your FormCreate() function:

```
void __fastcall TMainForm::FormCreate(TObject *Sender)
{
  TRACE("Entering FormCreate()");
  // intialization code
  TRACE("Leaving FormCreate()");
}
```

When this code is executed, two lines will be written to the OutDbg1.txt file. You can view the messages in the log file at any time—either during program execution or after the program terminates—simply by clicking on the OutDbg1.txt tab in the Code Editor.

NOTE

The diagnostic macros make use of C++ streams (remember when we used those way back on Day 1, "Getting Your Feet Wet"?). This makes it possible to create log messages like the following:
```
TRACE("Varible x = " << x);
```
This makes it extremely easy to log a wide variety of diagnostic messages.

The WARN macro is similar to TRACE except that it allows you to introduce conditions—the message will be output only if the condition is met. The following example sends a message to the message window only if the variable x is greater than 200:

```
WARN(x > 200, "x = " << x << ": Possible range error");
```

The WARN macro can reduce clutter in your log file by displaying messages only when necessary.

The diagnostic messages written to the log file include the source code module name, the line number in the source code, and the specified text. For example, let's say you had the following in a source code unit named MyApp.cpp:

```
int x = 100;
TRACE ("x = " << x);
WARN (x == 100, "x is now 100");
```

The text written to the OutDbg1.txt file would look like this:

```
Trace MyApp.cpp 18: [Def] x = 100
Warning MyApp.cpp 19: [Def] x is now 100
```

As you can see, the type of message (trace or warning), the source unit name, the line number, and text are all displayed. You can ignore the [Def] entry in the log message because it has no meaning in C++Builder (consider it a holdover from Borland C++).

NOTE	If no OutDbg1.txt file appears in the Code Editor, when a TRACE or WARN statement is executed, the OutDbg1.txt edit window will be created and the text displayed. If an OutDbg1.txt file is already displayed in the Code Editor, any new diagnostic messages are appended to the end of the existing file.

To use the diagnostic macros you must first enable them by defining __TRACE and __WARN. You can put the #defines at the top of one of your source files, but it would probably be better to add them at the project level. To add the #defines at the project level, choose Options | Project from the main menu. When the Project Options dialog box comes up, click on the Conditionals/Defines page and enter the following in the Conditional Defines field:

```
__TRACE;__WARN
```

Note that both defines are proceeded by a double underscore and that they are separated with a semicolon.

The diagnostic macros are declared in a file called checks.h, so you need to add the line

```
#include <checks.h>
```

to your source code as well. If you neglect to include checks.h, you will get a compiler error on any lines that contain TRACE or WARN.

Tracking Down GPFs

All Windows programmers have encountered general protection faults and general protection exceptions while developing their applications. For simplicity, I will refer to both universally as GPFs.

> **NOTE** The term GPF is a holdover from 16-bit Windows. Its use is still prevalent in the 32-bit Windows programming world even though 32-bit Windows actually generates access violation errors rather than general protection faults.

GPFs can be difficult to track down for beginning and experienced Windows programmers alike. Often, as programmers gain experience in writing Windows programs, they develop a sixth sense of sorts regarding locating the cause of GPFs. The following sections describe some things to look for when trying to track down the elusive GPF. These are not the only situations that cause a program to crash, but they are some of the most common.

Uninitialized Pointers

An *uninitialized pointer* is a pointer that has been declared but has not been set to point to anything meaningful in your program. An uninitialized pointer will contain random data. In the best case it points to some harmless spot in memory. In the worst cases the uninitialized pointer points to a random memory location somewhere in your program. This can lead to erratic program behavior because the pointer might point to a different memory location each time the program is run. Always set pointers to NULL both before they are used for the first time and after the object pointed to is deleted. If you try to access a NULL pointer, your program will GPF, but the offending line in the source code will be highlighted by the debugger, and you can immediately identify the problem pointer.

Deleting Previously Deleted Pointers

Deleting a pointer that has already been deleted will result in a GPF. The advice given for working with uninitialized pointers applies here as well: Set any deleted pointers to NULL or 0. In C++ it is perfectly safe to delete a NULL pointer. By setting your deleted pointers to NULL, you ensure that no ill effects will occur if you accidentally delete the pointer a second time.

Array Overwrites

Overwriting the end of an array can cause a GPF. In some cases the overwritten memory may not be critical, and the problem might not show up right away, but some time later the program crashes. When that happens you will likely be looking for a bug at the point where the program crashed when the actual problem occurred in a completely different part of the program. In other cases, the memory tromped on is critical, and the program GPFs immediately. In extreme cases you may even crash Windows. Check all arrays to be sure you are not overwriting the end of the array.

GPF on Program Termination

When a program GPFs on normal shutdown, it is usually an indication that the stack size is set too small. Although this is not likely in a 32-bit program, it could happen under extreme circumstances. A GPF on program termination can also be caused by deleting an already deleted pointer, as I've discussed.

Debug Quick Tips

In addition to the many tips offered on the preceding pages, you might want to implement some of these:

☐ For quick inspection of a variable without using breakpoints, change the form's Caption property to display the variable in question. Because placing a Label component on a form is so easy, you could use a label, too. Change the text in the label to show the value of a variable or any other information you might want to display.

☐ To slow down your program temporarily (possibly to view program effects in slow motion), enable a conditional breakpoint or a data watch breakpoint. These breakpoints slow down program execution while they check the condition of the breakpoint.

☐ Use the Evaluate/Modify dialog box to temporarily change the value of a variable at runtime. This will allow you to view the effects that different values have on your program without recompiling your code each time.

☐ Ordinarily you cannot use Trace Into with inline functions. To be able to trace into inline functions, you can turn on the Disable Inline Expansions option. Turn off the option again before your final build.

☐ To inspect the class that the debugger is currently stopped in, choose Run | Inspect from the main menu and enter this in the Expression field.

☐ Use MessageBeep(-1) as an audible indicator that a certain point in your program has been reached. This Windows API function beeps the PC speaker when called with a parameter of -1.

☐ You can stop an errant debuggee by choosing Run | Program Reset from the main menu or by pressing Ctrl+F2.

☐ Use temporary variables to break down long equations or chained function calls so that you can examine the results in more manageable pieces.

☐ Use the MessageBox() function to display program tracing information.

Summary

Debugging is a never-ending task. Debugging means more than just tracking down a bug in your program. Savvy programmers learn to use the debugger from the outset of a new project. The debugger is a development tool as well as a bug-finding tool. After today, you should at least have a basic understanding of how to use the debugger. You will still have to spend a lot of time actually using the debugger before you are proficient at it, but you've now got a place to start.

Workshop

The Workshop contains quiz questions to help you solidify your understanding of the material covered and exercises to provide you with experience in using what you have learned. You can find answers to the quiz questions in Appendix A, "Answers to Quiz Questions."

Q&A

Q My program used to run at regular speed when I ran it from the IDE. Now it's as slow as molasses in January. Why is that?

A More than likely you've got either a large number of breakpoints that you have disabled and forgotten about, or one or more conditional breakpoints in your code. Go to the breakpoint list and delete any breakpoints you are not currently using. Also, be sure you do not have a lot of variables listed in the Watch List.

Q **I have a variable that I want to view in both decimal and hexadecimal format. Can I do that with the Watch List?**

A Yes. First add the variable to the Watch List. When the Watch Properties dialog box comes up, choose the Decimal viewing option. Now add the variable again, but this time choose the Hexadecimal viewing option. Both items will be listed in the Watch List, one in decimal format and the other in hex format.

Q **I'm trying to add the Width property of a component on my form to the Watch List. I get some strange error like, "Pointer to structure required on left side of something or another." What am I doing wrong?**

A You can't inspect a property of a component using the Watch List. You can, however, inspect the component using the Debug Inspector and locate the FWidth data member rather than the Width property. (The FWidth data member holds the value of the Width property.)

Q **I want to stop at a breakpoint only when a variable reaches a certain value and after the breakpoint has been hit a certain number of times. Can I do that?**

A Sure. Enter a conditional expression in the Condition field of the Edit Breakpoint dialog box and a value in the Pass Count field. When the condition is met for the number of times indicated by the pass count, the program will pause at the breakpoint.

Q **I'm stepping through my code, and I get to a function in my program that I want to debug. When I press F8, the execution point jumps right over the function instead of going into it. What do I do to get into that function?**

A When the execution point is on the line where the function is called, press F7 (Trace Into) instead of F8. Now you can step through the function a line at a time.

Q **When I step through my code, the execution point jumps all over the place rather than proceeding through my code a line at a time. What causes that?**

A In a word: optimization. If you want to be able to debug your program one source code line at a time, sequentially, turn off all optimizations and then do a Build All to rebuild the project.

Q **I step through a function line by line. Sometimes when I get to the closing brace of the function I press F8 one more time and nothing happens. Why?**

A Because when that particular function returns, your program has nothing more to do, so it goes back into its idle state. Essentially, there is no more code to step through at that point, so the debugger returns control to the program being debugged.

Q **How do I use the CPU View when debugging?**

A Just choose View | CPU from the main menu to display the CPU View. Knowing what to do with the CPU View, however, is another matter entirely!

Quiz

1. How do you set a breakpoint on a particular line of code?
2. What is an invalid breakpoint?
3. How do you set a conditional breakpoint?
4. How can you change the properties of an item in the Watch List?
5. What's the quickest way to add a variable to the Watch List?
6. What tool do you use to view the data members and methods of a class?
7. How do you trace into a function call when stepping with the debugger?
8. How can you change the value of a variable at runtime?
9. What is the difference between the TRACE and WARN macros?
10. How do you view the output from the TRACE and WARN macros?

Exercises

1. Load the ScratchPad program that you created a few days ago. Place breakpoints in the FileOpenClick() and FileSaveClick() functions. Run the program. When program execution pauses, inspect the OpenDialog and SaveDialog classes, respectively.

2. Continuing with exercise 1, step through the program when you stop at a breakpoint and examine the program's operation as you step through the functions.

3. Load the DebugTst program you created earlier in this chapter. Place a breakpoint in the WatchBtnClick() function. Add the s and x variables to the Watch List. Add each variable to the Watch List four times. Edit each of the watches and change the display options. Run the program and step through the function to see the effects in the Watch List.

4. Add a conditional breakpoint to the function in exercise 3. Place it on the line immediately after the line that reads int x = Width. Make the condition x == 0 and run the program. What happens?

5. Continuing with exercise 4, edit the breakpoint and change the condition to x > 400. Run the program. Change the window's size and click the Watch Test button. Repeat this process several times, changing the window's size each time. What happens?

6. Load any program and switch to the Code Editor. Place the cursor on any line of code and choose the Run to Cursor item from the Code Editor speed menu. Experiment with the program until the breakpoint is hit.

7. Again load the DebugTst program you created earlier. Place a breakpoint in the WatchBtnClick() function and run the program. When the breakpoint is hit, use the Debug Inspector to inspect the WatchBtn.

8. Write a program that does some simple things when buttons are pressed (it doesn't matter what exactly). Place calls to TRACE in each function in the program. Run the program and try each button. Close the program. View the OutDbg1.txt file in the Code Editor to see the results of the TRACE macro.

9. Add several WARN calls to the program created in exercise 8. Run the program and again view the OutDbg1.txt file.

Day 12

C++Builder Tools and Options

by Kent Reisdorph

C++Builder comes with several tools to aid in your application development. Some of the tools are standard Windows GUI applications, and others are Win32 console applications. There are even some DOS applications in the mix. Today you will learn about some of the tools available to you. The tools include

- ☐ The Image Editor
- ☐ WinSight
- ☐ Command-line tools

We will begin today by looking at these tools. Toward the end of the chapter you will learn how to add your own tools to the C++Builder Tools menu. We will end the day with a look at the C++Builder Environment Options dialog box.

> **NOTE** In addition to the tools listed here, C++Builder also comes with a host of database tools such as Database Desktop. The database tools are covered in the chapters on C++Builder database operations.

The Image Editor

The C++Builder Image Editor is a program that allows you to create and edit bitmaps (.bmp), icons (.ico), and cursors (.cur). You can also create a resource project containing multiple bitmaps, icons, and cursors in a singe resource file (.res). The resource file can then be added to your C++Builder project, and the resources used as needed. Figure 12.1 shows the Image Editor while you're editing a bitmap.

Figure 12.1.

The Image Editor.

> **NOTE** All images are bitmaps whether they are actual bitmap files (.bmp) or are icons or cursors. I will refer to all images collectively as bitmaps in this chapter.

You can start the Image Editor by either double-clicking on the Image Editor icon in the C++Builder folder or choosing Tools | Image Editor from the C++Builder main menu. The Image Editor is a standalone program and does not have to be run from the C++Builder IDE.

12

Foreground and Background Colors

The Image Editor allows you to create 2-color, 16-color, and, in the case of bitmap files, 256-color images. You can choose from any of the available colors when drawing on a bitmap. In the bottom-left corner of the Image Editor are two boxes that contain the current foreground and background colors. (The foreground color is represented by the leftmost box.)

When using a drawing tool, you can draw with either the foreground color or the background color. To draw using the foreground color, use the left mouse button. For example, if you choose the filled rectangle tool and draw a rectangle on the bitmap, the rectangle will be filled with the foreground color. To draw a filled rectangle in the background color, use the right mouse button to drag your rectangle. The same is true for most of the other drawing tools.

NOTE
> The Text tool uses only the foreground color. You cannot place text with the background color. If you want to use the background color, you will have to change the foreground color and then place your text.

To change the foreground color, click on a color on the color palette with the left mouse button. (The color palette is located along the bottom of the Image Editor window.) When you choose a new foreground color, the square that represents the foreground color changes to show the new color selected. To change the background color, click on a color in the color palette with your right mouse button.

NOTE
> If you are editing a 256-color image, the color palette will have scroll buttons on either side so that you can scroll through the available colors.

The colors that appear in the color palette are determined by the bitmap itself if you are loading a bitmap that already exists. If you are starting a new 256-color image, the default 256-color palette is used.

You can also set the foreground or background colors using the Eyedropper tool. The Eyedropper allows you to set the foreground or background color by picking up a color that is already used on the image. To set the foreground color with the Eyedropper, choose the Eyedropper tool from the Tools palette, place the tip of the Eyedropper over a portion of the image that has the color you want to use, and then click the left mouse button. The foreground color changes to the color under the Eyedropper. To set the background color, click with your right mouse button rather than the left mouse button. The Eyedropper tool is invaluable when you want to exactly match a color previously used on your bitmap.

12

NOTE

The foreground and background colors may work differently in the Image Editor than in other bitmap editors you have used. For example, in some bitmap editors the outline of a filled rectangle will be drawn with the foreground color and filled with the background color. With the Image Editor, filled objects have no discernible border. A filled rectangle is in either the foreground or the background color.

Transparent and Inverted Colors

In the case of icons and cursors, you can also choose to use the transparent color (the word *color* is relative here). When you use the transparent color, the background beneath the icon shows through wherever the transparent color is used. That could mean the Windows background in the case of a shortcut, or it could mean the title bar of your application. Whether you use the transparent color is up to your personal tastes and the particular icon you are creating. In the case of cursors, you will almost always use the transparent color as the background for the icon. Rarely do you have a cursor that appears as a solid block.

Using the inverted color will cause the background underneath the icon to be inverted (like reverse video). Use of the inverted color is not common, but it is there if and when you need it.

Both the transparent and inverted colors are shown next to the Color Palette when you're editing icons and cursors. They are represented by color squares with a curved line running through them.

NOTE

By default, new icon and new cursor resources have the background filled with the transparent color.

Image Editor Drawing Tools

The Image Editor has drawing tools similar to most paint programs. Because these are common drawing tools, I'm not going to go over each and every one. Fifteen minutes of experimentation with the Image Editor will be more beneficial than what I could tell you anyway. Fire up the Image Editor and experiment with it for a while. I'll wait.

At the top of the Image Editor Tools palette, you will find the Marquee and Lasso tools. These tools work in essentially the same way, so I'll cover them together. Both of these tools allow you to select a region on the current image. The Marquee tool is used to define a rectangular region. Choose the Marquee tool and then drag a bounding rectangle on the image. When you stop dragging, a marquee is drawn around the region to mark it. The Lasso tool works in much the same way but allows you to drag a freehand region. A Lasso region is filled with a hatch pattern to identify it.

TIP   When using the Lasso tool, you don't have to close the region. When you release the mouse button, the Image Editor will automatically close the region by drawing a connection line between the start point and the end point.

Once a region is defined, you can cut or copy the image within the region and paste it somewhere else on the image or to another image you are working on (you can have multiple bitmaps open at one time). When you choose Edit | Paste from the main menu, the image within the marquee will be placed in the upper-left corner of the bitmap with a marquee around it. The pasted image can now be dragged into position. When you place your mouse cursor within the marquee, the cursor changes to a hand. Once you see the hand cursor you can drag the bitmap within the marquee to another location and drop it. You can continue to move the bitmap until you have it positioned exactly where you want it. Once you have the bitmap where you want it, click again on the image outside of the marquee and the bitmap within the marquee will be merged into the existing image.

TIP   The Image Editor has a shortcut method of doing cut and paste. Create a Marquee or Lasso region, place your mouse cursor inside the region, and drag. The image within the region will move as you drag.

When you cut a region or move it by dragging, the current background color will fill the area on the image the region originally occupied. Essentially, the background "shows through" the hole created by the cut operation.

TIP   You can copy portions of one bitmap to another using cut and paste. First, open both images in the Image Editor. Place a marquee around the portion of the original image you want to copy and then choose Edit | Copy from the main menu. Switch to the other image and choose Edit | Paste from the main menu. Move the pasted image as needed.

12

NOTE

If you have a marquee selected when you paste, the pasted image will shrink or stretch to fit the size of the marquee.

The Eraser tool works opposite of the other tools in regard to the left and right mouse buttons. With the Eraser, the left mouse button draws with the background color and the right mouse button draws with the foreground color.

The Text tool allows you to place text on the image. The text is drawn using the current text settings. The text settings can be changed by clicking on the Text item on the main menu. Here you can set the text alignment (left, right, or centered) or the font (typeface). To change the typeface, choose Text | Font from the main menu. Now you can choose a new typeface or make the font bold, italic, underlined, and so on.

The other drawing tools are pretty much self explanatory. As I said earlier, a little time behind the wheel of the Image Editor will teach you just about everything you need to know about those tools.

TIP

You can press and hold the Shift key while drawing rectangles to force the rectangle to a square. Likewise, you can draw a perfect circle by choosing the Ellipse or Filled Ellipse tool and holding the Shift key as you drag. Using the Shift key with the Line tool will allow you to draw straight lines (vertical, horizontal, or 45-degree angles).

Zooming

The Image Editor allows you to zoom in so that you can work on your bitmaps up close and personal. You can zoom either by using the Zoom tool or via the View menu. To zoom in on a particular part of your image using the Zoom tool, first select the Zoom tool from the Tools palette and then drag a bounding rectangle around the portion of the image you want to see up close. The magnification will change, depending on the size of the rectangle you created when you dragged. You can now see to change fine details in your bitmap.

To zoom using the menu, choose View | Zoom In or press Ctrl+I. When you choose Zoom In from the menu, the image is magnified by a predetermined amount. To zoom out again using the menu, choose View | Zoom Out (Ctrl+U) or View | Actual Size (Ctrl+A).

When you are creating a cursor or an icon, the Image Editor will set you up with a split view. Figure 12.2 shows an Image Editor window while you're creating an icon.

Figure 12.2.
Editing an icon.

Although you can zoom either side of the split window, you will typically work with a zoomed-in copy on the left side and an actual-size image on the right, as I have it in the figure.

The Line Width Palette

The Line Width palette is displayed immediately below the Tools palette. Depending on the currently selected tool, the Line Width palette may show line widths or brush shapes from which you can choose. To choose a line width, just click on one of the five widths displayed. Subsequent drawing operations will use the new line width until you change it. Similarly, to change a brush shape, just click on the brush shape you want to use. If you look back to Figure 12.1, you will see the Line Width palette showing brush shapes.

Working with Bitmap Files

You can create a bitmap from scratch or load an existing bitmap and modify it. To open an existing bitmap file, simply choose File | Open from the main menu. To create a new bitmap file, choose File | New from the main menu and then choose Bitmap File from the pop-up menu. The Bitmap Properties dialog box will be displayed, as shown in Figure 12.3.

Figure 12.3.
The Bitmap Proper-
ties dialog box.

Here you can set the initial size of the bitmap (in pixels) as well as the color depth. You can create a 2-color, 16-color, or 256-color bitmap.

NOTE

The Image Editor does not support bitmaps of more than 256 colors.

Select the size and color depth you want and click OK. A blank bitmap is displayed in an editor window. Do any drawing you want on the bitmap. When you are finished editing, choose File | Save or File | Save As to save the bitmap file to disk.

Anytime you are working with a bitmap file, the Image Editor main menu has a menu item called Bitmap. This menu has a single item under it called Image Properties. Choosing Bitmap | Image Properties will display the Bitmap Properties dialog box just like when you create a new bitmap file. The Bitmap Properties dialog box allows you to change the size and color depth of the bitmap. Select a new width, height, or color depth and click OK.

NOTE

There is one difference in the Bitmap Properties dialog box when it is displayed for an existing bitmap as opposed to when you're creating a new bitmap. When displayed for an existing bitmap, the Bitmap Properties dialog box has a check box labeled Stretch. This is used by the Image Editor when changing the size of the bitmap. If the Stretch option is off, the bitmap will not be stretched (either larger or smaller) when the bitmap size is changed. If the Stretch option is on, the bitmap will be stretched to fill the new bitmap size. Stretching a bitmap is an inexact science, so sometimes the effects of stretching are less than perfect.

All in all, there is not much to working with bitmap files. Although the Image Editor is fine for simple bitmaps, you will probably not find it adequate for sophisticated graphics. If you need high-quality bitmaps, you will probably want to consider purchasing a full-featured image-editing package or hiring a computer artist to create your bitmaps.

TIP

Don't forget to check out online sources for computer-graphic artists. These people know their craft far better than all but the most gifted of programmers and are often very reasonable in their pricing. Repeat this 10 times: "I am a programmer, not an artist." (Okay, maybe some of you are doubly blessed.)

Working with Icons

Creating icons is also an art form, but icons are not quite as demanding as full-color bitmaps. Most of the time you can create your own icons, but really great-looking icons still require some skill. If you flip back to Figure 12.2 you will see an icon as it is displayed in the Image Editor while editing.

TIP

Load icon files from any source you can find and zoom in on them to get tips on how the best-looking icons are created. Creating 3D icons takes practice. (And is something I never get quite right.)

An icon in 32-bit Windows is actually two icons in one. The large icon is 32×32 pixels in size. The large icon can be placed on a dialog box such as an About box. It is also the icon Windows will use when creating a shortcut to your application. The large icon is also used by Windows Explorer when the file list view is set to display large icons.

The small icon is 16×16 pixels in size and is the icon used by Windows on the title bar of your application, on the Windows taskbar, in the File Open dialog box, and in Windows Explorer when the view is set to small icons. Both the large and the small icons are stored in the same icon file (.ico).

NOTE

You do not have to supply both a large icon and a small icon. If you supply only the large icon, Windows will shrink the large icon when it needs to display a small icon. Sometimes, however, the results are not quite what you expect and may not be of high enough quality for your tastes. In those cases you can also create the small icon so that you are in control of how your application looks rather than relying on Windows to do the right thing.

To create a new icon resource, choose File | New from the main menu and then choose Icon from the pop-up menu. When you create a new icon in the Image Editor, you will see the Icon Properties dialog box, as shown in Figure 12.4.

Figure 12.4.

The Icon Properties dialog box.

12

This dialog box allows you to choose the icon you are creating (either the large or the small icon) and the number of colors to use for the icon. The default is to create the standard icon (the large icon) and to use 16 colors. (In reality, 2-color icons are rarely used. When was the last time you saw one?)

NOTE

Even if you are creating both the large icon and the small icon, you must choose one or the other to start with. For example, if you are creating a new icon you should start with the large icon. After creating the large icon, you can then create the small icon.

When you are editing an icon, the Image Editor menu bar has an item called Icon. The Icon menu has items called New, Delete, and Test. The New menu item allows you to create a new large or small icon. For instance, if you had already created the large icon you could choose Icon | New from the main menu in order to create the small icon.

TIP

The Image Editor window has a button called New that does the same thing and is faster than using the main menu. (Refer to Figure 12.2.)

When you choose New to create a second icon, the Icon Properties dialog box is displayed just as before. If you have already created the large icon, the small icon will be selected by default and all you have to do is click OK. The editor window will change to display the new, blank icon. The Image Editor will not let you create an icon that already exists in the icon file.

TIP

When both icons are present, you can switch between them using the combo box at the top of the Image Editor window.

The Delete item on the Icon menu allows you to delete either the large or the small icon from the icon resource. You cannot delete the last icon in the icon resource.

The Test item on the Icon menu displays the Icon Tester dialog box, which will show you what the icon will look like when displayed. Figure 12.5 shows the Icon Tester dialog box in action.

Figure 12.5.

The Icon Tester dialog box.

The Icon Tester allows you to change the background color so you can view the effect that different backgrounds have on the appearance of your icon. If you are currently editing the large icon, the large icon shows in the Icon Tester. If you are currently editing the small icon, the small icon will be displayed in the Icon Tester dialog box.

Working with Cursors

Working with cursors differs very little from working with icons. A cursor only has two colors: white and black. (Multicolor animated cursors are not supported by the Image Editor.) Simply draw the cursor as you want it to appear.

NOTE

A peculiarity of the cursor editor is that the transparent color is set to the color of your system's background color rather than the dark green color used for the icon editor. If you have your Windows background color set to a very light color, it can be difficult to see what is transparent and what is white. If you are having difficulty distinguishing the background color from white, set your Windows background color to a different value (such as dark green).

As when editing bitmap files and icons, the Image Editor menu displays a menu item called Cursor when you are editing a cursor. This menu item has two items: Set Hot Spot and Test.

The Set Hot Spot item allows you to specify the cursor's hot spot. The *hot spot* is the specific pixel of the cursor that Windows uses to report the mouse coordinates when your cursor is being used. To set the hot spot, choose Cursor | Set Hot Spot from the main menu. The Set Cursor Hot Spot dialog box appears where you can enter the x and y coordinates of the hot spot.

TIP

You must enter the exact x and y coordinates for the hot spot. To make this easier, prior to setting the hot spot, place the editing cursor over the point on the cursor where the hot spot will be placed. The Image

12

> Editor status bar will display the x and y coordinates of the point under the cursor. Make note of the x and y coordinates; then choose Cursor | Set Hot Spot from the main menu and enter the x and y coordinates.

The Test item on the Cursor menu gives you the opportunity to try out your new cursor. Choose Cursor | Test from the main menu, and the Cursor Tester dialog box will be displayed, as shown in Figure 12.6.

Figure 12.6.

Testing the cursor.

Hold down either mouse button to draw on the Cursor Tester window. If you haven't yet set the hot spot, you will probably notice that the hot spot is set to the lower-right corner of the cursor by default. You should always set the hot spot to a point on your cursor that will be logical to users of your application.

Image Editor Speed Menus

The Image Editor has speed menus for each of the editing modes (Bitmap, Cursor, and Icon). You might recall that the right mouse button is used for drawing, so you cannot bring up the speed menus by clicking the mouse button while over the image. To display the Image Editor speed menus, right-click when the mouse cursor is within the editor window but outside of the image itself. The speed menus contain the same items found on the individual menus as discussed in the previous sections.

Creating Resource Projects

The Image Editor also allows you to create a resource project file that can be used to store all of your bitmaps, icons, and cursors in a single file. To create a resource project, choose File | New from the main menu and then choose Resource File from the pop-up menu. A project window is displayed. The project window is a tree view control (much like the C++Builder Project Explorer) that shows the bitmaps, icons, and cursors in the project. Figure 12.7 shows the project window for a sample project.

Figure 12.7.

The Image Editor project window.

The project window has a speed menu that can be used to create new resources, edit resources, rename resources, and delete resources. The items on the speed menu are also duplicated on the main menu under the Resource menu item.

When you save the resource project, the Image Editor will compile it into a binary resource file (.res). You can then add the binary resource file to your C++Builder project.

Creating New Resources

To create a new resource for your project, choose New from the project window speed menu or Resource | New from the main menu. You can then choose to create a new bitmap, icon, or cursor as you did before when creating an individual resource file. A resource editor window will be displayed where you can create the resource using the drawing tools.

Editing Resources

Once you have a resource created, you may need to edit it in order to make changes to the resource. To edit a resource in a resource project, locate the resource in the project window tree and double-click on the resource name. A resource editor window will come up where you can edit the resource as needed.

Renaming Resources

Renaming resources can be accomplished using in-place editing on the tree view. Just click on the item you want to rename to select it and then click on it again to begin editing the item. You can also choose Rename from the speed menu to begin the in-place editing. After you have typed a new name for the resource, press Enter or click on another item in the tree view, and the name of the resource is changed.

Deleting Resources

To delete a resource from the resource project, just click on the resource name in the project tree to select it and then choose Delete from the speed menu. You will be prompted to be sure you want to delete the item, after which it will be deleted. There is no undo for deleting a resource, so be sure a resource is no longer needed before you delete it.

12

Adding Resources from Other Resource Files

Unfortunately, there is no simple way to add a resource contained in a separate file to a resource project. What you can do, however, is open your project file and then open the individual bitmap, icon, or cursor file that contains the resource you want to add to the project. Go to the individual file and choose Edit | Select All from the main menu to select the resource; then choose Edit | Copy to copy the object to the Clipboard. Create the new resource in the resource project. When the resource editor window is displayed, choose Edit | Paste from the main menu to paste the resource into the new resource.

NOTE

If the object you are adding to the resource project is a bitmap, be sure you check the bitmap attributes so that you know the width, height, and color depth of the bitmap. You will need those settings when you create the new bitmap in the resource project.

The Image Editor is not a high-end image editor, but it's good enough for many of your image-creation tasks. It's easy to use and is good enough for creating most icons and cursors.

WinSight: Spying on Windows

WinSight is a utility that allows you to spy on Windows. WinSight will show you every application running and every window running under that application. (Remember that controls are windows, too.) WinSight shows you every message generated by Windows (every message sent to a window, that is). You can elect to view all messages or just messages sent to a specific window. To start WinSight, choose Tools | WinSight from the C++Builder main menu. If you do not have a WinSight item on your Tools menu, see the section later in this chapter titled "Configuring Tools" to add WinSight to your Tools menu (the filename is WS32.exe). You can also run WinSight by double-clicking the WinSight32 icon in the C++Builder folder. WinSight, like the Image Editor, is a standalone program that can be run outside of the C++Builder IDE. Figure 12.8 shows WinSight spying on Windows Explorer.

As you can see from Figure 12.8, the WinSight window is split into two panes. The top pane lists the active windows, and the bottom pane shows the messages being sent to a particular window or to all windows. The size of the panes can be adjusted by dragging the sizing bar between the two windows. The default is for the windows to be split horizontally, but you can opt to split the windows vertically. To change the window layout, choose either Split Horizontal or Split Vertical from the Edit menu.

Figure 12.8.

WinSight in action.

We'll examine each of the two windows in more detail in just a bit, but first let's take a moment to talk about Windows messages.

The Windows Messaging System

Spying on Windows isn't very useful if you don't know what any of it means. (The thrill of being a legal Peeping Tom wears off rather quickly.) The truth is, you will have to spend a fair amount of time at Windows programming before you will understand all the information presented by WinSight.

Programs like C++Builder and Delphi are great for allowing you to write true standalone Windows applications in the shortest amount of time possible. If there is a disadvantage to this kind of programming environment, it is that you aren't given the opportunity to learn what really makes a Windows program run.

What makes a Windows program run is messages. Lots and lots of messages. Windows sends window messages to instruct the window to do something or to notify the window that some event has taken place. When a window is in need of repainting, for instance, Windows sends it a WM_PAINT message. The WM_PAINT message instructs the window to repaint itself. When a window is resized, Windows sends a WM_WINDOWPOSCHANGING message to notify the window that its size and/or position is changing. This message is followed by WM_WINDOWPOSCHANGED and WM_SIZE messages after the window has been sized. This sort of thing happens dozens or even hundreds of times each second in an average Windows environment.

There are well over 100 messages that Windows can send to an application. I talked about that a little on Day 5, "C++ Class Frameworks and the Visual Component Model," when I discussed events in VCL. Many of the events that a C++Builder program responds to are Windows messages. The OnCreate event is generated in response to a WM_CREATE message, the

12

OnSize event is generated in response to a WM_SIZE message, and the OnMouseDown event corresponds to both the WM_LBUTTONDOWN and WM_RBUTTONDOWN messages. The list goes on and on. C++Builder allows you to deal with messages at a higher level, thus freeing you to write the more important parts of your application.

Eventually you will want to learn about the ins and outs of what makes Windows tick. The great thing about C++Builder, though, is that you can write Windows programs now and learn about all of the low-level stuff a little at a time.

NOTE

Some very good Windows programmers would argue that you should first learn to write Windows programs in C like back in the good old days. The theory is that that kind of foundation is required to be an effective Windows programmer in any programming environment. While I would agree that that is the optimum scenario, I also recognize that very few programmers these days have the time for that kind of learning curve.

With that primer on Windows messages behind us, let's get back to WinSight and how it works.

The Window Tree

The top pane of WinSight is called the Window Tree. The Window Tree shows you all windows currently open. It also tells you some details about the window class of a specific window. For example, in Figure 12.8 you see that Windows Explorer is listed in the Tree Window. The detail looks like this (except that it appears all on one line onscreen):

```
Overlapped 00000D74 {ExploreWClass}
  EXPLORER.EXE (730,14)-(935,460) "Exploring - aTemplate"
```

The first item in this line shows the window style of the window. In this case, it is an overlapped window (WS_OVERLAPPED for you old Windows hackers). Other possibilities include child and pop-up windows. (There are other window types, but overlapped, child, and pop-up are the most common.) The second column shows the window handle (HWND) of the window. This correlates to the Handle property of a VCL-windowed component.

Next you see the window class name in curly braces. This is the class name that the application used to register this particular window with Windows. Frequently, windows share a class name. The common button control, for instance, has a class name of simply Button. Dozens of buttons may exist in different applications at any given time, but they are all of the same window class. In the case of C++Builder applications, forms and components will show the

VCL class that represents that component. For a button component, the class name in WinSight will show TButton.

Following the class name is the module name of the process that created the window. Typically the module is an executable program. In this example, the module name is EXPLORER.EXE. After the module name you see the window's size and position. Finally, you see the window text of the window. For overlapped windows, this usually means the text that appears in the title bar. For other types of windows, it means different things depending on the type of window. For a button, for instance, it will show the text on the button.

NOTE

A common practice with commercial applications is to create hidden windows to accomplish a specific task in the application. Hidden windows just show (hidden) after the module name. Because the window is hidden there is no size and position information, nor is there any window text.

The Window Tree is hierarchical. At the very top of the tree is the Windows Desktop. After that you will see any windows that are created as children of the desktop. An executable file, for instance, will appear under the desktop node. A given window may have other child windows under it. Lines connect the parents, their children, and any siblings.

Notice in Figure 12.8 that a diamond appears to the left of each item in the Tree Window. If a window has children, either a plus sign or a minus sign shows in the diamond. If the diamond has a plus sign, it means the node is contracted and can be expanded to reveal the child windows. If the node has a minus sign, the plus is already expanded. You can expand or contract a node by clicking anywhere to the left of the item. Diamonds that are blank indicate a window without children.

NOTE

If a particular window is enabled in the Window Tree, the diamond next to the item will flash whenever the window receives a message from Windows.

The Message Trace Window

The Message Trace window shows the individual messages as they are generated by Windows. A typical Message Trace item looks like this:

```
000684:00000854 {TMemo} WM_KEYDOWN Dispatched 48h 72d VK_H Scan 23h Down
```

It doesn't pay to analyze this in too much detail because the exact details vary so much from message to message. In this case, a memo component received a WM_KEYDOWN message with a parameter of VK_H. In other words, the user pressed the h key with the cursor in a memo component. As you can see, some of the information shown in a Message Trace item also is shown in the Window Tree. For example, the window handle is displayed as well as the class name.

You begin the message trace by choosing the Start! item in the main menu. The messages will begin appearing in the Message Trace window as they are received by the window or windows you have selected. To stop the message trace, choose the Stop! item in the main menu.

NOTE

> The Stop! and Start! items in the main menu occupy the same place on the menu bar. If the message trace is off, the menu item will say Start! If the trace is running, the menu item will say Stop!.

Messages scroll through the Message Trace window as they are received. You can always stop the message trace and scroll back through the list to view any messages that have scrolled out of view. Another option is to send the message output to a log file. WinSight options are discussed later, in the section "Message Trace Options."

Spying on a Window

WinSight allows you to view all messages sent to all windows or messages sent to just one window. To view all messages, choose Messages | All Windows from the main menu. Although you can choose to view all messages sent to all windows, it is not usually very productive. There are so many messages flying around that it is hard to pick out the specific messages you are looking for.

A better method is to select a specific window and then watch the messages for just that window. That will keep the clutter in the Message Trace window down to manageable levels. To view the messages for a specific window, locate the window in the Message Tree and click on it to select it. Now choose Messages | Selected Windows from the main menu. Choose Start!, and any messages sent to the selected window will show up in the Message Trace window.

TIP

> It's easiest to have a specific idea of what you are looking for when you are using WinSight. Because there are so many messages sent to an individual window, the specific message you are looking for will

probably scroll off the screen very quickly. To maximize the effective-
ness of WinSight, select the window for which you want to see messages, start the message trace, manipulate the window in any way you
need to, and turn the message trace off again.

Message Trace Options

You can control the messages that are displayed in the Message Trace window via the Message
Trace Options dialog box. (See Figure 12.9.) You can also change the way the message is
displayed. To view the Message Trace Options dialog box, choose Messages | Options from
the main menu.

Figure 12.9.

*The Message Trace
Options dialog box.*

The bulk of this dialog box is the section titled Messages to Trace. This section shows several
message groups on the left side and a list box displaying all Windows messages on the right
side. As you select or deselect message groups, the corresponding messages will be selected or
deselected in the list box.

NOTE

The messages in the list box that are all uppercase are the standard
Windows messages. The messages in lowercase are "undocumented"
Windows messages. Undocumented messages are messages that are
used by Windows, usually for internal use, but which are not documented in the Windows API help files.

When the All Messages option is checked, WinSight will trace all Windows messages. To
narrow things down a little and to reduce clutter in the Message Trace window, you can elect

to view only certain groups of messages. If, for instance, you only want to view mouse messages, you can turn off the All Messages check box and turn on the Mouse check box. To further narrow it down, you could turn off all options and then choose just the specific message you want to inspect from the list box on the right of the dialog box. For instance, if you only wanted to see the WM_LBUTTONDOWN message, you could turn off all options and then select just the WM_LBUTTONDOWN message from the list box. Then only the WM_LBUTTONDOWN messages would be reported in the Message Trace window.

Another group of options on the Message Trace Options dialog box controls how the messages are displayed in the Message Trace window. The Interpret Values option tells WinSight to break down each message's parameters into a more readable format. For example, given a WM_KEYDOWN message, would you rather see this:

```
0000309:00000474 {TMemo} WM_KEYDOWN Dispatched
```

or this:

```
0000309:00000474 {TMemo} WM_KEYDOWN Dispatched 44h 68d VK_D Scan 20h Repeat
```

Most of the time I opt to see more detail, so I generally leave the Interpret Values option on.

The Hex Values option tells WinSight to display the values in the Message Trace window in hexadecimal format. This is useful in some situations but probably isn't something you will use until after you've been programming for a while. The Show Times option is of limited use because it shows a system time that isn't generally meaningful.

The Log File option allows you to send the message trace output to a file on disk. When this option is on, the messages will still be displayed in the Message Trace window. This option is useful when you need a hard copy of the messages being generated.

 TIP

> Creating a log file has another advantage. After you have created a log file and have loaded it into a text editor, you can use the text editor's Find function to search for specific messages or message parameters you want to review.

Other WinSight Features

WinSight has other features that make finding and examining windows easier.

Viewing Window Details

The Detail feature of WinSight shows you all of the pertinent details of a particular window. To view a window's details, select the window in the Window Tree and then choose Spy | Open Detail from the main menu. You can also double-click on the window in the Message Tree or press Enter on the keyboard. Figure 12.10 shows the details of a main window from a C++Builder application.

Figure 12.10.

The WinSight Detail window.

As you can see, the Detail window shows you a great deal about the window you are examining. (Probably more than you want to know!)

Follow to Focus

This option allows you to select a window in an application and have that window become the active window in the Window Tree. The Window Tree usually contains dozens of windows. It is often difficult to find exactly the window you are looking for, so the Follow to Focus feature really comes in handy.

To use this feature, choose Spy | Follow to Focus from the main menu. Next, switch to the application that contains the window for which you want to view messages and, if needed, click on the specific control within the window the you want to spy on. WinSight automatically selects the window in the Window Tree. To begin spying on the window, choose Start! from the main menu.

12

TIP

> The Follow to Focus option stays on until you turn it off. Unless you want to view other windows or controls in your application, you should turn off Follow to Focus as soon as you locate the window you want to spy on.

Find Window

The Find Window feature of WinSight is the opposite of Follow to Focus. To use Find Window, you first locate the window you want to find in the Window Tree and then choose Spy|Find Window from the main menu. WinSight will place a thick frame around the window you are searching for and will flash the frame. The frame stays around the window until you click on the window or choose another window from the Window Tree. The thick frame is drawn on top of all windows so you can find a window even if it's hidden under other windows. A window located with Find Window does not come to the top or gain input focus; it is merely identified for you.

NOTE

> Find Window cannot find hidden windows or windows that are minimized.

The Find Window mode shuts off as soon as focus leaves the Window Tree. If you click on another application or anywhere else in WinSight, the Find Window mode will turn off.

Switch To

The Switch To feature allows you to switch to a particular window in an application. To switch to a window, just find the window in the Window Tree and then choose Spy|Switch To from the main menu. The window will come to the top and will have input focus. If the window is minimized, it will be restored to its previous location. Switch To has no effect on hidden windows.

It will take some time working with WinSight before you will understand each message sent and its significance. In time, though, you will pick it up.

Command-Line Tools

In addition to GUI tools like the Image Editor and WinSight, C++Builder also ships with a number of command-line tools. Some of the tools are used by C++Builder itself when it compiles your project. Others are supplemental tools that you can use as needed. A few of the more commonly used tools are discussed in the following sections. In some cases the tools can be added to the Tools menu so that you can access them from the IDE rather than having to run them from an MS-DOS prompt.

NOTE

The command-line tools all reside in the C++Builder bin directory. This directory is added to your system's PATH as part of the normal C++Builder installation. When running a given utility from an MS-DOS prompt, it should not be necessary to add the full path in addition to the filename. If, however, you get file not found errors, you may need to type the exact path to the bin directory when you run the utility.

grep.exe

grep (Global Regular Expression Print) is a text-searching utility. You can use grep to search for text in your source files (or any other text file for that matter). I frequently use grep to search the VCL source code for particular functions, variables, or classes. grep offers a good mix of speed and power. It is useful and convenient, and you should learn how to use it.

grep must be run from an MS-DOS prompt. The text you are searching for and any options are passed via the command line. The syntax for the grep command line looks like this:

```
[-options] searchstring [file(s) ... ]
```

If you are like me, you don't get too much out of syntax lines like this one, so an illustration might help. Let's say you wanted to search all source files in the current directory for the string AboutBox. At an MS-DOS prompt you would enter this:

```
grep AboutBox *.cpp
```

If you wanted to search the VCL source for the string TComponent, you would use

```
grep TComponent c:\CBuilder\source\vcl\*.pas
```

Search strings that include a space should be enclosed in double quotes. For example, let's say that you wanted to find out where in the Windows headers the SS_ETCHEDFRAME constant was defined. In that case, you would supply a command line of

```
grep -d "#define SS_ETCHEDFRAME" c:\CBuilder\include\*.h
```

In this example, grep will search all header files in the C++Builder Include directory and, because the -d switch was specified, all subdirectories as well. The results of any searches will

12

be output to the console. You can enter a single filename to search or use wildcards to search a group of files at one time. You can supply a path or leave the path off. If no path is specified, the current directory will be searched. When you specify files to search, all the usual wildcard characters apply.

TIP

Because the output from a grep search can be fairly long, you might want to redirect the output to a file. Take this line, for instance:

```
grep TComponent c:\CBuilder\source\vcl\*.pas > results.txt
```

This will produce an ASCII text file called results.txt that you can view with any text editor.

You can specify command-line options in addition to the search text and filename. There are a host of command-line options you can use, but I will touch on just a few here.

The -d switch tells grep to search the supplied directory and all subdirectories under that directory. If the -d switch is not used, only the specified directory will be searched. Specifying the -d switch will result in longer search times because more files will be searched.

The -i switch is used to indicate that the search should not be case sensitive. The search is case sensitive by default. Use the -i switch when you aren't sure whether the text you are searching for is capitalized. Generally speaking, using case-sensitive searches results in more accurate results being generated, but with slightly longer search times.

The -r switch tells grep to allow regular expressions in the search string. I discussed regular expressions briefly when I talked about the Find and Replace dialog boxes on Day 10, "More on Projects." See online help for a full description of how regular expressions can be used.

The default grep command-line options are user configurable. By default, only the -r switch is used by default when grep is run. All other command-line switches must be supplied each time grep is run. You can, however, change the default switches that grep uses by implementing the -u switch. Using this switch tells grep to add any switches in the command line to the default switch list. For example, if you always want to search subdirectories, you could add the -d switch to the defaults. From a DOS prompt, type

```
grep -u -d mygrep.exe
```

This will create a new file called MYGREP.EXE. Once you've done this you can delete the old GREP.EXE and rename the newly created file to GREP.EXE. Now, each time you run grep the -d switch will be automatically applied. To remove the -d switch from the defaults, run grep as follows:

```
grep -u -d-mygrep.exe
```

Once again, you will have to delete the existing `grep.exe` and rename the new file `grep.exe`.

To see which command-line options are on by default, you can run `grep` with a question mark (?) on the command line. Specifying the ? option will produce a help screen with instructions. The command-line options are all listed in the help screen. The options that are enabled by default will have a plus sign (+) after them, and the options that are not enabled by default will have a minus sign (-) after them. There are a total of 12 command-line options available. See the online help for `grep` for more information on other command-line options you can use.

implib.exe

This tool is used to create an import library file (`.lib`) for a dynamic link library (`.dll`). Before you can call functions in a DLL, the linker has to be able to "see" the functions exported from the DLL. An import library is read by the linker to determine what functions are contained in the DLL. Import libraries will be discussed more on Day 19, "Creating and Using DLLs."

`implib` is easy to use. Let's say that you have created a DLL named `MyStuff.dll` and you want to create a import library file for it. Open an MS-DOS box from Windows and switch to the directory where your DLL resides. From the MS-DOS prompt, type

```
implib MyStuff MyStuff.dll
```

An import library file called `MyStuff.lib` will be created, which you can then add to any of your C++Builder projects that reference that DLL.

NOTE   Microsoft and Borland use different name-mangling schemes for their compilers. If you buy a third-party control or library contained in DLLs, you may find that the import library file provided by the vendor does not work with your C++Builder project. If that happens, it is likely that the import library is in the Microsoft COFF format rather than the Borland OMF format. To produce an import library file that C++Builder can use, just run `implib` on the DLLs that came with the third-party library.

`implib` has a few command-line options that you can use if needed. For a complete list, run `implib -h` (the -h option is for help) from an MS-DOS prompt.

touch.exe

touch can be used to reset the time stamp on files. If you look at the files on the C++Builder CD-ROM, you will find that they all have the same file date and time. (The file time is sort of a code that identifies the version of C++Builder on the CD-ROM.) touch is pretty easy to use. Table 12.1 lists some of the touch command-line options.

Table 12.1. Selected touch command-line options.

Option	Description
-h	Prints a help screen. (Use -h2 for a more complete help screen.)
-s	Recurses through subdirectories.
-thh:mm:ss	Sets the time of the files to the time specified. (The seconds parameter is optional.)
-dmm/dd/yy	Sets the date of the specified files to the date specified.

For example, let's say that you were releasing version 2.12 of your project and you wanted to set all file dates to the current date with a time of 2:12 a.m. Further, let's assume that you have more than one directory and that you want to touch all of the files in all directories. The command line would look like this:

```
touch -t02:12 -s *.*
```

Note that you don't have to provide the date. If you do not use the -d option, the current date will be used. The same is true of the -t option.

tdump.exe

tdump could probably be considered an advanced programming tool. tdump will output the structure of an .exe (and other file types as well). By default, the output from tdump will go to the console, but it can be redirected to a text file that you can later examine to obtain information about the program. tdump will tell you about the structure of the file, what DLLs the program uses, what functions in those DLLs the program calls, and other information. For example, here is part of the results of a file dump on a program produced by C++Builder:

```
Portable Executable (PE) File

Header base: 00000200

CPU type              80386
Flags                 818E [ executable 32bit ]
DLL flags             0000 [ ]
Linker Version        2.19
```

12

```
Time stamp              00000000
O/S Version             1.0
User Version            0.0
Subsystem Version       4.0
Subsystem               0002 [ Windows GUI ]
Object count            00000008
Symbols offset          00000000
Symbols count           00000000
Optional header size    00E0
Magic #                 10B
Code size               0003C000
Init Data size          00009000
Uninit Data size        00001000

...(other information)...

Imports from OLEAUT32.dll
    SysAllocStringLen
    SysStringLen
    VariantChangeTypeEx
    VariantClear
    VariantCopyInd

Imports from MPR.dll
    WNetGetConnectionA

Imports from USER32.dll
    AdjustWindowRectEx
    BeginPaint
    CallNextHookEx
    CallWindowProcA
    CharLowerA

... (more DLL imports) ...
```

Typically you will run `tdump` from the command line. Because the output from `tdump` is usually fairly long, you will be better off if you redirect the output to a text file. The following illustrates:

```
tdump MyApp.exe > dump.txt
```

Now you have an ASCII text file that you can browse with the C++Builder Code Editor or any other text editor. Although you may not use `tdump` very often, it can be invaluable when you need it.

Configuring the C++Builder Tools Menu

The C++Builder Tools menu is configurable. By default, the C++Builder Tools menu has items for Database Desktop and Image Editor. You can add your own tools to the Tools menu, add other C++Builder tools, or add any other program you use frequently. You can also change the order of items on the Tools menu, or even delete items.

12

The Configure Tools Dialog Box

Just about any application you use frequently can be added to the Tools menu. By adding items to the Tools menu, you can quickly load any program you frequently use during program development. Adding a tool to the Tools menu is a trivial task and takes only a few minutes. Adding, deleting, and moving items on the Tools menu is accomplished through the Configure Tools dialog box. To display the Configure Tools dialog box, choose Tools|Configure from the main menu. (See Figure 12.11.)

Figure 12.11.

The Configure Tools dialog box.

The list box labeled Tools shows the current tools that appear on the Tools menu. The tools are listed in the order in which they appear on the Tools menu. To reorder the list of tools, simply click on the tool you want to move and click either the up or down arrow button. To remove a tool from the Tools menu, select the tool from the list box and click the Delete button. The tool will be removed.

To add a tool to the Tools menu, click the Add button. The Tool Properties dialog box is displayed and you can enter the properties for the tool you are adding. The Tool Properties dialog box is shown in Figure 12.12 with the properties for Windows Explorer displayed.

Figure 12.12.

The Tool Properties dialog box.

The Title field is where you type the title of the tool as you want it to appear on the Tools menu. You may use an ampersand to indicate the shortcut key character. The Program field is where you enter the path and filename of the tool. To ensure that the program will be found, you should enter the full path of the program. If you do not know the exact path and filename, you can click the Browse button and go hunting for the file. The Working dir field is used to set the working directory for the tool. If you browse to find the tool, the working directory will be automatically set to the directory where the program resides.

The Parameters field requires some explanation. In its simplest form, this field is used to set the command-line parameters for the tool. Simply type any parameters needed to run the tool. You can, however, use C++Builder's predefined macros in the Parameters field. If you click the Macros button in the Tool Properties dialog box, you will get a list of macros from which you can choose. To use a macro, you can type it in directly or you can choose it from the list and click the Insert button. Figure 12.13 shows the Tool Properties dialog box with the list of macros displayed.

Figure 12.13.

The Tool Properties dialog box showing macros.

The $EXENAME macro will return the full path of the project's target executable. For example, if you had a project named MyApp in a directory called Projects, the $EXENAME parameter would pass the string c:\Projects\MyApp.exe to the program. Some of the macros require parameters. To use just the path from your project's target without the filename, you would specify a parameters string of $PATH($EXENAME). Continuing with this example, that combination of parameters would yield c:\Projects\. For a complete list of the macros available, see the C++Builder online help.

Editing a tool on the Tools menu is as easy as clicking the Edit button on the Configure Tools dialog box. The Tool Properties dialog box is displayed, and you can change any of the fields as necessary.

When you are done adding, editing, or rearranging your tools, click the Close button. The changes will be reflected on the C++Builder Tools menu.

Setting the Environment Options

The C++Builder Environment Options allow you to make changes to the C++Builder IDE at the global level. (The Project Options dialog box controls settings at the project level.) To display the Environment Options dialog box, choose Options | Environment from the main menu. This is a tabbed dialog with six pages. You learned about the Editor, Display, and Colors pages when we looked at the Code Editor on Day 10. We will look at the Preferences, Library, and Palette pages now.

The Preferences Page

The Preferences page of the Environment Options dialog box is where you set general C++Builder preferences. Here you can set how the C++Builder IDE controls compiling, autosaving, and debugging processes. You can also set the Form Designer preferences on this page. (See Figure 12.14.)

Figure 12.14.

The Preferences page of the Environment Options dialog box.

The Compiling section has three options. The Show compiler progress option controls whether C++Builder displays the compiler progress dialog box when compiling projects. Most of the time you will leave this option on so that you can see what is happening with your project. Turning off this option will result in slightly faster compiles, although the difference will probably not be dramatic. The Beep on completion option will beep the PC speaker when compiling is finished. This is handy if you have a long compile running in the background and you want to know when it has finished. The Cache hdrs on startup option tells C++Builder to load the precompiled headers as soon as C++Builder loads. If you have lots of system RAM, this option can speed compilation times because the headers are already cached in memory before you start compiling. Without this option on, the precompiled headers are loaded from disk when needed. If you don't have an abundance of system RAM (probably 48MB or more), you will probably not want this option on.

The Autosave section allows you specify that either the Editor files or the Desktop be saved automatically every time the program is run. I do not like to have my editor files saved automatically; I want to have the ability to abandon current edits if necessary. Still, I know others who really like this feature. For one thing, if your application misbehaves and crashes the C++Builder IDE or Windows itself, you know that your last edits have been saved. The Desktop option saves the current size and position of the Code Editor, all forms, the Alignment Palette, the Object Inspector, and so on.

The Form Designer section is pretty much self-explanatory. The Display grid option turns the visible grid in the Form Designer on and off. This only affects the visible display of the grid, not whether objects snap to the grid. The Snap to grid option determines whether components placed and moved will snap to the grid points. The X and Y grid size fields allow you to set the size of the grid. By default, it is set at 8 pixels. The Show component captions option pertains to nonvisual components placed on your forms. When this option is on, the Form Designer displays the Name property of nonvisual components below the icon representing the component.

The Debugging section controls aspects of debugging at the global level. If the Integrated debugging option is on, the IDE debugger is used when you click the Run button. When this option is off, the program is run without going through the debugger. The Hide designers on run option will hide the Form Designer, Object Inspector, and other Form Designer support windows when the program is run via the Run button, but the C++Builder main window and Code Editor still will be visible. The Minimize on run option is similar. When this option is on, the entire C++Builder IDE minimizes whenever the target program is run through the debugger.

NOTE

When the Minimize on run option is on, any action in the program that requires the debugger (exceptions, breakpoints, and so on) will result in the C++Builder IDE being displayed again.

12

The Break on exception option controls how the debugger acts when a VCL exception is thrown. (You will learn about exceptions tomorrow.) When this option is on, the debugger will pause program execution when an exception is thrown. When this option is off, the VCL exception will be handled in the usual way—usually with a message box informing the user of what went wrong in the program. The Path for Source field indicates where the debugger can find the VCL source code. You don't normally have to change this field.

The Library Page

Whenever you add a component to the Component Palette, C++Builder rebuilds a file called cmplib32.lib. This happens independently of any specific project. The Library Page of the Environment Options dialog box controls how the compiler and linker behave when building cmplib32.lib. The options on this page are identical to those found on the Project

Options dialog box. Rather than repeat everything that was said earlier, I'll just refer you to Day 10, when project options were discussed.

The Palette Page

The Palette page of the Environment Options dialog box allows you to customize the Component Palette. The Palette page is shown in Figure 12.15.

Figure 12.15.

The Palette page of the Environment Options dialog box.

This page allows you to change the order in which the pages appear in the Component Palette. The Pages list box on the left side of the dialog box shows all the pages currently in the Component Palette. At the bottom of the list you see an item labeled [Library]. This item shows all the installed components in all pages of the Component Palette. The Components list box shows the components that appear in the page that is selected in the Pages list box.

To reorder the pages, just drag a page within the Pages list box to the position you want it to occupy in the Component Palette. For example, if you wanted the Samples page to appear first on the Component Palette, you could drag it to the top of the list in the Pages list box and drop it. You can also click on a page and use the up or down arrow button to move the page to a new location.

Pages can be added, deleted, or renamed, and those operations work exactly as you would expect them to. To add a page, just click the Add button. You will be prompted for a name for the page. After you supply the page name, the new page will be created. You might add a page if, for instance, you have created components of your own and you want them on their own page in the Component Palette. You could also take any of the VCL components that you use a lot and move them to a new page so you can get to them quickly.

NOTE

> You can move components from one page to another, but you cannot copy components. A component can only appear once in the Component Palette.

Deleting and renaming pages is pretty straightforward. As with the Object Repository, a page can be deleted only after it has been emptied of its components.

Components on a page can be rearranged just like pages can. To move a component, drag it to its new position in the Components list box or use the up and down arrow buttons. To move a component to a new page, drag-and-drop it on the name of the page in the Pages list box where you want it to appear. To delete a component, first select the component and then click the Delete button.

If you decide that you've goofed up the Component Palette beyond repair, don't despair—you can always click the Restore Defaults button. This button will reset the Component Palette to its installed configuration.

NOTE

> The Restore Defaults button will reset the Component Palette to the way it was when you originally installed C++Builder. This does not mean that it will revert the Component Palette back to the configuration in which you had last left the Component Palette.

12

Summary

So now you know a little bit more about the tools that are included as part of the C++Builder suite. Some of these tools are easy to miss, so it helps to have an overview of what is available to you. Some of the tools you may not use right away, but over time you may go back and take another look at what's available to you. We ended the day by going over the Environment Options dialog box. For the most part, you can leave these settings on their defaults. When you need to start customizing the IDE, you will have a better understanding of what the individual options do.

Workshop

The Workshop contains quiz questions to help you solidify your understanding of the material covered and exercises to provide you with experience in using what you have learned. You can find answers to the quiz questions in Appendix A, "Answers to Quiz Questions."

Q&A

Q **I'm creating an icon and I'm trying to get an ellipse with a black border and a yellow fill. I set the foreground color to black and the background color to yellow, but all I get is a black circle. What do I have to do to get what I want?**

A The Image Editor works differently than some bitmap editors in this regard. In order to accomplish what you're after, you first have to draw a black, hollow ellipse and then fill it with yellow.

Q **How can I draw perfect circles or straight lines in the Image Editor?**

A Hold down the Shift key as you draw the circle or line. The same is true for drawing perfect squares.

Q **I created my own arrow cursor, but when I click with it I can't seem to click with the point of the arrow. What's wrong?**

A You need to set the hot spot for the cursor. By default, the hot spot is in the lower-right corner. Edit the cursor in the Image Editor and change the hot spot to the pixel at the tip of the arrow.

Q **Am I required to create both a large version and a small version when I create an icon?**

A Not necessarily. If you supply only a large icon, Windows shrinks it when needed. If, however, you don't like the way your icon looks when Windows reduces it, you might want to design a small icon as well as the large one. When a small icon exists, Windows uses it.

Q **How can I copy part of one of my bitmaps to a new bitmap?**

A In the Image Editor, open the original bitmap in one editor window and a new bitmap in another editor window. Drag a marquee around the section of the original bitmap you want to copy and choose Edit | Copy from the Image Editor menu. Switch to the new bitmap and choose Edit | Paste. The bitmap in the Clipboard is pasted into the new bitmap you are creating.

Q **WinSight seems pretty slow on my system. Is that normal?**

A It can be, yes. WinSight has to monitor everything that is going on in Windows, and that takes a lot of processing power. On slower systems it will be more noticeable, of course. To reduce the effect as much as possible, be sure that only WinSight and the window you are spying on are open.

Q **I am looking for a specific message in my program, but all the other messages are cluttering up the Trace Window so I can't find the message I'm looking for. What can I do about that?**

A Two things. First, be sure that you are watching messages only for the specific window in which you are interested. Select the window in the Window Tree and then choose Messages | Selected Windows from the WinSight main menu. Second, you can go to the Trace Options dialog box and turn off all messages except the specific messages in which you are interested.

Q I want some components on the Component Palette to be in their original location but also to appear in a new page that I create. Can I do that?

A No. A component can appear only once in the Component Palette.

Quiz

1. How is the transparent color used for icons and cursors?
2. How do you choose a color in the Image Editor?
3. How do you select an area on a bitmap to cut or copy?
4. What is the maximum number of colors allowed in an Image Editor bitmap?
5. What is a cursor's hot spot?
6. Can WinSight spy on hidden windows?
7. What's the fastest way to locate a window in the Window Tree?
8. What is the grep tool used for?
9. How can you have your editor files automatically saved each time your program runs through the debugger?
10. How do you reset the Component Palette to its default layout?

Exercises

1. Using the Image Editor, create a bitmap that could be used as a splash screen for your company or for a specific application of yours.
2. Using the Image Editor, create an icon that has a transparent background and uses both large and small icons.
3. Create a cursor resource in the Image Editor. Be sure to set its hot spot and test the cursor with the Cursor Tester.
4. Create a new resource file. Create two bitmaps and a cursor. Save the file.
5. Using the resource file you created in exercise 4, create a new icon resource and copy the icon created in exercise 2 to the new icon.
6. Create a new program in C++Builder. Change its Name property to Test and its Caption property to Test Window. Run the program. Now start WinSight. Locate the Test Window program and set message tracing to Selected Windows. Arrange WinSight and Test Window side by side. Choose Start! in the WinSight main

menu. Move the Test Window, size it, click on it, minimize it, and so on. Observe the messages in the Message Trace window.

7. Continuing with exercise 6, go to WinSight, choose Messages|Options from the main menu, and turn off all messages except the Mouse message group. Again manipulate the Test Window program. Observe the output in the Message Trace window.

8. Open the Environment Options dialog box. Go to the Palette page. Create a new page in the Component Palette. Name it MyStuff. Move the Label, Image, and OpenDialog components to the new page. Close the Environment Options dialog box. Examine the new layout of the Component Palette.

9. Continuing with exercise 8, reset the Component Palette to its default layout.

10. Load a program in C++Builder. Open the Environment Options dialog box. On the Preferences page, turn on the Minimize on Run option. Click Run to run the program. Notice the behavior of the C++Builder IDE.

Day 13

Beyond the Basics

by Kent Reisdorph

Today you will learn about some of the things that can help turn a good Windows application into a great Windows application. Specifically, we will look at

☐ Window decorations: speedbars and status bars

☐ Command enabling

☐ Printing in C++Builder applications

☐ Using cursors

Tomorrow we will continue this discussion as we look at implementing advanced Windows programming features in your C++Builder applications.

Window Decorations

No, I'm not talking about pretty lights around the front window of your house. What I am talking about are things such as speedbars and status bars. These goodies are often called *window decorations.* This section deals with these types of decorations and how to implement them in your application.

Speedbars

A *speedbar* (also called a control bar or a toolbar) is almost standard fare for Windows programs today. Users expect certain amenities, and a speedbar is one of them. You've already seen just about all there is to a speedbar, but let's review. A speedbar has the following qualities and capabilities:

- ☐ Buttons that represent tasks that are also available on the application's menu.
- ☐ Enabling and disabling of buttons when appropriate.
- ☐ Dynamic adding and removing of buttons, depending on context.
- ☐ Tool tips that describe a button's function. Tool tips pop up when the user pauses over a button.
- ☐ Additional hint text that shows up in the application's status bar.
- ☐ Other controls such as combo boxes.
- ☐ Optional docking capabilities.

Obviously, a lot of these are optional features that not every speedbar needs to have. With C++Builder, creating much of this functionality is very easy to accomplish. Dockable toolbars are not a trivial task, however, so we won't attempt that today. I'll show you how to accomplish most of these features, however. (A little later in the chapter I will talk about command enabling in the section called, appropriately, "Command Enabling." For that reason I'll save discussion of command enabling for speedbar buttons for that time.)

Speedbar Review

As I mentioned on Day 9, "Creating Applications in C++Builder," the easiest way to construct a speedbar is to use the Application Expert. Even if you already have an application partially written, you can still use the Application Expert to create a speedbar. Just generate an application with the Application Expert, copy the panel with the speedbar to the Clipboard, reopen your original application (don't bother saving the Application Expert application), and paste the speedbar into your application from the Clipboard. Quick and easy.

13

Still, the Application Expert doesn't give you everything you could possibly need, so at times you might need to build your own speedbar from scratch (or maybe you're just a control freak!). We've done this before, but here are the steps required to create a speedbar (step 1 is optional, but I think it looks best):

1. Place a Bevel component on the form. Give its Height property a value of 2 and its Align property a value of alTop.

2. Place a Panel component on the form. Give its Height property a value of 33, its Align property a value of alTop, and its BevelOuter property a value of alNone. Remove the caption by making the value of the Caption property blank. Change the Name property to something meaningful (SpeedBar is customary).

3. Place each button on the panel and set its Glyph and Name properties as appropriate. If using hints, set the ShowHint property to true and supply text for the Hint property.

4. Nudge each control into place using the Ctrl+arrow key method. Add spacers to separate groups of buttons where appropriate.

5. Attach the OnClick event of each button to the corresponding menu item's OnClick event handler.

That's essentially it. As you might recall from Day 9, we have to do some things to get the hint text to show up in the status bar, but the basic speedbar is now functional.

NOTE

> This exercise assumes that you already have a menu for your application. It is considered good practice to place on the speedbar only buttons that have corresponding menu items. The speedbar is provided as an alternative to using the menu. It should not contain items not found elsewhere in the program. (There are exceptions to every rule, of course.)

Adding and Removing Speedbar Buttons

A high-quality Windows application will generally show only the speedbar buttons that are appropriate at any given time. For example, any program that deals with documents will usually have only a rudimentary speedbar when no document is open. You might show only the File Open, File New, Help, and About buttons when no document is open. When a document is open, all other buttons are shown. Achieving this effect can take quite a bit of work with traditional C++ programming tools. C++Builder makes it easy.

Simply put, dynamic adding and removing of buttons from speedbars is normally a pain in the rear. There are many different ways to approach the problem—one might be to have two arrays of speed buttons. One array would hold all available buttons, and the other array would hold the buttons that currently need to be shown. Each button's position would have to be calculated so that the buttons lie next to one another. To further add complication, the buttons should be placed in groups so that they will be easier for your users to locate. This means that the buttons cannot be simply placed one right next to another. Your button array could have 0s in it where spacers should be placed…as you can see, it starts to get pretty complicated.

Take heart! There's an easier way. You can take advantage of C++Builder's Notebook component to make this task easier. The Notebook component is a container component that is designed to hold other components. In this regard, it acts like a Panel component. The difference between a notebook and a panel, however, is that a notebook can have multiple pages. You can place different sets of components on the notebook pages at design time, and then at runtime, switch pages to display the particular group of components you want to see at that time.

As you have probably already figured out, we can use the Notebook component to perform our speedbar switching. What we will do is place a notebook on the form and create a notebook page for each speedbar we want to show. Then we will place the speed buttons on the individual pages as needed. Start with a blank form and we'll walk through this one step at a time. Here goes:

1. Place a Notebook component on your form (be sure you choose the Notebook component and not the Tabbed Notebook component). Change the value of the Height property to 33 and that of the Align property to alTop. This way the panel is always glued to the top of the form.

2. Locate the Pages property in the Object Inspector and double-click on its Value column. The Notebook editor dialog box will be displayed as shown in Figure 13.1. A notebook always has one page called Default. Click the Edit button and change the default page name to ShortSpeedBar.

3. Click the Add button to create a second page for the notebook. Name this page FullSpeedBar. After adding the second page, click the Close button to close the Notebook editor.

4. In the Object Inspector, change the value of the ActivePage property to ShortSpeedBar. Add some buttons or other components to the Notebook component. This is just a test, so it really doesn't matter what you put on the speedbar.

5. Be sure the Notebook component is selected and change the value of the ActivePage property to FullSpeedBar. Add other buttons or components to this page of the Notebook component.

6. Stand back and admire your work. Modify either the ActivePage or the PageIndex property to alternate between the pages so that you can edit the pages if needed.

7. Write code to modify either the `ActivePage` or the `PageIndex` property at runtime to alternate between the speedbars based on the program's state. (More on that in just a bit.)

Figure 13.1.

The Notebook editor dialog box.

This is a simple but effective solution to the problem of creating and implementing dynamic speedbars. The `Notebook` component is easy to work with at design time, which is a big advantage when you have several speedbars to design.

 NOTE

When you are using the notebook for speedbar switching, you will probably have duplicate buttons on two or more individual pages. Because the speed buttons are not windowed components, it doesn't hurt to keep a few extra buttons around. In other words, you are not using a window handle for each button, so the resource penalty for using this approach is negligible.

After you have the notebook set up, you can switch pages at runtime with ease. You can use either the `ActivePage` property or the `PageIndex` property. Given the preceding example, the following two lines have the same effect:

```
Notebook->PageIndex = 0;
Notebook->ActivePage = "ShortSpeedBar";
```

 The CD-ROM accompanying the book has a program called `SBarTest` that illustrates this technique. Load the program and work with it to gain an understanding of how to implement multiple speedbars.

Figure 13.2 shows the `SBarTest` program with the short speedbar in use, and Figure 13.3 shows the `SBarTest` program with the full speedbar displayed.

13

Figure 13.2.

The test program with the short speedbar.

Figure 13.3.

The test program with the full speedbar.

As you can see, multiple speedbars are almost ridiculously easy to implement with C++Builder. This is a perfect example of the power of the visual programming environment that C++Builder provides. If you have never had to do something like multiple speedbars using the raw Windows API, you won't have quite the appreciation that you would otherwise have, but you can take my word for it.

Tool Tips and Hints

Tool tips and hint text can also help to give your application a polished look. I've already covered just about everything there is to be said about tool tips and hints when I discussed components back on Day 8, "VCL Components," and again when adding hint text support for the ScratchPad program on Day 9. Go back and review the section on Day 9 titled "Adding a Function to Your Code" if you need to brush up on how to make hint text work in your applications.

TIP

Here again, the Application Expert comes in handy. Create a shell application using the Application Expert and turn on the option to enable hints. Application Expert will write the code needed to enable hints, and you don't have to do anything more than enable the ShowHint property and supply the hint text.

There is one thing I didn't talk about before, and that is changing the tool tip properties. The TApplication class has four properties that control how tool tips behave. Table 13.1 lists these properties and their descriptions.

13

Table 13.1. `TApplication` **properties pertaining to tool tips.**

Property	Description
HintColor	Sets the background color of the tool tip window.
HintHidePause	Controls how long to wait (in milliseconds) before hiding the tool tip if the mouse cursor remains stationary over the component.
HintPause	Controls the interval between the time the mouse cursor is paused over a component and the time the tool tip appears (in milliseconds).
HintShortPause	Controls the amount of time to wait before showing tool tips once they have already been shown—for instance, when the user is roaming over a group of speedbar buttons.

The default values for these properties are sufficient for most applications. Still, if you need to change any of the hint properties, you have that option.

HOUSE RULES: TOOLBARS AND HINTS

☐ Don't use tool tips on controls where they will be in the way when the user wants to read the text in the control. In particular, don't use tool tips for edit controls and combo boxes. At a very minimum, give the user the option to turn off tool tips for those types of controls.

☐ Keep your tool tip hint (the short hint) short and to the point.

☐ Make your status bar hint (the long hint) more descriptive and meaningful.

☐ Consider giving your users the option of turning off hints altogether.

Adding Other Controls to Speedbars

Because a panel is so versatile, there really isn't anything special that needs to be done to add other types of controls to your speedbar. The most common type of control to add to a speedbar is a combo box. A combo box on the speedbar can be used to select a font, a configuration option, or a zoom setting—the possibilities are endless.

To add a component to the speedbar, simply place the component on your SpeedBar panel. From there you can deal with the component just as you would a component on a form. I'd like to complicate this for you, but the truth is it's just that simple! Once again, if you've never tried to implement a combo box on a speedbar using the Windows API or even using OWL or MFC, you can't know how much work C++Builder saves you. Again, take my word for it—it's significant.

13

Speedbars come in many shapes and sizes. C++Builder makes creating and implementing speedbars very easy. With C++Builder you no longer have the excuse, "That's too hard!" In fact, you may even enjoy creating speedbars with C++Builder. (Heaven forbid!)

Status Bars

A status bar is another one of those features that can make an application more marketable. Not all applications can benefit from a status bar, but many can. Because C++Builder generates 32-bit applications, you can have the benefit of the Windows 32-bit status bar control in your applications. The VCL StatusBar component, which encapsulates the Win32 status bar control, makes creating status bars a breeze. First, let me give you a quick look at the major properties of the StatusBar component. (See Table 13.2.)

Table 13.2. StatusBar properties.

Property	Description
Panels	For status bars with multiple panels. This property defines the individual panels.
SimplePanel	Determines whether the status bar shows a simple panel or multiple panels.
SimpleText	The text for the status bar's simple panel.
SizeGrip	Determines whether the status bar displays the sizing grip in the lower-right corner. The size grip provides an area that the user can drag to size the window. The absence of the sizing grip does not prevent the window from being sized, but the presence of the size grip makes sizing a window easier.

As you can see from this table, a status bar can be a simple status bar or can have multiple panels. Let's discuss this choice next.

Simple or Complex?

A status bar can be either a simple status bar or a complex status bar. A *simple status bar* has a single panel that occupies the entire status bar. If you want a simple status bar, set the SimplePanel property to true.

 NOTE

By default, the StatusBar component has SimplePanel set to true, so you don't specifically have to set the SimplePanel property if you are using a simple status bar.

 13

The `SimplePanel` property acts as a toggle. You can switch between a simple and a complex status bar at runtime by setting `SimplePanel` to `true` or `false` accordingly.

A *complex status bar* is one with multiple panels. If you elect to use a complex status bar, you can use the StatusBar Panels Editor to set up the panels you want to see on your status bar. The StatusBar Panels Editor is invoked by double-clicking on the Value column of the `Panels` property. Figure 13.4 shows the StatusBar Panels Editor.

Figure 13.4.

The StatusBar Panels Editor.

The current panels are displayed in the Panels list box on the left side of the dialog box. To add a panel, fill in the Panel Properties fields on the right side of the dialog box and click the Add button. The new panel will show up in the Panels list box. To delete a panel, select the panel in the Panels list box and click the Delete button. To edit an existing panel, select the panel and then make changes to the panel's properties.

NOTE

> The individual panels in a complex status bar are instances of the `TStatusPanel` class.

Most of the properties are self-explanatory, but a couple require further note. The `Text` property contains the text that will be displayed in the panel. The `Text` property can also be used at runtime to change the text in the panel. Setting the status bar text is discussed a bit later; you do not need to supply text for the panel at design time if you are going to be changing the text at runtime.

The `Style` property can be set to either `Text` or `Owner Draw`. (When you choose one of these, the StatusBar Panels Editor sets the `Style` property to `psText` or `psOwnerDraw`, respectively.) If the `Style` is set to `Text`, the panel behaves as you would expect. The text is aligned in the panel according to the value of the `Alignment` property. If the `Style` is set to `Owner Draw`, it is up to you to draw any text or image that is displayed in the panel. Owner drawing of panel items is discussed a little bit later in the section titled "Owner-Drawn Status Bar Panels."

The `Width`, `Bevel`, and `Alignment` properties for the panel are pretty straightforward. Experiment with these properties to see what effect they have on the look of your status bar.

13

> **TIP**
>
> The effects of changes made to the status bar via the StatusBar Panels Editor can be seen immediately in the Form Designer. Position the StatusBar Panels Editor so that you can see the status bar as you work with the StatusBar Panels Editor. Each time you make a change, it will be reflected in the Form Designer when you move to the next field in the StatusBar Panels Editor or click the Apply button.

 The CD-ROM accompanying the book has a program called StatTest that illustrates some of the things you can do with status bars. Run the program and examine its source for tips on implementing status bars in your applications.

When you are done adding panels to the status bar, click OK to return to the Form Designer.

> **NOTE**
>
> When you modify the Panels property of a StatusBar component, the Form Designer automatically sets the SimplePanel property to false. The assumption is that if you are using multiple panels, you do not want to have a simple status bar.

Changing Text in the Status Bar

There are two ways to change text in a status bar:

☐ Manually modify the SimpleText property of the status bar (for simple status bars) or the Text property of an individual panel (for complex status bars).

☐ Respond to the OnHint event for the Application object.

Manually changing the text in the status bar is very easy, particularly if you have a simple status bar. When the SimplePanel property is true, you can just set the SimpleText property to the text you want displayed in the status bar:

```
StatusBar->SimpleText = "This shows up in the status bar.";
```

In the case of complex status bars, changing the text is only slightly more complicated. If you wanted to change the text for the first panel of a complex status bar, you would use something like this:

```
StatusBar->Panels->Items[0]->Text = "Status Bar Text";
```

Although this line gets a little strung out, it is not too difficult to understand. The Panels property of the StatusBar component has a property called Items that is an array of panels in the status bar. Setting the Text property for an element in the array changes the text for that panel. As you can see, the array is 0 based. The first panel in the status bar is array element 0.

Changing the text via the OnHint event requires a little more effort but is pretty simple after you've done it once. Back on Day 9 we added status bar hint support to the ScratchPad program. We don't need to go over all of that again, but let's review the steps we took:

1. Add a function declaration to the header for the main form for your own OnHint event:

```
void __fastcall OnHint(TObject* Sender);
```

2. Add the function implementation to the main form source unit. In the function body, set the Hint property of the Application object to the status bar's SimpleText property:

```
void _fastcall TMainForm::OnHint(TObject* Sender)
{
    StatusBar->SimpleText = Application->Hint;
}
```

3. In your OnCreate event handler for the main form, set the Application object's OnHint event handler to point to your own OnHint() function:

```
void __fastcall TMainForm::FormCreate(TObject *Sender)
{
    Application->OnHint = &OnHint;
}
```

4. Be sure all components that should display hints have their ShowHint property set to true and that there is valid hint text in the Hint property.

Like I said, it's not too terrible after you've done it a few times. This is easy enough for simple status bars, but if your application uses complex status bars, you need to modify your OnHint() function slightly:

```
void _fastcall TMainForm::OnHint(TObject* Sender)
{
  StatusBar->Panels->Items[0]->Text = Application->Hint;
}
```

To take it a step further, let's say your application switches between a simple status bar and a complex status bar, depending on the state of the program. In that case you need to check whether the status bar is currently set to a simple status bar or a complex status bar and set the text accordingly. This OnHint() function does it all:

```
void _fastcall TMainForm::OnHint(TObject* Sender)
{
  if (StatusBar->SimplePanel)
    StatusBar->SimpleText = Application->Hint;
  else
    StatusBar->Panels->Items[0]->Text = Application->Hint;
}
```

13

Now you've got it covered no matter what type of status bar you are using. Of course, this code assumes that you are using the first panel in the status bar to display the hint text. If you are using some other panel to display the hint text, change the code accordingly.

NOTE

> You can still modify the status bar's text manually even when using hints. There's nothing to stop you from changing the text manually, but remember that the text will get replaced the next time an OnHint event occurs.

Owner-Drawn Status Bar Panels

Earlier I said that a panel's style could be either text (psText) or owner draw (psOwnerDraw). When a panel's style is set to psOwnerDraw, you must take the responsibility of drawing anything in the panel that needs to be displayed there. It is unlikely that you are going to go to the trouble of using an owner-drawn panel just to display text, so usually it means you are going to display some sort of icon or bitmap in the status bar. Regardless of what is being drawn on the panel, the steps taken are the same:

1. Set the panel's Style property to psOwnerDraw (usually via the StatusBar Panels Editor).
2. Respond to the OnDrawPanel event.

Obviously, the real work here is going to take place in the event handler for the OnDrawPanel event. The function signature for the OnDrawPanel event handler looks like this:

```
void __fastcall TMainForm::StatusBarDrawPanel(TStatusBar *StatusBar,
    TStatusPanel *Panel, const TRect &Rect)
{
}
```

In this function, the StatusBar parameter is a pointer to the status bar. Usually you have a pointer to the status bar anyway (the Name property of the StatusBar component), so this parameter is not all that useful. The Panel property is a pointer to the particular panel that currently needs drawing. You can use this parameter to determine which panel needs to be drawn if you have more than one owner-drawn panel in your status bar. The Rect parameter contains the size and position of the panel. The Rect parameter is important because it tells you, in effect, the exact dimensions of the drawing area.

The OnDrawPanel event handler is called once for each panel that has its Style property set to psOwnerDraw. If you have only one panel to draw, you don't have to worry about much except the Rect parameter. If you have multiple panels to draw, you need to first determine which panel to draw and then do your drawing. An illustration might help to explain this.

13

Earlier I mentioned the StatTest program. Figure 13.5 shows the StatTest program running.

Figure 13.5.

The StatTest *program with owner-drawn status bar panels.*

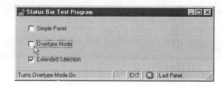

As you can see, the status bar in this program has multiple panels. The middle three panels are owner drawn. The panels marked OVR and EXT simulate the status bar on a word-processing program or code editor. In those types of programs, the Overtype or Extended Selection modes might be on or off. If the mode is on, the text in the status bar panel shows in black. If the mode is off, the text shows a 3D disabled-text look. The third owner-drawn panel displays a stock Windows icon to illustrate the use of a graphic on a status bar. Run the program from the CD-ROM and experiment with it to see how it works.

Listing 13.1 shows the OnDrawPanel event handler from the StatTest program. Examine it and read the comments to get an understanding of what is going on with the code.

Listing 13.1. The StatusBarDrawPanel() function of the StatTest program.

```
 1: void __fastcall TMainForm::StatusBarDrawPanel(TStatusBar *StatusBar,
 2:     TStatusPanel *Panel, const TRect &Rect)
 3: {
 4:   //
 5:   // Create a reference to the status bar Canvas so we
 6:   // don't have to do so much typing.
 7:   //
 8:   TCanvas& c = *StatusBar->Canvas;
 9:   //
10:   // Create a temporary TRect object. The Rect parameter
11:   // is const so we can't change it.
12:   //
13:   TRect temp = Rect;
14:   //
15:   // Check to see if panel 3 is the panel that needs
16:   // to be drawn. If so, draw an icon in the panel.
17:   //
18:   if (Panel->Index == 3) {
19:     //
20:     // Load one of the stock Windows icons. This time
21:     // using the API is easier than using VCL.
22:     //
23:     HICON icon = LoadIcon(NULL, IDI_HAND);
24:     //
25:     // Draw the icon and shrink it down to 15 x 15 pixels.
```

continues

Listing 13.1. continued

```
26:      // Center it in the panel, too.
27:      //
28:      DrawIconEx(c.Handle, Rect.Left + 6, 3, icon,
29:        15, 15, NULL, NULL, DI_NORMAL);
30:      //
31:      // Nothing more to do.
32:      //
33:      return;
34:    }
35:    //
36:    // This rather lengthy if statement checks to see if
37:    // either the Overtype Mode or Extended Selection
38:    // check boxes are checked. If so, then what we need
39:    // to do is to draw the text twice. First, we draw it
40:    // in white. Then we draw it again, offset by 1 pixel,
41:    // in gray. The effect is a 3D disabled-text look.
42:    //
43:    if ((Panel->Index == 1 && OvrMode->Checked == false) ||
44:      (Panel->Index == 2 && ExtendedSel->Checked == false)) {
45:        //
46:        // Move over and down one pixel for the offset.
47:        //
48:        temp.Left += 1;
49:        temp.Top += 2;
50:        //
51:        // Change the text color to white.
52:        //
53:        c.Font->Color = clWhite;
54:        //
55:        // Set the backround mode to transparent so the
56:        // text appears hollow and so that the white
57:        // text can be seen under the gray.
58:        //
59:        c.Brush->Style = bsClear;
60:        //
61:        // Draw the text using the API function DrawText().
62:        // I use DrawText() because it allows me to center
63:        // the text both horizontally and vertically within
64:        // the given rectangle.
65:        //
66:        DrawText(c.Handle, Panel->Text.c_str(),
67:          -1, temp, DT_CENTER | DT_VCENTER | DT_SINGLELINE);
68:        //
69:        // Set the color to gray because we're going to
70:        // draw the text in gray in a moment.
71:        //
72:        c.Font->Color = clGray;
73:        //
74:        // Set the rect back to the original size.
75:        //
76:        temp.Left -= 1;
77:        temp.Top -= 2;
78:    }
```

13

```
79:    //
80:    // Display the text. If the item is not disabled then
81:    // the default color (black) is used to draw the text.
82:    // If the item is disabled, then the text color has
83:    // been set to gray by the code above.
84:    //
85:    DrawText(c.Handle, Panel->Text.c_str(),
86:       -1, temp, DT_CENTER ¦ DT_VCENTER ¦ DT_SINGLELINE);
87: }
```

This code might seem a little intimidating, but most of it is just comment lines. The actual code is fairly simple. The comment lines explain what is happening at each step. As the comments explain, the 3D look for the disabled text is accomplished by drawing the text once in white and then drawing it again in gray with a slight offset. The effect is that the text looks recessed. The icon is displayed using the Windows API function `DrawIconEx()`.

NOTE

> Notice line 8 of Listing 13.1. Here I created a reference to the status bar's `Canvas` property to save some typing and to make the code less cluttered. After creating the reference, I can write code like this:
>
> `c.Font->Color = clWhite;`
>
> rather than like this:
>
> `StatusBar->Canvas->Font->Color = clWhite;`
>
> Granted, the use of c for the reference name is a little cryptic, but it illustrates how a reference can be used in a VCL application.

Owner drawing of status bar panels is a little daunting at first, but you'll soon find out that it's not all that bad. You might program for a long time and never need owner-drawn panels in your status bar, but if you ever need them, you'll know it's not impossible to accomplish.

Toolboxes

Toolboxes are not exactly window decorations, but they fit along the same lines, so I'll touch on them briefly. *Toolboxes* are simply secondary forms that contain speed buttons. You may have noticed that toolboxes like the C++Builder Alignment window and Object Inspector have smaller title bars than regular windows. You create this smaller title bar by setting the `BorderStyle` property to either `bsSizeToolWindow` (for sizable toolboxes) or `bsToolWindow` (for non-sizable toolboxes). Aside from that, a toolbox is just another form.

13

> **TIP**
>
> You may not be able to size your toolbox to the proper width at design time because of the standard buttons that are displayed on every form. For example, a toolbox with two buttons across should be about 54 pixels in width. The smallest the Form Designer will let you make the form is 112 pixels. The only thing you can do to get around this is to set the `Width` property of the toolbox at runtime before the toolbox is displayed.

Command Enabling

Command enabling is the process of enabling or disabling buttons depending on current conditions. For example, there's not much point in having the Cut or Copy button or menu item enabled for a text editor when no text is currently selected. Likewise, if there is no text in the Clipboard, the Paste button should be disabled.

Command enabling is not difficult, but it takes some time. It takes time because you have to pay attention to detail. (Sometimes it's attention to detail that separates the big dogs from the pups.)

Command-Enabling Ramblings

You can handle command enabling whenever and however you like. All you have to do to enable a menu item or speedbar button is to set its `Enabled` property to `true`. To disable a component, set its `Enabled` property to `false`. The actual enabling or disabling of a component really is as easy as that, but the real work comes in working out how and when to do the enabling or disabling. To put this into practice, let's go back to the `ScratchPad` program. What we will do is add command enablers for the menu items Cut, Copy, and Paste. (I say menu items, but I mean menu items, speedbar buttons, and pop-up menu items collectively.)

Before we dive into the code that does the command enabling, let's first lay the groundwork. First, let's assume that the Cut and Copy menu items should be enabled only when text is selected in the memo component. After all, if nothing is selected, there's nothing to cut or copy. In the case of pasting text, we want the Paste menu item to be enabled only if there is actually text in the Clipboard.

Okay—now we've got the ground rules laid, so we can get started. Well, not quite. There's still something that we need to work out: When and where do we do the enabling?

13

We could do the enabling for Paste when the user selects either Cut or Copy from the menu. If you recall, we have event handlers for the Cut, Copy, and Paste menu items. So we could do some enabling there:

```
void __fastcall TScratchPad::EditCutClick(TObject *Sender)
{
  Memo->CutToClipboard();
  EditPaste->Enabled = true;
}
```

If the user chooses Edit | Cut, we know something is in the Clipboard, so we can enable Paste. Okay—so when do we *disable* Paste? And what happens if the user uses Ctrl+X to cut rather than using the menu? Further, what if the user copies text to the Clipboard in some other application and wants to paste it into dear old ScratchPad? Looks like we've got some problems here that we have to work out. "Never do today what you can put off until tomorrow," I always say, so let's leave that problem on the back burner for now and see what we can do with Cut and Copy.

Cut and Copy should be enabled when text is selected. That's simple enough. If you dig through the VCL help files, you will discover that TMemo has a property called SelLength that will tell you the length of the selected text in a memo component. So if SelLength is greater than 0, the user has selected some text. "Great! This will be easy!" You think so? Bad news, I'm afraid. We don't have any way of knowing *when* the user selected the text. There is no event called OnTextSelected, so we can't use events to tell us. We could use a system timer, but that's a really messy solution. Besides, there are only so many system timers, and we can't be guaranteed that we'll get one when we want it. Well, we could catch the mouse messages for the memo component. That might work. But what if the user selected text with the keyboard rather than with the mouse? Then we'd have to catch all the mouse messages and all the keyboard messages and check to see if SelLength is greater than 0. Yech! This is getting complicated. And we still haven't solved the Paste problem we have simmering on the back burner. There's *got* to be a better way! Fortunately, there is.

OnIdle to the Rescue

When your application runs out of messages to process, Windows sends it a WM_ENTERIDLE message. Windows, in effect, tells your program, "I don't have anything for you to do right now, so relax and take it easy for a while." When a C++Builder application receives a WM_ENTERIDLE message, it triggers the Application object's OnIdle event. You can provide an OnIdle event handler that you can attach to the Application object's OnIdle event. This event handler will be called whenever the OnIdle event occurs. You put this into practice exactly like you did before when attaching an event handler to the Application object's OnHint event: Create a function in your main form's class and assign its address to the OnIdle event of the Application object.

13

So what's the benefit to us? The benefit is that we now have a function that will be called automatically at periodic intervals. We can use the function to check whether any text is selected in the memo component so we can enable or disable the Cut and Copy menu items as needed. Cool. That takes care of that.

But that still doesn't fix our problem with Paste, does it? Take heart—the Paste problem has a reasonable solution, too. VCL has a class called TClipboard that encapsulates Clipboard operations. One of the methods of TClipboard is HasFormat(). This method checks whether data of a particular format is currently in the Clipboard. If so, HasFormat() returns true. We can use this method to determine whether text is contained in the Clipboard with code like this:

```
if (Clipboard()->HasFormat(CF_TEXT)) PasteBtn->Enabled = true;
```

If text is in the Clipboard, we enable the Paste button and menu item. If no text is in the Clipboard, we disable the Paste items. Another world problem solved.

The use of the OnIdle() function means that our command enablers will be called regardless of whether the user selects text with the mouse, with the keyboard, or even from another application.

Okay, Let's Do It

As I said earlier, we have to create an event handler for the OnIdle event. That part is pretty simple, so let's do it first:

1. Open the ScratchPad program and switch to the Code Editor.

2. Open the header for the main form unit (SPMain.h) and add the following at the end of the other #includes near the top of the file:

   ```
   #include <vcl\Clipbrd.hpp>
   ```

3. Add the following to the private section of the class declaration:

   ```
   void __fastcall OnIdle(TObject* Sender, bool& Done);
   ```

4. Now switch to the SPMain.cpp file in the Code Editor. Add the following function to the end of the file:

   ```
   void __fastcall
   TScratchPad::OnIdle(TObject* Sender, bool& Done)
   {
   }
   ```

5. Locate the MainFormCreate() function and add this line to the function:

   ```
   Application->OnIdle = &OnIdle;
   ```

Now you have a function that will be called whenever your application enters its idle state. Obviously, the function doesn't do any good without any code in it, but we'll get to that in a minute. As long as we're at it, though, we'll go ahead and add command enablers for the Save, Save As, Undo, and Select All menu items. We'll use OnIdle to do it all. Listing 13.2 shows the complete OnIdle() function.

Listing 13.2. The ScratchPad OnIdle() function.

```
 1: void __fastcall
 2: TScratchPad::OnIdle(TObject* Sender, bool& Done)
 3: {
 4:   //
 5:   // Command enablers for Cut and Copy. If no text is
 6:   // selected then disable these items on the main menu,
 7:   // on the speedbar, and on the popup menu.
 8:   //
 9:   bool textSelected = Memo->SelLength > 0;
10:   EditCut->Enabled = textSelected;
11:   EditCutBtn->Enabled = textSelected;
12:   PopupCut->Enabled = textSelected;
13:   EditCopy->Enabled = textSelected;
14:   EditCopyBtn->Enabled = textSelected;
15:   PopupCopy->Enabled = textSelected;
16:   //
17:   // Command enablers for Paste. Is there text in the
18:   // clipboard? If not, disable Paste.
19:   //
20:   bool cbHasText = Clipboard()->HasFormat(CF_TEXT);
21:   EditPaste->Enabled = cbHasText;
22:   EditPasteBtn->Enabled = cbHasText;
23:   PopupPaste->Enabled = cbHasText;
24:   //delete clipBrd;
25:   //
26:   // Command enabler for Select All.
27:   //
28:   bool hasText = Memo->Lines->Count > 0;
29:   EditSelectAll->Enabled = hasText;
30:   //
31:   // Command enabler for Save and Save As.
32:   //
33:   bool modified = Memo->Modified;
34:   FileSave->Enabled = modified && hasText;
35:   FileSaveBtn->Enabled = modified && hasText;
36:   FileSaveAs->Enabled = modified && hasText;
37:   //
38:   // Command enabler for Undo
39:   //
40:   EditUndo->Enabled = modified;
41: }
```

13

Some of this code might look a bit odd if you haven't encountered it before. Take a look at line 9, for instance. This line assigns the result of Memo->SelLength > 0 to the bool variable, textSelected. If the SelLength property of the memo is greater than 0, the textSelected variable is assigned a value of true. If the SelLength property is less than or equal to 0 (meaning no text is selected), the variable is assigned a value of false. This value is then assigned to the Enabled property of the various Cut and Copy menu items and buttons. Other code in this function works in the same way. Examine Listing 13.2 and read the comment lines to see how the function works. Enter the code into the OnIdle() function of the ScratchPad program to convince yourself that it works.

NOTE

Debugging code in the OnIdle event handler is tricky. The problem is that any breakpoints in the OnIdle event handler will be immediately hit as soon as you run the program. You will have to use debugging methods other than breakpoints when debugging code in the OnIdle event handler (the TRACE and WARN macros, for instance).

NOTE

The OnIdle event handler could be called thousands of times per second. For that reason you must keep code in this function short and sweet.

And in Closing...

This is by no means the only way to handle command enablers in a C++Builder application. I think, however, that it is an elegant solution to the problems that command enablers present. Every situation is different, so don't be afraid to adapt if this particular solution doesn't fit with the way your application works. In some cases you might want to do command enabling in direct response to some action by the user. However you do it, command enabling is something that you should implement in your application when and where it's appropriate.

Printing in C++Builder Applications

Printing is an everyday necessity for most Windows users. Although there are plenty of programs that do not have printing capability, the majority of Windows applications have some form of printing support. We'll cover the basics of printing in this section.

Providing printing capabilities in a DOS application used to be a real chore. A DOS program had to provide and install printer drivers for every type of printer that the program supported. That put a huge burden on software developers, especially on small companies or shareware developers. Windows changed all that. For the most part, Windows takes on the burden of dealing with different printers, printer drivers, and so on. All you have to do is send output to the printer just as you would send output to a window. We'll get to that a little later.

Printing in C++Builder applications comes in several flavors. You'll probably be relieved to learn that in many cases printing is built into VCL and comes nearly automatically. In other cases, though, you'll have to do some specialized printing. For those times, you'll need to know how to go about it. Before I get into that, let's take a quick look at the common dialog boxes that pertain to printing. After that I'll discuss the different ways you can print from a C++Builder application.

The Common Printing Dialog Boxes

Windows provides the common Print and Print Setup dialog boxes that you can use in your applications. The Print dialog box is used just before printing begins, and the Print Setup dialog box is used to configure the printer. To use either one of these dialog boxes in your application, you first need to add the components to your form.

The Print Dialog Box

As mentioned, the Print dialog box is displayed just before printing begins, usually when the user chooses File | Print from the main menu. If the user clicks OK, printing should begin; if the user clicks Cancel, printing should be aborted. Figure 13.6 shows the Windows Print dialog box in its most basic form.

Figure 13.6.

The Windows Print dialog box.

13

No doubt this is not the first time you have seen this particular dialog box. The combo box at the top of the dialog box allows you to choose the particular printer to which you want to print. Clicking the Properties button will bring up a dialog box that is specific to the printer currently selected. The Properties dialog box allows you to set the orientation, resolution, and other properties specific to that printer. The Print Range section allows the user to print all pages, a page range, or any objects or text currently selected in the application. The Copies section allows the user to specify the number of copies to print, as well as whether to collate the copies.

The Print dialog box is encapsulated in VCL in the `PrintDialog` component. As with the other common dialog boxes, the Print dialog box is displayed by calling its `Execute()` method. You will probably not be too disappointed to learn that much of what the Print dialog box does is handled by Windows. The printer selection, number of copies, and collating options are all handled by Windows so you don't have to worry about them. Depending on your application, you might need to allow the user to print a specified range of pages or to print the current selection in the application. If you are providing that kind of support, you will need to examine some of the `PrintDialog` properties before printing begins.

The `PrintDialog` component has only the `Execute()` method and has no events. All the functionality of the `PrintDialog` component takes place through its properties. (See Table 13.3.)

Table 13.3. The `PrintDialog` properties.

Property	Description
Collate	If set to `true`, Windows will print so that the copies are collated.
Copies	Specifies the number of copies to print. You can set this property before calling the Print dialog box if you have the number of copies to print as one of your application's options. Windows takes care of printing the correct number of copies.
FromPage	Specifies the starting page when the option of printing a range of pages is enabled. Applications that support page-range printing should read this property to determine which pages to print.
MaxPage	Specifies the maximum page number that can be specified in the To field when printing a range of pages. The Print dialog box takes care of validating entry in the From and To fields.
MinPage	Specifies the minimum page number that can be specified in the From field when printing a range of pages.
Options	Contains a set of options that control which features of the Print dialog box are enabled. You can elect to have a Help button, to display the Print to File option, or to enable the page-range or print selection options.

Property	Description
PrintRange	Controls which of the Print Range radio buttons is selected when the Print dialog box is initially displayed.
PrintToFile	You read this property to determine whether the user has chosen the Print to File option. It is up to the application to write the output to a file.
ToPage	Specifies the ending page number when printing a range of pages. Applications that support page-range printing should read this property to determine which pages to print.

The application doesn't have much to do in response to the Print dialog box closing unless the Print Range and Print to File options are enabled. For example, if your application allows printing a range of pages, you need to read the FromPage and ToPage properties to determine which pages to print. Other than that, you simply begin printing if the user chooses OK.

The Print Setup Dialog Box

The Print Setup dialog box is used when the user wants to change printers, page size, paper source, or orientation. (See Figure 13.7.)

Figure 13.7.

The Print Setup dialog box.

The Print Setup dialog box is not necessary in most applications because the user can always press the Properties button on the Print dialog box to change the setup options (refer to Figure 13.6). On the other hand, implementing the Print Setup dialog box is so easy that you might as well include it in your applications. How easy is it? Well, the PrinterSetup component has no properties, methods, or events that are specific to it. As it is with the PrintDialog component, the Execute() method is the only method in which you are interested. To further simplify things, Windows handles everything that the Print Setup dialog box does. In fact,

13

the `Execute()` function does not even return a value because Windows handles everything for you. If the user clicks Cancel, Windows does nothing. If the user clicks OK, Windows makes the appropriate changes in preparation for printing. All you have to do is display the Print Setup dialog box and forget about it. A typical event handler for the File | Printer Setup menu item would look like this:

```
void __fastcall TScratchPad::FilePrintSetupClick(TObject *Sender)
{
  PrinterSetupDialog->Execute();
}
```

That's all there is to it. Like I said, implementing the Print Setup dialog box is so simple that you might as well add it to your application.

Printing the Easy Way

Printing is an application-specific task. That may not seem terribly profound, but it's true. Depending on what kind of application you have developed, printing can be as simple as one line, or it can entail hundreds of lines of code. Let me first discuss the easiest forms of printing, and then we'll progress to the more difficult printing operations.

The `Print()` Method for Forms

The `TForm` class has a method called `Print()` that can be used to print the contents of a form. Only the client area of the form is printed; the form's frame and menu bar are not. While this method works pretty well for a simple screen dump, it is pretty limited in its implementation. You can choose from three print options, which are controlled through the `PrintScaled` property. Table 13.4 lists the print scaling choices and their descriptions.

Table 13.4. The `PrintScaled` property options.

Option	Description
`poNone`	No special scaling is applied. The printed output of the form will vary from printer to printer.
`PoProportional`	This option will attempt to print the form in roughly the same size as it appears on the screen.
`poPrintToFit`	The image will be stretched or reduced in size to fit the current printer settings.

You can set the `PrintScaled` property at runtime or at design time. The `Print()` method's use is limited to simple screen dumps and is not likely to be used for any serious printing.

The `Print()` Method for the `RichEdit` Component

The `RichEdit` component is powerful. This is primarily due to the amount of work that is done by the underlying Windows rich edit control. Printing in the `RichEdit` component is accomplished via a call to the `Print()` method. This function takes a single parameter called `Caption` that is used by the print manager when it displays the print job. Printing the contents of a `RichEdit` component is as simple as this:

```
RichEdit->Print("MyApp.exe - readme.txt");
```

Everything is taken care of for you. Word wrapping and pagination are automatically implemented. If you are using a multiline edit control that requires printing, the `RichEdit` component is the way to go.

 TIP

> You can use the Windows API function `ShellExecute()` to print a text file. `ShellExecute()` is used, among other things, to run a program based on a filename extension. For example, by default Windows registers the `.txt` extension as belonging to Windows Notepad. If you double-click on a file with a `.txt` extension in Explorer, Windows will look up the `.txt` extension in the Registry, see that `Notepad.exe` is registered to handle `.txt` files, and will run Notepad. The file you double-clicked will be loaded automatically.
>
> You can use this behavior to your advantage. Take this line of code, for instance:
>
> ```
> ShellExecute(Handle, "print", "readme.txt", NULL, NULL, SW_HIDE);
> ```
>
> This code will load Notepad, print the file called `Readme.txt`, and then exit Notepad. In fact, you will never see the Notepad program's main window because the `SW_HIDE` style is specified for the `Show` parameter. Using this technique assumes that the user has not modified the default registration of the `.txt` extension and has not deleted Notepad from his system.

13

Printing via `QuickReport`

Database programs can use `QuickReport` to print reports. I mention `QuickReport` here because it obviously pertains to printing, but because `QuickReport` is one of the database components, I will leave the discussion about its actual implementation until a later chapter where `QuickReport` will be discussed in more detail.

Printing the Hard Way

Don't let the title of this section put you off too much. Printing really isn't all that difficult; it just takes some time and organization. First let's look at some of the things you need to know in order to implement printing in your applications. After that we will get into the actual code.

What's a Device Context?

A *device context* (DC) is sort of like a slate that Windows programs can draw on. A better word would be *canvas*. This canvas can be drawn on with text, lines, bitmaps, rectangles, ellipses, and so on. The line used when drawing on a device context depends on the current pen selected into the DC. The current fill color and fill pattern are taken from the brush that is currently selected into the device context. Device contexts have to be managed carefully. There are a limited number of DCs available to Windows, and you have to be careful to release the device context as soon as you are finished with it. Also, if you don't properly delete the objects you select into the device context, your program will leak memory and can even leave Windows itself in a precarious state. As you might imagine, working with DCs can be fairly complicated.

The good news is that VCL shields you from having to know every detail of device contexts. VCL encapsulates Windows DCs in the `TCanvas` class. Each form in C++Builder has its own canvas that is represented by the `Canvas` property. Any time you need to draw directly on a form, you can do so by accessing the `Canvas` property. For instance, the following code will draw a line diagonally on a form from the top-left corner to the bottom-right corner:

```
Canvas->MoveTo(0, 0);
Canvas->LineTo(ClientRect.Right, ClientRect.Bottom);
```

The line will be drawn using the current pen for the canvas as determined by the canvas's `Pen` property.

The nice thing about the `Canvas` property is that you don't have to worry about all the little details that can drive you nuts when dealing with Windows device contexts. VCL takes care of obtaining the DC, selecting the appropriate objects into the DC, and releasing the DC when it is no longer needed. All you have to do is draw on the canvas and let VCL worry about the rest.

So what does this have to do with printing? (Inquiring minds want to know.) Well, it's like this: Windows allows you to obtain a *printer* device context on which you can draw text, graphics, lines, and so on. In other words, you draw on a printer DC just like you draw on a screen DC. This concept represents quite a switch from the way printing was approached back in the good old days of DOS. In this case, it is Windows that comes to our rescue by allowing the use of a printer DC. VCL further aids us by encapsulating device contexts in the Canvas property. The bottom line is that printing is easier than it's ever been before.

The TPrinter Class and the Printer() Function

VCL aids in printing operations by providing the TPrinter class. This class encapsulates the whole of printing in Windows. TPrinter has a Canvas property that can be used to output lines, text, graphics, and other drawing objects to the printer. I don't want to make it sound too easy, but all you have to do to print in your C++Builder programs is include Printers.hpp, and then do something like the following:

```
Printer()->BeginDoc();
Printer()->Canvas->TextOut(20, 20, "Hello There!");
Printer()->EndDoc();
```

The Printer() function allows you access to a TPrinter object that is all set up and ready to go. All you have to do is put it to work for you.

Now let's take a quick look at TPrinter's properties and methods. Table 13.5 lists the primary TPrinter properties, and Table 13.6 shows the primary TPrinter methods.

Table 13.5. TPrinter properties.

Property	Description
Aborted	This property will be true if printing was started and then aborted before it was finished.
Canvas	The mechanism through which you can draw on the printer (the printer device context).
Fonts	A list of fonts supported by the current printer.
Handle	The handle to the printer device context (HDC). Use this property when you have to call a Windows API function that requires a handle to a device context.
Orientation	The printer orientation (poPortrait or poLandsacpe). This will be set automatically when the user chooses a printer or modifies the printer setup, but you can also set it manually.
PageHeight	The height of the page of the current printer, in pixels. This value will vary from printer to printer. In addition, this property will contain a different value based on the orientation of the printer. Further, some printers can use more than one resolution, which will also cause this value to vary.

13

continues

Table 13.5. continued

Property	Description
PageNumber	The page number of the page that is currently printing. This property is incremented each time you call NewPage() to begin printing a new page.
PageWidth	The width of the page, in pixels. As with the PageHeight property, this value can vary depending on the printer resolution, paper orientation, and paper size.
PrinterIndex	The index value of the currently selected printer in the list of available printers. Specify -1 to select the default printer.
Printers	A list of available printers on the system.
Printing	This property will be true if the printer is currently printing.
Title	The text that identifies this printing job in the Print Manager window.

Table 13.6. TPrinter() methods.

Method	Description
Abort	Used to abort the printing prior to normal completion.
BeginDoc	Begins the printing process. This method sets up the printer with Windows in preparation for printing.
EndDoc	Ends the printing process. Forces the current page to be printed and performs printing cleanup with Windows.
GetPrinter	Retrieves the current printer. Use the Printers property rather than using this method. (The Printers property is the preferred method of accessing printers because you can use it both for retrieving the current printer and for setting the current printer.)
NewPage	Used to force printing of the current page and start a new page. Increments the PageNumber property.
SetPrinter	Sets the current printer. Use the Printers property rather than using this method.

The TPrinter class has no design time interface. Everything is accomplished at runtime.

Putting It to Work

It's time to put your newly acquired knowledge to work. Once again, we'll dust off the ScratchPad program and spruce it up a bit. After all, what good is a text editor that doesn't print? We will add printing support to good old ScratchPad in this section. First, we need to modify the main form slightly. We already have menu items set up for the Print and Print Setup menu items, but we will need to enable them and add the Print and Printer Setup dialog boxes to the form. Here goes:

1. Double-click on the MainMenu component to bring up the Menu Designer.
2. Choose File | Print from the ScratchPad menu in the Menu Designer. Change the Enabled property to true.
3. Do the same for the File | Print Setup menu item. Close the Menu Designer.
4. Place a PrintDialog component on the form. Change its Name property to PrintDialog.
5. Place a PrinterSetupDialog on the form and change its Name property to PrinterSetupDialog.

Okay, now that we've completed the form we need to go to work modifying the code. To start with, we have to add a couple of items to the SPMain.h header file. Do this:

1. Open the ScratchPad project and switch to the SPMain.h file.
2. Add the following at the end of the other #includes near the top of the file:

```
#include <Windows.hpp>
#include <Printers.hpp>
```

3. Add this line to the private section of the class declaration:

```
void PrintFooter(TRect& rect, int lineHeight);
```

   This is the declaration for a function that will print the footer on each page.

That takes care of the header. Now we have to add code to the SPMain.cpp source code unit:

1. Switch back to the Form Designer and choose File | Print from the form's main menu. The FilePrintClick() function will be displayed. For now we will leave the function empty.
2. Switch back to the Form Designer and choose File | Print Setup from the main menu. Enter one line at the cursor so that the entire FilePrintSetupClick() function looks like this:

```
void __fastcall TScratchPad::FilePrintSetupClick(TObject *Sender)
{
  PrinterSetupDialog->Execute();
}
```

13

3. Still in the Code Editor, move to the end of the file and type the following:

```
void TScratchPad::PrintFooter(TRect& rect, int lineHeight)
{
}
```

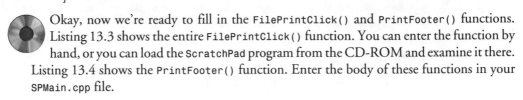 Okay, now we're ready to fill in the `FilePrintClick()` and `PrintFooter()` functions. Listing 13.3 shows the entire `FilePrintClick()` function. You can enter the function by hand, or you can load the `ScratchPad` program from the CD-ROM and examine it there. Listing 13.4 shows the `PrintFooter()` function. Enter the body of these functions in your `SPMain.cpp` file.

Listing 13.3. The `FilePrintClick()` function.

```
void __fastcall TScratchPad::FilePrintClick(TObject *Sender)
{
  //
  // Display the Print dialog.
  //
  if (PrintDialog->Execute()) {
    //
    // Set the title for the printer object.
    //
    Printer()->Title =
      "ScratchPad - " + OpenDialog->FileName;
    //
    // Set the printer font to the same font as the memo.
    //
    Printer()->Canvas->Font = Memo->Font;
    //
    // Determine the line height. Take the Size of the
    // font and and use the MulDiv() function to calculate
    // the line height taking into account the current
    // printer resolution. Use the abs() function to get
    // the absolute value because the result could be a
    // negative number. After that add 40% for leading.
    //
    int lineHeight = abs(
      MulDiv(Printer()->Canvas->Font->Size,
      GetDeviceCaps(Printer()->Handle, LOGPIXELSY), 72));
    lineHeight *= 1.4;
    //
    // Determine how many lines will fit on a page. Trim
    // it back by three lines to leave some bottom margin.
    //
    int linesPerPage =
      (Printer()->PageHeight/lineHeight) - 4;
    //
    // Start printing on line 4 rather than line 0 to leave
    // room for the header and to allow for some top margin.
    //
    int lineCount = 4;
```

13

```
//
// Tell Windows we're starting and print the header.
//
Printer()->BeginDoc();
TRect rect;
rect.Top = lineHeight;
rect.Left = 20;
rect.Right =  Printer()->PageWidth;
rect.Bottom = lineHeight * 2;
DrawText(Printer()->Handle,
  OpenDialog->FileName.c_str(), -1, rect, DT_CENTER);
//
// Loop through all of the lines and print each one.
//
for (int i=0;i<Memo->Lines->Count;i++) {
  //
  // When we get to the bottom of the page reset the
  // line counter, eject the page, and start a new page.
  //
  if (lineCount++ == linesPerPage) {
    PrintFooter(rect, lineHeight);
    lineCount = 4;
    Printer()->NewPage();
  }
  //
  // Get the next string and print it using TextOut()
  //
  String s = Memo->Lines->Strings[i];
  Printer()->Canvas->TextOut
    (0, lineCount * lineHeight, s);
}
//
// All done.
//
PrintFooter(rect, lineHeight);
Printer()->EndDoc();
}
}
```

Listing 13.4. The `PrintFooter()` function.

```
void TScratchPad::PrintFooter(TRect& rect, int lineHeight)
{
  //
  // Build a string to display the page number. We'll use the
  // C++ char* method rather than a String object because
  // DrawText() will want a char* anyway.
  //
  char buff[10];
  sprintf(buff, "Page %d", Printer()->PageNumber);
  //
  // Set up the rectangle where the footer will be drawn.
```

continues

Listing 13.4. continued

```
    // Find the bottom of the page and come up a couple of
    // lines.
    //
    rect.Top = Printer()->PageHeight - (lineHeight * 2);
    rect.Bottom = rect.Top + lineHeight;
    //
    // Display the text using DrawText so we can center the
    // text with no fuss.
    //
    DrawText(Printer()->Handle, buff, -1, rect, DT_CENTER);
    //
    // Draw a line across the page just above the Page x text.
    //
    Printer()->Canvas->MoveTo(0, rect.Top - 2);
    Printer()->Canvas->LineTo(rect.Right, rect.Top - 2);
}
```

This code illustrates how you can print directly through Windows rather than relying on the built-in printing that VCL provides. While I will always opt to do something the easy way when possible, there are times when the easy way just isn't flexible enough. In those times it's good to have the knowledge to get the job done without too much hassle.

Using Cursors

The use of cursors is not something that is difficult to implement, but I'll cover it here so that you have a basic understanding of how it works. This section deals with cursors that you change at runtime. (To change a cursor at design time, just select a new value for the component's Cursor property.) First, we will look at the basics of cursors and then I will discuss how to load stock cursors and custom cursors.

Cursor Basics

First of all, you can change the cursor for a particular component or form, or you can change it for the entire client area of your application. If you want to change the cursor for the entire application, you will need to change the Cursor property of the Screen object. The Screen object represents the screen of your application. By changing the Cursor property of the Screen object, you ensure that the cursor is the same, regardless of which component the cursor is over. Let's say, for instance, that you want to change the cursor to the hourglass cursor. If you change the Cursor property for the form only, the cursor will be an hourglass when over the form itself but will revert back to the default cursor when over any other components on the form. By changing the Cursor for the Screen object, you get the same cursor throughout.

Cursor management is the responsibility of the Screen object. All the cursors available for your use are contained in the Cursors property of the Screen object. Note that the name of this property is Cursors and is not the same as the Cursor property discussed in the previous paragraph. The Cursors property is an array that contains a list of available cursors for the application, and the Cursor property is the property that is used to display a particular cursor. Although this can be a bit confusing at first, you'll catch on to it soon enough. All it takes is a little experience working with cursors.

Windows provides several built-in cursors that you can use in your applications. In addition to these built-in cursors, VCL adds a few cursors of its own. Together these cursors are called the *stock cursors*. Each of the stock cursors has a named constant associated with it. For example, the arrow cursor is named crArrow, the hourglass cursor is named crHourglass, and the drag cursor is named crDrag. All these cursors are held in the Cursors array and occupy positions -17 through 0 in the array; the default cursor is at array index 0 (crDefault), no cursor is -1 (crNone), the arrow cursor is -2 (crArrow), and so on. The online help for the Cursors property lists all the cursors and their constant names, so check C++Builder help for a complete list of the available cursors.

To use one of the cursors in the Cursors array, assign the name of the cursor you want to use to the Cursor property of the Screen object:

```
Screen->Cursor = TCursor(crHourGlass);
```

At that point the VCL magic kicks in and the correct cursor is loaded and displayed. The use of the Cursors property is transparent to you because you don't access the Cursors property directly when you use a cursor. Instead, you simply make an assignment to the Cursor property and VCL takes care of looking up the proper cursor in the Cursors array and displaying it. The Cursor property of a component and the Cursors property of the Screen object work together to display different cursors in your application.

NOTE

> The preceding code snippet could have been written as follows:
>
> ```
> Screen->Cursor = crHourGlass;
> ```
>
> When written this way, the code will still work but the compiler will generate a warning that says Assigning int to Controls::TCursor. To keep the compiler happy, we create the temporary TCursor object.

13

You might have to change cursors in your applications for any number of reasons. You might want to display the wait cursor (the hourglass), you might have a drawing program that uses special cursors, or you might want to implement the help cursor in your application.

Now let's look at the two types of cursors you can use in your applications.

Loading and Using Stock Cursors

Windows provides several built-in cursors that you can use in your application. In addition to those, VCL adds a few more cursors from which you can choose. You can use these stock cursors anytime you like.

One of the most obvious reasons to change the cursor is when you have a lengthy process your application needs to perform. It is considered bad practice to tie up the program and not give the user some indication that the program is busy doing something. Windows provides the hourglass cursor (Windows calls it the wait cursor) for exactly this purpose. Let's say, for instance, that you have a processing loop in your application that might take a long time. You would do something like this:

```
//
// save the old cursor
//
TCursor oldCursor = Cursor;
//
// change the cursor to the hourglass cursor
//
Screen->Cursor = TCursor(crHourGlass);
//
// start the process
//
DoSomeReallyLongProcess();
//
// restore the original cursor
//
Screen->Cursor = oldCursor;
```

Because you don't always know which cursor your application is using at any given time, it is a good idea to save the current cursor prior to changing the Cursor property. After you are done with a particular cursor, you can restore the old cursor.

NOTE

Sometimes you will change the Cursor property before a lengthy processing loop and nothing appears to happen. The reason is that Windows didn't get a chance to change your cursor before your program entered the loop. Once in the loop, your application won't be able to process any messages—including the message to change the cursor. The fix is to pump the Windows message loop for waiting messages while you are in your loop:

```
Application->ProcessMessages();
```

Now your application will allow messages to flow, and the cursor will change when your loop starts.

You can, of course, change the cursor for an individual component. For instance, a drawing program might change the cursor of the client area depending on the current drawing tool. You don't want to change the cursor for the Screen object in that case because you want the arrow cursor to appear when the cursor is moved over the speedbar, status bar, or any other components that might be on the form. In that case you would set the cursor only for the component that represents the client window of your application:

```
PaintBox->Cursor = TCursor(crCross);
```

Now the cursor is changed for just this one component, and all other components use their own predefined cursors.

Loading and Using Custom Cursors

Loading custom cursors requires a little more work. As mentioned earlier, the Cursors property of the TScreen class contains the list of cursors available to your application. To use a custom cursor requires several steps:

1. Create a cursor in the Image Editor or other resource editor.
2. Create an .rc file that references the cursor and add it to your project. (An alternative to this is to compile the resource and add the resulting .res file to your project.)
3. Load the cursor into the Cursors array using the LoadCursor() function.
4. Implement the cursor by assigning the index number to the Cursor property for the form, the Cursor property for the Screen object, or the Cursor property for any other component.

The first two steps of this exercise were covered on Day 12, "C++Builder Tools and Options," when I talked about the Image Editor and also when I talked about projects. Once you have the cursor bound to the .exe, you can load it with the LoadCursor() function. Loading a cursor into the Cursors array is easy:

```
Screen->Cursors[1] = LoadCursor(HInstance, "MYCURSOR");
```

This code assumes that you have a cursor with the name MYCURSOR and that you are assigning the cursor to position 1 in the list of cursors (remember, positions -17 through 0 are used for the stock cursors). Loading the cursor only has to be done once, so you will probably do it in your main form's OnCreate event handler.

13

NOTE All cursors are loaded into the Screen object's Cursors property regardless of whether you are going to be using the cursor with the Screen object, with a form, or with a component. There is only one Cursors array, and it belongs to the Screen object.

To use the cursor, just assign it to the Cursor property of the Screen object or of any component:

```
PaintBox->Cursor = TCursor(1);
```

If you have several cursors, you might want to create global variables or #defines for each cursor so that you have meaningful names to use rather than integer values that are easy to mix up. Using that method, the preceding code would look something like this:

```
#define myCursor 1
Screen->Cursors[myCursor] = LoadCursor(HInstance, "MYCURSOR");
// later on...
PaintBox->Cursor = TCursor(myCursor);
```

As you can see, loading and implementing custom cursors is not too difficult once you know how to do it.

Summary

Today you have learned about some of the things that make up a top-quality Windows application and how to implement them in your own programs. I warn you that there does exist a temptation to overdo it with things like control bars, status bars, and cursors. Implement whatever decorations your application needs, but don't overuse them. You also learned about printing today. In some cases printing support is built into a particular component, and in those cases printing is incredibly easy. In other cases you will have to roll up your sleeves and go to work with the TPrinter class. Even for those times, though, printing is not something to be afraid of.

Workshop

The Workshop contains quiz questions to help you solidify your understanding of the material covered and exercises to provide you with experience in using what you have learned. You can find answers to the quiz questions in Appendix A, "Answers to Quiz Questions."

Q&A

Q Can I disable all the components on my speedbar at one time?

A Yes. If you disable the panel that contains the speedbar, all controls on the speedbar will be disabled as well. When you use this method, the controls will not show as disabled (grayed out)—they will just refuse to work.

Q **I want dockable toolbars like I see in other applications. Can I do that with C++Builder?**

A You can do anything you want with C++Builder; it's just a matter of how much work is involved. C++Builder has no built-in support for dockable toolbars, so you will have to create your own from scratch. You might want to look around on the various online sources to see what third-party or shareware dockable toolbar components are out there.

Q **How do I put a bitmap on my status bar?**

A Create a multipanel status bar. Change the style of the panel that should contain the bitmap to psOwnerDraw. Then, in your OnDrawPanel event handler, use the Draw() method of TCanvas to draw your bitmap on the panel.

Q **I had a simple status bar that I later converted to a complex status bar. Now my hints don't show up any more. What's wrong?**

A When you change to the complex status bar, you must change your code that displays hint text. Rather than using

```
StatusBar->SimpleText = Application->Hint;
```

you should use

```
StatusBar->Panels->Items[0]->Text = Application->Hint
```

This ensures that the text gets sent to the first panel of the status bar.

Q **Why should I bother with command enabling for my menu items and speedbar buttons?**

A Because users expect a consistent interface. When certain choices are not available (whether on menus or speedbars), they should be grayed out. This gives the user a visual cue that this command is sometimes available but is not currently applicable.

Q **I just want basic output of a large, multiline edit control in my application. What's the easiest way?**

A The easiest way is to use a RichEdit component and use its Print() method to print the contents of the component.

Q **I see that there is a Handle property for the Printer object and also a Handle property for the Canvas property of the Printer object. What's the difference?**

A In this case there is no difference. If you are calling a Windows API function that requires the printer device context handle, you can use either Printer()->Handle or Printer()->Canvas->Handle.

Q **When I change the cursor for my main form, the cursor is correct when over the form but reverts to the arrow cursor when over any of my buttons. Why?**

A You need to change the cursor for the Screen object and not just for the form. Changing the cursor for the Screen object ensures that the new cursor will be used whenever the cursor is over any part of your application.

13

Quiz

1. How do you attach an event to a speedbar button's OnClick event?
2. Can you put controls other than buttons on speedbars?
3. What component can you use to implement multiple speedbars in your application?
4. What does the SimplePanel property of the StatusBar component do?
5. How do you change the status bar text manually?
6. How do you enable and disable menu items and buttons?
7. How do you access the printer in a C++Builder application?
8. What method do you call to begin printing with the TPrinter class?
9. What method of TPrinter do you call when you want to start a new page when printing?
10. How do you change the cursor for a component at runtime?

Exercises

1. Create an application that has three speedbars, only one of which is visible at any one time. Place three radio buttons on the form. Write code so that when a radio button is pressed, the speedbar representing that radio button is displayed.

2. Write a program from scratch. Add a speedbar with five buttons and a status bar. Enable hints so that the speedbar buttons have both tool tips and hint text in the status bar.

3. Change the status bar for the ScratchPad program and add a second panel. In this panel display either Saved or Modified based on the value of Memo->Modified.

4. Make a copy of the ScratchPad program. Working with the copy, replace the Memo component with a RichEdit component and add printing support.

5. Change the About box of the ScratchPad program to read Version 1.05. Also change the Title property in the Project Options dialog box and the Caption of the main form. After all, we added features, so we must let the users know!

6. Create a custom cursor with the Image Editor. Write a program that displays the cursor when a button on the main form is pressed.

7. **Extra credit:** Modify the ScratchPad program from exercise 3 to display different bitmaps on the status bar depending on whether the current file is saved. (**Hint:** Look at the led1on.bmp and led1off.bmp bitmaps in the \Images\Buttons directory.)

8. **Extra credit:** Modify the ScratchPad program so that the user can specify a top margin, bottom margin, right margin, and left margin for printed output.

13

Day 14

Advanced Programming

by Kent Reisdorph

Today you will learn some of the more advanced aspects of Windows programming with C++Builder. Specifically, this chapter covers

☐ Implementing context-sensitive help

☐ Exception handling

☐ Using the Windows Registry

☐ Specialized message handling

We've got a lot to do today, so let's get right to it.

Implementing Context-Sensitive Help

Not too long ago you might have been able to get by with not providing context-sensitive help in your applications. In fact, for small applications you might have been able to get by without providing a help file at all. I wouldn't recommend that in today's market, though. Users are increasingly demanding when it comes to features. A help file is no longer an option, but a required component of a full-featured application.

Context-sensitive help means that when the user presses the F1 key, a particular page of the application's help file is displayed, depending on the program's current context. Take the C++Builder IDE, for example. Let's say you have the Project Options dialog box open and have the Application page displayed. When you press F1 (or press the Help button on the dialog box), WinHelp runs and displays the help topic for the Application page of the Project Options dialog box. Likewise, if you press F1 when the Object Repository Options dialog box is on the screen, you get help for that particular dialog box. Context-sensitive help works with menu items as well. If you highlight a menu item and press F1, you will be taken to the help file page regarding that menu item.

To implement context-sensitive help in your application, you must perform the following steps:

1. Create a help file for your application. The help file should contain context identifiers.
2. Assign the name of your help file to the `HelpFile` property of the `Application` object.
3. Set the `HelpContext` property of any forms or components for which context-sensitive help is supported. The `HelpContext` property is set to the context identifier in the help file corresponding to that component.
4. Create menu items for the Help menu so your users can invoke help from the menu.

Let's examine these steps one at a time.

Writing the Help File

Writing help files is a chore. I don't exactly hate it, mind you, but it's not one of the things I look forward to. If you are fortunate, you have a documentation department that writes the help files for you.

NOTE

> Even some limited-budget programmers have documentation departments that write help files for them. Frequently they refer to the doc writers as "Honey" or "Dear." For instance, a programmer might say to her documentation writer, "Honey, when you get done with that help page, would you put the kids to bed?"

14

Regardless of who writes the help file, there must be some coordination between the help-file writer and the programmer. The context identifiers in the help file must match those specified for the components in the program itself. Although this is not exactly a difficult task, coordination is still required so that everyone is on the same page (pun intended).

A Windows help file might be constructed from several individual files. The source for a Windows help file is called the *topic file*. The topic file is a rich text format (.RTF) file with lots of special codes that the help compiler understands. If your help file includes graphics, you might have one or more *graphics files*. Graphics files used in creating a help file include bitmap (.BMP), Windows metafile (.WMF), and some other specialized graphics files. Finally, you have the help *project file* (.HPJ). The project file contains a description of how the help compiler should go about merging the topic file, the graphics files, and any other specialized files the target help file needs. It also includes a [MAP] section that maps context ID numbers to particular help topics. After the project file is created, it is compiled with a help compiler such as the Microsoft Help Workshop (you can find it in the \CBuilder\Help\Tools directory). The Help Workshop takes the help project file and compiles it to produce the final help file (.HLP).

Although you can write help files with a word processor that supports .RTF files, I strongly recommend that you buy a help-authoring program. A good help-authoring package can take much of the frustration out of writing help files.

Context Identifiers and the HelpContext Property

Regardless of what method you use to create the help file, you need to have a context number associated with each major topic in the help file. The *context number* is used by the Windows help system, WinHelp.exe, to display a particular page in the help file. For example, let's say you have an Options dialog box in your application. When the user presses F1 with the Options dialog box open, your program passes the context ID for that dialog box to WinHelp. WinHelp will run and display the page in the help file that explains the application's Options dialog box. You don't need a context ID for each and every page in the help file, but you should have a help context ID for your main topic pages, dialog boxes, and other major components of your application.

Most components (forms, menu items, controls) have a property called HelpContext. This property contains the context ID that will be passed to WinHelp if the user presses the F1 key when that component has focus. By default, the HelpContext property is set to 0. If the HelpContext property is 0 for a component, the component will inherit the HelpContext value of its parent window. This allows you to set the HelpContext for a form and then, no matter which component on the form has input focus, the help context for the form will be used when F1 is pressed.

14

NOTE

> You may have noticed that the `SpeedButton` component does not have a
> `HelpContext` property. Because a `SpeedButton` is a non-windowed
> control, it can never gain input focus. Therefore, the F1 key cannot be
> used with speed buttons.

At a minimum, you should provide context-sensitive help for each form in your application
(a form being a dialog box or secondary window). Ultimately, it is up to you to decide which
items to provide context-sensitive help for. If you are going to err, you should probably err
on the side of providing too much context-sensitive help (if there is such a thing) rather than
not enough.

Implementing Context-Sensitive Help

Implementing context-sensitive help in your C++Builder applications is relatively easy. As
I said earlier, the real work in adding context-sensitive help to your C++Builder applications
is in the writing of the help file. The rest is child's play in comparison.

Setting the Help File

Regardless of how you implement context-sensitive help, you first have to tell Windows the
name of the help file for your application. To do that, you assign the help file name to the
`HelpFile` property of the `Application` class. You can do this one of two ways. The easiest way
is at design time via the Project Options dialog box. On Day 10, "More on Projects," we
looked at the project options. I discussed the fact that the Application page of the Project
Options dialog box has a field called Help File that is used to specify the name of the help
file for the application. Simply type the name of your help file in this field. VCL will assign
the help file name to the `HelpFile` property, and then the application will use that filename
each time help is requested.

You can also set the name of the help file at runtime. This might be necessary if you allow
your users to place the help file in a directory of their own choosing. You could store the
location of the help file in the Windows Registry (the Registry is discussed later, in the section
titled "Using the Registry") and then assign the help file's path and filename to the
`Application` object's `HelpFile` property. For instance, part of your `OnCreate` event handler
might look like this:

```
String filename = GetHelpFileName(); // user-defined function
Application->HelpFile = filename;
```

Although it's not very common, you can change the HelpFile property at runtime if you want. You might do this in order to switch between different help files, for instance. Once you have the help file name set up, you can go on to the actual implementation of the help system.

Adding F1 Key Support

To add F1 support for forms and components, all you have to do is set the HelpContext property to the matching context ID in the help file, and VCL takes it from there. Be sure that you have assigned a help file name to the HelpFile property of the Application class and that the help file contains valid context identifiers. After that, it's on autopilot.

Adding Menu Support for the Help File

In addition to F1 key support, most applications have one or two menu items under the Help menu (where else?) that can be used to start WinHelp. There will usually be a menu item called Contents. Choosing this item will display the contents page for the help file. The contents page is usually the main page for the help file. In addition to a Contents menu item, some applications have a Help menu item called Help Topics. Choosing this menu item displays the index for the help file (the index is created as part of the help file creation process).

To implement these and other Help items, you will have to do some programming. (It's only one line of code in each case.) VCL provides a method called HelpCommand() that can be used to display WinHelp in one of several modes. If you were to implement the Help | Contents menu item, the code would look like this:

```
void __fastcall TMainForm::HelpContentsClick(TObject *Sender)
{
  Application->HelpCommand(HELP_CONTENTS, 0);
}
```

The HelpCommand() method calls WinHelp with the specified command. (See the Windows API help under WinHelp() for a complete list of available commands.) In this case, WinHelp is invoked with the command HELP_CONTENTS. This command tells WinHelp to display the page that has been designated as the contents page. The final parameter of the HelpCommand() method is used to pass additional data to WinHelp. This parameter is not used with the HELP_CONTENTS command, so it is set to 0.

14

Conventional wisdom has it that you should no longer use the HELP_CONTENTS command to display the contents page, but rather should use the HELP_FINDER command along with the ID of the contents page. If, for example, your contents page had an ID of 1000, you could use the following:

```
Application->HelpCommand(HELP_FINDER, 1000);
```

I like the HELP_CONTENTS command because I can use it in any application without worrying about trying to remember the ID of the contents page for each of my applications.

Implementing a Help Topics menu item is nearly identical to implementing the Contents menu item, but involves a different command:

```
void __fastcall TMainForm::HelpTopicsClick(TObject *Sender)
{
  Application->HelpCommand(HELP_FINDER, 0);
}
```

The HELP_FINDER command, when used with the context ID 0, tells WinHelp to display the index for the help file. As I said earlier, you create the index when you create the help file.

A good index for your help file is invaluable. The quality of the help file—and the quality the help file's index—are directly proportional to the amount of technical support you will have to provide. Don't overlook this fact.

Context-Sensitive Help on Demand

Most of the time the two help implementations I just told you about are all you need for your application. At other times, however, you need to call WinHelp directly and with a specific context ID. For these times, VCL provides the HelpContext() method. This method takes, as its single parameter, the context ID of the page you want to see when WinHelp runs. For example, let's say you had a help page with a context ID of 99. To run WinHelp and display that specific page, you would do this:

```
Application->HelpContext(99);
```

By supplying a specific context ID, you can cause WinHelp to display any page of your help file on demand.

Using Help File Headers

Most of the time, setting the HelpContext properties for the forms or components for which you want to implement context-sensitive help is all you need to do. If, however, you need to call specific help pages in your application, you might consider using #defines to create constants for your help identifiers. Using a named constant is much easier than trying to remember an integer value for a particular help context ID.

In the last section I talked about using the HelpContext() method to call WinHelp with a particular context ID. I used the example of a help context ID of 99. Rather than using the numerical value of the context identifier, you could use a constant like this:

```
Application->HelpContext(IDH_FILEOPEN);
```

Obviously, the string is easier to remember than its integer value equivalent. The context-sensitive help #defines can all be kept in a separate header file that is included in your application where needed (using the #include directive). Listing 14.1 shows a typical header containing context-sensitive help identifiers.

Listing 14.1. HELP.H.

```
#define IDH_FILENEW           1
#define IDH_FILEOPEN          2
#define IDH_FILESAVE          3
#define IDH_FILESAVEAS        4
#define IDH_FILEPRINT         5
#define IDH_FILEPRINTSETUP    6
#define IDH_FILEEXIT          7
#define IDH_EDITUNDO          8
#define IDH_EDITCOPY          9
#define IDH_EDITCUT          10
#define IDH_EDITPASTE        11
#define IDH_EDITSELECTALL    12
#define IDH_EDITWORDWRAP     13
#define IDH_HELPABOUT        14
```

At the top of your source file you can add a line that includes the help file header:

```
#include "help.h"
```

Now you can use the name of the context ID when needed rather than the actual integer value.

How the help file header is created depends on the tools you are using to write your help files. Most help-authoring software includes an option to generate a header of some description that contains the named constants. The specific implementation depends on whether the

14

help file is being written by you or by a coworker and what help-authoring software you are using. If you are not using help-authoring software, you can simply type in the #defines by hand.

Putting It to Work

It's time to put your newly acquired knowledge into practice. In this section we'll add context-sensitive help to the ScratchPad program. (You knew we'd come back to old ScratchPad, didn't you?)

 The CD accompanying the book contains a simple help file for the ScratchPad program. Copy the help file, Scratch.hlp, from the CD to your working directory so C++Builder can find it when you build the ScratchPad application.

Context-sensitive help should take about 10 minutes to implement. (I told you C++Builder was cool!) Here we go:

1. Load the ScratchPad project. Go to the Application page of the Project Options dialog box and type Scratch.hlp in the Help File field. Click OK to close the dialog box. (Be sure you have moved the Scratch.hlp file into the project's directory.)

2. Display the ScratchPad main form in the Form Designer. Double-click on the MainMenu icon to invoke the Menu Designer.

3. In the Menu Designer, select the File | New menu item from the MainMenu component (not the C++Builder main menu, of course). Locate the HelpContext property in the Object Inspector and change its value to 1.

4. Repeat with the remaining menu items. Use the values from Listing 14.1 to set the HelpContext properties of the menu items.

5. Add a menu item under the Help menu called Help Topics. Change its Name property to HelpTopics. Add a separator under the Help Topics item to separate the Help items from the About menu item. Close the Menu Designer.

6. In the Form Designer, choose Help | Contents from the main menu. The Code Editor displays the HelpContentsClick() function. Type this line at the cursor:

   ```
   Application->HelpCommand(HELP_CONTENTS, 0);
   ```

7. Switch back to the Form Designer. Choose Help | Help Topics from the main menu. When the Code Editor is displayed, enter this line at the cursor:

   ```
   Application->HelpCommand(HELP_FINDER, 0);
   ```

8. Change the HelpContext property of the main form to 1000 (the context ID of the contents page).

Run the program and experiment with it. If you press F1 when the cursor is in the memo window, the Contents page of the help file will be displayed. If you highlight a menu item and press F1, help for that menu item will be displayed. Also check out the Contents and Help Topics items on the main menu to see if they work as expected.

 If you compile and run the ScratchPad program on the CD for Day 14, you will see that it has a feature not discussed here. The program has a Help Mode that can be used to get help on a specific speedbar button or menu item. To start the Help Mode, press the Help button on the speedbar. The cursor changes to the help cursor. Now select any menu item or speedbar button. The help topic for the item selected will be displayed. The Help Mode turns off automatically after you choose an item. Browse the source code to see how the Help Mode is implemented. This feature also makes use of special message handling, as discussed later in the chapter.

Context-sensitive help is no longer a luxury. Whether your users are members of the general public or your coworkers, they are still your users. They demand certain features, and context-sensitive help is one of those features. As easy as context-sensitive help is to implement in a C++Builder application, there is no reason for it to be missing from your applications.

Exception Handling

Even in the most well-designed program, things can go wrong that are beyond the control of the program. Users make mistakes. For instance, a user might input a bad value into a data field, or he could open a file of the wrong type for your application. Whatever the scenario, you should be prepared to handle these types of errors wherever and whenever possible. You can't anticipate your users' every move, but you can anticipate some of the more common blunders and handle them gracefully.

Exception handling is essentially a sophisticated form of error checking. While any program can implement and use them, exceptions are of primary benefit to users of components and other C++ classes. For instance, if you are using a component and something nasty happens within the component, you need to know about it. A well-written component will throw an exception when something goes wrong. You can catch that exception and handle it however you want—maybe by terminating the program or by allowing your user to correct the problem and try again.

NOTE

There are two types of exception handling. First, there is true C++ exception handling, which is what we are discussing here. In addition, 32-bit Windows implements what it calls *structured* exceptions. These two types of exception handling are not exactly the same thing. I won't

14

> go into the differences, but I just want to point out that you might encounter two different discussions on exception handling as you get further into Windows programming. You are not likely to use structured exceptions, since C++ has its own exception-handling mechanism.

You may not write a lot of exception handling into your day-to-day code. Your primary use of exceptions will be in handling exceptions that VCL throws when things go wrong within a component. If you write components, you will probably use exception handling with more frequency.

NOTE

> The use of exceptions in your programs should be reserved for extreme error conditions. You should throw an exception if the error condition is serious enough to make continued use of the program difficult. Most runtime errors can be handled with parameter checking, validation of user input, and other more traditional error-checking techniques.

A full discussion of exception handling could easily take an entire chapter, so I will limit this discussion to how you can handle exceptions thrown by VCL components.

Exception-Handling Keywords: try, catch, and throw

Exception-handling syntax is not terribly complicated. The three exception-handling keywords are try, catch, and throw. The try and catch keywords are used when handling exceptions, and the throw keyword is used to initiate (throw) an exception. Let's look at these in more detail.

SYNTAX

The try and catch keywords:

```
try {
    TryStatements
}
catch (TypeToCatch)
{
    CatchStatements
}
```

The try keyword marks the beginning of the try block. The statements in *TryStatements* are executed. If any exceptions of type *TypeToCatch* are thrown during the execution of *TryStatements*, *CatchStatements* is executed. If no exception is thrown, *CatchStatements* is

14

ignored and program execution proceeds to the statement following the `catch` block. *TypeToCatch* can be one of the integral data types (`int`, `char`, `long`, and so on), an instance of a class, or an ellipsis (...). If *TypeToCatch* is an ellipsis, then all exceptions are caught, regardless of the type of exception thrown.

Catching Exceptions with `try` and `catch`

Before I attempt to explain the `try` and `catch` keywords, let's look at a simple example. Listing 14.2 contains a short code snippet that illustrates exception handling. This code attempts to load a picture file (`.bmp`, `.wmf`, or `.ico`). If the file chosen by the user is not a picture file, VCL will throw an exception. If that happens, you catch the exception and display a message box telling the user that the file was not a picture file.

Listing 14.2. An exception-handling example.

```
 1: try {
 2:    TImage* image = new TImage(0);
 3:    image->Picture->LoadFromFile(OpenDialog->FileName);
 4:    TChild* child = new TChild(this);
 5:    child->Parent = this;
 6:    child->Image->Picture = image->Picture;
 7:    child->ClientWidth = child->Image->Picture->Width;
 8:    child->ClientHeight = child->Image->Picture->Height;
 9: }
10: catch (...)
11: {
12:    Application->MessageBox(
13:      "This file is not a Windows image file.",
14:      "Picture Viewer Error", MB_ICONHAND | MB_OK);
15: }
```

In this code you see a `try` block and a `catch` block. The `try` block is used to define the code for which an exception might be thrown. The `try` statement tells the compiler, "Try this and see if it works." If the code works, the `catch` block is ignored and program execution continues. If any of the statements inside the `try` block throws an exception, the code within the `catch` block will be executed. The `catch` block must immediately follow the `try` block, with no other code in between.

It is important to realize that as soon as an exception is thrown, program execution jumps immediately to the `catch` block. In this example, the code on line 3 is likely to be the code that throws an exception. If an exception is thrown on line 3, program execution will jump to line 12. In that case, lines 4–8 will never be executed.

14

Throwing Exceptions

As you can see, the `catch` statement catches an exception that was thrown somewhere in the program. Most of the time this will mean an exception thrown in VCL somewhere.

An exception is thrown using the `throw` keyword. The code that throws the exception will throw an exception of a particular type. For example, a typical `throw` statement might look like this:

```
if (badParameter) throw("A bad parameter was passed");
```

The `throw` statement throws an object of the type passed as its parameter. In this case a `char*` is thrown, but any type of object can be thrown. Let's say you had an error code 111 for a particular type of error. In that case, you could write the `throw` statement like this:

```
if (badParameter) throw(111);
```

Here an integer is being thrown. The compiler makes a copy of the object being thrown and passes it on to the `catch` statement immediately following the `try` block (we'll get back to that in a moment).

Most class libraries throw an instance of an exception-handling class. VCL defines several exception-handling classes for exactly this purpose. There are several reasons to throw an instance of a class. First of all, the class can contain data members and/or functions that describe everything you need to know to deal with the error. A basic exception-handling class might have data members called `Error` and `Msg` that would contain the error number and a text string describing the error. Then you could check the error number in order to properly handle the error or display the message string (or both).

Hey! Catch!

As I said, for starters, your involvement with exceptions will likely be in catching VCL exceptions. If something goes wrong in a VCL component, VCL is going to throw an exception. If you do not handle the exception, VCL will handle it in the default manner. Usually this means that a message box will be displayed that describes the error that occurred. By catching these exceptions in your code, you can decide how they should be handled, rather than accepting the default behavior.

Take a look at Listing 14.2 again. On line 10 you will see this:

```
catch (...)
```

This tells the compiler that you want to catch all exceptions of any type. If any type of exception is thrown in the `try` block, the `catch` block will be executed. This is convenient if you don't know what type of exception a particular piece of code will throw or if you want to catch any and all exceptions, regardless of the type. In the real world, though, you will probably need to be more specific in what exceptions you catch.

For example, let's go back to Listing 14.2 again. The code on line 3 might throw an exception if the file the user is trying to open is not a graphics file. If that happens, VCL will throw an EInvalidGraphic exception. More specifically, VCL will throw an exception and will throw an instance of the EInvalidGraphic class. You can catch only that type of exception and let all others be handled in the default manner:

```
catch (EInvalidGraphic&)
{
  Application->MessageBox(
    "This file is not a Windows image file.",
    "Picture Viewer Error", MB_ICONHAND | MB_OK);
}
```

Notice that this is catching a reference to an EInvalidGraphic class. This is the preferred method of catching exceptions. Catching a class passed by reference is equivalent to passing a class by reference, as I discussed back on Day 4, "Totally Immersed: C++ Classes and Object-Oriented Programming." Now any exceptions of this type will be caught by the catch block, and all other exception types will be handled in the default manner.

NOTE

VCL will handle many types of exceptions automatically, but cannot account for every possibility. An exception that is not handled is called an *unhandled exception*. If an unhandled exception occurs, Windows will generate an error message and your application will be terminated. Try to anticipate what exceptions might occur in your application and do your best to handle them.

You can have multiple catch blocks following a try statement. For example, let's say that you have written code that calls some VCL methods and also calls some functions in your program that might throw an exception. If a VCL EInvalidGraphic exception occurs, you want to handle it. In addition, your own code may throw a exception of type MyOwnException (a class you have written for handling exceptions). In that case, you would write the code like this:

```
try {
  OneOfMyFunctions();
  Form->Image->Picture->LoadFromFile(filename);
  AnotherOfMyFunctions();
}
catch (EInvalidGraphic&) {
  // do some stuff
}
catch (MyOwnException&) {
  // do some stuff
}
```

14

In this case you are preparing to catch either a VCL exception or an exception of your own type. You want to handle each type of exception differently so that you can catch each type of exception independently.

You can have as many catch statements as you want following a try statement. You must, however, have at least one catch statement, and it must immediately follow the try block. If you have multiple catch statements, they must follow each other, and there can be no other code between the catch statements. The compiler will issue a compiler error if you violate the try/catch syntax rules.

Note that in the preceding examples we are catching a reference to a VCL exception class, but we aren't actually doing anything with the class instance passed to the catch block. In this case we don't really care what information the EInvalidGraphic class contains because it is enough to simply know that the exception occurred. You should check the online help for the specific type of VCL exception-handling class you are interested in for more information about what properties and methods are available for that class.

TIP

The VCL exception classes all have a Message property that contains a textual description of the exception that occurred. You can use this property to display a message to the user:

```
catch (EInvalidGraphic& info)
{
  // do some necessary stuff since an error
  // occurred, and then...
  Application->MessageBox(
   info.Message.c_str(),
   "My Program - Error", MB_ICONHAND ¦ MB_OK);
}
```

Sometimes the VCL messages may not be descriptive enough for your liking. In those cases you can create your own error message, but often the Message property is sufficient.

Catching Unhandled Exceptions at the Application Level

Your application can also handle exceptions at the application level. TApplication has an event called OnException that will occur any time an unhandled exception is thrown in your application. By responding to this event you can catch any exceptions thrown by your applications.

NOTE

> This event occurs when an unhandled exception is thrown. Any exceptions you catch with try and catch are handled; therefore, the OnException event will not occur for those exceptions.

You hook the OnException event just like you do when hooking the OnHint or OnIdle events as we did earlier:

1. Add a function declaration to the main form's header:

   ```
   void __fastcall OnException(TObject *Sender, Exception *E);
   ```

2. Add the function implementation to the main form's source unit:

   ```
   void __fastcall
   TMainForm::OnException(TObject *Sender, Exception *E)
   {
     // do whatever necessary to handle the exception here
   }
   ```

3. Assign your OnException() function to the OnException event of the Application object:

   ```
   Application->OnException = &OnException;
   ```

Now your OnException function will be called when an unhandled exception occurs.

WARNING

> If you do not handle an exception properly, you could lock up your program and possibly even crash Windows. It is usually best to let VCL and Windows handle exceptions unless you know exactly how to handle them.

The ShowException() function can be used to display a message box that describes the error that occurred. This function is usually called by the default OnException handler, but you can use it in your applications as well. One of the parameters of the OnException event handler is a pointer to an Exception object (Exception is VCL's base exception-handling class). To display the error message box, pass the Exception object to the ShowException() function:

```
void __fastcall
TMainForm::OnException(TObject *Sender, Exception *E)
{
  // do whatever necessary to handle the exception here
  // then display the error message
  //
  Application->ShowException(E);
}
```

14

Now the error message box will be displayed just as it would if VCL were dealing with the unhandled exception.

As you can see, handling exceptions at the application level is an advanced exception-handling technique and is not something you should attempt unless you know exactly what you're doing.

Debugging and Exception Handling

Simply put, debugging when using exception handling can be a bit of a pain. Each time an exception is thrown, the debugger will pause program execution at the catch block, just as if a breakpoint were set on that line. If the catch block is in your code, the execution point will be displayed as it would be if you had stopped at a breakpoint. You can restart the program again by clicking the Run button, or you can step through your code.

NOTE

> You may not be able to continue execution of your program after an exception is thrown. Whether you can continue debugging depends on what went wrong in your program.

Sometimes the catch block is in the VCL code. This will be the case for VCL exceptions that you don't handle in your code. In this circumstance, the CPU view will show the execution point.

Another aspect of debugging with exceptions is that the VCL exception message box will be displayed even when you are handling the exception yourself. This can be confusing and somewhat annoying if you haven't encountered it before. To prevent the VCL message box from being displayed and the debugger from breaking on exceptions, go to the Preferences page of the Environment Options dialog box and clear the Break on Exceptions check box. With this option off, the debugger will not pause program execution when an exception is thrown.

As with many other aspects of C++Builder and VCL, learning exception handling takes some time. Remember to use exception handling when necessary, but use traditional error-handling techniques for the minor errors.

The CD that accompanies the book contains a program called EHTest. This program demonstrates throwing and catching several kinds of exceptions. Note that this project has the Break on Exceptions option turned off. Figure 14.1 shows the EHTest program running.

Figure 14.1.

The EHTest *program running.*

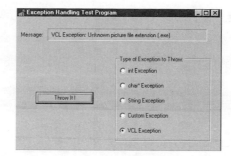

Using the Registry

Once upon a time, Windows programs used configuration files (.INI files) to store application-specific information. The master configuration file, as you probably know, is called WIN.INI. Applications could store systemwide information in WIN.INI or application-specific configuration data in a private .INI file. This approach has several advantages, but also some disadvantages.

Somewhere along the line someone smarter (presumably) than I decided that the new way to do things would be to use the Registry to store application-specific configuration information. Throughout the land, knaves everywhere bowed to the king and said, "The Registry is good." Whether good or bad, conventional wisdom has it that the use of .INI files is out and the use of the Registry is in.

The term *Registry* is short for the Windows Registration Database. The Registry contains a wide variety of information about your Windows configuration. Just about every option and setting in your Windows setup is stored in the Registry. In addition to the system information stored in the Registry, you will find data specific to installed applications. The type of information stored for each application depends entirely on the application, but can include things like the last size and position of the window, a list of the most recently used documents for the application, the last directory used when opening a file, and on and on. The possibilities are endless.

Windows 95 and NT come with a program called the Registry Editor (REGEDIT.EXE) that can be used to browse the Registry and make changes to the entries in the Registry. Figure 14.2 shows the Registry Editor while examining the C++Builder Form Designer options.

As you can see, the Registry is hierarchical. You can approach the Registry exactly as you approach files and directories on a hard drive.

14

Figure 14.2.
The Windows Registry Editor.

Registry Keys

Each item in the Registry is called a *key*. A key can be likened to a directory on your hard drive. To access a particular key, you first have to open the key. After the key is opened, you can write to it or read from it. Take a look at Figure 14.2. The key that is being displayed is

```
\HKEY_CURRENT_USER\Software\Borland\C++Builder\1.0\FormDesign
```

You can't see every branch of the Registry tree, but if you look at the status bar of the Registry Editor you can see the current key displayed. Also notice that the C++Builder\1.0 key has several *subkeys*. You can create as many keys and subkeys as you want for your application.

An individual key can store data in its *data items*. Every key has a data item called (Default). The default value is not normally used because you will almost always create your own data items for a particular key. By looking at Figure 14.2 you can see that the FormDesign key has the following data items:

```
DisplayGrid
GridSizeX
GridSizeY
ShowComponentCaptions
SnapToGrid
```

If you've been paying attention, you will recognize that these data items correspond to the Form Designer options on the Preferences page of the Environment Options dialog box. Each data item has an associated value. You can write to the Registry to change the data item or you can read the data item.

Registry Data Types

The Registry has the capability to store several different types of data in the data items. The primary types of data that you are interested in are the binary data, string, and integer data types. The *binary data type* can be used to store any type of binary data. You could, for instance, store an array of integers in a binary data item. You probably won't directly use the binary data type very often, if ever.

For most of your purposes, you will probably only be concerned with reading and writing strings or integer values. As you can see from Figure 14.2, even numerical data can be stored as strings. It's really up to you to decide how to store data in the Registry.

Up to this point we have discussed what you can do with the Registry but not *how* you do it. Let's look at that next.

The TRegistry **Class**

The Windows API provides several functions for Registry manipulation. These functions include RegCreateKey(), RegOpenKey(), RegQueryValue(), RegSetValue(), RegDeleteKey(), and many more. Dealing with the Registry at the API level is a bit tedious. I am thankful (and you should be, too) that the folks at Borland thought to provide a VCL class called TRegistry that encapsulates registry operations. This class (along with a derived class, TRegIniFile) provides everything you need to write to and read from the Registry. Before I get into how to use the TRegistry class, let's go over the properties and methods of this class.

TRegistry **Properties**

TRegistry has just four properties. The CurrentKey property contains the value of the current key. This value is an integer value that identifies the key. When you call a TRegistry method, that method acts on the current key. The CurrentKey property is set for you when you open a key. This property can be read, but reading it is of dubious value.

The RootKey and CurrentPath properties work together to build a text string to the current key. The CurrentPath property contains a text description of the current key's path excluding the RootKey value. For example, the current path of the key open in Figure 14.2 is Software\Borland\C++Builder\1.0\FormDesign. The RootKey property in this example would contain the value \HKEY_CURRENT_USER.

NOTE

> By default, the RootKey has the value \HKEY_CURRENT_USER. This is where you should store application-specific data, so it is not normally necessary to change the root key. If you need to change the root key, you can assign a new value to the RootKey property.

The LazyWrite property determines how the application writes the data to the specific key. If LazyWrite is true, control is immediately returned to the application when you close the key. In other words, the writing of the key begins and then your application goes on its way. If LazyWrite is false, control will not return to the application until the writing of the key is completed. By default, LazyWrite is true, and you should leave it set to true unless you have some critical data that needs to be written before your application resumes operation.

TRegistry **Methods**

The TRegistry class has several methods that you will use to read from and write to the Registry. Table 14.1 lists the primary methods and their descriptions.

Table 14.1. Primary methods of TRegistry.

Method	Description
CloseKey	Closes the key and writes the data to the key. You should close a key as soon as you are done with it, but you don't have to specifically call CloseKey() because the TRegistry destructor will close the key for you.
CreateKey	Creates a key but does not open it for use. Use the OpenKey() method rather than CreateKey().
DeleteKey	Deletes the specified key. You can specify any key to delete. To delete the current key, pass an empty string to DeleteKey().
GetKeyNames	Returns all the subkeys for the current key in a TStrings object. You can use this method if you need to iterate all the subkeys for a given key.
GetValueNames	Returns the names of all the data items for the current key. Use this method if you need to iterate the data items of a given key.
KeyExists	Returns true if the key passed exists or false if it does not exist. You can use this method to check for the existence of a key before attempting to read the key.
LoadKey	Loads a key previously stored on disk. See the C++Builder online help for specific details.
OpenKey	Opens the specified key. If the key does not exist, the value of the CanCreate parameter determines whether the key will be automatically created. Use this method rather than CreateKey() if you are going to create the key and begin writing data to it because OpenKey() creates the key and then opens it.
ReadBinaryData	Reads binary data from the specified data item.
ReadBool	Reads a boolean value from the specified data item.

Method	Description
ReadDateTime	Reads a date and time value from the specified data item. The returned value is an instance of the TDateTime class. To retrieve just a date value, use ReadDate(); to retrieve just a time value, use ReadTime().
ReadFloat	Reads a floating-point value from the specified data item.
ReadInteger	Reads an integer value from the specified data item.
ReadString	Reads a string value from the specified data item.
SaveKey	Saves a key to disk so that it can be loaded later with LoadKey(). See the C++Builder online help for full details.
ValueExists	Returns true if the specified data item exists.
WriteBinaryData	Writes a binary data item to the specified key. Use this item to store arrays or other types of binary data.
WriteBool	Writes a boolean value to the specified data item. The value is converted to an integer and then stored in the data item.
WriteDateTime	Writes a TDateTime object to the specified data item. To store just a date object, use WriteDate(). To store just a time object, use WriteTime(). The TDateTime object is converted to a binary data type before being stored.
WriteFloat	Writes a floating-point value to the specified data item after converting it to binary data.
WriteInteger	Writes an integer value to the specified data item.
WriteString	Writes a string to the specified data item.

Although there are a lot of methods listed here, many of them perform the same operations—they just use different data types. Once you know how to use one of these methods, you pretty much know how to use them all. Notice that several of these methods convert the value passed to binary data and then store it in the Registry.

Using TRegistry

Using TRegistry is really pretty easy. Most of your interaction with the Registry will require just these four steps:

1. Create an instance of the TRegistry class.
2. Open a key using the OpenKey() method.
3. Read or write data using one or more of the Read() or Write() functions.
4. Close the key using CloseKey().

14

NOTE

Before you can use TRegistry, you must first #include the header for the Registry classes. Add the following line to your main form's header beneath the other headers listed there:

`#include <Registry.hpp>`

Failure to do this will result in a compiler error stating Typename expected or Undefined symbol.

The following code illustrates these steps:

```
TRegistry& regKey = *new TRegistry();
bool keyGood = regKey.OpenKey(
    "Software\\SAMS\\C++Builder in 21 Days", false);
if (keyGood) {
  int top = regKey.ReadInteger("Top");
  int left = regKey.ReadInteger("Left");
  int width = regKey.ReadInteger("Width");
  int height = regKey.ReadInteger("Height");
  SetBounds(left, top, width, height);
}
delete &regKey;
```

This code opens a key and reads values for the top and left coordinates and the width and height of a form. It then calls the SetBounds() function to move and/or size the window. I want you to notice a couple of things about the code. First, notice how I use a reference when I create the TRegistry instance. Doing so reduces clutter in the rest of the code. I don't particularly like the indirect member operator (->), so I avoid its use when I can.

Next, notice that the result of the OpenKey() method is assigned to a bool variable. OpenKey() returns true if the key was successfully opened and false if it was not. If the key was successfully opened, the individual data items are read. You should always check the return value of OpenKey() if there is any doubt that opening the key might fail.

NOTE

VCL will throw exceptions if reading data from or writing data to a key fails. If you attempt to read data from an unopened key, you will get an exception. Either be prepared to handle the exception or be sure to check the return value from OpenKey() before reading or writing data items.

Finally, notice that the key is not specifically closed in the preceding code. If you fail to close the key, the TRegistry destructor will close the key for you. In that case, the destructor will be called (and the key closed) as soon as the regKey object is deleted, so an explicit call to CloseKey() is not necessary.

14

NOTE

The OpenKey() function automatically assumes a root key of HKEY_CURRENT_USER, so you don't have to include the root when opening a key.

We've got the cart just slightly before the horse here because we are talking about reading from the Registry when we haven't yet written to it. No matter—writing to the Registry is just as simple:

```
TRegistry& regKey = *new TRegistry();
regKey.OpenKey(
    "Software\\SAMS\\C++Builder in 21 Days", true);
regKey.WriteInteger("Top", Top);
regKey.WriteInteger("Left", Left);
regKey.WriteInteger("Width", Width);
regKey.WriteInteger("Height", Height);
delete &regKey;
```

This code simply opens a key and writes the form's Top, Left, Width, and Height properties to the key, using the WriteInteger() method. Notice that the last parameter of the OpenKey() method is true. This specifies that the key should be created if it does not yet exist. If you use this construct, you should never need to call the CreateKey() method at all.

That's basically all there is to reading values from and writing values to the registry. The other data reading and writing methods are just variations on the previous code snippet. Listings 14.3 and 14.4 contain a program that uses the Registry to store application-specific data. This program stores several items in the Registry: the last size and position of the window; the window state (normal, minimized, or maximized); the last directory, last file, and last filter index used when opening a file with the File Open dialog box; and the date and time the program was last run. To clear out the Registry key created by the RegTest program, you can click the Delete Key button on the main form (see Figure 14.3).

This program is also on the CD that accompanies the book.

Listing 14.3. RegMain.h.

```
1: //---------------------------------------------------------
2: #ifndef RegMainH
3: #define RegMainH
4: //---------------------------------------------------------
5: #include <vcl\Classes.hpp>
6: #include <vcl\Controls.hpp>
7: #include <vcl\StdCtrls.hpp>
8: #include <vcl\Forms.hpp>
9: #include <vcl\Menus.hpp>
```

14

continues

Listing 14.3. continued

```
10: #include <vcl\Dialogs.hpp>
11: #include <vcl\Registry.hpp>
12: #include <vcl\ExtCtrls.hpp>
13: //---------------------------------------------------------
14: class TMainForm : public TForm
15: {
16: __published:    // IDE-managed Components
17:     TMainMenu *MainMenu;
18:     TMenuItem *File1;
19:     TMenuItem *FileExit;
20:     TMenuItem *FileOpen;
21:     TOpenDialog *OpenDialog;
22:     TPanel *Panel1;
23:     TLabel *Label1;
24:     TButton *DeleteKey;
25:     TPanel *Panel2;
26:     TLabel *Label2;
27:     TLabel *Label3;
28:     TLabel *TimeLabel;
29:     TLabel *DateLabel;
30:     TLabel *Label4;
31:     void __fastcall FileOpenClick(TObject *Sender);
32:     void __fastcall FormCreate(TObject *Sender);
33:
34:     void __fastcall FormClose
35:         (TObject *Sender, TCloseAction &Action);
36:     void __fastcall FileExitClick(TObject *Sender);
37:     void __fastcall DeleteKeyClick(TObject *Sender);
38: private:         // User declarations
39:     void ParseFileName(String& path, String& fname);
40:     bool keyDeleted;
41: public:          // User declarations
42:     virtual __fastcall TMainForm(TComponent* Owner);
43: };
44: //---------------------------------------------------------
45: extern TMainForm *MainForm;
46: //---------------------------------------------------------
47: #endif
```

Listing 14.4. RegMain.cpp.

```
1: //---------------------------------------------------------
2: #include <vcl\vcl.h>
3: #pragma hdrstop
4:
5: #include "RegMain.h"
6: //---------------------------------------------------------
7: #pragma resource "*.dfm"
8: TMainForm *MainForm;
9: //---------------------------------------------------------
10: __fastcall TMainForm::TMainForm(TComponent* Owner)
11:     : TForm(Owner)
```

```
12: {
13:    //
14:    // Initialize the keyDeleted variable to false. This
15:    // variable is used if the user deletes the key from
16:    // the program. See the MainFormClose() function.
17:    //
18:    keyDeleted = false;
19: }
20: //------------------------------------------------------------
21: void __fastcall TMainForm::FormCreate(TObject *Sender)
22: {
23:    //
24:    // Create a TRegistry object to access the registry.
25:    //
26:    TRegistry& regKey = *new TRegistry();
27:    //
28:    // Open the key.
29:    //
30:    bool keyGood = regKey.OpenKey(
31:      "Software\\SAMS\\C++Builder in 21 Days", false);
32:    //
33:    // See if the key is open. If not, then this is the first
34:    // time the program has been run so there's nothing to do.
35:    // If the key is good then read all of the data items
36:    // pertinent to application startup.
37:    //
38:    if (!keyGood) return;
39:    int top = regKey.ReadInteger("Top");
40:    int left = regKey.ReadInteger("Left");
41:    int width = regKey.ReadInteger("Width");
42:    int height = regKey.ReadInteger("Height");
43:    SetBounds(left, top, width, height);
44:    WindowState =
45:      TWindowState(regKey.ReadInteger("WindowState"));
46:    //
47:    // The TDateTime class is a handy item to have around
48:    // if you are doing date and time operations.
49:    //
50:    TDateTime dt;
51:    dt = regKey.ReadDate("Date and Time");
52:    DateLabel->Caption = dt.DateString();
53:    TimeLabel->Caption = dt.TimeString();
54:    delete &regKey;
55: }
56: //------------------------------------------------------------
57: void __fastcall TMainForm::FileOpenClick(TObject *Sender)
58: {
59:    //
60:    // This function displays the File Open dialog but
61:    // doesn't actually open a file. The last path, filter,
62:    // and filename are written to the registry when the
63:    // user presses OK.
64:    //
65:    // Create a TRegistry object to access the registry.
```

14

continues

Listing 14.3. continued

```
66:   //
67:   TRegistry& regKey = *new TRegistry();
68:   //
69:   // Open the key.
70:   //
71:   regKey.OpenKey(
72:     "Software\\SAMS\\C++Builder in 21 Days", true);
73:   //
74:   // Read the values. If these items have not yet been
75:   // created then we will get an exception.
76:   //
77:   try {
78:     OpenDialog->InitialDir = regKey.ReadString("LastDir");
79:     OpenDialog->FileName = regKey.ReadString("LastFile");
80:     OpenDialog->FilterIndex =
81:       regKey.ReadInteger("FilterIndex");
82:   }
83:   //
84:   // We know what the exception is and it's no big deal
85:   // so we'll just catch it and ignore it.
86:   //
87:   catch (...) {}
88:   //
89:   // Display the File Open dialog. If the user presses OK
90:   // then save the path, filename, and filter to the
91:   // registry.
92:   if (OpenDialog->Execute()) {
93:     String path;
94:     String fname;
95:     //
96:     // A function to separate the path from the filename.
97:     //
98:     ParseFileName(path, fname);
99:     regKey.WriteString("LastDir", path);
100:    regKey.WriteString("LastFile", fname);
101:    regKey.WriteInteger
102:      ("FilterIndex", OpenDialog->FilterIndex);
103:   }
104:   delete &regKey;
105: }
106:
107: void TMainForm::ParseFileName(String& path, String& fname)
108: {
109:   //
110:   // This function separates the path from the filename.
111:   //
112:   int pos = 0;
113:   String s = OpenDialog->FileName;
114:   int x = 1;
115:   while (x) {
116:     x = s.Pos("\\");
117:     s = s.SubString(x + 1, s.Length() - x);
118:     pos += x;
119:   }
```

14

```
120:   fname = s;
121:   path = OpenDialog->FileName.SubString(0, pos);
122: }
123: //------------------------------------------------------------
124: void __fastcall TMainForm::
125: FormClose(TObject *Sender, TCloseAction &Action)
126: {
127:   //
128:   // If the user pressed the button to delete the key
129:   // then we don't want to write out the information.
130:   //
131:   if (keyDeleted) return;
132:   //
133:   // Create a TRegistry object to access the registry.
134:   //
135:   TRegistry& regKey = *new TRegistry();
136:   //
137:   // Open the key.
138:   //
139:   regKey.OpenKey(
140:     "Software\\SAMS\\C++Builder in 21 Days", true);
141:   //
142:   // Write out the values.
143:   //
144:   regKey.WriteInteger("WindowState", WindowState);
145:   if (WindowState != wsMaximized) {
146:     regKey.WriteInteger("Top", Top);
147:     regKey.WriteInteger("Left", Left);
148:     regKey.WriteInteger("Width", Width);
149:     regKey.WriteInteger("Height", Height);
150:   }
151:   TDateTime dt;
152:   regKey.WriteDate("Date and Time", dt.CurrentDateTime());
153:   delete &regKey;
154: }
155: //------------------------------------------------------------
156: void __fastcall TMainForm::FileExitClick(TObject *Sender)
157: {
158:   //
159:   // Bye!
160:   //
161:   Close();
162: }
163: //------------------------------------------------------------
164: void __fastcall TMainForm::DeleteKeyClick(TObject *Sender)
165: {
166:   //
167:   // The user pressed the Delete Key button so delete the
168:   // key. Set a flag so that we don't re-create the key
169:   // when the program closes.
170:   //
171:   TRegistry& regKey = *new TRegistry();
172:   regKey.DeleteKey("Software\\SAMS");
173:   keyDeleted = true;
174:   delete &regKey;
175: }
```

14

By examining this listing and by running the RegTest program, you can learn a lot about using the Registry in your applications. Figure 14.3 shows the RegTest program running; Figure 14.4 shows the Registry key that is created by the program.

Figure 14.3.
The RegTest
program running.

Figure 14.4.
*The Registry Editor
showing the* RegTest
key.

NOTE

> The TRegIniFile class is a specialized Registry-manipulation class that can be used for applications that are moving from storing data in .INI files to storing data in the registry. See the online help for TRegIniFile for complete information.

NOTE

> Although conventional wisdom has it that the Registry is the place to store application-specific data, you still can use .INI files if you like. One advantage to .INI files is that less-sophisticated users can edit them with a text editor when necessary (which is also a disadvantage in some cases). To make using .INI files easier, VCL includes the TIniFile class. Be sure to check out this class if you intend to use .INI files in your application.

Specialized Message Handling

On Day 11, "Using the Debugger," I talked about Windows messages as part of the discussion of the WinSight program. For the most part, C++Builder makes message handling easy through its use of events. As I have said, an event is usually generated in response to a Windows message being sent to an application. There are times, however, when you may want to handle messages yourself. There are two primary scenarios that require that you handle messages outside of the normal C++Builder messaging system:

- ☐ Windows messages that VCL does not handle
- ☐ User-defined messages

Handling messages on your own requires a few extra programming techniques; you'll learn about those techniques in this section.

More on Windows Messages

How do Windows messages get sent? Some messages are sent by Windows itself to instruct the window to do something or to notify the window that something has happened. At other times messages are sent by the programmer or, in the case of VCL, OWL, or MFC, by the framework the programmer is using. Regardless of who is sending the messages, you can be guaranteed that a lot of messages are flying around at any given millisecond.

Message Types

Basically, messages fall into two categories:

- ☐ Command messages
- ☐ Notification messages

Command messages cause something to occur either in Windows or within a particular control. Notification messages are sent by Windows to notify you that something has happened. To illustrate the difference between these two types of messages, let's take a look at the standard edit control.

The standard Windows edit control has almost 80 command messages and nearly 20 notification messages. Surprised? It's true, and don't forget that the edit control is just one control out of dozens of Windows controls.

14

NOTE

I lied to you back on Day 5, "C++ Class Frameworks and the Visual Component Model," when I talked about events. (Well, not exactly.) At that time I said that there are more than 175 messages that

Windows could send to an application, and that is essentially true. But when you consider messages specific to controls as well as messages that can be sent to main windows, the count goes to something like 700 messages. Whoa! And that includes only command messages, not notification messages. You should have a new appreciation for VCL after reading this section.

A programmer writing a Windows program in C has to send a lot of messages to accomplish tasks. For example, to get the length of the currently selected text in an edit control requires the following code:

```
int start;
int end;
long result = SendMessage(hWndEdit, EM_GETSEL, 0, 0);
start = LOWORD(result);
end = HIWORD(result);
int length = end - start;
```

This is how C programmers (or C++ programmers not using frameworks) spend their days. Contrast that with the VCL way of doing things:

```
int length = Edit->SelLength;
```

Which do you prefer? Regardless of who is doing the sending, command messages are used heavily, both by programmers and by Windows itself.

Notification messages, on the other hand, are sent only by Windows itself. Notification messages tell Windows that something has happened within a control. For example, the EN_CHANGE message is sent when the contents of an edit control have changed. VCL has an event for the Edit, MaskEdit, and Memo components—called OnChange—that is triggered in response to the EN_CHANGE notification message (as well as some others). Programmers using traditional Windows programming tools have to "catch" these messages and deal with them as needed. Which brings us to the next subject: message parameters.

NOTE   Traditional C Windows programs have long switch statements that are used to determine which message was sent to the window.

WPARAM, LPARAM, and Message Cracking

Every Windows message has two parameters: the WPARAM (short for word parameter) and the LPARAM (short for long parameter).

In 32-bit Windows these parameters are both 32-bit values. In 16-bit Windows the WPARAM is a 16-bit value (a word), and the LPARAM is a 32-bit value (a double word, or a long). And that ends your history lesson on the names WPARAM and LPARAM. And now back to our program...

These two parameters could be likened to the parameters sent to a function. When a Windows message is received, the parameters are examined to obtain information specific to the message being sent. For example, the WM_LBUTTONDOWN message is a notification message that is sent when the left mouse button is clicked on a window. For a WM_LBUTTONDOWN message, the WPARAM contains a special code that tells which of the other mouse buttons were pressed and also what keys on the keyboard were pressed when the event occurred. The LPARAM contains the coordinates of the mouse cursor when the mouse button was clicked. The x position is contained in the low-order word, and the y position is contained in the high-order word.

To get at these nuggets of information, the message must be *cracked* to reveal what's inside. The code for cracking a WM_LBUTTONDOWN message might look like this:

```
int Shift = wParam;
int X = LOWORD(lParam);
int Y = HIWORD(lParam);
```

This is a fairly simple example, but it's indicative of what goes on each time a message is handled in a Windows application.

You'll be relieved to know that VCL performs message cracking for you for all VCL events. For instance, if you set up a message handler for the OnMouseDown event, C++Builder will generate a function in your code that looks like this:

```
void __fastcall TScratchPad::FormMouseDown(TObject *Sender,
  TMouseButton Button, TShiftState Shift, Integer X, Integer Y)
{
  // put your code here
}
```

As you can see, the event handler generated by C++Builder contains all the information you need. VCL will crack the WPARAM and LPARAM for you and hand them to you in sensible pieces you can deal with more easily. This same thing happens for every message for which VCL creates an event.

14

VCL takes messaging and message cracking one step further in the case of the mouse button messages. Windows actually generates up to three different mouse down messages: one for the left button being pressed,

> one for the middle button (if one exists), and yet another when the
> right button is pressed. VCL handles all these messages in a single
> event. The TMouseButton parameter of the OnMouseDown event tells you
> which of the three buttons was pressed.

With that primer on Windows messaging under your belt, let's take a brief look at exactly how to send messages.

Sending Versus Posting

The Windows API provides two functions for sending messages: PostMessage() and SendMessage(). The PostMessage() function posts the message to the Windows message queue and immediately returns. This function simply hands the message to Windows and goes on its way. PostMessage() returns 1 if the function call succeeded or 0 if it did not. (About the only reason for PostMessage() to fail is if the message is sent to an invalid window.)

The SendMessage() function, on the other hand, sends the message to Windows and waits until the message is carried out before returning. The return value from SendMessage() depends on the message being sent. Sometimes the biggest reason to use SendMessage() over PostMessage() is because you need the return value from a particular message.

NOTE

> The differences between situations when you use PostMessage() versus
> SendMessage() are subtle. For example, due to timing issues within
> Windows there are times when sending a message will fail to have the
> effect you expected. In those cases you'll have to use PostMessage().
> The reverse is also true: Sometimes PostMessage() is wrong for a given
> set of circumstances and you'll have to use SendMessage(). Although
> this is not something you really need to be concerned with right now, it
> is something to file away for future reference.

You can use both PostMessage() and SendMessage() in your C++Builder applications. For instance, to post yourself a message you would do something like this:

```
PostMessage(Handle, WM_QUIT, 0, 0);
```

The first parameter of both PostMessage() and SendMessage() is the window handle of the window to which you want to send the message. In this case we are sending the message to the main form (assuming this code was written in the main form's source code unit).

In addition to the Windows API functions, VCL provides a method called `Perform()` that you can use to send messages to any VCL window. `Perform()` bypasses the Windows messaging system and sends the message directly to the message-handling mechanism for a given window. The `Perform()` equivalent of the preceding example is

```
Perform(MW_QUIT, 0, 0);
```

You can use any of these three functions to send messages to your application and to other windows within your application.

Handling Events

We've already discussed handling VCL events, but a short review can't hurt. When a particular component receives a Windows message, it looks up the message and checks to see if there is an event handler assigned for that particular message. If an event handler has been assigned for that event, VCL calls the event handler. If no event handler was assigned, the message is handled in the default manner. You can handle any messages you like and ignore the rest.

What happens in your event handlers depends on a variety of factors: the particular message being handled, what your program does in response to the message, and whether you are modifying the incoming message or just using the event handler as notification that the event occurred. As you get further into Windows programming, you will see that there are literally hundreds of things you might do in response to events.

Most of the time you will be using the event handler for notification that a particular event occurred. Take the `OnMouseDown` event, for instance. If you handle the `OnMouseDown` event, you are simply asking to be notified when the user clicks on the component with the mouse (remember that forms are components, too). You probably are not going to modify the message parameters in any way; you just want to know that the event occurred. A great number of your event handlers will be used for notification purposes.

Sometimes, however, you want to change one or more of the message parameters before sending the message on its way. Let's say, for instance, that you wanted to force the text in a particular edit control to uppercase. (You could set the `CharCase` property to `ecUpperCase`, of course, but we'll stick with this example for now.) To change all keystrokes to uppercase, you could do something like this in your `OnKeyPress` event handler:

```
void __fastcall TScratchPad::EditKeyPress(TObject *Sender, Char &Key)
{
  if (Key >= 'a') Key -= 32;
}
```

In this way you are actually modifying some aspect of the message before it gets sent on to VCL for processing. The parameters sent in the event handler are often passed by reference for exactly this reason.

14

NOTE

> C++Builder protects you a bit by passing message parameters that you should not change by value rather than by reference. This is also true of message parameters for which changing the value has no effect. Take the OnMouseDown event discussed earlier. This event is for notification only. There is no point in modifying the Button, Shift, X, or Y parameters, so all are passed by value.

Whether you change one or more of the parameters sent depends entirely on the message and what you intend to do with the message. Over time, you will likely run into situations where modification of a particular message is required to cause Windows to behave in a particular way. At other times, you will not modify the parameters at all, but will inspect them to determine what is happening with your application. Since the possibilities are so numerous, I'll have to leave further exploration of message parameters as an exercise for the reader.

Handling Other Windows Messages

There will undoubtedly be some point when you need to respond to a Windows message for which VCL provides no event. When that time comes, you are going to want to know how to handle those messages, and that is what this section is about.

VCL provides events for the most commonly used Windows messages. Obviously, with more than 700 Windows messages, VCL does not provide events for them all. The 80/20 theory says, among other things, that 20 percent of the people do 80 percent of the work. The same is probably true of Windows messages. VCL may provide events for only 10 percent or 20 percent of Windows messages, but they are the messages you will use 90 percent of the time. Still, there are plenty of Windows messages that VCL does not provide events for, and you need to know how to handle those messages when the time comes.

You'll be glad to know that you can handle just about any Windows message once you know how. When you've got the basics down, each message is just a variation on the same theme. The mechanism that C++Builder uses to handle messages not covered by VCL events is called the *message map table*. The message map table is used to associate a certain Windows message with a function in your code. When your window receives that message, the function is called. Hmmm...sounds like events, doesn't it? There are certainly some similarities.

Implementing message handling at this level is a three-step process:

1. Create the message map table in the class declaration and add the message you want to handle to the message map table.
2. Add the function declaration for the message handler to the class declaration.
3. Add the definition of the message handler to your form's source code unit.

14

First, let me show you the code to implement a message map for your class; then we'll look at the message-handling function.

The C++Builder Message Map Table

The message map table goes at the end of your class definition. A message map table begins with BEGIN_MESSAGE_MAP and ends with END_MESSAGE_MAP. Between these two items are one or more MESSAGE_HANDLER declarations. You pass the name of the base class as the single parameter in END_MESSAGE_MAP. Even with today's inflation, a picture is still worth a thousand words, so let me show you a sample message map table. It looks like this:

```
BEGIN_MESSAGE_MAP
  MESSAGE_HANDLER(WM_NCHITTEST, TWMNCHitTest, WMNCHitTest)
  MESSAGE_HANDLER(WM_ERASEBKGND, TWMEraseBkgnd, WMEraseBkgnd)
END_MESSAGE_MAP(TForm)
```

This message map table sets up the program to handle two Windows messages: WM_NCHITTEST and WM_ERASEBKGND.

NOTE

The WM_ERASEBKGND message is sent just prior to the WM_PAINT message (which is when Windows paints the window). In VCL programming, this means that WM_ERASEBKGND is received *before* the OnPaint event occurs. You can catch the WM_ERASEBKGND message to do any painting on the window that must be done independent of the OnPaint event handler. (When you respond to a Windows message, you are said to *catch* or *handle* the message.)

NOTE

You might be wondering, "So why all the caps?" The reason for the caps is that BEGIN_MESSAGE_MAP, END_MESSAGE_MAP, and MESSAGE_HANDLER are all macros, and macro names are traditionally written in all upper-case characters. Macros are text placeholders that expand to actual C++ code when the parser (part of the compiler) encounters them. The macro definitions for the message map table are tucked away somewhere in the VCL source code.

For those of you who can't live without knowing more, read on. All the message map table macros work together to create a function called Dispatch(). Because the message map table is contained in the class declaration, that automatically makes the function an inline function.

14

For the preceding example it would look something like this, once the macros were all expanded:

```
virtual void __fastcall Dispatch(void *Message)
{
  switch  (((PMessage)Message)->Msg)
  {
    case WM_NCHITTEST :
      OnNCHitTest((TWMNCHitTest&)*Message);
      break;
    case WM_ERASEBKGND :
      OnEraseBkgnd((TWMEraseBkgnd&)*Message);
      break;
    default:
      TForm::Dispatch(Message);
      break;
  }
}
```

It's not so mysterious once you break it down. Pretty cool, really. If you want to see what the macros look like, take a look in \CBuilder\include\ vcl\sysdefs.h.

Let's break down the MESSAGE_HANDLER handler macro and examine its pieces. Here I'll use one of those syntax lines I despise so much:

```
MESSAGE_HANDLER(<message>, <message struct>, <message handler>)
```

The message parameter is the Windows message you want to handle. Windows messages names are always in uppercase (the documented messages, anyway).

The message struct parameter is used to pass the name of the message-handling structure that will be used to pass the parameters once VCL has cracked the message. VCL has declared a message-cracker structure for most Windows messages. The structure name is the Windows message name, preceded by T, minus the underscore. For example, the Windows message WM_ERASEBKGND gets translated into the structure named TWMEraseBkgnd. You sort of have to guess at the capitalization, but for the most part it makes perfect sense. This structure gets passed along to the message handler (more on that in just a bit).

The message handler parameter is for the actual name of the message-handling function. You can use any name you like, but tradition has it (I'm starting the tradition right now) that you remove the leading TWM from the structure name and add the word On. So, again using WM_ERASEBKGND as an example, the function name of the message handler would be OnEraseBkgnd.

To put this in perspective, you need to see the entire class declaration for a class that implements a message map table. Listing 14.5 shows a typical main form class declaration for a class that uses a message map table.

Listing 14.5. Message.h.

```
 1: //---------------------------------------------------------
 2: #ifndef MsgMainH
 3: #define MsgMainH
 4: //---------------------------------------------------------
 5: #include <vcl\Classes.hpp>
 6: #include <vcl\Controls.hpp>
 7: #include <vcl\StdCtrls.hpp>
 8: #include <vcl\Forms.hpp>
 9: #include <vcl\ExtCtrls.hpp>
10:
11: #define MYMESSAGE WM_USER + 1
12:
13: //---------------------------------------------------------
14: class TMainForm : public TForm
15: {
16: __published:      // IDE-managed Components
17:     TButton *ShowTBar;
18:     TButton *Button1;
19:     TLabel *Label;
20:     TBevel *Bevel1;
21:     TCheckBox *Hatched;
22:     TCheckBox *LetVCLHandle;
23:     void __fastcall ShowTBarClick(TObject *Sender);
24:
25:     void __fastcall Button1Click(TObject *Sender);
26:     void __fastcall HatchedClick(TObject *Sender);
27:
28: private:          // User declarations
29:     void __fastcall OnNCHitTest(TWMNCHitTest& Message);
30:     void __fastcall OnEraseBkgnd(TWMEraseBkgnd& Message);
31:     void __fastcall OnGetMinMaxInfo(TWMGetMinMaxInfo& Message);
32:     void __fastcall OnMyMessage(TMessage& Message);
33: public:           // User declarations
34:     virtual __fastcall TMainForm(TComponent* Owner);
35: BEGIN_MESSAGE_MAP
36:   MESSAGE_HANDLER(MYMESSAGE, TMessage, OnMyMessage)
37:   MESSAGE_HANDLER(WM_NCHITTEST, TWMNCHitTest, OnNCHitTest)
38:   MESSAGE_HANDLER(
39:     WM_GETMINMAXINFO, TWMGetMinMaxInfo, OnGetMinMaxInfo)
40:   MESSAGE_HANDLER(WM_ERASEBKGND, TWMEraseBkgnd, OnEraseBkgnd)
41: END_MESSAGE_MAP(TForm)
42: };
43: //---------------------------------------------------------
44: extern TMainForm *MainForm;
45: //---------------------------------------------------------
46: #endif
```

Notice in particular the message map table at the end of the class declaration and the function declarations for the message-handling functions. (Don't let lines 11, 32, and 36 throw you. These lines implement a user-defined message that I'll talk about a little later.)

14

The Message-Handling Function

The *message-handling function* (or just *message handler*) is the function that will be called whenever the message you are responding to is received by your application. The message handler has a single parameter—the message-cracker structure I discussed earlier. The message handler for the WM_ERASEBKGND message would look like this:

```
void __fastcall
TMainForm::OnEraseBkgnd(TWMEraseBkgnd& Message)
{
  // your message handling code here
}
```

As I said, the message-cracker structure will contain all the parameters necessary to handle the message. The message cracker structure for the WM_ERASEBKGND message is as follows:

```
struct TWMEraseBkgnd
{
  unsigned int Msg;
  HDC DC;
  long Unused;
  long Result;
};
```

All message-cracking structures have two data members in common: Msg and Result. The Msg member contains the message that is being sent. This parameter is used by VCL and is not something you will be concerned with.

The Result data member, however, is important. This is used to set the return value for the message you are handling. The return value varies from message to message. For instance, the return value from your message handler for WM_ERASEBKGND should return true if you erase the background prior to drawing, or false if you do not erase the background. (Check the Win32 API online help for the individual message you are processing to determine what to set the Return data member to.) Set the Return data member of the message-cracker structure as needed:

```
void __fastcall
TMainForm::OnEraseBkgnd(TWMEraseBkgnd& Message)
{
  // do some stuff
  Message.Return = false;
}
```

Any other data members of the message-cracking structure will vary from message to message.

Sometimes you will need to call the default message handler for a particular message in addition to performing your own handling. In that case, you can call DefaultHandler() or call the base class's Dispatch() method. Which one you use depends on the behavior you are after. For instance, you might want to paint on the background of your window in some circumstances but not in others. If you don't paint the background, you want VCL to paint the background in the default way. So, you would do this:

```
void __fastcall
TMainForm::OnEraseBkgnd(TWMEraseBkgnd& Message)
{
  if (LetVCLDoIt) {
    TForm::Dispatch(&Message); // pass it on to VCL
    return;
  }
  else {
    // do some painting stuff here
  }
  Message.Return = false;
}
```

In other cases you will use DefaultHandler() to perform some default processing for you. Whether you call DefaultHandler() before you do your processing or afterward depends, again, on what you are trying to accomplish.

User-Defined Messages

Besides the normal Windows messages, Windows allows you to create what is called a *user-defined message*. A user-defined message is nothing more than a private message that you can send to yourself or to one of the other windows in your application. There are a variety of reasons you might want to use user-defined messages in your application. Truthfully, VCL events reduce the need for user-defined messages, but there still may be times when you need to use them. For example, let's say you are performing a lengthy calculation that your application created in another thread. (We won't try to tackle threads today.) If something occurs in that thread that the application should know about, the thread can send a user-defined message back to the application to inform it that something noteworthy happened.

Implementing and catching a user-defined message is nearly identical to handling a Windows message. The one exception is that you need to first define the message. You define a user-defined message like this:

```
#define MYMESSAGE WM_USER + 1
```

This line sets up a user-defined message called MYMESSAGE.

NOTE

> The symbol WM_USER is a special symbol that marks the beginning of the range of numbers that can be used for user-defined messages. You can use anything up to WM_USER + 31,743 for user-defined messages. I usually just pick something in the WM_USER + 100 range. The exact number you use is not important; just be sure that you do not accidentally use the same value for two different messages.

14

If you look back to Listing 14.5, you will notice the declaration for the user-defined message on line 11. Once you have the message defined, you can add it to the message map table as follows:

```
MESSAGE_HANDLER(MYMESSAGE, TMessage, OnMyMessage)
```

Notice that the message-cracker structure passed is of the TMessage type. This is the generic message-cracker structure. It is defined as follows:

```
struct TMessage
{
  unsigned int Msg;
  long WParam;
  long LParam;
  long Result;
};
```

> **NOTE**
>
> The actual declaration of TMessage looks slightly different, but the structure shown here is the end result.

When you send a user-defined message, you pass any parameters you want in the WParam and LParam members. For instance, let's say you were sending a user-defined message indicating that error code 124 occurred on iteration 1019 of a processing loop. The call to Perform() would look like this:

```
int result = MainForm->Perform(MYMESSAGE, 124, 1019);
```

You could use either PostMessage() or SendMessage() to send the message, too, of course. For user-defined messages, you can probably use Perform() for most of your messaging.

Okay, so the message is defined and sent. Now you need to write code to handle it. The message handler for the MYMESSAGE message might look like this:

```
void __fastcall
TMainForm::OnMyMessage(TMessage& Message)
{
  char msg[100];
  sprintf(msg,
    "Error #%d occurred on iteration number %d.",
    Message.WParam, Message.LParam);
  Application->MessageBox(msg, "Error Message", MB_OK);
  Message.Result = true;
}
```

The return value from Perform() will be the value of the Result member of the TMessage structure. It's up to you whether you send parameters and whether your message handler returns a result.

The CD that accompanies the book contains a program called Message that illustrates the use of handling Windows messages not covered by VCL events. It also illustrates the use of a user-defined message. This program illustrates the implementation of a Windows programming trick: You can drag the window by clicking and dragging anywhere on the client area of the form.

Summary

Wow, we have covered a lot of ground today. You started with a look at context-sensitive help and how to put it to use. Remember that creating context-sensitive help is not necessarily easy, but it is something you should implement. After that you looked at exception handling and how you can use it to trap VCL exceptions. You have also gotten some insights into the Windows Registry. The Registry is something that can and should be used to store application-specific data. Knowing how to use the Registry can help you to implement those little features that make users smile. Finally, we ended with a discussion on how to handle messages other than through the use of events. All in all, it was a long day but a rewarding one.

Workshop

The Workshop contains quiz questions to help you solidify your understanding of the material covered and exercises to provide you with experience in using what you have learned. You can find answers to the quiz questions in Appendix A, "Answers to Quiz Questions."

Q&A

Q Writing help files with a word processor is kind of tedious. What do you suggest?

A Get a commercial help-authoring program. These programs take care of all the little stuff that drives you crazy when trying to write help files "the hard way." Writing help files is not much fun for most of us, but using a good help-authoring program can really ease the pain.

Q Do I have to put context identifiers in my help file?

A Not necessarily. You can just have your users invoke help from the main menu. You won't be able to support context-sensitive help without help context IDs in the help file, though.

14

Q Why should I bother with exception handling?

A Using exception handling allows you to be in control of what your program is doing as much as possible. By using exception handling, you can more closely control what happens when errors occur in your program.

Q I've caught a VCL exception. How can I reproduce the error message box that VCL creates when it throws an exception?

A Call `Application->ShowException()`, and VCL will display the error message.

Q Do I have to use the Registry to store my program's preferences and settings?

A No. You can use `.INI` files or any other type of configuration file. However, the Registry is the preferred location for application-specific data. The `TRegistry` class makes it easy to use the Registry, so you might as well put it to work for you.

Q I get exceptions every time I try to create a key and then use `WriteString()` to write a data item to the key. What could be wrong?

A You are probably using `CreateKey()` to create the key. `CreateKey()` creates the key but does not open it. Use `OpenKey()` to create your keys, rather than `CreateKey()`.

Q What is a user-defined message?

A A user-defined message is a message defined by you, the user, for private use in your application. Contrast this with Windows messages that are defined and used by Windows on a global level.

Q What should I do to get the default message-handling behavior for a particular Windows message?

A Call the base class's `Dispatch()` method:

```
TForm::Dispatch(&Message);
```

Quiz

1. How do you set up the help file that your application will use?
2. How do you implement F1 key support for a particular form or dialog box?
3. What function do you call to display the index for your help file?
4. What types of objects can an exception throw?
5. Is it legal to have more than one `catch` statement following a `try` statement?
6. How do you throw an exception?
7. What is the default `RootKey` for the `TRegistry` class?
8. Must you call `CloseKey()` when you are done with a key?

14

9. What is the difference between SendMessage() and PostMessage()?

10. What is the name of the VCL function that is used to send a message directly to a component?

Exercises

1. Research the availability of help-file authoring tools. Although this might seem like a strange exercise, it might be the most beneficial exercise you can do in regard to help files.

2. Create a new project. Add some components to the main form. Give each a different HelpContext number.

3. Attach a help file to the project (any help file will do). If you have help-authoring software, create a simple help file for the program to use. Run the program and press F1 when a component has focus.

4. Create a new project. Add a button to the main form. Place the following code in the OnClick handler for the button:

```
TImageList* list;
delete list;
```

Run the program and click the button. What happens?

5. Write a try/catch pair for the two lines of code in exercise 4 to catch any exceptions. Display a message when the error occurs, but allow the program to continue to function.

6. Modify the ScratchPad program to use the Windows Registry. Save the filename and path of the last file opened.

7. Modify the ScratchPad program to use the filename and path retrieved from the Registry when the File Open and File Save dialog boxes are displayed.

8. Write a program that sends itself a user-defined message when a button is clicked. Display a message box when the message is received.

9. Add a message handler for the Windows MW_MOVE message to the program in exercise 8. When the window is moved, beep the speaker and display the new coordinates on the form.

10. **Extra credit:** Modify the PictureViewer program from Day 6, "The C++Builder IDE Explored: Projects and Forms," to catch an exception if the user attempts to open a file other than a graphics file.

14

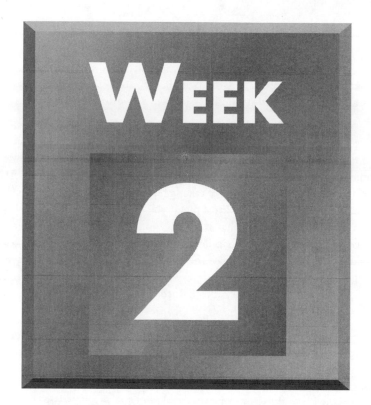

WEEK 2

In Review

Wow, that was intense, wasn't it? But did you enjoy yourself? Are you starting to get the fever? By now I'll bet the wheels are really turning in your head! Likely, you have already envisioned an application or two of your own. Maybe you have even begun work on an application. I hope you have because, as I have said many times, that is where you really learn. If you haven't yet developed an idea for an application, don't worry about it. It will come to you in good time.

This week included a mixture of material. Early in the week you found out the basics of building a C++Builder application. You can drop components on a form all you want, but someday you have to get into writing code. It can be a little daunting to branch out on your own. C++Builder has sort of taken you by the hand up to this point. But now it's time to leave the nest. You found out how to add your own functions and data members to your code. You found out how to add resources like bitmaps and sounds to your programs. This is good stuff! Before long you'll be doing all these things on your own like a pro.

This week's less-than-exciting material dealt with more on C++Builder projects and how to use the debugger. The chapters might not have been flashy, but they still contained vital information that you need when developing applications. It's all about maximizing your time. Learning how to use the debugger takes a few hours or even a few days, but it will save you weeks of work in the long run. Trust me! If you know how to use the debugger, you can really get in there and find out what is going wrong when you encounter a bug in your program. If you don't have a good handle on the debugger, I urge you to go back and review Day 11. Like I said, the debugger is not the most thrilling thing you will learn about in this book, but it will certainly be one of the most valuable. Learning how to effectively use your projects falls into this same category. Proper project management will save you time in the long run, too.

Toward the end of the week you learned about some of the things that can take an average program and turn it into a great program. Let's face it, window decorations like status bars and speedbars cannot take a weak programming idea and turn it into a great program. No amount of gadgetry can do that. But if you have a good program to start with, adding bells and whistles can really make your program stand out from the competition. There's nothing stopping you from adding these kinds of goodies to your applications because C++Builder makes it easy! That's not hype, folks. It's the honest truth.

You also got a chance to do some printing. Printing is, by nature, nonvisual. C++Builder's great visual programming tools can't help you here. Still, VCL makes printing much less frustrating than it would be with the straight API. Once you get into printing, you will find that it is not all that difficult. Once again, experiment as much as you can. Playing around can be the best teacher you can have. Don't worry about the boss—tell him or her that I said it was okay to play around. (That's *play around* not *play a round*. Don't blame me if you get caught playing golf on company time!)

Finally, you ended the week with some more in-depth programming techniques. Implementing context-sensitive help is something you will just have to do in today's competitive market. The good news is that C++Builder makes it easy. The bad news is that there is no shortcut to writing good help files. It can't be helped. Take my advice and get a good help authoring program. Such a program can take the frustration out of creating help files. If you write help files "the hard way," you will probably get bogged down in the tedium and will start skimping on the details. Using a good help authoring program can help you avoid that situation. Remember that the help file is as important as the program itself. After all, what good is a Maserati if you can't figure out how to get it out of first gear?

Using the Registry is something that can really put a shine on your program, too. Oh, it won't make your program look any different, but when you give the users options, you are increasing the value of your program. Storing these options in the Registry makes your job easier, too. There's no excuse for omitting features that users have come to expect. Sure, it takes a little time and you have to pay attention to detail, but there's no substitute for quality.

We ended the week with a discussion on message handling. This is a lower level of programming than you have encountered thus far. Handling messages is not something that you may have to do often, but when you must handle messages, knowing how will be more than half the battle. Hopefully the section on message handling will benefit you down the road if not immediately.

Listing R2.1 is the listing for the main form of the ScratchPad program; it shows the SPMain.h header and Listing R2.2 contains the SPMain.cpp file. Look over these listings to gain further understanding of the concepts covered this week.

Listing R2.1. SPMain.h.

```
 1: //----------------------------------------------------
 2: #ifndef SPMainH
 3: #define SPMainH
 4: //----------------------------------------------------
 5: #include <Classes.hpp>
 6: #include <Controls.hpp>
 7: #include <StdCtrls.hpp>
 8: #include <Forms.hpp>
 9: #include <ExtCtrls.hpp>
10: #include <Buttons.hpp>
11: #include <ComCtrls.hpp>
12: #include <Menus.hpp>
13: #include <Dialogs.hpp>
14: #include <Clipbrd.hpp>
15: #include <Windows.hpp>
16: #include <Printers.hpp>
17: //----------------------------------------------------
18: class TScratchPad : public TForm
19: {
20: __published:      // IDE-managed Components
21:     TPanel *SpeedBar;
22:     TBevel *Bevel1;
23:     TSpeedButton *FileOpenBtn;
24:     TSpeedButton *FileSaveBtn;
25:     TStatusBar *StatusBar;
26:     TMainMenu *MainMenu;
27:     TMenuItem *FileMenu;
28:     TMenuItem *FileOpen;
29:     TMenuItem *FileSave;
```

continues

Listing R2.1. continued

```
30:        TMenuItem *FileSaveAs;
31:        TMenuItem *N1;
32:        TMenuItem *FilePrintSetup;
33:        TMenuItem *N2;
34:        TMenuItem *FileExit;
35:        TMenuItem *FilePrint;
36:        TMenuItem *Edit1;
37:        TMenuItem *EditReplace;
38:        TMenuItem *EditFind;
39:        TMenuItem *N4;
40:        TMenuItem *EditPaste;
41:        TMenuItem *EditCopy;
42:        TMenuItem *EditCut;
43:        TMenuItem *N5;
44:        TMenuItem *EditUndo;
45:        TMenuItem *Help1;
46:        TMenuItem *HelpAbout;
47:        TMenuItem *HelpContents;
48:        TMenuItem *EditSelectAll;
49:        TMenuItem *N3;
50:        TMenuItem *EditWordWrap;
51:        TOpenDialog *OpenDialog;
52:        TSaveDialog *SaveDialog;
53:        TMenuItem *FileNew;
54:        TPopupMenu *MemoPopup;
55:        TMenuItem *PopupCut;
56:        TMenuItem *PopupCopy;
57:        TMenuItem *PopupPaste;
58:        TSpeedButton *EditCutBtn;
59:        TSpeedButton *EditCopyBtn;
60:        TSpeedButton *EditPasteBtn;
61:        TSpeedButton *AboutBtn;
62:        TPrintDialog *PrintDialog;
63:        TPrinterSetupDialog *PrinterSetupDialog;
64:        TMemo *Memo;
65:        TSpeedButton *HelpBtn;
66:        void __fastcall FileOpenClick(TObject *Sender);
67:        void __fastcall FileSaveClick(TObject *Sender);
68:        void __fastcall FileSaveAsClick(TObject *Sender);
69:        void __fastcall FileExitClick(TObject *Sender);
70:        void __fastcall EditSelectAllClick(TObject *Sender);
71:        void __fastcall EditCutClick(TObject *Sender);
72:        void __fastcall EditCopyClick(TObject *Sender);
73:        void __fastcall EditPasteClick(TObject *Sender);
74:        void __fastcall EditWordWrapClick(TObject *Sender);
75:        void __fastcall FileNewClick(TObject *Sender);
76:        void __fastcall EditUndoClick(TObject *Sender);
77:        void __fastcall HelpAboutClick(TObject *Sender);
78:        void __fastcall FormCreate(TObject *Sender);
79:
80:        void __fastcall FilePrintClick(TObject *Sender);
81:        void __fastcall FilePrintSetupClick(TObject *Sender);
82:        void __fastcall HelpBtnClick(TObject *Sender);
83:
```

```
84:      void __fastcall HelpContentsClick(TObject *Sender);
85:      void __fastcall HelpTopicsClick(TObject *Sender);
86: private:          // User declarations
87:      void __fastcall OnSetCursor(TWMSetCursor& Message);
88:      void __fastcall OnHint(TObject* Sender);
89:      void __fastcall OnIdle(TObject* Sender, bool& Done);
90:      void PrintFooter(TRect& rect, int lineHeight);
91:      void DoHelp(int contextID);
92:      bool HelpMode;
93: public:           // User declarations
94:      virtual __fastcall TScratchPad(TComponent* Owner);
95:
96:   BEGIN_MESSAGE_MAP
97:      MESSAGE_HANDLER(WM_SETCURSOR, TWMSetCursor, OnSetCursor)
98:   END_MESSAGE_MAP(TForm)
99: };
100: //-------------------------------------------------------------
101: extern TScratchPad *ScratchPad;
102: //-------------------------------------------------------------
103: #endif
```

Listing R2.2. SPMain.cpp.

```
 1: //-------------------------------------------------------------
 2: #include <vcl.h>
 3: #pragma hdrstop
 4:
 5: #include "SPMain.h"
 6: #include "SPAbout.h"
 7: #include "SPHelp.h"
 8: //-------------------------------------------------------------
 9: #pragma resource "*.dfm"
10:
11: TScratchPad *ScratchPad;
12: //-------------------------------------------------------------
13: __fastcall TScratchPad::TScratchPad(TComponent* Owner)
14:   : TForm(Owner)
15: {
16:   //
17:   // Set the help mode to false initially.
18:   //
19:   HelpMode = false;
20: }
21: //-------------------------------------------------------------
22: void __fastcall TScratchPad::FileNewClick(TObject *Sender)
23: {
24:   //
25:   // Check each menu item to see if the HelpMode is on.
26:   // If so, call the DoHelp() function to display the
27:   // specific help file for this menu item. We have to
28:   // do it this way so that the help mode works for the
```

continues

Listing R2.2. continued

```
29:    // speed buttons as well as the menu items. Also, if
30:    // help mode is on then the user doesn't want to choose
31:    // this menu item so return after displaying WinHelp.
32:    //
33:    if (HelpMode) {
34:      DoHelp(IDH_FILENEW);
35:      return;
36:    }
37:    //
38:    // Open a file. First check to see if the current file
39:    // needs to be saved.
40:    //
41:    if (Memo->Modified) {
42:      //
43:      // Display a message box.
44:      //
45:      int result = Application->MessageBox(
46:        "The current file has changed. Save changes?",
47:        "ScratchPad Message", MB_YESNOCANCEL | MB_ICONWARNING);
48:      //
49:      // If Yes was clicked then save the currnt file.
50:      //
51:       if (result == IDYES) FileSaveClick(Sender);
52:      //
53:      // If No was clicked then do nothing.
54:      //
55:      if (result == IDCANCEL) return;
56:    }
57:    //
58:    // Delete the strings in the memo, if any.
59:    //
60:    if (Memo->Lines->Count > 0) Memo->Clear();
61:    //
62:    // Set the FileName property of the Save Dialog to a
63:    // blank string. This lets us know that the file has
64:    // not yet been saved.
65:    //
66:    SaveDialog->FileName = "";
67: }
68: //------------------------------------------------------------
69: void __fastcall TScratchPad::FileOpenClick(TObject *Sender)
70: {
71:    if (HelpMode) {
72:      DoHelp(IDH_FILEOPEN);
73:      return;
74:    }
75:    //
76:    // Open a file. First check to see if the current file needs
77:    // to be saved. Same logic as in FileNewClick() above.
78:    //
79:    if (Memo->Modified) {
80:      int result = Application->MessageBox(
81:        "The current file has changed. Save changes?",
82:        "ScratchPad Message", MB_YESNOCANCEL | MB_ICONWARNING);
```

```
 83:      if (result == IDYES) FileSaveClick(0);
 84:      if (result == IDCANCEL) return;
 85:    }
 86:    //
 87:    // Execute the File Open dialog. If OK was pressed then
 88:    // open the file using the LoadFromFile() method. First
 89:    // clear the FileName property.
 90:    //
 91:    OpenDialog->FileName = "";
 92:    if (OpenDialog->Execute())
 93:    {
 94:      if (Memo->Lines->Count > 0) Memo->Clear();
 95:      Memo->Lines->LoadFromFile(OpenDialog->FileName);
 96:      SaveDialog->FileName = OpenDialog->FileName;
 97:    }
 98:  }
 99:  //------------------------------------------------------------
100:  void __fastcall TScratchPad::FileSaveClick(TObject *Sender)
101:  {
102:    if (HelpMode) {
103:      DoHelp(IDH_FILESAVE);
104:      return;
105:    }
106:    //
107:    // If a filename has already been provided then there is
108:    // no need to bring up the File Save dialog. Just save the
109:    // file using SaveToFile().
110:    //
111:    if (SaveDialog->FileName != "")
112:    {
113:      Memo->Lines->SaveToFile(SaveDialog->FileName);
114:      //
115:      // Set Modified to false since we've just saved.
116:      //
117:      Memo->Modified = false;
118:    }
119:    //
120:    // If no filename was set then do a SaveAs().
121:    //
122:    else FileSaveAsClick(Sender);
123:  }
124:  //------------------------------------------------------------
125:  void __fastcall TScratchPad::FileSaveAsClick(TObject *Sender)
126:  {
127:    if (HelpMode) {
128:      DoHelp(IDH_FILESAVEAS);
129:      return;
130:    }
131:    //
132:    // Display the File Save dialog to save the file.
133:    // Set Modified to false since we just saved.
134:    //
135:    SaveDialog->Title = "Save As";
136:    if (SaveDialog->Execute())
137:    {
```

continues

Listing R2.2. continued

```
138:      Memo->Lines->SaveToFile(SaveDialog->FileName);
139:      Memo->Modified = false;
140:    }
141: }
142: //-----------------------------------------------------------
143: void __fastcall TScratchPad::FileExitClick(TObject *Sender)
144: {
145:   if (HelpMode) {
146:     DoHelp(IDH_FILEEXIT);
147:     return;
148:   }
149:   //
150:   // All done. Close the form.
151:   //
152:   Close();
153: }
154: //-----------------------------------------------------------
155: void __fastcall TScratchPad::EditUndoClick(TObject *Sender)
156: {
157:   if (HelpMode) {
158:     DoHelp(IDH_EDITUNDO);
159:     return;
160:   }
161:   //
162:   // TMemo doesn't have an Undo method so we have to send
163:   // a Windows WM_UNDO message to the memo component.
164:   //
165:   SendMessage(Memo->Handle, WM_UNDO, 0, 0);
166: }
167: //-----------------------------------------------------------
168: void __fastcall
169: TScratchPad::EditSelectAllClick(TObject *Sender)
170: {
171:   if (HelpMode) {
172:     DoHelp(IDH_EDITSELECTALL);
173:     return;
174:   }
175:   //
176:   // Just call TMemo::SelectAll().
177:   //
178:   Memo->SelectAll();
179: }
180: //-----------------------------------------------------------
181: void __fastcall TScratchPad::EditCutClick(TObject *Sender)
182: {
183:   if (HelpMode) {
184:     DoHelp(IDH_EDITCUT);
185:     return;
186:   }
187:   //
188:   // Call TMemo::CutToClipboard().
189:   //
190:   Memo->CutToClipboard();
191: }
```

```
192: //------------------------------------------------------------
193: void __fastcall TScratchPad::EditCopyClick(TObject *Sender)
194: {
195:   if (HelpMode) {
196:     DoHelp(IDH_EDITCOPY);
197:     return;
198:   }
199:   //
200:   // Call TMemo::CopyToClipboard().
201:   //
202:   Memo->CopyToClipboard();
203: }
204: //------------------------------------------------------------
205: void __fastcall TScratchPad::EditPasteClick(TObject *Sender)
206: {
207:   if (HelpMode) {
208:     DoHelp(IDH_EDITPASTE);
209:     return;
210:   }
211:   //
212:   // Call TMemo::PasteFromClipboard().
213:   //
214:   Memo->PasteFromClipboard();
215: }
216: //------------------------------------------------------------
217: void __fastcall TScratchPad::EditWordWrapClick(TObject *Sender)
218: {
219:   if (HelpMode) {
220:     DoHelp(IDH_EDITWORDWRAP);
221:     return;
222:   }
223:   //
224:   // Toggle the TMemo::WordWrap property. Set the Checked
225:   // property of the menu item to the same value as WordWrap.
226:   //
227:   Memo->WordWrap = !Memo->WordWrap;
228:   EditWordWrap->Checked = Memo->WordWrap;
229:   //
230:   // If WordWrap is on then we only need the vertical scroll
231:   // bar. If it's off, then we need both scroll bars.
232:   //
233:   if (Memo->WordWrap) Memo->ScrollBars = ssVertical;
234:   else Memo->ScrollBars = ssBoth;
235: }
236: //------------------------------------------------------------
237:
238: void __fastcall TScratchPad::HelpAboutClick(TObject *Sender)
239: {
240:   if (HelpMode) {
241:     DoHelp(IDH_HELPABOUT);
242:     return;
243:   }
244:   //
245:   // Show the About box.
246:   //
```

continues

Listing R2.2. continued

```
247:    AboutBox->ShowModal();
248: }
249: //------------------------------------------------------------
250: void __fastcall TScratchPad::FormCreate(TObject *Sender)
251: {
252:    Application->OnIdle = &OnIdle;
253:    Application->OnHint = &OnHint;
254: }
255: //------------------------------------------------------------
256: void __fastcall TScratchPad::OnHint(TObject* Sender)
257: {
258:    StatusBar->SimpleText = Application->Hint;
259: }
260:
261: void __fastcall
262: TScratchPad::OnIdle(TObject* Sender, bool& Done)
263: {
264:    //
265:    // If help mode is on then enable all buttons and
266:    // menu items so the user can pick any menu item or
267:    // speed button to get help.
268:    //
269:    if (HelpMode) {
270:      EditCut->Enabled = true;
271:      EditCutBtn->Enabled = true;
272:      PopupCut->Enabled = true;
273:      EditCopy->Enabled = true;
274:      EditCopyBtn->Enabled = true;
275:      PopupCopy->Enabled = true;
276:      EditPaste->Enabled = true;
277:      EditPasteBtn->Enabled = true;
278:      PopupPaste->Enabled = true;
279:      EditSelectAll->Enabled = true;
280:      FileSave->Enabled = true;
281:      FileSaveBtn->Enabled = true;
282:      FileSaveAs->Enabled = true;
283:      EditUndo->Enabled = true;
284:      return;
285:    }
286:    //
287:    // Command enablers for Cut and Copy. If no text is
288:    // selected then disable these items on the main menu,
289:    // on the speed bar, and on the popup menu.
290:    //
291:    bool textSelected = Memo->SelLength > 0;
292:    EditCut->Enabled = textSelected;
293:    EditCutBtn->Enabled = textSelected;
294:    PopupCut->Enabled = textSelected;
295:    EditCopy->Enabled = textSelected;
296:    EditCopyBtn->Enabled = textSelected;
297:    PopupCopy->Enabled = textSelected;
298:    //
299:    // Command enablers for Paste. Is there text in the
300:    // clipboard? If not, disable Paste.
```

```
301:    //
302:    bool cbHasText = Clipboard()->HasFormat(CF_TEXT);
303:    EditPaste->Enabled = cbHasText;
304:    EditPasteBtn->Enabled = cbHasText;
305:    PopupPaste->Enabled = cbHasText;
306:    //delete clipBrd;
307:    //
308:    // Command enabler for Select All.
309:    //
310:    bool hasText = Memo->Lines->Count > 0;
311:    EditSelectAll->Enabled = hasText;
312:    //
313:    // Command enabler for Save.
314:    //
315:    bool modified = Memo->Modified;
316:    FileSave->Enabled = modified && hasText;
317:    FileSaveBtn->Enabled = modified && hasText;
318:    //
319:    // Command enabler for Undo
320:    //
321:    EditUndo->Enabled = modified;
322: }
323: void __fastcall TScratchPad::FilePrintClick(TObject *Sender)
324: {
325:    if (HelpMode) {
326:      DoHelp(IDH_FILEPRINT);
327:      return;
328:    }
329:    //
330:    // Display the Print dialog.
331:    //
332:    if (PrintDialog->Execute()) {
333:      //
334:      // Set the title for the printer object.
335:      //
336:      Printer()->Title =
337:        "ScratchPad - " + OpenDialog->FileName;
338:      //
339:      // Set the printer font to the same font as the memo.
340:      //
341:      Printer()->Canvas->Font = Memo->Font;
342:      //
343:      // Determine the line height. Take the Size of the
344:      // font and and use the MulDiv() function to calculate
345:      // the line height taking into account the current
346:      // printer resolution. Use the abs() function to get
347:      // the absolute value because the result could be a
348:      // negative number. After that add 40% for leading.
349:      //
350:      int lineHeight = abs(
351:        MulDiv(Printer()->Canvas->Font->Size,
352:        GetDeviceCaps(Printer()->Handle, LOGPIXELSY), 72));
353:      lineHeight *= 1.4;
354:      //
355:      // Determine how many lines will fit on a page. Trim
```

continues

Listing R2.2. continued

```
356:     // it back by three lines to leave some bottom margin.
357:     //
358:     int linesPerPage =
359:       (Printer()->PageHeight/lineHeight) - 4;
360:     //
361:     // Start printing on line 4 rather than line 0 to leave
362:     // room for the header and to allow for some top margin.
363:     //
364:     int lineCount = 4;
365:     //
366:     // Tell Windows we're starting and print the header.
367:     //
368:     Printer()->BeginDoc();
369:     TRect rect;
370:     rect.Top = lineHeight;
371:     rect.Left = 20;
372:     rect.Right =  Printer()->PageWidth;
373:     rect.Bottom = lineHeight * 2;
374:     DrawText(Printer()->Handle,
375:       OpenDialog->FileName.c_str(), -1, (RECT*)&rect, DT_CENTER);
376:     //
377:     // Loop through all of the lines and print each one.
378:     //
379:     for (int i=0;i<Memo->Lines->Count;i++) {
380:       //
381:       // When we get to the bottom of the page reset the
382:       // line counter, eject the page, and start a new page.
383:       //
384:       if (lineCount++ == linesPerPage) {
385:         PrintFooter(rect, lineHeight);
386:         lineCount = 4;
387:         Printer()->NewPage();
388:       }
389:       //
390:       // Get the next string and print it using TextOut()
391:       //
392:       String s = Memo->Lines->Strings[i];
393:       Printer()->Canvas->TextOut
394:         (0, lineCount * lineHeight, s);
395:     }
396:     //
397:     // All done.
398:     //
399:     PrintFooter(rect, lineHeight);
400:     Printer()->EndDoc();
401:   }
402: }
403:
404: void TScratchPad::PrintFooter(TRect& rect, int lineHeight)
405: {
406:   //
407:   // Build a string to display the page number. We'll use the
408:   // C++ char* method rather than a String object because
409:   // DrawText() will want a char* anyway.
```

```
410:    //
411:    char buff[10];
412:    sprintf(buff, "Page %d", Printer()->PageNumber);
413:    //
414:    // Set up the rectangle where the footer will be drawn.
415:    // Find the bottom of the page and come up a couple of
416:    // lines.
417:    //
418:    rect.Top = Printer()->PageHeight - (lineHeight * 2);
419:    rect.Bottom = rect.Top + lineHeight;
420:    //
421:    // Display the text using DrawText so we can center the
422:    // text with no fuss.
423:    //
424:    DrawText(Printer()->Handle, buff, -1, (RECT*)&rect, DT_CENTER);
425:    //
426:    // Draw a line across the page just above the Page x text.
427:    //
428:    Printer()->Canvas->MoveTo(0, rect.Top - 2);
429:    Printer()->Canvas->LineTo(rect.Right, rect.Top - 2);
430: }
431: //------------------------------------------------------------
432: void __fastcall
433: TScratchPad::FilePrintSetupClick(TObject *Sender)
434: {
435:    if (HelpMode) {
436:      DoHelp(IDH_FILEPRINTSETUP);
437:      return;
438:    }
439:    //
440:    // Just display the Printer Setup dialog. Windows takes
441:    // it from there.
442:    //
443:    PrinterSetupDialog->Execute();
444: }
445: //------------------------------------------------------------
446: void __fastcall TScratchPad::HelpBtnClick(TObject *Sender)
447: {
448:    //
449:    // Toggle the help mode.
450:    //
451:    HelpMode = !HelpMode;
452: }
453: //------------------------------------------------------------
454: void TScratchPad::DoHelp(int contextID)
455: {
456:    //
457:    // Display WinHelp with the context ID passed to us.
458:    //
459:    Application->HelpContext(contextID);
460:    //
461:    // As soon as the user chooses an item then help mode
462:    // shuts off so reset everything.
463:    //
464:    HelpBtn->Down = false;
```

continues

Listing R2.2. continued

```
465:   HelpMode = false;
466: }
467: void __fastcall TScratchPad::HelpContentsClick(TObject *Sender)
468: {
469:   //
470:   // Display the Contents page of the help file.
471:   //
472:   Application->HelpCommand(HELP_CONTENTS, 0);
473: }
474: //-----------------------------------------------------------
475: void __fastcall TScratchPad::HelpTopicsClick(TObject *Sender)
476: {
477:   //
478:   // Display the index for our help file.
479:   //
480:   Application->HelpCommand(HELP_FINDER, 0);
481: }
482: //----------------------------------------------------------------------
483:
484: //---------------------------------------------------
485: // NOTE: The code below uses Windows::SetCursor() to
486: // access the Win API SetCursor() function. This may
487: // change later to make the use of the 'Windows'
488: // namespace unneccessary. If this code does not
489: // compile as-is then change Windows::SetCursor() to
490: // ::SetCursor().
491: //---------------------------------------------------
492: void __fastcall
493: TScratchPad::OnSetCursor(TWMSetCursor& Message)
494: {
495:   //
496:   // We'll handle the cursor change ourself rather than
497:   // depending on VCL. We have to do it this way to get
498:   // the help cursor over the menu.
499:   //
500:   if (HelpMode) {
501:     //
502:     // If the cursor is over the client window then
503:     // display the 'NO' cursor.
504:     //
505:     if (Message.CursorWnd == Memo->Handle)
506:       ::SetCursor(LoadCursor(NULL, IDC_NO));
507:     else
508:     //
509:     // Otherwise display the Help cursor.
510:     //
511:       ::SetCursor(LoadCursor(NULL, IDC_HELP));
512:     Message.Result = true;
513:   }
514:   //
515:   // If help mode is not on return false to tell Windows
516:   // that we didn't handle the message.
517:   //
518:   else TForm::Dispatch(&Message);
519: }
```

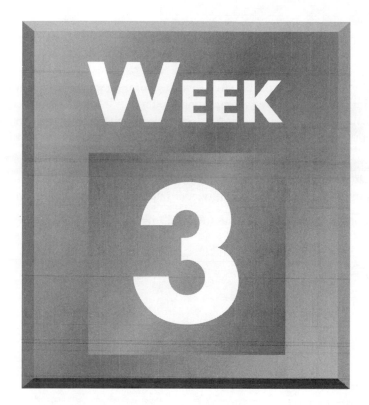

WEEK 3

15

16

17

18

19

20

21

At a Glance

This week we change gears a little. First we'll tackle ActiveX controls and OLE programming. ActiveX is a hot topic right now. After that discussion you will get into database programming. You will learn about database architecture and how C++Builder and VCL implement database operations. You will start out with the basics and work toward more advanced database programming techniques.

After our discussion of database programming, we will tackle the subject of dynamic link libraries, or DLLs. DLLs are there for the taking. You can use them if you want, or not use them. But it is important that you make an informed decision on DLLs. In order to do that, you will have to learn what DLLs are and how you can use them in your applications. Day 19 will tell you all about it. After going through Day 19, you can decide whether DLLs are for you. No doubt you will find that you can use DLLs at some point in your programming journeys.

On Day 20 you will tackle the big stuff—writing components. Writing components is not for the faint of heart. It is real programming. You might love it…you never know (I know I do). Creating a component requires a deeper understanding of properties, methods, and events than you presently have.

Finally, you will learn how to use C++Builder with other programming environments. One of the great things about C++Builder forms is that you can call them from just about any programming environment. This ability opens up a whole new world to you.

So, one more week to go! Are you up for it? All right, then, let's go!

Day 15

OLE, ActiveX, and OCX Controls

by Ken Henderson

There was a time that *OLE* had a very simple meaning: object linking and embedding. These days, however, OLE has come to represent an entire network of interprocess communication systems. Many of these systems can be used independently of one another. I'll take you through a few of the subsystems that make up OLE, and we'll talk about how you can use them in your applications.

> With regard to OLE buzzwords and terms, I should point out that, as the song goes; "the times they are a changin'." OLE is the old term now; ActiveX is the new one. Rather than speak of OLE documents, Microsoft wants us to talk about ActiveDocs. And rather than using OLE controls (OCXs) in our applications, I'm now told that we use ActiveX controls. Use the buzzwords you like best—the technology they refer to is the same.

Out of the box, C++Builder comes with basic support for constructing OLE containers and automation servers. An OLE container can house OLE objects in such a way that they appear to belong to its host application. An OLE automation server provides an interface to the outside world that allows it to be controlled and queried externally. OLE automation objects are provided by OLE automation servers for use by other processes. An automation object can be embedded or linked by an OLE container and can be used to control its host server. I'll take you on a tour of OLE containers and OLE automation servers.

The best way to delve into OLE is to see how it's actually used in applications. Rather than construct a bunch of OLE applications from scratch, we can look at those that come with C++Builder. These demos illustrate just how easy it is to get up and running with OLE using C++Builder.

Autosrv and Autocon

The first pair of applications we'll explore illustrates OLE automation. Autosrv is an automation server that allows itself to be queried and controlled externally. Autocon instantiates an OLE automation object exposed by Autosrv in order to set and retrieve the value of a TEdit control in Autosrv.

To see how this works, follow these steps:

1. Start C++Builder and load the Autosrv project. It should be located in your C:\Program Files\Borland\CBuilder\Examples\Apps\Autosrv directory.

2. Press Ctrl+F9 to compile the application without running it.

3. Once the application is compiled, load the Autocon project. It will be located in your C:\Program Files\Borland\CBuilder\Examples\Apps\Autocon directory by default.

4. With the Autocon application still loaded in C++Builder, run the Autosrv application from outside C++Builder. To do this in Windows 95 and Windows NT 4.0, select the Run option from the Start menu, type C:\ProgramFiles\Borland\

15

CBuilder\Examples\Apps\Autosrv\Autosrv.exe, and press Enter. Once Autosrv starts, drag it so that it won't be obscured when you switch back to C++Builder.

5. Return to C++Builder and press F9 to run Autocon. You should see a display similar to the one shown in Figure 15.1. Once both applications are running, observe what happens in Autosrv when you click the buttons in Autocon.

Figure 15.1.

The Autosrv and Autocon OLE applications.

As you can see, Autocon is able to control (or automate) Autosrv via OLE. Let's look more closely at the code in Autocon to see how this happens. Listing 15.1 shows the source code behind Autocon's lone form.

Listing 15.1. Autocon's one and only form.

```
1: //-------------------------------------
2: //Borland C++ Builder
3: //Copyright (c) 1987 Borland International Inc. All Rights Reserved.
4: //-------------------------------------
5: //-------------------------------------
6: #include <vcl.h>
7: #pragma hdrstop
8:
9: #include "auto1.h"
10: //-------------------------------------
```

continues

Listing 15.1. continued

```
11: #pragma resource "*.dfm"
12: TForm1 *Form1;
13: //----------------------------------
14: __fastcall TForm1::TForm1(TComponent *Owner)
15:   : TForm(Owner)
16: {
17:   try
18:   {
19:       AutoServer = CreateOleObject("BCBAutoSrv.EditServer");
20:   }
21:   catch (...)
22:   {
23:       ShowMessage("Please build and run the AutoSrv example before this one.");
24:       Application->Terminate();
25:   }
26: }
27: //----------------------------------
28: void __fastcall TForm1::Button1Click(TObject *Sender)
29: {
30:   AutoServer.OlePropertySet("EditStr", Edit1->Text);
31: }
32: //----------------------------------
33: void __fastcall TForm1::Button2Click(TObject *Sender)
34: {
35:   Edit1->Text = AutoServer.OlePropertyGet("EditStr");
36: }
37: //----------------------------------
38: void __fastcall TForm1::Button3Click(TObject *Sender)
39: {
40:   AutoServer.OleProcedure("Clear");
41: }
42: //----------------------------------
```

The following is the key line of code:

```
AutoServer = CreateOleObject("BCBAutoSrv.EditServer");
```

AutoServer is a variable of type Variant that's defined in AUTO1.H. Autocon establishes its communication link with Autosrv by instantiating Autosrv's BCBAutoSrv.EditServer OLE automation object. Where does BCBAutoSrv.EditServer come from? Load the Autosrv project and examine its Auto2.CPP module. The source is shown in Listing 15.2.

Listing 15.2. Autosrv's Auto2.CPP OLE automation object source.

```
1: //----------------------------------------
2: //Borland C++ Builder
3: //Copyright (c) 1987 Borland International Inc.
4: //All Rights Reserved.
5: //----------------------------------------
```

```
 6: //-----------------------------------
 7: #include <vcl.h>
 8: #pragma hdrstop
 9: #undef RegisterClass
10:
11: #include "Auto2.h"
12: #include "Auto1.h"
13: //-----------------------------------
14: int Initialization();
15: static int Initializer = Initialization();
16: //-----------------------------------
17: __fastcall ButtonServer::ButtonServer()
18:     : TAutoObject()
19: {
20: }
21: //-----------------------------------
22: String __fastcall ButtonServer::GetEditStr()
23: {
24:     return Form1->Edit1->Text;
25: }
26: //-----------------------------------
27: void fastcall ButtonServer::SetEditStr(AnsiString NewVal)
28: {
29:     Form1->Edit1->Text = NewVal;
30: }
31: //-----------------------------------
32: int fastcall ButtonServer::GetEditNum()
33: {
34:     int val;
35:
36:     sscanf(Form1->Edit1->Text.c_str(), "%d", &val);
37:     return val;
38: }
39: //-----------------------------------
40: void fastcall ButtonServer::SetEditNum(int NewVal)
41: {
42:     Form1->Edit1->Text = NewVal;
43: }
44: //-----------------------------------
45: void __fastcall ButtonServer::Clear()
46: {
47:     Form1->Edit1->Text = "";
48: }
49: //-----------------------------------
50: void fastcall ButtonServer::SetThreeStr(AnsiString s1,
51:     AnsiString s2, AnsiString s3)
52: {
53:     Form1->Edit1->Text = s1 + ", " + s2 + ", " + s3;
54: }
55: //-----------------------------------
56: void __fastcall ButtonServer::SetThreeNum(int n1,
57:                                 int n2, int n3)
58: {
59:     AnsiString s1(n1), s2(n2), s3(n3);
```

continues

Listing 15.2. continued

```
60:
61:     Form1->Edit1->Text = s1 + ", " + s2 + ", " + s3;
62: }
63: //----------------------------------
64: void __fastcall RegisterButtonServer()
65: {
66:     TAutoClassInfo AutoClassInfo;
67:
68:     AutoClassInfo.AutoClass = __classid(ButtonServer);
69:     AutoClassInfo.ProgID = "BCBAutoSrv.EditServer";
70:     AutoClassInfo.ClassID = "{61E124E1-C869-11CF-9EA7-00A02429B18A}";
71:     AutoClassInfo.Description =
72:                 "Borland C++Builder AutoSrv Example Server Class";
73:     AutoClassInfo.Instancing = acMultiInstance;
74:
75:     Automation->RegisterClass(AutoClassInfo);
76: }
77: //----------------------------------
78: int Initialization()
79: {
80:     RegisterButtonServer();
81:     return 0;
82: }
83: //----------------------------------
```

If you look closely at the source, you can see that EditServer is defined in Auto2.CPP. Notice the reference to the TAutoObject class in this line:

```
fastcall ButtonServer::ButtonServer()
  : TAutoObject()
```

The ButtonServer class implements several methods. The GetEditStr(), SetEditStr(), and Clear() methods are called by Autocon to communicate with Autosrv. For example, in Autosrv, the implementation of the GetEditStr() method looks like this:

```
String __fastcall ButtonServer::GetEditStr()
{
  return Form1->Edit1->Text;
}
```

While in Autocon, GetEditStr() is called using this code:

```
Edit1->Text = AutoServer.OlePropertyGet("EditStr");
```

Because GetEditStr is defined as the read function for the EditStr property (see AUTO2.H), querying EditStr causes the GetEditStr function to execute and return a value. The name of the property is passed as a parameter to AutoServer's OlePropertyGet() method. When EditStr is queried in its host OLE automation object, the GetEditStr function in Autosrv is called and the value of Autosrv's Edit1->Text property is returned. Once this happens, the

15

process reverses itself. The value returned by GetEditStr is passed back to Autocon and assigned to the Text property of Autocon's Edit1 component. The net result is that Autocon can reference values in Autosrv as though they were its own, thanks to Autosrv's OLE automation object.

The Initialization() function registers EditServer with Windows so that other OLE-savvy applications can utilize it. This is a necessary step if you intend to do much with OLE automation objects. Initialization() calls RegisterButtonServer(), which establishes the relationship between the ButtonServer class and BCBAutoSrv.EditServer. Listing 15.3 shows the source of RegisterButtonServer().

Listing 15.3. RegisterButtonServer().

```
1: void __fastcall RegisterButtonServer()
2: {
3:    TAutoClassInfo AutoClassInfo;
4:
5:    AutoClassInfo.AutoClass = __classid(ButtonServer);
6:    AutoClassInfo.ProgID = "BCBAutoSrv.EditServer";
7:    AutoClassInfo.ClassID = "{61E124E1-C869-11CF-9EA7-00A02429B18A}";
8:    AutoClassInfo.Description =
9:    "Borland C++Builder AutoSrv Example Server Class";
10:    AutoClassInfo.Instancing = acMultiInstance;
11:
12:    Automation->RegisterClass(AutoClassInfo);
13: }
```

Notice the assignment of AutoClass and ProgID. These assignments link BCBAutoSrv.EditServer and ButtonServer and allow OLE applications to reference the ButtonServer automation object using BCBAutoSrv.EditServer.

Creating Your Own Automation Server

You can create your own OLE automation server using the Automation Object Wizard included with C++Builder. Follow these steps to create a simple OLE automation server:

1. Select File | New Application from the C++Builder main menu to start a new application. This application will become your OLE automation server. It will provide an Automation object that other applications can use to query and control it.

2. Change the Caption property of the new application's main form to My OLE Automation Server. This will make your application's purpose a little more obvious.

3. Select the File | Save Project As menu option and save the new application. Save its main form as unit1.CPP and the project itself as MyAuto.MAK.

4. Drop a single TEdit component on to the new application's only form.

5. Select File | New... from C++Builder's main menu, then double-click Automation Object in the New Items dialog. You should then see a dialog like the one shown in Figure 15.2.

Figure 15.2.

The OLE Automation Object Wizard dialog.

6. The first item you need to specify is the new object's class name. This must be a valid C++ class name. Type TMyOLEEditServer and press Tab.

7. The next item that needs to be specified is the OLE class name. This is the name the outside world will use to create instances of your automation object. This should already be set to the name of the project, followed by a period and the C++ class name (minus the T prefix). In this case, it should be set to MyAuto.MyOLEEditServer. Press Tab to continue.

8. Next you need to type in a description for the new object. The value you type here will be stored in the system Registry. Type A Test OLE Automation Server into the Description field.

9. The last item in the Automation Object Wizard is the Instancing entry. For in-process servers (implemented via DLLs), you'll set this to Multiple Instance. For applications, you'll usually set it to Single Instance. For the time being, let's leave it unchanged and click OK to generate the automation object source code. Figure 15.3 shows the completed dialog.

Figure 15.3.

Your completed Automation Object Wizard dialog.

Now that source code for your new automation object has been generated, you're ready to add methods that you want to be usable by the outside world. Just as Autosrv implemented special functions that other applications could access via OLE, so must the functions that your automation object is to provide be added.

In the interest of expediency, you can copy code from the Autosrv demo program to your new automation server. What you need from Autosrv is its EditStr property and all supporting code. Follow these steps to copy EditStr to your new automation object:

1. Place the cursor under unit2.h in #include "unit2.h" (within unit2.CPP) and press Ctrl+Enter to load it into the Code Editor.

2. Load the Auto2.CPP source file from the Examples\Apps\Autosrv subdirectory of your C++Builder main directory (this will be C:\Program Files\Borland\CBuilder\ Examples\Apps\Autosrv, by default) into the C++Builder Code Editor.

3. Place the cursor under Auto2.h in #include "Auto2.h" and press Ctrl+Enter to load it into the Code Editor.

4. Copy these lines:

```
AnsiString __fastcall GetEditStr();
void __fastcall SetEditStr(AnsiString NewVal);
```

from the private section of the ButtonServer class definition in Auto2.h to the private section of your TMyOLEEditServer class definition in unit2.h.

5. Copy this line:

```
__property AnsiString EditStr = {read=GetEditStr, write=SetEditStr};
```

from the __automated section of the ButtonServer class definition in Auto2.h to the __automated section of TMyOLEEditServer's class definition in unit2.h.

6. Add the following line to unit2.CPP, just below #include "unit2.h":

```
#include "unit1.h"
```

This will allow unit2 (which defines your automation object) to access unit1's form, specifically its Edit1 component.

7. Copy these lines:

```
//------------------------------------------------------------------
String __fastcall ButtonServer::GetEditStr()
{
  return Form1->Edit1->Text;
}
//------------------------------------------------------------------
void __fastcall ButtonServer::SetEditStr(AnsiString NewVal)
{
  Form1->Edit1->Text = NewVal;
}
```

from `ButtonServer`'s class implementation in `Auto2.CPP` to `TMyOLEEditServer`'s class implementation in `unit2.CPP`. When you do this, replace every occurrence of `ButtonServer` with `TMyOLEEditServer`, like so:

```
//--------------------------------------------------------------
String __fastcall TMyOLEEditServer::GetEditStr()
{
  return Form1->Edit1->Text;
}
//--------------------------------------------------------------
void __fastcall TMyOLEEditServer::SetEditStr(AnsiString NewVal)
{
  Form1->Edit1->Text = NewVal;
}
```

8. Now save your project and press Ctrl+F9 to compile it.

In order to test your new OLE automation server, you'll need a client program to create an instance of your automation object and attempt to call its methods. Once again, you can avoid creating a whole new application by making use of one of C++Builder's demo programs. Load the Autocon project that you compiled and ran earlier into C++Builder. Once the project is loaded, make a duplicate of this line:

```
AutoServer = CreateOleObject("MyAuto.MyOLEEditServer");
```

just below it and comment it out, like so:

```
AutoServer = CreateOleObject("BCBTestOLE.EditServer");
//AutoServer = CreateOleObject("BCBTestOLE.EditServer");
```

Once you've duplicated the line, change the reference (in the uncommented line) to `BCBTestOLE.EditServer` to `MyAuto.MyOLEEditServer` instead, like so:

```
AutoServer = CreateOleObject("MyAuto.MyOLEEditServer");
//AutoServer = CreateOleObject("BCBTestOLE.EditServer");
```

This will cause Autocon to create an instance of your new automation object instead of the one defined in Autosrv.

Once you've finished changing which object is instantiated, start the MyAuto application outside C++Builder, and then run your newly modified Autocon application. Arrange the applications so that you can see them both simultaneously.

You're now ready to test whether Autocon can call the methods you set up for `TMyOLEEditServer`. You can do this by clicking the buttons in Autocon. Click the Get Val button to retrieve the current contents of the `Edit1` component in MyAuto. Now, type a value into Autocon's `TEdit` control and click the Set Val button. You should see the value appear in `Edit1` in MyAuto. Finally, click Autocon's Clear button.

15

You should get an error when you click the Clear button because we didn't implement the Clear method when we copied Autosrv's code to MyAuto. Since C++Builder's implementation of OLE automation relies on late binding, you often won't know about miscues like this until you actually test your application.

You've now completed your own OLE automation server. As you can see, the process is really quite simple once you've gone through it a time or two.

Listings 15.4 through 15.8 show the complete source for MyAuto.

Listing 15.4. The `unit1.h` source code.

```
 1: //----------------------------------------
 2: #ifndef unit1H
 3: #define unit1H
 4: //----------------------------------------
 5: #include <vcl\Classes.hpp>
 6: #include <vcl\Controls.hpp>
 7: #include <vcl\StdCtrls.hpp>
 8: #include <vcl\Forms.hpp>
 9: //----------------------------------------
10: class TForm1 : public TForm
11: {
12: __published:    // IDE-managed Components
13:     TEdit *Edit1;
14: private:     // User declarations
15: public:         // User declarations
16:     virtual __fastcall TForm1(TComponent* Owner);
17: };
18: //----------------------------------------
19: extern TForm1 *Form1;
20: //----------------------------------------
21: #endif
```

Listing 15.5. The `unit1.cpp` source code.

```
 1: //----------------------------------------
 2: #include <vcl\vcl.h>
 3: #pragma hdrstop
 4:
 5: #include "unit1.h"
 6: //----------------------------------------
 7: #pragma resource "*.dfm"
 8: TForm1 *Form1;
 9: //----------------------------------------
10: __fastcall TForm1::TForm1(TComponent* Owner)
11:     : TForm(Owner)
12: {
13: }
14: //----------------------------------------
```

Listing 15.6. The `unit1.dfm` source code.

```
 1: object Form1: TForm1
 2:   Left = 200
 3:   Top = 108
 4:   Width = 435
 5:   Height = 300
 6:   Caption = 'My OLE Automation Server'
 7:   Font.Charset = DEFAULT_CHARSET
 8:   Font.Color = clWindowText
 9:   Font.Height = -11
10:   Font.Name = 'MS Sans Serif'
11:   Font.Style = []
12:   PixelsPerInch = 96
13:   TextHeight = 13
14:   object Edit1: TEdit
15:     Left = 128
16:     Top = 72
17:     Width = 121
18:     Height = 21
19:     TabOrder = 0
20:     Text = 'Edit1'
21:   end
22: end
```

Listing 15.7. The `unit2.h` source code.

```
 1: //----------------------------------------
 2: #ifndef unit2H
 3: #define unit2H
 4: //----------------------------------------
 5: #include <vcl\oleauto.hpp>
 6: #include <vcl\Classes.hpp>
 7: //----------------------------------------
 8: class TMyOLEEditServer : public TAutoObject
 9: {
10: private:
11:     AnsiString __fastcall GetEditStr();
12:     void __fastcall SetEditStr(AnsiString NewVal);
13: public:
14:     virtual __fastcall TMyOLEEditServer();
15: __automated:
16:     __property AnsiString EditStr =
17:        {read=GetEditStr, write=SetEditStr};
18: };
19: //----------------------------------------
20: #endif
```

15

Listing 15.8. The `unit2.cpp` source code.

```
 1: //------------------------------------
 2: #include <vcl\vcl.h>
 3: #pragma hdrstop
 4:
 5: #include "unit2.h"
 6: #include "unit1.h"
 7: //------------------------------------
 8: __fastcall TMyOLEEditServer::TMyOLEEditServer()
 9:     : TAutoObject()
10: {
11: }
12: //------------------------------------
13: String __fastcall TMyOLEEditServer::GetEditStr()
14: {
15:    return Form1->Edit1->Text;
16: }
17: //------------------------------------
18: void __fastcall TMyOLEEditServer::SetEditStr(AnsiString NewVal)
19: {
20:    Form1->Edit1->Text = NewVal;
21: }
22: //------------------------------------
23: void __fastcall RegisterTMyOLEEditServer()
24: {
25:     TAutoClassInfo AutoClassInfo;
26:
27:     AutoClassInfo.AutoClass = __classid(TMyOLEEditServer);
28:     AutoClassInfo.ProgID = "MyAuto.MyOLEEditServer";
29:     AutoClassInfo.ClassID = "{1B0BA200-7C66-11D0-B9C3-0080C82BD9D5}";
30:     AutoClassInfo.Description = "A Test OLE Automation Server";
31:     AutoClassInfo.Instancing = acMultiInstance;
32:
33:     Automation->RegisterClass(AutoClassInfo);
34: }
35: //------------------------------------
36: #pragma startup RegisterTMyOLEEditServer
37: //------------------------------------
```

Olemdi and Olesdi

Now that you've seen how OLE automation servers work, let's take a look at OLE containers. An OLE container allows an application to host an object type that actually belongs to another application. The object can be inserted either as an icon (and viewed/edited in its source application via out-of-place activation) or exactly as it would appear in its source application, allowing it to be viewed or edited via in-place activation. The focus when working with OLE documents shifts from their source applications to the documents themselves.

C++Builder supports OLE containers via the TOLEContainer component. TOLEContainer provides special methods for creating OLE objects. You can use CreateObject or CreateObjectFromFile to create an embedded OLE object, while CreateLinkToFile will create a linked OLE object. An embedded OLE object actually resides in its host. A linked OLE object, on the other hand, resides on disk—its host contains only a reference to it. The advantage to embedded objects is that their host documents are self-contained—they don't need any auxiliary or support files. You can distribute a document containing embedded OLE objects without having to worry about including additional files. Conversely, using linked objects requires including supporting source documents. This results in smaller host documents since they only contain references to linked objects, not the objects themselves.

C++Builder includes two demo applications that vividly demonstrate the power of OLE containers. The Olemdi (OLE multiple-document interface) and Olesdi (OLE single-document interface) applications illustrate how easy it is to embed objects from a variety of sources into C++Builder applications.

For our purposes, exploring Olemdi is sufficient, so open the Olemdi.MAK project file in the C++Builder IDE (it's located in the C:\ProgramFiles\Borland\CBuilder\Examples\ Doc\Olectnrs directory, by default).

To take Olemdi on a test drive, press the F9 key to run it. Once the application starts, click the Open button on its toolbar and open some OLE documents (for example, a Microsoft Word document or a Microsoft Excel spreadsheet). Figure 15.4 shows Olemdi with a Word document, an Excel spreadsheet, and an HTML file loaded.

Figure 15.4.

Olemdi can host OLE objects from other applications.

NOTE

The ability to open HTML files (Web pages) depends heavily on the Web browser that's been set up as the default. In my case, that's Netscape Navigator. If you use Microsoft's Internet Explorer 3.0 instead, you won't be able to view HTML files within Olemdi. This is because Internet Explorer 3.0, despite being a Microsoft product, doesn't support in-place activation of OLE documents, whereas Netscape Navigator does. Instead, the object will be represented by an icon that you'll then have to double-click to view. When you double-click it, the linked HTML file will be loaded into Internet Explorer outside of your OLE container application.

As you load OLE-enabled documents into Olemdi, you'll notice that double-clicking them will cause Olemdi's appearance to change dramatically. While viewing a given OLE document, you'll see its source application's menus and toolbar added to Olemdi. For example, when you're viewing a Word document in Olemdi, the Word menu system and toolbar will appear at the top of the Olemdi screen. It will appear as though Word itself is loaded, but the Window title will still read Olemdi. If you then switch to an Excel spreadsheet, the menus and toolbar will change to those of Excel. Since my default Web browser is Netscape Navigator, I get Navigator's menus and toolbar when I view HTML files. The idea behind OLE's document linking and embedding is that you should feel right at home when viewing "foreign" document types in an OLE container application. The OLE object brings with it all that's necessary to successfully view and edit it.

Olemdi Behind the Scenes

For all its power, Olemdi is really a very simple application. Most of its functionality is provided by the `TOLEContainer` component on its MDI child form. For example, the code attached to `TMainForm`'s `OpenButton` component looks like this:

```
void __fastcall TMainForm::Open1Click(TObject *Sender)
{
    if (OpenDialog1->Execute()){
        TMDIChildForm* ch = new TMDIChildForm(this);
        ch->CreateFromFile(OpenDialog1->FileName, False);
        CutButton->Enabled = True;
        CopyButton->Enabled = True;
    }
}
```

In this code, three basic things happen:

- ☐ A File Open dialog is displayed.
- ☐ A new MDI child form is created.
- ☐ The new form's TOLEContainer's CreateFromFile method is called to insert the OLE object.

This is the heart of the Olemdi application—objects are linked and embedded using this very straightforward approach. You can create your own OLE container applications by simply dropping a TOLEContainer component onto a form and calling its CreateObject, CreateFromFile, and CreateLinkToFile methods as necessary.

OCX Controls

An OCX (or OLE or ActiveX) control is similar to a C++Builder component in that it consists of a component-based interface to a modular piece of code. C++Builder supports OCX controls by importing them and providing a VCL class "wrapper" so that they look and work like regular components. To import an OCX control, select the Install option from the Component menu, and then click the ActiveX button. For example, to import the OCX that makes up most of Microsoft's Internet Explorer 3.0 Web browser, follow these steps:

1. Select Component | Install from the C++Builder main menu.
2. Click the ActiveX button.
3. When the Import OLE Control dialog box displays, select Microsoft Internet Controls in the Registered Controls list.
4. Make sure the Palette page entry is set to Internet so that the new control will be installed onto the Internet page of the C++Builder Component Palette.
5. Click OK and then click OK again. You should see a new control named TWebBrowser on the Internet page of C++Builder's Component Palette. You can now build your own applications that have the same basic functionality as Internet Explorer 3.0.

Summary

Today's discussion focuses on C++Builder's support for OLE and related technologies. C++Builder provides native support for building OLE automation servers and OLE containers and for using OCX controls (also known as OLE or ActiveX controls) in your applications.

Workshop

The Workshop contains quiz questions to help you solidify your understanding of the material covered and exercises to provide you with experience in using what you have learned. You can find answers to the quiz questions in Appendix A, "Answers to Quiz Questions."

Q&A

Q Does C++Builder support a Variant data type for interacting with OLE?

A Yes, see the Autocon application (covered earlier today) for an example.

Q What component do I use to link and embed OLE objects in my applications?

A The TOLEContainer component.

Q How do I access the OLE Automation Object Wizard?

A Click File | New... in the C++Builder menu system, and then double-click Automation Object.

Quiz

1. What happens when an OLE application calls a non-existent method in an OLE automation object?

2. What menu choice would you use to install an OCX component into the C++Builder Component Palette?

Exercises

1. Add an OLE automation object to an existing C++Builder application and set up methods to query/set various elements within the application via OLE.

2. Import an OLE control and install it on the C++Builder Component Palette.

3. Using the Olemdi or Olesdi application, open a number of different OLE documents and see how they affect the appearance of the menus and toolbar of the host application.

Day 16

C++Builder Database Architecture

by Ken Henderson

Today's work consists of exploring the C++Builder database component hierarchy. I'll discuss in detail the classes that make up the C++Builder database architecture and point out the key properties, methods, and events of each one. By the end of the day, you'll be thoroughly familiar with how the various classes fit together in the grand scheme of things and how they're used to build applications.

Specifically, you'll learn

☐ How the C++Builder database architecture is constructed

☐ Which components are essential to building database applications

☐ The purpose of the TSession component

☐ TDatabase's key elements

☐ How to use the TDatasource component

☐ The properties, events, and key methods of the `TTable`, `TQuery`, and `TStoredProc` components

☐ How to use the `TBatchMove` component to copy rows and create tables

Some Terms You'll Need to Know

Throughout this chapter, I'll refer to various elements of the C++Builder database architecture by name when describing them or how they inter-operate with other elements. So, before we begin, I need to define some terms so that you'll understand what I'm saying as we go. Some of these are C++Builder terms; some are database terms. These may or may not be terms with which you're already familiar. Table 16.1 summarizes today's key terms.

Table 16.1. Common C++Builder database access terms.

Term	Description
Table	A collection of rows (or entities) in a database. For example, you might construct an `INVOICE` table to store invoice entities or rows.
Row	A record or an entity in a table. For example, a `CUSTOMER` table would contain rows of customer data. Each row would contain information for a different customer.
Column	A field or an attribute that's contained in the rows of a table. For example, your `INVOICE` table might contain a `CustomerNumber` column. The `CustomerNumber` column would be present in every row in the table.
Borland Database Engine	The set of DLLs and support files that allows C++Builder (and other Borland products) to access databases. The Borland Database Engine (BDE) saves much of the work normally associated with building full-featured database applications by providing a high-level database API that is consistent across all the DBMS platforms it supports. This developer-friendly interface is provided in C++Builder's database controls so that you rarely have to work directly with the BDE itself.
IDAPI	Borland's Independent Database Application Programming Interface. It's the interface whereby applications (including C++Builder apps) talk to the BDE. Because nearly all necessary IDAPI calls are made for you by C++Builder's database components, you'll rarely write code that directly references IDAPI. Instead, you'll interact with the methods, properties, and events of C++Builder's database components, which, in turn, make the necessary IDAPI calls.

16

Term	Description
BDE Driver	A DLL (or set of DLLs) that allows the BDE to communicate with a particular DBMS platform. The client/server version of C++Builder includes drivers to connect with Sybase, Microsoft, Oracle, InterBase, Informix, DB2, Paradox, dBASE, and any 32-bit ODBC data source. C++Builder programs don't communicate directly with BDE drivers. Instead, they utilize BDE aliases, which are themselves based on BDE drivers.
BDE Alias	A collection of configuration parameters that tells the BDE how to connect to a given database. Aliases are based on BDE database drivers. You create aliases using either the BDE Configuration program or C++Builder's Database Explorer. Aliases are usually database specific. For example, you might create one alias to reference the Microsoft Access Northwind database and another to reference its Orders database. Both drivers would be based on the Access ODBC driver because they both reference Access databases. However, each would differ in that it would connect to a *different* Access database. This is what distinguishes BDE aliases from BDE drivers—a driver references a particular DBMS platform; an alias references a single database on a given DBMS platform.
SQL Links drivers	High-performance database access drivers that the BDE can use to connect with client/server DBMSs. The client/server version of C++Builder ships with SQL Links drivers for the Sybase, Microsoft, Oracle, InterBase, Informix, and DB2 platforms. Because these drivers are included with C++Builder, you don't need to use alternative methods such as ODBC to access these DBMS platforms, although you still can if you want to.
ODBC drivers	Database access drivers based on Microsoft's Open Database Connectivity specification. C++Builder can use 32-bit ODBC drivers to connect with database back ends. You set up and manage ODBC data sources (which are similar to BDE aliases) via the ODBC Administrator applet in the Windows Control Panel.
Data access control	A nonvisual (invisible at runtime) component that provides database access to your application. Data access controls are located on the Data Access page of the C++Builder Component Palette. TDatabase, TTable, and TDatasource are all data access controls.

continues

16

Table 16.1. continued

Term	Description
TDataset	The C++Builder class that provides access to database tables and table-like query result sets. Because the TTable, TQuery, and TStoredProc components indirectly descend from the TDataset class, you'll often see me refer to them collectively as TDatasets.
TTable	The C++Builder component that provides access to database tables. You use TTable's TableName property to reference the actual table that you want to access in your database.
TQuery	The C++Builder component that allows you to construct, execute, and process your own SQL queries.
TStoredProc	The C++Builder component that allows you to run compiled SQL procedures that reside on a database server (also known as *stored procedures*).
Data-aware control	A visual (visible at runtime) component that uses the data access provided by your app's data access controls to allow the user to see and modify data in a database. Data-aware controls reside on the Data Controls page in C++Builder's Component Palette. For the most part, you can think of them as "data smart" versions of the controls on the Palette's Standard page. TDBGrid, TDBNavigator, and TDBEdit are examples of data-aware controls.
TDatasource	The C++Builder component that facilitates linking TDatasets with data-aware controls. Data-aware components reference TDatasource components that, in turn, reference TDataset controls.
TField	The C++Builder class that provides access to fields in a database table. C++Builder creates TField descendants such as TStringField and TIntegerField when you use the Fields Editor to add field components to a form. TField components that have been added to a form are owned by the form, not by their associated Tdataset.

An Overview of the Architecture

C++Builder applications communicate with local and remote databases using the Borland Database Engine. In the case of local formats such as Paradox and dBASE tables, the BDE makes use of its own, built-in, local DBMS drivers. In the case of remote formats like Oracle and Sybase, the BDE communicates with back-end database servers using SQL Links and/or ODBC drivers. Often these drivers make calls to native driver libraries supplied by the DBMS vendor. Figure 16.1 illustrates this relationship.

Figure 16.1.

C++Builder implements a simple, yet flexible, database-access architecture.

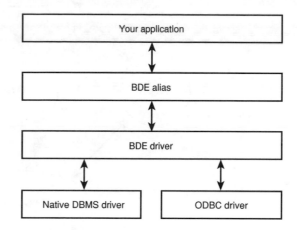

Within your applications, data-aware controls reference TDatasource components. Usually, a given form makes use of only a handful of TDatasource controls, although it may include numerous data-aware components. These components reference one or more TDatasource controls that, in turn, reference one or more TDatasets. It's not unusual for a form to include just one TDataset and one TDatasource. Figure 16.2 illustrates how these elements relate to one another.

The flexibility inherent in this multilevel architecture makes it quite easy to develop database applications that are not only robust, but also scalable. Thanks to the separation of the back-end BDE drivers from your front-end application components, it's at least theoretically possible to change an application's database back end without even recompiling the app. The architecture's modularity allows individual pieces of it to be replaced without having to reengineer it or rebuild applications based on it.

Now that I've given you a broad overview of the architecture, let me make a few general statements that may help reinforce the concepts I've just discussed. You may be saying, "This architecture stuff sounds nifty, but how do I use it? How does it apply to me? What does all this *really* mean?" If this sounds like you, hopefully the following tips will help crystallize the discussion thus far.

Figure 16.2.

Database access from the perspective of a C++Builder app.

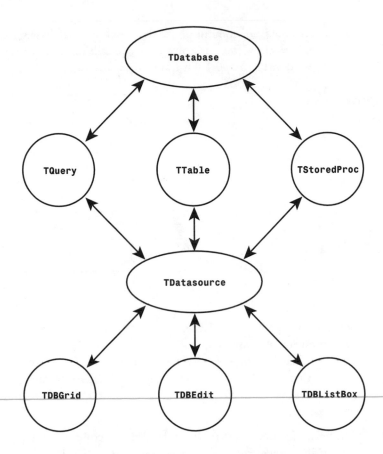

☐ You do not need to use the TDatabase component to access databases. The TDatabase component provides some additional features and controls that you may or may not need, but it's not required to build C++Builder database applications.

☐ You will probably not access the TSession component unless you're developing multithreaded database applications. A multithreaded application opens multiple execution "pipelines" simultaneously. This means that several operations can occur at the same time. Normal database applications are not multithreaded, so, as a rule, you won't need to concern yourself with the TSession component. C++Builder automatically creates a TSession (stored in a global variable named Session) for database apps when they start up. This means that for single-threaded apps, you can just reference the Session variable when you need access to TSession's properties or methods.

- ☐ You do not need the TQuery or TStoredProc components unless you're writing your own SQL or accessing server-based stored procedures. You can open database tables in any of the local or remote formats supported by C++Builder using just the TTable component.

- ☐ You'll normally use the TTable component to send/receive data from databases. As mentioned, TTable is the centerpiece of C++Builder's database access. You use it to reference database tables and to exchange data with data-aware controls.

- ☐ The components on the Data Controls page are visual, data-aware controls—they allow data to be displayed and allow users to change the data visually. They're "data smart" versions of the controls you often see in Windows applications. You'll use these components to build the user interface of database applications. They interact with data access controls such as TTable to provide users with database access.

- ☐ TDataset descendants (for example, TTable, TQuery, and TStoredProc) retrieve data from databases, but they cannot supply this data directly to data-aware components (such as TDBEdit); they need TDatasource to function as the conduit between them and your application's data-aware controls. This means that data-aware components such as TDBEdit do not refer directly to the TDataset that provides their data access. Instead, they reference a TDatasource that, in turn, references a TDataset.

- ☐ So, to build a simple data-aware form you need three things: a TTable, a TDatasource, and whatever data-aware controls the form requires (TDBEdit, TDBMemo, and so on).

A Tour of the C++Builder Database Components

Now that you've received a basic overview of the C++Builder database architecture, let's cover the components individually. I'll go through C++Builder's database components one by one and discuss the key elements of each. I'll build on the general discussion of the database architecture by giving you a thorough tour of the C++Builder database components that encompass it.

I've intentionally omitted components that act only as support classes. If a class is not actually a component—that is, if it's merely an ancestor of a component—I don't include it. This includes the TDataset and TDBDataSet classes, for example. They're class ancestors of the TTable, TQuery, and TStoredProc components. My emphasis here is on components that you can manipulate using C++Builder's visual tools. Although the ancestor class hierarchy is important, most of the properties, events, and methods you'll need to be aware of are provided in C++Builder's components by design.

Each component narrative consists of three sections:

- A description of the component, its module, and class ancestor, as well as tables listing its key properties, methods, and events
- A key elements section
- A tasks section

The key properties, methods, and events tables are by no means exhaustive—see the C++Builder documentation, or, better yet, the VCL source code, for complete lists of these. The idea is to give you a thorough baptism into the C++Builder database architecture without venturing into every nook and cranny of the VCL.

TSession

Module: DB   Class ancestor: Tcomponent

Because C++Builder automatically creates a TSession component for you each time your application runs, you won't normally need to create one yourself. This built-in TSession can be referenced using C++Builder's global Session variable.

As a rule, you won't need more than one TSession per application. The only exception to this is when you're building multithreaded database applications. When doing that, you may need to use TSession components to open extra connections into your server in order to keep database access in one thread from interfering with that in another. You can drop as many TSession components as you need onto a form or data module and then utilize them in your Database and TDataset components. In a multithreaded database application, you typically set up one TSession per thread. Note that C++Builder defines another global variable, Sessions, for tracking multiple Session components in a single application. Sessions is of type TSessionList and contains an entry for each Session component in the application.

Table 16.2 lists the key properties, Table 16.3 lists the key methods, and Table 16.4 lists the key events for TSession.

Table 16.2. TSession key properties.

Property	Description
DatabaseCount	Returns a count of the number of active TDatabases.
Databases	Returns the array of active TDatabases.
Handle	Provides access to the BDE handle—used for direct BDE calls.
KeepConnections	Determines whether inactive connects are retained.

Property	Description
NetFileDir	Specifies the location of PDOXUSRS.NET.
PrivateDir	Specifies the location of temporary files.
SessionName	Specifies the session name to publish to other components.

Table 16.3. TSession **key methods.**

Method	Function
AddPassword	Adds a password to the current session (for Paradox connections).
CloseDatabase	Explicitly closes a TDatabase component.
DropConnections	Drops all inactive TDatabase connections.
FindDatabase	Locates a TDatabase by name.
GetAliasNames	Returns the available BDE aliases.
GetAliasParams	Returns the parameters for a given alias.
GetDatabaseNames	Lists all available aliases, including local ones.
GetDriverNames	Lists the available BDE drivers.
GetDriverParams	Returns the parameters for a given driver.
GetPassword	Prompts for a password; returns true if successful.
GetTableNames	Lists all tables in a given database.
GetStoredProcNames	Lists all stored procedures in a given database.
OpenDatabase	Explicitly opens a TDatabase.
RemoveAllPasswords	Removes all Paradox-related passwords.
RemovePassword	Removes a given Paradox-related password.

Table 16.4. TSession **key events.**

Event	Catalyst
OnPassword	Occurs when the BDE needs a Paradox table password.
OnStartup	Occurs when the session becomes active.

16

Key Elements

TSession is the central control facility for an application's database connections. Use the DatabaseCount property to determine the number of active TDatabases; use the Databases property to access them by index.

Similar to the Database component's DatabaseName property, the Session component's SessionName property enables you to specify a name to publish to other components. In a multithreaded application, you would set this property to a name of your choice and then set the SessionName property of an associated Database and TDataset component (a Table, Query, or StoredProc) to match. By setting SessionName of a Database and, say, a Query component to match the one used in a TSession, you specify which database connection the Query is to use. By extension, if you then interact with Query from within a process thread, you've effectively specified which database connection the thread is to utilize. On some servers, this is a must because database access in one thread interferes with that of another.

The KeepConnections property determines whether inactive database connections are retained for temporary TDatabase components. Use DropConnections to drop all inactive database connections. Keep in mind that if all the current connections to a database server are inactive and you drop them, you'll have to log back into the server the next time you need to access it. There is, however, a way to set KeepConnections to false and still avoid being prompted for a username and password each time the BDE reconnects to your back end. (This is covered in the discussion of the Database component later today.)

The location of the BDE network control directory is stored in the NetFileDir property. Note that this is used for Paradox tables only. The directory path in which temporary files are located is stored in the PrivateDir property.

Tasks

Use the TSession component when you need to get at the internals of the BDE. You can access information such as alias lists, alias parameters, and driver settings. You can also make direct BDE API calls using TSession's Handle property.

You can use the predefined Session instance variable to call TSession methods. The following three code excerpts are examples of TSession method calls.

This method call replaces the contents of ListBox1.Items with the list of currently defined BDE aliases:

```
Session->GetAliasNames(ListBox1->Items);
```

This method call replaces the contents of ListBox1.Items with the list of all BDE and application-specific aliases:

```
Session->GetDatabaseNames(ListBox1->Items);
```

This tells your application to drop inactive temporary database connections:

```
Session->KeepConnections=false;
```

Note that this affects only temporary database connections—those constructed by the BDE itself, not those you've explicitly created. Databases that have their own TDatabase component use that component's KeepConnections property instead.

The main advantage of dropping inactive database connections is the conservation of network bandwidth. On local area networks (LANs), this may be barely perceptible. However, over wide area networks or dial-up connections, the difference this makes can be huge. Note that releasing unused database connections also frees up connections on the server and local PC resources, although this rarely justifies having to log back in to the server repeatedly.

As mentioned previously, you can set up the OnLogin event of a TDatabase component such that the user is not actually required to log in to the server each time the TDatabase reconnects, so dropping inactive connections is perhaps not as bad as it sounds. (See the "Tasks" section for the Tdatabase component for instructions on how to do this.)

TDatabase

Module: DB   Class ancestor: TComponent

Although the explicit use of a TDatabase component is not required for database access, it does provide access to certain aspects of database connections that you cannot otherwise reference. Typically, you have only one TDatabase per application. C++Builder instantiates a temporary TDatabase component internally if you do not include one yourself.

Table 16.5 lists the key properties, Table 16.6 lists the key methods, and Table 16.7 lists the key events for TDatabase.

Table 16.5. TDatabase **key properties.**

Property	Description
AliasName	Refers to the BDE alias used.
Connected	Reflects whether the TDatabase is open.
DatabaseName	Defines an application-specific database alias.
DriverName	Specifies a driver type to use.
KeepConnection	Toggles retention of inactive database connections.
LoginPrompt	Toggles whether the user is prompted to log in.

Table 16.6. TDatabase **key methods.**

Method	Function
Open	Explicitly opens a database connection.
Close	Explicitly close a database connection.

Table 16.7. TDatabase **key events.**

Event	Catalyst
OnLogin	Occurs when a SQL TDatabase is opened and LoginPrompt is true.

Key Elements

You use the DatabaseName property to define an application-specific, or local, BDE alias. Once you've specified a name here (it can be the same as the component's Name property, if you like), you'll see it "published" in the drop-down DatabaseName property list of TDataset components like TTable and TQuery. You can then select it from those lists to link the associated TDataset component with your Tdatabase.

AliasName specifies the BDE alias you want this TDatabase to use. It refers to an alias you've already defined using the BDE Configuration utility and uses it to get default settings. Note that this property and the DriverName property are mutually exclusive. Setting one automatically clears the other.

If you elect not to set AliasName, use the DriverName property to identify a BDE driver that you want to use instead. This can include the STANDARD driver for local tables (dBASE and Paradox), or the INTERBASE, SYBASE, ORACLE, or MSSQL drivers for SQL database servers. As mentioned previously, the DriverName property and the AliasName property are mutually exclusive.

Toggling the Connected property opens and closes the database connection. You can set it to true in the C++Builder Object Inspector to open a database connection while you're designing. If you open a TDataset that refers to your TDatabase, the TDatabase will automatically be opened. If you close a TDatabase that has associated TDatasets, you'll close them as well.

 TIP

> Note that if you define an application-specific alias, the form or data module that contains the associated TDatabase must be currently loaded in order for you to open TDatasets that reference it.

To avoid logging in each time the database is opened, set the KeepConnection property to true.

If the LoginPrompt property is set to true, the user will be prompted for login information when connecting to the database server. You can override this using the OnLogin event (detailed in the following section, "Tasks").

Set the TransIsolation property to specify the *transaction isolation level* (TIL) to establish on the database server. The TIL you select affects both your ability to see transactions originated by other users and their ability to see transactions you initiate.

Tasks

Your application must include a Database component to do any of the following:

- Establish a permanent database connection
- Establish local, application-specific database aliases
- Change server login parameters
- Manipulate server-based transaction-control mechanisms

Establishing Database Connections

C++Builder applications connect to SQL servers using the SQL Links drivers for the Borland Database Engine. These drivers provide access to the InterBase, Sybase, Oracle, and Microsoft DBMSs.

Typically, you'll use the Database Explorer or the BDE Configuration utility to construct database *aliases* through which your application will connect to these back-end servers. A BDE alias is no more than a named parameter list—a set of connection information that the BDE uses to connect you to your database. Once you've set up an alias, it appears in the DatabaseName property list of TDataset components such as TTable and TQuery. You can override the defaults provided by a BDE alias by editing TDatabase's Params property. The settings you make in Params override the parameters that are embedded in the alias definition.

Retaining Database Connections

You set the KeepConnection property of a TDatabase component to true to cause database connections to be retained even when no TDatasets are open. This is necessary if you want to avoid having to log in the next time a connection is needed.

> **NOTE**
>
> Don't confuse TDatabase's KeepConnections property with TSession's property of the same name. TSession's property affects only temporary TDatabase components, not those you create. Setting TSession's KeepConnections property will have no effect on whether your explicit TDatabase connections are retained.

Changing Server Login Parameters

You can use TDatabase's OnLogin event handler to keep the default password dialog box from displaying when a connection is initiated. OnLogin gets passed two parameters: a TDatabase component that points to the database the user is trying to log on to, and a TStrings object for storing the required login parameters. Here's the header definition for a typical OnLogin event method handler:

```
void __fastcall TForm1::Database1Login(TDatabase *Database, TStrings
*LoginParams)
```

From inside the OnLogin method handler, you can use TStrings's indexed Values property to access individual parameters, like so:

```
LoginParams->Values["SERVER NAME"] = "VH1";
LoginParams->Values["USER NAME"] = "dave";
LoginParams->Values["PASSWORD"] = "ureally";
```

To prevent the default login dialog box from displaying, you'll have to at least set the PASSWORD parameter. You can gather the parameters you need from a dialog box of your own, retrieve them from another Database component, or hard-code them—it doesn't matter. If they leave your OnLogin method handler with values, C++Builder will attempt to use them to establish a connection.

Application-Controlled Transaction Processing

A *transaction* is a unit of database work—a set of data modifications that you want to treat as a single unit. It may consist of a single data-modification command; it may consist of thousands. When you group a series of data changes together as a single transaction, you ensure that either all the changes occur or none of them do. If a transaction consists of 1,000 changes and the 999th one fails, they all fail, and the database behaves as though none of them ever occurred. Normally, C++Builder handles transaction-related issues for you automatically by starting and committing transactions when your application attempts to make changes to a database. If this level of control isn't sufficient, you can guide transaction processing yourself using the TransIsolation property and the StartTransaction, Commit, and Rollback methods.

The TransIsolation property controls the transaction isolation level (TIL) on the database server. The TIL on the server controls the accessibility of concurrent transactions to changes made by one another.

TransIsolation has three possible values: tiDirtyRead, tiReadCommitted, and tiRepeatableRead (default is tiReadCommited). These TransIsolation values have the following effects:

- [ ] tiDirtyRead—Uncommitted changes by other transactions are visible.
- [ ] tiReadCommitted—Only committed changes by other transactions are visible.
- [ ] tiRepeatableRead—Changes by other transactions to previously read data are not visible, which means that every time a transaction reads a given record, it always gets the *exact same* record.

The StartTransaction method marks the beginning of a group of database changes that you want to be treated as a unit. They will either all be applied to the database or none of them will be.

Commit makes permanent the database changes that have occurred since the transaction was started. Think of it as a database save command.

Rollback discards the database changes that have been made since the transaction began. Think of it as a database undo command.

NOTE

You can also control transaction processing on your server using Passthrough SQL. To do this, you issue SQL commands that change the transaction processing on your server. Be aware that doing this with SQLPASSTHRUMODE set to SHARED AUTOCOMMIT or SHARED NOAUTOCOMMIT could cause your new TIL setting to affect other transactions initiated by your application.

TTable

Module: DBTables   Class ancestor: TDBDataSet

TTable is a direct descendant of the TDBDataSet class and an indirect descendant of the TDataset class. You access database tables using the TTable component. When you open a TTable, you establish a connection between your application and the table. You add, change, and delete rows in database tables using the TTable component.

Table 16.8 lists the key properties, Table 16.9 the key methods, and Table 16.10 the key events of TTable.

Table 16.8. `TTable` **key properties.**

Property	Description
Active	Toggles whether the `TDataset` is open.
AutoCalcFields	Determines how calculated fields are calculated.
Bof	Reflects whether the `TDataset` is at its beginning.
CachedUpdates	Toggles whether updates are cached.
Database	Identifies the `TDatabase` in use by the `TDataset`.
DatabaseName	Names the alias used to connect to the database.
Eof	Reflects whether the `TDataset` is at its end.
Exclusive	Toggles whether other users can access the `TDataset`.
FieldCount	Returns the number of fields in the `TDataset`.
FieldDefs	Lists important information about fields in the `TDataset`.
Fields	(Indexed) returns a specific field from the `TDataset`.
Filter	Specifies an expression to filter records by.
Filtered	Toggles whether the filtering specified by `Filter` or `OnFilterRecord` is active.
FilterOptions	Controls the behavior of filters.
IndexDefs	Lists important information about the `TDataset`'s indexes.
IndexFieldCount	Returns the number of fields in the current index key.
IndexFieldNames	Specifies a set of fields as an index key.
IndexName	Specifies the name of the index to use.
IndexFields	(Indexed) returns a specific index field from the `TDataset`.
KeyExclusive	Reverses the effect of the range and search functions.
KeyFieldCount	Specifies the number of key fields to use in a search.
MasterFields	Specifies the master fields in a master/detail relationship.
MasterSource	Specifies the master `DataSource` of a master/detail relationship.
Modified	Reflects whether the current record has been changed since the last `Post` or `Cancel`.
ReadOnly	Determines whether the `TDataset` can be changed.
RecordCount	Returns the number of rows in the `TDataset`.
SessionName	Specifies the `TSession` component to use to connect to the database.

16

Property	Description
State	Returns the state of the TDataset (for example, dsEdit or dsBrowse).
TableName	Specifies the physical name of the associated table.
TableType	Specifies the type of (local) table.
UpdateMode	Determines the type of SQL used to perform data changes.
UpdateObject	Specifies the UpdateSQL component to use in conjunction with cached updates.

Table 16.9. TTable **key methods.**

Method	Function
AddIndex	Creates a new index.
Append	Appends a blank row to the TDataset and puts it in edit mode.
AppendRecord	Appends a row to the TDataset using specified values.
ApplyRange	Activates the range established by the Set/EditRange methods.
ApplyUpdates	Saves cached updates to the database.
BatchMove	Copies a batch of rows between TDatasets.
Cancel	Discards pending modifications to the current row.
CancelRange	Cancels the effects of the Set/EditRange methods.
CancelUpdates	Discards pending cached updates.
ClearFields	Sets the current row's fields to their default values.
Close	Closes the TDataset.
CreateTable	Creates a new table.
Delete	Deletes the current record.
DeleteIndex	Deletes a secondary index.
DeleteTable	Deletes the associated physical database table.
Edit	Puts the TDataset in edit mode.
EditKey	Allows search key values to be modified.
EditRangeEnd	Allows editing of the upper key limit of a range.
EditRangeStart	Allows editing of the lower key limit of a range.
EmptyTable	Deletes all the rows in the TDataset.
EnableControls	Enables associated data-aware controls.

continues

Table 16.9. continued

Method	Function
FetchAll	Reads all pending rows from the database.
FieldByName	Returns a TField using its database field name.
FindFirst	Finds a record using the filter conditions you specify.
FindNext	Finds the next record that meets the filter criteria.
FindKey	Performs an exact search on the TDataset.
FindNearest	Performs an inexact search on the TDataset.
GetFieldNames	Returns a list of the fields in the TDataset.
GetIndexNames	Returns a list of the TDataset's indexes.
GotoKey	Performs an exact SetKey-based search on the TDataset.
GotoNearest	Performs an inexact SetKey-based search on the TDataset.
Insert	Inserts a blank row and allows it to be edited.
InsertRecord	Inserts a row using supplied column values.
Locate	Finds a record in a TDataset.
LockTable	Locks a local table.
Lookup	Finds a record in a TDataset and returns values from it.
MoveBy	Moves the TDataset cursor by a given number of rows.
Open	Opens the TDataset.
Post	Saves pending modifications to the current row.
RenameTable	Renames a local table.
RevertRecord	Discards cached updates to the current row.
SetKey	Puts the TDataset in a key-based search mode.
SetRange	Puts the database in a range-based search mode.
SetRangeEnd	Sets the upper limit of a range.
SetRangeStart	Sets the lower limit of a range.
UnlockTable	Unlocks a local table.

Table 16.10. TTable key events.

Event	Catalyst
AfterCancel	Occurs following a Cancel.
AfterClose	Occurs following the close of the TDataset.

Event	Catalyst
AfterDelete	Occurs following a Delete.
AfterEdit	Occurs following an Edit.
AfterInsert	Occurs following an Insert or Append.
AfterOpen	Occurs after a TDataset is opened
AfterPost	Occurs following a Post.
BeforeCancel	Occurs prior to a Cancel.
BeforeClose	Occurs before the close of the TDataset.
BeforeDelete	Occurs prior to a Delete.
BeforeEdit	Occurs prior to an Edit.
BeforeInsert	Occurs prior to an Insert or Append.
BeforeOpen	Occurs before a TDataset is opened.
BeforePost	Occurs prior to a Post.
OnCalcFields	Occurs when calculated fields need values.
OnDeleteError	Occurs when there is a problem deleting a record.
OnEditError	Occurs when there is a problem editing a record.
OnFilterRecord	Occurs when filtering is active and the TDataset needs a row.
OnNewRecord	Occurs when a new record is added to the TDataset.
OnPostError	Occurs when there is a problem posting a record.
OnUpdateError	Occurs when there is a problem while applying cached updates.
OnUpdateRecord	Occurs for each row saved by a call to ApplyUpdates.

Key Elements

You use the DatabaseName property to specify the database you want to access. It points either to a local application-specific alias or to one that you've defined using the Database Explorer or the BDE Configuration utility.

The TableName property points to the physical database table. On some platforms it may also include the name of the table's home database and/or that of the table's owner or schema.

Set the IndexName or IndexFields property to make use of a secondary index with the table. To establish a master/detail relationship with another table, set the MasterSource property to reference a TDataset that shares a common key with this one. Once MasterSource is set, specify the key fields in the master DataSource using the MasterFields property. These keys must correspond with those of the current index, as specified by IndexName or IndexFields.

Note that you can double-click `MasterFields` to invoke C++Builder's Field Link Designer, which enables you to establish master/detail relationships visually.

Setting the `Active` property to `true` is identical to calling the `TDataset`'s `Open` method—it opens the `TDataset`. Likewise, setting `Active` to `false` is the same as calling the `TDataset`'s `Close` method—it closes the `TDataset`.

You can check the current status of a `TDataset` with the `State` property. It will have one of the following values:

- [ ] `dsInactive`—The `TDataset` is closed.
- [ ] `dsBrowse`—The `TDataset` is in `Browse` mode. The `TDataset` can be navigated, but changes can't be made to the data until `State` is switched to `dsEdit`.
- [ ] `dsEdit`—The `TDataset` is in `EUdit` mode and allows changes to the data.
- [ ] `dsInsert`—The `TDataset` is in `Insert` mode.
- [ ] `dsSetKey`—The `TDataset` is in `SetKey` mode because `SetKey` has just been called. When values are assigned to columns while in this mode, they are interpreted as search values. A subsequent `GotoKey` will search for a record using these values.
- [ ] `dsCalcFields`—The `OnCalcFields` event handler is being called.

Tasks

The `First` method moves the current record pointer (also known as the `cursor`) to the top of the `TDataset`, and the `Last` method moves to the bottom. The `Prior` and `Next` methods move to the previous and next rows, respectively. Use the `MoveBy` method to move a number of rows forward or backward from the current row.

The `SetKey`, `FindKey`, `GotoKey`, `FindNearest`, and `GotoNearest` methods can be used to search the `TDataset` for a given set of field values.

You use the `Bof` property to determine whether the `TDataset` cursor is at its beginning. You use the `Eof` property to determine whether the cursor has reached the `TDataset`'s end. These two properties can be useful in looping through the rows in a `TDataset`. For example, here's a simple routine that loops through a table's rows, displaying a field from each as it goes:

```
Table1->First();
while (!(Table1->Eof)) {
  ShowMessage("Category is: "+Table1->FieldByName("Category")->Value);
  Table1->Next();
}
```

WARNING

Be careful that you don't make bad assumptions about the Bof and Eof properties. You can't assume that Bof will be true just because you're on the first row of a table. Nor can you assume that Eof will be true when you're on the last row of a table. Typically, an additional Prior or Next is required to set Bof or Eof to true. For example, the sequence First, Next, Prior won't reset Bof to true, but First, Next, Prior, Prior will. Note that Bof is true immediately after opening a table or calling the First method, and Eof is true immediately after calling the Last method.

16

The Append and Insert methods are used to add blank rows to a TDataset. Append adds a record to the end of the TDataset, whereas Insert adds it at the current cursor position. Append and Insert both put the TDataset in dsEdit mode. The AppendRecord and InsertRecord methods are used to add non-blank rows to a TDataset using a supplied set of field values.

The Delete method deletes the row at the current cursor position. The Edit method allows modification of rows in the TDataset, placing the TDataset in dsEdit mode. The Post method saves these changes to the database, whereas Cancel discards them. This is also true of the Append and Insert methods—you can Post or Cancel them as well.

Local Filters

The Filter, Filtered, and FilterOptions properties facilitate setting up local filters on the TDataset. *Local filtering* enables you to filter a TDataset from within the application. This can be advantageous with TDatasets that have a small number of rows; the entirety of the TDataset will typically be cached by the BDE anyway, so filtering it locally saves interaction with the database server or network.

Filter enables you to specify a filter expression for restricting the rows that are visible in the TDataset. The syntax supported in the expression is similar to that of a SQL WHERE clause. Fields can be compared to each other and to static values. The operators shown here can be used to build your filter expressions:

Operator	Use
<	Less than
>	Greater than
>=	Greater than or equal to
<=	Less than or equal to
=	Equal to
<>	Not equal to

continues

Operator	Use
()	Encloses individual elements of a compound expression
[]	Encloses field names with spaces
AND, OR, NOT	Joins individual elements of compound expressions

You can also filter records using the `OnFilterRecord` event. `OnFilterEvent` looks like this:

```
void __fastcall TForm1::Table1FilterRecord(TDataset *TDataset,
    Boolean &Accept)
{
  Accept=(dlr==vhlead);
}
```

The `OnFilterRecord` event handler sets the value of the `Accept` parameter to indicate whether a row meets the filter criteria. Note that the `TDataset` to which the filter corresponds is also passed in as a parameter. In the previous example, only those properties with gas heat are visible when the filter is active. Note the use of the `Value` variant property to set the `Accept` parameter.

You can also use the `FindFirst`, `FindNext`, `FindPrior`, and `FindLast` methods to search an unfiltered `TDataset` using a filter expression. `FindFirst` locates the first row matching the filter expression; `FindNext` locates the next one that does. `FindPrior` locates the previous row matching the filter expression, and `FindLast` locates the last one that does.

`FilterOptions` is a set variable that can include two possible elements:

Element	Meaning
foCaseInsensitive	The filter ignores the case of the `TDataset`'s data
foNoPartialCompare	Partial field matches aren't allowed

You can set them using C++Builder's Object Inspector.

Ranges

The `SetRangeStart`, `SetRangeEnd`, `EditRangeStart`, `EditRangeEnd`, `ApplyRange`, and `SetRange` methods also allow you to limit the set of rows visible to your application. Unlike C++Builder's more flexible local filters, the rows within the set must correspond to a consecutive set of keys within an index when you're dealing with local tables. For SQL tables, the fields can be any listed in the `IndexFieldNames` property. The `CancelRange` method makes all rows again visible to your application.

Locate/Lookup

The `Locate` and `Lookup` methods allow you to search for rows in a table. They're much more flexible than the `FindKey`/`SetKey` family of functions because they do not require the use of an index and can therefore be used with `Query` and `StoredProc` components in addition to `Table` components. You choose the data you want, and the BDE finds the best way to access it.

Locate

The Locate method takes three parameters: a string that identifies the field(s) you want to search, a variant that lists the values to search for, and a TLocateOptions set variable that specifies options for the search. Here's the syntax for the Locate function:

```
System::Boolean __fastcall Locate(const System::AnsiString KeyFields,
const System::Variant &KeyValues, TlocateOptions Options);
```

You separate multiple field names with semicolons in Locate's KeyFields parameter and pass their values as a variant array in its KeyValues parameter. Locate's Options parameter is of type TLocateOptions and enables you to specify options that control the search. The parameter is a set variable and can have two possible values, loCaseInsensitive and loPartialKey. The first option, loCaseInsensitive, tells Locate to perform a search that is not case sensitive. The second one, loPartialKey, allows for partial key searches. You can pass either one or both of these by assigning them to a set variable like so:

```
TLocateOptions SearchOpts
SearchOpts << loPartialKey;
Table1->Locate("NAME","Cri",SearchOpts);
```

Locate uses the fastest available means of satisfying your search criteria. If an index exists that can satisfy the search request, Locate uses it. If an index does not exist that can service the search, a BDE filter is constructed. Either way, the fastest possible path to your data is taken.

Locate returns true if it's able to locate the data you request, and false if it isn't.

Lookup

Similarly to the Locate function, the Lookup function takes three parameters: a string parameter specifying a semicolon-delimited list of columns to search for, a variant or variant array specifying the column values to search for, and a string parameter listing the names of columns to return in the function's result. Here's the syntax for the Lookup function:

```
System::Boolean __fastcall Lookup(const System::AnsiString KeyFields,
const System::Variant &KeyValues,const System::AnsiString ResultFields);
```

In addition to performing a TDataset search, Lookup returns values from the operation as well. If a matching row cannot be found, Lookup returns a null variant. If a matching row is found, Lookup first processes any lookup fields you've defined for its associated TDataset, and then returns the values of the fields you've specified in ResultColumns. If ResultColumns lists multiple fields, the result is a variant array; otherwise, it's just a simple variant.

Cached Updates

C++Builder's cached updates mechanism enables you to delay applying updates to your database back end. You can decide when to apply updates, and then apply them all at once. Normally, updates are applied as soon as you make them. For client/server applications, this results in increased network utilization because your app must negotiate with the back end every time you make even the slightest change. By using cached updates, you take control of when and how often this negotiation takes place. Updates are cached locally until you apply them, so using cached updates can have a dramatic impact on performance, especially when you're communicating over extremely slow wide area network (WAN) connections.

A side benefit of using cached updates is the ability to update read-only TDatasets. Because you can control the SQL that's generated to update a TDataset, you can set up code to modify result sets that would otherwise be read-only.

Four methods relate to cached updates: ApplyUpdates, CancelUpdates, CommitUpdates, and RevertRecord. I've summarized what each one does in the following:

Method	Function
ApplyUpdates	Saves cached updates to the database.
CancelUpdates	Discards cached updates.
CommitUpdate	Notifies the cache that updates have been applied.
RevertRecord	Returns a row to the state it was in prior to cached updates to it.

There are also a couple of properties that relate directly to cached updates:

Property	Description
CachedUpdates	Toggles cached updates for a TDataset.
UpdateRecordTypes	Controls the visible rows in a cached update set.

The following is the process for making use of cached updates in an application:

1. Set the CachedUpdates property of the TDataset whose updates you want to cache to true.

2. Set the UpdateRecordTypes property to control which rows should be visible in the cached set. UpdateRecordTypes is a set property that can have the following values: rtModified, rtInserted, rtDeleted, and rtUnmodified. Each of these control the type of rows that are visible in a TDataset whose updates are being cached.

3. Set up an OnUpdateError event handler to handle any errors during a call to ApplyUpdates.

4. Make changes to the TDataset's data.

5. Call the ApplyUpdates method to save your changes, or CancelUpdates to discard them.

A good application of cached updates is in data-entry forms. There are three basic types of database forms: decision-support forms, transaction-processing forms, and data-entry forms. Because users of data-entry forms will typically add several rows in succession, it makes sense to cache these additions locally and then save them in one pass. This will reduce table locking on your database and speed up the application.

Updating read-only TDatasets is covered in the discussion of the UpdateSQL component later today.

On...Error

The OnEditError, OnDeleteError, and OnPostError events allow you to react to errors that occur while modifying the data in a TDataset. These events all send the same three parameters to handlers you define for them: the TDataset in which the error occurred, the exception class raised by the error, and a var parameter that lets you specify what action to take once the handler finishes. Here's a sample of the method handler that C++Builder generates for the On...Error events:

```
void __fastcall TForm1::Table1DeleteError(TDataset *TDataset,
EDatabaseError *E, TDataAction &Action)
{
}
```

You can set Action to one of three values: daFail, daAbort, or daRetry.

TQuery

Module: DBTables   Class ancestor: TDBDataSet

Like TTable, TQuery is a direct descendant of the DBDataSet class and an indirect descendant of the TDataset class. You use TQuery to send explicit SQL statements to the database engine. This SQL either operates on local tables or is passed directly to your database server. You execute a query that returns a result set using TQuery's Open method or by setting its Active property to true. Provided that the query adheres to C++Builder's restrictions on "live" queries, you can then treat the result set as if it were a table, which is similar to the way a SQL VIEW works on many database servers. You can update, add to, and delete the rows in this live result set, just as you can when using a TTable component.

Table 16.11 lists the key properties, Table 16.12 lists the key methods, and Table 16.13 lists the key events for the TQuery component.

16

Table 16.11. TQuery **key properties.**

Property	Description
Active	Toggles whether the TDataset is open.
AutoCalcFields	Determines how calculated fields are calculated.
Bof	Reflects whether the TDataset is at its beginning.
CachedUpdates	Toggles whether updates are cached.
Constrained	Controls allowable updates to live result sets.
Database	Identifies the TDatabase in use by the TDataset.
DatabaseName	Names the alias used to connect to the database.
DataSource	Specifies a TDataSource from which to retrieve query parameters.
DBHandle	Returns the low-level BDE connection handle.
Eof	Reflects whether the TDataset is at its end.
FieldCount	Returns the number of fields in the TDataset.
FieldDefs	Lists important information about fields in the TDataset.
Fields	(Indexed) returns a specific field from the TDataset.
Filter	Specifies an expression to filter records by.
Filtered	Toggles whether the filtering specified by Filter or OnFilterRecord is active.
FilterOptions	Controls the behavior of filters.
Handle	Returns the low-level BDE cursor handle.
Modified	Reflects whether the current record has been changed in a live result set.
ParamCount	Reflects the number of parameters for the SQL query.
Params	Specifies the parameters to use with the SQL query.
Prepared	Reflects whether the query has been prepared.
RecordCount	Returns the number of rows in the TDataset.
RequestLive	Specifies whether you want the query result to be updatable.
SessionName	Specifies the TSession component to use to connect to the database.
SQL	Specifies the SQL statements to execute on the server.
State	Returns the state of the TDataset (such as dsEdit or dsBrowse).
StmtHandle	Returns the low-level BDE handle for the last query result.
UniDirectional	Specifies that the cursor moves in only one direction.

16

Property	Description
UpdateMode	Determines the type of SQL used to perform data changes.
UpdateObject	Specifies the UpdateSQL component to use in conjunction with cached updates.

Table 16.12. TQuery key methods.

Method	Function
Append	Appends a blank row to the TDataset.
AppendRecord	Appends a row to the TDataset using specified values.
ApplyUpdates	Saves cached updates to the database.
Cancel	Discards pending modifications to the current row.
CancelUpdates	Discards cached updates that are pending.
ClearFields	Sets the current row's fields to their default values.
Close	Closes the TDataset.
Delete	Deletes the current record.
Edit	Puts the TDataset in edit mode.
ExecSQL	Executes the SQL without returning a cursor.
FetchAll	Reads all pending rows from a database server connection.
FieldByName	Returns a TField using its database field name.
FindKey	Performs an exact search on the TDataset.
GetFieldNames	Returns a list of the fields in the TDataset.
Insert	Inserts a blank row and allows it to be edited.
InsertRecord	Inserts a row using supplied column values.
Locate	Finds a record in a TDataset.
Lookup	Finds a record in a TDataset and returns values from it.
MoveBy	Moves the TDataset cursor by a given number of rows.
Open	Opens the TDataset.
ParamByName	Returns a query parameter using its name.
Post	Saves pending modifications to the current row.
RevertRecord	Discards changes to the current record when using cached updates.

16

Table 16.13. TQuery **key methods.**

Event	Catalyst
AfterCancel	Occurs following a Cancel.
AfterClose	Occurs following the close of the TDataset.
AfterDelete	Occurs following a Delete.
AfterEdit	Occurs following an Edit.
AfterInsert	Occurs following an Insert or Append.
AfterOpen	Occurs after a TDataset is opened.
AfterPost	Occurs following a Post.
BeforeCancel	Occurs prior to a Cancel.
BeforeClose	Occurs before the close of the TDataset.
BeforeDelete	Occurs prior to a Delete.
BeforeEdit	Occurs prior to an Edit.
BeforeInsert	Occurs prior to an Insert or Append.
BeforeOpen	Occurs before a TDataset is opened.
BeforePost	Occurs prior to a Post.
OnCalcFields	Occurs when calculated fields need values.
OnDeleteError	Occurs when there is a problem deleting a record.
OnEditError	Occurs when there is a problem editing a record.
OnFilterRecord	Occurs when filtering is active and the TDataset needs a row.
OnNewRecord	Occurs when a new record is added to the TDataset.
OnPostError	Occurs when there is a problem posting a record.
OnUpdateError	Occurs when there is a problem while applying cached updates.
OnUpdateRecord	Occurs for each row saved by a call to ApplyUpdates.

Key Elements

SQL statements that do not return a result set can also be executed. This includes calls to the SQL INSERT, UPDATE, and DELETE commands, for example. Use the ExecSQL method for these types of queries.

The DatabaseName property specifies the database you want to query. The SQL property specifies the single SQL statement that you want to use in the query. When you query local tables, use Local SQL. When querying server tables, you can use any SQL syntax that your database server supports, unless you intend for the result set to be updatable. If you want an updatable result set, you must use Local SQL syntax so that the database engine can determine which database tables to actually update.

The SQL statement can be a static SQL statement or one that includes parameters that are dynamically replaced with real values. A query that uses replaceable parameters (known as a *dynamic* SQL query) uses a colon to delineate those parameters, like so:

```
SELECT * FROM ORDERS
WHERE CustomerNumber=:CustNo
```

In this example, CustNo is the name of the replaceable parameter. You supply these named parameters using TQuery's Params property.

> **TIP**
>
> When editing TQuery's SQL property, you can edit your SQL using C++Builder's full-blown Code Editor. You do this by clicking the Code Editor button from within the SQL property editor. You'll find C++Builder's Code Editor to be much more versatile than the TMemo component that's used to edit the property by default.

The Constrained property enables you to control what updates may be made to a live result set. If you set Constrained to true, updates that would cause a row to be excluded from the result set are not permitted. That is, if you set up a Query component to return only those customers whose last names begin with A, an attempt to change the LastName column in a row to start with B will fail. This works much the same as the WITH CHECK option on SQL VIEWs.

Tasks

To establish a live, or updatable, result set, two things must happen. First, you must set TQuery's RequestLive property to true. Second, the SQL you use to define the query must conform to certain rules. These rules are different, depending on whether you are querying local tables. For local tables, the SQL must

- [ ] Use Local SQL syntax only.
- [ ] Involve only one table.
- [ ] Not have an ORDER BY clause.
- [ ] Not contain aggregate functions.
- [ ] Not contain calculated fields.
- [ ] Use a WHERE clause involving comparisons of column names to scalar constants only. Operators supported include LIKE, >, <, >=, and <=. Individual elements of the clause may be joined by ANDs and ORs as well.

For server tables, the SQL must

☐ Use Local SQL syntax only

☐ Involve only one table

☐ Not contain aggregate functions

NOTE

The TLiveQuery component that's included on the CD-ROM accompanying this book provides an alternative method of acquiring updatable result sets from database servers. Basically, it creates and opens a temporary view on your server that you may then update as though it were a table. The updates you can make to this "live" result set are limited only by the restrictions your server places on updatable views.

The First method moves to the top of the TDataset, and the Last method moves to the bottom. The Prior and Next methods move to the previous and next rows, respectively. You use the MoveBy method to move a number of rows forward or backward from the current row.

Use the Bof property to determine whether the TDataset cursor is at its beginning. Use the Eof property to determine whether the cursor has reached the TDataset's end. These two properties can be useful in looping through the rows in a TDataset.

WARNING

Be careful that you don't make bad assumptions about the Bof and Eof properties. You can't assume that Bof will be true just because you're on the first row of a query result set, nor can you assume that Eof will be true when you're on the last row of a result set. Typically, an additional Prior or Next is required to set Bof or Eof to true. For example, the sequence First, Next, Prior won't reset Bof to true, but First, Next, Prior, Prior will. Note that Bof is true immediately after you open a query or call the First method, and Eof is true immediately after you call the Last method.

The Append and Insert methods are used to add blank rows to a TDataset. Append adds a record to the end of the TDataset, whereas Insert adds it at the current cursor position. Along these same lines, the AppendRecord and InsertRecord methods are used to add non-blank rows to a TDataset using a supplied set of field values.

16

The Delete method deletes the row at the current cursor position. The Edit method allows you to modify rows in the TDataset, placing the TDataset in dsEdit mode. The Post method saves these changes to the database, whereas Cancel discards them.

See the previous discussion on the Table component for information on other TDataset-based properties, methods, and events.

TStoredProc

Module: DBTables   Class ancestor: TDBDataSet

Like TTable and TQuery, TStoredProc is a direct descendant of the DBDataSet class and an indirect descendant of the TDataset class. This means that, in addition to the methods, properties, and events defined by the class itself, TStoredProc inherits several class elements from the DBDataSet class. This establishes a lot of common ground between the three TDataset-based components, TTable, TQuery, and TStoredProc.

You use the TStoredProc component to execute stored procedures from within your C++Builder applications. A stored procedure is a compiled set of SQL statements executed as a single program. TStoredProc enables you to interact with the result sets returned by these stored procedures.

Table 16.14 lists the key properties, Table 16.15 lists the key methods, and Table 16.16 lists the key events for the TStoredProc component.

Table 16.14. TStoredProc key properties.

Property	Description
Active	Toggles whether the TDataset is open.
AutoCalcFields	Determines how calculated fields are calculated.
Bof	Reflects whether the TDataset is at its beginning.
CachedUpdates	Toggles whether updates are cached.
Database	Identifies the TDatabase in use by the TDataset.
DatabaseName	Names the alias used to connect to the database.
Eof	Reflects whether the TDataset is at its end.
FieldCount	Returns the number of fields in the TDataset.
FieldDefs	Lists important information about fields in the TDataset.
Fields	Returns a specific field from the TDataset. (Requires an index parameter to be passed in.)

continues

Table 16.14. continued

Property	Description
Filter	Specifies an expression by which to filter records.
Filtered	Toggles whether the filtering specified by Filter or OnFilterRecord is active.
FilterOptions	Controls the behavior of filters.
Modified	Reflects whether the current record has been changed in updatable result sets.
Overload	Specifies the overload procedure to use on the Oracle platform.
ParamBindMode	Determines how Params will be bound to proc parameters.
ParamCount	Reflects the number of parameters for the SQL query.
Params	Specifies the parameters to use with the SQL query.
Prepared	Reflects whether the query has been prepared.
RecordCount	Returns the number of rows in the result set.
SessionName	Specifies the TSession component to use to connect to the database.
State	Returns the state of the TDataset (such as dsEdit or dsBrowse).
StmtHandle	Returns the low-level BDE handle for the last result set.
StoredProcName	Specifies the name of the procedure to execute.
UpdateObject	Specifies the UpdateSQL component to use in conjunction with cached updates.

Table 16.15. TStoredProc key methods.

Method	Function
Append	Appends a blank row to the TDataset.
AppendRecord	Appends a row to the TDataset using specified values.
ApplyUpdates	Saves cached updates to the database.
Cancel	Discards pending modifications to the current row.
CancelUpdates	Discards cached updates that are pending.
Close	Closes the TDataset.
Delete	Deletes the current record.
Edit	Puts the TDataset in edit mode.
ExecProc	Executes the stored procedure.

Method	Function
FetchAll	Reads all pending rows from a database server connection.
FieldByName	Returns a TField using its database field name.
FindKey	Performs an exact search on the TDataset.
GetFieldNames	Returns a list of the fields in the TDataset.
GetResults	Returns Sybase stored procedure output parameters.
Insert	Inserts a blank row and allows it to be edited.
InsertRecord	Inserts a row using supplied column values.
Locate	Finds a record in the result set.
Lookup	Finds a record in the result set and returns values from it.
MoveBy	Moves the TDataset cursor by a given number of rows.
Open	Opens a stored procedure that returns a result set.
ParamByName	Returns a query parameter using the parameter's name.
Post	Saves pending modifications to the current row.

Table 16.16. TStoredProc **key events.**

Event	Catalyst
AfterCancel	Occurs following a Cancel.
AfterClose	Occurs following the close of the TDataset.
AfterDelete	Occurs following a Delete.
AfterEdit	Occurs following an Edit.
AfterInsert	Occurs following an Insert or Append.
AfterOpen	Occurs after a TDataset is opened.
AfterPost	Occurs following a Post.
BeforeCancel	Occurs prior to a Cancel.
BeforeClose	Occurs before the close of the TDataset.
BeforeDelete	Occurs prior to a Delete.
BeforeEdit	Occurs prior to an Edit.
BeforeInsert	Occurs prior to an Insert or Append.
BeforeOpen	Occurs before a TDataset is opened.
BeforePost	Occurs prior to a Post.

continues

16

Table 16.16. continued

Event	Catalyst
OnCalcFields	Occurs when calculated fields need values.
OnDeleteError	Occurs when there is a problem deleting a record.
OnEditError	Occurs when there is a problem editing a record.
OnFilterRecord	Occurs when filtering is active and the TDataset needs a row.
OnNewRecord	Occurs when a new record is added to the TDataset.
OnPostError	Occurs when there is a problem posting a record.
OnUpdateError	Occurs when there is a problem while applying cached updates.
OnUpdateRecord	Occurs for each row saved by a call to ApplyUpdates.

Key Elements

Use the DatabaseName property to specify the database you want to access. It points to either a local, application-specific alias or one that you've defined using the Database Explorer or BDE Configuration utility.

The StoredProcName property points to the stored procedure on the server that you want to execute.

The Params property enables you to specify parameters for the stored procedure. You can edit this information at design time using the C++Builder Object Inspector. If the information is available from the server, the Object Inspector will list the parameters that the stored procedure expects.

You can set these parameters at runtime by assigning values to the Params property. For example, you could use the following code to assign the parameter named CustomerNumber for the stored procedure associated with the TStoredProc:

```
StoredProc1->ParamByName("CustomerNumber")->AsString = "123";
```

Note that stored procedure return values are accessed using the Params property, as well. That is, if you've defined an output parameter named Balance in the Params property, you can reference its return value using ParamByName("Balance")->AsFloat following the execution of the procedure.

 NOTE

If you intend to return output parameters from a Sybase stored procedure that also returns a result set, you'll need to call TStoredProc's GetResults method in order to retrieve them. Normally, the

 16

> StoredProc component handles this automatically, but Sybase SQL Server does not return stored procedure output values until all results are read, so you'll need to call GetResults yourself.

Tasks

If a stored procedure returns only one row, or no rows, execute it with the ExecProc method. If it returns multiple rows, use the Open method instead.

Note that you'll need to prepare a stored procedure before executing it. At runtime, you do this using the Prepare method. At design time, you do so by editing the Params property.

The First method moves to the top of the result set; Last moves to the bottom. The Next and Prior methods move to the previous and next rows, respectively. You use the MoveBy method to move a number of rows forward or backward from the current row.

The Append and Insert methods are used to add blank rows to the result set of a TStoredProc component. AppendRecord and InsertRecord add non-blank rows to the result set, using a supplied set of field values.

The Delete method deletes the row at the current cursor position. The Edit method allows modification of the row at the current cursor position, placing the result set in dsEdit mode. The Post method saves these changes to the database, whereas Cancel discards them.

Cached Updates

As mentioned previously, you can only update stored procedure result sets by using cached updates and a TUpdateSQL component. Basically, you set up the InsertSQL, DeleteSQL, and ModifySQL properties of a TUpdateSQL component to handle the TDataset modifications for you. When you then call the ApplyUpdates method of your TStoredProc, the relevant SQL is executed. Because you can control the SQL that's generated to update a TDataset, you can set up code to modify result sets that would otherwise be read-only.

You do this using an UpdateSQL component that defines SQL statements for handling, inserting, modifying, and deleting rows. These SQL statements can be complex SQL queries that update multiple tables or even other stored procedure calls, so you should be able to update a stored procedure's underlying tables. You reference UpdateSQL objects using TStoredProc's UpdateObject property.

TStoredProc has two methods that relate directly to cached updates: ApplyUpdates and CancelUpdates. ApplyUpdates saves changes you've made to the database. In the case of the StoredProc component, this means that the relevant INSERT, UPDATE, or DELETE SQL statements are executed in the linked UpdateSQL component. Note that you can set up the OnUpdateError event to handle errors that occur during a call to ApplyUpdates.

There are also a couple properties that relate directly to the use of cached updates with stored procedures: CachedUpdates and UpdateRecordTypes. CachedUpdates toggles cached update support for the StoredProc component. Unless CachedUpdates is enabled and you've linked and set up an UpdateSQL component properly, you won't be able to update stored procedure result sets. UpdateRecordTypes determines which types of updates remain visible in a TDataset with CachedUpdates set to true.

Updating read-only TDatasets is discussed further in the section on the UpdateSQL component later today.

TBatchMove

Module: DBTables   Class ancestor: TComponent

The TBatchMove component enables you to work with sets of records in operations between two tables. These sets can range from a few records to all the records in a TDataset. When working with TBatchMove, you specify both a source and a destination table. You can append, update, and delete rows in the target table. You can even replace the target table completely if you want to. The actual operation carried out when you call the component's Execute method depends on the setting of the Mode property.

Table 16.17 lists the key properties and Table 16.18 lists the key methods of the TBatchMove component. This component has no key events.

Table 16.17. TBatchMove key properties.

Property	Description
Destination	Specifies the destination of the batch move operation.
Mapping	Specifies column-to-column mappings between Source and Dest. If your source and destination tables are not identical, you'll need to provide field mappings so that the BDE can figure out where to put your data. If you neglect to do this with tables that aren't identical, the batch move will fail.
Mode	Specifies the type of move (such as batAppendUpdate or batCopy).
Source	Specifies the source of the batch move operation.

16

Table 16.18. TBatchMove **key methods.**

Method	Function
Execute	Initiates the batch move operation.

Key Elements

You set the Source property to the TDataset from which you want to copy. You set the Destination property to the target TDataset. You set Mode to one of the following values, depending on what you want to do:

- [ ] batAppend—Appends rows to a preexisting target TDataset.

- [ ] batUpdate—Updates rows in a preexisting target TDataset with their counterparts in the source table. The mode requires an index in order to locate the rows to update.

- [ ] batAppendUpdate—Appends new rows to a preexisting target TDataset and updates existing rows. This mode requires an index in order to locate the rows to update.

- [ ] batCopy—Copies rows in the source TDataset to the target TDataset. It creates the target table when executed, so an existing target table will be overwritten. Be aware that, because existing tables are deleted and replaced, any dependent objects such as indexes and triggers are deleted as well. *Note that these secondary objects are not re-created.*

- [ ] batDelete—Deletes records from the target table that match the source table. This mode requires an index in order to locate the rows to delete.

Tasks

When Mode is set appropriately, call the Execute method to perform the copy. If there are problems, TBatchMove will behave differently based on the settings of various properties:

- [ ] If AbortOnProblem has been set to true, the copy will abort the moment any errors occur.

- [ ] If AbortOnKeyViol is set to true, the operation will abort when any key violation error occurs.

- [ ] If the ProblemTableName property has been set, any rows causing errors will be placed in it. Obviously, if AbortOnProblem is also set to true, this table will contain no more than one record.

□ If the `KeyViolTableName` property has been specified, any rows causing key violation errors will be placed in it.

□ If the `ChangedTableName` property has been specified, `TBatchMove` will move updated or changed rows to it from the target table rather than discard them.

TDataSource

Module: `DBTables`   Class ancestor: `TComponent`

The `TDataSource` component is the link between data-aware controls and the `TDataset` components (`TTable`, `TQuery`, and `TStoredProc`). It's what allows data-aware components to interact with physical database objects.

Data-aware controls reference a common `TDataSource` through their `DataSource` properties. It, in turn, references the `TDataset` that supplies them with data. The `TDataset` supplies data to the `TDataSource`, which is then passed to the data-aware controls. When data is modified in a data-aware control, the change is passed to the `TDataSource`, which then passes it to the `TDataset`.

By abstracting the data control level from the `TDataset` level, C++Builder allows the interaction between the `TDataset` and data-aware controls to be more easily coordinated. It enables you, for example, to change the `TDataset` for a number of components without changing them individually. That is, if you want to change the `TDataset` to which a form's data-aware controls refer, you don't have to change the controls themselves. Instead, you change the `TDataset` property of the `TDataSource` to which they refer. This three-tiered approach allows the access of a group of controls to a given `TDataset` to be more easily controlled.

Table 16.19 lists the key properties, Table 16.20 lists the key methods, and Table 16.21 lists the key events for `TDataSource`.

Table 16.19. `TDataSource` **key properties.**

Property	Description
Autoedit	Determines whether modifying the contents of a data-aware control automatically starts Edit mode.
Dataset	References the TDataset that provides data to this TDataSource.
Enabled	Specifies whether the display of associated data controls is updated.
State	Returns the state of the linked TDataset component.

Table 16.20. TDataSource **key methods.**

Method	Function
Edit	Switches the associated TDataset into Edit mode.

Table 16.21. TDataSource **key events.**

Event	Catalyst
OnDataChange	Occurs when data is changed or the record pointer moves.
OnStateChange	Occurs when the State property changes.
OnUpdateData	Occurs when Post or UpdateRecord is called.

Key Elements

The TDataset property identifies the TTable, TQuery, or TStoredProc that supplies the component with data. The AutoEdit property determines whether modifying the contents of a data-aware control will automatically switch the TDataset into Edit mode, allowing changes to be made to the underlying data.

Tasks

You can monitor changes to a TDataset and its associated data-aware controls by assigning an event handler to the OnDataChange event.

The OnStateChange event occurs when the State of the TDataset changes. For example, if you switch the TDataset's State from dsBrowse to dsEdit by calling the Edit routine, this event will be triggered. Because OnStateChange can occur for nil TDatasets, be sure to check for a nil TDataset before attempting to reference it.

If you want to change the data in the current row before it is posted, set up an OnUpdateData event. It's triggered when Post or UpdateRecord is called.

TUpdateSQL

Module: DBTables   Class ancestor: TDataSetUpdateObject

The TUpdateSQL component enables you to control the way that TDatasets are updated. Because you have complete control over the update process, you can even update read-only TDatasets. You do this via TUpdateSQL's InsertSQL, DeleteSQL, and ModifySQL properties, which allow you to specify the SQL to execute for row insertions, deletions, and updates.

Table 16.22 lists the key properties and Table 16.23 lists the key methods of the `TUpdateSQL` component. There are no key events for the `TUpdateSQL` component.

Table 16.22. `TUpdateSQL` key properties.

Property	Description
DeleteSQL	Specifies the SQL to execute when a row is deleted.
InsertSQL	Specifies the SQL to execute when a row is added.
ModifySQL	Specifies the SQL to execute when a row is updated.

Table 16.23. `TUpdateSQL` key methods.

Method	Function
Apply	Replaces parameters in and calls the SQL you specify (DeleteSQL, InsertSQL, or ModifySQL). Calls both SetParams and ExecSQL.
ExecSQL	Executes DeleteSQL, InsertSQL, or ModifySQL, as specified.
SetParams	Replaces the parameters in DeleteSQL, InsertSQL, or ModifySQL, as specified.

Key Elements

The `InsertSQL`, `ModifySQL`, and `DeleteSQL` properties provide the means of controlling updates to `TDatasets`. These `TDatasets` can be `TTables`, `TQuery` result sets, or `TStoredProc` result sets. The SQL you specify can be a simple SQL `INSERT`, `UPDATE`, or `DELETE` statement. It can be a complex SQL query and can even consist of a call to a stored procedure. This flexibility gives you the control you need to update almost any type of result set.

Tasks

To make use of a `TUpdateSQL` component, follow these steps:

1. Drop a `TUpdateSQL` component on a form and set its `InsertSQL`, `DeleteSQL`, and `ModifySQL` statements to update the database object(s) referenced by your `TDataset`.
2. Set the `TDataset`'s `UpdateObject` property to point to your `TUpdateSQL` component.
3. Set the `TDataset`'s `CachedUpdates` property to `true`.
4. Call the `ApplyUpdates` command from within your application when you want to invoke the SQL specified in the `TUpdateSQL` component.

16

Updates that you make via the DeleteSQL and ModifySQL statements will, of course, need to be qualified by a SQL WHERE clause. Both of these properties support a special extension to SQL that enables you to refer to a field's original value by prefixing its name with Old_. This is similar to InterBase's Old. context variable. For example, the ModifySQL statement you set up for the CUSTOMER table might look like this:

```
UPDATE CUSTOMER SET Name=:Name
WHERE CustomerNo=:Old_CustomerNo
```

Though this query doesn't actually change CustomerNo, it's a good idea to get into the habit of using the Old_ prefix anyway, because some updates aren't possible without it.

TIP

When editing the SQL associated with the TUpdateSQL component, you can edit your SQL using C++Builder's full-blown Code Editor. You do this by clicking the Code Editor button from within the InsertSQL, DeleteSQL, and ModifySQL property editors. You'll find C++Builder's Code Editor to be much more powerful than the TMemo component that's used to edit the three properties by default.

Use your TDataset's OnUpdateRecord event when you want to perform additional processing before sending rows to TUpdateSQL. Once you've completed this additional processing, you can call TUpdateSQL's Apply method to replace the parameters embedded in your SQL and execute the SQL against your database. Here's a sample OnUpdateRecord handler:

```
void __fastcall TForm1::Table1UpdateError(TDataset *TDataset, EDatabaseError *E,
TUpdateKind,TUpdateAction &UpdateAction)
{
#define DEFAULTRATE 5.00
  if (UpdateKind == ukInsert)
    StoredProc1->FieldByName("Rate")->Value=DEFAULTRATE;
  UpdateSQL1->Apply(UpdateKind);
  UpdateAction=uaApplied;
}
```

Notice that the routine sets the UpdateAction parameter to tell the cached updates ApplyUpdates routine that no further action is necessary.

TField

Module: DBTables   Class ancestor: TComponent

The TField component is used to access the columns in a TDataset's rows. Everything that C++Builder enables you to configure at the field level is done with the TField component.

You can toggle a database field's visibility in a grid, determine what its valid values are, and control whether it can be changed—all using the TField component.

Table 16.24 lists the key properties, Table 16.25 lists the key methods, and Table 16.26 lists the key events for TField.

Table 16.24. TField key properties.

Property	Description
Calculated	Reflects whether a field is a calculated field.
TDataset	Returns the TDataset to which this TField belongs.
EditMask	Specifies an input mask that limits text typed into the control.
FieldName	Specifies the associated database field name.
Lookup	Reflects whether a field is a lookup field.
Value	Returns the TField's underlying data value as a variant.
Visible	Determines whether the TField is visible (by default) in DBGrid controls.

Table 16.25. TField key methods.

Method	Function
Assign	Copies the value in one field to another.
AssignValue	Assigns a literal value to a TField.
Clear	Empties a TField.
GetData	Returns the data from a field in raw format.
SetData	Assigns raw data to a field.

Table 16.26. TField key events.

Event	Catalyst
OnChange	Occurs when any modification is made to a TField.
OnValidate	Occurs when a field's value is changed.

Key Elements

If you do not specifically create a set of TFields using the Fields Editor in C++Builder, field objects are automatically created for you each time a TDataset is opened. This list of TFields that's created reflects the columns as they appear in the TDataset.

By creating your own list of TFields using the Fields Editor, you ensure that your application is indeed accessing the TDataset columns it intends to access. Without such a list, changing the underlying table automatically changes the columns your application works with. Using TField components makes your application immune to column reordering and causes an exception to be raised if a column's name or data type changes. The only time you shouldn't make use of TField components is when you're building a generic table browser. On all other occasions, you'll want to be sure to establish TField components to service your TDatasets.

When you establish your own TField list, referencing a field that's been renamed or removed from the underlying table raises an exception. This is preferable to allowing the application to possibly work with the wrong data.

A TField component itself is never actually created in C++Builder applications—it's an abstract class and, therefore, parts of it must be overridden before it can be instantiated. You must create a descendant of TField and fill in some of its abstract gaps in order to create a TField instance. In OOP parlance, you do this via *inheritance*. The TField class type can also be used to typecast and manipulate its descendants. The technical term for this OOP concept is *polymorphism*. TField's descendant classes are detailed in Table 16.27.

Table 16.27. TField **descendants.**

TField Descendant	Type of Data Stored
TStringField	Fixed-length text data up to 255 characters.
TIntegerField	Whole numbers from -2,147,483,648 to 2,147,483,647.
TSmallintField	Whole numbers from -32,768 to 32,767.
TWordField	Whole numbers from 0 to 65,535.
TFloatField	Real numbers from $5.0*10^{-324}$ to $1.7*10^{308}$.
TCurrencyField	Currency values accurate to 15 to 16 digits; represented as a binary value with a range of $\pm 5.0*10^{-324}$ to $1.7*10^{308}$.
TBCDField	Binary Coded Decimal values with accuracy to 18 digits.
TBooleanField	Boolean values.

continues

Table 16.27. continued

TField **Descendant**	**Type of Data Stored**
TDateTimeField	Date and time values.
TDateField	Date values.
TTimeField	Time values.
TBlobField	Variable-length field with no size limit.
TBytesField	Variable-length field with no size limit.
TVarBytesField	Variable-length field up to 65,535 characters.
TMemoField	Variable-length text field with no size limit.
TGraphicField	Variable-length graphics field with no size limit.

You never specifically drop a TField descendant on a form. As mentioned, these are created for you, either via the Fields Editor or automatically when a TDataset is opened.

Tasks

TFields support a number of column-based settings that you can use to customize your applications. You specify these settings using the Fields Editor of a TDataset. You access the Fields Editor by right-clicking a TDataset component and selecting Fields Editor from the pop-up menu.

For example, to prevent modifications to a field, right-click its TDataset, select Fields Editor, and then set the field's ReadOnly property to true in the Object Inspector. To make a field invisible in a DBGrid, set its Visible property to false. If you want to control the types of characters allowed in the field, specify a mask in its EditMask property. To change the database field to which the TField is linked, change its FieldName property to the field you want to reference.

NOTE

Note that TField's Visible property only controls whether a column appears in a DBGrid component if no columns have been defined using the grid's Columns property.

16

You can drag TFields from the Fields Editor directly onto a form. This will create a data-aware control and a corresponding label on the form. You can configure which data-aware component is dropped onto the form using the TControlClass property in the Database Explorer.

16

TFields also support implicit data conversions. That is, you don't have to know what type of data a TField actually stores to convert it to another data type. This is facilitated by TField's Value property. Value is a variant type that is implicitly converted when it is assigned or receives a value. For example, you can assign a string to a boolean field using its Value variant, like so:

```
TBooleanField MyBoolean;
...
MyBoolean->Value="T";
```

You can also assign a numeric field to a string control using its Value property:

```
TCurrencyField MyMoney;
...
Edit1->Text=MyMoney->Value;
```

TField's amazing ability to implicitly convert between different data types makes it chameleon-like in its capacity to adapt to varying data requirements. This simplifies your applications and makes for less work when an application's underlying data structure changes.

Summary

As you can see, the C++Builder database class hierarchy is rich, yet easy to use. Great attention has been given to making the hierarchy not only extensive, but also coherent. The VCL database classes strike a good balance between functionality and ease of use.

Workshop

The Workshop contains quiz questions to help you solidify your understanding of the material covered and exercises to provide you with experience in using what you have learned. You can find answers to the quiz questions in Appendix A, "Answers to Quiz Questions."

Q&A

Q **What property of the TQuery component determines whether a result set is updatable?**

A The RequestLive property.

Q **What property of the TDatabase component is used to set up an application-based alias?**

A The DatabaseName property.

Q **At a minimum, what components on the Data Access page must be in a C++Builder app that needs to include data-aware user interface controls?**

A The TTable and TDatasource components.

Quiz

1. What's the purpose of the TSession component?

2. What are the advantages of using a TDatabase component in your applications?

3. What conditions must be true in order for a TQuery result set to be updatable?

4. What component is used to copy rows from one TDataset to another?

Exercises

1. Construct a sample form using a TTable, a TDataSource, and data-aware components from the Data Controls page of the Component Palette.

2. Modify the form you constructed in exercise 1 to include a TDatabase component.

3. Create a new table by copying rows from an existing one using the TBatchMove component.

4. Set up a TQuery component to return rows from the BIOLIFE table in the DBDEMOS sample database.

5. Configure this TQuery so that its result set is updatable.

16

Day 17

Building Database Forms

by Ken Henderson

Yesterday you took a brief tour of the C++Builder database architecture. Today I'll reinforce what you learned with a discussion of how C++Builder's database components are used to build database forms. We'll take the knowledge you gained on Day 16, "C++Builder Database Architecture," and see how it applies to real applications.

You'll learn the following today:

- ☐ How to construct a database form using the Database Form Wizard
- ☐ What the essential properties of the TTable, TDataSource, and TDBEdit components are
- ☐ How to construct a database form using conventional form-design techniques
- ☐ Why data-aware controls must reference TDataSet controls indirectly through TDataSource components

A Simple Form

Let's begin today's lesson by building a simple database form. By actually going through the process of building a working database form, you'll begin to see how C++Builder's database architecture manifests itself in real applications.

There are two basic ways to build a database form in C++Builder. You can build it manually, dropping components onto your new form one at a time and linking them to each other, or you can let C++Builder's Database Form Wizard build the form for you. Let's begin with the Database Form Wizard. If you haven't already done so, start C++Builder and begin a new project.

The Database Form Wizard

The purpose of the Form Wizard is to construct a form based on your responses to a few simple questions. Choose New from the File menu; then click on the Forms tab in the New Items dialog box. Next, double-click on the Database Form icon on the Forms page. Figure 17.1 shows the New Items dialog box.

Figure 17.1.

You can access the Database Form Wizard via the New Items dialog box.

> **TIP**
>
> You can also start the Database Form Wizard from C++Builder's Database menu. To do this, simply choose Form Wizard from C++Builder's Database menu.

The first dialog box of the C++Builder Database Form Wizard asks whether you'd like to build a simple or master/detail form and whether to base the new form on TTable components

17

or TQuery components. For now, just take the defaults and click the Next button. Figure 17.2 illustrates the first step of the Database Form Wizard.

Figure 17.2.

Select the type and basis of the new form you're building.

The wizard then asks what table you'd like to make use of on the form. Begin by selecting the DBDEMOS alias in the Drive or Alias name drop-down list box. This will establish the database server or disk location from which you'll access tables. Once you select DBDEMOS, the list of table names shows those tables located in the directory referenced by the DBDEMOS BDE alias. Double-click the BIOLIFE table near the top of the list. Figure 17.3 shows the Database Form Wizard's second dialog box.

Figure 17.3.

Select the table you want your new form to use.

Next, you're presented with a list of fields from the BIOLIFE table. You can select them one at a time with the > button, or all at once using the >> button. Click the >> button; then click Next to proceed. Figure 17.4 illustrates the field-selection process.

The next form presented by the wizard asks you to select an orientation for the fields on the new form. You have three choices: Horizontal, Vertical, and Grid. Take the default, Horizontal, by clicking the Next button. Figure 17.5 illustrates.

Figure 17.4.

Selecting fields in the Database Form Wizard.

Figure 17.5.

Use this dialog box to select your new form's orientation.

The next—and final—form presented by the Database Form Wizard asks whether you want to generate the form as your application's main form. As you may recall, an application's *main form* is the form that's first displayed when the application starts. Note the check box at the top of the form that enables you to select whether to generate a main form. We'll accept the default for now and allow this new form to become the application's main form. Obviously, as you add forms to an application you may not want each new one to become the application's main form. To avoid this, simply uncheck the check box at the top of the form.

This final dialog box also asks whether you'd like to create the new form and a corresponding data module or create the new form alone. Let's accept the default and leave the Form Only option selected. Figure 17.6 shows the Database Form Wizard's final step.

Now that you've answered all the prompts provided by the Database Form Wizard, click the Finish button. You should see your new form loaded into the C++Builder Form Designer. The form should have its own TTable and TDataSource components, along with a collection of data-aware visual controls. Figure 17.7 shows what the new form should look like.

Figure 17.6.

You can select whether to create a main form by itself or to include a data module form.

Figure 17.7.

Your new form as it appears in the Form Designer.

Now that your new form is complete, let's see how it appears at runtime. Press F9 to execute your project now. Because the new form you built was designated as your application's main form, you should see it first when the application runs. Figure 17.8 shows what your new form should look like.

Once the application is onscreen, you can navigate the BIOLIFE table using the DBNavigator control at the top of the form. With this tool you can add, change, and delete rows in the table. Click the + button on the DBNavigator to add a record; click the – button to delete one. Type in a field to begin editing it. Click the Post button (the button with a check mark on it) to save any changes you make. With a minimal amount of effort, you've just created a fully functional data entry form for the BIOLIFE table.

Once you've finished viewing the new form, close it to return to C++Builder.

Figure 17.8.

The new form you built appears when you run your application.

NOTE

Note that you can customize forms generated by the Database Form Wizard. They're regular C++Builder forms in every sense of the word. As you work, you may find that creating a form using the Database Form Wizard and then tailoring it to your specific needs makes the most sense.

The New Form Analyzed

Before we move on, let's inspect the form we just generated to learn how it works. Click on the form's TTable component (it should be near the top of the form) to select it. Now press F11 to switch to the C++Builder Object Inspector. There are two key properties to note here. First, notice the DatabaseName property. It's set to the DBDEMOS BDE alias that you selected in the Database Form Wizard. It provides the information the BDE needs to locate the table specified by the second key property, TableName. The TableName property lists the BIOLIFE table you selected in the Database Form Wizard. Figure 17.9 illustrates what you should see in the Object Inspector.

Figure 17.9.

The TTable *component on closer inspection.*

Now that we've examined the TTable component, let's have a closer look at the TDataSource component as well. It should be adjacent to the TTable component on your form. Click on it now to select it.

As with the TTable component, there are two key TDataSource properties of which you should take special note. First, note the DataSet property—it references the form's TTable component, Table1. This means that as the TDataSource couriers data to and from data-aware controls, it will send and receive this data from Table1's underlying database table.

Second, notice the AutoEdit property. It's set to true (true is the property's default setting). As mentioned yesterday, setting the AutoEdit property to true causes the TDataSource to automatically switch to Edit mode when data is modified in a linked data-aware control. Figure 17.10 shows the two properties in the C++Builder Object Inspector.

Figure 17.10.

Your TDataSource *component under the microscope.*

The last form elements that beg further examination are the form's data-aware controls. They're the controls responsible for allowing data to be visually entered and modified. Click the topmost TDBEdit control on your form to select it; then select a couple other TDBEdit components along with it. Once you have a few TDBEdits selected, press F11 to bring up the C++Builder Object Inspector.

TIP

> Once you've selected a single component, you can add other components to your selection by holding down the Shift key while you click on them with the left mouse button.

Similarly to the TTable and TDataSource components, there are two key TDBEdit properties that you should consider. First, note the DataSource property. It's set to the form's TDataSource component. This means that data you enter into the form's visual controls is sent to its underlying table by way of the DataSource1 component. Second, notice the DataField property. It establishes *which* field in the underlying table a particular data-aware control services.

Now that we've inspected the TTable, TDataSource, and TDBEdit components a little more closely, the relationship between them becomes more evident. TTable components provide the basic link between a form and tables in a database. TDataSource components function as messengers between these TTable components and their linked controls. Data-aware controls, like TDBEdit, send and receive data from TDataSource components. The bottom line is that C++Builder takes a flexible three-tiered approach to providing database access to applications.

You might be wondering why the TDataSource component is even needed. Consider the following: If data-aware controls such as TDBEdit could refer directly to TDataSet components, what would be involved if you wanted to change all the controls on a form to refer to a different TDataSet? You'd have to select each of them and set its DataSet property accordingly. That said, what's involved with changing the underlying TDataSet when controls are instead linked to a TDataSource? You simply change the TDataSource's DataSet property. You change a single property of a single control. It couldn't be much simpler.

You might respond, "But I can select all the controls at once and change their DataSource properties just as easily." To which I might respond, "What about at runtime? How would you change a group of them at runtime?" You'd have to change each control individually. You might construct a loop to do the work for you, but you'd be changing each control separately, nonetheless. Perhaps now you can see some of the logic behind C++Builder's database architecture.

A Simple Form the Hard Way

Now that you've created a basic form the easy way, let's create one manually so that you can see the process in more detail. Click the New form button on C++Builder's toolbar to begin constructing a new form.

Next, drop two TPanel components onto the new form. Drop one near the top of the form and set its Align property to alTop. This causes the TPanel to occupy the topmost area of the form. No matter how large or small the form becomes, the TPanel will always occupy its top region. Drop the second TPanel near the bottom of the form and set its Align property to alClient. This will cause the TPanel to occupy all the area not taken up by the first TPanel. No matter how the form is sized, the second TPanel will always cover all the area not occupied by the first TPanel.

Next, let's remove the text that each TPanel displays by default. We don't want either TPanel to display a caption of any type, so we need to reset their Caption properties. Select both TPanel controls; then press F11 to bring up the Object Inspector. Next, delete the contents of the Caption property they share. Figure 17.11 shows the form with its TPanels selected and the Caption property erased.

Figure 17.11.

In the Object Inspector, clear the Caption *property of both* TPanel*s.*

The next order of business is to drop a TScrollBox control onto the lower TPanel. The reason you need to do this is to allow more controls than will fit on the form to be displayed. If a table has lots of fields, you might need to place more data-aware controls on your form than will physically fit. TScrollBox allows you to do this by providing an area that can be scrolled at runtime to display more controls as needed. Click the lower TPanel to select it; then drop a TScrollBox control onto it. Set the TScrollBox control's Align property to alClient. This will cause the TScrollBox to occupy all the space on its host TPanel that's not taken by other controls. Because it's the only control on the TPanel, this means that it will take all the TPanel's client area. Figure 17.12 shows what your new form might look like with the TScrollBox in place.

Figure 17.12.

Your new form with its TScrollBox *in place.*

Now that the form's visual foundation has been established, you're ready to begin dropping components on it. Let's begin with two nonvisual controls: a TTable and a TDataSource. Place one of each anywhere you'd like on the form. Their locations on the form are unimportant because they're both nonvisual controls—they're invisible at runtime. I recommend, though, that you place them near the top of the form so that they can be easily accessed no matter how you size the form.

Set the TTable component's DatabaseName property to the DBDEMOS BDE alias. Set its TableName property to the BIOLIFE.DB table located in the DBDEMOS alias.

Next, set the TDataSource component's DataSet property to the name of the TTable component you dropped on the form (it will be named Table1 by default). This creates the link between the TTable and the data-aware controls the TDataSource will service.

TIP

You can double-click on the TDataSource component's DataSet property to quickly set it to your form's lone TTable component. Because there's only one TDataSet descendant on the form (your TTable component), C++Builder will automatically supply it to your TDataSource's DataSet property when you double-click on the property.

17

Figure 17.13 shows your `TTable` and `TDataSource` components in place.

Figure 17.13.
Your new form with its nonvisual components.

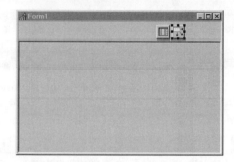

Now that the form's nonvisual components have been set up, you're ready to set up its data-aware controls. *Data-aware controls* are user interface controls that are linked to database tables. They're similar to the controls you normally see in Windows applications, but provide specialized support for sending and receiving data from databases. For example, you often see C++Builder's `TEdit` control included in Windows applications for editing strings of one type or another. C++Builder includes a data-aware version of `TEdit`, called `TDBEdit`, that works just like `TEdit` except that its whole purpose is to service a given column in a database table. It displays data currently contained in the column and sends any changes a user makes to the data back to the column.

The first data-aware control you'll drop is the `TDBNavigator` control. It's located on the Data Controls page in the C++Builder Component Palette. Select your form's top `TPanel` component; then drop a `TDBNavigator` onto it. Set the `TDBNavigator`'s `DataSource` property to your form's `TDataSource` component. Figure 17.14 illustrates.

Figure 17.14.
Your form with its `TDBNavigator` *in place.*

Now that the form's TDBNavigator has been set up, you're ready to move on to dropping the other data controls. There are two basic ways of doing this. The first way is the more tedious of the two. It consists of dropping TDBEdits, TDBMemos, and other data-aware controls onto the form, one at a time, and then setting each of their DataSource and DataField properties individually. Once the data-aware controls are in place, you then drop TLabel components to label each of them. Although this will certainly work, there is a much easier way.

The second, and much quicker, method involves the use of the C++Builder Fields Editor. Essentially, you can drag field components right from the Fields Editor onto a form. C++Builder will then create a data-aware control and label for each field dropped. To do this, follow these steps:

1. Right-click on your TTable component to bring up its context menu.
2. Select the Fields Editor option from the Context menu.
3. Right-click the Fields Editor and select Add fields.
4. When the list of fields is displayed, click OK to add all of them.
5. With all fields still selected in the Fields Editor, drag them as a group onto your form. You should now see a data-aware control and a TLabel component for each field.

Figure 17.15 illustrates what your form might look like.

Figure 17.15.

Your new form, after its data-aware controls have been placed.

At this point, your form is basically complete. You've just manually built what the Database Form Wizard did for you automatically. Perhaps this can help you appreciate the time saved by using the wizard to create new forms rather than building them all by hand.

The one thing that remains to be done with your new form is to decide how and when to open your TTable. There are two easy ways of doing this. First, you could simply toggle the TTable's Active property to true at design time. Setting it to true will open the TTable while you work on it as well as when the application is executed. Second, you could set the form's OnCreate or OnShow event handler to open the TTable at runtime. This, in fact, is how the Database Form Wizard does things—it sets up the form's OnCreate event handler to open the table at runtime.

Let's mimic the Form Wizard for now and set up your new form's OnCreate handler so that it opens your table when the form is created. Press F11 to bring up the C++Builder Object Inspector; then click the drop-down box and select your form from the list of component classes. Next, click on the Object Inspector's Events page and then double-click on its OnCreate event. Type the following code into the C++Builder Code Editor:

```
Table1->Open();
```

This will cause the table to open when the form is created. By default, an application's forms are automatically created when it runs, although you can change this behavior.

Running the New Form

Your form is now complete, and you're ready to run it. In order to ensure that your new form is the first one displayed when the application runs, you need to identify it as the application's main form. To do this, follow these steps:

1. Select the Options item on the C++Builder Project menu.
2. On the Forms page of the Options dialog box, click the Main form drop-down list and select your form. This will make it your application's main form.
3. Click OK to save your changes.

Now that your new form is the application's main form, press F9 to execute the application. You should see your new form displayed when the application loads. Figure 17.16 shows what you might see.

Figure 17.16.

Your new form as it might appear at runtime.

When you've finished viewing your new form, close it to return to C++Builder.

Summary

In this chapter you have learned to build database forms using both the Database Form Wizard and conventional form-construction techniques. You have seen the easy way and the hard way of doing things. More importantly, you have learned *why* certain elements of the C++Builder database architecture are constructed the way they are. You have also learned to utilize the C++Builder database architecture to construct basic table edit/entry forms.

Workshop

The Workshop contains quiz questions to help you solidify your understanding of the material covered and exercises to provide you with experience in using what you have learned. You can find answers to the quiz questions in Appendix A, "Answers to Quiz Questions."

Q&A

Q **What property of the TQuery component determines whether a result set is updatable?**

A The RequestLive property.

Q **What property of the TDatabase component is used to set up an application-based alias?**

A The DatabaseName property.

Q **At a minimum, what components must be in a C++Builder application in which you want to include data-aware user interface controls?**

A One TTable, Tquery, or TStoredProc component along with a TDatasource component.

Quiz

1. What are the two methods of starting the C++Builder Database Form Wizard?
2. What are the key properties of the TTable component?
3. What are the key properties of the TDataSource component?
4. What component do data-aware controls require in order to reference a TDataSet descendant such as TTable?

Exercises

1. Build a database form completely by hand, without using the Fields Editor drag-and-drop technique I showed you today.

2. Construct a database form that involves a master/detail relationship between two tables.

3. Create a new form using the Database Form Wizard and then customize it to your liking.

4. Construct a new form using the Database Form Wizard that is based on a TQuery instead of TTable component.

Day 18

Building Database Applications

by Ken Henderson

Yesterday you learned the basics of building database forms. Today you'll learn more about building database forms and constructing database applications. Specifically, today's topics are

- [ ] Using the TDatabase component in your apps
- [ ] Defining BDE aliases
- [ ] Setting up data modules
- [ ] Creating master/detail forms
- [ ] Making use of the TQuery component
- [ ] Designing reports

The TDatabase **Component**

If you haven't already done so, start C++Builder and load the second form you created yesterday. We'll begin today's work by changing this form to make use of a TDatabase component.

Using a TDatabase component in your database apps isn't required, but it is the best way to manage your app's database access from a single vantage point. For example, to switch your application's transaction isolation level, you can change the value of TDatabase's TransIsolation property. To override the default login sequence, you can attach code to TDatabase's OnLogin event. And to specify driver-specific parameters, you can add entries to TDatabase's Params property.

Locate the TDatabase component on the Data Access page of C++Builder's toolbar and drop one onto the form. As with the TTable and TDataSource controls, the physical location of the TDatabase component on your form is unimportant. It's a nonvisual control—it won't be displayed at runtime.

Set the TDatabase's AliasName property to the DBDEMOS alias that you used earlier on the form. Set its DatabaseName property to dbTest. The DatabaseName property specifies the name by which other components will reference your TDatabase. They do so via their own DatabaseName properties. That is, in order to use your TDatabase with a TTable component, you'll set the TTable's DatabaseName property to the name you specified in the DatabaseName property of your TDatabase.

Now that your TDatabase is set up, change your TTable to reference it. Bring up the Object Inspector and click on the drop-down list next to Table1's DatabaseName property. You should see dbTest in the list. Click on it to select it. You've now switched your form to funnel its database access through a single control, your TDatabase component. Figure 18.1 shows your form with its TDatabase component set up.

Figure 18.1.

You can channel your database access through a TDatabase *component.*

Be sure to save the changes you've just made to your form before proceeding.

BDE Aliases

C++Builder's Database Explorer has a variety of uses—you'll use it here to create a Borland Database Engine (BDE) alias. You need a BDE alias in order to access database objects from C++Builder.

I've never liked the term *alias*. To me, the word implies that the name is false—that it's a pseudonym. Implications aside, a BDE alias is analogous to an ODBC data source. It's a collection of parameters that define how to connect to a given database or DBMS.

Yesterday we made use of the built-in demo alias, DBDEMOS. C++Builder includes it by default to support some of its database demo applications. Today I'll show you how to define your own BDE aliases. When you build real applications, you'll likely require custom alias definitions.

Select the Explore option from C++Builder's Database menu to start the Database Explorer. Click on the Database tab, if it isn't already selected, then click on the Databases entry in the treeview below it. Next, right-click on the Database entry and select New on the ensuing menu.

You're then prompted to select a database driver for your new BDE alias. The alias you'll build today will be Paradox based, so select Standard and click OK.

Next, you're prompted for the name of the new database alias. Type PDOXDEMO and press Enter. Next, click on the Path entry in the right-hand pane and type the name of the directory where C++Builder's demo database files are stored (in my case that's C:\Program Files\Borland\CBuilder\Examples\Data) and then press Enter.

NOTE

> By pointing your new alias to C++Builder's demo data directory, you're basically duplicating the DBDEMOS alias. This makes testing the new alias easier, because tables are already present in the directory. In your own apps, though, you'll no doubt specify a different directory.

Next, click the Apply button in Database Explorer's toolbar. It's the blue arrow that curves to the right. This saves your new alias definition.

Figure 18.2 illustrates what the screen should look like when you're done.

Figure 18.2.

Your new alias definition.

Now that you've built a new BDE alias, let's change your form to use it. To do so, follow these steps:

1. Close the Database Explorer and return to the C++Builder Form Designer.
2. Click your TDatabase component; then press F11 to bring up the Object Inspector.
3. Change TDatabase's AliasName property to reference your new alias.

Figure 18.3 shows what you should see in the Object Inspector.

Figure 18.3.

Your TDatabase references your new BDE alias.

Save your work now and run your app. You should see that it opens the BIOLIFE Paradox table as it did before. When you're finished viewing the app, close it and return to C++Builder.

Data Modules

NEW TERM   A *data module* is a special type of form designed for holding nonvisual controls such as database access controls. It allows you to centrally locate all your nonvisual data controls for easy access and management.

I recommend that you create a data module for every database that you might want to access with C++Builder applications. You don't have to put all the tables in a given database in a single data module. I recommend you do so when possible, however, because this enables you to save the data module to the C++Builder Object Repository, where you and others can reuse it when building applications. This helps ensure consistency across your applications and enables you to manage C++Builder's database access from a single vantage point—the Object Repository.

So select File | New Data Module. You'll be presented with a small form onto which you can drop nonvisual components. You may want to resize your data module so that it's a bit larger before proceeding. Its default size is quite small.

Now that you have a data module, we'll move your form's nonvisual data access components to it. If you were building an entire application, you'd place as many of your data access components on the app's data module as possible.

Begin by selecting the TTable, TDataSource, and TDatabase components on your BIOLIFE form and pressing Ctrl+X to cut them to the Windows Clipboard. Next, select your new data module and press Ctrl+V to paste your components from the Clipboard onto your data module. Your data access components have now been moved to your data module. Figure 18.4 shows what the new data module should look like.

Figure 18.4.

*Your new data
module houses data-
access components.*

When you've finished this cut-and-paste operation, you need to return to your BIOLIFE form and repair the references to your data access components that were broken when you moved them. That is, the data-aware controls (for example, TDBEdit) on your form referenced the TDataSource that you removed from the form. Now that the TDataSource has been moved, the reference is invalid, and C++Builder has cleared it. You'll need to repair these broken references before proceeding.

Before you can make use of the components on your new data module, you'll have to include the module form's header file in your form's source code so that the form can "see" the data module's components. To do this, load your BIOLIFE form into the Form Designer; then select the Include Unit option on the File menu and choose your data module's source code unit. Now the objects on the data module are available in your form just as if they'd been dropped onto the form itself.

18

Next, select all the data-aware components on your form (including the TDBNavigator), and then press F11 to bring up the Object Inspector. When the Object Inspector is up, click on the drop-down list next to the DataSource property and select your data module's TDataSource. You'll notice that the TDataSource component's name is now qualified with the name of the data module unit. Figure 18.5 shows the form modified to reference your new data module.

Figure 18.5.

Your form now references the data module you created.

 TIP

You can quickly select several components at once by dragging a selection rectangle over them. You do this by positioning the mouse pointer to the left and above the leftmost component, holding down button one, and then dragging the rectangle that subsequently appears so that it encompasses the controls that you want to select. When you release button one, the controls within the rectangle are selected.

Because we used source code to open the TTable when the BIOLIFE form was created, we'll have to fix that reference as well. Press F11 to bring up the Object Inspector; then select your form from the drop-down list of components. Next, click on the Events page and double-click on the OnCreate event. You should see this code:

```
Table1->Open();
```

Because there's no longer a Table1 component on this form, this code won't compile. You could change this to

```
DataModule1->Table1->Open();
```

But this would create an interunit dependency that you don't need and should avoid when possible. That is, you'd have to be sure that your data module were created before your BIOLIFE form; otherwise, calling Table1's open method might generate an access violation. The better method is not to open the table with source code at all. It's easier (and, I think, far more preferable) to open the table at design time than to do so via method calls in your source code. By opening the table at design time, you get to view your data while working on forms that reference it and you also get to avoid having to explicitly open the TTable in program source code. Basically, it's less work and more flexible.

Delete the Table1->Open() line from the form's OnCreate event and save the form. Next, load your data module into the C++Builder Form Designer and select its TTable component. Now, press F11 to bring up the Object Inspector and double-click on the Active property to open the TTable. Once you've done this, save your project.

You can run your app now, if you'd like, to see that it still works as expected. Once you've finished, close it to return to C++Builder.

Now that the data module is completed, let's save it to the Object Repository. You'll often find that storing a form you design, whether it's a data module or just a "regular" form, makes a lot of sense. By storing a form in the Object Repository, you can later inherit from it to create new forms or include it as is in other projects.

Right-click on the data module itself and select Add to Repository from the Context menu. Type dmBIOLIFE for the title and BIOLIFE data module form for the description. Select Data Modules in the Page drop-down list box and type your name into the Author entry box; then click OK. Figure 18.6 illustrates the Add To Repository dialog box.

Figure 18.6.

The completed Add To Repository dialog box.

on the right margin: **18**

> **NOTE**
>
>
>
> You can also select an icon to represent your data module in the Object Repository. As you add more data modules to the Repository, you'll probably find that assigning a unique bitmap to each one makes them easier to distinguish from one another. To choose a special icon for your new data module, click the Browse button in the Add To Repository dialog box.

If you haven't already saved your data module form, you'll next be asked whether you want to save the data module to disk before adding it to the Object Repository. If so, click Yes and enter a pathname for the file.

Now that you've added the dmBIOLIFE data module to the Object Repository, you'll be able to use it whenever an application needs access to the BIOLIFE table.

Creating a Master/Detail Form

NEW TERM A *master/detail* form usually browses at least two tables that are related to one another. It normally displays one table in one portion of the form and the other in a second portion. For example, you might browse the ORDERS table at the top of a master/detail form and its related LINEITEM table at the bottom. As each row in ORDERS is perused, the associated rows in LINEITEM will be displayed. You see this type of form quite often in real database applications.

The next item to cover today is the construction of a master/detail form. I'll show you how to build one for inclusion in your apps.

You'll also get acquainted with the TQuery component. The database forms you've built thus far have all been based on the TTable component. The master/detail form you're about to build will instead utilize the TQuery component.

Begin by starting the Database Form Wizard (choose Database | Form Wizard from the main menu). When the Form Wizard starts, click the Create a master/detail form and the Create a Form using TQuery objects radio buttons; then click Next.

In the Database Form Wizard's second dialog box, click on the Drive or Alias drop-down list and select the PDOXDEMO alias you defined earlier, then double-click on the CUSTOMER.DB table in the Table Name list. This will select the CUSTOMER table (a Paradox table) in the C++Builder demo data directory as your master/detail form's master table.

When you double-clicked on the CUSTOMER table, the Database Form Wizard automatically moved you to its next step. Now you're ready to select which fields from the CUSTOMER table to include on the form. Click the >> button to select all of them, and then click Next.

The next Database Form Wizard dialog box asks what layout you'd like to use for your master table's fields. Your choices are Horizontal, Vertical, and Grid. Click the Next button to accept the default (Horizontal).

Now that you've chosen your master table, you're ready to select the form's detail table. The alias you selected earlier for your master table is selected by default for you—you need only select a table. Double-click on the ORDERS table to select it as your form's detail table.

After you've selected a detail table, the Database Form Wizard asks which fields you'd like to include from it. Click the >> button to select them all; then click on the CustNo field in the Ordered Selected Fields list and click the < button to remove it from the list. Because the master table's CustNo field will be displayed in the form's top region, there's no reason to include it in the bottom region as well. Click the Next button to proceed.

TIP

> You can also select the order in which the fields will appear from this dialog box. You can drag-and-drop fields in the list to move them, or you can use the up- and down-arrow buttons beneath the Ordered Selected Fields list to move a single field one position at a time.

Figure 18.7 shows what the dialog box should look like before you click Next.

Figure 18.7.

Selecting all but the CustNo *field.*

As with the master table, the Database Form Wizard next prompts for the layout you'd like to use with your detail table's fields. The default is Grid. Click Next to accept the default and proceed.

Next, you're asked to select pairs of fields that will join your master and detail tables. When databases are designed intuitively, these fields will have the same names in both tables. In this particular case, you'll be joining your master and detail tables using their CustNo columns. Click the CustNo column in both lists, and then click Add. Figure 18.8 illustrates how the join definition should appear. When you've finished setting up the join, click Next to proceed.

Figure 18.8.

Joining your tables using the CustNo *column.*

The final dialog box of the Database Form Wizard allows you to choose whether to generate a main form and whether to also generate a data module. Click the Form and DataModule radio button; then click the Finish button. This will have the effect of making your new form the app's main form because the wizard generates a main form by default. Figure 18.9 shows your completed form in the C++Builder Form Designer.

Figure 18.9.

Your finished master/ detail form.

Before we execute your app to view the new form at runtime, let's study it a bit to see how it works. Understanding how the generated form works will help you build your own master/ detail forms.

You should have noticed two new forms when the Database Form Wizard finished. You should have a master/detail form and a data module form. Load the data module now in the visual designer, and then click its leftmost TQuery component. Press F11 to bring up the Object Inspector, and then double-click on the SQL property. You can click the Code Editor button to view the SQL in C++Builder's Code Editor. Figure 18.10 illustrates what you might see.

Figure 18.10.

Some SQL generated by the Database Form Wizard.

This SQL query retrieves all the columns and all the rows in the CUSTOMER.DB table. It names the columns individually, but because you selected them all in the Database Form Wizard, it's actually retrieving all the table's columns. Because the SQL doesn't have a WHERE clause to qualify it, it retrieves all the table's rows as well. Press Ctrl+F4 to close the Code Editor window when you're through viewing the SQL.

Now that you've viewed the SQL for the master table, let's have a look at the SQL generated for the detail table. Click the rightmost TQuery component and then double-click on its SQL property in the Object Inspector. You should see the following SQL:

```
Select
    ORDERS."OrderNo",
    ORDERS."SaleDate",
    ORDERS."ShipDate",
    ORDERS."EmpNo",
    ORDERS."ShipToContact",
    ORDERS."ShipToAddr1",
    ORDERS."ShipToAddr2",
    ORDERS."ShipToCity",
    ORDERS."ShipToState",
    ORDERS."ShipToZip",
    ORDERS."ShipToCountry",
    ORDERS."ShipToPhone",
    ORDERS."ShipVIA",
    ORDERS."PO",
    ORDERS."Terms",
    ORDERS."PaymentMethod",
    ORDERS."ItemsTotal",
    ORDERS."TaxRate",
    ORDERS."Freight",
    ORDERS."AmountPaid"
From "ORDERS.DB"
As ORDERS
Where
    "ORDERS"."CustNo" =:"CustNo"
```

18

The most remarkable thing about this SQL is its WHERE clause. It restricts the rows returned from the ORDERS table to just those whose CustNo column matches a variable named :CustNo. Where is :CustNo defined?

To find the answer to this question, return to the Object Inspector and check out the detail TQuery's DataSource property. You should see that it's set to the master TQuery's DataSource. What does this mean? This means that as the CustNo field changes in the master table (when the current row cursor moves, for example), the detail TQuery will be reexecuted and requalified by the new value. In this way, the two queries are automatically kept in sync by C++Builder. And the only rows that are visible in the detail table are those that correspond to the current row in the master table.

To check out how this works, run the app now. Figure 18.11 shows what you should see.

Figure 18.11.

Your master/detail form as it appears at runtime.

When you've finished viewing your new form, close it and return to C++Builder.

Reports

C++Builder provides a couple easy ways to construct reports. You can build them using the QuickReport components, which you can find on the QReport page of the C++Builder Component Palette. You can also construct reports using C++Builder's client/server report writer, ReportSmith. Today I'll take you through the process of building a report using the QuickReport components. Consult the C++Builder documentation for information on building reports with ReportSmith.

C++Builder includes a couple handy report templates that you can appropriate for your own use. You'll find them on the Forms page of the Object Repository. Select the New option on the C++Builder File menu, and then click the Forms page. Locate the QuickReport List form on the page and double-click on it. Figure 18.12 shows what you should see.

Select the File | Include Unit menu option, and then choose the unit containing the BIOLIFE data module that you built earlier today. This will make the TDataSource you defined on the data module available to the report.

Figure 18.12.

You can create a new report using C++Builder's report templates.

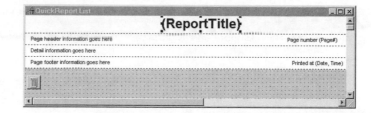

Figure 18.12.

You can create a new report using C++Builder's report templates.

Next, click the TQuickReport component on the report form; then press F11 to bring up the Object Inspector and set the component's DataSource property to the TDataSource on your BIOLIFE data module. Click on the ReportTitle property and set it to BIOLIFE.

Now that the TQuickReport component is set up, select the three placeholder TQRLabel components on the left side of the report form and delete them. (The text in each component ends with ...goes here.)

Next, drop four TQRDBText components onto the report's detail band (the middle one) and space them equally across the band. Select all four of them; then bring up the Object Inspector and set the TDataSource property they share to the TDataSource on your data module. Next, select just the first TQRDBText component and set its DataField property to the Species No field in the BIOLIFE table. Click the second TQRDBText and set its DataField property to the Category BIOLIFE field. Set the third TQRDBText field to reference the Common_Name field and the fourth to reference the Length_In field.

When all the fields are set up, drop TQRLabel components onto the form's PageHeader band (the top one) to correspond with each TQRDBText. These will serve as column headings, so set each control's Caption property to match the column under it in the report's detail band. You might also consider bolding or underlining the column headings to make them stand out. Figure 18.13 shows what your report might look like.

Figure 18.13.

Your report with columns and column headings in place.

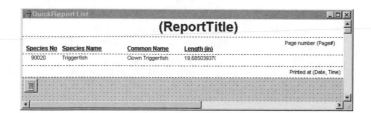

You've now finished the basic report we were building to list the BIOLIFE table. Now you're ready to link the report into your application so that it can be displayed and printed at runtime.

Load the BIOLIFE form you created yesterday into the Form Designer and select its top TPanel component. Locate the TButton component on the Standard page of the C++Builder Component Palette, and then drop one onto the right side of the your form's top TPanel control. Change the button's Caption to &Report, and then double-click it to set the button's OnClick event. Type the following code into the C++Builder Code Editor:

```
QRListForm->QuickReport->Preview();
```

Next, select the Include Unit option on the File menu and double-click on your report form's unit file to add it to the include list of your BIOLIFE form. This makes the QRListForm report form and its QuickReport component visible to your BIOLIFE form—it's what enables you to call the Preview() method.

Next, select Options from the Project menu and set your BIOLIFE form as the app's main form. This way, when you run the app, you'll see the BIOLIFE form first.

You're now ready to run the app and test your report. Press F9 to execute your application, and then click the Report button on the BIOLIFE form. Figure 18.14 shows what you might see.

Figure 18.14.

Your report as it might appear at runtime.

NOTE

Running a QuickReport report form that uses a TDataSource that's also in use by a form has the unfortunate side effect of scrolling the TDataSource as it places rows on the report. This means that the form will scroll with it. When the report finishes printing, you may not be at the same row you were when the report started. You can work around this via TTable's GetBookmark and GotoBookmark methods. See the C++Builder documentation for more information.

When you've finished viewing your report, close it and your application, and return to C++Builder.

Summary

In this chapter you have learned to use data modules in your data applications. You have also learned to define your own BDE aliases and make use of them in your apps. You have learned to build master/detail forms and to design simple reports using C++Builder's QuickReport components.

Workshop

The Workshop contains quiz questions to help you solidify your understanding of the material covered and exercises to provide you with experience in using what you have learned. You can find answers to the quiz questions in Appendix A, "Answers to Quiz Questions."

Q&A

Q What property is used to set up link queries in C++Builder?

A The DataSource property.

Q What facility within C++Builder can be used to define BDE aliases?

A The Database (or SQL) Explorer.

Q What are two ways C++Builder provides of constructing reports?

A Using the QuickReport components and using ReportSmith.

Q **What's the best way to create tables and other database objects for use by my applications?**

A The Database Desktop (included with C++Builder) is a stripped-down version of Borland's popular Paradox for Windows local DBMS. You'll find it well suited to creating tables, indexes, and related database elements.

Quiz

1. What property of the TDatabase component determines the name other components will use to refer to a given TDatabase?
2. What option on the File menu allows one unit to reference another?
3. Where are C++Builder's report form templates located?
4. What are some of the advantages of using data modules?

Exercises

1. Construct a BDE alias using the BDE Configuration program rather than the C++Builder Database Explorer.
2. Build a master/detail report using the C++Builder master/detail report template and the CUSTOMER and ORDERS tables you used today.

18

Day 19

Creating and Using DLLs

by Ken Henderson

If you use Windows, you can't escape DLLs. Just take a look in your \Windows and \Windows\System directories. I count more than 350 DLLs in those directories on my system. So, let's not debate the question. DLLs are a fact of everyday life in Windows.

The question, then, gets to be do *you* need to create and use DLLs? That's what you will find out today. Specifically, you will look at the following today:

- ☐ What DLLs are and why you should use them
- ☐ Calling functions and using classes in DLLs
- ☐ Writing DLLs
- ☐ Using resource DLLs

By the end of the day you will have a better idea of whether DLLs are for you. I suspect that you will see that DLLs can fit into your game plan somewhere along the line.

DLL Overview

DLLs are very useful critters. To shed more light on that subject, I will have to discuss the benefits of DLLs and how that translates to you, the C++Builder programmer. But before we get into that, let's talk about what exactly a DLL is.

What Is a Dynamic Link Library?

Simply put, a DLL (dynamic link library) is one or more pieces of code stored in a file with a .dll extension. The code in the DLL can be called from executable programs, but the DLL itself is not a standalone program. A DLL could be considered a helper file for a main program.

There are essentially two types of DLLs: code DLLs and resource DLLs. This is not an exclusive arrangement. You can have both code and resources in the same DLL, and there's no problem with that whatsoever. In some cases, though, it is convenient to store your code in one DLL and your resources in another. In just a bit I'll talk about *why* you might want to do that (it's in the section titled "Using Resources in DLLs").

Code contained in a DLL can be of two primary forms. The first form is a standalone function that you call from your main application. You have already done that several times up to this point in your journey through this book. "Huh? Whazzat?" Yes, it's true. Remember this code from Day 14, "Advanced Programming":

```
Screen->Cursors[myCursor] = LoadCursor(HInstance, "MYCURSOR");
```

Or how about this, also from Day 14:

```
DrawText(c.Handle, Panel->Text.c_str(),
  -1, temp, DT_CENTER | DT_VCENTER | DT_SINGLELINE);
```

Both LoadCursor() and DrawText() are Windows API functions. You probably knew that. But did you know that these functions are called from DLLs? When you think about it, those functions have to be stored somewhere. But where? In this case, both LoadCursor() and DrawText() are contained in the Windows DLL called User32.dll.

And what about all of those common dialog boxes we've been using? Things like the File Open dialog box, the Print dialog box, and the Printer Setup dialog box? They have to come from somewhere. In this case, those dialog boxes are stored as resources in the file called Comctl32.dll. So, without knowing it, you have been using DLLs all along.

The second form of code that can be contained in a DLL consists of C++ classes. Rather than accessing individual, standalone functions as I've discussed, you can create an instance of a class and call member functions of that class, all of which are contained in the DLL. I discuss this aspect of DLLs a little later on, in the section titled "Importing and Exporting Functions and Classes."

Using DLLs in this manner is one thing, but using and creating your own DLLs is another story entirely, right? Not really. Once you've got a DLL created, you can call functions from the DLL just like you do when calling Windows API functions. Creating DLLs is not too tough, so there's really nothing stopping you from putting DLLs to work for you.

Why Should I Use a DLL?

Ah, a good question. After all, what does a DLL give you over just putting all that stuff in your executable file? Using DLLs has these benefits:

- ☐ Effective code reuse
- ☐ The capability to easily share code among many applications
- ☐ The capability to compartmentalize code
- ☐ Internationalization of your application
- ☐ Effective use of Windows resources

Let's take a look at these selling points individually, and we'll see if I can convince you that DLLs are a good thing.

Effective Code Reuse

Code reuse is a big part of object-oriented programming. After all, why keep reinventing the wheel? DLLs can aid in code reuse in a very big way. For example, let's say you had a set of classes that you wrote to handle multimedia in your programs. The classes might include a base class that handles basic multimedia operations and derived classes that include specialized handling of wave files, MIDI files, CD audio, and AVI video. Sounds like you've put a lot of work into this! Now that you've gone to all that trouble, it would be nice if you could reuse all of that code in any of your applications that need it. DLLs allow you to do exactly that.

What you would do is compile all your classes into a DLL. Once that is done, all you have to do to use the class in any of your programs is #include the header file for the classes contained in the DLL and start creating class instances. (Actually, there are a couple of other steps required, but they are simple and I don't want to get ahead of myself, so I won't go into them right now.) What could be easier?

Now you have those classes at your fingertips any time you need them. Better yet, you can give the DLL to your best programming pal and he can use the classes, too. Hey, this is starting to sound pretty good! Better yet, you can *sell* the DLL to other programmers. Hey—you put all of that work into it, so you might as well get out of it what you can!

NOTE

> You can even create DLLs that can be called from applications written in Delphi, Borland C++, Visual Basic, Visual C++, or other programming environments. Of course it depends on the code contained in the DLL and how that code is called, but it can be done.

So do you see where this is heading? Once you've got a DLL written, you can use it whenever and wherever you want with ease. Getting at all the goodies contained in a DLL is just a few mouse clicks away.

Sharing Code Among Applications

Sharing code ties in with code reuse, but takes it a step further. Let's say that you are a programmer for a large corporation. You might have hundreds of users, each with his own system (we'll ignore networking considerations for this example). Let's say that you've written five different applications for those users. Further, let's assume that each of those five applications uses your multimedia classes (discussed earlier) and that the multimedia classes compile to 100KB of code (a modest figure). If you do not use a DLL, you will have 100KB of code repeated five times (once for each of the five applications) for a total of 500KB of code. That's code waste, folks.

A better approach is to put the multimedia classes in a DLL. Each of the five programs can use the same DLL when the multimedia stuff kicks in. That's part of the beauty of DLLs: Once the DLL is written, all of your applications can share it. Each of your users will get an additional 100KB DLL on his machine, *but* each of the five applications will be reduced in size by 100KB. The bottom line is that each user saves 400KB of disk space. Saving 400KB might not sound like a lot, but if you multiply it times hundreds of users, it starts to add up from a corporate perspective (bean counters tend to look at those types of things). And this is just a simple example. In a real-world situation, you could easily save several megabytes per user by using DLLs.

But what if three of the five programs are running simultaneously? No problem. Each program pulls code from the DLL as needed, and there are no conflicts. Windows keeps track of who's calling whom and that sort of thing. All you do is write the DLL and start using it.

Compartmentalizing Code

By keeping your code compartmentalized, you can deal with it more easily when it comes time to update your code. I am not advocating a separate DLL for each aspect of your program, but when and where it is sensible to break up your program into related chunks of code, you should do so. There is not much benefit in breaking an application into DLLs just for the sake of compartmentalizing the code. But if you have libraries of classes that you have written, it makes sense to keep those libraries in separate DLLs. Again, this is most obvious when creating libraries that can be used by any of your programs.

NOTE

As you develop a class or component, you should always be thinking about how you can reuse that object at some point in the future. In other words, plan ahead and design code for reuse from the beginning. Even if you feel that the code you are working on today will not likely be used again in the future, you should still write it with reuse in mind. You never know when you will need that same type of code at a later date. Once you are into the OOP mind-set, programming for reuse becomes second nature.

One advantage to this approach is that your applications can be more easily upgraded if necessary. Let's face it; even the best of programs goes to market with bugs. It's more a question of how many or how severe rather than a question of whether there are bugs at all. If you discover bugs in your DLL, you can fix the bug and ship just a new DLL to your users rather than having to recompile and ship an entire executable file. At first, this might not appear to have much benefit for the types of applications you have written up to this point. On the other hand, you may eventually write programs several megabytes in size with dozens of source modules. In these cases, compartmentalizing makes much more sense.

Internationalization

Just a few years ago you could write a program and not really worry too much about the international market. You would write the program and create menu items, dialog boxes, hint text, error messages, and so forth in your native language and that was that. You put the program on the market and didn't think about it after that.

Haven't you noticed? The world is getting smaller. With the explosion of the Internet and the World Wide Web, things are completely different than they were just a couple of years ago. You might create a demo of your program, or maybe a shareware version, and put it on the Net. Within hours, minutes even, people all around the world can have access to your

19

program. It's exciting and frightening all at the same time. This phenomenon means that you must plan ahead and prepare for translating your program into different languages.

One of the ways you can do that is to create resource DLLs that contain string resources in various languages. You can have a separate DLL for each language, or as an alternative you could have all of the string resources in a single DLL and load the correct language version of each string at runtime. At runtime, you can use the Windows API function LoadString() to load the strings and assign them to various components as needed.

NOTE
One of the disadvantages to the C++Builder programming model is that it does not use traditional resources as other programming environments do. Things like menus are not loaded as resources, but rather are contained within the form's resource. This makes internationalization more difficult and is one of the few times that this model works against you.

Again, planning ahead can save you a lot of work later on. If you plan your application with internationalization in mind, it can be much easier to translate your application into different languages when necessary.

Effective Use of Windows Resources

Today's systems are faster, have more RAM, and have more hard disk space. It's easy to fall into the mode of, "Hey, I'm only using 2MB of system RAM, so what's the big deal?" The truth is, you should always be conscious of how much of your users' system resources you are consuming. Here again, DLLs can help.

This is really a continuation of the discussion on sharing code among different applications. Let's go back to the example I used earlier. (Remember, you have five applications all using some common code.) If you do not use DLLs, then when several of your programs are running at the same time they all load some of the same code into memory. You are wasting system resources because each program loads its own copy of the exact same code. Rather than having each program load the exact same code, you can use a DLL and load the code just once. All of your applications can use the same code in memory and reduce the drain on the system.

Calling Functions and Using Classes in DLLs

In just a bit I'll talk about how to call functions contained in DLLs. But before you can use a function in a DLL, you first have to load the DLL into memory. Let's take a quick look at how you go about loading a DLL.

Loading DLLs

Loading DLLs can be accomplished in one of two ways. The first is via static loading and the second is via dynamic loading. Both methods have their advantages and disadvantages.

Static loading means that your DLL is automatically loaded when the application that calls the DLL is executed. Your DLL will have functions that it exports. The description of these functions is contained in a special file called an *import library file*. The import library file has the same filename as the DLL it represents and has a filename extension of .lib.

To use static loading, you link the .lib file for the DLL with your project during the link phase. In a C++Builder application, that means adding the .lib file to the project via the Project Manager. The DLL is loaded when the application loads, and you can call any functions exported from the DLL just as you would any other function. This is by far the easiest way to use code contained in a DLL. The disadvantage to this approach is that if a DLL that the program references is missing, the program will refuse to load.

Dynamic loading means that you specifically load the DLL when needed and unload it when you are done with it. This type of DLL loading has its advantages and disadvantages, too. One advantage is that the DLL is only in memory as long as you need it, so you are making more efficient use of memory. Another advantage is that your application will load more quickly when using dynamic loading because not all of the code needed to run the program is loaded when the application initially loads.

The primary disadvantage to using the dynamic loading approach is that it is a lot more work for you. First, you need to load the DLL with the Windows API function LoadLibrary(). Then, when you are done with the DLL, you unload it with FreeLibrary(). Further (and this is where the work comes in) you need to use the GetProcAddress() function to obtain a pointer to the function you want to call. To say that this approach can be a tad confusing would be an understatement. To illustrate, let's look at calling functions from DLLs.

19

Calling Functions Located in DLLs

The method you use to call a function in a DLL depends on whether the DLL was statically or dynamically loaded. Calling functions from DLLs that are dynamically loaded is not a lot of fun. It requires that you set up a pointer to the function in the DLL, and pointers to functions can be confusing. For example, let's say you had a function in a DLL called SayHello(). It would look like this in the DLL's source code:

```
void _export __stdcall SayHello(HWND hWnd)
{
  MessageBox(hWnd, "Hello There!!",
    "Message From a DLL", MB_OK);
}
```

To call this function from your program, you first have to declare the function pointer:

```
void (__stdcall *SayHello)(HWND);
```

Now that you've done that, you can load the DLL, use GetProcAddress() to get a pointer to the function, call the function, and, finally, unload the DLL. It goes like this:

```
// load the DLL
HINSTANCE dllInstance = LoadLibrary("mystuff.dll");
// get the address of the function
SayHello = (void(__stdcall*)(HWND))
    GetProcAddress(dllInstance, "_SayHello");
// call the function
SayHello(Application->Handle);
// unload the DLL
FreeLibrary(dllInstance);
```

Man, that's *ugly*, isn't it? Function pointers are one of the most confusing aspects of C++ when you look at it from a syntax standpoint. Still, when you need to load a DLL at runtime, that's the way you have to do it. I should add that this code is pared down a bit. You would almost always add some error-checking code to be sure that the DLL loaded correctly and that GetProcAddress() returned a good address. As you can see, you probably won't use dynamic loading of DLLs unless you absolutely have to.

Calling functions from DLLs that are statically loaded is a breeze. First, you must have a function declaration for the function. After that, you call the function like any other function:

```
extern "C" __import void SayHello(HWND);
// later on...
SayHello(Application->Handle);
```

Unless you really need the flexibility that dynamic loading provides, you will almost always opt for static loading.

19

Some third-party tools and libraries come in the form of DLLs. To use these tools or libraries, you place the DLL or DLLs that contain the libraries in your application's directory. Then in your source code you will use the `#include` directive to include the headers that come with the library. Each library should come with complete instructions on how to implement it.

Creating a DLL

Creating a DLL is not particularly difficult. There are a couple of things to be aware of, but most of it is just straight C++ programming. From the earlier discussion you can see that static loading is probably the method you will use most often. For DLLs that are statically loaded, you will have four or more files:

- [ ] One or more source code files. These files do not need to be distributed with the DLL.
- [ ] One or more header files. This header will contain the declarations or classes that can be called from the DLL.
- [ ] The import library file. This file allows the linker to resolve calls in the application with addresses in the DLL.
- [ ] The DLL itself.

Of these files, the header (`.h`), import library (`.lib`), and final dynamic link library (`.dll`) must be shipped with the DLL.

NOTE

You don't need an import library for DLLs that you load with `LoadLibrary()`.

NOTE

If you are an experienced DLL user, you might be surprised to find out that C++Builder does not support module definition files (DEF files). Use an import library and specifically export any functions you need from the DLL.

19

Let's start with a discussion on the basics of creating DLLs. After that, we'll put together a DLL.

Importing and Exporting Functions and Classes

Functions in a DLL fall into three basic categories:

☐ Functions that are called from within the DLL

☐ Functions that can be called from outside the DLL

☐ Functions that are members of a class contained in the DLL

Functions that are called within a DLL require no special handling. You declare this type of function just like you do any function. The function can be called by other functions within the DLL, but it cannot be called from outside the DLL. In other words, a calling application will not have access to these functions. These functions could be considered to be private to the DLL, much as private class member functions are private to the class in which they reside. In effect, your application won't be able to "see" the functions to even know they exist.

NOTE　　Attempting to use a function in a DLL that is private to the DLL may or may not result in a compiler error but will always result in a linker error. The linker error will say something like `Unresolved external 'MyFunction()' referenced from module unit1.cpp`.

NOTE　　In addition to functions, a DLL may contain global data that all functions in the DLL can access. In 16-bit Windows, global data in a DLL is shared among all instances of the DLL. In other words, if one program changed the global variable x to 100, x would have the value 100 for all other applications calling the DLL as well. In 32-bit Windows this is not the case. In Win32, a separate copy of a DLL's global data is created for each process that loads the DLL.

Exporting Functions and Classes

Another class of functions is those that can be referenced from outside the DLL. These are functions that are made public by *exporting* them from the DLL. These functions can be called by other functions in the DLL, or they can be called by applications outside the DLL.

NOTE

Functions in a DLL can be called by executable applications and also by other DLLs. In other words, one DLL can call functions in another DLL.

Once a function has been exported, you can call it from your application. To export a function, you use the __export keyword when you build the DLL. The DLL source code for a simple function contained in a DLL might look like this:

```
void __export SayHello(HWND hWnd)
{
  MessageBox(hWnd, "Hello from a DLL!",
    "DLL Message Box", MB_OK | MB_ICONEXCLAMATION);
}
```

This function is now exported and can be called from any application.

Exporting a class works in essentially the same way, except that the __export modifier is placed in the class declaration. The class declaration for an exported class looks something like this:

```
class __export MyClass {
  public:
    MyClass(HWND hwnd);
    void SaySomething(char* text);
    void Beep();
  private:
    HWND hWnd;
};
```

Notice that the __export modifier is placed between the class keyword and the class name.

TIP

If you are having trouble with exporting functions or classes, you can run the TDUMP utility on the DLL. The information produced by TDUMP will have a section on symbols that are exported from the DLL. By examining that section of the output from TDUMP, you can get a better idea of where the problem lies.

Importing Functions and Classes

Exporting a function is only half the story. When you build the application that calls the function, you must *import* the functions you want to call from the DLL. As you might guess, importing a function is done with the __import modifier.

The __import and __export keywords both have double leading underscores preceding the keywords. This practice is commonly used by compiler vendors to distinguish a compiler-specific keyword from a C++ language keyword.

To import a function contained in a DLL, you use the __import modifier in the function declaration. For example, given the SayHello() function shown earlier, part of the calling application would look like this:

```
extern "C" void __import SayHello(HWND hWnd);
//
// later on...
//
SayHello(Handle);
```

The __import modifier tells the compiler that the function being declared can be referenced in an import library file. The actual function call looks no different than any other function call.

This code marks the second time you have seen the extern "C" statement. extern "C" is used to prevent name mangling of the function name. Any time you use a standalone function in a DLL, you should use the extern "C" modifier. This will allow the function to be imported by any calling application, including those compiled with compilers other than Borland compilers.

Importing classes works exactly the same way. Before you use a class that lives in a DLL, you must first declare it with the __import modifier:

```
class __import MyClass {
  public:
    MyClass(HWND hwnd);
    void SaySomething(char* text);
    void Beep();
  private:
    HWND hWnd;
};
```

Now you may create an instance of this class and access any of its public functions or data members as needed:

```
MyClass Billy(Handle);
Billy.SaySomething("Hi, there!");
Billy.Beep();
```

The trick in writing and using DLLs, then, is in getting the imports and exports right. After that, there's nothing to it.

Forget All That

Forget everything I just told you about __import and __export. Okay, so I'm being a little facetious. The __import and __export modifiers are a big part of writing and using DLLs, and you need to understand how they are used. But C++Builder applications have a new method of importing and exporting classes and functions. Rather than using __import and __export in your C++Builder applications, it is a better idea to use the __declspec() keyword.

This keyword gives you more flexibility in where you place the import and export modifiers. Previously you had to be sure that you placed the __import or __export modifier in exactly the correct place in the function definition or compiler errors would result. Using the __declspec() keyword, you can place the modifier anywhere you like in the function declaration (within reason, of course). For instance, the following two lines are both legal:

```
__declspec(dllexport) void SaySomething(HWND hWnd);
void __declspec(dllexport) SaySomething(HWND hWnd);
```

If you were using __export, you would have to make sure that you placed the __export keyword between the return type and the function name. By using __declspec() you don't have to worry about it.

 TIP

> The __declspec() keyword, as with __import and __export, has two underscores preceding it. Because __declspec() is a keyword, it will be highlighted in bold when typed correctly. This is a trait of the C++Builder Code Editor's syntax highlighting feature. If you only use a single underscore, the keyword will not be bold. You can use syntax highlighting to confirm that you have typed a keyword correctly.

You will notice from the preceding example that __declspec() takes a single parameter. To export a function, use __declspec(dllexport); to import a function, use __declspec(dllimport). That's all there is to it. (Don't think that I led you down the wrong path earlier; understanding the __import and __export modifiers is a good thing to know. It is a good thing to know because at some point in your programming journey you might wind up programming with a compiler other than C++Builder and might have to use __import and __export with that compiler.)

19

The Secret of DLL Headers

You might have picked up on a potential problem in the previous discussion. If you are required to export a function or class when building the DLL and you must import the function or class when building the .exe, you will have to have two separate headers: one with all exported functions using the __export modifier and one with all exported functions using the __import modifier. Right? Actually, no. You can put macros to use so that you need only one header.

The header for just about every DLL will contain something like this:

```
#if defined(BUILD_DLL)
#   define DLL_EXP __declspec(dllexport)
#else
# if defined(BUILD_APP)
#   define DLL_EXP __declspec(dllimport)
# else
#   define DLL_EXP
# endif
#endif

extern "C" void DLL_EXP SayHello(HWND);

class DLL_EXP MyClass {
  public:
    MyClass(HWND hwnd);
    void SaySomething(char* text);
    void Beep();
  private:
    HWND hWnd;
};
```

The group of pre-processor directives at the top of the header works like this: If the symbol BUILD_DLL is defined, the DLL_EXP symbol will expand to the text __declspec(dllexport). If BUILD_APP is defined, the DLL_EXP symbol will expand to __declspec(dllimport).

So what does that mean? It means that you can use a single header whether you are building the DLL or the calling application. When you build the DLL, you will do this:

```
#define BUILD_DLL
#include "mydll.h"
```

In this case, all the classes and functions that use DLL_EXP will be exported. On the other hand, when you build the application you will use this code:

```
#define BUILD_APP
#include "mydll.h"
```

Here DLL_EXP expands to __declspec(dllimport), and all functions and classes that use the DLL_EXP symbol will be imported. This allows you to use just one header for building both the application that calls the DLL and the DLL itself.

Creating a DLL with the Object Repository

Creating a DLL in C++Builder is accomplished through the Object Repository. Choose File | New from the main menu to display the Object Repository. Next, click on the DLL icon to create a new DLL and click OK. The Code Editor is displayed and the file in the edit window looks like this:

```
 1: //----------------------------------------------------------------
 2: #include <vcl\vcl.h>
 3: #pragma hdrstop
 4: //----------------------------------------------------------------
 5: //    Important note about DLL memory management: ShareMem must be the
 6: //    first include file in your library and in your project (select:
 7: //    View / Project Source) if your DLL exports any functions that pass
 8: //    String objects as parameters or function results. This applies to all
 9: //    String objects passed to and from your DLL--even those that
10: //    are nested in records and classes. ShareMem is the interface unit to
11: //    the DELPHIMM.DLL shared memory manager, which must be deployed along
12: //    with your DLL. To avoid using DELPHIMM.DLL, pass string information
13: //    using PChar or ShortString parameters.
14: //----------------------------------------------------------------
15: USERES("Project1.res");
16: //----------------------------------------------------------------
17: int WINAPI DllEntryPoint(HINSTANCE hinst, unsigned long reason, void*)
18: {
19:     return 1;
20: }
21: //----------------------------------------------------------------
```

First let's talk about the comments on lines 5 through 13. This message is telling you that if your DLL has exported functions that take an instance of the String class as a parameter, you must do the following:

☐ Add a line to the source of both the DLL and the .exe that calls the DLL to #include the ShareMem.hpp header. Be sure that this #include comes before other includes in the file.

☐ Ship the Delphimm.dll file with your DLL.

To avoid this requirement, just be sure your DLL functions don't have any String instances as parameters. For instance, rather than using this:

```
MyFunction(String& s)
{
}
```

use this:

```
MyFunction(char* buff)
{
}
```

19

This odd situation is easy enough to work around, so you should never have the need for Delphimm.dll. You just need to be aware of the restrictions placed on using the String class in DLL functions. Note that you can use String objects within the DLL itself without the need for Delphimm.dll. This applies only to exported functions that pass a String object, whether as a parameter or as the return value.

Now look at line 2. Notice that #include <vcl/vcl.h> is automatically added for you. This is for your convenience; it is not a requirement. If your DLL contains only your own code (no VCL classes or forms), you should remove this #include. This also applies to the code on line 15. If you are not using VCL forms in your DLL, you can remove this line. (I'll talk about VCL forms in DLLs in just a bit.)

Finally, notice the DllEntryPoint() function. This function is the entry point into the DLL. This function will be called when the DLL is initially loaded. It will also be called when another process (program or DLL) references the DLL. Further, it will be called whenever a process detaches itself from the DLL and, ultimately, when the DLL is unloaded. You might need to account for all of that, but most of the time you don't have to worry about it. If you do need to keep track of those things, you can use the reason parameter to determine what is going on with your DLL. Most of the time you can just leave the default DllEntryPoint() function as is.

NOTE

The DllEntryPoint() function's first parameter is hinst. This is the instance handle (HINSTANCE) of the DLL. If you have any functions that require the instance handle of the DLL (such as LoadIcon() or LoadCursor()), you can use the hinst parameter to create a global variable. You can then access the global variable any time the instance handle to the DLL is required. (Using the instance handle is discussed later in the chapter, in the section titled "Using Resources in DLLs.")

Now that you have the Code Editor displaying the DLL's source code unit, all you have to do is start adding code. Be sure to use a header file for the DLL and follow the techniques I've mentioned for any exported functions or classes. Write any standalone functions or classes that you need in your DLL. When you are done, you can choose Run | Build All or Run | Make to compile and build the DLL.

Let's take this one step at a time so that it makes more sense:

1. Choose File | New from the main menu. When the Object Repository is displayed, double-click on the DLL icon to create a new DLL project. A new, blank DLL project is created for you.

2. In the Code Editor, change the line that reads `#include <vcl\vcl.h>` to read

   `#include <windows.h>`

   (We won't be using VCL classes in this DLL, but we will need the `Windows.h` file.)

3. Delete all the comment lines about `ShareMem.h` and `Delphimm.dll`.

4. Add these two lines just above the `DllEntryPoint()` function:
   ```
   #define BUILD_DLL
   #include "MyDll.h";
   ```

5. Add the code below the `DllEntryPoint()` function until your code matches Listing 19.1. (The `DllEntryPoint()` function and the text above it will already be in the Code Editor window.)

6. Save the project with the filename `MyDll`.

Listing 19.1. `StaticLd.cpp`.

```cpp
//----------------------------------------------------------
#include <windows.h>
#pragma hdrstop

#define BUILD_DLL
#include "StaticLd.h"

int WINAPI DllEntryPoint(HINSTANCE, unsigned long, void*)
{
  return 1;
}
//----------------------------------------------------------
void DLL_EXP SayHello(HWND hWnd)
{
  MessageBox(hWnd, "Hello from a DLL!",
    "DLL Message Box", MB_OK | MB_ICONEXCLAMATION);
}

MyClass::MyClass(HWND hwnd)
{
  hWnd = hwnd;
}

void MyClass::SaySomething(char* text)
{
  MessageBox(hWnd, text,
    "A Text Message From a DLL Class", MB_OK);
}

void
MyClass::Beep()
{
  MessageBeep(-1);
}
```

19

This file is called StaticLd.cpp because the DLL produced by this code will be loaded at runtime using static loading. The CD-ROM accompanying the book contains a sample program called CallDll.mak that calls functions in a DLL using static linking and also calls functions in a different DLL using dynamic loading. The filenames are meant to be as descriptive as possible while still complying within the standard 8-character rule. Remember that you can use long filenames with your own programs and DLLs, but I use the 8.3 convention in this book for reasons related to electronic publishing.

Now we have to create the header file for the DLL. Here goes:

1. Choose File | New from the main menu. When the Object Repository comes up, choose Text to create a new text file and click OK. The new text file is displayed in the Code Editor.

2. Choose File | Save from the main menu. Save the file as StaticLd.h. (We save the file first because that way the syntax highlighting works. Syntax highlighting does not work for a file with a .txt extension.)

3. Enter the code from Listing 19.2.

4. Choose File | Save All from the main menu.

Listing 19.2. StaticLd.h.

```
#ifndef _STATICLD_H
#define _STATICLD_H

#if defined(BUILD_DLL)
#  define DLL_EXP __declspec(dllexport)
#else
# if defined(BUILD_APP)
#  define DLL_EXP __declspec(dllimport)
# else
#  define DLL_EXP
# endif
#endif

extern "C" void DLL_EXP SayHello(HWND);

class DLL_EXP MyClass {
  public:
    MyClass(HWND hwnd);
    void SaySomething(char* text);
    void Beep();
  private:
    HWND hWnd;
};

#endif
```

Now that you've entered the source code and the header, you can build the project. Choose Project | Build All from the main menu to build the project.

NOTE

A function in a DLL does not need a function declaration to compile successfully. If you find that a function does not appear to be exported, check to be sure that you have not forgotten to include it in the DLL's header file.

Creating an Import Library File

Now that you have the DLL compiled, you need to create an import library for the DLL (unless you want to use dynamic loading). An import library is a file that contains a list of the functions that are exported from the DLL. The linker needs the import library file to resolve function references in the source code with actual addresses in the compiled code. To create an import library, you will have to use the command-line tool, IMPLIB. Do this:

1. In Windows, open an MS-DOS prompt window.
2. Switch to the directory where your DLL resides.
3. Type the following at the command line and press Enter:

```
\CBuilder\bin\implib MyDll.lib MyDll.dll
```

   (Be sure to type the exact path where C++Builder resides.)

That's it! You now have a DLL, a header, and an import library. Sounds like you're ready to create the calling application.

19

NOTE

If you are coming from a programming environment like Borland C++, you may find the requirement to build the import library manually a little cumbersome. Look for improvements in this area in future versions of C++Builder.

TIP

You can configure your Tools menu to run IMPLIB if you like. Refer to Day 12, "C++Builder Tools and Options," for more information on configuring the Tools menu.

NOTE

As of this writing, there is a problem with the $NAME macro, which can be used in configuring tools. The problem makes it impossible to configure IMPLIB to be called from the Tools menu. For that reason, I have written a simple console application that executes IMPLIB and creates a .lib file for the current DLL project. You can add this tool to your Tools menu to make creating a .lib file more convenient.

The program is called MakeLib.exe and can be found on the CD-ROM accompanying this book. To add MakeLib to your Tools menu, do the following:

1. Copy MakeLib.exe from the CD-ROM to your \CBuilder\bin directory.

2. Choose Tools | Configure Tools from the main menu.

3. Click the Add button to add a new tool.

4. Enter the information as shown in Figure 19.1. Be sure you enter the drive and directory where you have C++Builder installed.

5. Click OK to close the Tool Properties dialog box and then click the Close button to close the Configure Tools dialog box.

Figure 19.1.

*The tool
properties for*
MakeLib.exe.

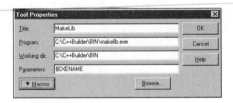

Now you can choose Tools | MakeLib from the main directory and, provided you have a DLL project open, a .lib file will be created for your DLL in the project's directory.

Creating the Calling Application

Okay, you've now got a working (we hope) DLL. A DLL doesn't do much good without an application to call it, so let's get to work creating the application. Creating an application that uses a DLL requires only two steps in addition to the regular things you do when you create an application (assuming dynamic loading):

☐ Add the #include for the DLL's header file.

☐ Add the DLL's import library file to the project.

As I've said, once you have the header created properly, the rest is easy. To prove it, let's create a program that uses our DLL:

1. Create a new application.

2. Place a button on the form and change the button's Caption property to Say Hello.

3. Double-click the button to display the OnClick handler for the button. Type the following at the cursor:

   ```
   SayHello(Handle);
   ```

4. Place another button on the form. Make the Caption of this button MyClass Test. Double-click the button and type the following code at the cursor:

   ```
   MyClass mc(Application->Handle);
   mc.SaySomething("Uh... Hello, there.);
   mc.Beep();
   ```

   This will allow us to test the class that we exported from the DLL.

5. Save the unit as CDMain.cpp and the project as CallDll.mak.

Okay, now the calling app is nearly written. Before the file will compile, however, we need to add the #include for the DLL's header.

Adding the #include for the DLL's Header

Adding the #include for the DLL's header is simple:

1. Move to the top of the file and place the following lines just below the line that reads #pragma hdrstop:

   ```
   #define BUILD_APP
   #include "MyDll.h"
   ```

2. Save the project.

There! That was easy. That's all we have to do in the calling app. One more step and we'll be done.

NOTE

> You might have several headers for a single DLL. For example, if your DLL exports five different classes, you might have five headers, one for each class. Just be sure that you add all the needed headers. If you forget one, don't worry—the compiler will remind you.

You will have to #include the header in each of your units that uses functions or classes from the DLL. Now let's add the import library file to the project.

Adding the Import Library File

You can add the import library for the DLL to the project in one of several ways. Without question, the easiest way is through the Project Manager:

1. Choose View | Project Manager from the main menu.
2. Click the Add Unit button or choose Add File from the Project Manager speed menu.
3. When the Add to Project dialog box comes up, choose the MyDll.lib file and click OK.
4. The library file will be displayed in the Project Manager window.

That wasn't too difficult, either. As you can see, using DLLs is not very complicated once you get the rules down.

You can also add the library file directly to the project source file. If you view the project source after adding the .lib file (View | Project Source), you will see a line that looks like this:

```
USELIB("MyDll.lib");
```

When you added the .lib file through the Project Manager, C++Builder automatically added this line to the project source. If you want, you can add a line similar to this on your own rather than going through the Project Manager. Going through the Project Manager is easier than doing it yourself, though—plus, it has the added benefit of allowing you to choose the file rather than depending on your memory to get the filename typed correctly.

Finally, you can add the .lib file directly into the project makefile. There really isn't any reason for you to do this, but you certainly can if you want to. If you look at the project makefile (View | Project Makefile), you will see a line that looks something like this:

```
LIBFILES =
```

Just add the name of the import library to the end of this line:

```
LIBFILES = mydll.lib
```

As I said, the easiest way is to add the .lib file through the Project Manager.

Now you are ready to compile and run the program. Click the Run button and test the program. When you click the buttons, the functions contained in the DLL are executed.

Using Forms in DLLs

You can place forms in a DLL just as you can place code in one. There really isn't a lot of difference in the way the form is created as compared to the way a form in an application is created. To begin, you create a new DLL through the Object Repository just as you did before. When the project is displayed, create a new form by clicking the New Form button or by going through the Object Repository. Add components to the form and write code for the form's source unit just as you would when creating a form in an application.

There are essentially two types of applications from which you might call the form contained in the DLL:

- ☐ C++Builder applications
- ☐ Non-C++Builder applications

These two situations must be handled differently. First, let's take a look at the easy route: calling a form in a DLL from a C++Builder application.

Calling a Form in a DLL from a C++Builder Application

If you want to call forms contained in a DLL, you need to make sure the form's class is exported from the DLL. To do that, you have to implement the technique described earlier for exporting classes (in the section titled "Exporting Functions and Classes"). Specifically, you will have to add macros that either export or import the form's class based on whether you are building the DLL or the calling application. This means manually editing both the form's header and the form's source unit.

Writing the DLL and the DLL Header

First, you need to add the macros for importing or exporting the class. Open the header for the form and add code similar to the following before the class declaration (I say *similar to* because you could use any identifier you want where I have DLL_EXP here):

```
#if defined(BUILD_DLL)
#  define DLL_EXP __declspec(dllexport)
#else
# if defined(BUILD_APP)
#  define DLL_EXP __declspec(dllimport)
# else
#  define DLL_EXP
# endif
#endif
```

NOTE   The symbol name used in the preceding code is DLL_EXP. I borrowed this name from a sample program that ships with Borland C++. The symbol name can be anything you want. For instance, you might find the name BUILD_TYPE more descriptive. Use any name you are comfortable with.

Now you need to add the macro name to the form's class declaration. The class declaration begins with this line:

```
class TMyForm : public TForm
```

Place the macro name between the `class` keyword and the name of the form:

```
class DLL_EXP TMyForm : public TForm
```

Now that the header is done, switch to the form's source unit. Locate the line that `#includes` the unit's header and add this line above it:

```
#define BUILD_DLL
```

Now that section will look something like this:

```
#define BUILD_DLL
#include "MyForm.h"
```

You now have a form class that will be exported from the DLL. You can now build the DLL. Be sure that you create an import library file when you are done building the DLL.

NOTE

> You don't have to export the form's class if you don't want to. You could use the technique used when calling a form from a non-C++Builder app if you like (I'll discuss this in the section titled "Calling a Form from a Non-C++Builder Application"). In that case, though, you would pass the form's `this` pointer to the DLL function that creates and displays the form. That way the form in the DLL is properly parented to the main form in the calling application.

Writing the Calling Application

In your calling application, you will have to perform the same two steps that you performed earlier plus a third step:

1. Add the `#include` for the DLL's header file.
2. Add the DLL's import library file to the project.
3. Create the form before showing it.

The steps to `#include` the form's header and add the `.lib` file to the project are identical to those outlined earlier. Just be sure that you add the `#define BUILD_APP` prior to the line that `#includes` the form's header. After that, add the `.lib` file to the project.

On Day 10, "More on Projects," I discussed the auto-creation of forms. Because a form in a DLL is not part of the calling application's project, the form cannot be auto-created by the program when the program loads. You will have to explicitly create the form before displaying it. I've discussed this already, but not in this context, so let's go over it again. The code to display and execute the form looks like this:

```
TMyForm* form = new TMyForm(this);
form->ShowModal();
delete form;   // optional
```

Aside from the fact that you need to create the form before displaying it, there is no difference between a form in the application's file and a form in a DLL from the perspective of the calling application.

 NOTE

The preceding code snippet deletes the form's pointer after the form returns. This is not required, but you may delete the form's pointer to free up memory if you want. If you do not delete the form, the calling form will delete it when the calling form itself is deleted (usually when the application terminates). When you specified this in the form's constructor, you made the form a child of the main form, and VCL parent objects take care of deleting their child objects.

Calling a Form from a Non-C++Builder Application

If you want to call a form from a non-C++Builder application, you will have to do a little more work. Because the calling app knows nothing about VCL, you can't import a VCL class and call its ShowModal() method as you did when calling the form from a C++Builder application. What you have to do is create a standalone function in the DLL that is called by the calling application. This function can be called from any program if you specify extern "C" when declaring the function. Within the function body you can then create and execute the form.

You create the form in the DLL as described earlier except that you do not have to export the form's class. Instead, create a function in the main form's source unit that looks like this:

```
void ShowForm()
{
  TMyForm* form = new TMyForm(0);
  form->ShowModal();
  delete form;   // must do this
}
```

19

Notice that NULL is passed for the parent of the form. This has to be done because the non-C++Builder application does not have a VCL object that can be passed as the parent of the form. You need to delete the TMyForm object in this case because the form is not parented to a VCL object.

Next you have to create a separate header for the DLL. Remember that the form's class is not going to be exported, so the form's header is meaningless to the calling application. All the calling application wants to see is a header that contains the ShowForm() function. Create a header that includes a declaration for the ShowForm() function and then #include it in the calling application's source file. (Be sure to write the macro to ensure proper importing and exporting of the function.) As before, you will have to link the .lib file for the DLL to the calling application when you build the calling application. You can also use runtime loading if you prefer. Which method you use depends on your preference and the language in which the calling application is written.

Using Resources in DLLs

Sometimes it's convenient to have resources contained in a DLL. I've already mentioned internationalization and how a DLL can be used to make your program more easily ported to languages other than the one for which it was designed. For example, let's say you had an instructions screen for your application and that those instructions were contained in five strings in a DLL. The strings might be named IDS_INSTRUCTION1, IDS_INSTRUCTION2, and so on. You could load and display the strings like this:

```
char buff[256];
LoadString(dllInstance, IDS_INSTRUCTION1, buff, sizeof(buff));
InstructionLabel1->Caption = buff;
```

The first parameter of the LoadString() function contains the instance handle (HINSTANCE) of the module where the strings can be found. You could have DLLs created in several different languages and just load the DLL in the appropriate language based on a user selection. The code might look something like this:

```
String dllName;
witch (language) {
  case french : dllName = "french.dll"; break;
  case german : dllName = "german.dll"; break;
  case spanish : dllName = "spanish.dll"; break;
  case english : dllName = "english.dll"; break;
}
dllInstance = LoadLibrary(dllName.c_str());
```

You only have to load the correct DLL; the rest of the code remains the same. This is just one example of using resources contained in a DLL. You might find many uses for this technique.

Creating a Resource DLL

You can create a DLL that contains only resources, or you can mix code and resources in the same DLL. There are no restrictions on DLLs in this regard.

NOTE

> If your DLL contains only resources, you should remove the following lines from the default DLL project source unit:
>
> ```
> #include <vcl/vcl.h>
> #pragma hdrstop
>
> USERES("MyDLL.res");
> ```
>
> You may also be able to delete the DllEntryPoint() function from the DLL depending on whether you are loading statically or dynamically (more on that later). You will have to #include the Windows.h file if you remove the #include for vcl.h.

Placing resources in a DLL is essentially the same as adding resources to an application. From the Project Manager, click the Add Unit button and add the name of a resource script (.rc) or binary resource file (.res) where the resources can be found. When you build the DLL, the resources will be bound to the DLL.

You may have to perform one other step if you are loading a resource statically (at load time). As you can see from the preceding code snippet, you must have the instance handle of the DLL before you can access resources contained in the DLL. When you load the DLL dynamically, this step is easy because LoadLibrary() returns the instance handle:

```
int dllInstance = LoadLibrary("resource.dll");
```

Now you can use the instance handle wherever required. In this case, using dynamic loading is actually easier. When using static loading, you need to have some way of obtaining the instance handle of the DLL (remember, the DLL will be loaded when the application starts). To prepare for dynamic loading, you have to perform these steps when building the DLL:

1. Declare a global variable in the DLL that will hold the instance handle.
2. Assign the DLL's instance handle to the global variable in the DllEntryPoint() function.
3. Write a function to return the instance handle to the calling application.

Rather than walking you through this step by step, let me just show you the complete source code for a DLL that uses this technique. (See Listing 19.3.)

19

Listing 19.3. `Resource.cpp.`

```
 1: //----------------------------------------------------------
 2: #include <windows.h>
 3: #pragma hdrstop
 4:
 5: #define BUILD_DLL
 6: #include "resource.h"
 7:
 8: HINSTANCE hInstance;
 9:
10: //----------------------------------------------------------
11: int WINAPI DllEntryPoint(HINSTANCE hinst, unsigned long, void*)
12: {
13:   hInstance = hinst;
14:   return 1;
15: }
16: //----------------------------------------------------------
17:
18: HINSTANCE GetDllInstance()
19: {
20:   return hInstance;
21: }
```

As you can see, I have removed much of what the default C++Builder DLL source code file initially contains when the DLL is created from the Object Repository. Notice that on lines 5 and 6 I #include the header file for the DLL. The header will only contain the declaration for one function in this case. Following that, line 8 declares a global variable called hInstance. Line 13 assigns the instance handle passed in the DllEntryPoint() function to the global variable.

NOTE

> The instance handle of the DLL is created by Windows and passed to the DllEntryPoint() function when the DLL is loaded.

Finally, lines 18 through 21 contain the function, called GetDllInstance(), that returns the DLL instance to the calling application. This function can be used in the calling application any time the instance handle of the DLL is required:

```
LoadString(
  GetDllInstance(), IDS_TEXT, buff, sizeof(buff));
```

The cast from HINSTANCE (which the DLL returns) to an int is required because VCL and Windows handle the HINSTANCE type differently.

Remember to create a static library for your DLL if you are using static loading. If you are not using static loading, it is not necessary to create a .lib for the DLL.

Implementing Resources in DLLs

Actually, there's not much left to say. I've pretty much covered how to use resources contained in a DLL through the discussion on creating resource DLLs. To review, though, you know that you can load resource DLLs either statically or dynamically. If you load statically, you will have to use an exported function to get the instance handle of the DLL to get at the resources. If you load dynamically, you can get the instance handle from the LoadLibrary() function. Don't forget to call FreeLibrary() when you are done with the DLL or before your application closes.

In the case of resource DLLs, dynamic loading is actually easier than static loading because you don't have to write any code in the DLL if you don't want to. It's also easier because you don't have to create an import library for the DLL. Just use LoadLibrary() and go to it.

NOTE

Using dynamic loading has the added advantage of allowing your application to load faster. In many cases you load the resource DLL only when it's needed and unload it when it is no longer needed. This results in your application using less memory than when the resources are contained in the executable file. The downside to static loading is that your users might see a slight pause when the resource DLL loads. Try to anticipate as much as possible and load the resource DLL when it is least likely to be noticed.

When using static loading, you need to remember to add the .lib file to the project of the calling application and also to #include the header for the DLL. The advantage of static loading is that you don't have to worry about LoadLibrary()/FreeLibrary(). The disadvantage is that it's a little more work to set up initially. Also, your program takes longer to load and uses more memory when you use static loading.

Remember JumpingJack from Day 9, "Creating Applications in C++Builder"? The CD-ROM accompanying the book has a version of JumpingJack that loads the bitmap, sound, and string resources from a DLL. Check out that program for an example on using resources in a DLL.

Summary

Using dynamic link libraries is not terribly difficult, but it can be frustrating until you get the combination of export and import correct. This is made easier by using the __declspec keyword, as described in this chapter. Placing VCL forms in a DLL and then calling those forms from a non-C++Builder application is a powerful feature. This means that you can create forms that others can call from just about any type of Windows application whether it be an application written in OWL, MFC, straight C, Visual Basic, Delphi, and on and on. Using resources in DLLs is effective if you have a lot of resources in your application and you want to control when and where those resources are loaded.

Workshop

The Workshop contains quiz questions to help you solidify your understanding of the material covered and exercises to provide you with experience in using what you have learned. You can find answers to the quiz questions in Appendix A, "Answers to Quiz Questions."

Q&A

Q I've got a relatively small program and I don't really see the need to use DLLs. Should I reevaluate my structure?

A Probably not. For small applications, DLLs are often not necessary. Any time you have classes that can be reused, you might as well use a DLL, but don't go out of your way looking for a way to use DLLs in a small application.

Q I'm beginning work on what should be a fairly large class. Should I plan on putting it in a DLL?

A Regardless of whether the class ends up in a DLL, you should always try to write the class with reuse in mind. If you do that from the start, putting the class in a DLL later is a trivial undertaking.

Q That `GetProcAddress()` thing is a little weird. Do I have to use that to call functions in my DLL?

A No. Just use static loading and you won't have to worry about the `LoadLibrary()`, `GetProcAddress()`, and `FreeLibrary()` functions. Using static loading will require that you use an import library (`.lib`) for your DLL, but it's much easier to use in the long run.

Q My program compiles fine, but I keep getting a linker error that says, `Undefined external MyFunction() in module MyUnit.cpp`. What's wrong?

A You have either not exported the function from the DLL or are not properly importing the function from the DLL. This could be as simple as forgetting to add the `.lib` file for the DLL to the project, or it could be that you didn't properly set up your DLL's header and something is going wrong when you build either the DLL or the calling application.

Q **I have a form contained in a DLL, and my calling app is a C++Builder program. The size of the DLL is pretty large. Is there any way I can reduce that?**

A Unfortunately, no. This is where the power of programming in C++Builder works against you a little. Both the calling application and the DLL contain some of the same VCL code. In other words, the code is being duplicated in both the `.exe` and the `.dll`. You'll just have to live with the larger overall program size if you are using forms in DLLs.

Q **I have a lot of wave files for my application. Right now they are all contained in separate files, but I would like to place them all in one file. Is a resource DLL a good idea here?**

A Absolutely. The only disadvantage is that if you just need one wave file you must load the entire DLL. Still, by using dynamic loading you can load and unload the DLL as required. The `PlaySound()` function makes it easy to play sounds from a DLL.

Q **I live in a French-speaking country. Why should I bother with internationalization of my program?**

A It depends entirely on who your target audience is. If you know that your program will never be used by people in countries where French is not the native language, you don't have to worry about internationalization at all. But if there is even the slightest possibility that your program could be marketed in other countries, you should plan on international support from the beginning. It's much easier to do it right the first time than it is to go back and fix it later.

Q **Will C++Builder automatically create an import library file for me when I create a DLL?**

A No. You must run IMPLIB on the DLL to create a `.lib` file.

Quiz

1. How do you load a DLL using static loading?
2. How do you load a DLL using dynamic loading?
3. How do you call a function from a DLL that has been loaded statically?
4. What steps do you have to take to ensure that a function in your DLL can be called from outside of the DLL?
5. In the case of a DLL that has been dynamically loaded, can you unload the DLL at any time or only when the program closes?
6. What must you do to display a C++Builder form contained in a DLL from a non-C++Builder program?

7. What is the advantage of using import/export macros when building DLLs and the applications that call them?

8. How do you add resources to a DLL?

9. Does a resource DLL need to contain code as well as the resources?

10. Can a DLL containing resources be loaded statically (when the program loads)?

Exercises

1. Create a DLL that contains a function that displays a message box when called.

2. Create a calling application that calls the DLL in exercise 1.

3. Create a DLL containing a form and a calling application that will display the form.

4. Create a DLL that has two bitmap resources.

5. Create a program that will display either of the bitmap resources in your new DLL on demand. (**Hint:** Use a TImage component and the LoadFromResource() method.)

6. **Extra credit:** Write five DLLs, each of which contains the same strings but in different languages.

7. **Extra credit:** Write a calling application that displays the strings you created in exercise 6. Allow the user to choose the language to be used in the application. Display the strings in the language chosen.

Day 20

Creating Components

by Kent Reisdorph

C++Builder provides a wide assortment of components that you can use in your applications. These components include basic Windows controls as well as some specialty components not inherent in Windows itself. Still, you might run into a situation where you need a component to perform a task not provided by any of the pre-installed components. In that case, you can write the component yourself. Creating a component requires these steps:

1. Use the Component Wizard to begin the creation process (or create the component from scratch using a blank editor file).

2. Add properties, methods, and events to the component's class.

3. Test the component.

4. Add the component to the Component Palette.

Today you will learn how to create components. As with most of what you have encountered in C++Builder, it's not so bad once you've done it a couple times.

Getting Started

Writing components requires a higher level of programming expertise than you have used up to this point. First, you have to create a class for your new component. The class needs to be designed so that some of its properties will show up in the Object Inspector (assuming that you are writing a visual component). Then you have to provide properties for the component. In addition, you will have to write methods for your component. Some of these will be private to the component; others will be made public so they can be accessed by users of the component. Finally, you may also have to write events for the component.

As you can see, there is some work involved. As great as C++Builder's visual programming environment is, it won't help you here. Writing components is pure programming.

There are two basic ways to create components:

☐ Modify an existing component
☐ Write the component from scratch

The method you use depends on the type of component you are writing. Let's say, for instance, that you wanted to create a label component that flashes the label's text (call it the FlashingLabel component). In that case, the standard Label component has everything you need to get started, so you could start with a TLabel and modify it to create the flashing effect. If, on the other hand, you wanted to create a label that allowed you to create Windows shortcuts, you would have to write the component from scratch because there is no VCL component that gives you a base from which to work.

NOTE

C++Builder provides several classes that you can use as base classes for new components. The names of these classes all start with TCustom. For example, the base class for a TLabel is TCustomLabel. You can derive from one of these classes whenever you are creating an original control. The custom classes already provide the properties you are most likely to need for that type of component (a custom label component in this case). All you have to do is redeclare the property in the published section of your component's class declaration. This is explained more fully in the section titled "TFlashingLabel: A Component Example," later in this chapter.

To modify an existing component, you use the Component Wizard. You invoke the Component Wizard through the Object Repository. To start the Component Wizard, choose File | New from the C++Builder main menu. When the Object Repository is displayed, double-click on the Component icon, and the Component Wizard will appear. You can then choose the component you want to use for a base class. (The Component

20

Wizard is explained in detail in the section titled "The Component Wizard.") If you choose a class name that already exists in the component library, the Component Wizard will tell you. You will have to choose a unique class name before you can go on.

NOTE

> There's no reason that you have to start the name of the class with a T; it just happens to be customary for Borland classes. (The use of T in Borland classes is a Borland tradition that goes back to the early days of Turbo Pascal. It is used in both OWL and VCL.) Some people use the T when deriving from a Borland class but don't use the T when creating their own classes. It's entirely up to you.

The Ancestor Type field of the Component Wizard is used to specify the base class of the component. This field is a combo box that contains the names of all classes currently registered in the component library (about 150 class names for the default installation, plus any others you add). You can choose one of the classes from the list or, if you already know the class name, you can type it in directly. Choosing the base class name from the list is preferable because it eliminates the chance that you might mistype the base class name.

Modifying Existing Components

To modify existing components, you use the C++ feature called *inheritance*. It's been a while since I talked about inheritance, so refer to Day 4, "Totally Immersed: C++ Classes and Object-Oriented Programming," if you need a refresher course. Inheriting from a component says, in effect, "Give me everything that component has and then I'll add some stuff of my own." The class you are inheriting from is the *base class* and the new class is the *derived class*. In the previous example, TLabel would be the base class and TFlashingLabel would be the derived class. When deriving from an existing component, you can use the Component Wizard to set up the initial source file and header (more on that in just a bit).

Creating Components from Scratch

Modifying existing components is the easiest way to create a component. Sometimes, though, you have to create the component from the ground up without the benefit of deriving from an existing component. If you create a component from scratch, you need to do the following:

1. Create a header that contains the component's class declaration.
2. Create a source code unit for the component.
3. Register the component with C++Builder.

20

After you have taken these steps, you can proceed to write the component, test it, and add it to the Component Palette. There is nothing too mysterious about creating a new source file and header.

TIP

> If you must build a component from scratch, you can use the header from an existing component as a pattern. Just copy the class declaration from one of the VCL classes and paste it into a new editor window. Gut the class to remove all the code, but leave the basic shell of the class declaration to build on.

Registering the Component

Registering the component is necessary for C++Builder to know what components to place in the component library. This step is performed for you when you use the Component Wizard to create the new component. If you are creating a component from scratch, you will need to perform the registration yourself.

To register a component, place a function called `Register()` in your component's source code unit. A typical `Register()` function looks like this:

```
namespace Mycomponent {
void __fastcall Register()
{
  TComponentClass classes[1] = {__classid(TMyComponent)};
  RegisterComponents("Samples", classes, 0);
}
}
```

First notice that the `Register()` function is wrapped in a *namespace*.

 NEW TERM   A *namespace* is a C++ feature that allows sections of code to be distinguished by name.

Namespaces are a C++ feature I haven't talked about yet. A namespace is used to keep this `Register()` function separate from the `Register()` functions of all the other components in the component library.

NOTE

> The name of the namespace for a C++Builder component must follow a specific design. The namespace name must be the name of the file in which the component is contained, in all lowercase letters except for

> the leading character. For example, let's say you had a component called TFancyEdit and that it was contained in a file called FancyEdit.cpp. The namespace name for the Register() function in this case would be Fancyedit.
>
> If you use the Component Wizard to create your component, you don't have to worry about setting the namespace name. The name will be set for you when you save the file and will be changed if you happen to change the name of the file using File | Save As.

The first line in the Register() function creates an array of components to be registered and places this component in the array. If you were creating an entire library of components, you could register them all at one time by placing them all in the TComponentClass array. Most of the time, though, you will be dealing with one component at a time.

The second line in the Register() function tells C++Builder on which page of the Component Palette the icon for the new component should be placed. After the component has been written and fully tested, you can add the component to the component library. Adding the component to the component library is discussed in detail later in the chapter in the section titled "Adding the Component to the Component Library."

The Component Wizard

The Component Wizard gives you a head start on writing a component. It is invoked from the Object Repository. To start the Component Wizard, choose File | New to display the Object Repository and then double-click on the Component icon. The Component Wizard dialog box will be displayed, as shown in Figure 20.1.

Figure 20.1.

The Component Wizard dialog box.

Type the name of your class in the Class Name field. The class name should begin with a T and should be descriptive of the function the class performs. For instance, going back to an earlier example, if you have a label that flashes, you could call it TFlashingLabel.

TIP

> You can quickly jump to a particular class name in the Ancestor Type combo box. First click the drop-down arrow to expose the list of class names. Then type the first two or three characters of the class name you are looking for. The list of class names will scroll as you type characters.

The Palette Page field allows you to specify the page on the Component Palette where you want the icon for this component to appear. (The component's icon won't actually appear on the Component Palette until you install the component.)

As you might have guessed, now we're going to write a sample component. As long as we're discussing the Component Wizard, you might as well get started with the task of creating a component. We'll create the `TFlashingLabel` component I used as an example in the "Getting Started" section. This component is a regular `Label` component that flashes (or blinks, if you prefer) the label's text on the screen. Later I'll give you the details, but this should give you an idea of what we'll be trying to accomplish. So with that in mind, let's get started with creating the component.

Creating the Component

In this case we are going to create a component derived from an existing component. To do that we can use the Component Wizard, of course. Follow these steps:

1. Choose File | New from the main menu to invoke the Object Repository.

2. Double-click on the Component icon in the Object Repository. The Component Wizard dialog box is displayed.

3. Type `TFlashingLabel` in the Class Name field.

4. From the Ancestor Type combo box, choose the `TCustomLabel` class to use as the base class.

5. The Palette Page field contains `Samples`. Leave this field as is. The new component will be added to the Samples page of the Component Palette when we install the component.

6. Click OK to close the Component Wizard dialog box. The Code Editor comes to the top and displays a new source code unit.

7. Save the unit as `FlashingLabel.cpp`.

NOTE

> You should save the unit generated by the Component Wizard right away. When you save the unit, the reference to the unit's header is updated, as is the namespace name.

Listings 20.1 and 20.2 show the source unit and header as they appear at this point.

Listing 20.1. `FlashingLabel.h.`

```cpp
//-------------------------------------------------------------
#ifndef FlashingLabelH
#define FlashingLabelH
//-------------------------------------------------------------
#include <vcl\sysutils.hpp>
#include <vcl\controls.hpp>
#include <vcl\classes.hpp>
#include <vcl\forms.hpp>
#include <vcl\StdCtrls.hpp>
//-------------------------------------------------------------
class TFlashingLabel : public TCustomLabel
{
private:
protected:
public:
__published:
};
//-------------------------------------------------------------
#endif
```

Listing 20.2. `FlashingLabel.cpp.`

```cpp
//-------------------------------------------------------------
#include <vcl\vcl.h>
#pragma hdrstop

#include "FlashingLabel.h"
//-------------------------------------------------------------
static inline TFlashingLabel *ValidCtrCheck()
{
  return new TFlashingLabel(NULL);
}
//-------------------------------------------------------------
__fastcall TFlashingLabel::TFlashingLabel(TComponent* Owner)
  : TLabel(Owner)
{
}
//-------------------------------------------------------------
namespace Flashinglabel
{
  void __fastcall Register()
  {
     TComponentClass classes[1] = {__classid(TFlashingLabel)};
     RegisterComponents("Samples", classes, 0);
  }
}
//-------------------------------------------------------------
//-------------------------------------------------------------
```

20

By looking at Listing 20.1, you can see that the TFlashingLabel class is derived from TCustomLabel. The class declaration is empty except for the access keywords (private, public, protected, and __published). We'll fill in the blanks a little later, after I've had a chance to go over some of the details of what makes up a component.

As you can see, the Component Wizard gives you a head start by filling out some of the header and some of the source unit for you. You still have to do the hard stuff, but at least the Register() function is written and the class declaration is started.

Before we can go on, I need to spend some time explaining what makes up a component. After that we'll get back to writing the rest of the TFlashingLabel component. Keep the component that you just created handy (such as it is) because you'll need it a little later.

Writing Properties

A big part of writing components is writing the component's properties. You have been using properties in your journey up to this point, so you know what properties are from a user's perspective. Now you need to understand properties from a component writer's perspective. Before you can write components, you need to understand what properties are—and what they are not.

Specifically, properties are not data members. It is natural to think of properties as data members of the class to which they belong. After all, you treat properties just like data members when you do things like this:

```
int width = Width;
Height = width * .7;
```

But properties are *not* data members, and you need to keep that in mind when writing components. Properties differ from data members in many ways. But properties have at least one thing in common with regular data members: They have a specific data type. A property's type could be one of the integral data types (int, long, double, enum, and so on), a class (String, Tfont, and so on), or a structure (TRect, for example).

What properties are, then, is a special type of object that meets the following criteria:

- [ ] Properties have an underlying data member that is used to store the property's value.
- [ ] Properties can implement a write method.
- [ ] Properties can implement a read method.
- [ ] Properties can use direct access rather than using read and write methods.
- [ ] Properties can be read-only or write-only.

☐ Properties can have a default value.

☐ Properties can be published or nonpublished.

To help this make more sense, let's take a look at the features of properties one at a time.

Properties Have Underlying Data Members

Each property has an underlying data member associated with it. It is this data member that holds the actual value associated with a property. Take a simple assignment, for example:

```
Label->Caption = "McGarry & Mahar";
```

This statement assigns a string to the Caption property of a Label component. What happens behind the scenes is more than just a simple assignment. Because a Caption property is of the String type, it has a String object as its underlying data member. When an assignment is made like this one, the underlying data member is given the value of the assigned string. Using an underlying data member is necessary because a property does not have the capability to store data.

The underlying data member can be named anything you want, but tradition has it that the data member associated with a property has the same name as the property with a leading F. For instance, the data member associated with the Caption property would be named FCaption.

NOTE

> This associate between the property and its underlying data member can be the source of much confusion when you start writing components. It's not that it's difficult to understand; it's just that you might mix up the two when writing code for the component. For example, you might accidentally write
>
> ```
> Left = 20;
> ```
>
> when you meant to write
>
> ```
> FLeft = 20;
> ```
>
> This can lead to all sorts of interesting behavior in your component. You'll see why when I discuss write methods in the next section.

20

The underlying data member is almost always declared as a private data member. You want your users to modify the data member through the property or by calling a method, but never directly. This way you are in control of the data member as much as possible, which leads us to the next feature of components.

Properties Have Write Methods

When you make an assignment to a property, a lot of things can happen behind the scenes. Exactly what happens depends on the specific property. For instance, this code looks pretty simple:

```
Left = 20;
```

But several things happen when this line is executed. First, the underlying data member, FLeft, is changed to the new value. Next, the form (assuming this code was executed from a form) would be moved to the new left position using the Windows API function MoveWindow(). Finally, the form will be repainted by calling Invalidate() for the form. How does all that happen? It happens through the Left property's write method. The write method is a method that is called any time the property is assigned a value. You can use the write method to do validation of the assigned value or to perform special processing.

You declare a property's write method when you declare the property. For example, here's an example of a typical property declaration:

```
__property int FlashRate = {read=FFlashRate, write=SetFlashRate};
```

This declaration has some syntax that you haven't seen before because it is syntax specific to properties and doesn't exist in standard C++. First of all, notice that the property is declared with the __property keyword and that following the declaration is an equal sign and additional code. The code following the declaration tells the compiler that the write method for the property is called SetFlashRate(). You can name the write method anything you want, but tradition has it that you name the write method the same name as the property prepended with the word Set. (Notice also that this declaration assigns a value to the read method. I'll get to the read method in just a bit.)

When the property is written to (assigned a value), the write method associated with the property will be called automatically. The write method must return void. The write method must have one parameter, and that parameter must be of the same type as the property itself. For example, the write method's declaration for the FlashRate property would be

```
void __fastcall SetFlashRate(int AFlashRate);
```

The value passed to the write method is the value that was assigned to the property. So, given this line

```
FlashingLabel->FlashRate = 1000;
```

you end up with the value of 1000 passed to the SetFlashRate() function. What you do with the value within the write method depends on a wide variety of factors. At a minimum, you would assign the value to the associated data member. In other words, the write method would look something like this:

```
void __fastcall TFlashingLabel::SetFlashRate(int AFlashRate)
{
  FFlashRate = AFlashRate;    // FFlashRate now equals 1000
  // do some other stuff;
}
```

NOTE

The use of the leading A for the parameter name in a write method is another tradition.

You will almost always do something more than assign the value to the underlying data member. If you are only assigning the value to the data member associated with the property, you don't need a write method for the property at all. I'll explain that in just a moment. First let's look at read methods.

NOTE

The value passed to the write method can be passed by value or by reference. You should pass classes and structures by reference to reduce overhead. You can pass the integral data types by value.

Properties Have Read Methods

The read method works exactly like the write method (aside from the obvious difference). When a property's value is read, the read method is executed and the value of the underlying data member is returned.

The name of the read method is the property name preceded by Get. The read method takes no parameters and returns the type of the property. For example, if you were to use a read method for the FlashRate property, it would be declared like this:

```
int __fastcall GetFlashRate();
```

The read method might perform some processing and then return the value of the underlying data member, FFlashRate in this case. The reading of a property happens in many different ways. Sometimes it's the result of an assignment to a variable:

```
int rate = FlashingLabel->FlashRate;
```

At other times it is used within a C++ statement:

```
switch (FlashingLabel->FlashRate) {
  case 1000 : SpeedUp(); break;
  // etc.
}
```

20

Regardless of how the property is read, the read method is called each time a read takes place.

Notice that above I said *if* you are using a read method. Frequently you won't use a read method at all, but will instead use direct access to retrieve the value of the data member associated with a property. Let's take a look at direct access right now.

Properties Can Use Direct Access

You don't have to use read and write methods at all for your properties. If you are simply assigning a value to the underlying data member or reading the value of the underlying data member, you can use direct access. The declaration for a property using direct access looks like this:

```
__property int FlashRate = {read=FFlashRate, write=FFlashRate};
```

This code assigns the data member itself (`FFlashRate`) to both the read and the write specifiers rather than calling a read method or a write method. When the property is written to, the data member is changed and nothing more takes place. When the property is read, the value of the underlying data member is returned. It's as simple as that.

NOTE

> It is common to use direct access when reading the property and a write method for writing to the property. Writing to a property often has side effects, as I explained in the previous section. In fact, the ability to spawn side effects is one of the big strengths of properties. In order to cause side effects when your property is written to, you must use a write method. Reading a property, on the other hand, is usually just a matter of returning the value of the underlying data member. In this case direct access makes the most sense.

Properties Can Be Read-Only or Write-Only

You can specify a property to be read-only or write-only. Making a property read-only is a useful feature. (VCL has many read-only properties.) For instance, you may have a property that you want the user to be able to read but not to modify. It could be that modifying the property directly could have adverse effects on the component, so you need to protect against that.

Making a property read-only is easy: You simply omit the write specifier in the property's declaration:

```
__property int FlashRate = {read=FFlashRate};
```

20

If the user attempts to write to a property that is declared as read-only, you will get a compiler error that says `TFlashingLabel::FlashRate is not accessible`. As you can see, making a property read-only is very simple.

You can make a property write-only by omitting the read specifier from the property's declaration. It's difficult to imagine a use for a property that can be written to but not read, but you certainly may write such a property if you ever find the need.

Properties Can Have Default Values

A *default value* is another useful feature of properties. You will notice that when you place a component on a form, many of the properties that are displayed in the Object Inspector already contain values. These are the default values as defined by the writer of the component. Assigning default values makes things easier for the user of the component. All properties should have a default value if possible. This allows the user to change only the properties he or she wants and to leave the rest alone. Certain types of properties do not lend themselves to default values, but most do.

Like the read and write methods, the default value is set when the property is declared. Let's go back to the `FlashRate` property of the component. Declaring the `FlashRate` property with a default value would look like this:

```
__property int FlashRate =
    {read=FFlashRate, write=SetFlashRate, default=800};
```

Now, when the `FlashingLabel` component is displayed in the Object Inspector, the value of `800` (milliseconds in this case) will already be displayed for the `FlashRate` property.

NOTE

Setting a default value for the property only displays the default value in the Object Inspector. It does *not* set the value of the underlying data member for the property. You must still assign the default value to the data member in the component's constructor. For example, the constructor for the `FlashingLabel` component would look like this:

```
__fastcall TFlashingLabel::TFlashingLabel(TComponent* AOwner)
  : TCustomLabel(AOwner)
{
  FFlashRate = 800;
  // other things here
}
```

Be sure to set the appropriate values for all data members that correspond to properties with default values.

20

If you do not want to use a default value for a property, simply omit the default specifier in the property's declaration.

Properties Can Be Published or Nonpublished

Some properties are available at design time. These properties can be modified at design time through the Object Inspector and can also be modified or read at runtime. Other properties are *runtime-only* properties, which cannot be accessed at design time (they do not show up in the Object Inspector). Properties available at design time are said to be *published*; properties not available at design time are *nonpublished*.

Simply put, a published property is one that shows up in the Object Inspector at design time. You can declare a property as published by placing its declaration in the __published section in the component's class declaration. To declare a property as a runtime property, place the property's declaration in the public section of the class's declaration. Any properties that are located in the __published section will be displayed in the Object Inspector at design time.

Writing Methods for Components

Writing methods for components is really no different than writing methods for any C++ class. The one exception to this statement is that a component's methods must use the __fastcall modifier. Other than that, your component's methods can be either private, protected, or public. Let's review what you know about these access levels.

Access Levels for Components

Back on Day 4, I talked about access levels for classes. In that discussion I said that there were three access levels: private, protected, and public. C++Builder extends C++ in this regard by also allowing for the published section. I discussed the published section briefly just a moment ago. Let's take a moment to review these access levels. Table 20.1 lists the access levels and gives a brief description of each.

Table 20.1. Component class access levels.

Access Level	Description
Private	The private level is the most restrictive. The method is only available for use in this class. Users of the component cannot call these methods, nor can classes derived from this class. Only other methods within the class can call a private method.
Protected	The method cannot be used by users of the component, but classes derived from this component can call protected methods.

Access Level	Description
Public	The public method is available to the public and can be called by users of the class or by other methods of the class.
Published	The published specifier is for properties only and does not apply to methods. A published property shows up in the Object Inspector at design time.

This table pretty much sums up what you need to know about access levels. It pays to keep access levels in mind as you write components. Determining what methods to make public is fairly easy. A public method is one that users of your component can call to cause the component to perform a specific action.

NOTE Keep the use of methods to a minimum in your components. Use a property to perform some action when possible. When it is not possible, that is the time to use a public method instead.

The use of private versus published methods is a little more difficult to sort out. After programming for a while, you will be able to better recognize the situations when protected access should be used over private access.

NOTE Read and write methods for properties will usually be made protected. By making these methods protected, you allow classes derived from your component to modify the behavior of the read and write methods by overriding the method.

As I said earlier, methods of components are just methods and, for the most part, can be treated as regular class member functions.

20

TFlashingLabel: **A Component Example**

A little later I'll talk about events and how to write them, but for now you have enough information to write your first component. As I said earlier, the FlashingLabel component is a component that flashes its text on the screen. It has these features:

- [ ] A property called FlashRate that controls the blink rate.
- [ ] A property called FlashEnabled that turns the flashing on or off.

☐ Write methods for the two properties.

☐ Default values for the two properties.

☐ A private class member (a TTimer class instance) to control the timing of the flash.

☐ All the characteristics of a regular Label component.

First I'll show you the complete program listings for the header and the source unit. (See Listings 20.3 and 20.4.) After that we'll go over what is happening with the code.

Listing 20.3. FlashingLabel.h.

```
 1: //---------------------------------------------------------------
 2: #ifndef FlashingH
 3: #define FlashingH
 4: //---------------------------------------------------------------
 5: #include <vcl\sysutils.hpp>
 6: #include <vcl\controls.hpp>
 7: #include <vcl\classes.hpp>
 8: #include <vcl\forms.hpp>
 9: #include <vcl\StdCtrls.hpp>
10: //---------------------------------------------------------------
11: class TFlashingLabel : public TCustomLabel
12: {
13: private:
14:   //
15:   // Private data members.
16:   //
17:   bool  FFlashEnabled;
18:   int   FFlashRate;
19:   TTimer* Timer;
20: protected:
21:   //
22:   // Protected write methods for the properties.
23:   //
24:   void __fastcall SetFlashEnabled(bool AFlashEnabled);
25:   void __fastcall SetFlashRate(int AFlashRate);
26:   //
27:   // OnTimer event handler.
28:   //
29:   void __fastcall OnTimer(TObject* Sender);
30: public:
31:   __fastcall virtualTFlashingLabel(TComponent* AOwner);
32: __published:
33:   //
34:   // The component's properties.
35:   //
36:   __property bool FlashEnabled =
37:     {read=FFlashEnabled, write=SetFlashEnabled, default=true};
38:   __property int FlashRate =
39:     {read=FFlashRate, write=SetFlashRate, default=800};
40: };
41: //---------------------------------------------------------------
42: #endif
```

20

Listing 20.4. `FlashingLabel.cpp.`

```
 1: //-----------------------------------------------------------
 2: #include <vcl\vcl.h>
 3: #pragma hdrstop
 4: #include "FlashingLabel.h"
 5: //-----------------------------------------------------------
 6: static inline TFlashingLabel *ValidCtrCheck()
 7: {
 8:    return new TFlashingLabel(NULL);
 9: }
10: //-----------------------------------------------------------
11: __fastcall TFlashingLabel::TFlashingLabel(TComponent* AOwner)
12:    : TCustomLabel(AOwner)
13: {
14:    //
15:    // Set the data members to their default values.
16:    //
17:    FFlashEnabled = true;
18:    FFlashRate = 800;
19:    //
20:    // Initialize the timer object.
21:    //
22:    Timer = new TTimer(this);
23:    //
24:    // Set the timer interval using the flash rate.
25:    //
26:    Timer->Interval = FlashRate;
27:    //
28:    // Assign our own OnTimer event handler to the
29:    // TTimer OnTimer event.
30:    //
31:    Timer->OnTimer = &OnTimer;
32: }
33: void __fastcall
34: TFlashingLabel::SetFlashEnabled(bool AFlashEnabled)
35: {
36:    //
37:    // Set FFlashEnabled data member.
38:    //
39:    FFlashEnabled = AFlashEnabled;
40:    //
41:    // Don't start the timer if the component is on a form
42:    // in design mode. Instead, just return.
43:    //
44:    if (ComponentState.Contains(csDesigning)) return;
45:    //
46:    // Start the timer.
47:    //
48:    Timer->Enabled = FFlashEnabled;
49:    //
50:    // If flashing was turned off be sure that the label
51:    // is visible.
52:    //
53:    if (!FFlashEnabled) Visible = true;
54: }
```

continues

Listing 20.4. continued

```
55: void __fastcall TFlashingLabel::SetFlashRate(int AFlashRate)
56: {
57:   //
58:   // Set the FFlashRate data member and the timer interval
59:   // all at the same time.
60:   //
61:   Timer->Interval = FFlashRate = AFlashRate;
62: }
63: void __fastcall TFlashingLabel::OnTimer(TObject* Sender)
64: {
65:   //
66:   // If the component is on a form in design mode then
67:   // stop the timer and return.
68:   //
69:   if (ComponentState.Contains(csDesigning)) {
70:     Timer->Enabled = false;
71:     return;
72:   }
73:   //
74:   // Toggle the Visible property each time the timer
75:   // event occurs.
76:   //
77:   Visible = !Visible;
78: }
79: namespace Flashinglabel {
80: //
81: // Register the component.
82: //
83: void __fastcall Register()
84: {
85:   TComponentClass classes[1] = {__classid(TFlashingLabel)};
86:   RegisterComponents("Samples", classes, 0);
87: }
88: }
```

 ANALYSIS First, let's take a look at the header (Listing 20.3). Notice the private section beginning on line 13. This section declares three data members. The first two, FFlashEnabled and FFlashRate, are the data members associated with the FlashEnabled and FlashRate properties. The last declaration, on line 19, looks like this:

```
TTimer* Timer;
```

This declares a pointer to a TTimer object. The TTimer object will be used to regulate the flash rate.

> **NOTE** We haven't discussed timers yet. A timer is set up to fire at a specified interval (in milliseconds). Each time the timer fires, a WM_TIMER message is sent to the window that owns the timer. As a result, the OnTimer

20

> event is triggered. For example, if you set the timer interval to 1,000 milliseconds, your OnTimer event will be called roughly every second. I should point out that the WM_TIMER message is a low-priority message and can be preempted if the system is busy. For this reason you can't use a regular timer for mission-critical operations. Still, for noncritical timings the TTimer does a pretty good job. (See the C++Builder online help under TTimer or the WM_TIMER message for more information on timers.)

The protected section of the class declaration, which begins on line 20, contains the write methods for the FlashRate and FlashEnabled properties. The protected section also declares the OnTimer() function. This function will be called each time a timer event occurs. It is protected and declared as virtual so that derived classes can override it to provide other special handling when a timer event occurs. For instance, a derived class might want to change the color of the text each time the label flashes. Making this method virtual allows overriding of the function to add additional behavior.

Finally, notice the __published section beginning on line 32. Line 36 declares the FlashEnabled property. The read specifier uses direct access, the write specifier is assigned to the SetFlashEnabled() method, and the default value is set to true. The FlashRate property uses a similar construct.

Now turn your attention to the component's source unit, shown in Listing 20.4. First, on lines 17 and 18 you see that the default values for the data members representing the FlashEnabled and FlashRate properties are assigned. Remember that we declared default values for these properties, but that only affects the way the property is displayed in the Object Inspector. So we must assign the actual values in the constructor.

Now notice these three lines, which begin with line 22 (comments removed):

```
Timer = new TTimer(this);
Timer->Interval = FlashRate;
Timer->OnTimer = &OnTimer;
```

The first line creates an instance of the TTimer object. The second line assigns the value of the FlashRate property to the Interval property of the Timer component. This sets the timer interval that will be used to flash the text on the label. Finally, the last line assigns the address of the OnTimer() function to the OnTimer event of the Timer object. This ensures that when a timer event occurs, you will get notification.

The SetFlashEnabled() function (beginning on line 34) is the write method for the FlashEnabled property. On line 39, the FFlashEnabled data member is set to the value of AFlashEnabled. On line 48, the Enabled property of the Timer object is set according to the

20

value of `AFlashEnabled`. By writing to the `FlashEnabled` property, the user of our component can turn the flashing on or off. This function also contains a line of code that sets the `Visible` property to `true` when flashing is disabled. This eliminates the situation in which the flashing could be turned off in mid-flash and, as a result, keep the text hidden.

Beginning on line 55, you will see the `SetFlashRate()` function. This is the write method for the `FlashRate` property. The user can assign a value to the `FlashRate` property to control how fast the component flashes. (A rate of `1200` is fairly slow, and a rate of `150` is very fast.) This function contains just a single line:

```
Timer->Interval = FFlashRate = AFlashRate;
```

This line contains syntax that you may not have seen before. This is basic C++ syntax that assigns the value of `AFlashRate` first to the `FFlashRate` data member and then to the `Interval` property of the `Timer` object.

The `OnTimer()` function doesn't require much explanation. This function is called in response to an `OnTimer` event. All you do is toggle the component's visible state each time a timer event occurs. In other words, if the `FlashRate` were set to 1000, the timer events will occur roughly every second. When the first timer event occurs, the component is hidden. A second later the next timer event occurs and the component is shown. This continues until the `FlashEnabled` property is set to `false` or until the application closes. Finally, lines 83 through 88 contain the registration of the component.

Enter the code from Listings 20.3 and 20.4 into the `FlashingLabel.h` and `FlashingLabel.cpp` files created earlier by the Component Wizard. Don't worry about typing the comment lines if you don't want to. Remember to use the cut-and-paste method when it comes time to add all of the `TCustomLabel` published properties. The `TCustomLabel` class declaration can be found in the `Stdctrls.hpp` file. After you have the code typed in, we'll test the component to see if it works.

Planning Ahead

I am getting ahead of myself just a little here, but I wanted to point out some code that I didn't discuss in the analysis of Listing 20.4. There is one important line in the `SetFlashEnabled()` function that requires some explanation. On line 44 you will see this code:

```
if (ComponentState.Contains(csDesigning)) return;
```

This line checks whether the component is being used on a form at design time. If the form is being used at design time, you need to prevent the timer from starting. When a component is placed on a form in the Form Designer, it does not necessarily have full functionality—the Form Designer cannot fully approximate a running program. In this case you don't want the timer to run while the component is being used in design mode.

All visual components have a property called ComponentState. The ComponentState property indicates, among other things, whether the component is being used at design time. A flag, csDesigning, is either set (on) or not set (off). If the csDesigning flag is set, the component is being used on a form in the Form Designer. You can use the Contains() function to determine whether the csDesigning flag is set. If the flag is set, you can return from the OnTimer() function without starting the timer.

NOTE

In Delphi, the ComponentState property is implemented in the form of a set (a set is a Pascal language feature). A set is a collection of like objects. A simple analogy would be a basket of fruit. The basket (the set) can contain an apple, an orange, a peach, or a plum. It might contain one or more of these objects, or it might contain all of them. The ComponentState property, then, is a set of flags that indicate the current state of the component.

The C++ language does not support the notion of a set. Instead, the C++Builder designers implemented sets as C++ templates. I won't go into the details of templates right now, but I will simply say that you can use the Contains() function to determine whether a particular object exists in the set.

Lines 69 through 72 of Listing 20.4 check whether the component is being used on a form in the Form Designer. If the component is being used in the Form Designer, the timer is turned off and the function returns without performing the remaining code in the function. The timer, by default, will be started in the TFlashingLabel constructor, so it needs to be immediately turned off if the component is being use at design time.

Testing the Component

Ultimately, you will add your newly created component to the component library and to the Component Palette. First, though, you must test your component to be sure it compiles and to be sure it functions as you intended.

NOTE

When you add a component to the component library, C++Builder will rebuild the entire VCL library. Depending on your hardware, this can be a fairly time-consuming operation the first time you add a new component (it takes about 10 minutes on my old 486). After the initial build, subsequent builds take only a couple minutes. In any case, be sure that your component is thoroughly tested before adding it to the component library.

To test your component, you need to write an application that will serve as a testing ground. Because you can't drop the component on a form from the Component Palette, you have to create the component manually. In this case, because our `FlashingLabel` component has two properties, we want to make sure that each of the properties works. For that reason, our test program will need to turn the flashing mode on and off. In addition, the test program should allow us to set several flashing rates to see if the `FlashRate` property performs as designed. Figure 20.2 shows the test program running. This will give you an idea of what we're going for before we begin.

Figure 20.2.

The test program running.

Now that you've had a peek at the test program, let's create it. As always, start with a blank form. First we will add the check box and radio group components as you see them in Figure 20.2:

1. Change the Name property of the form to MainForm and the Caption property to FlashingLabel Test Program.

2. Using Figure 20.2 as a pattern, add a CheckBox component to the form. Change its Name property to FlashBox, its Caption property to Flash, and its Checked property to true.

3. Switch to the Events page of the Object Inspector and double-click in the Value column next to the OnClick event. The Code Editor displays the OnClick handler for the FlashBox component. Type this code at the cursor (the name of the FlashingLabel component will be Flasher):

   ```
   Flasher->FlashEnabled = FlashBox->Checked;
   ```

   This will enable or disable flashing, depending on the state of the check box.

4. Place a `RadioGroup` component on the form. Change its `Name` property to `Group` and its `Caption` property to `Flash Speed`.

5. Double-click on the Value column next to the `Items` property. When the String Editor is displayed, type these lines:

```
Slow
Medium
Fast
LightSpeed
```

Click OK to close the String Editor. The strings you typed will be displayed as radio buttons in the group box.

6. Set the `ItemIndex` property to `1`. The Medium radio button will be selected.

7. With the radio group box selected, switch to the Events page in the Object Inspector. Double-click in the Value column next to the `OnClick` event. The Code Editor will display the `OnClick` event handler for the group box.

8. Type the following code at the cursor:

```
switch (Group->ItemIndex) {
    case 0 :  Flasher->FlashRate = 1200; break;
    case 1 :  Flasher->FlashRate = 800; break;
    case 2 :  Flasher->FlashRate = 400; break;
    case 3 :  Flasher->FlashRate = 150; break;
}
```

This will set the `FlashRate` value of the `FlashingLabel` component, based on the radio button selected.

9. Save the project in the same directory where your `TFlashingLabel` component resides. Save the main form's unit as `FTMain.cpp` and the project as `FlashTst.pof`.

Okay, now we need to add the component itself. Because this component is not yet visual (we can't add it from the Component Palette), we need to add it manually. It goes like this:

1. Click the Add to Project button (from the speedbar, from the main menu, or from the Project Manager window). When the Add to Project dialog box is displayed, choose the `FlashingLabel.cpp` file and click OK.

2. Switch to the main form's source unit in the Code Editor and choose File | Include Unit Hdr from the main menu. Choose FlashingLabel from the Include Unit dialog box and click OK.

3. Switch to the `FTMain.h` file and add this declaration in the `private` section of the `TMainForm` class:

```
TFlashingLabel* Flasher;
```

20

4. Switch to the Code Editor and locate the main form's constructor. Type the following code in the constructor:

```
Flasher = new TFlashingLabel(this);
Flasher->Parent = this;
Flasher->SetBounds(20, 20, 200, 20);
Flasher->Font->Size = 16;
Flasher->Caption = "This is a test";
Flasher->FlashRate = 800;
```

You are now ready to test the component. Click the Run button to compile and run the test program. If you encounter any compiler errors, carefully check your code and fix any errors the compiler points out.

When the program runs, you can click on the Flash check box to turn the flashing on or off. Change the flash rate by choosing one of the radio buttons in the group box. Hey, it works! Congratulations, you've written your first component!

Adding the Component to the Component Library

After the component is working properly and you are satisfied with it, you can add it to the component library. When you add the component to the component library, you are also adding it to the Component Palette. Before we install the FlashingLabel component, though, let's take a quick look at the Install Components dialog box.

The Install Components Dialog Box

To add the component to the component library, choose Component | Install from the main menu. The Install Components dialog box will be displayed. This dialog box allows you to add and remove components, and also to add OCX controls. The Install Components dialog box is shown in Figure 20.3.

Figure 20.3.

The Install Components dialog box.

Let's take a moment to go over this dialog box. The first field contains the name of the library source file. You should never need to change this field. The next field contains the search path that C++Builder will use to locate the components it will compile when it rebuilds the component library. Keep in mind that the component library can contain components from a variety of sources: the C++Builder default components, components from third-party developers, your own components, and so on. C++Builder must know where to find all the installed components each time it rebuilds the component library.

NOTE   You shouldn't need to change the Search Path field directly. When you add a component using the Add button, the location of the new component will be added to the search path automatically. Take care when modifying this field.

In the middle of the Install Components dialog box are two list boxes. The list box on the left contains the registered groups of components. When you click on one of the registration groups, the list box on the right will show you which component classes are installed under that registration group.

To remove an installed component, select the component from the Component Classes list box and click the Remove button. The component is removed from the list of installed components.

NOTE   Any time you make a change in the Install Components dialog box, the component library will automatically be rebuilt. This is true whether you add a component or remove one. A removed component will not actually be removed until the library has been rebuilt. Likewise, a newly installed component will not show up in the Component Palette until C++Builder has finished rebuilding the library.

20

If you want to revert to the installed configuration, click the Revert button and then click OK. The library will be rebuilt to the way it was when you first installed C++Builder.

What you really want to know about, though, is the Add button. The Add button, as you would expect, allows you to install a new component in the component library. Let's illustrate that by adding the `FlashingLabel` component.

TIP

> You might want to put all the components you create in a central location. By having all your components in the same directory, you eliminate the need to go hunting for them if you ever need to modify a component.

Installing the `FlashingLabel` Component

Now we're ready to install the `FlashingLabel` component. First, however, close any project you currently have open.

NOTE

> If you have a project open, C++Builder will close it before continuing with the component installation. If the project needs to be saved, C++Builder will prompt you to save the project.

Okay, we're ready to go. Perform the following steps:

1. Choose Component | Install from the main menu. The Install Components dialog box is displayed.

2. Click the Add button. The Add Module dialog box is displayed. Click the Browse button and locate the `FlashingLabel.cpp` file. Click OK to select the file, and click OK again to close the Add Module dialog box.

3. Now the Installed Components list box of the Install Components dialog box shows `FlashingLabel` at the bottom of the list. You are ready to install the component.

4. Click OK to close the Install Components dialog box. C++Builder begins rebuilding the component library.

5. Sit back and take a breather while C++Builder rebuilds the component library (it only takes a couple of minutes on most systems).

If you have thoroughly tested your component, the library rebuild will go off without a hitch. If any errors occur, the compile status dialog box will indicate the number of errors, and the Messages window will open to display whatever errors occur. (The Messages window is a special window seen only when errors occur during the component library build.) You will have to fix any errors encountered before you can rebuild the library. This is why you want to be sure your components are fully tested before attempting to install them to the component library.

When C++Builder is done rebuilding the component library, you can search for your newly installed component. Check on the Samples page; you should see a button that looks like the

Label component button, or maybe the C++Builder default component button. If you pause over the button, the tool tip should say FlashingLabel. Start a new project and test the FlashingLabel component by dropping it on the form. Note that all the usual properties of a Label component are present in the Object Inspector, as are the FlashRate and FlashEnabled properties. Note that the default values we specified for these properties are displayed in the Object Inspector.

Adding a Custom Bitmap to the Component's Button

I don't want to detract from your newfound success, but you might have noticed a problem. The button for the FlashingLabel component on the Component Palette looks like the regular Label component. We can't have that!

NOTE   If a bitmap for a new component cannot be found, C++Builder will use the bitmap of the component's base class or the default Component Palette bitmap.

You can specify a bitmap for your new component if you want to (and you usually will). The bitmap must be contained in a .dcr file and must follow a specific naming convention. (A .dcr file is a compiled resource file similar to a .res file.) The file must be named the same as the source file for the component and must reside in the same directory as the component. In addition, the .dcu file must have a bitmap resource that exactly matches the class name of the component. For example, to create a bitmap for the FlashingLabel component's button, you would create a file called FlashingLabel.dcr that would contain a bitmap resource called TFLASHINGLABEL. Case does not matter for the resource name, but uppercase is traditional.

TIP   Sometimes you might want to take the button for the base class and modify it slightly to represent your new component. In that case, you can start the Image Editor and open one of the .dcr files in the \CBuilder\Lib\Obj directory. (You'll have to hunt around a little to find the exact bitmap.) For example, the bitmap for the Label component is in the file called Stdreg.dcr. Open that file, copy the TLABEL bitmap to the Clipboard, begin a new .dcr file, and paste the bitmap in the Clipboard to a new bitmap resource called TFLASHINGLABEL. Modify the bitmap as desired and then save the resource project.

20

The bitmap for the component's button must by 24×24 pixels in size. Most of the time a 16-color bitmap is sufficient. C++Builder uses the dark yellow color as the transparent color, so keep that in mind when designing bitmaps for your buttons.

If you want to add a bitmap to the button for your component as described in this section, first create a `.dcr` file as instructed. Place the `.dcr` in the directory where you have the `FlashingLabel.cpp` file and rebuild the component library (choose Component | Rebuild Library from the main menu). If the button doesn't show up correctly, you may have to first remove the `FlashingLabel` component and then reinstall it. If you've done everything correctly, the bitmap you created for the button will show up in the Component Palette.

Writing Events for Components

Writing events requires some planning. When I speak of events, I am talking about two different possibilities. Sometimes an event occurs as the result of a Windows message, and sometimes an event occurs as a result of some change in the component. An event triggered by a Windows message is, more or less, out of your control. You can respond to this type of event, but you generally do not initiate the event. The second type of event is triggered by the component itself. In other words, as the component writer you are in control of when this type of event occurs.

Working with events at this level can be pretty confusing at times. I'll try to get past all that and show you how events can be used on a practical level. To do this, we'll add an event to the `TFlashingLabel` class. Before we do that, however, let's cover a few of the event basics.

Events Overview

First of all, you should understand that events are properties. As such, they have all the features that a "regular" property has; for instance, you can assign values to the read and write specifiers. Also, events use a private data member to store their values, as do other properties. In the case of an event, the underlying data member contains the address of a function that will be called when the specified event occurs. Like properties, events can be published or non-published. Published events show up in the Object Inspector just as published properties do.

Secondly, events are *closures*. A closure is a special type of function pointer that contains the address of a function to call when an event occurs. Closures are sort of like function super-pointers—not only can they can point to a function in a class instance, but they can also point to a function in an instance of an unrelated class. As long as the function declarations match (the same return type and the same function parameters), the closure happily calls the function, regardless of where it's located. For example, the `OnClick` event of a `TLabel` object can point to an event-handling function in a TEdit object, a TForm object, a TListBox object, and so on. Closures are a little more complicated than that, but we don't need to go into the gory details. (By the way, for those of you who are wondering, closures are not found in standard C++.)

> **NOTE**
>
> Events always have a return type of void. The event might pass one or more parameters, depending on the type of the event, but it cannot return a value. You can get information back from the event handler, though, by passing one or more parameters by reference and allowing the user to change those parameters to achieve a particular behavior.

You might deal with events on any one of several levels. For instance, you might want to override the base class event handler for a particular event to add some functionality. Let's say you want something special to happen if the user clicks on your component with the mouse. In that case, there's no use going to all the trouble of creating a new event for a mouse click because the event already exists in the form of the base class's OnClick event. You can just tag onto that event, rather than creating a new event to catch the mouse click.

Another way you might deal with events is by creating an event that you trigger from within the component. It is this type of event we will deal with first. As I said, we're going to add an event to the TFlashingLabel component that you created earlier. Adding this event will require that we add a new property, too. The event will be called OnLimitReached, and the new property will be called FlashLimit. This event will be fired after the component flashes the number of times specified by FlashLimit. If FlashLimit is 0 (the default), the OnLimitReached event will never be fired. So let's get to it.

Parts Is Parts

Writing a user-defined event for a component can be broken down into five basic tasks:

1. Determine the event type.
2. Declare the event.
3. Declare the underlying data member.
4. Create a virtual function that is called when the event is to be triggered.
5. Write code to trigger the event.

Let's walk through this so you can better understand what is involved.

20

Determining the Event Type

Earlier, when I discussed properties, I said that a property is of a specific type. The same is true of events. In the case of events, though, the type is a function pointer that includes a description of the event handler's parameters. Yesterday I talked a little about function pointers when I discussed DLLs (in the section titled "Calling Functions Located in DLLs").

As I have said several times, there are two basic types of events. One is the *notification event*. This event simply tells you that something happened; it doesn't give you any other details. The function declaration of the event handler for a notification event looks like this:

```
void __fastcall Clicked(TObject* Sender);
```

The only information you get in a notification event is the sender of the event. C++Builder provides the TNotifyEvent type for notification events. TNotifyEvent is actually a typedef that equates to a function pointer. Don't get too hung up on that right now; just make a mental note that any events you create that are notification events should be of the TNotifyEvent type.

The other type of event is an event that has more than one parameter and that actually passes information to the event handler. If you want to, you can create this type of event for your components, too. For example, let's say you wanted to use an event handler that is prototyped like this:

```
void __fastcall LimitReached(TObject* Sender, bool& Stop);
```

Using this type of event handler allows the user to modify the Stop parameter, thereby sending information about the event back to the component. If you are going to create events that have parameters, you will need to declare your own function type. For example, let's say you wanted to write an event type for the preceding function declaration and that the event type would be named TMyEvent. It will look something like this:

```
typedef void __fastcall
  (__closure *TMyEvent)(System::TObject *Sender, bool& Stop);
```

Although that's kind of confusing, all you have to do is copy this pattern and then add or remove parameters as needed. Then you could declare an event to be of the type TMyEvent. (This won't make a lot of sense until we work through the whole thing, so bear with me.)

NOTE

> Declare a new event type just above the class declaration in the component's header file. See Listing 20.5 if you want a sneak peek.

Try to determine, to the best of your ability, what type of events (if any) you will need for your component. If you only need notification events, you can create your events to be of the

`TNotifyEvent` type. If your events will pass parameters to the event handler, you will need to define your own event type.

Declaring the Event

Now that you have the event type determined, you can declare the event for the component. The declaration for an event looks almost identical to the declaration for any other property. Here's a typical declaration for an event:

```
__property TNotifyEvent OnSomeEvent =
    {read=FOnSomeEvent, write=FOnSomeEvent};
```

For the most part, this looks like the property declarations that you dealt with earlier. Notice that there is no default specifier. Notice also that the read and write specifiers both point to the `FOnSomeEvent` data member. This illustrates that events use direct access and do not use read and write methods. Finally, notice that in this example the event's type is `TNotifyEvent`. If your event passes parameters, you will need to define your own type, as discussed in the section titled "`TFlashingLabel`: A Component Example."

Our `OnLimitReached` event will pass parameters, so we need to define a special type and apply it to the event. Given that, our declaration for the `OnLimitReached` event looks like this:

```
__property TMyEvent OnLimitReached =
    {read=FOnLimitReached, write=FOnLimitReached};
```

A little later I'll show you the entire header so you can see it in perspective. (If you want to look ahead, you can check out Listing 20.5.)

Declaring the Underlying Data Member

Declaring the underlying data member is the simple part. All we have to do is declare a private data member with the same type as our event. It looks like this:

```
TMyEvent FOnLimitReached;
```

As with properties, the data member's name is the same as the event name, with the `F` on the front.

Creating a Virtual Function to Trigger the Event

Creating a virtual function to trigger the event is the part that requires some explanation. You will trigger the event as a result of some change within the component. In this case we are going to trigger the event when the number of times the component has flashed reaches the value of the `FlashLimit` property. You can trigger an event by simply calling the event:

```
bool stop = false;
OnLimitReached(this, stop);
```

20

You might trigger the event from one of several places in the component, based on different factors. To centralize things, we will create a virtual function that triggers the event. The virtual function will have the same name as the event, minus the On part. First, we declare the event in the class declaration:

```
virtual void __fastcall LimitReached();
```

Then we must write the function body that actually triggers the event:

```
void __fastcall TFlashingLabel::LimitReached()
{
  //
  // Set the default value for the Stop parameter. If the
  // user doesn't do anything to modify the parameter then
  // this value will be returned.
  //
  bool stop = false;
  //
  // If an event handler has been attached to this event
  // then call it. (Event is triggered here.)
  //
  if (OnLimitReached) OnLimitReached(this, stop);
  //
  // Set the value of the FlashEnabled property based
  // on the value of the Stop parameter.
  //
  FlashEnabled = !stop;
}
```

There are several things to note here. First, notice that we set up the default value of the Stop parameter. If the user doesn't modify the parameter, the value of Stop will be false. The Stop parameter is used to determine whether the flashing should stop when the FlashLimit value is reached. In the event handler for the event (in the application that uses the component), the user can set Stop to true to cause the flashing to stop or leave the Stop parameter as is to allow the flashing to continue.

Now notice the line that triggers the event:

```
if (OnLimitReached) OnLimitReached(this, stop);
```

If the user of the component has attached an event handler to the event, you call the event handler. If no event handler has been attached, you just do the default handling for the event. (In this case, there is no default handling.) It is important to allow the user to ignore the event if he so chooses. This code allows that.

NOTE

> One of the things that is difficult to grasp when writing events is that the component itself does not provide the event handler. The application using our component provides the event handler; we only provide

> the mechanism by which the event handler can be called when the
> event occurs.

As mentioned earlier, this function is a virtual function. It is a virtual function because derived
classes might want to redefine the default behavior of the event. Because we were kind enough
to make the function virtual, any components derived from our component only have to
override the `LimitReached()` function to change the default event-handling behavior.
This makes it easy to change the behavior of the event without having to hunt through the
code and locate every place the event is triggered. The event is triggered here only in the
`LimitReached()` function.

Writing Code That Triggers the Event

Somewhere in the component must be the code to call the `LimitReached()` function (which,
in turn, triggers the event). In the case of the `TFlashingLabel` component, we will call
`LimitReached()` from the `OnTimer()` function. Here's how the function looks after being
modified to trigger the event:

```
void __fastcall TFlashingLabel::OnTimer(TObject* Sender)
{
  //
  // If the component is on a form in design mode then
  // stop the timer and return.
  //
  if (ComponentState.Contains(csDesigning)) {
    Timer->Enabled = false;
    return;
  }
  //
  // Toggle the Visible property each time the timer
  // event occurs.
  //
  Visible = !Visible;
  //
  // Trigger the event if needed. Only increment the counter
  // when the label is visible (on, if you prefer).
  //
  if (FFlashLimit && Visible)  {
    //
    // Increment the FlashCount data member.
    //
    FlashCount++;
    //
    // If the FlashCount is greater than or equal to the
    // value of the FlashLimit property then reset the
    // FlashCount value to 0 and trigger the event.
```

20

```
  //
  if (FlashCount >= FFlashLimit) {
    FlashCount = 0;
    LimitReached();
  }
 }
}
```

As you can see, when the FlashLimit is reached, the LimitReached() function is called and the event is triggered. By the way, you only count every other OnTimer event. If you incremented the counter every time the OnTimer() function was called, you would get an inaccurate count because the OnTimer event is fired twice for every flash (on and off).

Overriding Base Class Events

The preceding discussion ties in with something else I wanted to mention briefly. If you want to override the default behavior of one of the events defined in the base class, all you have to do is override its event-triggering function as I've described. For example, let's say you wanted to override the default OnClick event to make the speaker beep when the component is clicked. All you have to do is override the Click() function of the base class, like this:

```
void __fastcall TFlashingLabel::Click()
{
  //
  // Beep the speaker and then call the base class
  // Click() method for the default handling.
  //
  MessageBeep(-1);
  TCustomLabel::Click();
}
```

Because this function is declared as virtual in the base class, it will be called automatically any time the component is clicked with the mouse (it will only work when the component is visible, so keep that in mind if you try to click the component while it is flashing). We just make the speaker beep to prove that it works.

Putting It All Together

You got a peek at most of the new and improved TFlashingLabel component in the preceding pages, but let's look at the entire thing to put it all in perspective. Listing 20.5 shows the TFlashingLabel header, and Listing 20.6 shows the source file for the component. Study the implementation of the OnLimitReached event to gain an understanding of how events should be implemented in your components. Listing 20.7 shows the source unit for the FlashTst test program with the OnLimitReached event handler in use.

Listing 20.5. `FlashingLabel.h` (new and improved).

```
 1: //--------------------------------------------------------------
 2: #ifndef FlashingH
 3: #define FlashingH
 4: //--------------------------------------------------------------
 5: #include <vcl\sysutils.hpp>
 6: #include <vcl\controls.hpp>
 7: #include <vcl\classes.hpp>
 8: #include <vcl\forms.hpp>
 9: #include <vcl\StdCtrls.hpp>
10: //--------------------------------------------------------------
11:
12: //
13: // Define a new type for our event handler. This type takes
14: // a TObject* and a bool reference.
15: //
16: typedef void __fastcall
17:   (__closure *TMyEvent)(System::TObject *Sender, bool& Stop);
18:
19: class TFlashingLabel : public TCustomLabel
20: {
21: private:
22:   //
23:   // Private data members.
24:   //
25:   bool  FFlashEnabled;
26:   int   FFlashRate;
27:   int   FFlashLimit;
28:   int   FlashCount;
29:   TMyEvent FOnLimitReached;
30:   TTimer* Timer;
31: protected:
32:   //
33:   // Protected write methods for the properties.
34:   //
35:   void __fastcall SetFlashEnabled(bool AFlashEnabled);
36:   void __fastcall SetFlashRate(int AFlashRate);
37:   //
38:   // The LimitReached() function to trigger the event.
39:   //
40:   virtual void __fastcall LimitReached();
41:   //
42:   // An overridden Click() method just for an example
43:   // of overriding a base class event. This function will
44:   // be called whenever the component is clicked becuase
45:   // it is a virtual function.
46:   //
47:   virtual void __fastcall Click()
48:   {
49:     //
50:     // Beep the speaker and then call the base class
51:     // Click() method for the default handling.
52:     //
```

continues

Listing 20.5. continued

```
53:      MessageBeep(-1);
54:      TCustomLabel::Click();
55:    }
56:    //
57:    // OnTimer event handler.
58:    //
59:    virtual void __fastcall OnTimer(TObject* Sender);
60: public:
61:    __fastcall virtual TFlashingLabel(TComponent* AOwner);
62: __published:
63:    //
64:    // The component's properties.
65:    //
66:    __property bool FlashEnabled =
67:      {read=FFlashEnabled, write=SetFlashEnabled, default=true};
68:    __property int FlashRate =
69:      {read=FFlashRate, write=SetFlashRate, default=800};
70:    __property int FlashLimit =
71:      {read=FFlashLimit, write=FFlashLimit, default=0};
72:    //
73:    // The OnLimitReached event.
74:    //
75:    __property TMyEvent OnLimitReached =
76:      {read=FOnLimitReached, write=FOnLimitReached};
77: };
78: //------------------------------------------------------------
79: #endif
```

Listing 20.6. `FlashingLabel.cpp` (new and improved).

```
 1: //------------------------------------------------------------
 2: #include <vcl\vcl.h>
 3: #pragma hdrstop
 4:
 5: #include "FlashingLabel.h"
 6: //------------------------------------------------------------
 7: static inline TFlashingLabel *ValidCtrCheck()
 8: {
 9:   return new TFlashingLabel(NULL);
10: }
11: //------------------------------------------------------------
12: __fastcall TFlashingLabel::TFlashingLabel(TComponent* AOwner)
13:   : TCustomLabel(AOwner)
14: {
15:   //
16:   // Set the data members to their default values.
17:   //
18:   FFlashEnabled = true;
19:   FFlashRate = 800;
20:   FFlashLimit = 0;
```

```
21:    FlashCount = 0;
22:    //
23:    // Initialize the timer object.
24:    //
25:    Timer = new TTimer(this);
26:    //
27:    // Set the timer interval using the flash rate.
28:    //
29:    Timer->Interval = FlashRate;
30:    //
31:    // Assign our own OnTimer event handler to the
32:    // TTimer OnTimer event.
33:    //
34:    Timer->OnTimer = &OnTimer;
35: }
36:
37: void __fastcall
38: TFlashingLabel::SetFlashEnabled(bool AFlashEnabled)
39: {
40:    //
41:    // Set FFlashEnabled data member.
42:    //
43:    FFlashEnabled = AFlashEnabled;
44:    //
45:    // Don't start the timer if the oomponent is on a form
46:    // in design mode. Instead, just return.
47:    //
48:    if (ComponentState.Contains(csDesigning)) return;
49:    //
50:    // Start the timer.
51:    //
52:    Timer->Enabled = FFlashEnabled;
53:    //
54:    // If flashing was turned off be sure that the label
55:    // is visible.
56:    //
57:    if (!FFlashEnabled) Visible = true;
58: }
59:
60: void __fastcall TFlashingLabel::SetFlashRate(int AFlashRate)
61: {
62:    //
63:    // Set the FFlashRate data member and the timer interval
64:    // all at the same time.
65:    //
66:    Timer->Interval = FFlashRate = AFlashRate;
67: }
68:
69: void __fastcall TFlashingLabel::OnTimer(TObject* Sender)
70: {
71:    //
72:    // If the component is on a form in design mode then
73:    // stop the timer and return.
74:    //
75:    (ComponentState.Contains(csDesigning)) {
76:      Timer->Enabled = false;
```

20

continues

Listing 20.6. continued

```
 77:    return;
 78:  }
 79:  //
 80:  // Toggle the Visible property each time the timer
 81:  // event occurs.
 82:  //
 83:  Visible = !Visible;
 84:  //
 85:  // Trigger the event if needed. Only increment the counter
 86:  // when the label is visible (on, if you prefer).
 87:  //
 88:  if (FFlashLimit && Visible)  {
 89:    //
 90:    // Increment the FlashCount data member.
 91:    //
 92:    FlashCount++;
 93:    //
 94:    // If the FlashCount is greater than or equal to the
 95:    // value of the FlashLimit property then reset the
 96:    // FlashCount value to 0 and trigger the event.
 97:    //
 98:    if (FlashCount >= FFlashLimit) {
 99:      FlashCount = 0;
100:      LimitReached();
101:    }
102:  }
103: }
104:
105: void __fastcall TFlashingLabel::LimitReached()
106: {
107:   //
108:   // Set the default value for the Stop parameter. If the
109:   // user doesn't do anything to modify the parameter then
110:   // this value will be returned.
111:   //
112:   bool stop = false;
113:   //
114:   // If an event handler has been attached to this event
115:   // then call it. (Event is triggered here.)
116:   //
117:   if (OnLimitReached) OnLimitReached(this, stop);
118:   //
119:   // Set the value of the FlashEnabled property based
120:   // on the value of the Stop parameter.
121:   //
122:   FlashEnabled = !stop;
123:   //
124:   // Beep just because.
125:   //
126:   MessageBeep(-1);
127: }
128:
129: namespace Flashinglabel {
130:   //
```

20

```
131: // Register the component.
132: //
133: void __fastcall Register()
134: {
135:   TComponentClass classes[1] = {__classid(TFlashingLabel)};
136:   RegisterComponents("Samples", classes, 0);
137: }
138: }
```

Listing 20.7. FlashTst.cpp.

```
 1: //----------------------------------------------------------
 2: #include <vcl\vcl.h>
 3: #pragma hdrstop
 4:
 5: #include "FlashingLabel.h"
 6: #include "FTMain.h"
 7: //----------------------------------------------------------
 8: #pragma resource "*.dfm"
 9: TMainForm *MainForm;
10: //----------------------------------------------------------
11: __fastcall TMainForm::TMainForm(TComponent* Owner)
12:   : TForm(Owner)
13: {
14:   Flasher = new TFlashingLabel(this);
15:   Flasher->Parent = this;
16:   Flasher->SetBounds(20, 20, 200, 20);
17:   Flasher->Font->Size = 16;
18:   Flasher->Caption = "This is a test";
19:   Flasher->FlashRate = 800;
20:   Flasher->FlashLimit = 5;
21:   Flasher->OnLimitReached = OnLimitReached;
22: }
23: //----------------------------------------------------------
24: void __fastcall TMainForm::FlashBoxClick(TObject *Sender)
25: {
26:   Flasher->FlashEnabled = FlashBox->Checked;
27: }
28: //----------------------------------------------------------
29: void __fastcall TMainForm::GroupClick(TObject *Sender)
30: {
31:   switch (Group->ItemIndex) {
32:     case 0 :  Flasher->FlashRate = 1200; break;
33:     case 1 :  Flasher->FlashRate = 800; break;
34:     case 2 :  Flasher->FlashRate = 400; break;
35:     case 3 :  Flasher->FlashRate = 150; break;
36:   }
37: }
38: //----------------------------------------------------------
39: void __fastcall
40: TMainForm::OnLimitReached(TObject* Sender, bool& Stop)
41: {
42:   //
```

20

continues

Listing 20.7. continued

```
43:   // The OnLimitReached event handler. Set Stop to true to
44:   // stop flashing or leave as-is to continue flashing.
45:   //
46:   Stop = true;
47: }
```

 This component and the `FlashTst` test program are included on the CD that accompanies the book. However, the component's source is called `Flashing.cpp` and the header is `Flashing.h`.

Run the test program to see if the event works as advertised. Experiment with the test program to get a better feeling for how the event and the event handler work. Notice that the speaker beeps when you click on the label (as long is it is visible). This is because of the inline function called `Click()` in the component's class declaration. I added this function to illustrate overriding a base class event.

 NOTE

> If you want to install the new `FlashingLabel` component on the Component Palette, choose Component | Rebuild Library from the main menu, and the old version of `FlashingLabel` will be updated to the new version.

Writing events takes some time to master. You must kiss a lot of frogs before being rewarded with the prince (or princess). In other words, there's no substitute for experience when it comes to writing events. You just have to get in there and do it. You'll probably hit a few bumps along the way, but it will be good experience and you'll find yourself a better programmer for it.

Summary

Well, you're in the big leagues now. Writing components is not for the faint of heart. Once you've got a basic understanding of writing components, the world is at your fingertips. If you are anything like me, you will learn to enjoy your nonvisual programming time as much as you enjoy the visual programming you do. If you are feeling a bit blown away by this chapter, don't feel bad. You may have to let it soak in for a few days and then come back to it later. You may have to read several different documents on writing components before it all comes together. Keep at it and it will eventually make sense.

Workshop

The Workshop contains quiz questions to help you solidify your understanding of the material covered and exercises to provide you with experience in using what you have learned. You can find answers to the quiz questions in Appendix A, "Answers to Quiz Questions."

Q&A

Q Is there any reason I must know how to write components?

A No. You can use the basic components that C++Builder gives you in your applications. You might never find the need to write components.

Q Can I buy components?

A Yes. A wide variety of sources exist for third-party component libraries. These libraries are sold by companies that specialize in VCL components. In addition, many freeware or shareware components are available from various online sources. Be sure to search the Internet for sources of VCL components.

Q Can I use my Delphi components with C++Builder?

A Yes. C++Builder has the capability to compile and install Delphi components. Just install them like you would a C++Builder component.

Q Do I have to use read and write methods to store my property's value?

A No. You can use direct access and store the property's value directly in the underlying data member associated with the property.

Q What's the advantage of using a write method for my properties?

A Using a write method allows you to perform other operations when a property is written to. Writing to a property often causes the component to perform specific tasks. Using a write method will allow you to carry out those tasks.

Q Why would I want a property to be public but not published?

A A published property is displayed in the Object Inspector at design time. Some properties do not have a design-time interface. Those properties should be made public so the user can modify or read them at runtime but not at design time.

Q How do I test my component to be sure it works correctly before I install it?

A Write a test program and add the component's source file to it. In the constructor of the main form, create an instance of your component. Set any properties that you need to set prior to the component being made visible. In the test program, manipulate the public properties of your component to see if everything works properly.

20

Q Do I have to write events for my components?

A Not necessarily. Some components make use of events; others do not. Don't go out of your way to write events for your components, but by the same token don't shy away from writing events when you need them.

Quiz

1. Must a property use a write method?

2. Must a property have an underlying data member?

3. Can you create a component by modifying an existing component?

4. What happens if you do not specify a write specifier (either a write method or direct access) in a property's declaration?

5. What does direct access mean?

6. Must your properties have a default value?

7. Does the default value of the property set the underlying data member's value automatically?

8. How do you install a component on the Component Palette?

9. How do you specify the button bitmap your component will use on the Component Palette?

10. How do you trigger a user-defined event?

Exercises

1. Review the FlashingLabel component source in Listing 20.5 and 20.6. Study it to learn what is happening in the code.

2. Remove the FlashingLabel component from the component library. Reinstall the FlashingLabel component.

3. Write a test program that uses three FlashingEdit components, all with different flash rates.

4. Change the bitmap for the FlashingLabel button on the Component Palette to one of your own design.

5. Write a write method for the FlashLimit property of the FlashingLabel component so that the user cannot enter a number greater than 100.

6. Change the OnLimitReached event for the FlashingLabel component to a regular notification event (**Hint:** TNotifyEvent).

7. **Extra credit:** Write a component of your own design.

8. **Extra credit:** Test your new component and install it on the Component Palette.

Day **21**

C++Builder and Delphi

by Ken Henderson

One of the first things people notice about Borland C++Builder is how similar it looks to Borland's Delphi. Naturally, questions arise about what differences there are between the products and why two separate products exist in the first place. Today I'll attempt to provide some answers to these questions and cover how C++Builder relates to and can be used in conjunction with Delphi.

Major Differences Between C++Builder and Delphi

The biggest difference between C++Builder and Delphi is that Delphi is based on the Object Pascal programming language, while C++Builder is (obviously) based on C++. Object Pascal is the latest rendition of the highly successful Turbo Pascal language that Borland originally introduced in the 1980s. Although many developers knew and loved Pascal in the '80s, until Delphi was released, the Pascal language was nearing extinction. Delphi saved the language from certain oblivion, and now more developers are using it than ever. Despite this, C has been, and probably always will be, more popular than Pascal. If you were one of those who declined to give Delphi a try because it was based on Object Pascal, you're in luck. Borland C++Builder gives you most of Delphi's good points in a C++-based product.

I should point out that Delphi has benefited significantly because it's based on Object Pascal rather than C++. Borland essentially defines the standard for the Object Pascal programming language; it doesn't answer to a committee regarding compatibility with other vendors or compilers. This has allowed it to extend Object Pascal for the express purpose of supporting Delphi's visual development model. Whereas C++ tool vendors must answer to the ANSI standards committee regarding changes they make to the language, the people who modify Delphi are shackled by none of this. The end result is that Borland has been able to craft Object Pascal to perfectly suit visual development, all the while retaining the ability to compile it into machine language. Being a nonconformist can have its advantages.

However, nonconformity can also have its drawbacks. For one thing, third-party libraries for Borland's Pascal dialects have historically been scarce compared to the wealth of offerings out there for the C and C++ programming languages. For another, should Borland ever decide to inexplicably goof up Object Pascal in some horrendous way (I rather doubt this will ever happen), no standards group would be present to challenge it. Because there's no real competition in the Object Pascal arena, Borland's implementation *is* the de facto standard.

I couldn't care less about the lack of involvement with a standards body or the occasional dearth of add-on libraries for Object Pascal or Delphi. However, this is a *huge* deal to some people. Those people will be pleased to know that underneath all C++Builder's glamour and glitz is the same standards-based C++ implementation they've come to know and love in Borland's C++ product line. You can think of C++Builder as a cross between Delphi 2.0 and Borland C++ 5.0. Yes, it's a RAD (rapid application development) tool, but it's also a standards-based tool. This is yet another way that C++Builder differs from Delphi. Delphi is definitely the maverick of the two.

Other Differences Between C++Builder and Delphi

Now that I've covered the major ways that C++Builder and Delphi differ from one another, let's regress and cover some of their minor differences. This is primarily for the benefit of those people coming from Delphi to C++Builder.

Project Files

C++Builder stores project options in project *makefiles* (files ending with the extension .MAK). Delphi, by contrast, stores its project options in files with the extension .DOF.

The makefile in which C++Builder stores compiler/linker options is fully functional—you can use it outside of C++Builder with the supplied command-line tools. You can even edit C++Builder's makefiles to set up advanced compiler or linker options not supported by the C++Builder IDE.

WARNING

> Any outside modifications to these makefiles must employ valid C++Builder makefile syntax if you want to continue using them with the C++Builder IDE.

The Component Library

Another small way in which C++Builder and Delphi differ is the way the Visual Component Library (VCL) is implemented. Object file DLLs form the basis of the C++Builder VCL. Delphi 2.0, by contrast, implements its VCL through DCU (Delphi Component Unit) files.

Multiple Language Support

Although it is strictly C++ based, C++Builder will still compile Delphi Object Pascal modules. You can also open Delphi forms in C++Builder and install Delphi-based components. This is in stark contrast to Delphi itself, which supports Object Pascal exclusively. In C++Builder, you can freely mix .PAS and .CPP source code modules in the applications and DLLs you build.

Header Files

Unlike Delphi, C++Builder uses a separate header file to publish a form's class definition. Delphi always stores the class definitions that correspond with forms you build in the interface section of the form's source file. C++Builder, by contrast, stores this information in a separate header (.H file), which it then includes in the form's main source code module.

21

C++Builder Emulation of Delphi Elements

There are several areas in which C++Builder emulates features originally pioneered by Delphi. This helps ensure that the two environments are as compatible as possible and helps produce the same magic in C++Builder that has made Delphi so popular.

Compiler Changes

One area in which changes have been made is the C++Builder compiler, to which several changes have been made to make it more Delphi-like. For example, the compiler has been changed to support native properties and native closures as well as a number of new Delphi-related keywords. For example, `__declspec`, `delphiclass`, `delphireturn`, `__automated`, `__published`, `__closure`, `__property`, `__classid(class)`, and `__dispid(int)` are all new keywords added specifically for compatibility and interoperability with Delphi.

New Classes

A number of new C++ classes have also been added on Delphi's behalf. The `AnsiString`, `Variant`, `ShortString`, `Currency`, `TDateTime`, and `Set` classes have all been added to C++Builder for compatibility with Delphi.

Component Support

Because C++Builder's linker supports linking Delphi DCUs, you can install and use Delphi 2.0 components with C++Builder. If you have source code for these components, you can install them on the C++Builder Component Palette and use them in your own applications or base new components on them.

Open Arrays

Delphi features complete support for *open arrays*—arrays whose exact number and type of elements is unknown at compile time. C++Builder also supports this powerful facility and provides several helper macros to assist with using it. The following helper macros are provided for working with open arrays in C++Builder: `OPENARRAY`, `ARRAYOFCONST`, `EXISTINGARRAY`, and `SLICE`.

Development Environment

Other than the title at the top of the screen, you'll notice that the C++Builder Integrated Development Environment (IDE) is nearly identical to that of Delphi 2.0. The Object

Inspector, Form Designer, and Component Palette are, for all intents and purposes, identical between the two products. If you've used Delphi before, you should be right at home in C++Builder. Figures 21.1 and 21.2 illustrate the striking similarities between the two environments.

Figure 21.1.

The C++Builder IDE.

Figure 21.2.

The Delphi 2.0 IDE.

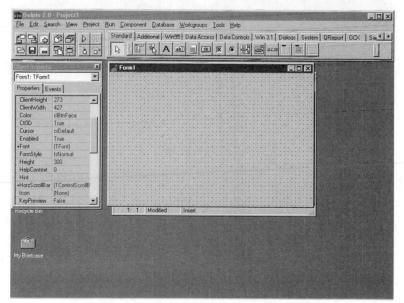

21

Database Access

Because both Delphi and C++Builder utilize the Borland Database Engine to access databases, they are extremely similar when it comes to database app development. Concepts that apply to Delphi's database access apply equally well to C++Builder.

Summary

Today's brief discussion focuses on the similarities and differences between C++Builder and Borland's Delphi, including their language elements, component issues, compiler nuances, and advanced features. I hope this discussion will help you understand the relative strengths and weaknesses of the two environments well enough to work with them effectively.

Workshop

The Workshop contains quiz questions to help you solidify your understanding of the material covered and exercises to provide you with experience in using what you have learned. You can find answers to the quiz questions in Appendix A, "Answers to Quiz Questions."

Q&A

Q Can I compile Delphi's Object Pascal in C++Builder?

A Yes, C++Builder can compile Object Pascal source code modules.

Q Can I compile my C++Builder source modules in Delphi?

A No, Delphi can compile only Object Pascal source code modules.

Q Can components designed for Delphi also be used with C++Builder?

A Yes.

Quiz

1. What are some of the new Delphi-related keywords in C++Builder?
2. Does C++Builder support Object Pascal open arrays?
3. What are some of the new Delphi-related classes that have been added to C++Builder?
4. What version of Delphi does C++Builder most closely resemble?
5. When you create a new form and begin dropping components onto it, where is the form's class definition stored as you build it visually?

Exercises

1. Install a component in C++Builder that was originally designed for Delphi.

2. Open a Delphi-based form in C++Builder.

3. Open one of C++Builder's .MAK files in its Code Editor and inspect the make syntax it uses.

4. Design a simple one-form app in both Delphi and C++Builder; then compare the number of lines of code that must be compiled in each case to produce an executable.

21

In Review

That was a pretty productive week, wasn't it? You probably had no idea that database operations could be so easy. Easy is a relative thing. I wouldn't go so far as to say that database programming is ever simple, but C++Builder certainly makes it easier than it would be in other C++ frameworks.

I told you that you would learn about DLLs and that you could then decide whether to use DLLs in your applications. Regardless of what you decide, you can now see the benefit of DLLs and can make an informed decision. If you plan on calling C++Builder forms from programs not written in C++Builder, you will have to use DLLs. DLLs can be frustrating to get working at first. Like I said, the secret is to get the headers designed correctly. Once you've got that done, the rest is just regular old C++ programming. DLLs are not difficult, but here again, a little experience will go a long way.

On Day 20 you learned about creating your own components. You either loved it or you were left scratching your head. If the latter, don't worry about it. You may never have to write your own components. There are plenty of sources for good, commercial-quality components out there. Plus, you can always go back and tackle Day 20 again after you've got some time in your C++Builder log book. If you enjoyed learning about writing components, it was probably difficult to get you to read the last chapter! I'd be willing to bet that at some time during Day 20 you could have been overheard saying, "Cool!" Writing your own components is cool, no question. We only had time to scratch the surface of writing components. There is a lot more to learn, and much of that can be learned by experience only. Hopefully, this chapter gave you enough to get you started.

Finally, you learned about how you can use C++Builder code (forms and DLLs, for instance) in applications written in other programming environments. The ability to call C++Builder forms from other applications is an important part of C++Builder. Understanding how to use C++Builder with other programming environments makes you a more valuable programmer.

Bonus Day

Day 22

Building Internet Applications

by Ken Henderson

Today you'll explore building Internet applications with C++Builder. Because C++Builder ships with a suite of Internet-related OCX controls, it's ideally suited for building applications that access the Internet. In this chapter you'll learn the purpose of the Internet controls and use them to build your very own Web browser. Specifically, today's lesson will consist of

- [ ] An introduction to building Internet applications with C++Builder
- [ ] A tour of the Internet page of the C++Builder Component Palette
- [ ] A tutorial session that takes you through the process of building your own Web browser using C++Builder

The Basics

Because C++Builder's underlying language is C++, and C++ is such a popular programming language, you can do almost anything you'd like in C++Builder, including build Internet applications. The specifications have been published and the necessary interfaces established to build Internet applications from scratch using C++Builder, if that's your pleasure. Like any other natively compiled C++ environment, you could include the appropriate header files and code whole Internet applications in C++ if you really wanted to.

But that would remove the biggest and best reason for using a tool like C++Builder in the first place—its expediency. You use RAD (rapid application development) tools like C++Builder because they're fast. At the same time, you don't want something that's just thrown together—you want a tool that generates *efficient* executables efficiently.

C++Builder really shines in its capability to construct natively compiled executables through dragging and dropping components. Like its elder sister Delphi, C++Builder combines the best of the object-oriented and component-based development models to provide a development platform that is easy to use and extremely powerful.

What does this have to do with Internet development? Well, for starters, it means that, thanks to C++Builder's Internet component set, you can build Internet-related applications as easily as any other type of application—by dropping components on a form. It also means that you can extend these components to enhance them, while still being able to manipulate low-level API details, if you need to, because C++Builder is natively compiled and C++ based.

To work directly with the low-level APIs (for example, ISAPI) that are required to build Internet client and server applications, your tool of choice must be able to use and construct DLLs and to utilize the published interfaces to these DLLs. C++Builder is natively compiled and can both use and create DLLs. Also, because it's C++ based, interfaces to all the major Internet-related APIs are readily available for it. What you have in C++Builder is the Swiss Army Knife of Win32 development. Whether it's a game, a database program, or an Internet application, you'll find that C++Builder takes you where you want to go and even makes the trip somewhat enjoyable.

A Tour of the Internet Component Palette Page

Before we get started building your Web browser, let's take a brief tour of the components on the Internet page of the C++Builder Component Palette. Although you'll only use one of these components in today's sample project, it's helpful to know what's available to you. Table 22.1 lists each component and describes its function.

Table 22.1. C++Builder's Internet components and their respective functions.

Component	Description
FTP	Supports exchanging files with remote machines
THTML	Supports parsing and layout of HTML data and provides a scrollable view of the current HTML page
THTTP	Provides access to the Hypertext Transfer Protocol
TNTTP	Provides the ability to read and post to newsgroups
TPOP	Provides access to the POP3 electronic mail protocol
TSMTP	Supports sending Internet mail messages to SMTP servers
TTCP	Provides access to the WinSock Transfer Control Protocol (both client and server side)
TUDP	Provides access to the WinSock User Datagram Protocol (both client and server)

Some of these components provide access to popular Internet elements with which you're probably familiar. For example, if you were going to build an FTP utility, you would use the FTP component. If you were building a newsreader, you'd use the NTTP component. If you were constructing a Web browser (as we are today), you'd make use of the THTML control. If you wanted to send mail over the Internet, you might make use of the POP or SMTP component. This bevy of high-level controls makes much of the WinSock coding of yesteryear obsolete and makes developing sophisticated Internet-related applications a snap.

Building Your Web Browser

Now that I've introduced you to C++Builder's Internet components, let's build a simple Web browser. It's not like the world really needs yet another Web browser; the purpose of this exercise is to demonstrate how easy it is to put together Internet apps that would have been major undertakings just a couple of years ago. C++Builder's component-based approach to development allows you to concentrate on what you want to do rather than on how to do it.

Let's begin by starting a new project in C++Builder. Choose File | New Application from the C++Builder menu system to initialize a new application project. When the new project is started, you'll be presented with a new, blank form on which you can drop components. This form will be your Web browser. Set its Caption property to Surf and its Position property to poScreenCenter. Before you proceed, go ahead and save the new application as Surf.CPP and its associated form as Surf00.CPP. I suggest you use these similar yet different filenames for project and form files because a project file and a form file cannot have the same name. For single-form applications, naming the project and its one form differently may seem a bit strange, but C++Builder requires it nonetheless.

Begin constructing your Web browser form by dropping a TTabControl component on the top of the form. This control will list URLs as you browse them so that you can easily return to one you've already visited. Set the control's Align property to alTop. This will make it expand to occupy the top of the form. Thanks to alTop, your TTabControl will always occupy the topmost region of the form, no matter how large or how small the form becomes. You can drag the TTabControl's bottom border to size it vertically.

Next, change the TTabControl component's TabWidth property to something in the neighborhood of 145 pixels. This will ensure that each tab is large enough to display simple URLs without allowing any one tab to take up too much space. Figure 22.1 shows what your TTabControl might look like.

Figure 22.1.

*Your Web browser
form with
TTabControl
in place.*

Now that the top of the browser form is in place, let's set up the bottom. Drop a TPanel component onto the bottom of the form and set its Align property to alBottom. As with the TTabControl component, this will cause the TPanel control to always occupy the bottom of the form, regardless of how the form is resized.

Press F11 to bring up the Object Inspector; then delete TPanel's Caption property. Set its TabOrder property to 0. This will cause TPanel's default component (which you'll drop in place momentarily) to be the form's default when it first displays.

After you've set up the TPanel, you're ready to drop its child controls onto it. Begin by dropping another TPanel component onto the first TPanel's right edge. Set the new TPanel's Align property to alRight and delete its Caption property. This will allow you to position controls so that they are always on the form's far right, no matter how the form is resized.

Next, drop two TBitBtn components onto the new TPanel. Set the Caption property of the first button to Go! and the Caption property of the second to Home. You can set the Glyph property of each button to the bitmap of your choosing. Set the Go! button's Default property to true. This will allow the user to simply type a URL and then press Enter to jump to it. The Go! button will cause your browser to attempt to open a URL you supply, while the Home button will cause it to jump directly to your home page. I'll show you how to specify a home page in the browser's source code in a moment.

When your buttons are in place, drop a TComboBox onto the left edge of your bottom TPanel, stretch it so that it's as wide as possible, and then delete its Text property. You'll use this combo box to supply Web page addresses that you want to browse. When the application runs, you'll type a URL into the TComboBox and click the Go! button to browse it. Figure 22.2 shows what your form should look like so far.

Figure 22.2.

Your Web browser form with its bottom and top sections in place.

Now that the top and bottom of your Web browser form are complete, let's supply the middle. Drop a THTML component onto the form's middle and set its Align property to alClient. This will cause it to take all the form space not already occupied by the top TTabControl or the bottom TPanel. When the form is resized, minimized, maximized, or restored, the area of the form that renders HTML will expand or shrink with it. Figure 22.3 shows your form with all its controls in place.

Figure 22.3.

Your new form as it appears with all its visual controls.

Giving the New Form Life

When your form is all set up visually, you still need to attach code to its events in order for it to do anything. The biggest event that you'll customize is the OnBeginRetrieval event of the THTML component. Of course, you'll also attach custom code to the OnClick event of both your buttons and also to the OnChange event of your TTabControl.

Begin by clicking on your TTabControl and then double-clicking its OnChange event in the Object Inspector. Type the following code into the C++Builder Code Editor:

```
cbURL->Text=tcURL->Tabs->Strings[tcURL->TabIndex];
cbURL->SelectAll();
bbGo->Click();
```

NOTE

> This code sample and the others in this chapter assume you've adopted some sort of naming conventions for the objects in your application. I always prefix identifier names with a two-character mnemonic that allows me to identify the type of component represented by the identifier. Here, cbURL refers to the TComboBox control you placed on the bottom TPanel, tcURL refers to the TTabControl at the top of the form, and bbGo refers to the Go! TBitBtn component.

Setting cbURL's Text property to the text of the tab that was clicked when the OnChange event fired ensures that the cbURL control and the tcURL control stay synchronized. Calling the SelectAll() method ensures that the TComboBox's Text property value is highlighted. The call to bbGo's Click() event simulates actually clicking the button. This allows clicking a tab and clicking the Go! button to behave identically.

Now that the tab control is set up, click on the THTML component and then double-click on its OnBeginRetrieve event in the C++Builder Object Inspector. Type this code into the Code Editor:

```
Cursor=(TCursor)crHourGlass;
if (cbURL->Items->IndexOf(htBrowser->URL)==-1) {
    cbURL->Items->Add(htBrowser->URL);
    cbURL->Text=htBrowser->URL;
    cbURL->SelectAll();
    tcURL->Tabs->Add(htBrowser->URL);
    tcURL->TabIndex=tcURL->Tabs->Count-1;
    bbGo->Click();
}
```

This code checks whether the list of URLs maintained by the TComboBox contains the one about to be browsed. If the URL isn't there, the code adds it to both the TComboBox and the TTabControl.

Notice the assignment of the form's `Cursor` property. This is done to show that the form is in the process of loading a Web page.

Of course, once the cursor is set to an hourglass, it needs to be reset to its normal representation at some point. The place to do this is in the `THTML` component's `OnEndRetrieve` event. Type this code into the `OnEndRetrieve` method handler:

```
Cursor=(TCursor)crDefault;
```

This will reset the cursor once the selected Web page loads.

Now that the `TTabControl` and `THTML` controls are set up, you're ready to configure your buttons. Double-click the Go! button in the Form Designer to bring up its `OnClick` method handler. Type the following code into it:

```
htBrowser->RequestDoc(cbURL->Text);
```

This simply tells the `THTML` control (named `htBrowser` here) to open whatever URL is specified in the `TComboBox` (named `cbURL` here).

When you're finished with the Go! button, double-click the Home button to set it up. Type the following code into the C++Builder Code Editor:

```
htBrowser->RequestDoc(HomePage);
```

This code relies on a constant named `HomePage`, which you'll need to define in advance. Go to the top of `Surf00.CPP` and type in a declaration for the `HomePage` variable like so:

```
String HomePage = "http://www.borland.oom";
```

You can place the `HomePage` declaration right after your form's instance variable declaration if you want—it helps keep the form's global variables together.

After you've set up this constant, you're finished with your very basic browser. Listings 22.1 through 22.3 show what your new application's source code should look like thus far.

Listing 22.1. The header file to your Web browser's main form, Surf00.

```
 1: //----------------------------------------------------------------
 2: #ifndef Surf00H
 3: #define Surf00H
 4: //----------------------------------------------------------------
 5: #include <vcl\Classes.hpp>
 6: #include <vcl\Controls.hpp>
 7: #include <vcl\StdCtrls.hpp>
 8: #include <vcl\Forms.hpp>
 9: #include <vcl\ComCtrls.hpp>
10: #include <vcl\ExtCtrls.hpp>
```

continues

Listing 22.1. continued

```
11: #include <vcl\Buttons.hpp>
12: #include <vcl\ISP.hpp>
13: #include <vcl\OleCtrls.hpp>
14: //----------------------------------------------------------------
15: class TfmBrowser : public TForm
16: {
17: __published:      // IDE-managed Components
18:     TTabControl *tcURL;
19:     TPanel *paHeader;
20:     TComboBox *cbURL;
21:     TBitBtn *bbGo;
22:     THTML *htBrowser;
23:     TBitBtn *bbHome;
24:     void __fastcall bbGoClick(TObject *Sender);
25:     void __fastcall htBrowserBeginRetrieval(TObject *Sender);
26:     void __fastcall tcURLChange(TObject *Sender);
27:     void __fastcall bbHomeClick(TObject *Sender);
28:     void __fastcall htBrowserEndRetrieval(TObject *Sender);
29: private:          // User declarations
30: public:           // User declarations
31:     virtual __fastcall TfmBrowser(TComponent* Owner);
32: };
33: //----------------------------------------------------------------
34: extern TfmBrowser *fmBrowser;
35: //----------------------------------------------------------------
36: #endif
```

Listing 22.2. The C++ source file of your Web browser's main form, Surf00.

```
 1: //----------------------------------------------------------------
 2: #include <vcl\vcl.h>
 3: #pragma hdrstop
 4:
 5: #include "Surf00.h"
 6: //----------------------------------------------------------------
 7: #pragma resource "*.dfm"
 8: TfmBrowser *fmBrowser;
 9: String HomePage = "http://www.borland.com";
10:
11: //----------------------------------------------------------------
12: __fastcall TfmBrowser::TfmBrowser(TComponent* Owner)
13:     : TForm(Owner)
14: {
15: }
16: //----------------------------------------------------------------
17: void __fastcall TfmBrowser::bbGoClick(TObject *Sender)
18: {
19:    htBrowser->RequestDoc(cbURL->Text);
```

```
20: }
21: //------------------------------------------------------------
22: void __fastcall TfmBrowser::htBrowserBeginRetrieval(TObject *Sender)
23: {
24:   Cursor=(TCursor)crHourGlass;
25:   if (cbURL->Items->IndexOf(htBrowser->URL)==-1) {
26:     cbURL->Items->Add(htBrowser->URL);
27:     cbURL->Text=htBrowser->URL;
28:     cbURL->SelectAll();
29:     tcURL->Tabs->Add(htBrowser->URL);
30:     tcURL->TabIndex=tcURL->Tabs->Count-1;
31:     bbGo->Click();
32:   }
33: }
34: //------------------------------------------------------------
35: void __fastcall TfmBrowser::tcURLChange(TObject *Sender)
36: {
37:   cbURL->Text=tcURL->Tabs->Strings[tcURL->TabIndex];
38:   cbURL->SelectAll();
39:   bbGo->Click();
40: }
41: //------------------------------------------------------------
42: void __fastcall TfmBrowser::bbHomeClick(TObject *Sender)
43: {
44:   htBrowser->RequestDoc(HomePage);
45: }
46: //------------------------------------------------------------
47: void __fastcall TfmBrowser::htBrowserEndRetrieval(TObject *Sender)
48: {
49:   Cursor=(TCursor)crDefault;
50: }
51: //------------------------------------------------------------
```

Listing 22.3. The text version of your Web browser's main form, Surf00, as text.

```
 1: object fmBrowser: TfmBrowser
 2:   Left = 249
 3:   Top = 183
 4:   Width = 500
 5:   Height = 337
 6:   Caption = 'Surf'
 7:   Font.Color = clWindowText
 8:   Font.Height = -13
 9:   Font.Name = 'MS Sans Serif'
10:   Font.Style = []
11:   Position = poScreenCenter
12:   PixelsPerInch = 120
13:   TextHeight = 16
14:   object tcURL: TTabControl
15:     Left = 0
```

continues

Listing 22.3. continued

```
16:      Top = 0
17:      Width = 492
18:      Height = 33
19:      Align = alTop
20:      TabOrder = 1
21:      TabWidth = 145
22:      OnChange = tcURLChange
23:    end
24:    object paHeader: TPanel
25:      Left = 0
26:      Top = 264
27:      Width = 492
28:      Height = 41
29:      Align = alBottom
30:      TabOrder = 0
31:      object cbURL: TComboBox
32:        Left = 16
33:        Top = 8
34:        Width = 353
35:        Height = 24
36:        ItemHeight = 16
37:        TabOrder = 0
38:      end
39:      object bbGo: TBitBtn
40:        Left = 368
41:        Top = 8
42:        Width = 51
43:        Height = 25
44:        Caption = 'Go!'
45:        Default = True
46:        TabOrder = 1
47:        OnClick = bbGoClick
48:        Glyph.Data = {
49:          78010000424D780100000000000076000000280000002000000010000000100
50:          0400000000000000000000120B0000120B00000000000000000000000000000000
51:          80000080000000808000800000008000800080800000F7F7F00BFBFBF000000
52:          FF0000FF000000FFFF00FF000000FF00FF00FFFF0000FFFFFF00555555555555
53:          555555FFFFFFFFFF55555000000000055555577777777775FFFF00B8B8B8B8B0
54:          0000775F5555555777770B0B8B8B8B8B8B0FF07F75F555555575F70FB0B8B8B8B8
55:          B0F07F575FFFFFFFF7F70BFB0000000000F07F557777777777570FBFBF0FFFFF
56:          FFF07F55557F5FFFFFF70BFBFB0F000000F07F55557F777777570FBFBF0FFFFF
57:          FFF075F5557F5FFFFFF750FBFBF0F000000F0575FFF7F777777575700000FFFFF
58:          FFF05577777F5FF55FF75555550F00FF00005555557F775577775555550FFFFF
59:          0F055555557F55557F755555550FFFFF00555555557FFFFF7755555555000000
60:          055555555577777775555555555555555555555555555555555555550000}
61:        NumGlyphs = 2
62:      end
63:      object bbHome: TBitBtn
64:        Left = 424
```

```
65:        Top = 8
66:        Width = 65
67:        Height = 25
68:        Caption = 'Home'
69:        Default = True
70:        TabOrder = 2
71:        OnClick = bbHomeClick
72:        Glyph.Data = {
73:          780100004244D78010000000000000076000000280000002000000010000000000100
74:          040000000000000000000120B0000120B00000000000000000000000000000000000
75:          8000008000000080800080000000800080008080000007F7F7F00BFBFBF000000000
76:          FF0000FF000000FFFF00FF000000FF00FF00FFFF0000FFFFFF00330000000000
77:          03333377777777777F33330111111111110333337F333333337F33330111111111
78:          0333337F333333337F33330111111111110333337F333333337F33330111111111
79:          0333337F333333337F33330111111111110333337F333333337F33330111111111
80:          0333337F3333333F7F3333011111111B10333337F333333737F33330111111111
81:          0333337F333333337F33330111111111110333337F33FFFFF37F3333011EEEEE11
82:          0333337F377777F37F3333011EEEEE110333337F37FFF7F37F3333011EEEEE11
83:          0333337F377777337F33330111111111110333337F333333337F33330111111111
84:          0333337FFFFFFFFF7F33330000000000003333377777777777773330000}
85:        NumGlyphs = 2
86:      end
87:    end
88:    object htBrowser: THTML
89:      Left = 0
90:      Top = 33
91:      Width = 492
92:      Height = 231
93:      Align = alClient
94:      ParentColor = False
95:      ParentFont = False
96:      TabOrder = 2
97:      OnBeginRetrieval = htBrowserBeginRetrieval
98:      OnEndRetrieval = htBrowserEndRetrieval
99:      ControlData = {
100:        2143341208000000AE2800001A13000000001010100011E0000000100000000
101:        C0C0C000000000000000FF00FF00FF00010000009001C0D401000F54696D6573
102:        204E657720526F6D616E010000009001007701000B436F7572696572204E6577
103:        01000000BC0280A903000F54696D6573204E657720526F6D616E01000000BC02
104:        20BF02000F54696D6573204E657720526F6D616E01000000BC02101B02000F54
105:        696D6573204E657720526F6D616E01000000BC02C0D401000F54696D6573204E
106:        657720526F6D616E01000000BC02007701000F54696D6573204E657720526F6D
107:        616E01000000BC02B03001000F54696D6573204E657720526F6D616E}
108:    end
109: end
```

Now that your new Web browser is complete, you're ready to run it. Save your work; then press F9 to run your new application. Figure 22.4 illustrates what your browser might look like at runtime.

Figure 22.4.
Your new Web
browser at runtime.

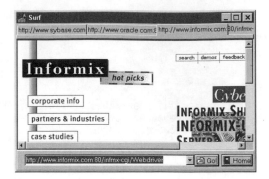

Summary

Today you have learned the purpose of each of the components on the Internet page of the C++Builder Component Palette. You have learned the process involved with taking one of these components, the THTML control, and using it to build an Internet utility—in this case, a Web browser. If you wanted to build an e-mail client or a newsreader, the process would be much the same. C++Builder's component-based architecture allows you to focus on what you want to build rather than on how to build it.

Workshop

The Workshop contains quiz questions to help you solidify your understanding of the material covered and exercises to provide you with experience in using what you have learned. You can find answers to the quiz questions in Appendix A, "Answers to Quiz Questions."

Q&A

Q Who authored the Internet components that ship with C++Builder?

A Borland licensed C++Builder's Internet components from NetManage.

Q If I already have Microsoft Internet Explorer 3.0 installed, is there a way I can utilize it in my browser application rather than the NetManage HTML control?

A Yes—to do so, follow these steps:

    1. Select Component | Install from the C++Builder main menu.

    2. Click the OCX button.

22

3. When the Import OLE Control dialog box appears, select Microsoft Internet Controls in the Registered Controls list.

4. Make sure the Palette page entry is set to Internet so that the new control will be installed onto the Internet page of the C++Builder Component Palette.

5. Click OK and then click OK again. You should see a new control named TWebBrowser on the Internet page of C++Builder's Component Palette. This is the Microsoft Internet Explorer 3.0 browser implemented as an OLE control. Browser applications that you build using it will have the same basic functionality as Microsoft Internet Explorer 3.0 itself.

Quiz

1. What C++Builder component would you use to build your own Internet newsreader application?

2. What event is fired by the THTML control before a document is retrieved?

3. What property of the THTML control contains the address of the current Web page?

4. What component would you use to construct an FTP utility?

Exercises

1. Change the browser you created today to use the Microsoft Internet Explorer 3.0 OCX control instead.

2. Construct a C++Builder application that allows you to subscribe and post to newsgroups.

3. Construct a C++Builder exception handler than sends e-mail when an application exception is thrown.

4. Construct server and client WinSock applications that talk to one another using the TCP component.

5. Build an application that automatically attaches to a given FTP site and downloads any files that you don't already have.

Day 23

C++Builder Extensions to C++

by Kent Reisdorph

C++Builder is a powerful RAD tool. It is largely the PME (properties, methods, and events) model that gives C++Builder its power. The C++ language, however, lacks some language features necessary to fully implement the PME model. In just a moment we'll take a look at the C++Builder extensions to C++, but first I think it would help to talk about what brought us to this point.

What Brought Us Here?

For the past couple years, Borland C++ users and C++ users in general have been crying for a RAD tool that is based on C++. As great as Borland's Delphi is, it is based on ObjectPascal. ObjectPascal is no less a language than C++ in the hands of the average developer, but, as they say, image is everything. There are many organizations (public, private, and government) that flatly refuse to use a product based on Pascal. Obviously, a C++ RAD tool was needed.

So Borland began working on a solution to the problem. It made sense to leverage both the popularity of Delphi and the existing Delphi IDE. After all, people were asking for "Delphi for C++," so why not give them what they ask for? It was obvious that using the Delphi IDE would present no real problem. In fact, it was an immediate solution. There was no point in trying to modify the Borland C++ IDE (or in trying to hybridize the Delphi and Borland C++ IDEs) when the Delphi IDE had most of what users were asking for, not to mention the fact that it was a ready-made solution. So that part was easy.

The hard part came when Borland began looking at the PME model and at how to implement it and still stay 100 percent ANSI C++ compliant. This was a dilemma for Borland because Borland C++ has been one of the few PC-based C++ compilers that has maintained ANSI C++ compliance over the years. (Microsoft has many extensions to Visual C++ that preclude it from making such a claim.) It didn't take long to come to the realization that it just couldn't be done—there was no way to implement the PME model, as it exists in Delphi, and stay within current C++ standards. The solution was to extend C++ in order to leverage the power of the PME model and the already-existing Visual Component Library. At that point the question was not How can we do this? but rather Do we dare do this?

When in doubt, ask the public. Borland conducted marketing surveys in an attempt to determine what developers wanted. The surveys were extensive. One important question Borland wanted answered was, "What is more important to you: rapid application development or maintaining C++ standards?" The results of the survey indicated that strict compliance with C++ standards was not as important to many C++ programmers as it once was. Apparently the overall feeling is that RAD is more alluring than strict adherence to C++ standards. Armed with that information, Borland proceeded to add to the C++Builder implementation of C++ those extensions that it would need in order to implement the PME model.

NOTE

It is important to note that there is nothing to preclude compiling 100 percent ANSI-compliant C++ code with C++Builder. The C++Builder extensions to C++ are there if you need them, but that does not in any way affect C++Builder's ability to compile standard C++ code. If you want strict adherence to C++ standards, you can still use C++Builder to compile your code. If, however, you want to use the RAD aspect of C++Builder, you will have to accept the extensions C++Builder makes to C++. In the long run I'm confident you will find the extensions something you can easily live with.

Language Extensions: The Great Debate

Back in 1994 or so Borland began working on a RAD tool that they codenamed Delphi. Once it was decided that the component model architecture was the best way to implement RAD, it was then necessary to settle on the programming language that would be the heart of the system. At that time Borland was the only compiler vendor mass marketing a Pascal compiler. They were known as the company that produced the best Pascal tools. If you were a Pascal programmer, you probably used Borland's TurboPascal in one flavor or another. Borland more or less "owned" Pascal. While Borland didn't own the Pascal language in a legal sense, they no doubt felt that because of their position in the Pascal world, they could take considerable liberties in implementing new language features and enhancements. In addition, there was no Pascal standards committee to deal with. So Borland created Delphi.

Before Delphi came into being, Borland had already been modifying the Pascal language in positive ways. For instance, Borland had already extended Pascal by creating a new language called ObjectPascal. It could be said that ObjectPascal is to Pascal what C++ is to C. ObjectPascal added classes to Pascal, thereby hurling Pascal into the world of object-oriented programming languages. When Delphi came along, it was easy enough to add new keywords and new language behavior to deal with the component model. Keywords such as `published` and `property` were added, as were others. This allowed Borland to fully implement the power of the component model. By modifying the Pascal language to suit the component model, Borland was able to do RAD right. In essence, the ObjectPascal language was modified as needed when design issues came up during the development of the then-unknown product called Delphi. The result is a language that works seamlessly with the PME model (the component model).

While modifying Pascal could be considered a bold step for Borland, it was not without precedent. Previously Microsoft had taken the BASIC language and modified it to produce a new language called Visual Basic. This new language was nearly unrecognizable when compared to the BASIC language that served as its base. While it could be said that Microsoft took a risk in modifying BASIC to create Visual Basic, Microsoft is after all Microsoft, and they could afford to take the risk. The BASIC language was not being used to any great degree and so there was little or no hue and cry when Microsoft came out with Visual Basic (there was hue and cry, but it was not of the negative type). Borland took more of a risk in modifying Pascal. After all, they had a loyal base of customers that might not take kindly to enhancements to the language they had come to know and love. Still, Borland was in a solid position in the Pascal market and went ahead with their plans. The result was the smash hit Delphi (the Borland internal code name stuck and became the official product name).

But modifying C++ is another matter entirely. As I said at the beginning of the chapter, the world had been crying for a RAD C++ product for a long time, so it was not a question of whether such a product was needed, but more a question of how to go about it. Simply put, the component model that was so brilliantly implemented in Delphi could not be emulated in C++ given the current structure of the language. Something had to give.

The problems associated with modifying the C++ language are many. First, there is a C++ standards committee. It is this committee's job to decide what features should be in the C++ language and how those features should be implemented (there is no such committee for Pascal or BASIC). I could write an entire chapter on whether this system actually works, but I'll spare you the details. Suffice it to say that simply because a C++ standards committee exists means that messing with the C++ language can be expected to be met with some criticism. On the other hand, compiler vendors all implement extensions to the C++ language in some form or another. The theory is that you should be able to take an MFC program, for example, and compile it with any C++ compiler. After all, that's why there is a standard, right? Unfortunately, it doesn't work that way. For whatever reason, MFC contains a fair number of nonstandard extensions to C++ so you cannot, for instance, compile MFC with the Borland compiler without some tweaking (Borland C++ 5.0 does have the ability to compile MFC programs, although Borland had to bend a lot of C++ rules to allow compiling of MFC programs). So, as you can see, it's a less-than-perfect world in which C++ operates to begin with. Since all C++ compiler vendors extend C++ in one way or another, the debate then gets to be one of degree. Company A extended C++ more than did Company B, so Company A has the better C++ compiler. A pointless debate, in my opinion.

One of the other problems with extending the C++ language is public perception. Since C++ is rumored to have a "standard" (yes, I use the word loosely), modifying it in any way might unnerve some dyed-in-the-wool C++ programmers. This is probably a better reason to tread lightly when thinking about C++ language extensions than the standards issue. After all, those people are your customers and you better have a handle on what they think before you start extending their programming language of choice. As I said before, Borland conducted surveys to determine the public's feelings on this issue. Rest assured that they did not arrive at their decision without a great deal of corporate soul searching. The result of the surveys indicated that many programmers would be willing to accept language extensions to have a true RAD product for C++. To them the language debate was not as important as the prospect of increased productivity.

Another problem with extending C++ is the actual implementation. While such an undertaking was no doubt monumental, there is no question in my mind that the engineers at Borland handled it with relative ease. Borland has some of the best minds in the software industry. Once the decision was made to extend the C++ language to take advantage of the component model, I have no doubt that the Borland people got right down to business. So the bottom line is that Borland felt it was worth the risk to extend C++ in order to fully leverage the PME model.

It should be pointed out (again) that the extensions to C++ that exist in C++Builder are just that: extensions. They are there for you to use if you want to take advantage of rapid application development in C++. At its heart, the C++Builder compiler is a standards-compliant C++ compiler, implementing some of the latest features announced by the C++ standards committee. If you don't want to use the C++Builder extensions to C++, you certainly don't have to. If that is the case, however, you probably won't use C++Builder very much (and you probably wouldn't be reading this book!).

New C++ Keywords in C++Builder

So C++Builder does, in fact, extend the C++ language in order to gain the most from the component model. In order to implement the new language extensions, C++Builder introduces several new keywords. The new keywords are

```
__automated
__classid
__closure
__declspec (modified)
__int8
__int16
__int32
__int64
__property
__published
```

Of these new keywords the most obvious, and probably the most important, are the __closure, __property, and __published keywords. Let's take a look at all the new keywords individually.

__automated

The __automated keyword is similar to the public keyword except that the compiler generates automation-type information for functions and data members declared in the __automated section of the class declaration. This is needed when the class is used as an OLE automation server. This is an advanced topic and is not covered in detail here.

__classid

The __classid keyword generates a pointer to a class's virtual function table (vtable). __classid is for C++Builder's internal use and it is not recommended that you use this keyword in your applications.

__closure

A closure is a special type of function pointer. A regular function pointer is a 4-byte value that points to a function within the program's code segment. A closure, on the other hand, is an 8-byte value that contains not only the function address (in the first 4 bytes), but also the address of the specific object in which the function resides (in the last 4 bytes). This type of function pointer is vital to the way C++Builder programs operate. In Pascal this is termed a *method pointer*. A closure is the mechanism that allows you, at design time or runtime, to assign an event handler in one class (in your main form's class, for instance) with an event that occurs in another class (such as in a menu class or a button class). While this is very common in C++Builder programming, it might come as a surprise to learn that the C++ language does not inherently have this ability. The __closure keyword extends C++ to allow events and event handlers to work as they do.

A closure, then, is used with events. An event is a property that uses a function pointer as its data type. So an event *is* a closure. You can declare a closure just as you do a regular function pointer, only with the addition of the __closure keyword:

```
void __fastcall  (__closure *TMyEvent)(System::TObject *Sender);
```

You will generally only use the __closure keyword when writing events for components. While your day-to-day use of C++Builder will rarely make direct use of the __closure keyword, you will still use closures heavily whether you realize it or not. Closures are something that should, in my opinion, be in the C++ language standard.

__declspec

The __declspec keyword is not new to Borland C++ compilers, but it has been extended for use in C++Builder. The delphiclass and delphireturn arguments are new to C++Builder.

You use __delcspec(delphiclass) any time you forward declare a class derived from TObject (whether derived directly or indirectly). You use __delcspec(delphireturn) any time you make a forward declaration of a class derived from Currency, AnsiString, Variant, TDateTime, or Set.

__int8, __int16, __int32, and __int64

The new integer keywords allow you to specify the size of an integer variable: either 8, 16, 32, or 64 bits. In 32-bit Windows a regular int will be 32 bits in size (as will a long). By using one of these new keywords you can specify the size of the variable you want. If, for instance, you only need an integer value between 0 and 255, you could use the __int8 keyword as follows:

```
__int8 x = GetResult();
```

As with the standard int keyword, all integers declared with the new keywords are signed. To make a variable unsigned, precede the integer keyword with the unsigned keyword. For example, to create a 16-bit unsigned integer you would use this:

```
unsigned __int16 left = MainForm->Left;
```

Use the new integer keywords any time you need an integer variable to be a specific size.

__property

The __property keyword is used to declare a property in a class declaration. It is easy to confuse a property with a regular class data member, but a property has several features that distinguish it from a class data member:

- [ ] The ability to associate a read method with the property
- [ ] The ability to associate a write method with the property
- [ ] The ability to set a default value for the property
- [ ] The ability to store itself in the form file
- [ ] The ability to extend a property declared in a base class

Read and Write Methods

Writing to a property often causes something to happen within the component to which the property belongs. For example, changing the Color property of a component causes the background color of the component to be changed immediately without further action from the user. Side effects such as this are implemented through the read and write methods associated with a property. Take the Color property example, for instance. A Color property might be declared like this:

```
__property int Color { read=GetColor, write=SetColor };
```

This declaration tells the compiler to call the GetColor() method of the class (the read method) when the Color property is read, and to call the SetColor() method of the class (the write method) when the Color property is written to. The exact implementation of the GetColor() and SetColor() methods is entirely up to the component writer.

Properties can use direct access rather than read or write methods. A property almost always has a private class data member that is used to store the actual value of the property. It is common to use a write method to effect some change in the component when the property is written to, but no such method when the property is read. In that case you would specify a write method for the property but use direct access to read the property directly from the class data member that holds the property's value. In that case the property's declaration would look something like this:

```
__property int Color { read=FColor, write=SetColor };
```

Now when the property is written to, the SetColor() method is called as before, but when the property is read, the value of the FColor variable is returned rather than a read method being called. (The FColor variable would have been declared in the private section of the component's class declaration.)

A property need not declare either a read or write specifier. If no write specifier is included, the property will be a read-only property (a valuable option at times). If no read specifier is included, the property will be a write-only property (of dubious value). If neither a read nor a write specifier are included, the property can neither be read nor written to, making it a worthless property.

Default Values

Properties can specify the default value that the property should have when it is displayed in the Object Inspector. For instance, let's say that your Color property should default to white (clWhite). In that case, the declaration of the property would look like this:

```
__property int Color { read=FColor, write=SetColor, default=clWhite };
```

This tells the Form Designer to display the default value clWhite in the Object Inspector next to the property. Note that this does not automatically set the underlying data member's value to clWhite. You must still set the underlying data member to the value clWhite in the component's constructor. The use of the default specifier is optional. If you do not specify a default value, 0 will be used (or false in the case of bool properties) as the default value.

Storing the Property

The stored specifier controls how a property is stored in a form's form file. Storing the property refers to storing the property's value in the form file when the project is saved. The value is loaded again from the form file when the form is loaded in the Form Designer, or when the form is displayed in the application. By default all properties in the __published section of the class declaration will be stored automatically. Properties that are contained in the public section of a component's class declaration are not automatically stored. To specifically store a property, you set the stored property to true:

```
__property int Value { read=FValue, write=SetValue, stored=true };
```

As I said, all properties in the __published section of the class declaration will be stored automatically. This is almost always what you want, so you may never have to use the stored specifier for your published properties. But if, for some reason, you want to specifically preclude a property from being stored, you can specify a value of false for the stored specifier:

```
__property int Value { read=FValue, write=SetValue, stored=false };
```

Most of the time you can allow C++Builder to use the default storage action for your properties.

Extending Base Class Properties

It is common to extend a property that is provided in the base class of the component you have created. One of the most common reasons to do so is to change the default value of the property. For instance, let's say you had derived a new component from the TLabel component and that this new component needed to have its text centered. In that case you could redeclare the Alignment property as follows:

```
__property Alignment = { default=taCenter };
```

When your new component is placed on a form in the Form Designer, the Alignment property will now default to taCenter. Note that you only need to add whatever specifiers are needed to change the property. In this example the default specifier is the only one that is changed, so it is the only one listed.

Another common need is to override the default behavior of a component when a particular property is written to. In that case you could redeclare the property and just change the write specifier:

```
__property Alignment = { write=MyWriteAlignment };
```

When you redeclare a published property, be sure that you place the redeclaration in the __published section of the class declaration.

23

__published

The `__published` keyword is used when you want a property to be displayed in the Object Inspector at design time. This keyword is used in a class declaration just like the `public`, `private`, and `protected` keywords are used. For example, a typical class declaration for a C++Builder component might look like this:

```
class TFlashingLabel : public TCustomLabel
{
private:
  //
  // Private data members and functions here.
  //
protected:
  //
  // Protected data members and functions here.
  //
public:
  //
  // Public data members and functions here.
  //
__published:
  //
  // The component's published properties here.
  //
__property int FlashLimit = {read=FFlashLimit, write=FFlashLimit, default=0};
  // more property declarations
};
```

Any properties in the `__published` section will be displayed in the Object Inspector at design time. Although the implementation of the `__published` keyword is trivial, this keyword is one of the major keywords from the standpoint of C++Builder extensions to the C++ language.

Summary

Programming languages evolve based on many factors. One of the most viable reasons for a language to evolve is because programmers require a language feature not found in the current incarnation of that language. That's the way it should be: Ask and ye shall receive—or at least have a chance of receiving at some point in the future. Programming languages are rarely static. They are almost always changing to some degree or another. Changes to a language frequently challenge the comfort level of many of the users of that language. While I don't promote change just for the sake of change, I am certainly open to language extensions when they make sense.

The fact is that Borland decided to add extensions to the C++ language. Those extensions give C++Builder much of its power. It is pointless to debate the language extensions. You can either use C++Builder with all its power and accept the extensions to the C++ language, or you can stick with standard C++ and write Windows programs the hard way. The decision is yours to make. I'm fairly confident that if you are still reading this book at this point, you have decided that the RAD that C++Builder provides outweighs the perceived problem of Borland's extensions to C++. So if you are an existing C++ programmer, you may have to ponder the ramifications of language extensions and decide whether you can live with them. If you are new to C++, you probably don't understand what the fuss is all about. Whichever camp you are from, you can almost certainly be more productive if you use the power that C++Builder offers. That power comes at a price, but I think that the price is a very small one.

23

Workshop

The Workshop contains quiz questions to help you solidify your understanding of the material covered and exercises to provide you with experience in using what you have learned. You can find answers to the questions in Appendix A, "Answers to Quiz Questions."

Q&A

Q I really like C++Builder, but I don't know if I like the language extensions. What are my choices?

A Your choices are fairly simple: Either use C++Builder and learn to accept the language extensions or don't use C++Builder and give up RAD.

Q Is the practice of extending C++ common?

A To a degree, yes, but generally not on the scale of the extensions that C++Builder introduces. The C++Builder extensions are fairly significant.

Q The C++ extensions in C++Builder make C++Builder a nonstandard C++ compiler, right?

A Wrong. The extensions do not prevent C++Builder from being an otherwise standard C++ compiler. C++Builder is a standard C++ compiler *plus* it gives you RAD through language extensions.

Quiz

1. What is the name of the keyword that is used to declare a property?
2. Is an event a closure?
3. What does the `__published` keyword do?
4. Is the `declspec` keyword new to C++Builder?

Exercises

1. Write a short paragraph on whether you think C++ language extensions are acceptable to gain RAD in Windows programming.

2. Search the various online source for a copy of the C++ standard draft. Read portions of the draft to gain a better understanding of what is involved in maintaining a language like C++.

3. **Extra Credit**: Write a component that uses a published property.

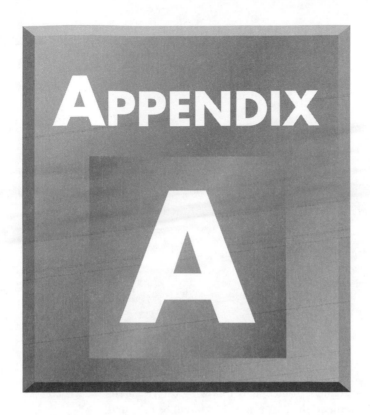

APPENDIX A

Answers to Quiz Questions

Day 1

1. There is no main() function. Every program must have a main() function.
2. One. A function can have many parameters but can return only one value.
3. The strcpy() function copies the contents of one string to another.
4. You never know. A variable will contain random data until it is initialized.
5. There is no limit to the number of functions a program can have.
6. Yes.
7. There is no function declaration for the doSomething() function.
8. One.
9. 19 characters plus the terminating NULL.
10. Zero.

Day 2

1. The statement immediately following the if statement. If a code block follows an if statement, the entire code block will be executed.
2. The first parameter is the starting value, the second parameter is the test expression, and the final parameter is the increment parameter.
3. A while loop checks the conditional expression at the beginning of the loop. A do-while loop checks the conditional expression at the end of the loop.
4. The break statement is used to break out of a loop. The statement following the loop will be executed following a break statement. The continue statement forces program execution back to the top of the loop.
5. A global variable is one that is in scope anywhere in the program. It can be accessed by any functions in the program.
6. Yes. A structure can contain any number and type of data members.
7. With the direct member operator (.). Here's an example:

```
record.LastName = "Noble";
```

8. Yes.

Day 3

1. A pointer is a variable that holds the address of another variable or an object in memory.

2. To de-reference a pointer means to get the value of the variable that the pointer points to and not the value of the pointer itself (which is just a memory location).

3. The memory address where the newly created object resides.

4. Usually classes and structures should be passed by reference to eliminate unnecessary overhead.

5. The const keyword prevents a variable from being modified.

6. No. Overloaded functions must vary by the type and number of parameters. These two functions vary only by return type.

7. It depends on the situation. No one situation is best every time. This is a trick question.

8. A class member function is a function that belongs to a class.

9. The compiler will place the entire contents of the inline function in the compiled code each time the inline function is encountered in the source code. In the case of a regular function, the function exists in the compiled code only once and the compiler places a call to the function each time the function is encountered in the source code.

10. The function should use the delete[] form of operator delete:

```
delete[] buff;
```

Day 4

1. In C++ a structure is simply a class in which all data members and functions have public access by default. Aside from that, there is no difference.

2. Private data members protect data from being modified directly by users of the class. Private data members can be modified through public member functions but not directly.

3. By using getters and setters, which are public member functions that can be called to change the value of a private data member.

4. The destructor is called when the object is destroyed. For local objects this will occur when the object goes out of scope. For dynamically allocated objects this will occur when the object is deleted.

5. To override a function means to replace a function in the base class with a function in your derived class. The new function must have the exact same name, parameters, and return type to override the base class function.

6. Call the base class function from within the overridden function:

```
void MyClass::DoIt()
{
  BaseClass::DoIt();
  // do some other stuff
}
```

7. An initializer list initializes a class's data members and calls any base class constructors prior to the body of the constructor being entered.

8. Yes. It's very common.

9. Multiple inheritance. Derive the class from two separate base classes.

Day 5

1. No. Only visual components can be seen at design time.

2. None is best. All have their own strengths and weaknesses.

3. No. VCL objects must be allocated dynamically (using operator new).

4. Yes and no. For the most part they are equivalent. Since VCL is written in Object Pascal, there are no overloaded VCL methods.

5. Yes.

6. TOpenDialog, TSaveDialog, TRegistry, TColorDialog, TTimer, TImageList, TFontDialog, and many more.

7. Yes. All components are ultimately derived from TComponent, so they all have the properties found in TComponent like Name and Owner, for instance.

8. Top, Left, Owner, Parent, Width, Height, and so on.

9. Yes.

10. A canvas. VCL encapsulates device contexts through the TCanvas class.

Day 6

1. Right-click on the toolbar and choose Properties from the ToolBar speed menu.

2. Drag them to the toolbar and drop them where you want them.

3. Drag unwanted buttons off the bottom of the toolbar and drop them.

4. Hold the Shift key when you click on the component in the Component Palette. Each time you click on the form a new component will be placed.

5. Double-click the component's button in the Component Palette.

6. `.mak`, `.cpp`, `.h`, `.dfm`, and `.res`.

7. `Show()`.

8. `ShowModal()`.

9. In the Object Inspector, switch to the Events page. In the value column next to the event, click the drop-down arrow button. A list of compatible event handlers is displayed. Choose one.

10. Click on a component in the Form Designer and press the Tab key on the keyboard. Each time you hit the Tab key, the next component on the form is selected and will be displayed in the Object Inspector.

Day 7

1. When selecting components that are children of another component (components on a panel, for example).

2. It is the anchor component. It will retain its position, and all other components are aligned to it.

3. Drag a bounding rectangle around (or just touching) them.

4. Select all the components you want to modify. Then choose Edit | Size from the main menu and choose the Grow to Largest radio button.

5. The default event handler for that component is displayed in the Code Editor. In the case of many components the `OnClick` event handler will be displayed. In some special cases (like the `Image` component, for instance) a dialog is displayed.

6. It forces the component to fill the entire client area of its parent, regardless of how the parent (a form, usually) is sized.

7. Traditionally, it means that choosing that menu item will result in a dialog being displayed.

8. In the Menu Designer you can drag the menu to a new location or you can use Cut and Paste.

9. When typing the caption for the menu item, add an ampersand (&) before the shortcut key you want to be the shortcut for that menu item. For instance, the `Caption` for the File | Exit menu item would read `E&xit`.

10. Set its `Enabled` property to `false`.

Day 8

1. Yes, but it's a very bad idea.
2. The `Enabled` property.
3. Its text is grayed out.
4. The long hint is used for the status bar text and the short hint is used for the tool tip text.
5. `Invalidate()`, `Repaint()`, `Refresh()`, and `Update()`.
6. Three: simple, drop-down, and drop-down list.
7. When a button with a `ModalResult` property set to a whole number is clicked, the form will close. The value of the `ModalResult` property for the button clicked will be the return value from the `ShowModal()` method.
8. The `Panel` component. Several others qualify, too.
9. `true`.
10. Just change its `Title` property to `Save As`.

Day 9

1. When you want all the features of the base object and you want the inherited object to change if the base object ever changes.
2. Choose Project | Add to Repository from the main menu or Add Project to Repository from the Project Manager speed menu.
3. All the inherited forms change to reflect the change made to the base form.
4. In the `private` or `public` sections. Never in the __published section (unless you know what you are doing).
5. In any source unit, but usually in the same unit as the rest of the code for that form.
6. If you switch to the Details view, the author of the object is listed.
7. In the Object Repository configuration dialog box (which you get by selecting Options | Repository from the main menu).
8. By using the Application Expert in almost all cases.
9. Add the `.res` file or the `.rc` file to the project via the Project Manager, or use the `#pragma resource` preprocessor directive.
10. Yes, easily.

Day 10

1. F12.

2. No. It is only removed from the project.

3. On the Forms page of the Project Options dialog.

4. You will have to take the responsibility of creating the forms before using them.

5. It's hard to say, but probably 32MB for Windows 95 and 40MB for Windows NT.

6. When debug info is generated, you will be able to step through your code during debugging sessions.

7. In the directory where the project file resides.

8. Ctrl+S.

9. Set a bookmark with Ctrl+K+0 through Ctrl+K+9. There are 10 bookmarks available.

10. Choose Read Only from the Code Editor speed menu.

Day 11

1. Click in the gutter (the left margin) on that line of code. You can also press F5 or choose Toggle Breakpoint from the Code Editor speed menu.

2. A breakpoint that is inadvertently set on a source code line that generates no compiled code.

3. Set the breakpoint, choose View | Breakpoints from the main menu, click on the breakpoint in the Breakpoint List window, and then choose Properties from the Breakpoint List speed menu. Set the condition in the Condition field of the Edit Breakpoint dialog.

4. Double-click the watch in the Watch List window. The Watch Properties dialog is displayed. Modify the properties as needed.

5. Click on the variable and type Ctrl+F5 (or choose Add Watch at Cursor from the Code Editor speed menu).

6. The Debug Inspector.

7. F7.

8. Click on the variable and then choose Evaluate/Modify from the Code Editor speed menu. Change the value in the Evaluate/Modify dialog.

9. TRACE unconditionally displays a message. WARN only displays the message if the provided expression evaluates to true.

10. In the OutDbg1.txt file in the Code Editor.

Day 12

1. The background shows through wherever the transparent color is used on the icon or cursor.

2. Click on a color in the color palette.

3. Choose the Marquee tool and then drag a rectangle with the mouse. You could also use Edit | Select All to select the entire image or the Lasso tool.

4. 256.

5. The exact pixel in the cursor that is used to report the screen coordinates to Windows when the mouse is clicked.

6. Yes.

7. Choose Window | Follow to Focus from the main menu and then click on the window you wish to spy on.

8. grep is used to search for text in source files.

9. Turn on the Editor Files option on the Preferences page (Autosave Options section) of the Environment Options dialog.

10. Click the Reset Defaults button on the Palette page of the Environment Options dialog.

Day 13

1. In the Object Inspector click on the Event tab. Click the drop-down arrow next to the OnClick event. Choose an event handler from the list.

2. Yes.

3. A Notebook component works nicely.

4. Forces the status bar to have a single panel.

5. For a simple status bar:

   ```
   StatusBar->SimpleText = "Text";
   ```

6. Set the component's Enabled property to true to enable the component and false to disable the component.

7. Through the Printer() function.

8. BeginPrint().

9. NewPage().

10. Modify the component's Cursor property.

Day 14

1. Through the Project Options dialog (Application page) or by setting the `HelpFile` property of the `Application` object at runtime.

2. Just assign a nonzero value to the `HelpContext` property. Make sure there is a corresponding help context ID in the help file and that the help file has been set for the application.

3. `HelpCommand()`,

4. Any type: integral data types, classes, or structures.

5. Yes. You can have as many as needed.

6. With the `throw` keyword.

7. `\HKEY_CURRENT_USER`.

8. No. The `TRegistry` destructor will close the key for you. You shouldn't leave a key open indefinitely, though.

9. `PostMessage()` posts the message to the Windows message queue and returns immediately. `SendMessage()` sends the message and doesn't return until the message has been carried out.

10. `Perform()`.

Day 15

1. An error message is generated that indicates that the method is not implemented in the automation object.

2. Click Component | Install, and then click ActiveX.

Day 16

1. Multithreaded database applications.

2. Additional controls (for example, transaction isolation levels, transaction control statements, and greater flexibility when changing back ends).

3. For local tables, the SQL must

  ☐ Use Local SQL syntax only.

  ☐ Involve only one table.

  ☐ Not have an `ORDER BY` clause.

A

☐ Not contain aggregate functions.

☐ Not contain calculated fields.

☐ Use a WHERE clause involving comparisons of column names to scalar constants only. Operators supported include LIKE, >, <, >=, and <=. Individual elements of the clause may be joined by ANDs and ORs as well.

For server tables, the SQL must

☐ Use Local SQL syntax only.

☐ Involve only one table.

☐ Not contain aggregate functions.

4. TBatchMove.

Day 17

1. Select the Form Expert option from the Database menu or by clicking File | New and selecting the Database Form option from the Forms page of the ensuing dialog.

2. The DatabaseName and TableName properties.

3. The DataSet and AutoEdit properties.

4. TDataSource.

Day 18

1. DatabaseName.

2. The Include Unit Hdr option.

3. On the Forms page of the New Items dialog (you can access the New Items dialog via the File | New menu option).

4. One advantage of using data modules is the ability to save them to the C++Builder Object Repository where you and others can reuse them in other applications. Another advantage to data module use is consistency across your applications as far as database access goes. A final advantage is the ability to manage C++Builder's database access from a single vantage point. Instead of having your database-related components spread throughout an application, you house them all in a single location from which you can easily administer and configure them.

Day 19

1. Add the DLL's import library (.lib file) to the project. The DLL will load when the application starts.

2. Use the Windows API function LoadLibrary().

3. Just call the function as you would a regular function.

4. The function has to be exported from the DLL and must use the extern "C" modifier.

5. You can unload the DLL any time you wish (with the FreeLibrary() function).

6. Create an exported function that the calling application can call. In this function write code that creates the form and displays it.

7. You can use a single header when building both the DLL and the calling application.

8. Add an .res or .rc file to the DLLs project via the Project Manager.

9. No. If the DLL uses static loading, it doesn't need any code at all.

10. Yes. Create a .lib file for the DLL just as you would a DLL containing code, and add the .lib file to the calling application's project.

Day 20

1. No. You can use direct access instead.

2. No, but they usually do. A property that does not store a value is pretty unusual.

3. Absolutely. That's the easiest way to create a new component.

4. Then the property becomes read-only.

5. The underlying data member for the property is modified and/or read directly (no read method and no write method).

6. No. Default values are optional. Published properties should have a default value, though.

7. No. The default value only displays a value in the Object Inspector at design time. You must set the underlying data member to the default value in the component's constructor.

8. Choose Component | Install from the main menu.

9. Create a .dcr file with the same name as the component's source. The .dcr should contain a 24×24 bitmap with the same name as the component's class name. Be sure the .dcr is in the same directory as the .cpp file for the component.

10. Just call the event after checking to see if an event handler exists for the event:

```
if (OnMyEvent) OnMyEvent(this);
```

Day 21

1. `__declspec`, `delphiclass`, `delphireturn`, `__automated`, `__published`, `__closure`, `__property`, `__classid(class)`, and `__dispid(int)`.

2. Yes, via helper macros.

3. The `AnsiString`, `Variant`, `ShortString`, `Currency`, `TDateTime`, and `Set` classes.

4. Version 2.0.

5. In the header file corresponding to the form's main source module.

Day 22

1. The NTTP component.

2. `OnBeginRetrieve`.

3. The `URL` property.

4. The FTP component.

Day 23

1. `__property`.

2. Yes, an event is a closure as well as a property.

3. The `__published` keyword causes the property to be displayed in the Object Inspector at design time.

4. No. It was in previous Borland compilers. Its use has been extended for C++Builder, though.

INDEX

Symbols

MACMILLAN COMPUTER PUBLISHING USA

A VIACOM COMPANY

Technical

Support:

If you cannot get the CD/Disk to install properly, or you need assistance with a particular situation in the book, please feel free to check out the Knowledge Base on our Web site at **http://www.superlibrary.com/general/support**. We have answers to our most Frequently Asked Questions listed there. If you do not find your specific question answered, please contact Macmillan Technical Support at **(317) 581-3833**. We can also be reached by email at **support@mcp.com**.

Delphi 2 Developer's Guide, Second Edition

Steve Teixeira & Xavier Pacheco

This book empowers the reader with the ability to capitalize on the growing movement toward GUI (graphical user interface)-based applications. The reader will become adept at exploiting Delphi 2's tools and commands and will learn how to create object-oriented programs.

Price: $59.99 USA/$81.99 CDN
ISBN: 0-672-30914-9

User level: Accomplished—Expert
1,368 pages

Tom Swan's Mastering Borland C++ 5, Premier Edition

Tom Swan

The new release of Borland C++ 5.0 includes valuable tools developers are craving. These tools include new object-oriented scripting, a new C++ language environment that lets you control the IDE completely, and debugger control. With all those and many other new features, developers will turn to *Tom Swan's Mastering Borland C++ 5.0, Premier Edition* to receive the latest, most accurate information on how to exploit these new features in their programs.

Price: $59.99 USA/$81.99 CDN
ISBN: 0-672-30802-9

User level: Casual—Accomplished—Expert
1,088 pages

Teach Yourself Delphi 2 in 21 Days

Dan Osier, Steve Grobman, & Steve Batson

This unique book presents Delphi programming in logical, easy-to-follow sequences that have made the *Teach Yourself* series a best-seller. The reader begins learning the basics of Delphi and then moves on to more advanced topics.

Price: $35.00 USA/$47.95 CDN
ISBN: 0-672-30863-0

User level: New—Casual—Accomplished
800 pages

Teach Yourself Borland C++ 5 in 21 Days, Third Edition

Craig Arnush

Updated and revised, this book shows readers how to use the language and how to write beginning-level programs. The author is a member of Team Borland and has access to the most frequently asked questions from the Borland help line.

Price: $39.99 USA/$53.99 CDN
ISBN: 0-672-30756-1

User level: New—Casual
864 pages

Delphi 2 Unleashed

Charles Calvert

This book helps every programmer get the most from the latest version of Delphi. It reveals all the latest information, including how to develop client/server applications, multimedia programs, and advanced Windows programs in an easy-to-understand style.

Price: $59.99 USA/$81.99 CDN User level: Casual—Accomplished—Expert
ISBN: 0-672-30858-4 1,440 pages

Borland's Official No-Nonsense Guide to Delphi 2

Michelle Manning

This book contrasts itself against others by providing an in-depth, no-nonsense study of Delphi—just the facts. Written for casual programmers, *Borland's Official No-Nonsense Guide to Delphi 2* gives readers the essential information they need on topics as varied as developing client/server applications, multimedia programs, and advanced Windows programs.

Price: $25.00 USA/$34.95 CDN User level: New—Casual
ISBN: 0-672-30871-1 416 pages

Database Developer's Guide with Delphi 2

Ken Henderson

This is the only book that focuses on advanced database development. Readers will learn the intricacies involved in developing robust database applications with Delphi 2.

Price: $55.00 USA/$74.95 CDN User level: Accomplished—Expert
ISBN: 0-672-30862-2 912 pages

Database Developer's Guide with Borland C++ 5

Mike Cohn, Jay Rutten, Kristen Hill, Mark Gee, & James Moran

This unique reference not only details the preliminary design steps essential for effective database creation, but also delves deeply into the various programming methods available for implementation. Sample databases are developed with IDAPI, ODBC, and Borland's new Visual Database tools. Also included is a solid introduction to SQL.

Price: $59.99 USA/$81.99 CDN User level: Accomplished—Expert
ISBN: 0-672-30800-2 736 pages

Add to Your Sams Library Today with the Best Books for Programming, Operating Systems, and New Technologies

The easiest way to order is to pick up the phone and call
1-800-428-5331
between 9:00 a.m. and 5:00 p.m. EST.
For faster service please have your credit card available.

ISBN	Quantity	Description of Item	Unit Cost	Total Cost
0-672-30914-9		Delphi 2 Developer's Guide, Second Editon (book/CD-ROM)	$59.99	
0-672-30802-9		Tom Swan's Mastering Borland C++5, Premier Edition (book/CD-ROM)	$59.99	
0-672-30863-0		Teach Yourself Delphi 2 in 21 Days	$35.00	
0-672-30756-1		Teach Yourself Borland C++ 5 in 21 Days, Third Edition	$39.99	
0-672-30858-4		Delphi 2 Unleashed (book/CD-ROM)	$59.99	
0-672-30871-1		Borland's Official No-Nonsense Guide to Delphi 2	$25.00	
0-672-30862-2		Database Developer's Guide with Delphi 2 (book/CD-ROM)	$55.00	
0-672-30800-2		Database Developer's Guide with Borland C++ 5 (book/CD-ROM)	$59.99	
		Shipping and handling: See information below.		
		TOTAL		

Shipping and handling: $4.00 for the first book, and $1.75 for each additional book. If you need to have it NOW, we can ship product to you in 24 hours for an additional charge of approximately $18.00, and you will receive your item overnight or in two days. Overseas shipping and handling adds $2.00. Prices subject to change. Call between 9:00 a.m. and 5:00 p.m. EST for availability and pricing information on latest editions.

201 W. 103rd Street, Indianapolis, Indiana 46290

1-800-428-5331 — Orders   1-800-835-3202 — Fax   1-800-858-7674 — Customer Service

Book ISBN 0-672-31020-1

Installing the CD-ROM

The companion CD-ROM contains all the source code and project files developed by the authors, plus an assortment of evaluation versions of third-party products. To install, please follow these steps:

Windows 95/NT 4 Installation Instructions

1. Insert the CD-ROM into your CD-ROM drive.
2. From the Windows 95 or NT 4 desktop, double-click on the My Computer icon.
3. Double-click on the icon representing your CD-ROM drive.
4. Double-click on the icon titled setup.exe to run the CD-ROM installation program.

This program will create a program group with the icons to run the programs on the CD. No files will be copied to your hard drive during this installation.

NOTE If you have Windows95 and the Autoplay feature is enabled, the setup.exe program is executed automatically when the CD is inserted into the drive.

Windows NT 3.51 Installation Instructions

1. Insert the CD-ROM into your CD-ROM drive.
2. From the File Manager or Program Manager, choose Run from the File menu.
3. Type <drive>\setup.exe, where <drive> corresponds to the drive letter of your CD-ROM drive, and press Enter. For example, if your CD-ROM drive is d:, type d:\setup.exe and press Enter.
4. Installation creates a program group named Teach Yourself Cpp Builder. This group will contain icons to browse the CD-ROM.